Contemporary International Relations

Frameworks for Understanding

Sixth Edition

Daniel S. Papp
University System of Georgia

New York San Francisco Boston
London Toronto Sydney Tokyo Singapore Madrid
Mexico City Munich Paris Cape Town Hong Kong Montreal

Publisher: Priscilla McGeehon
Senior Acquisitions Editor: Eric Stano
Associate Editor: Anita Castro
Marketing Manager: Megan Galvin-Fak
Production Manager: Mark Naccarelli
Project Coordination, Text Design, and Electronic Page Makeup: WestWords Inc.
Cover Design Manager: John Callahan
Cover Designer: Joan O'Connor
Cover Photos: Large photo: © Photonica; Small Photos: © PhotoDisc
Photo Reseacher: Photosearch, Inc.
Manufacturing Buyer: Roy Pickering
Printer and Binder: Hamilton Printing
Cover Printer: John P. Pow

Library of Congress Cataloging-in-Publication Data

Papp, Daniel S., 1947–
    Contemporary international relations : frameworks for understanding / Daniel S.
  Papp.—6th ed.
      p. cm.
    Includes bibliographical references and index.
    ISBN-0-321-08999-5
      1. International relations. I. Title.

  JZ1305 .P37 2001
  327—dc21   00-054575

Please visit our website at http://www.ablongman.com

ISBN-0-321-08999-5

  2 3 4 5 6 7 8 9 10—HT—04 03 02

Contents

PART 2   THE SYSTEMIC FRAMEWORK: THE ACTORS IN THE INTERNATIONAL SYSTEM   137

PART 4   THE INSTRUMENTAL FRAMEWORK: THE TOOLS OF POWER IN INTERNATIONAL POLITICS   295

Preface

In the opening years of the twenty-first century, international relations are complex and confusing. No new international system has emerged to replace the tense order imposed by the defunct East–West conflict, and competing political, economic, military, social and technological forces render the future of international relations uncertain.

In many peoples' eyes, whatever degree of certainty and stability exists in international relations in the early twenty-first century results from economic forces. Economic interdependence influences many international political actors to recognize that they have shared interests. The volume of world trade continues to increase as many areas of the world develop free trade areas and move toward regional integration. And some people believe that a global economic system is imminent, fueled by the new technologies of the Information Age and the breakdown of international barriers to the movement of people, goods, capital, and ideas.

Nevertheless, major sources of instability and disorder exist. Indeed, economics itself is a source of uncertainty and change as new economic relationships disrupt old patterns of economic activity. Meanwhile, nationalism runs rampant in many countries, tearing old states apart and creating new nation-states. Violence and warfare are endemic in many regions of the world. Health, the environment, drugs, and gender issues have also emerged as major concerns for the international community.

The objective of this text, *Contemporary International Relations,* is to assist students in their efforts to understand the complex world in which we live. Like preceding editions of *Contemporary International Relations (CIR),* the sixth edition approaches the task by using six frameworks which together provide a comprehensive understanding of the complexity, interdependence, and diversity of the twenty-first century world.

The first framework proceeds from the assumption that before students can understand contemporary international relations, they must first know who the actors are and what objectives and interests they have. Therefore, *CIR*'s first framework analyzes the major types of international actors and their interests: states, international governmental organizations (IGOs), multinational corporations (MNCs), and non-governmental organizations (NGOs).

The interactions of these actors and their interests form the international system, which itself has an impact on the actors' objectives, perceptions, capabilities, and actions. Recognizing this, *CIR*'s second framework studies how actors make the policies through which they interact and explores the dimensions of the international systems that actors and their interactions over time have created and are creating.

Regardless of each actor's place in the international system, the policies and actions of all international actors are based on how they see themselves, their own situations, the positions of others, and the international system. *CIR*'s third framework therefore first discusses the importance of perceptions. It then examines the perceptions of several major states, grouping them into two categories—developed states and developing states.

Framework four studies the different instruments and tools that international actors have at their disposal to implement policies and undertake actions. This framework concentrates on economic, military, sociopolitical, diplomatic, and legal parameters of power and influence. The rationale behind this framework is straightforward: regardless of whether an international actor is a state, an MNC, an IGO, or an NGO, it requires certain instruments or tools to achieve its objectives. Students of international relations therefore need to understand those tools and how international actors use them.

This leads directly to the fifth framework, which explores the more important problems and issues that international actors both create and confront in their international interactions. International political economy, war and violence, human rights, and conflicts of values, and the environment and health are presented and analyzed as separate issues which confront the international community.

Finally, in framework six, *Contemporary International Relations* speculates about the future. In the final analysis, all actors plan for the future and implement policies to try to bring about the world they desire. With this in mind, framework six ponders how the world might change as the twenty-first century progresses.

The sixth edition has been completely updated. Its organization remains substantially the same as earlier editions, but to conserve space, the framework on perceptions has been shortened. This does not imply that the perceptions of international actors are less important in the twenty-first century than they were in the twentieth. Indeed, in the Information Age, the perceptions of international actors may well be more important than ever.

At the same time, given that the present era is often described as "the Information Age," the sixth edition includes a new and distinctive feature. Each chapter discusses how new and emerging information and communication technologies may influence the primary actors and issues under discussion in that chapter. This not only helps bind the study together, but also provides a sometimes surprising look at what information and communication technologies are doing and might do to the world we call home.

Like preceding editions, this edition is written for introductory students. It assumes only a basic knowledge of international affairs. It avoids esoteric language and concepts, but provides a rigorous understanding of international affairs by blending the theories of academia with the realities of everyday international life.

This edition of *Contemporary International Affairs* also continues to stress that in international affairs, change is inevitable. Events of the last century made this exceedingly evident. But one of the reasons that international affairs is studied is because change and the forces that lead to change can be understood. Hopefully, once understood, change and its causes can be shaped in ways that lead to improvements in the human condition.

So to use once again the words that ended the prefaces of the twentieth century's editions of *CIR,* there remains hope—hope that with understanding, skill, and perhaps a little luck, we may yet fashion a safer, saner, and more humane world for ourselves, our children, and future generations.

NEW TO THIS EDITION

- Updating of data and examples throughout.
- Short vignettes on the impact of information and communication technology on aspects of IR have been added to every chapter.
- Shortened and more concise discussion of national perceptions.
- Expanded discussion of foreign policy decision-making (Ch. 6).
- Expanded discussion of human rights (Ch. 8).
- Expanded discussion of health issues in international relations (Ch. 19).
- Expanded discussion of environmental issues in international relations (Ch. 19)
- Website references have been added to every chapter.
- New theoretical discussions have been added throughout text where appropriate.
- Key Term definitions have been added to the end of each chapter.

SUPPLEMENTS

Microsoft® Encarta® Interactive World Atlas 2001 CD-ROM. Available at 60% of the retail price when ordered bundled with Papp's Text! This powerful, state-of-the-art CD-ROM maps every corner of the earth in rich, engaging detail. Offering students an unparalleled database of information about countries across the world, the CD-ROM provides a dynamic tour of the counties being studied in class, while helping students develop geography skills.

Discount Subscription to Newsweek magazine. For more then 80% off the regular price, your students can receive 12 issues of *Newsweek* magazine delivered to their door! Ask your local Allyn & Bacon/Longman representative how to order the text packaged with the discount subscription card.

New Signet World Atlas. From Penguin-Putnam, this pocket-sized yet detailed reference features 96 pages of full-color maps, plus statistics, key data, and much more. Available at 60% off the retail price when ordered packaged with the text.

Longman Atlas of War and Peace. Adapted from *The Penguin Atlas of War & Peace,* this unique booklet contains ten full-color maps with explanatory notes, examining forces changing the world today. FREE when ordered packaged with the text.

ACKNOWLEDGMENTS

I wish to acknowledge the valuable contributions of Donald Ray, Ferris State University, Uk Heo, University of Wisconsin—Milwaukee, Bernard-Thompson Ikegwuaha, Western Washington University, Earl Contieh-Morgan, University of South Florida, James F. Hollifield, Southern Methodist University, Robert E. Williams, Pepperdine University, Philip Meeks, Creighton University, Marc Simon, Bowling Green State University, Elizabeth Smytue, Concordia University College of Alberta, Peter Schraeder, Loyola University Chicago, Joseph Lepgold, Georgetown University, Gary Prevost, St. John's University, Henry A. Schockley, Boston University.

Chapter 1

International Relations in the Twenty-First Century

- How do international relations affect you?
- What is the twenty-first century world like?
- What causes international change?
- How can international relations best be understood?
- How can international relations best be studied?

As you begin this course in international relations, you are probably asking yourself two questions: "How does international relations affect me, and why should I study it?"

There are many answers to these questions.

If you drive a car, the gas in your car may have begun as oil pumped somewhere in the Middle East. A war in the Middle East will increase the price you pay for gas, as occurred in 1991. So too will a decision by Middle Eastern governments to cut back oil production, as occurred in 2000.

If you live in the United States or Canada and eat fruits or vegetables in the winter, some of your food was probably grown in Mexico, Central America, or South America. Bad weather, drought, or political unrest there could make it difficult or impossible to get your favorite food. A bad hurricane season was the primary reason that the price of bananas and other tropical fruits went up in 1999.

If you look at the labels in your clothes, you probably will find some were made in China. A trade war with China or an embargo on imports from China because of its human rights practices could mean that you spend more on clothes. This is one reason why in 2000, many Americans supported granting China permanent trading status. On the other hand, others opposed granting China permanent trade status because there would be fewer textile jobs in the U.S. Others opposed permanent trade relations because of China's violations of Western standards of human rights.

If you plan to buy a car, chances are strong that a major part of it, or perhaps the whole vehicle, was built or will be built in Korea or Japan. If you intend to buy a computer, the likelihood is that many of its components will also be produced somewhere in

East Asia. The exchange rate between the dollar and East Asian currencies will affect how much you pay for your car or your computer.

If you are African American, Asian, Caucasian, or Hispanic and live in North America, you probably trace your cultural traditions and ethnic heritage to a region of the world outside North America. Many of those traditions and heritages play a large role in popular culture today, especially in music, entertainment, and food.

If you use a computer, chances are strong that you have gone on-line with an international internet site. In 2000, your computer may also have been affected by the Love Bug virus, created half a world away in the Philippines but spread globally overnight.

If you pay taxes in the United States, about twenty cents out of every tax dollar is spent on defense. If you have not talked with your grandparents or parents about World War II, the Vietnam War, or growing up during the Cold War with the fear of nuclear war in the background, please do. All these events had a significant impact on their lives, and as a result, on who you are today.

Many other examples could also be used to show how international relations affect you, and almost everyone else as well. Sometimes the effects are relatively small, like having less money to spend because the price of gas went up or having more money to spend because the price of clothes went down. Sometimes the effects are large, as when a terrorist attack shatters a city's peace or when a country goes to war.

With only a moment's reflection, the impacts of international relations can easily be found. Those impacts are everywhere, and many affect us directly both in our everyday lives and our longer term futures. It is therefore important that we understand contemporary international relations.

WHAT THE TWENTY-FIRST CENTURY WORLD IS LIKE

The twenty-first century world and the international relations that go with it can best be described as complex, interdependent, diverse, and rapidly changing. Examining a few illustrations of these points is a good place to start.

Global Complexity

There are many dimensions to the complexity of twenty-first century international relations. For example, many different countries and companies play a major role in international affairs. These countries and companies have many different interests, pursue many different objectives, and interact in many different ways. For our purposes, the twenty first century's **global complexity** can best be illustrated in two ways.

First, during the nineteenth century and most of the twentieth century, almost all major international events and issues were centered on and revolved around states. This is no longer true. Today, several different types of actors are important players in the international arena. Without denying the continued importance and dominance of the state as the primary type of international actor, it is nevertheless impossible to gain an accurate picture of international relations without taking into account the presence of and the actions by other types of international actors.

Chapter 1

INFORMATION TECHNOLOGY (IT) AND
INTERNATIONAL RELATIONS: THE INFORMATION AGE

The era in which we live is often described as the Information Age, and for good reason. During the last decade, a large number of new information technologies have emerged. These technologies provide humans new capabilities to overcome barriers on communications imposed by time, distance, and location. They also increase human ability to store, process, and analyze data and to make decisions based on the information that is developed. Their implications for international relations are immense.

Many technologies led to the Information Age, but eight stand out: 1. advanced semiconductors, which greatly expanded human ability to store, process, and communicate data and information; 2. computers, central to all facets of automated data and information storage, dissemination, analysis, and use; 3. fiber optics, which immensely increase the rate at which data and information can be sent and received; 4. wireless and cellular technologies, which allow users to send and receive data and information without being tied to a location; 5. advanced networking, which enhances "connectivity," that is, the ability of information technologies to talk to each other; 6. communication satellites, which provide the ability to communicate globally; 7. improved human-computer interaction, which makes it easier for people to use computers; and 8. digital technologies, which use binary numbers—one and zero—carried as electrical pulses to represent data and information.

Together, these technologies increase the speed at which data and information can be transmitted and received. They expand the amount of data and information that can be sent and received. They enhance the flexibility of data and information flow since senders and receivers no longer must be tied to a location. Together, they also increase the types of data and information that can be sent.

The implications of these capabilities for international relations are immense. Information is available at more places than ever before. It flows faster and more freely than ever, enabling decisions to be made in more places than ever before. Boundaries between states and other international actors are becoming more permeable. Existing power relationships are being disrupted and changed. Trends toward regionalization and globalization are accelerating (and so too is opposition to both). And the distribution of wealth within and between states is becoming even more skewed as a digital divide increasingly separates creators and users of information technologies—many of whom are becoming wealthy—from those who are not knowledgeable, many of whom are falling economically behind.

Yet the implications of information technology for international relations are rarely discussed, especially in introductory courses and texts. *Contemporary International Relations* remedies this by including in each chapter a discussion of how advanced information technologies affect the issues under discussion in that chapter.

What are the other types of actors? In addition to states, international governmental organizations (IGOs), multinational corporations (MNCs), and nongovermental organizations (NGOs) are all important players on the international scene. Their importance is recognized and detailed in *Contemporary International Relation's* second framework, where each type of actor is studied.

A second measure of complexity is that each type of international actor has a growing number of individual actors within it. For example, in 1950, there were perhaps 75 independent states. In 2000, there were approximately 200. Similarly, in 1950, there were perhaps 100 IGOs. In 2000, there were over 250. The number of NGOs and MNCs has also increased dramatically over the years. As the twenty-first century begins, there are about nineteen thousand NGOs and perhaps 40 thousand MNCs.[1] Not all are of great significance, but many play major role in international relations. Their numbers alone complicate international relations immensely.

All of the above mean that international relations have become exceedingly complex. It is no longer possible to understand international relations by studying exclusively the actions and interests of a few states. Using only the proliferation of the types and numbers of international actors, the world in the twenty-first century is an exceedingly complex place.

Global Interdependence [2]

The world is also quite interdependent. As used here, interdependence has both a general and a specific meaning.

In general terms, **global interdependence** refers to the fact that events and actions in one region of the world often over time affect other events and actions in other regions of the globe. More specifically, **economic interdependence** also refers to the mutual dependence of national economies on one another. Economic interdependence is a reality of twenty-first century international relations for all but a few of the world's poorest countries. Both versions of interdependence have been spurred by two factors.

First, during the late twentieth century, many states instituted policies that consciously sought to remove barriers to the movement of people, capital, goods, services, and ideas across state boundaries. These policies have been highly successful in many locations, most notably Europe, where what began as the European Economic Community evolved first into the European Community and then the European Union.

Second, technology, especially transportation technology and information and communication technology, spurred the growth of interdependence. Technology expanded human ability to move people, capital, goods, services, and ideas reliably and inexpensively over long distances in short periods of time, so growth of interdependence was virtually inevitable. Thus, with the removal of policy barriers and the advance of technology, interdependence is a reality of twenty-first century international relations.

Global Diversity

Despite global interdependence and the new policies and new technologies that promote it, the world is incredibly diverse. This **global diversity** is the result of several factors.

There are thousands of ethnic groups, nationalities, languages, cultures, and value sets. Most people remain wedded to the ethnicity, nationality, language, culture, history, and values of their homeland or locality. Most French remain ardently pro-French in their preferences, most Germans pro-German, most Indians pro-Indian, most Chinese pro-Chinese, and most Japanese pro-Japanese. The list of course goes on.

The perceptions that different people hold are also often vastly different. Sometimes, perceptions of international actors, events, and issues vary widely from country to country and from type of actor to type of actor, as we will see in framework three. Indeed, perceptions of a single event can and do vary so widely that it is sometimes difficult to believe that different observers viewed the same event. This is as true in international relations as it is in traffic accidents.

Is this changing? As people travel more, as they move from one country to another, as barriers to international movement are reduced, and as technology makes international communications easier, the possibility exists that the world will become increasingly homogenized and diversity will eventually disappear.

Some people see this as a desirable objective to pursue, while others fear it as a future to be avoided at all costs. Regardless of whether this is seen as a desirable objective or feared future, today's world remains incredibly diverse. And more and more people are becoming more aware of that diversity.

At the same time, diversity has a downside. Differences in ethnicity, nationality, language, culture, values and perceptions sometimes lead people to believe they are superior to others and to try to control or dominate them. Sometimes differences influence people to resent, fear, or hate those who do not have the same background. This sometimes has tragic results, as the world saw in the 1990s in Bosnia, Kosovo, Rwanda, East Timor, and elsewhere as well. Unfortunately, violence, death, and destruction are parts of the diversity of twenty-first century international relations, just as they were parts of the diversity of preceding centuries.

Global Change

The twentieth century was a century of **global change,** the speed and dimensions of which will probably be dwarfed by the speed and dimensions of twenty-first century change. The twentieth century began with a few European states dominating most of the world with their global colonial empires. It ended with about 200 sovereign states, each of which pursued its own interests and objectives. The twentieth century also began with little electricity, few cars, and no nuclear weapons. Today, many people consider electricity and cars necessities, while leaders of many states consider nuclear weapons a primary measure of national power regardless of whether or not their country has any.

What is more, the rate of change may be accelerating. As Table 1-1 shows, many people are using major technological advances more and more rapidly. Without implying that technology is the only force for change, it is nevertheless striking that it took 46 years for 25 percent of all Americans to use electricity after it became available, and only seven years for the same percentage of Americans to use the Internet once it was available.

TABLE 1-1   Years For a New Technology to Reach 25% of U.S. Population

Year of Introduction	Invention	Years Until 25% Use
1873	Electricity	46
1876	Telephone	35
1886	Gas Automobile	55
1906	Radio	22
1926	Television	26
1953	Microwave Oven	30
1975	Personal Computer	16
1983	Cellular Phone	13
1991	Internet	7

Source: Newsweek, April 13, 1998

Conversely, our awareness of change should not obscure the fact that traditions, and traditional values, are powerful forces in many societies. Usually, established social, religious, or economic groups are the staunchest defenders of tradition and traditional values. As a result, tensions often develop between those who emphasize tradition and traditional values and those who emphasize change and modernization.

Often, these tensions lead to clashes between defenders of tradition and traditional values on the one hand and proponents of change and modernization on the other. These clashes can unleash powerful emotions that lead to conflict, fighting, and even war. This too is a reality of twenty-first century international relations.

 ## FORCES BEHIND CHANGE

Change, however, is inevitable. As the 1990s began, several forces converged that together overturned the international system that had existed since shortly after World War II. Those forces remain in place today as we begin the twenty-first century.

Chief among those forces were the collapse of communism in Eastern Europe and the Soviet Union, the reemergence of economics as a critical concern in international affairs, the development of trends toward democratization and privatization, the movement toward regional and global integration, the emergence of new information and communication technologies, renewed nationalist demands by many ethnic groups and nationalities for their own independent states, and the emergence of global problems that crossed national and regional boundaries. These seven forces were not and are not only causes of change, but together they are revolutionizing contemporary international relations.

The Collapse of Soviet and Eastern European Communism

Throughout the post–World War II era, one of the main features of international relations was the conflict between the Soviet Union and its communist allies on the one hand and the United States and its allies on the other. Even at times when there was little tension be-tween the superpowers, no one really challenged the basic assumption that rivalry and competition remained central to the superpower relationship. And no one expected the **collapse of communism.**

However, throughout the late 1970s and early 1980s, the Soviet economy deterio-rated and many Soviet citizens were becoming disenchanted with their lot in life.[3] Then, in 1985, a new Soviet leader, Mikhail Gorbachev, assumed power and began a series of reforms unparalleled in Soviet history. Gorbachev reduced censorship, permitted social and political debate, decentralized the economy, introduced democracy into the Soviet political system, and promoted "new thinking" in Soviet foreign policy.[4] Gorbachev in-troduced these reforms for a basic reason. He understood that past policies had to be changed radically or the USSR would decline both politically and economically.

In some areas, Gorbachev's reforms succeeded. But in others, particularly econom-ics, they failed. In addition, the Soviet leader's attempt to change his country led to immense political struggles within the USSR over his reforms and contributed to height-ened ethnic tensions between the Soviet Union's diverse nationalities. By 1989, even though East–West tensions had declined immensely, it was not at all clear if Gorbachev's reforms were helping or hurting the people of the Soviet Union. Nor was it clear whether Gorbachev could withstand the pressures from hard-line conservatives who wanted to end his reforms and return to traditional Soviet policies. Gorbachev also faced pressures from radical reformers who wanted him to accelerate change.

By 1989, the impacts of Gorbachev's reforms had also spread beyond the Soviet Union. Nowhere outside the USSR were the impacts greater than in Eastern Europe. The people of Eastern Europe, who had fallen under communist control following World War II and afterward had twice been subjected to Soviet invasions to maintain that control (Hungary in 1956 and Czechoslovakia in 1968), considered Gorbachev's reforms a godsend. Eastern Europeans took special note of Gorbachev's position that the Soviet Union would no longer use military force to keep other countries under communist rule.

With Gorbachev's rejection of the use of force to impose communism, the resentment of the peoples of Eastern Europe toward their governments poured out. In 1989, popular resentment, street demonstrations, and elections toppled governments in all six of the Soviet Union's Eastern European allies. These were incredible events that ended Eastern Europe's subservience to the USSR, led to the unification of East and West Germany, and shook the structure of the entire international system. Was the Cold War over, or was it just in temporary remission?

The question became more important as change accelerated in the Soviet Union in 1990 and 1991. As the USSR's economy continued to decline and ethnic conflict wors-ened, the political struggle over Gorbachev's reforms increased. Finally in August 1991, conservative Communist Party and military hard-liners staged a coup and removed Gorbachev from power.

But the coup was short-lived. Thousands of Soviet citizens led by Russian President Boris Yeltsin refused to submit to the hard-liners, and significant numbers of the Soviet military sided with Yeltsin and his supporters as well. The coup collapsed, Gorbachev re-turned to Moscow, the hard-liners were arrested, and all that they stood for was disgraced.

No two people played more important roles in the collapse of the Soviet Union than Mikhail Gorbachev, the last President of the USSR, and Boris Yeltsin, the first President of independent Russia. Here, Gorbachev and Yeltsin address the Russian parliament on August 23, 1991, shortly after the failed coup.

After the coup failed, events unfolded even more rapidly. Gorbachev, although still Soviet president, lost prestige and influence because of the coup. Conversely, Russian President Yeltsin gained prestige and influence. In December 1991, Yeltsin and the presidents of two of the other most important Soviet republics, Ukraine and Belarussia (now Belarus), declared that the USSR would cease to exist on January 1, 1992. Gorbachev protested, but could do nothing. And the Soviet Union passed into history.

These were momentous events for the people who lived in the former USSR. And they were momentous events for the world as well. For almost half a century, since shortly after World War II, the East–West conflict, with the East centered around the Soviet Union and the West around the United States, had defined much of international relations. With the dissolution of the Soviet Union, that conflict was over.

The Reemergence of Economics

But what might replace it? What might become the dominant organizing concept in contemporary international affairs?

One answer to these questions was economics. For years, the superpowers and their allies concentrated on military power, while economic considerations played an important but secondary role. Occasionally, world leaders such as former U.S. President Dwight Eisenhower emphasized the role of economics as an important component of national strength, but these references were infrequent and quickly forgotten. Newly independent Developing World states focused on economics as a critical issue, but rarely succeeded in achieving economic success. For most of the Cold War period then, guns, bombs, and missiles were the stuff of high politics and high importance. Trade, foreign aid, economic development, and debt remained secondary priorities.

Slowly, international economic issues during the 1980s began to acquire greater importance. The **reemergence of economics** as a major force in international affairs cannot be traced to a single event or a single trend. Rather, it was the culmination of a series of events and trends that made it impossible to overlook the importance that international economic issues have. These events and trends included but were not limited to (1) increased U.S., Western European, and Japanese awareness of their dependence on foreign sources of energy and other nonfuel mineral resources; (2) burgeoning Developing World debt; (3) the emergence of Japan as a major international economic actor; (4) the transformation of the United States from the world's greatest creditor state to the world's greatest debtor state; (5) the economic collapse of the Soviet Union and the beginning of the integration of the postcommunist Eastern European and Soviet successor states into the Western economic system; (6) the movement of international economic growth to the Western Pacific; (7) the decision by Western Europe to create a single European market; (8) the continuing inability of large segments of the Developing World to grow economically; and (9) the transformation by electronic banking of much of the world into a single financial market.

By the 1990s, economic concerns had become as important as military concerns on the agendas of many international actors. Thus, when Iraq invaded Kuwait in 1990, many countries feared not only that Iraqi expansionism might threaten their geopolitical interests, but also, as a result of Iraq's control of a large percentage of the world's oil reserves, their economies. This linkage between economic concerns and military concerns was not new, but the Iraqi invasion of Kuwait provided the linkage with a poignancy that it had not had for some time. At the same time, much of the world had become economically linked. American-built aircraft flew Japanese businesspeople to Indonesia to secure oil for Japanese industries, and French financiers tracked their investments in stock markets in London, New York, Tokyo, and Hong Kong. American consumers purchased inexpensive East Asian textile products, forcing U.S. textile manufacturers to lay off workers and invest in high-technology German textile machines purchased with money deposited in Italian banks by Saudi princes. Many people debated whether this economic interdependence was a blessing or a curse, but no one debated its reality.

The reemergence of economics as a critical concern in international affairs raised important questions. Who would benefit from the growth in international trade? Would only a few states or would many states? Or would multinational corporations and other types of international actors begin to become more important than states in international affairs? How long could any state, even one as wealthy as the United States, run huge balance-of-trade deficits? Could individual states maintain their sovereignty in an economically interdependent world? What duty do developed states have to aid economic growth in underdeveloped states? Where do domestic economic concerns end and international economic concerns begin? What responsibility does one state have to citizens of another so that its own citizens and corporations do not take economic advantage of them? And if the first state concludes that it has no responsibility to protect the economic interests of citizens of another state, what actions may that other state take to defend its citizens'—and its own—interests?

Democratization and Privatization

During the late 1980s and 1990s, two other trends also accelerated. These processes were democratization and privatization.

Democratization is the political process of replacing dictatorial and autocratic governments with freely elected governments of one form or another. This simple definition is complicated because there is no clear answer to the question, "When is a government democratic?"

For example, if a country holds a free election, is that enough to declare that the country is democratic? What if voting in the election is restricted to one class, gender, or race? Is the government democratic then? Must multiple parties contest an election for democracy to be in place or can there be democracy when there is only one party? Is a country democratic if the electoral process favors one party or candidate? If a freely elected government becomes politically repressive, violates human rights, favors the economic interests of only a few people, or cancels elections, is it still democratic? These are difficult questions, and there are no easy answers.[5]

Despite the complexity of defining democracy, most analysts agree that the world is experiencing a trend toward democratization. In many respects, the trend toward democratization began during the 1980s in Latin America as country after country moved away from authoritarian and dictatorial governments and instituted democratic governments. With the restoration of a freely elected government to power in Haiti in 1994, 34 of the 35 states in the Western Hemisphere were governed by freely elected governments.

The trend toward democratization was not restricted to Latin America. As we have already seen, in Eastern Europe in 1989, communist governments fell and in most instances were replaced by freely elected governments. The same thing happened in the Soviet Union in 1991, where one state became fifteen states, many of which instituted free elections. Democratization proceeded in Africa as well, where countries such as Benin, Mozambique, Namibia, Sao Tome and Principe, and South Africa all held free elections. In Asia, Cambodia, South Korea, Taiwan, and Thailand all serve as examples of states where free elections have been newly instituted.[6]

But the trend toward democratization should not be overstated. Many countries did not and do not have democratic governments. In some countries such as China in 1989, democracy had been brutally repressed. And in some states where free elections have been held, democracy's hold is tenuous as economic problems, ethnic unrest, civil strife, and extremist movements on the political left and right threaten to undermine freely elected governments.

Democratization is primarily a domestic issue, but it has several implications for international affairs. First, democracies rarely go to war with each other. Second, because in today's era of instant communications ideas can be easily transmitted on a global basis, more and more people than ever before are aware that self-government is possible. Many want that possibility as their right. This, too, means that democracy—and other ideas as well—have international implications. Third, some countries, including the United States, have pressured other states to adopt democracy, sometimes even intervening militarily to achieve this end. This again has clear international implications. Fourth, some analysts have argued that the global trend toward democracy is the beginning of a new global democratic age, or as one put it, "the end of mankind's ideological evolution and the universalization of Western liberal democracy as the final form of government."[7]

Whether this is true is open to debate, but there is no doubt that another trend often closely linked to democratization, **privatization,** is also gaining strength. Privatization is the economic process of turning state-owned and -operated businesses, industries, and services over to the private sector. Linked to democratization because it is so pronounced in Latin America and the former communist states where democratization has made great strides, it is a trend that also exists in countries such as China and Cuba where democratization has made little progress.

The concept of privatization is based on two major arguments, both grounded in the fact that with few exceptions, the market economies of East Asia, Europe, and North America grew more rapidly during the 1970s and 1980s than did the centrally planned and regulated economies of the Developing World and the former communist states. The first argument is that businesses, industries, and services can be operated more efficiently and economically by the private sector than by government. The second argument is that market economic forces allocate resources and determine prices better than government bureaucrats.

The scope of privatization varies widely from country to country. In some countries such as Argentina, privatization was pursued vigorously as the operation and ownership of roads, defense industries, power industries, airlines, and consumer goods industries were turned over to the private sector. Other countries such as China maintained a large government role in the economy even as they encouraged individuals and privately owned businesses to become more active.

Privatization also has several international implications. First, private businesses often find it easier to work with other private businesses than with governments. Some analysts argue that privatization therefore encourages international trade. Second, when states encourage private ownership, they often make it easier for multinational corporations to expand. This means that privatization encourages the growth of types of international actors other than the state. Third, when states privatize, they also often enact policies that make it easier for foreign direct investment to take place. This encourages transnational economic linkages.[8]

Democratization and privatization are thus two important factors that are helping reshape the world we live in. Both are primarily domestic phenomena, but their international implications are considerable.

Regional and Global Integration

In many areas of the world, the 1990s also witnessed the emergence of a trend toward **regional integration.** Spurred primarily by economic advantage, this trend was most evident in the development of **free trade areas,** or groups of states between which all economic barriers were removed, in several geographical areas of the world. Based on the argument that the removal of such barriers would accelerate economic growth and improve economic vitality, major free trade areas or near free trade areas had been negotiated by the early 1990s in Europe (the European Union, with at first 12 and by 1995 15 members), North America (the North American Free Trade Area, with three members), South America (MERCOSUR, with four members), and Southeast Asia (the Association of Southeast Asian Nations, which expanded to seven states when Vietnam joined in 1995).

In the mid–1990s, the basis for more extensive regional integration was laid with the initiation of plans for extremely large free trade areas in the Pacific and the Americas. In 1994, 18 Asian and American countries, including the United States, approved the Asian–Pacific Economic Cooperation (APEC) agreement, which committed all signatory states to dismantle barriers to international trade between member states by 2020. With China, Japan, the United States, and fifteen other countries in APEC, this free trade area by itself includes approximately 40 percent of all the people in the world and nearly half of the world's economic production. And for the United States, whose trans-Pacific trade is already about 50 percent larger than is trans-Atlantic trade, the implications of APEC are immense.

Shortly after APEC was signed, regional integration in the Americas was boosted when 34 Western Hemisphere states concluded the Free Trade Area of the Americas (FTAA), at the Summit of the Americas in Miami in December 1994. Under FTAA, Western Hemisphere states pledged to work to eliminate all trade barriers between them by 2010. For the United States, the implications of FTAA were again sizable, with U.S. exports to Latin America even in the absence of FTAA projected to surpass U.S. exports to Europe as early as 2005.

The trend toward regional integration was accompanied by a trend toward **global integration.** Again, the primary impetus was economics. On the global level, the clearest evidence of a trend toward global integration was a new General Agreement on Tariffs and Trade (GATT) concluded in 1994. Negotiated over many years, the new GATT agreement was originally signed by 123 states and projected to reduce tariffs by an estimated $750 billion during its first ten years. The GATT agreement over time will eliminate many quotas and other noneconomic barriers to trade and has the potential to alter significantly international economic relations.[9]

Trends toward regional and global integration were well in place by 2000. Some analysts concluded that certain regions and even the world had already become integrated, but others were more skeptical, arguing that neither regionalization nor globalization had become irreversible. Nevertheless, by 2000, no one could deny that such trends were firmly in place.

Advances in Information and Communication Technologies

Advances in information and communication technologies were critically important in spurring democratization, privatization, regionalization, and globalization. But their impacts stretched far beyond these areas as well into virtually every human endeavor, changing the ways people lived, worked, played, and thought. Indeed, the changes that these technologies brought about and promised to bring about in the late twentieth and early twenty-first century led many scholars and analysts to call the present era the Information Age.[10]

A host of different technologies created the Information Age. Fiber optic, wireless, computer advances, better human-computer interaction, improved satellites, digital signal processing, digital compression, and advanced networking all increased the capacity, flexibility, and speed of global communications. The Internet and World Wide Web also made it easier for people in widely separate locations to communicate.

Some observers maintained that the growth of transborder electronic data, information, and financial flows had become so great by the early twenty-first century that a single global marketplace existed. On an individual level, electronic mail and facsimiles link many people. Much of the personal use of these technologies is for social, educational, and business purposes, but on two occasions, during the Tiananmen Square massacre in China in 1989 and during the Soviet coup attempt in 1991, electronic mail and facsimiles played a major political role keeping people in the outside world connected to individuals in China and the USSR. At the same time, the international media provided foreign perspectives and outlooks to every major media outlet in the world, thereby creating a degree of global connectivity, if not community, to a greater extent than even before.[11]

The Resurgence of Nationalism

Nationalism also reemerged in the 1980s and 1990s as a potent force for reshaping international affairs. However, unlike economics and technology, which appeared to be forces that linked international actors together via trade, the **resurgence of nationalism** appeared to be a force that often—but not always—drove states apart. Indeed, in cases such as Czechoslovakia, the Soviet Union, and Yugoslavia, nationalism in the 1990s even broke up established states when ethnic groups that had long been members of a multinational state demanded—and sometimes fought for—their own independent state.

Nationalism comes from the concept of a "nation," which is simply a grouping of people who view themselves as linked to one another. People who consider themselves to be ethnically, culturally, linguistically, religiously, or in some other way linked may be considered a nation. Nationalism in turn is the psychological force that binds such people together. Specifically, nationalism is the feelings of attachment to one another that members of a nation have, and the sense of pride that members of a nation have in themselves and their nation.

Nationalism is not a new arrival on the international scene. It has been a potent force for several centuries, and it remained important during the post–World War II era both in contributing to the dissolution of colonial empires and in adding to the rivalry in the East–West conflict.

But paradoxically, both the struggle against colonialism and the existence of the East–West conflict in some ways dampened the expression of nationalism. With the struggle against colonialism identifying the colonial country as the primary enemy, national groups in colonial areas sometimes temporarily set aside their differences, concentrating instead on the struggle against the colonial power. And for countries centrally involved in the East–West conflict, the dangers of that conflict often influenced national groups to accept their inclusion in the state in which they found themselves.

As traditional colonial empires disappeared in the 1970s and as the East–West conflict dissipated in the late 1980s, this situation began to change. As a result, long-repressed nationalist sentiment began to emerge in states that included several ethnic, cultural, linguistic, or religious groups.

In several cases, this resurgence of nationalism led to the breakup of established states. This occurred in Yugoslavia and Czechoslovakia. The resurgence of nationalism among its diverse peoples was also one of the leading causes of the dissolution of the Soviet Union.

In other states such as India, Spain, Pakistan, and Iraq, separatist ethnic groups fought the established state government in efforts to establish their own independent states. Even in Belgium, Canada, and Great Britain, separatist ethnic groups made known their desire to obtain independence and establish separate ethnically based states, although in these cases, the efforts were usually peaceful.

By 2000, then, it was not a certainty that the world would move toward regional or global integration based on economic advantage or technical advances. In many regions, a resurgence of nationalism indicated that smaller nationally based international actors might be the hallmark of the emerging new international system rather than larger economically based or technically created international actors.

The Emergence of Global Problems

Throughout the 1990s, widespread awareness about problems whose solutions had to be global in scope grew in the international community. These problems included terrorism, drugs, and environmental deterioration. As was the case with the rediscovery of economics, the emergence of trends toward regional and global integration, and the resurgence of nationalism, it is not possible to point to a single event or trend as the beginning of the growth of awareness about the **emergence of global problems.** Nevertheless, such awareness has grown. It has immense implications for contemporary international relations.

Terrorism is particularly vexing. No single source of terrorism exists. Sometimes, states support terrorism. U.S. officials frequently point to North Korea, Libya, and Iran as states that plan and sponsor terrorist attacks.[12] Other times, sub-state actors such as drug cartels, religious fundamentalists, and radical political movements or individuals launch terrorist attacks to further their own political agendas. From the U. S. perspective, the single most dangerous source of terrorism in the early twenty-first century was the terrorist network established and funded by Ossama bin Ladn, a wealthy Saudi Arabian former businessman.

At the same time, defining terrorism is a difficult task. Indeed, several countries throughout the world consider the United States, several Western European states, and Israel as undertaking terrorist actions. We will return to the question of defining terrorism later.

Here, we will concentrate simply on the issues of identifying and coping with terrorism, which are two completely different things. Given the necessity to acquire and collate large amounts of timely information about terrorist intentions and movements and to coordinate responses against planned terrorist attacks or terrorists themselves, an international response to the terrorist problem is clearly required. Single states by themselves rarely have the wherewithal to respond effectively to terrorist activity.

Even this simple observation gives rise to several difficult questions. When is it legitimate for a state to use military power to defend its interests? What is terrorism, and is it only a weapon that the weak use against the strong? Are terrorists sometimes more powerful than states, or does it only seem that way? To what extent should governments act to protect their citizens living or traveling overseas?

The international drug situation presents similarly difficult issues, and it, too, transcends national boundaries. Although the United States probably has the world's most serious drug problem, the abuse of drugs is widespread in Europe, Russia, China, and many Developing World states as well.

Again, identifying the problem is not enough. With drugs originating in South America, Southeast Asia, and elsewhere; with billions of dollars involved in illegal international drug traffic; with drug traffickers willing to use both directed and indiscriminate violence; and with demand for drugs apparent in most societies, stemming the tide of drugs is a multifaceted problem that requires the cooperation and integration of domestic and international policies from the entire international community. Whether the international community is up to the challenge remains to be seen.

The international community's response to yet another emerging global problem, environmental deterioration, gives cause for both optimism and pessimism. On the optimistic side of the ledger, within two years of the confirmation that the release of manmade chloroflourocarbons into the atmosphere played a major role in creating a hole in the earth's ozone layer over the South Pole, the states of the world in the 1987 Montreal Protocol agreed to limit the production and use of chloroflourocarbons. Quick international cooperation on global problems is thus demonstrably possible.

On a more pessimistic note, international disagreement on environmental issues is often more prevalent than agreement. For example, in 1990, the United States, the Soviet Union, and Japan opposed international efforts to limit carbon dioxide emissions into the atmosphere to prevent global warming, arguing that more research had to be undertaken before a link between global warming and carbon dioxide emissions could be established. The U.S. continued to oppose significant reductions in carbon dioxide emissions at the Rio Earth Summit in 1992. But by the time the United States and most developed states at the 1997 Kyoto Environmental Summit supported the reduction of emissions, many developing states had changed their position, concluding that reducing carbon dioxide emissions would curtail their economic development.[13] No significant agreement was thus possible.

Despite these difficulties in moving toward a broad international commitment to environmental protection and improvement, there is widespread recognition that the global environment is deteriorating. There is equally widespread recognition that unprecedented international cooperation is needed to halt and reverse that deterioration. A certain sense of "global consciousness" may thus be developing, not only on environmental issues, but also on terrorism, drugs, and other global problems.

Does this imply that the concept of national sovereignty may be increasingly challenged? May it even portend that states may curtail their own short-term growth or economic well-being in the interests of securing a greater long-term global good? We are a long way from answering these and related questions, but until recently, these questions could not even be seriously asked.

Altogether, the collapse of Eastern European and Soviet communism, the reemergence of economics, democratization and privatization, the movement toward regional and global integration, the emergence of new information and communication technologies, the resurgence of nationalism, and the emergence of global problems are revolutionizing international relations. What will emerge as the new international system is not clear, but it is clear that the old system is no more.

The purposes of this text flow directly from these forces for change, the questions they raise, and the need to move students of international affairs closer to answers to these and other questions. Before we clarify how this text handles these tasks, we first discuss other attempts that have been made to make the study of international relations more comprehensible.

ANALYZING CONTEMPORARY INTERNATIONAL RELATIONS

Without doubt, international relations appear at times bewildering. Students may at times feel that their efforts to understand the complexities of international affairs today are futile.

The task is difficult, but not futile. It requires patience and persistence as well as logical inquiry and flexible perspectives. As argued earlier, contemporary international relations are interdependent. Our task to achieve understanding is complicated because seemingly unrelated actions and events in different areas of the world over time combine to affect actions and events in other regions of the world. Actions and events are demonstrably interdependent, and as we improve our ability to understand the causes of and reasons behind this interdependence, we improve our ability to understand contemporary international relations.

How can this task best be approached? There is no single answer to this question. Throughout history, analysts of international relations have differed in their approach to their field. Here, we will present only the most important.

Diplomatic History and Strategic/Geopolitical Analyses

During the late nineteenth and early twentieth centuries, the study of international relations centered around **diplomatic history.** Who did what to whom at a particular time and place were the main features of diplomatic history. This methodology concentrated on states as the main actors in international relations and included the study of the major diplomats and ministers of the period. Detailed accuracy was required and obtained, but seldom, if ever, were causal connections or comprehensive analyses sought. As a means for understanding a particular series of events, diplomatic history was (and is) excellent; as a means for understanding broader sweeps of international relations or for developing a theoretical basis for the study of international relations, diplomatic history was (and is) of limited utility.

Other methodologies that were developed during the nineteenth and early twentieth centuries viewed international relations on a global scale. **Strategic and geopolitical analyses,** methodologies in wide use even today, trace their roots to concepts developed by U.S. Admiral Alfred Mahan during the late nineteenth century and British geographer Sir Halford Mackinder during the early twentieth century. To Mahan, the world's oceans were its highways, and whoever controlled them could control the course of international relations. Mahan was therefore a major proponent of sea power and advocated the development of a powerful American navy and the acquisition of overseas bases to support that navy. Not surprisingly, Mahan based most of his analysis on Great Britain and its Royal Navy.[14]

Sir Halford Mackinder, on the other hand, emphasized the importance of land power. To Mackinder, whichever country dominated the center of the Eurasian land mass would dominate world politics. Mackinder called this area the "heartland." The heartland was in turn surrounded by coastal areas that Mackinder termed the "rimland." The state that controlled the heartland, Mackinder believed, could exert power as it desired against rimland areas and, because of its central position, could emerge victorious. Mackinder interpreted European history as a record of different countries attempting to achieve control of the heartland and of other countries attempting to prevent that from occurring.[15]

Socioeconomic Theories of International Relations

Other scholars and analysts in the nineteenth and twentieth centuries adopted more comprehensive approaches to understanding international relations. Some such as Karl Marx and Vladimir Ilyich Lenin developed theories that claimed to explain not just the way international relations worked, but also the way all human societies developed and operated.

Marxism was the most influential socioeconomic theory.[16] To Marx, the history of humankind was the history of the struggle of economic classes. Every human society, Marx believed, reflected the economic structure that dominated within it. All human activities—politics, law, religion, sports, business, war, the arts, and so on—were products of the dominant economic structure, he argued.

Marx maintained that the economic class that owned the means of production used any means that it could, but particularly the state, to maintain control. Marx predicted that in all societies except communist ones, those who owned the means of production would exploit those who worked for them, getting richer while the working class became poorer and more desperate. Class conflict was inevitable in all noncommunist societies, Marx said.

Marx interpreted all human history, not just international relations, in light of his theory. History, Marx theorized, began with a primitive form of communism that dissolved into an owner/slave relationship in which a few strong men subjugated the many weak. The strong then set up a complicated system of social relationships including the state and religion to assure their dominance.

Gradually, however, means of production changed. Intensive agriculture allowed a new class of nobility to develop, the lords and kings of the Middle Ages. Lords and kings owned the land, and serfs and peasants worked it for them and made them rich. The state and religion were used by lords and kings to assure their control.

In time, industrial production replaced agricultural production as the primary economic activity. Industrial capitalists—the bourgeoisie—replaced lords and kings as the owners, while the industrial worker—the proletariat—replaced serfs and peasants. But one thing remained constant, Marx asserted: owners grew wealthy off the sweat of the workers' brow. Eventually, Marx predicted, the workers' condition would deteriorate so much that they would rise up in revolution against the capitalists, overthrow them and their unjust institutions, and create a new just society.

This just society would be based on socialism, where each worked according to ability and received according to work. Over time, socialism would evolve into communism, where each worked according to ability and received according to need. This, Marx predicted, would end "the exploitation of man by man."

Lenin, a Russian revolutionary and eventually the founder of the Soviet Union, accepted most of Marx's theories and developed one of his own that applied specifically to the international relations of the early twentieth century. This was Lenin's theory of **imperialism,** which he set forth in his 1912 study *Imperialism—The Highest Stage of Capitalism.*[17]

To Lenin, the capitalist economic system was the driving force behind colonization, global empires, and war. Lenin believed that capitalist states needed new markets, inexpensive resources, and cheap labor to keep their economies going. Thus, they divided the world into vast colonial holdings to acquire these needs and to increase their profits. Imperialism was therefore the product of the capitalist system, Lenin argued. And as imperialist states struggled for new markets, inexpensive resources, and cheap labor, all to increase profits, they came into conflict with one another.

This, Lenin believed, was why World War I occurred. Capitalism inevitably led to imperialism, the Soviet Union's founder asserted, and imperialism inevitably led to war. Until recently, communists almost universally accepted both Marx's views of history and economics and Lenin's views of imperialism.

Political Idealism and National Socialism

The catastrophy of World War I brought forth new methods of analyzing international relations. Two new schools of thought were particularly important, one centered around the question of how best to prevent another major international conflict, the other centered around the question of how best to assert and establish national power. These two new major schools of thought were generally labeled **political idealism** and **national socialism** (or fascism), and they dominated Western analysis of international relations between World War I and World War II.

Both schools of thought were heavily policy-oriented, but they reached totally different conclusions. To the political idealists (there were many variations of them), human beings were basically good and generally sought the welfare of others as well as themselves.[18] The idealists for the most part believed that bad structural and institutional arrangements on a worldwide basis created bad human behavior on an individual basis. Therefore, they argued, war was not inevitable, but was caused by bad structural and institutional arrangements.

War could be prevented, political idealism taught, only if proper structures could be created. Political idealists, as a result, advocated one or more of a number of policy prescriptions, all of which were implemented to one degree or another during the interwar years. To some, international cooperative institutions would help prevent war. The League of Nations in particular would serve as a forum to which nations could bring their disputes, and in extreme cases, all of the nations of the League would act against an aggressor nation to ensure peace. This principle of collective security required joint action and a clear ability to define an aggressor. The events that led up to World War II showed the League could not successfully undertake either task.

To other political idealists, the rule of international law would bring peace. The Kellogg–Briand Pact of 1928 was one such attempt. It declared that all signatory nations had renounced war as an instrument of national policy except in cases of self-defense. Here, it is worth noting that before World War I, international conventions such as the Hague Conferences of 1899 and 1907 sought to establish laws *of* war, whereas the postwar political idealists sought to create laws *against* war.

Still other political idealists believed that weapons themselves were the cause of war. A number of studies in the interwar era asserted that the major arms manufacturers such as Krupp had instigated World War I for profit. As a result of these studies, some political idealists argued that if the "merchants of death" could be curbed and the number of weapons reduced, then war would not occur. The Washington Naval Treaties of 1921–1922, the most successful of which established a ratio of capital ships that each nation could have in relation to other nations, were the highwater marks for this approach.

Numerous other political idealists advocated reform of internal social systems, redistribution of wealth and ownership, creation of an international system of free trade, or establishment of universally accepted criteria for self-determination.

Again, however, caution must be exercised, for the political idealist school was neither as unified, as organized, nor as simplistic as the preceding discussion might suggest. Sophisticated men and women, appalled by the horror of modern war, sought ways to prevent its recurrence, and if the competing school of national socialism (fascism) had not developed as rapidly as it did, they might have been successful for a longer period of time.

National socialism was also policy-oriented, but it advocated the growth and enhancement of national power. Under national socialism, the German variant of which was called Nazism, the entire industrial and productive capacity of the nation-state and all the energies of its population were to be devoted to strengthening the state. The national leader was deified and the military was glorified. Territorial expansion was considered proof of the superiority of the system. As a school of analysis of international relations, fascism in all of its variants stated simply that "might makes right," and that the most powerful nation-state should rightfully dictate to weaker nation-states. The fascist leaders of Germany and Italy believed war was inevitable, and if it was inevitable, they meant to win it.[19]

With militarism rampant in Germany, Italy, and Japan, the 1930s became a decade of conflict. Japan attacked Manchuria in 1931, Italy invaded Ethiopia in 1935, and Germany repudiated numerous provisions of the Treaty of Versailles, which formally concluded World War I. By 1939, Germany had remilitarized the Rhineland, taken over Austria, and annexed much of Czechoslovakia following the 1938 Munich Agreement. The appeasement at Munich, where Great Britain and France agreed to the German annexation of the Sudetenland portion of Czechoslovakia, convinced Hitler that neither Great Britain nor France would fight. On September 1, 1939, German forces attacked Poland, and World War II began. Political idealism had proven insufficient to the task of preventing war.[20]

Political Realism

To some political idealism had failed because it had not been universalized. To others, it had failed because it had not been given long enough a time to succeed. But to many others, political idealism's failure to prevent war was the inevitable result of what they believed were political idealism's naive and erroneous assumptions. Human beings were *not* inherently good, argued the post–World War II **political realists,** led in the United States by Hans Morgenthau, Reinhold Niebuhr, George Kennan, and Henry Kissinger.[21] At best, humans had equal capacities for bad and good; at worst, they had an instinctive desire to dominate each other. War, therefore, was always a possibility and in many instances a probability.

The responsibility of each state, according to this outlook of **realpolitik,** was to provide for its own defense and security. Collective security became a theoretical nicety that could be used in alliances and international organizations to enhance a state's security, but collective security could not be relied on to guarantee it. The measure of the wisdom of a proposed national policy or action, to the political realist, was whether that policy or action furthered the national interest, most often defined by proponents of realpolitik as the acquisition of power in any of its various forms, but most particularly as the acquisition of military power. The logic of realpolitik dictated that peace could never be assured, but it could be attained because in a world where national policies were based on realpolitik's worldview, a balance of power would result as different states sought to assure their own security and self-interest by aligning against any state that appeared too powerful.

Realpolitik urged primacy of foreign policy over domestic policy, maintenance of large and capable military forces, and emphasis on nationalism. It also asserted the primacy of states as international actors, considered states to be unitary actors with a single decision-making process, maintained that states were essentially rational in their actions, and argued that national security was the most important international issue.

The language and policy prescripts of realpolitik have dominated U.S. government policy since World War II. Every American president since that war, with the possible exceptions of Jimmy Carter and Bill Clinton, has based his policies on its conceptual tenets. But questions were raised about realpolitik in academia, the government, and other circles as well. In a nuclear era, did realpolitik's emphasis on the military make national annihilation a likely outcome? How could realpolitik explain the move in Western Europe and elsewhere toward regional integration? In a world in which national borders and national interests were becoming increasingly less well-defined, who could tell what did and what did not further the national interest? Indeed, as more and more colonial areas sought and received their independence, and as several major states broke up as a result of internal ethnic demands for national self-determination, the question of whether or not an area was a nation-state became increasingly relevant. In all cases, realpolitik failed to determine who within a nation-state should define the national interest. Realpolitik too often relied on simple assertions, and thus, in skeptical minds, its shortcomings became increasingly clear. Critics of realpolitik argued that more scientific and less assertive methodologies were needed to enhance the study of international relations.

Behavioralism

The new emphasis on the scientific study of international relations was call **behavioral-ism.** During the 1950s and 1960s, more and more scholars and analysts accepted the need for rigorous, systematic, and scientific study of international relations, but few agreed how to do this.[22]

To behavioralists, the study of international relations had to include a clear statement of a problem, an analysis of the variables in the problem, additional analysis of the relationships between those variables, and a discussion of the conditions under which those relationships would hold. The results had to be replicable and free from biases introduced by external factors. The behavioral revolution demanded that theories derived from behavioral analysis be consistent with all available facts and not solely with those that fit the theories. "The exception that proved the rule" was not acceptable to the behavioralist.

Behavioralism itself has been regularly criticized, at least in part because of the inability of its proponents to agree on anything other than the broadest methodologies. Also, behavioralists have tended to study quantifiable events, a fact that has led some to criticize behavioralists as having limited relevance to the "real world" of international relations. Other critics argue that although the objectives of behavioral analysis are laudable, its findings are irrelevant because the rapidity of change in the modern world has altered the conditions of interrelationships between the variables the behavioralists study even before they complete their analysis. Historical accuracy thus yields policy irrelevance, critics of behavioralism often maintain.

More Recent Schools

Other schools of analysis of international relations emerged during and after World War II. Some were new theories and methods of analysis, but others were refinements of old theories and methods of analysis that resulted from criticism directed toward the old theories.

Neorealism, also called **structural realism**, emerged as a "new and improved" version of realism. According to neorealists, international events can best be explained by examining the international distribution of power rather than the power that each individual state actor has. Neorealists often use **game theory**, that is, an approach to decision-making based on the assumption that states act rationally in situations of competition to achieve their objectives, as a method of analysis. With their emphasis on the structure of the international system, many neorealists de-emphasize the role of willpower, diplomacy, and other elements central to realism. Nevertheless, their central focus remains on power.

Functionalism also emerged after World War II as an influential way to explain how international affairs worked. According to functionalists, the chances for peace and stability are promoted by transnational political and economic institutions that help states work together to achieve objectives and overcome differences. Functionalists—and much of the international commmunity—thus put their hopes in the United Nations, the World Bank, and other international institutions as mechanisms that would promote peace and stability.

The development of U.S.–Soviet rivalry and the Cold War proved the predictions and hopes of functionalists to be overly optimistic. However, as happened with realism, a "new and improved" version of functionalism emerged during the later decades of the twentieth century. Called **neofunctionalism**, the new theory argued that while specialized agencies may be insufficient by themselves to promote peace and stability, those objectives could be achieved by the creation of more generalized political bodies with greater degrees of political and economic authority such as the European Union.

Other scholars took more radical approaches to the study of international affairs, arguing that even the new approaches overlooked or ignored key elements or were based on false premises. One such approach centered on gender and provided a **feminist perspective on international relations**.[23] It pointed out that both the analysis and the practice of international relations had historically been based on male-dominated thinking. Indeed, until relatively recently, few females obtained leading roles in international diplomacy or in the international policy community, and few females entered academic or analytical professions concerned with international relations. Most feminist perspectives on international relations argue further that this male dominance leads states to be aggressive and favorably disposed toward conflict.

On the analytical side, male dominance produces a male-oriented bias, most proponents of gender studies argue, that skewed and distorted one's ability to understand international relations and frustrated the ability of states and other international actors to produce and implement more balanced policies. Only the entrance of more females into the study and practice of international relations can overcome the errors introduced by male oriented biases, proponents of gender based studies of international relations maintain.

Critics of feminist perspectives on international relations cannot and do not disagree with the observation that until recently, the analysis and the practice of international relations has been male dominated. Rather, they argue that male domination of analysis and policy has no real importance. Instead, those who reject feminist critiques of international relations maintain that as females enter the international policy and analytical communities, they will respond to the same inputs and reach the same conclusions and policy preferences as their male counterparts. The debate thus continues.

Other scholars argue that in the post–Cold War world, the study of international interactions of states and other international actors should be identified simply as **foreign policy analysis.** This is an all-encompassing approach that has as its central thrust the analysis and understanding of "the intentions, statements, and actions of an actor—often but not always a state—directed toward the external world and the response of other actors to those intentions, statements, and actions."[24] Foreign policy analysis uses diverse approaches and methods including comparative foreign policy analysis and events data analysis;[25] social and political psychology, perception, and culture;[26] bureaucratic politics; the analysis of domestic policies as inputs to foreign policy; area studies; decision theory; economic and strategic analysis; and a host of other analytical methods and tools. Foreign policy analysis can be descriptive, explanatory, or predictive.

Critics of foreign policy analysis sometimes assert that it is not a "real" school of analysis because of its eclectic and all-encompassing nature. How can something be considered a "school," they ask, when it is willing to accept virtually any method of analysis? Conversely, defenders argue that by including all issues pertaining to the interactions of international actors within a single field of study and by applying a variety of different approaches, methods, and tools to that study, foreign policy analysis provides the best opportunity to understand fully the way international affairs and the international system work.

Historically, then, the last century has provided no definitive answer to the original question: "How can we best improve our ability to understand contemporary international relations?" Numerous methodologies claim to be most accurate but, as before, little empirical evidence supports any of their claims. The methodologies discussed here coexist today, and probably will coexist in the future as well. Some political idealists and political realists now prefer to be identified as traditionalists, and some behavioralists believe they have moved into a postbehavioral era, but the fundamental fact remains that analysts of international relations themselves do not agree on how best to improve their own understanding. Table 1-2 provides a useful representation of the differences between some of the more prominent methods of analyzing international relations.[27]

LEVELS OF ANALYSIS AS AN ANALYTICAL TOOL

One analytical tool that is widely accepted in international affairs is the concept of **levels of analysis.** In its simplest form, the levels-of-analysis concept forces students of international affairs to recognize that international events flow from many different sources, and that there is rarely a single "correct" way to examine an international event.

Clarifying the Need

A few examples may clarify the point. For example, the Libyan government under Muammar Qadhafi has actively aided and abetted anti-American terrorist attacks around the world. Many Americans therefore condemn Libya and all Libyans. But is this actually a valid response? Is Libyan state-supported terrorism a result of the Libyan people's

TABLE 1-2   Differences between Several Prominent Methods of Analyzing International Relations

	Diplomatic History	Marxism	Realism	Idealism	Behavior-ialism	Foreign Policy Analysis
Primary actors	Nation-states; diplomats	Economic classes	Nation-states	Many	Many	Many
Primary issues	Personalities; national security	Economics; others subsidiary	National security	Morality	Many	Many
Method of analysis	Historical record	Economic class	Capabilities of state	Values	Quantitative	Many
Perspective	Primarily national	National and global	National	National, regional, or global	National, regional, or global	Many

animosity toward the United States, the Libyan government's dislike of the United States, or Muammar Qadhafi's own personal predilections?

Another example is also helpful. In May 1987, the U.S. Navy frigate *Stark,* on patrol in the Persian Gulf, was attacked by an Iraqi warplane. Thirty-seven American sailors were killed, and the *Stark* was severely damaged. Was the attack intentionally planned by the Iraqi government, perhaps to indicate Iraq's displeasure with earlier U.S. arms sales to Iran? Was it the result of a decision by an individual Iraqi pilot to "get even" with the United States for a real or imagined U.S. slight? Or was it as both the United States and Iraqi governments asserted, simply a "ghastly error"?

A final example is equally poignant. In 1999, the United States during the war in Kosovo bombed the Chinese embassy in Belgrade, Yugoslavia. Several people were killed, and China was incensed. The U.S. said that the bombing was an accident, the result both of planners at NATO headquarters using old and outdated information and of a breakdown in NATO procedures to make sure that mistakes did not occur. The U.S. defense was that the attack was a ghastly mistake caused by individual human error and oversight.

China rejected these explanations. To China, the attack was a clear and conscious effort by the United States to punish China for a number of disagreements that it had with the United States on issues ranging from arms sales to trade to human rights. From Beijing's perspective, the attack was not the result of human error, but the result of government policy.

Who was right, the United States or China?

Levels of Analysis

These uncertainties are sometimes referred to as "the levels-of-analysis problem."[28] The concept is best viewed and used as a tool to help us understand international affairs. Levels of analysis help us comprehend that all individuals, whether they be the ruler of Libya or the president of the United States, may be acting on purely individualistic motives or they may be acting on a broad-based statewide consensus on national interest. Between the extremes of action for the individual and action for even a global system, numerous levels exist at which foreign policy can be made and studied. Figure 1-1 illustrates several of these other levels.[29]

Each level of analysis casts different light on why international actors act as they do. At the individual level of analysis, individual decision makers are studied. Important factors

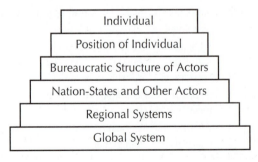

FIGURE 1-1   **Levels of analysis in international relations.**

considered here are the values that a decision maker holds; the views that a decision maker has of himself or herself, the actor that he or she acts for, and the world; and how the decision maker makes decisions. Traditionalists classify these studies as memoirs or biographies, whereas behavioralists class them as studies of "elite ideosyncratic behavior" or "operational codes." At this level of analysis, the unifying factor is that the individual decision maker is the primary—and sometimes exclusive—unit of analysis. This level of analysis, for example, helps us to understand that Jimmy Carter's strong Christian beliefs and values were important inputs to U.S. human rights policies during the Carter presidency.

A second level of analysis is the position that an individual holds in the decision-making structure. This level of analysis takes into account that positions of responsibility often influence a person's views of life, the world, domestic and international issues, and so on. It recognizes the reality that when it comes to issues, "where you stand depends on where you sit." For example, this level of analysis allows us to understand why Thomas Jefferson opposed an expansion of power by the national government before he became president, but when he became president he sought greater power for the national government so the Louisiana Purchase could take place. Traditionalists and behavioralists both find this level of analysis useful.

A third level of analysis is the bureaucratic structure of actors. This level emphasizes the competition for power and influence between organizations and bureaucracies at the subactor level as a primary variable in understanding the policy of actors. Analyzing policy at the bureaucratic structure level helps the student understand, for example, why the U.S. Army and U.S. Air Force both had long-range missile programs during the 1950s. It also offers one explanation why both Air Force bombers and Navy jets were used in the 1986 U.S. air raid against terrorist training centers in Libya. Traditionalists rarely use this approach, whereas behavioralists use it in a variety of forms, most notably under the terminology of "bureaucratic rivalry" or "linkage politics."

A fourth level of analysis is the international actor itself. In its purest form, this level views each actor as a monolithic entity with neither internal divisions nor external attractions. It sees each actor's policy as the result of a rational decision-making process that keeps interests and objectives paramount throughout the decision-making process. Sometimes called the "rational actor" model, this level of analysis is used most often by traditionalists. Behavioralists deride it as the "billiard ball" approach to international affairs.

A fifth level of analysis is that of the regional system. Those who approach issues from a regional system perspective argue that actor-level analyses and subactor analyses do not allow enough scope to understand the actual dimensions of a given problem. The regional level of analysis, for example, would argue that the Vietnam War could best be understood not as a localized war, but as one that was regional in scope; the El Salvador insurgencies of the 1980s and 1990s could also best be understood as part of a regional Central America-wide phenomenon. Regional analysis is not confined to military issues; the problem of how to cope with acid rain, for example, may well require regional analyses.

A sixth level of analysis centers around the global system. The global level of analysis asserts that even the regional level is too confining. For example, a global level of analysis indicates that world hunger is a problem caused not by too little food in the world, but by the uneven distribution of food. A global level of analysis also would emphasize the global environmental consequences of the "greenhouse effect," or global warming, as well as the global impact of the deterioration of the ozone layer. Analysis at the global system level is often used in economics. For example, in 1997 and 1998, as the economies of East Asian states declined precipitously, economists developed global models that predicted where and how the effects of East Asian's economic trauma would spread throughout the world. Policymakers in individual countries and at international institutions like the World Bank and the International Monetary Fund then used these models to implement policies to minimize the effects of East Asia's economic woes both in the region and beyond. Traditionalists and behavioralists alike have found this level of analysis useful.

Summation

Again, each level of analysis casts a different light on why actors act as they do. Thus, for analysts of international affairs, an understanding of the levels-of-analysis problem is important because it allows them to improve their understanding of how and why an international actor acts as it does. It allows them to understand, for example, that John Kennedy put a naval quarantine around Cuba during the 1962 Cuban Missile Crisis both because he believed that the United States' national interest demanded that Soviet missiles be withdrawn and because Robert Kennedy, in response to an Air Force plan that the missiles be removed by an air attack, declared that he did not want his brother to go down in history as "another Tojo." (Tojo was the Japanese Minister of War who initiated the attack on Pearl Harbor.[30])

An understanding of the levels-of-analysis problem is critical if the student of international affairs hopes to understand the forces of change that affect contemporary international affairs. The seven forces for change with which we began our analysis in this chapter provide excellent examples. Unless a student understands that Mikhail Gorbachev had his own perspective on change within the former USSR and Eastern Europe (Level 1), that Gorbachev's own perspective was influenced by his position as Soviet leader (Level 2), and that different organizations and bureaucracies within the former USSR competed to promote and defend their own positions (Level 3), that students cannot understand events in the former USSR and Eastern Europe, nor how those events interacted with the international system. Similarly, unless a student understands that national economic concerns including employment, debt, and the balance of trade often drive policy at the state level (Level 4), he or she will overlook major forces in international affairs. Finally, unless a student understands that acid rain requires at a minimum regional responses (Level 5) and other types of environmental deterioration may require global responses (Level 6), that student will not understand emerging regional and global perspectives on contemporary international relations. Importantly, given that all these forces and levels of analysis interact with one another, unless all levels are understood, none can be truly understood.

 ## FRAMEWORKS FOR UNDERSTANDING

Students may still feel that their efforts to understand international relations are futile. However, they are not. In reality, students are not much worse off than analysts, and in some ways, they are better off. Students may not yet have a grasp of some of the more esoteric issues and concepts involved in international relations, and in most instances they still may be willing to balance and assess the conflicting types of models, or paradigms, that different schools of analysis use.

To maximize our understanding of contemporary international relations, this text borrows heavily from many schools of analysis. It is wedded to none. By avoiding identification with a particular school of thought, this text proceeds from the assumption that many methods of analysis provide useful insights into the state of the world, but none provide perfect insight.

With this assumption in mind, the following 19 chapters are organized into six frameworks based on the questions that were asked following our discussion earlier in this chapter of some of the forces for change in contemporary international relations. Each framework examines a particular set of concepts critical to understanding international relations.

The first framework identifies and examines international actors. It discusses who and what they are, how they came to be what they are, and what their objectives are in international affairs. Nation-states, multinational corporations, international government organizations, nongovernmental organizations, and private individuals are all analyzed as actors in the international arena. The rationale for this framework is a simple one; one must understand who the participants are before international relations in its broader contexts can be understood. Some of the questions that the first framework approaches are:

- Who are the major actors in international affairs?
- What objectives do they seek?
- Who determines those objectives?
- Where did these actors come from?
- How important are they today?
- How are they changing?

Together, the actors that we examine in the first framework form an international system. We examine international systems in the second framework. First, the ways in which major international actors interact are explored in a chapter on how they make policy. Next, the evolution of international systems in the twentieth century is traced, with special emphasis on the bipolar system of the Cold War. Finally, the North–South conflict is examined. The second framework examines questions such as:

- How do states and other international actors formulate and implement their foreign policies?
- How did the international system evolve in the twentieth century?
- How did the East–West conflict begin and evolve?
- How and why did it end?
- What caused the North–South conflict, and how has it evolved?

Understanding who the actors are and how they form and fit into the international system is not enough. Because each of the actors has its own vantage point, each individual actor views itself—and others—as being somewhat different from other actors. In some instances, perceptions clash to such an extent that it is difficult to realize that the same actor or event is being described. Anyone who seeks to understand world politics must be aware of those differing perceptions and their impacts on the different policies of the various actors. Thus, the third framework stresses perceptual outlooks. Although the points of view of all types of actors are presented, the greatest emphasis is placed on the perceptions of states. Obviously, with almost 200 states in the international community, not all state outlooks are provided. Rather, outlooks are grouped into those of developed states and those of developing states. Although significant differences in perceptions exist between states in each group, there are also significant similarities between the outlooks of many states in each group. Questions that this framework analyzes are:

- How do actors view each other?
- How do actors view themselves?
- What has influenced the development of these perceptions?
- How do these perceptions affect policy?

The fourth framework analyzes the instruments that the various actors use as they seek to achieve their diverse objectives. It also discusses the utility of different instruments of power in different settings and details what constraints, if any, may operate on the use of a particular instrument. Economic capabilities, military power, sociopolitical influence, international law, and diplomacy are all examined as tools that are employed by international actors as they pursue their objectives. The questions examined in this framework include:

- What are the constituents of power?
- Why is one type of power useful in one instance but not in another?
- What constrains the employment of power?
- What are the differences between military, economic, and sociopolitical parameters of power?
- How do international law and diplomacy affect an actor's power?

The fifth framework discusses several contemporary global issues both as a statement of concern and an agenda for discussion. These issues are grouped into four chapters: 1. international political economics; 2. war, peace, and violence; 3. human rights and conflicts of values; and 4. the environment and health. Additional issues could also have been included, but exigencies of space prevent a more comprehensive listing and discussion. This framework discusses questions such as:

- Why are some countries economically underdeveloped and how can their development be speeded?
- Why do resource shortages exist and can their impact be lessened?
- How serious are global environmental problems?
- What causes war and how can war be avoided?
- What types of conflicts of values exist and why?

The sixth and final framework delves into what is sometimes called "futurology," that is, an effort to delineate the shape of both probable and preferable international futures and how we can move from one to the other. It is the only framework in this text that is speculative. Nonetheless, it is a significant chapter, for without having at least some understanding of the alternative futures we face and can fashion, even a comprehensive and detailed understanding of the present is a sterile and vacuous possession. In some respects, it approaches the most important questions in this or any other book:

- Where is the international community heading?
- Where do we want it to go?
- How can we help it get there?

With study, skill, work, and luck, this and subsequent generations will be able to answer these questions.

 KEY TERMS AND CONCEPTS

global complexity   many different countries, companies, and organizations play major roles in twenty first century international affairs, and they all have different interests, different objectives, and interact in different ways

global interdependence   the fact that events and actions in one region of the world often over time affect other events and actions in other regions of the world

economic interdependence   the mutual dependence of national economies on one another

global diversity   despite global interdependence and the new policies and technologies that promote it, the world remains incredibly diverse, with thousands of ethnic groups, nationalities, languages, value sets, etc.

global change   the twentieth century witnessed immense change in international affairs, and all indications are that this will continue in the twenty first century

collapse of communism   during the 1970s and 1980s, the Soviet economy deteriorated, Soviet citizens became disenchanted, and communism no longer motivated. To cope with this, Soviet leader Gorbachev instituted reforms that led to the fall of communism in Eastern Europe and eventually to the collapse of the U.S.S.R.

reemergence of economics   during the 1970s and 1980s, leaders increasingly recognized that economics played a major role in international relations. This was long understood, but for most of the post-World War II era, military and strategic affairs were of greatest importance and economic issues were lesser priorities

democratization   the process of moving from an autocratic or dictatorial political system to a democratic political system

privatization   the process of divesting governments of property and returning it to private ownership

regional integration   spurred by economics, a trend which became apparent in the 1980s and 1990s with the creation of regional trading zones such as the European Union, the North American Free Trade Area, and the Asia-Pacific Economic Cooperation agreement

free-trade area   a group of states between which all economic barriers to trade are removed

global integration   the trend toward globalization of markets

advances in information and communication technologies   advances in fiber optics, computers, human-computer interface, satellites, cellular capabilities, and other technologies that accelerated trends toward regional and global integration

resurgence of nationalism   in the 1980s and 1990s, many people reemphasized their ties to their ethnic and national groups, helping bring about the collapse of the Soviet Union and Yugoslavia and the growth of separatist trends in many countries in the world

emergence of global problems   in the late twentieth century, several international problems emerged such as terrorism, drugs, and the environment that could only be approached on a global basis

diplomatic history   a way to analyze international affairs that emphasizes who did what to whom at a particular time and place and stresses countries, individual leaders, and diplomats

strategic and geopolitical analyses   efforts to explain the course of international affairs on a global scale that stress military, economic, and geographical influences on state behavior

socioeconomic theories of international relations   theories that purport to explain international affairs as results of the interaction of social and economic forces, with Marxism as a leading example

Marxism   a socioeconomic theory that emphasizes historical stages, economic and material forces, and class analysis, and that predicts that contradictions in each historical era lead to a new dominant class

political idealism   a method of analysis of international relations that argues that defective structural and institutional arrangements on a global basis lead to flawed human behavior

national socialism   a political-economic system emphasizing political totalitarianism, economic centralization, and state direction of the means of production, also called fascism or nazism

political realism (realpolitik)   a method of analysis of international relations that argues that at best humankind has equal capacities for bad and good and at worst humankind desires to dominate. Realpolitik concludes that states must therefore provide their own security to the best of their ability

behavioralism   a method of analysis of international relations that advocates a rigorous and systematic study of international relations, including a specific statement of the problem and a scientific, often quantitative analysis of the variables involved and their relationship

feminist perspectives on international relations   an analytical method that explores how we think, do not think, or avoid thinking about gender in international relations

foreign policy analysis   an analytical method that examines the intentions, statements, and actions of an international actor directed toward the external world

levels of analysis   the concept that the policies of an international actor may be based on the goals and outlooks of an individual decision-maker; on internal political or bureaucratic needs; on "national interest;" or on other factors

 ## WEBSITE REFERENCES

democratization: *www.democracy.stanford.edu*   the website of Stanford's Comparative Democratization Project

privatization: *www.public-policy.org/~ncpa/pd/private*   discussions of privatization from the National Center for Policy Analysis

theories of international relations: *www.IRTHEORY.COM/KNOW.HTM*   an index and set of definitions of many prominent international relations theories

Marxism: *www.marxists.org*   an impressive set of archival materials from many major Marxists thinkers

behavioralism: *www.valt.helsinki.fi/vol/projects/behavior/htm*   a discussion of the history, nature, intellectual background, and legacy of behavioralism

feminist perspectives: *www.umbc.edu/cwit/syl_pol.html*   a listing of syllabi on the web for courses on feminism and international relations

 ## NOTES

1. *Yearbook of International Organizations 1999–2000*, pp. 2356–2357.

2. For more detailed discussions of interdependence, see Harold K. Jacobson, *Networks of Interdependence: International Organizations and the Global Political System* (New York, NY: Knopf, 1979); R.J. Barry Jones, *Globalisation and Interdependence in the International Political Economy: Rhetoric and Reality* (London: Pinter, 1995); and Robert O. Keohane and Joseph S. Nye, Jr., *Power and Interdependence,* 3d ed. (New York, NY: Addison-Wesley, 2001).

3. See Daniel S. Papp, "From the Crest All Directions Are Down: The Soviet Union Views the

1980s," *Naval War College Review* (July–August 1982), pp. 50–68.

4. See Daniel S. Papp, *The End of the Soviet Union* (Atlanta: The Southern Center for International Studies, 1999); David Lane, *Soviet Society Under Perestroika* (New York: Routledge, 1992); and Stuart H. Loory and Ann Inse, *Seven Days that Shook the World* (Atlanta: Turner Publishing, 1991).

5. See Alain Touraine, "What Does Democracy Mean?," *International Social Science Journal* (1991), pp. 259–268.

6. The process of democratization is discussed in greater detail in Larry Diamond and Mark F. Plattner, eds., *The Global Resurgence of Democracy* (Baltimore, MD: Johns Hopkins University Press, 1993); Laurence Whitehead, ed., *The International Dimension of Democratization: Europe and the Americas* (New York, NY: Oxford University Press, 1996); Lisa Anderson, ed., Transitions to Democracy (New York, NY: Columbia University Press, 1999); and Mark Robinson and Gordon White, ed., *The Democratic Developmental State: Political and Institutional Design* (New York, NY: Oxford University Press, 1999).

7. Francis Fukuyama, "The End of History?," *National Interest* (1989), pp. 3–18. For discussions of Fukuyama's thesis, see Timothy Burns, ed., *After History? Francis Fukuyama and His Critics* (Lanham, Md.: Rowman and Littlefield, 1994).

8. For more detailed discussions of privatization, see Kazimierz Z. Poznanski, *The Evolutionary Transition to Capitalism* (Boulder, CO: Westview Press, 1995); and Olivier Blanchard, *The Economics of Post–Communist Transition* (New York, NY: Oxford University Press, 1997).

9. The 1994 GATT agreement also created the World Trade Organization (WTO). The WTO superceded GATT and now is the chief international institution responsible for resolving international trade disputes and reducing international barriers to trade. See Chapter 13.

10. See for example David S. Alberts and Daniel S. Papp, eds., *The Information Age Anthology, Volume 1* (Washington, D.C.: National Defense University Press, 1997), especially Parts 1 and 2.

11. *Ibid.,* especially Part 4.

12. See U.S. Department of State, *Patterns of Global Terrorism 1999* (April 2000).

13. See Chapter 19 for a more detailed discussion of the Kyoto Environmental Summit.

14. See Alfred Thayer Mahan, *The Influence of Seapower Upon History 1600–1783* (Boston: Little, Brown, 1890).

15. For Mackinder's own analysis, see Halford Mackinder, *Democratic Ideals and Reality* (New York: Holt, Rinehart, and Winston, 1919). See also Christopher J. Fettweis, "Sir Halford Mackinder, Geopolitics, and Policymaking in the 21st Century," *Parameters* (Summer 2000), pp. 58–71.

16. One of the best introductory explanations of Marxism is R.N. Carew-Hunt, *The Theory and Practice of Communism* (Baltimore: Penguin Books, 1963). See also Theodore Dan, *The Origins of Bolshevism* (New York: Schocken Books, 1970).

17. Vladimir Ilyich Lenin, *Imperialism–The Highest Stage of Capitalism, Selected Works,* Vol. V (New York: International Publishers, 1943).

18. Most political idealists rejected the outlook that man's selfishness, aggressiveness, or stupidity caused war and international conflict. For a discussion of this outlook, see Kenneth N. Waltz, *Man, the State, and War* (New York: Columbia University Press, 1959). See also Konrad Lorenz, *On Aggression* (New York: Harcourt Brace Jovanovich, 1963). See also David Long and Peter Colin Wilson, *Thinkers of the Twenty Years Crisis: Interwar Idealism Reassessed* (New York: Oxford University Press, 1995).

19. Adolf Hitler detailed his view of the world in *Mein Kampf* (Boston: Houghton Mifflin, 1943).

20. For a superb overview of this entire period of world history, see William R. Keylor, *The Twentieth Century World* (New York: Oxford University Press, 1992).

21. For some of the most prominent works of these political realists, see Hans J. Morgenthau, *Politics Among Nations* (New York: Alfred A. Knopf, 1948); Reinhold Niebuhr, *Moral Man and Immoral Society* (New York: Charles Scribner's Sons, 1947); George Kennan ("X"), "The Sources of Soviet Conduct," *Foreign Affairs* (July 1947), pp. 566–582; and Henry A. Kissinger, *Nuclear Weapons and Foreign Policy* (New York: Harper & Row, 1957). For other discussions of realpolitik, see Frank W. Wayman and Paul F. Diehl,

eds., *Reconstructing Realpolitik* (Ann Arbor: University of Michigan Press, 1994); and Martin Griffiths, *Realism, Idealism, and International Politics* (New York: Routledge, 1995).

22. Some of the more prominent analysts of international affairs closely identified with the behavioralist revolution were J. David Singer, James N. Rosenau, and Dina Zinnes. See, for example, J. David Singer, ed., *Human Behavior and International Politics* (Chicago: Rand McNally, 1965); James N. Rosenau, *The Scientific Study of Foreign Policy* (New York: The Free Press, 1971); and Dina Zinnes, *Contemporary Research in International Relations: A Perspective and a Critical Appraisal* (New York: The Free Press, 1976). See also Karl W. Deutsch and Richard L. Merritt, "Effects of Events on National and International Images," in Herbert C. Kelman, ed., *International Behavior* (New York: Holt, Rinehart and Winston, 1965), pp. 132–187; Dean G. Pruitt and Richard C. Snyder eds., *Theory and Research on the Causes of War* (Englewood Cliffs, NJ: Prentice Hall, 1969); and Robert C. North, Ole R. Holsti, M. George Zaninovich, and Dina A. Zinnes, *Content Analysis* (Evanston, IL: Northwestern University Press, 1963). This is only a partial listing.

23. For feminist perspectives on international relations, see V. Spike Peterson, ed., *Generated States: Feminist (Re)Visions of International Relations Theory* (Boulder, CO: Lynne Rienner Publishers, 1992); Christine Sylvester, *Feminist Theory and International Relations in a Postmodern Era* (New York: Cambridge University Press, 1994); Georgina Waylen, *Gender in Third World Politics* (Boulder, CO: Lynne Rienner Publishers, 1996); and V. Spike Peterson and Anne Sisson Runyan, *Global Gender Issues* (Boulder, CO: Westview Press, 1998).

24. Deborah J. Gerner, "Foreign Policy Analysis: Exhilarating Eclecticism, Intriguing Enigmas," *International Studies Notes* (Fall 1991–Winter 1992), p. 4.

25. For good discussions of the advantages and disadvantages of comparative foreign policy analysis and events data analysis, see, for example, James N. Rosenau, "Introduction: New Directions and Recurrent Questions in the Comparative Study of Foreign Policy," and Charles F. Hermann and Gregory Peacock, "The Evolution and Future of Theoretical Research in the Comparative Study of Foreign Policy," both in Charles F. Hermann, Charles W. Kegley Jr., and James N. Rosenau, eds., *New Directions in the Study of Foreign Policy* (Boston: Allen and Unwin, 1987). See also Maurice A. East, "The Comparative Study of Foreign Policy: We're Not There Yet But ...," *International Studies Notes* (Spring 1987), p. 31; James A. Caporaso et al., "The Comparative Study of Foreign Policy: Perspectives on the Future," *International Studies Notes* (Spring 1987), pp. 32–46; and Richard L. Merritt et al., *International Event-Data Development* (Ann Arbor: University of Michigan Press, 1993).

26. For an overview of several approaches from the field of political psychology, see, for example, Eric Singer and Valerie M. Hudson, eds., *Political Psychology and Foreign Policy* (Boulder, CO: Westview Press, 1992).

27. For excellent surveys of different theories of international relations, see James E. Dougherty and Robert L. Pfaltzgraff, Jr., *Contending Theories of International Relations: A Comprehensive Survey* (New York: Harper & Row, 1990); and John A. Vasquez, ed., *Classics of International Relations* (Englewood Cliffs, NJ: Prentice Hall, 1996).

28. See, for example, J. David Singer, "The Level-of-Analysis Problem in International Relations," in Klaus Knorr and Sidney Verba, eds., *The International System: Theoretical Essays* (Princeton: Princeton University Press, 1961), pp. 77–94.

29. James N. Rosenau, for example, identifies six levels of decision: (1) individual decision makers and their personalities; (2) individual decision makers and their positions; (3) governmental structure; (4) the structure of society; (5) the relations that exist between one nation-state and other international actors; and (6) the international system itself. See James N. Rosenau, *The Scientific Study of Foreign Policy* (New York: The Free Press, 1971), esp. Chap. 5.

30. For a fascinating application of the levels-of-analysis concept to the Cuban Missile Crisis, see Graham Allison, *Essence of Decision: Explaining the Cuban Missile Crisis* (Boston: Little, Brown, 1971).

PART 1

The Participants' Framework: Actors and Interests in International Politics

We are stranded between old conceptions of political conduct and a wholly new conception, between the inadequacy of the nation-state and the emerging imperative of global community.

—HENRY A. KISSINGER

In the twenty-first century world, it is increasingly difficult to identify the international actors without a scorecard.

For years, the primary actor in international affairs was the state. It still is, but its primacy is no longer absolute. Increasingly, other types of international actors are playing greater and greater roles in the international arena. These other types of international actors include international governmental organizations, multinational corporations, nongovernmental organizations, and even individuals. During the last 30 years, all have steadily increased the roles that they play in the global community.

Multinational corporations, for example, often operate in five, ten, or even twenty or more states with little regard to the national interests of the states that serve as their hosts. Often, they wield considerable economic clout. Indeed, as long ago as 1978 General Motors and Exxon individually had more annual income than all but 22 individual states. And in at least one instance during the same decade, a multinational corporation played a fundamental role in changing the government of a state (ITT in Chile).

International governmental organizations also can challenge the dominance of the state. The European Union (EU), for example, evolved out of the European Community (EC) and has as its objective the political and economic unity of its 15 member states. Under the EC, member states had already surrendered a limited amount of their sovereignty to the European Council, and when the EU was created in 1993, member states surrendered even more decision-making authority to that and other EU bodies. There is little doubt that the EU challenges the state system in Europe. The question is, "How much?"

Yet another class of actor, the nongovernmental organization (NGO), also challenges the primacy of the state. NGOs include many types of organizations ranging from national liberation movements, which seek to establish new governments within existing states or to create new states from either the colonial dependencies or internal territory of existing states, to organizations such as Amnesty International and Greenpeace, which seek to mobilize international public opinion to apply pressure to national governments to alter a particular policy or policies.

Even individuals occupy prominent places, as individuals, in contemporary international relations. Until his death in 1989, Soviet physicist Andrei Sakharov's statements and views about the USSR had a major impact on Western perceptions of the Soviet Union. Similarly, Mother Teresa's services to the poor in India captured the admiration of the international community throughout the 1990s. Meanwhile, former U.S. President Jimmy Carter, acting as a private citizen, traveled to Africa, Asia, and Latin American to try to assure fair elections and to end wars and conflicts.

None of this means the state is dead or dying. Indeed, the state as a class of actor still reigns supreme just as it has for most of the past three and a half centuries. But new and influential actors have joined it on the international stage, and if an accurate understanding of contemporary international relations is to be developed, it is also necessary to understand who they are, what their objectives are, and how they seek to achieve them.

The purposes of the next four chapters, then, are to explore the following questions:

- Who are the major actors in international relations?
- What objectives do they seek?
- Who determines these objectives?
- Where did these actors come from?
- How important are they today?
- How are they changing?

Chapter 2

The State, Nationalism, and the National Interest

- What are the differences between a state and a nation?
- How has the international system of states evolved over time?
- What is nationalism?
- What is the national interest?
- How does the balance of power work?
- How secure is the future for the nation-state?

The state has dominated global politics for over 300 years. Arising in Western Europe from the feudal system that preceded it, the state's dominance is generally traced back to the **Peace of Westphalia** of 1648. The Westphalian Peace ended the Thirty Years' War in Europe and established a system of sovereign entities that rejected subservience to the political authority of the pope and the Roman Catholic Church. The old system of papal authority over the principalities of Europe had been overthrown, and a new system of geographically fixed self-ruling political entities that accepted no higher authority than themselves had been born.

The birth of the state system evolved over centuries. Whereas previous rulers accepted their subservience to the Pope in Rome, even sometimes allowing the church to dictate what weapons could be used in combat, the Westphalian system of states placed the rulers of states in control of their own destinies. Without a higher authority to dictate their actions or determine their ranking, rulers were free to maximize their power by whatever means they saw fit within the confines of a broadly defined system of international law laid down by the Peace of Westphalia.

 ## SOVEREIGNTY, LEGITIMACY, AND DUTY

The concepts of sovereignty, legitimacy, and duty were central to the state system created by the Peace of Westphalia. Although the exact definition of each has changed since 1648, the core concepts remain the same today as then.

As interpreted at Westphalia, **sovereignty** meant that no higher authority than the state existed. States and their kings could pursue the objectives that they thought proper by whatever means they chose. In addition, rulers of states did not have to accept any authority higher than their own. Rulers ruled in whatever way they wanted to.

Sovereignty was a fundamental departure from the practices of earlier years. Before Westphalia, European princes and kings followed the dictates of the pope. After Westphalia, sovereignty asserted the primacy of states and rulers and rejected external controls on and rules over them.

The concept of sovereignty carries great weight even today. For example, when Iraq invaded Kuwait in 1990, the U.S. maintained that Iraq had violated the sovereignty of an independent state. The U.S. used Iraq's violation of Kuwait's sovereignty as one of its major rationales to assemble a coalition of countries and expel Iraq from Kuwait. Similarly, during the 1990s, the U.S. often criticized China's human rights policies. China, however, rejected the criticism, arguing that China was a sovereign country and that the U.S. was meddling in its domestic affairs. As a sovereign state, China said, it had the right to implement whatever domestic policies it chose.

Legitimacy is closely linked to sovereignty. Under Westphalia, it meant that a king's right to rule within his own country was unquestioned, rightfully his, and supreme. No one within or outside a country could legitimately challenge the right of a king to rule. In the years since Westphalia, this concept has been extended beyond kings to include governments, regardless of the form they may take or the policies they may implement. The example of China used above to illustrate sovereignty could equally well be used to demonstrate legitimacy. According to the Chinese government, because it is sovereign, its human rights policies are by definition legitimate.

Sovereignty and legitimacy are also closely linked to the concept of **duty.** Put simply, duty means that states must follow certain rules of behavior in their relations with one another. This eventually developed into the concept of international law. Laws were established and frequently followed for declaring and fighting wars, for adhering to treaties and alliances, for recognizing the legitimacy of foreign rulers and the territorial integrity of their states, and for exchanging and treating diplomatic representatives.

The concepts of sovereignty, legitimacy, and duty carry great weight in international relations even today. Nevertheless, sovereignty, legitimacy, and duty raise issues that often do not have clear cut answers.

For example, when does a state become a state? In the case of Iraq's invasion of Kuwait, Iraq maintained that Kuwait was not really an independent state, but rather an Iraqi province that had been torn away by Great Britain during the nineteenth century. Was Iraq right, or was the U.S. right?

Similarly, do sovereignty and legitimacy really mean that a government can do whatever it wants to its people? Or are certain human rights so fundamental that the international community has a responsibility to intervene if a government is systematically denying and violating those rights? If so, which rights are fundamental, and which are not? In China throughout the 1990s, the U.S. maintained that China was violating its citizen's rights, but responded only with words. In Kosovo in 1999, the United States maintained that Serbia was violating its Kosovar citizens' rights, but responded with military

Chapter 2

IT AND THE STATE:
A GROWING CHALLENGE

For three centuries, states have dominated international relations. Today, however, information technologies are raising new and serious challenges to the primacy of the state in international relations. This challenge comes from three directions.

First, information technologies are reducing the state's ability to guarantee security. Given the reliance of developed states on information technology in areas such as business, communications, defense, finance, and resource delivery, disruption of these technologies could raise havoc. Many of these technologies are not secure, as demonstrated in 2000 by the Love Bug computer virus, denial of service attacks on government and business web sites, and hacker alterations of numerous government and business web sites.

This is not the first time that new technologies have raised questions about the ability of states to protect their citizens, so threats posed by the vulnerability of information technologies should not be exaggerated. But neither should they be dismissed. As we will see later, as information technologies are increasingly applied to the tools of war, the ability of states to provide security will be challenged even more.

Second, economic activity is increasingly being conducted beyond individual states. A growing percentage is in information-related goods and services, with information becoming a chief commodity. The volume and importance of international trade in information is increasing as more people and organizations use information technologies, with trillions of dollars of trade already being in information. This leads some to question whether states are losing their ability to provide economic well being for their population as multinational corporations increasingly operate beyond the control of single states.

Third, the same question may be asked regarding the nation-state's ability to provide a sense of belonging to a nationality. There is little doubt that nationalism is on the rise. It contributed to the dissolution of the Soviet Union, Yugoslavia, and Czechoslovakia, and is creating problems in Belgium, Canada, India, Malaysia, and elsewhere. At first appearance, nationalism virtually guarantees the survival of the state.

This may be so. However, nations do not always need states to consider themselves nations. Sometimes individuals who comprise a nation see themselves linked to one another in the absence of their controlling land. Advanced information technologies increase the ability of the people of a nation to be geographically remote from one another but still retain a sense of identity. For example people of all nationalities use email, chat rooms, online newspapers, and even video-streaming to remain "connected" to their home countries when they are overseas or in remote locations. The extent to which advanced information technologies allow this to occcur will have a significant impact on the extent to which states retain their dominant international role.

None of this means that states are in danger of disappearing. But the new capabilities that information technologies provide and the new dependencies that they bring raise questions about the extent to which states will be the dominant form of international actor late in the twenty-first century.

action. In both cases, the U.S. adopted the position that sovereignty was not absolute. China and Serbia disagreed. Who was right?

Sovereignty, legitimacy, and duty are fluid concepts whose precise meanings are open to debate. Perhaps surprisingly, even the meaning of the term "state" is less than precise. Thus, before we examine the evolution of the Westphalian state system, we must clarify the meaning of state, nation, and nation-state.

 ## STATE, NATION, AND NATION-STATE

The terms *state, nation,* and *nation-state* are usually used interchangeably in discussions of international relations. However, these terms have different meanings. In certain contexts, the differences in meaning have great significance. Therefore, an understanding of the more precise definitions is important.

A **state** is a geographically bounded entity governed by a central authority that has the ability to make laws, rules, and decisions, and to enforce those laws, rules, and decisions within its boundaries. A state is also a legal entity, recognized under international law as the fundamental decision-making unit of the international legal system. States determine their own policies (at least in theory) and establish their own forms of government, which may differ significantly from state to state. Those people who inhabit the territory of a state may or may not be citizens of that state, depending on the laws passed by the government of that state. Regardless of their citizenship status, inhabitants of the territory of a state are subject to the laws of that state.

A **nation,** by contrast, need not necessarily be either geographically bounded or legally defined. A nation is a grouping of people who view themselves as being linked to one another in some manner. A nation is therefore as much a psychological fixation as anything else. Groupings of people who consider themselves to be ethnically, culturally, or linguistically related may thus be considered a nation. Nations may exist without territorial control, as did the Jewish nation before 1947 (when the *state* of Israel was founded), Ukrainians in the former Soviet Union, and various Indian tribes in the United States. Other groups calling themselves national liberation movements also exist and seek to establish territorial control in a certain area, thereby becoming a state. The Palestine Liberation Organization (PLO) in the Middle East and the Sendero Luminoso in Peru are examples of self-styled national liberation movements.

The term **nation-state** means a state whose inhabitants consider themselves to be a nation. It is a geographically bounded legal entity under a single government, the population of which psychologically considers itself to be in some way, shape, or form related. The term *nation-state* is historically more recent than either state or nation and reflects the growing convergence in recent years between the two older terms.

However, many countries are commonly called nation-states even though they are not. For example, in Africa, territory included in most states that received independence during the 1950s and 1960s was based on what had been the old colonial boundaries. In some cases, several different ethnic groups were included in one country. Thus, some of these states count many nations as their inhabitants. In other cases, ethnic groups were divided by state boundaries and found themselves inhabiting several different states. The same was true of the former Soviet Union. Technically, such entities that include large percentages of more than one nationality are states, not nation-states.

Despite the extremely important differences between the terms *state, nation,* and *nation-state,* these terms are often used interchangeably. This practice is so widespread that in the minds of most casual observers of international affairs, there are no differences among the three terms. However, the significant differences in meaning that are hidden by the modern practice of interchanging terms should be kept in mind.

NATIONALISM

Nationalism is closely related to the concept of a nation. In its most basic form, "nationalism" is a psychological force that binds people together who identify with each other. It refers both to the feelings of attachment to one another that members of a nation have and to the sense of pride that members of a nation have in themselves and their nation.

Over time, nationalism has in many cases also become closely related to the concept of a state, or more precisely, to a nation-state. But this was not always so. When the Westphalian system of states was first emerging in Europe during the mid-seventeenth century, nationalism was only rarely associated with states. Rather, citizens of states pledged allegiance to the individual who ruled the state. *"L'état, c'est moi"* ("The state, it is I"), said Louis XIV of France, and he was right, at least in most of Europe until the end of the eighteenth century.

Gradually, however, people who lived in certain states came to believe that the state was theirs as much as the king's. Further, as peoples who lived in a state began to identify more and more with each other as well as—and in some cases, instead of—the king, modern nationalism and the modern nation-state was born.

Nationalism may be expressed in many ways. Efforts to raise standards of living, to win more gold medals than other nations at the Olympics, and to conquer adjoining territories are all different manifestations of nationalism. From these few examples alone, it may be seen that depending on how it is expressed, nationalism may be constructive and helpful, benign and moderate, or destructive and dangerous.

As a psychological force that binds people who identify with one another, nationalism has played and continues to play an immense role in international affairs. Since the eighteenth century, and at an accelerated pace during the nineteenth and twentieth centuries, nationalism has manifested itself most visibly in the desire of the members of a nation to control and govern the territory in which they live. It may thus be argued that in one sense, nationalism is what brought about events and trends as diverse as the American Revolution, in which British subjects rejected kingly rule and sought to govern themselves; the collapse of European colonial empires, during which peoples throughout the world struggled against European imperialism and demanded self-government; and the end of the Soviet Union, fomented to a great extent by the demands of different ethnic groups that they, not Moscow, rule themselves.

There is another side to nationalism as well. In its more extreme form, nationalism does more than simply psychologically bind people together who identify with one another, instill them with pride in who and what they are, and lead them to seek self-rule.

In its more extreme form, nationalism can also lead a people to ascribe superiority to themselves over others, and create a desire to control and exploit other peoples, their territories, and their wealth. This extreme form of nationalism was one of the main driving forces, along with economics, behind European colonial expansion during the eighteenth, nineteenth, and early twentieth centuries. It also contributed significantly to the national rivalries that led to World War I and to the German and Japanese territorial expansion that precipitated World War II.

Regardless of how nationalism is expressed, it requires individuals to identify with a larger group. Often, as in Germany, Japan, France, and elsewhere, this larger group is based on ethnicity. Sometimes, as in the case of the United States, it is not. In the U.S., few would deny that a "U.S. nationalism" exists, but it is a multi-ethnic and theoretically inclusive nationalism, tied to the U.S. government, U.S. citizens, and the ideals that the United States espouses.

Technically, the United States—and other states that have large percentages of more than one nationality living within them—may or may not be nation-states. Nevertheless, citizens of such states may be "nationalists" about the state in which they live. Indeed, in some cases, the United States included, the citizens of multiethnic states may exhibit more nationalism toward and about their state than the citizens of "true" nation-states. In these instances, theoretical and definitional differences between "states" and "nation-states" become moot.

Recognizing this, governments of multiethnic states often attempt to transfer the loyalty of their citizens from the old group of identification to the new state, thereby creating a sense of state nationalism, and in so doing, the equivalent of a nation-state. Sometimes, it is difficult to tell if this effort has succeeded.

This was the case in the former Soviet Union. For years, the Soviet government and most people around the world believed that the USSR had successfully created "Soviet nationalism," that is, a sense of Soviet nationhood. But as Soviet citizens became increasingly free to express their real sentiments as a result of Mikhail Gorbachev's reforms, it became clear that most Soviet citizens still identified more with their ethnic nationality than with the USSR. Hence, "nationalism," in the traditional sense of identification with one's own ethnic group, contributed immensely to the dissolution of the Soviet Union.

Much the same thing happened in Yugoslavia and Czechoslovakia, where ethnic loyalty proved stronger than the loyalty of peoples to either the Yugoslavian or Czechoslovakian states. In the Yugoslav case, ethnic nationalism led to ethnic conflict, civil war, and thousands of deaths. In the Czechoslovakian case, ethnic nationalism led to cordial discussions and the decision by the Czech and Slovak peoples to create peacefully two separate nation-states from what formerly had been one state that included two nations.

Elsewhere around the world, the pull of nationalism grew in the 1990s. In many states, some of which have long been considered nation-states, ethnic nationalism has gained new strength, calling into question whether currently established states will survive as presently constituted. In addition to those states already discussed, other states as diverse as Belgium, Canada, India, Iraq, Spain, and Turkey are challenged by internal national groups, some of which call themselves "national liberation movements," that seek to break away to set up their own independent nation-states.

Nationalism, then, has been and remains a powerful force in international affairs. It is a major part of today's international system of states. But it is not a force that necessarily supports the status quo. As the following sections show, nationalism has been and remains a powerful force for change in the evolution of the international system of states.[1]

THE EVOLUTION OF THE STATE SYSTEM TO 1870

The Westphalian system of states was a European system that eventually expanded to include all corners of the globe. (See Table 2-1.) However, even before the state system became firmly established in Europe, European powers had begun to expand their empires outside Europe. By the beginning of the seventeenth century, Dutch, English, French, Portuguese, and Spanish adventurers had explored every inhabited continent. Their parent countries followed their explorations by using military power to create overseas colonial empires.

TABLE 2-1   The Evolution of the Modern State System

1648	Treaty of Westphalia establishes modern state system.
16th, 17th, 18th cent.	European states establish colonial empires, especially in North and South America; this is the first round of empire.
1775–1790	American and French revolutions challenge the rule of kings; nationalism emerges as a powerful international force.
1804–1815	Napoleon's French empire threatens to overturn the European state system.
1815–1870	The Concert of Europe protects the legitimacy of the state and royal rule.
1870–1914	European states divide Africa and much of the Middle East and Asia in the second round of empire; the United States and Japan also acquire overseas colonial holdings.
1914–1918	World War I shakes the world system of states.
1870–1930	The number of states in Europe expands from about 15 to over 35; this is the first proliferation of states.
1918–1939	The coming to power of the Bolsheviks in Russia and the Nazis in Germany challenges the legitimacy of the state system.
1939–1945	World War II.
1945–1990	The second proliferation of states takes place as old colonial empires fall; the number of states increases from about 54 in 1945 to about 170 in 1990; this period also marks the longest uninterrupted time of peace among major powers since the inception of the state system. State formation slows markedly during the last decade of this period as decolonization is achieved on virtually a universal basis.
1991–Today	The third proliferation of states takes place as established states break up. Czechoslovakia, the Soviet Union, and Yugoslavia dissolve and form at least 21 new states, and dissolution threatens other states around the world as well.

The First Round of Empire

European states built their empires during the sixteenth, seventeenth, and eighteenth centuries to increase their wealth, power, and prestige. Vast colonial empires were created in North and South America, and gold, silver, furs, and other forms of wealth flowed from the New World to the courts of European kings and royalty.

A general pattern of colonization was followed by most European states. After the adventurers proved the feasibility of a journey or the existence of a new (for Europeans) land, European merchants examined the possibility of commercial profit. European governments, aware of the possibility of increasing their own power and wealth and thereby enhancing their position in the competition between states, quickly claimed the new lands as colonies, and chartered and funded commercial companies to explore and develop the opportunities for wealth. Conflicts between states over colonial holdings broke out, and naval and army forces financed and manned by states became necessary adjuncts of the drive for empire.

The economic philosophy that led to this **first round of empire** was **mercantilism.** First espoused by Jean Baptiste Colbert, Minister of Finance to Louis XIV of France, mercantilism taught that state power was derived from wealth. To maximize power, wealth had to be maximized in any way possible. Gold, silver, and furs were important, but rulers of the day considered it equally necessary to maintain a positive balance of trade, that is, to export more than they imported. Colonies became important not only as sources of valuable resources, but also as captive markets.

If mercantilism provided the economic rationale for the first round of empire building, then scientific-technical innovations in navigation and transportation, as well as in the military, provided the capabilities. In navigation, widespread use of the sextant permitted seafarers to chart their courses accurately, and the European development of the square-rigger allowed ships to point closer into the wind and increased their cargo space. The marriage of gunpower and heavy cannon with the square-rigged sailing vessel permitted European powers, Great Britain in particular, to bring heavy firepower to bear on enemy ships and enemy shores. Although often overlooked, these and other scientific-technical innovations allowed Europeans to travel beyond the confines of their home continent and carry their living requirements and military capabilities with them.

Attacks on Regal Legitimacy

By the end of the eighteenth century, the mercantilist philosophy was decreasing in popularity and persuasiveness and was gradually being replaced by an international trading system that stressed free trade, that is, trade with little or no government intervention. This logic was persuasively argued by Adam Smith in his *Wealth of Nations.* Bullion was not the determinant of national power and prestige, Smith maintained, but capital and goods were. Thus, free trade became a logical adjunct to Smith's laissez-faire economic philosophy.

With the supporting logic of mercantilism removed, colonies became less important. European states continued to maintain their overseas empires, but they became increasingly distracted from non-European affairs by events closer to home. The existence of the

During the fifteenth and sixteenth centuries, European explorers ventured to
every inhabited continent, and European countries established large overseas
empires in their wake. Here, from a 1590 stamp engraved in copper in the collection of "New Voyages," Christopher Columbus lands on the island of Guanahani
in the West Indies on May 12, 1492, early in the first round of empire.

European system of states itself was challenged, first by the French Revolution and then
by the revolution's offspring, Napoleon.

Following the Peace of Westphalia, the answer to the question of who was to rule the
state was considered a given: the king. Within any state, the king's word was law. The regal mantle would be passed from father to son, and the state's fortunes would follow the
skills and fortunes of the king. If a king proved unable or unwilling to exercise his authority within his state and was forced to share it, as had occurred in Great Britain, that was
acceptable to the royal families of Europe as long as neither the legitimacy of the king nor
of his state was challenged, and as long as his realm did not challenge the legitimacy of
other kings and their states.

To some extent, the revolt of Great Britain's thirteen North American colonies and
their Declaration of Independence in 1776 challenged the self-perpetuating continuity of
the Westphalian system. By declaring their independence, the North American colonies
rejected King George's right to rule them. Some Europeans recognized this challenge.
Others did not. In either case, North America was an ocean away, and the actions of the
North Americans did not threaten the fundamental stability of the European state system

and its rulers. By the early nineteenth century, most Spanish possessions in South America followed the North American lead and declared their independence as well. Regal legitimacy had been rejected in North and South America, but the legitimacy of the state had not been. The European state system was now in the Americas.

The French Revolution was another matter. France was in the heart of Europe and at the core of the state system. Louis XVI was the legitimate heir to the throne, and he exercised his regal rights as kings had done within their respective states for nearly a century and a half. The French Revolution of 1789 rejected the legitimacy of regal authority, asserted that the people of the state were sovereign, and called on French nationalism to raise France to preeminence in Europe.

France was thus a real and immediate problem for other European states. Louis XVI was beheaded, and a reign of terror swept France. In 1804, after a series of dazzling military victories throughout Europe, Napoleon Bonaparte emerged as Emperor of France.

Napoleon's dream was to create another Roman Empire in Europe. If the French Revolution challenged the legitimacy of kings to govern, Napoleon threatened the very existence of the concept of the state. After establishing his empire throughout most of western Europe, Napoleon overextended his reach and attacked Russia in 1812. Defeated by the Russian winter, Napoleon's empire declined, and within three years a coalition of states destroyed it. Napoleon's last defeat came at Waterloo in 1815.

In Europe, regal legitimacy was again restored, and the state system had been preserved. But in some states, nationalism had been joined to the state, and the era of the modern nation-state was about to begin.

The Second Round of Empire

After the defeat of Napoleon, European states, with the exception of Great Britain, joined together in the so-called Concert of Europe, which consciously sought to preserve and protect the state and regal legitimacy. To a great extent, the concert succeeded for a half century. Great Britain, meanwhile, acted as an independent entity that sought to preserve a balance of power among the states of Europe.[2]

Beginning in about 1870, a second wave of empire building swept Europe and eventually the United States and Japan. Explanations for the new wave of imperial conquest varied. Diplomatic historians and later political realists declared that traditional politics was at work, with states either seeking to improve their status in the international ranking of states or attempting to maintain the European balance of power. Lenin, as we have seen, believed that imperialism was simply the highest stage of capitalism, brought about by capitalism's need for more markets, less expensive resources, and cheaper labor. Whatever the causes, by the early twentieth century, European states again had built colonial empires. The empires were created primarily by superior European military power. By 1900, nearly all of Africa with the exceptions of Liberia and Ethiopia had been divided by seven European states. Asia, including the "Inner Kingdom" of China, had been similarly dismembered. The British Empire was immense. By 1900, Great Britain governed one-fifth of the world's land mass and one-fourth of its population.

Non-European states also joined the rush to empire. The United States annexed Hawaii, leased the Panama Canal Zone "in perpetuity" from the American-created state of

Panama, acquired the Philippines from Spain, and granted Cuba its independence only after having an amendment added to the Cuban constitution that permitted American armed intervention in Cuban affairs when the United States deemed it necessary.[3] Meanwhile, Japan acquired Korea and Taiwan. Imperialism had become the order of the day, and European-style nation-states dominated international affairs.

THE EVOLUTION OF THE STATE SYSTEM: 1870 TO TODAY

At the beginning of the twentieth century, the nation-state's position in international affairs seemed secure, and the international state system appeared stable. However, appearances were deceiving. Lurking below the calm surface of the European state system were forces that soon unleashed the cataclysm of World War I.

The First Proliferation of States

The second wave of imperial expansion inevitably led to economic exploitation of colonial holdings and increased rivalry among European states themselves. One manifestation of this was a major arms race among the European powers. For the most part, the struggle for prestige and territory was confined to Asia and Africa. In some instances, however, territorial struggles occurred in Europe as well. Following France's defeat by Prussia in the 1870 Franco-Prussian War, Prussia annexed the French province of Alsace-Lorraine. This annexation, as well as the military defeat itself, was a humiliating blow to French national pride, and revanchist sentiment swelled within the French nation. In addition, particularly in the Austrian-Hungarian and Ottoman empires, national groups accelerated their struggles for national independence from the remaining old and crumbling multinational dynastic empires.

In Europe, a subtle change was taking place in the state system. It was acquiring new members. During the half century before the beginning of World War I, the number of states in Europe grew from about 15 to over 25. This proliferation occurred in two ways. In some cases, as in Albania and Serbia, new states were born as national groupings broke away from traditional empires. In other cases, as in Germany and Italy, smaller territorial units formed modern nation-states. Concurrently with this proliferation of nation-states, the countries of Europe led by the militarily more powerful among them sought to protect themselves and their possessions, and to either maintain the existing distribution of power in Europe or change it by establishing a rather rigid network of alliances that stretched throughout the continent, and as a result of their colonial holdings, beyond.

Alliances had long been a part of the European state system. In the past, however, alliances had been relatively flexible. For example, Great Britain regularly aligned itself with different countries throughout the nineteenth century in an effort to maintain the existing distribution of power in Europe (which, not coincidentally, significantly favored

Britain). The two major alliances of the early twentieth century, the Triple Entente, including Great Britain, France, and Russia, and the Triple Alliance, including Germany, Austria-Hungary, and Italy, were much more rigid in character. In addition, several of the states in the two major alliances were tied by secret treaties to other states not in the Entente or Alliance.

The slide toward World War I would have been comic if its results were not so tragic. Following the assassination of Archduke Ferdinand of Austria-Hungary at Sarajevo, Austria-Hungary demanded that Serbia permit it to enter Serbia to search for the assassins. Serbia refused. Austria-Hungary prepared to march into Serbia anyway, and Russia, committed by secret treaty to Serbia's defense, began to mobilize. Czar Nicholas at first ordered a partial mobilization of Russian forces, intending only to show the Austro-Hungarians that Russia would in fact defend Serbia. However, the Russian military leadership informed him that partial mobilization would hopelessly complicate full mobilization, and urged him to proclaim full mobilization immediately because the Russian mobilization rate was slower than that of any other European power. The Czar complied with his generals' urgings.[4] Germany, viewing the Russian action with alarm, began its mobilization. Meanwhile, Austria-Hungary, fearing that Germany would renege on its "blank check" promise of support for Austria-Hungary in the event of an Austro-Hungarian conflict with Russia, refused to respond to a series of urgent diplomatic communications from Berlin and marched into Serbia. World War I had begun.

The savagery of World War I appalled rational men and women everywhere, but the destruction went on for four bloody years. Blame for the war was variously attributed, depending on which model of international relations was used. Following the war, collective security, international law, and arms control were all proposed as remedies for the scourge of modern war. But by far the most powerful single concept emerging from the war was the principle of national self-determination, espoused most forcefully by the American President Woodrow Wilson. Under this principle, nationalities themselves would determine who would rule them. Theoretically, self-rule would minimize the thrust for territorial expansion and make war less likely. Actually, self-determination further accelerated the growth in numbers of new nation-states.

As a result of the acceptance of self-determination, the number of nation-states in Europe leaped to over 35 by the early 1930s. Six new states—Austria, Czechoslovakia, Hungary, Poland, Romania, and Yugoslavia—were formed from the old Austro-Hungarian Empire alone. Other states were carved from the Russian Empire, which had evolved into the Bolshevik-ruled Soviet Union. Under the League of Nations' mandate system, land in former German-held colonial territories and in the former Ottoman Empire was transferred to other nation-states with the specific intent of eventual self-rule and creation of still additional new states.[5] Thus, in Africa, Great Britain received most of Tanganyika and shared Cameroons and Togoland with France, whereas the Union of South Africa was mandated Southwest Africa. In the Middle East, France received Syria, whereas Iraq, Transjordan, and Palestine all became subject to the British crown. In the Pacific, Australia, New Zealand, and Japan were all beneficiaries of the league's mandate system. World War I had shaken the state system, but it had also spread seeds for its further proliferation.

Attacks on Bourgeois Legitimacy

Whereas the collapse of dynastic rule in Austria-Hungary and the Ottoman Empire paved the way for the creation of additional traditional nation-states, the collapse of Czarist Russia led to the formation of a state that proclaimed itself to be of a fundamentally new type. Czar Nicholas II abdicated in February 1917. He was replaced by a provisional government that intended to keep Russia in the war and planned to hold Western-style free elections to form a new government. However, in 1917, the Bolshevik party under V. I. Lenin seized power and proclaimed the creation of a Soviet state under the control of the Russian working class.

Lenin's Bolshevism was one of several varieties of Russian Marxism. As a Marxist, Lenin believed in the inevitability of class conflict and the idea that the dominant class controlled the state, as we saw in Chapter 1. And again as we have seen, Lenin also believed that capitalism led directly to imperialism and war. With the overthrow of capitalism, Lenin concluded, class conflict, imperialism, and war would disappear.

Leaders of other states viewed Lenin and his Bolshevik government and state as a real threat to the international community and acted to suppress it. They extended limited support to Russian groups that opposed the Bolsheviks, and small contingents of Western European, U.S., and Japanese combat forces landed in the czar's old empire. However, after the four bloody years of World War I, none of the interventionist states was seriously committed to the conflict. All eventually withdrew.

Soviet rhetoric and actions gave other states cause for concern. Asserting hostility to the "exploitive" governments of other states, Soviet propaganda called for the proletariat of other nations to rise up against their oppressors. In 1920, Bolshevik forces invaded Poland and attempted to establish a "proletariat dictatorship" there but failed. Although Soviet rhetoric and actions became less revolutionary during the 1920s, hostility remained between the Soviet Union and most other states throughout the 1920s and 1930s. Bourgeois legitimacy had been challenged, and an allegedly new type of state had come into existence in the Soviet Union. This fact would have tremendous significance for the future of the international system of states.

Similarly, in Germany, another allegedly new type of state came into existence. Based on theories of racial superiority and the subservience of non-Germanic people, national socialism, or Nazism, preached a philosophy of expansion. It was an assault both on all non-Germans and on the system of nation-states, for it sought to reduce Europe and beyond to vassals of Hitler and his minions. From this perspective, World War II in Europe was a result of Nazism's offensive against the state system in Europe.

The Second Proliferation of States

As we have seen, World War I shattered the old European empires of Austria-Hungary, Czarist Russia, and the Ottoman Empire, and led to the creation of a number of new states. Following World War II, a similar phenomenon occurred as the states of Europe gradually granted or were forced to grant independence to their former colonial territories. By 1980, with the exception of some 40 dependencies most of which were inhabited by fewer than 100,000 people, European empires were a thing of the past.

With the end of the Belgian, British, French, Portuguese, and Spanish empires, the European-style state had conquered the world. As Table 2-2 shows, the number of states increased drastically in the post–World War II era. Over 50 new states were in Africa alone. Some of the new states remained closely tied to their old colonial masters, sometimes for economic reasons and other times for psychological or cultural reasons. In other cases, the governments of newly independent territories rejected any ties with the former colonial ruling power.

Colonialism, then, was the vehicle that led to the second proliferation of states. Colonialism also left its mark in other ways. Almost invariably, former colonial territories, that is, those states that received their independence following World War II, are the countries of the Developing World, the poor nations of the earth. Although perceptions differ as to the causes of that poverty, few analysts anywhere rejected the assertion that the disparity in wealth that exists between the rich "Northern" states (the established industrial states, primarily located in the Northern Hemisphere) and the poor "Southern" states (the Developing World, primarily located in the Southern Hemisphere) is a cause for concern and potential conflict.[6]

Similarly, in many newly independent states, old colonial boundaries were followed as new states received their independence. In some instances, because of this practice, one nation or tribe sometimes found itself divided among several states, whereas in other instances, one nation or tribe found itself in a multinational state, in the minority, and powerless to

TABLE 2-2   Independent States, 1945–2000

Year	No. of Independent States
1945	54
1950	75
1955	84
1960	107
1965	125
1970	135
1975	155
1980	165
1985	170
1990	170
1995	190+
2000	195+

Source: 1945–1960, from Michael Wallace and J. David Singer, "Intergovernmental Organization in the Global System, 1815–1964: A Quantitative Description," *International Organization,* Vol. 24 (Spring 1970), p. 272; 1965–2000, United Nations' and author's estimates.

Note: These figures are estimates. The international community does not accept a universal definition for "independent state." Therefore, some states are viewed as independent by one government, but not by another.

influence governmental policy decisions. Thus, colonialism not only led to the second proliferation of states, but also carried with it the seeds of instability that plague so much of the world today.

The Third Proliferation of States

The end of the colonial era led many people to conclude that the number of independent states in the international community by the 1980s had reached a relatively stable maximum of about 170. As Table 2-2 shows, during the entire decade of the 1980s, the number of independent states increased only from 165 in 1980 to 170 by 1990. This was a marked decrease in the rate of growth from the preceding 35 years, when during no decade did the number of independent states grow by fewer than 28 new states.

Many people were wrong. As Chapter 1 has shown, the struggle against colonialism sometimes influenced national groups to set aside temporarily their differences as they struggled against colonialism, and the dangers of the East–West conflict usually influenced national groups to accept their inclusion in the state in which they found themselves. With traditional colonial empires having disappeared in the 1970s and the East–West conflict having ended in the early 1990s, the two factors that held nationalism in check were removed.

As a result, the early 1990s witnessed yet another proliferation of states as the Soviet Union, Yugoslavia, and Czechoslovakia all broke up.[7] The Soviet Union's dissolution led to the creation of fifteen nation-states out of the USSR's former fifteen republics. The actual breakup of the Soviet Union occurred reasonably peacefully, but violence nevertheless sometimes flared between ethnic groups within former Soviet republics as smaller ethnic groups fought for their own independence from several of the newly independent states. The most notable case was in Russia where the region of Chechnya fought for independence from Russia. In 1999, Russia launched an assault against Chechnya in an effort to reassert control, and thousands were killed. Even so, the possibility remains that the collapse of the Soviet Union will lead to the creation of more than 15 new states.

Similarly, in the former Yugoslavia, it was not clear how many new states would finally emerge. Slovenia and Macedonia seceded relatively peacefully, but when Croatia seceded, civil war broke out, and thousands of people died in the fighting. It was even worse in Bosnia, where hundreds of thousands died when warfare erupted following Bosnia-Herzegovina's attempt to withdraw from the remains of the Serbian-dominated former Yugoslavia. Even more died in Kosovo in 1998 and 1999 as the Kosovo Liberation Army fought for independence for Kosovo, Yugoslavia resorted to ethnic cleansing of Albanians living in Kosovo, and the North Atlantic Treaty Organization (NATO) launched air attacks against Yugoslavia and eventually occupied Kosovo. None of this resolved Kosovo's status as a state.

Conversely, in Czechoslovakia, Czechs and Slovaks peacefully formed two separate nation-states out of what had been one state. By the dawn of the new century, then, 21 new states had been formed out of what 10 years earlier had been only three states. How many more states might be created was not certain.

The struggle by ethnic groups to create their own self-ruled independent states was not confined to the Soviet Union, Yugoslavia, and Czechoslovakia. Many other ethnic groups throughout the world also either launched or accelerated drives for national independence from the states in which they were included. Sometimes these drives were peaceful, as in some Scots' efforts to secede from Great Britain and some *Québecois'* efforts to withdraw from Canada. In other cases, these drives were violent, as in some Basques' efforts to secede from Spain; the Kurds' efforts to establish their own state out of Iraq, Iran, and Turkey; or the Sikhs' efforts to withdraw from India.

In still other instances, as in Angola and Afghanistan, it became clear that wars that had once been considered part of the East–West conflict were in fact at least as much— and probably more—civil wars between different ethnic groups or tribes seeking to assert their own national power and identity.

The proliferation of states also led to another problem, namely, the multiplication of the number of decision-making units in the world. This often complicated the conduct of foreign policy by states. For example, during the height of European colonial power each European government had to take into account the reaction of only 20 to 30 states to a particular policy. In the 1990s, however, governments needed to take into account the reaction of as many as 190 states to a policy.

Obviously, some states are more important than others to a particular government, and many states may even be ignored. Nevertheless, the point to be made is simple: The proliferation of states has tremendously complicated the conduct of foreign policy. In 1918, perhaps 50 states existed throughout the world, and perhaps 1,225 sets of bilateral political relations existed between and among them. If only 150 states existed, then 11,175 sets of bilateral political relations would be possible. With approximately 200 states in existence, the number of possible bilateral political relationship far exceeds even this.[8]

Indeed, then, the world has become far more complex than it has been, if only because so many states now exist.

THE NATIONAL INTEREST

Throughout the evolution of the state, states have recognized no higher authority than themselves. Obviously, then, the state is the entity that defines its own interests and that determines how it will attempt to achieve them. A state's interests are called the **national interest,** and the methods and actions it employs to attempt to achieve its national interests are called national policy.

What is National Interest?

Unfortunately, the concept of national interest is extremely ambiguous. Who within a state defines the national interest? Do national interests change when governments change either peacefully or by force? Which group or groups within a state define who the friends and enemies of a state are? When serious internal disagreements exist concerning national interests and national policy, which view of interest and policy is truly national? Does a state in fact have long-term interests determined by geography, resource base, population, cultural ties, and other factors that transcend short-term or midterm definitions of national interest that are influenced by the politics of the day? The ambiguities are many.

These questions are more than academic inquiries relevant only to the classroom. Throughout history, individuals and groups have appealed to the national interest to justify the policies that they preferred. Hannibal believed that the national interest of Carthage dictated war against Rome; he may have been correct, but because of his failure to defeat Rome in the Punic Wars, the Romans eventually sacked and destroyed Carthage. Thomas Jefferson, despite his reputation as pro-French and despite his opposition to a strong central government, upon hearing that Napoleon intended to occupy New Orleans as part of a secret agreement with Spain, informed the French emperor that the United States considered whoever possessed New Orleans to be "our natural and habitual enemy." Jefferson then promptly expanded the power of the central government by buying not only New Orleans, but also the entire Louisiana Territory. Nine years later, Napoleon determined that France's national interest dictated he should initiate a disastrous invasion of Russia.

National interest is variously defined today as well. In 1999, President Clinton believed that the American national interest was served by launching air attacks against Serbian-controlled Yugoslavia in retaliation for Serbian brutality against ethnic Albanians living in the Yugoslavian province of Kosovo, but many Americans disagreed. Similarly, Russian President Vladimir Putin in 1999 and 2000 believed that Russia's national interests were served by assaulting Chechnya to prevent it from seceding from Russia. Many Russians disagreed. And in many European states, the turn of the century witnessed continuing debates about whether political and economic unity within the European Union served their country's national interest or undermined its sovereignty.

What, then, is national interest, and who is to define it? What factors should be considered when an attempt is made to define it? With roughly 200 states in the world today, these and other related questions are of great importance. Perhaps the most significant question, however, is what should "count" when national interest is being defined. Inevitably, different individuals give different answers.

Criteria of National Interest

To some, *economic criteria* is the answer. Any policy that enhances a state's economic position is seen to be in the national interest. Improving a country's balance of trade, strengthening a country's industrial base, and guaranteeing a country's access to oil, natural gas, or other energy or nonfuel mineral resources may all be considered to be in its national interest. Often, however, economic criteria may conflict with other criteria. For example, should one country continue to trade with another country if the second country uses the materials it buys to subjugate other countries? Such was the dilemma the United States found itself in the years immediately before World War II, both in its relations with Germany and with Japan. Similarly, should one country seek to maintain access to the mineral resources that a second country has if that second country has an internal social system that is repugnant to most of the citizens of the first country? Such was the dilemma in which the United States found itself in its relations with South Africa when apartheid was in place.

Ideological criteria are sometimes used as an important determinant of national interest. Most countries either formally or informally use an ideology to justify both their legitimacy and their policies. For example, until relatively recently, most Marxist states generally considered their interests to be quite similar to one another. Likewise, Western liberal-democratic states often saw their interests paralleling one another's, whereas poverty-stricken Developing World states regularly sided with one another in efforts to restructure the international economic system. But with the collapse of Soviet and Eastern European communism and the rediscovery of economics, ideological criteria have become less important in the struggle to define national interest in many states. Ideological criteria still influence states to adopt certain ways of looking at the world and of looking at their national interest, and in some states, ideological criteria remain extremely important. But on the whole, the use of ideological criteria to define national interest has declined.

The augmentation of *power* is another method of defining national interest. Power was defined by Hans Morgenthau, perhaps the leading proponent of the realpolitik school of thought, as anything that allows one state to establish and maintain control over another.[9] Any policy that enhances a state's power is therefore in its national interest. Power, of course, may be augmented in a variety of ways, such as by improving economic strength, by using ideological persuasion, or by enhancing military capabilities. To Morgenthau, power permits a state to survive, and therefore it is in the interest of all states to acquire power.

Military security and/or advantage is another prominent criterion for determining national interest. With force playing such a prominent role in international relations, states

In 1994, the United States contemplated invading Haiti to restore democratically elected Haitian President Jean-Bertrand Aristide to power after he had been overthrown by a military coup several years earlier. This led to a debate in the United States whether such an action was in the U.S.' national interest. Here, Aristide is shown meeting with President Bill Clinton.

perhaps only naturally look to military security as a minimum determinant of their national interest. Proponents of military security argue that a chief responsibility of any state is to provide safety for its inhabitants; proponents of military advantage argue that the best way to achieve that safety is through military advantage.

Morality and legality are similarly contentious issues when attempts are made to determine national interest. Although in many instances the "right" or "wrong" of an issue may be at first apparent, closer examination often clouds what at first glance may have been a clear moral or legal conclusion. The 1994 debate over whether the United States should invade Haiti to restore its democratically elected President Jean-Bertrand Aristide to power provides a perfect example of the complexities that spring up when one attempts to define national interest through morality and legality. On the one hand, it was clear that the Haitian military had overthrown a fairly elected president and was terrorizing and violating the human rights of many Haitians. But on the other hand, did these facts, as outrageous as they were, give the United States the right to invade Haiti, remove the military from power, and restore Aristide? And did the United Nations eventual approval of the use of "all means necessary" to restore the rightful government to power in Haiti provide such justification if it was not there previously?

Numerous other criteria also exist for determining the national interest. Some people argue that national interest should be determined by *cultural affinity,* that is, by defining a state's interests to coincide with the interests of other states whose language or traditions may be the same as one's own. Others argue that *ethnic* or *race* issues should play a large role in determining national interest. Still other individuals see national interest as any action or set of actions that allow a country to make all its decisions for itself, regardless of what the economic, military, or other implications of that total independence would be.

Summation

What, then, "counts" when national interest is being defined? The answer, obviously, depends on who is doing the defining. In the minds of some, so-called objective factors such as economic strength, military capabilities, or the size of the resource base may prove dominant when national interest is being defined. Others may view subjective factors such as morality, legality, or ideology as more important. National interest therefore must be viewed less as a constant set of national objectives than as a changing approximation of what the leaders of a country or other significant individuals or groups within a country view as important. Even this general observation must be qualified, however, for the rate of change of these approximations of national interest may differ considerably from one country to the next.

Even the type of government that a state has may play a major role in determining how a state's national interests are defined. Governments of Western-style democracies, for example, often take into account the wishes and desires of various interest groups that wield domestic political power; more autocratic or dictatorial governments define their national interests with less concern for inputs from domestic interest groups. This does not necessarily mean, however, that the foreign policies of autocratic states have the universal support of those who implement policies; sometimes leaders of autocratic states must accommodate disagreements among themselves to arrive at and implement policy.

National interest, then, is a difficult term with which to come to grips. Within a single state, different individuals and different groups define the national interest in different ways, even at the same time. It is a concept that has no universal meaning. Even with those shortcomings, however, national interest is a useful concept, for it provides us with a tool with which we can understand, at least in general terms, the objectives that states seek in international affairs.

THE STATE AND THE "BALANCE OF POWER"

Fashioning an appropriate policy is only part of the problem that national decision makers face when they undertake international activities. They must also have appropriate means at their disposal to enable them to undertake their policy. Put simply, they must have *power* to implement their policy.

Unfortunately, the exact meaning of power is a matter of considerable debate. It is discussed in detail throughout Framework Four (Chapters 12 to 15). Here, however, we must detail the concept of the **balance of power** for it has played and continues to play a major role in the relations between and among states.

Balance of power is used to denote several types of interstate relations. In some cases, it means that two states have approximately equal capabilities. Thus, the statement that "a balance of power existed between the United States and the Soviet Union" meant just that—U.S. and Soviet capabilities were approximately equal. This balance of power relationship is depicted in Figure 2-1(a).

In other cases, balance of power means that an imbalance exists! Thus, the statement that "the balance of power is in the U.S. favor over Iraq" implies that U.S. capabilities are greater than Iraqi capabilities, and no balance exists. This balance of power relationship is depicted in Figure 2-1(b).

Both these meanings of balance of power envision a relatively static and nonchanging relationship. But the concept of balance of power may also be used to envision a dynamic and changing relationship. Thus, when Israel moved into Lebanon during the summer of 1982 and destroyed much of the Syrian military there and forced the Palestine Liberation Organization out of Lebanon, "the balance of power in the Middle East shifted toward Israel." Imbalance replaced relative balance. This meaning of balance of power is illustrated in Figure 2-1(c). Of course, the dynamic nature of this third meaning of balance of power can also be used to describe a movement from imbalance to balance. For example, as the Soviet Union strengthened its military forces during the 1960s and 1970s, "the balance of Soviet–American power moved toward equilibrium." Figure 2-1(d) depicts this transformation.

The concept of balance of power need not apply only to the relationship between two individual actors. Several actors or groups of actors may be included. Thus, it is possible to have a balance of power between organizations, as existed between the North Atlantic Treaty Organization (NATO) and the Warsaw Pact through most of the post–World War II era. Similarly, regional and even global balances of power may exist. Thus, in the Middle East, a regional balance of power is sometimes said to exist between Israel and neighboring Arab states.

The nature of the balance of power system in international relations warrants closer examination, and will be presented in some detail in Chapter 7.[10] Here, two final points must be made about the concept of balance of power. First, there is no single answer to the question, "How is power measured?" Chapter 12 explores power in some detail, but here, suffice it to say that there are many ways to measure and to acquire power. For example, during most of the balance-of-power era that existed during the 19th century, the balance of power was almost universally assumed to mean military capabilities. The same assumption prevailed during most of the era of bipolarity. Today, however, economic strength, moral and ideological example, and other factors are often assumed to be important ingredients in determining whether a balance of power exists.

Second, regardless of which definition of the concept of balance of power is used, the fulcrum (i.e., the balancing point) is almost always viewed as a single point, as shown in

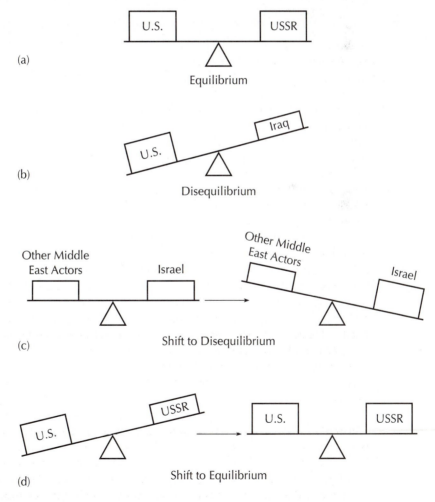

FIGURE 2-1 Meanings of balance of power.

Figure 2-2(a). Envisioned in this manner, the addition of even a small quantity of "power" to one side or the other may change the balance, as illustrated in Figure 2-2(b). However, if the fulcrum is viewed as a widely based central area rather than a single point, as in Figure 2-2(c), even significant additions of "power" to one side or the other may be insufficient to change the balance. Figures 2-2(d) and (e) illustrate this change. The degree of threat that analysts and policy makers see when one side in a balance-of-power relationship enhances its power is thus a function not only of power, but also of the width of the fulcrum. A conceptual model, that is, the type of balancing device that we mentally create, therefore may determine the degree of balance or imbalance that we see. Unfortunately, however, no objective method exists to determine how wide the fulcrum should be in a

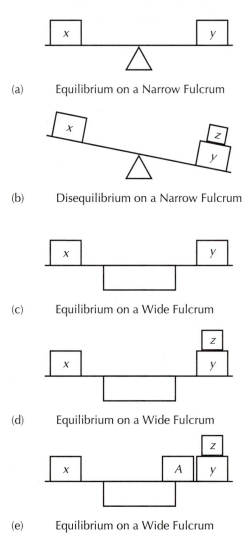

(a)   Equilibrium on a Narrow Fulcrum

(b)   Disequilibrium on a Narrow Fulcrum

(c)   Equilibrium on a Wide Fulcrum

(d)   Equilibrium on a Wide Fulcrum

(e)   Equilibrium on a Wide Fulcrum

FIGURE 2-2   The balance of power and the fulcrum.

"balance-of-power" construct. Nevertheless, the "balance of power" has been and continues to be widely used by analysts and policy makers as an analytical tool. Despite its shortcomings, no replacement has found wide acceptance.

 ## CHALLENGES TO THE STATE

The state has dominated international political affairs for over 350 years. In recent years, however, the utility of the state as we currently know it has been increasingly questioned. As we have already seen, some groups identify the state as the cause of war, whereas others maintain that increased global economic interdependence has rendered the state an obsolete organizational concept. In other cases, transnational ideological or religious movements assert that beliefs supercede the parochial interests of states.

Here, the point to be made is a simple one, specifically, that the primacy of the state in international relations *is* being challenged. The most significant challenges come from five separate directions: 1. economic interdependence; 2. technical advances; 3. international governmental organizations; 4. transnational movements and thought systems; and 5. internal fragmentation.

The Challenge of Economic Interdependence

In the not-too-distant past, one of the primary objectives of states was to attain as great a degree of economic self-sufficiency as was feasible. Within the past 30 years, however, fewer and fewer states have pursued economic self-sufficiency as a primary objective of national policy.

This has led to a situation where economic interdependence exists between and among most states, that is to say, a situation where states do not produce everything that they need for themselves, but depend on other states to produce some of the goods and services that they need. The reason that this situation has developed is in many instances one of simple economic self-interest. Goods and services may be obtained more cheaply elsewhere than they can be obtained domestically.

Thus, few finished products in today's world are made entirely in one country. Whether it be automobiles, computers, aircraft, or almost any other manufactured product, raw materials, component parts, and even final assembly often come from and take place in many countries. Economic interdependence has become a present-day reality. Indeed, given the increased volume of world trade, the vital nature of much of that trade, and the international linkages that have developed in manufacturing processes, the challenge of economic interdependence is a serious one for the contemporary state. Why, critics of the state ask, need the state continue to exist if trade is so vital, if economic self-sufficiency is a thing of the past, and if economic and manufacturing efficiency can be improved by an international division of labor?

As shown in Chapter 1, some trade barriers created by states to assure national economic autonomy already have been removed in Europe, North America, South America, and Southeast Asia, and if the Asian–Pacific Economic Cooperation area and the Free Trade Area of the Americas are eventually implemented, even more will disappear. The

1994 General Agreement on Tariffs and Trade also contributed immensely to the reduction of barriers to trade between states. And as advances in information and communication technologies ease the electronic movement of money, data, and information across borders, regional and global marketplaces move closer to reality. In an economic sense, then, it is possible to argue that the world may be moving toward a poststate era.

There is another side to the coin. Many people are concerned that the growth of economic interdependence will lead to unemployment, and the leaders of some states are unwilling to become even more dependent on external resources to meet critical economic needs. Thus, in 1999 and 2000, tens of thousands of American workers and other concerned citizens turned out in Seattle and Washington to express their opposition to the World Trade Organization and its efforts to increase economic interdependence by reducing trade barriers. This sentiment is not restricted to the United States. Similarly, American and Japanese leaders often bemoan their respective country's dependence on external sources of oil to meet much of their national needs for energy.

Nor should it be overlooked that some states are "more interdependent" than others. For example, Japan must import almost all its raw materials, and in turn must export finished products to pay for these imports. In comparison, the Soviet Union was self-sufficient in most resources, and therefore was less reliant on foreign raw materials. Degree of interdependence is thus an important factor in conditioning the international behavior of a state.

Thus, although the world may be moving toward a poststate era in economic relations, the state can marshal persuasive arguments of its own that economic autarchy and independence are still desirable objectives. The challenge of economic interdependence to the state is a real challenge, however, and will not easily be overcome.[11]

The Challenge of Technology

Technology, particularly advanced information and communication technologies and military technologies, also challenges the state's dominant place in international affairs.

As discussed in Chapter 1, fiber-optic cables, wireless communications, computer advances, easier human-computer interface, improved satellites, cellular and digital communication technologies, and advanced networking are information and communication technologies that increase the capacity, flexibility, and speed of communications, and the Internet and World Wide Web also make it easier for people in widely separated locations to communicate. These technologies challenge the state from three directions.

First, the increased importance of information and communication technologies has rendered states vulnerable if information and communication flows are disrupted. Given the reliance of industrial states on electronic transfer of financial data and information, any disruption of such transfers could raise havoc. Similarly, given the reliance of most governments on electronic communications to maintain contact with their peoples, disruption of communications could significantly degrade a government's ability to govern.

Second, because economic activity is increasingly conducted across international boundaries, the question arises whether states are losing their ability to provide for the economic well-being of their populations. This phenomenon is already occurring. International finance and banking have been transformed by global electronic fund transfers at a moment's notice. Other service sector industries are also internationalizing their capabilities with these technologies. This leads to the question of whether states are losing their ability to provide economic well-being for their population. If they are, why need states exist?

The same question may be asked about nation-states' provision of a sense of belonging to the dominant nationality within them. Even though nationalism is on the rise, nations have not always needed states to consider themselves nations. Indeed, advanced information and communication technologies open possibilities for peoples of a single nation to be geographically remote from one another but still retain a sense of identity. Put differently, advanced information and communication technologies may allow individuals to overcome boundaries of time and distance, raising questions about whether states remain necessary for nations to have an identity.

As for military technologies, there is no doubt that the state is vulnerable as never before. Barring perfection of a new exotic technology defensive system that would render nuclear weapons and intercontinental ballistic missiles (ICBMs) ineffective, the advent of nuclear weapons and ICBM delivery systems removed the state's rationale that it could provide effective security for its citizens. Even at the conventional level, modern weapons are appallingly effective and have a long reach; it is doubtful that even the victorious side in a large-scale war could assure its population's security.

Despite the end of the Cold War, uncertainty remains about whether states can defend their citizens from external attack. More and more countries are obtaining the capability to build nuclear weapons, and the danger of sub-state actors including terrorists obtaining nuclear weapons is real. Similarly, many states and other international actors have the ability to make or to obtain chemical and biological weapons.

Just as in the case of nuclear weapons, there is no definite and certain defense against these other weapons of mass destruction. The question thus remains for states, how well can they actually protect their citizens given the challenge of advanced military technologies?[12]

The Challenge of International Governmental Organizations

Although international governmental organizations (IGOs) are not new, the challenge they present to established states is. Many of the political, economic, social, and military problems that confront contemporary states cut across national boundaries, and in response to this reality, governments of states created IGOs to enable them better to meet their problems. In some cases, primarily in Western Europe, states have surrendered effective decision-making and policy-implementing powers to IGOs. Both the European Council and the Nordic Council, for example, can determine export and import prices for selected products. With the creation of the European Union (EU) in 1993 and the drive for political and economic unity in the EU continuing, the possibility is strong that more and more European states will surrender more and more of their decision-making prerogatives to the EU.

There remains continuing concern in many quarters in Europe about the impact of the EU on state sovereignty. Nevertheless, the EU remains a major challenge to the primacy of the state in Europe. It is ironic that even though the concepts of the nation-state and national sovereignty were first born in Europe, the most serious challenge to their continuation is there.[13]

The Challenge of Transnational Movements and Thought

The state system that currently dominates international affairs arose from the ruins of a European wide religious empire that pledged its allegiance to the pope. It is somewhat ironic that one of the most serious challenges confronting the current state system comes from transnational movements and thought that claim the allegiance of individuals and groups. Some of these movements are specifically religious, as is fundamentalist Islam, whereas others are specifically antireligious, as is Marxism.

The resurgence of fundamentalist Islam may be traced to the fall of the shah of Iran and the coming to power of Ayatollah Khomeini in 1979. After a series of fits and starts, Khomeini proclaimed Iran an Islamic republic, and announced that he and his followers sought to convert other states to Islamic republics. Although territorial designs on neighboring states were denied, other Arab states interpreted Khomeini's message as a direct assault on their legitimacy and sovereignty. To them, Khomeini's Iran represented a direct threat. Khomeini's continuing calls for a return to fundamentalist Islamic teachings only solidified their perception that he sought to establish a transnational political–religious entity following his version of the Shiite Islamic faith.

Marxism also rejected the legitimacy of the state. In the *Communist Manifesto,* Karl Marx and Friedrich Engels argued that the nation-state and nationalism were tools of the ruling bourgeois class to divide and weaken the proletariat. Eventually, Marx believed, the proletariat would develop international class consciousness and see through the sham of nationalism perpetuated by the bourgeoisie. Following the proletariat revolution, Marx concluded, the state would "wither away." Even today, Marxists maintain that the state will eventually disappear.

In a practical sense, proponents of both fundamentalist Islam and revolutionary Marxism found it necessary to create their own bases of power in states. Both, however, deny that their states are traditional. To Khomeini, Iran was subservient to Allah and the Koran; to the Soviet leadership, the USSR was subservient to its working class. Even more strikingly, Soviet ideologues saw fit to declare that communism could develop differently in different countries, taking into account local history, culture, levels of economic development, and other factors.

The collapse of communism in Eastern Europe and the Soviet Union as well as the movement toward moderation in Iran following Khomeini's death in 1989 lead some observers to conclude that Marxism and fundamentalist Islam were ideas whose time had come and gone. But this does not mean that the challenge of transnational movements and thought to the state has passed into history.

Indeed, in one sense, the American insistence in 1999 that Yugoslavia's treatment of its Albanian citizens in Kosovo violated international standards of human rights may be seen as the most recent challenge presented by transnational ideas to the state. In essence, the U.S. argument was that certain human rights are more important than sovereignty. If this argument becomes widely accepted, it clearly will present a significant challenge to the continued primacy of the state.

The Challenge of Internal Fragmentation

As defined earlier in this chapter, a nation-state is a geographically bounded legal entity under a single government, the population of which psychologically considers itself to be in some way, shape, or form related. As shown earlier, there are many indications that nationalism, the very force that led to the existence of nation-states, remains strong and is growing. However, this very nationalism is leading to further fragmentation of states, and the creation of new "ministates," which by themselves may not be viable political-economic units. In a certain sense, then, nationalism itself presents a challenge to the state because of its potential to fragment existing states and create nonviable new ministates.

To one extent or another, countries on every continent are beset by separatist pressures. Africa has been particularly affected. In Nigeria during the late 1960s, the Ibo tribe attempted to secede and establish the state of Biafra. A bloody civil war ended the Ibos' effort. The Angolan Civil War was and is as much the product of tribal conflict as ideological antipathy. In Zimbabwe in the 1970s, Robert Mugabe's rule was challenged by Joshua Nkomo; both men based their prestige and influence on their own ethnic groups within Zimbabwe. In Ethiopia, Eritrean secessionist movements fought for over 30 years against two different governments in Addis Ababa. Finally, in 1993, a referendum was held in Eritrea and the Eritreans voted nearly unanimously for independence. In the Western Sahara, the Polisario guerillas began their struggle for independence from Morocco in the 1970s, and fought on into the 1990s until the United Nations arranged a precarious peace.

In recent years, many European countries have also experienced extensive growth of separatist pressures. Since 1991, these pressures have led to the dissolution of Czechoslovakia, the Soviet Union, and Yugoslavia. But these were not the only countries where the impacts of nationalism within established states have been felt. In Great Britain, Scotland and Wales the local self-government, and Italy have established an autonomous provincial government in South Tyrolea. The Basques seek independence from Spain, and some Normans seek independence from France. Belgium has changed its constitution so that the Flemings and the Walloons now enjoy cultural autonomy.

In Asia, Bangladesh received its independence from Pakistan after India defeated Pakistan in full-scale warfare. Meanwhile, in Australia, the sporadic Westralia movement again flickered to life during the 1970s and 1980s.

Even North America is not immune to this challenge of fragmentation. Quebec continues to flirt with secession from Canada and has consuls in a number of European and American cities. Puerto Rican nationalists periodically demand independence from the United States. Perhaps most subtly, throughout the 1990s, more and more American states and even cities established trade offices overseas to seek external foreign investment. In addition, governors of many states led trade delegations overseas for the same purpose. Although these examples present no threat of secession, they do indicate that even within the United States, concern for state identity and wealth is influencing changes in policy.

Internal fragmentation, then, is a genuine challenge to many states. In some states, the challenge is a crisis. In others, it is little more than a joke. The point, however, is that the state must face another challenge to its three centuries of international domination.

CONCLUSION

Despite these challenges to the dominance of the state in the international arena, nothing indicates that the state is in imminent danger of demise. Questions are being raised, however, about the reasons for its existence. If it can no longer offer economic independence, provide military security, or cope with transnational problems, why then does it continue to exist? One answer to that question is that the state may provide a sense of identity to its inhabitants, but even that is not a satisfactory response by itself. Ayatollah Khomeini was not alone in giving his allegiance to a movement, thought system, or organization that transcends the state, and the Ibos, Basques, and *Québecois* are not alone in their resentment of and opposition to the governments of the states in which they currently reside.

Perhaps Hans Morgenthau had the best and simplest answer to the question of why the state continues to exist despite its obvious shortcomings—*power,* defined in its broadest terms. Except for those in Antarctica, every person on the earth lives on land that is controlled or claimed by a state, and all the land on the face of the earth, Antarctica again excepted, has been divided by states. International law and common practice recognize the right of states to use force both internationally and domestically, to control their own citizens and citizens of other states living within their territorial confines (except diplomats), and to make laws that determine how and whether other actors will operate on their territory. The sovereignty of states may be less absolute than it once was, but states still dominate the international system.

KEY TERMS AND CONCEPTS

Peace of Westphalia   the treaty that ended the Thirty Years War in 1648 and established the European System of States

sovereignty   the concept that no international authority higher than the state exists

legitimacy   the concept that all states have the right to exist and that within each state's boundaries, authority belongs only to the ruler

duties (of states)   the belief that in their relations with each other, states have responsibilities to fulfill and rules to follow

state   a geographically bounded entity governed by a central authority that has the ability to make laws, rules, and decision, and to enforce laws, rules, and decisions within its boundaries

nation   people who view themselves as linked to each other in some manner; any grouping of people who consider themselves a nation

nation-state   a state whose inhabitants consider themselves a nation

nationalism   the psychological force that binds people who identify with one another together

first round of empire   the period during the sixteenth, seventeenth, and eighteenth centuries when European States built vast colonial empires to increase their wealth, power, and prestige

mercantilism   an economic philosophy that says state power comes from wealth; hence, state policy should maximize wealth through colonial acquisitions, trade, war, etc.

regal legitimacy   the belief that a king had a divine right to rule

second round of empire   the period from about 1870 until early in the twentieth century when European States, Japan, and the United States as well expanded their overseas empires

first proliferation of states   following World War I, several European Empires including Russia, Austria-Hungary, and the Ottoman Empire broke up, creating many new states

bourgeois legitimacy   the belief that states should be ruled by democratically elected governments

second proliferation of states   following World War II, many European States divested themselves of their colonies; as a result, many new states were formed

colonialism   the practice followed by European and other States from the sixteeenth to mid twentieth centuries of establishing control over land and people, often in distant lands; also called imperialism

third proliferation of states   in the early 1900s, the Soviet Union, Czechoslovakia, and Yugoslavia broke up, creating many new states

national interest   a vague term intended to reflect the interests, desires, goals, and objectives that a nation-state seeks

balance of power   a concept that refers to a balanced distribution of capabilities between two states or groups of states

challenges to the state   the text identifies economic interdependence, military technologies, international governmental organizations, transnational movements and thought systems, and internal fragmentation as challenges to the state

 ## *WEBSITE REFERENCES*

Peace of Westphalia: *www.yale.edu/lawweb/avalon/westphal.htm*   the treaty text

sovereignty: *www.sovereignty.net*   the website of Sovereignty International which "exists to promote the belief that the best government is empowered only by the consent of those governed"

nation-state: *campus.northpark.edu/history/WebChron/World/Nation-State*   a useful discussion of the development of the nation-state from 1789 to 1914

nationalism: *www.wisc.edu/nationalism/*   a collection of resources on nationalism from the University of Wisconsin's Nationalism Project

colonialism: *www.nsu.edu/history/European_Colonialism2.htm*   discussions of European colonialism

challenges to the state: *www/globalpolicy.org.nations.indexfut.htm*   a discussion of the future of states

 ## *NOTES*

1. For several studies of nationalism, see Charles Kupchan, ed., *Nationalism and Nationalities in the New Europe* (Ithaca, NY: Cornell University Press, 1995); Geoffrey Howe, *Nationalism and the Nation-State* (New York: Cambridge University Press, 1995); and Wolfgang Danspeckgruber, ed., *The Self-Determination of Peoples: Community, Nation, and State in an Interdependent World* (Boulder, CO: Lynne Rienner Publishers, 2000).

2. René Albrecht-Carrie's *A Diplomatic History of Europe Since the Congress of Vienna* (New York: Harper & Row, 1958), uses the methodology of diplomatic history to detail this period.

3. American expansionism during this period is chronicled in Foster R. Dulles, *Prelude to World Power: American Diplomatic History, 1860–1900* (New York: Macmillan, 1965); Walter LaFeber, *The New Empire: An Interpretation of American Expansion*

1860–1898 (Ithaca, NY: Cornell University Press, 1963); and H. Wayne Morgan, *America's Road to Empire* (New York: John Wiley, 1965).

4. For details of the Russian fiasco, see David MacKenzie and Michael W. Curran, *A History of Russia and the Soviet Union* (Homewood, IL: Dorsey Press, 1977), pp. 434–436.

5. See "Covenant of the League of Nations," Article 22, in *Essential Facts about the League of Nations* (Geneva: League of Nations, 1935).

6. No less an authority than Henry Kissinger proclaimed in 1975 that "poverty levels may be more of a threat to the security of the world than anything else."

7. For several recent studies on this third proliferation of states, see, for example, Anthony W. Birch, *Nationalism and National Integration* (New York: Unwin Hyman Academic Press, 1989); Uri Ra'anan et al., eds., *State and Nation in Multi-Ethnic Societies: The Breakup of Multinational States* (Manchester: Manchester University Press, 1992); and R. B. J. Walker and Saul H. Mendlovitz, eds., *Contending Sovereignties: Redefining Political Community* (Boulder, CO: Lynne Rienner, 1990).

8. The mathematical formula that determines the number of bilateral relations x that may exist between n variables is $x = n!/r \, (n - 4)!$, where r is the number of members in each combination. Thus, for a world in which 50 states exist, $x = 1,225$. In a world in which 150 states exist, $x = 11,175$.

9. See Hans J. Morgenthau, *Politics Among Nations* (New York: Alfred A. Knopf, 1948), esp. Chap. 3.

10. For interesting discussions of balance of power concepts and theories, see Charles W. Kegley and Gregory Raymond, *A Multipolar Peace? Great Power Politics in the Twenty-First Century* (New York, NY: St. Martin's Press, 1994); and Michael Sheehan, *The Balance of Power: History and Theory* (New York, NY: Routledge, 1996).

11. For further discussion of interdependence, see Lester Brown, *The Interdependence of Nations* (New York: Foreign Policy Association, 1972); Robert O. Keohane and Joseph S. Nye, *Power and Interdependence* (Boston: Little, Brown, 1989); Bruce Russet et al., *Choices in World Politics: Sovereignty and Interdependence* (New York: W. H. Freeman, 1989); and Peter B. Kenen, *Understanding Interdependence: The Macroeconomics of the Open Economy* (Princeton: Princeton University Press, 1995). See also Herman M. Schwartz, *State Versus Markets: History, Geography, and the Development of the International Political Economy* (New York: St. Martin's Press, 1994).

12. For further discussion of the role that technology plays in international affairs, see James N. Rosenau, *Turbulence in World Politics: A Theory of Change and Continuity* (Princeton: Princeton University Press, 1990); Eugene B. Skolnikoff, *The Elusive Transformation: Science, Technology, and the Evolution of International Politics* (Princeton: Princeton University Press, 1992); and Dennis Pirages, *Global Technopolitics: The International Politics of Technology and Resources* (Pacific Grove, CA: Brooks-Cole, 1989).

13. For a discussion of the challenge presented to states by international government organizations, nongovernmental organizations, and multinational corporations, see Hendrik Spruyt, *The Sovereign State and Its Competitors* (Princeton: Princeton University Press, 1994).

Chapter 3

International Governmental Organizations

- What is an IGO and what does it do?
- How have IGOs changed over time?
- What does the UN do and how is it structured?
- How effective has the UN been?
- What does the European Union actually accomplish?

International governmental organizations (IGOs) are so named for a basic reason: They are organizations that are created by two or more sovereign states. They meet regularly and have full-time staffs. They are organizations in which the interests and policies of the member states are put forward by the representatives of the respective states. Membership in IGOs is voluntary, and therefore in a technical sense, IGOs do not challenge state sovereignty. In an actual sense, however, they may in fact challenge sovereignty.

IGOs may be categorized according to breadth of membership or scope of purpose. Membership may be globally, regionally, or otherwise defined. Thus, for example, both the League of Nations and the United Nations sought to be global organizations with as wide a membership as possible. Regional IGOs are geographically defined, such as the Organization of American States (OAS), the Organization of African Unity (OAU), the Association of Southeast Asian Nations (ASEAN) and the European Union (E. U.). Otherwise defined IGOs include the British Commonwealth, which is restricted to former colonies of the British Empire, and the International Wool Study Group, whose membership includes only those states that seek to cooperate in improving their wool production.

IGOs may be described as broad-purpose or limited-purpose. Broad-purpose IGOs operate in a variety of political, economic, military, cultural, social, technical, legal, or developmental milieus; their membership may be globally, regionally, or otherwise defined. The United Nations is an example of a global broad-purpose organization; the North Atlantic

TABLE 3-1   **Examples of Types of International Government Organizations**

Membership	Broad-Purpose	Limited-Purpose
Global	UN	WHO
Regional	NATO, ASEAN, OAU	COMECON, Desert Locust Control Organization of East Africa
Other	British Commonwealth	International Wool Study Group

Treaty Organization (NATO) is a regional broad-purpose organization, although its primary function is military in nature; and the British Commonwealth is an otherwise-defined broad-purpose IGO. Limited-purpose IGOs, also called functional IGOs, concentrate their activities in a single area; their membership may again be globally, regionally, or otherwise defined. The World Health Organization (WHO), for example, is a global narrow-purpose IGO; the Desert Locust Control Organization of East Africa is a regional narrow-purpose IGO; and the International Wool Study Group is an otherwise-defined narrow-purpose IGO. Table 3-1 schematically groups these IGOs. It must be stressed, however, that this is an extremely simplistic scheme for grouping them.

Why do states find IGOs so useful and continue to create them even though, as we saw at the end of Chapter 2, some IGOs challenge the dominance of the state? A number of answers exist and are explored in the following section. In addition, the next section examines some institutional structures of modern IGOs.

THE STRUCTURE AND FUNCTION OF MODERN IGOS

As a rule, IGOs are established by treaty or executive agreement between two or more states. States create IGOs to provide a means and a forum for cooperation among states in functional areas where cooperation offers advantages for all or most of the member states. These areas of cooperation may be political, economic, military, cultural, social, technical, legal, or developmental in nature. There is practically no area of human endeavor that could benefit from cooperation from which IGOs have been excluded.

IGOs are therefore sometimes called transnational institutions, that is, they are institutions whose membership transcends traditional state boundaries, but that have no clear authority to enforce their decisions on their members. A very few IGOs have moved from transnational status to supranational status and do have authority over even member states that disagree with the IGOs' decisions. One such supranational IGO is the European Union, discussed later in this chapter.

Regardless of which areas they function in, IGOs generally share a number of institutional characteristics. All have permanent headquarters, often in major Western cities such as Brussels, Geneva, London, New York, Rome, or Paris. Regional IGOs are headquartered most regularly in a major city within the affected region's domain, such as Bangkok,

Chapter 3

IT AND IGOS:
STRENGTHENING INTERNATIONALISM

Since they are created by states, IGOs in most respects are hostage to the desires of states. This will not change as a result of increased use of advanced information technologies. Nevertheless, since IGOs operate across state boundaries and often must cope with problems imposed by time and distance, the capabilities provided by advanced information technologies will help IGOs overcome constraints imposed by time and distance. In the process, they may also expand the influence of IGOs. An example may help illustrate the point.

The UN's associated agencies have outposts and operating arms scattered around the world. As these outposts and operating arms become increasingly connected both to each other and to UN headquarters in New York via advanced telecommunications networks, the quality of the data and information they collect, report, and analyze is improving and becoming more easily accessible. For example, the UN already collects large quantities of environmental information, more and more of it in real time. Assuming the countries of the world look increasingly to the UN to provide accurate information to them about global issues such as those discussed in Chapters 17, 18, and 19—war and peace, human rights, and health and the environ-

ment, among others, this will undoubtedly lead to greater influence for the United Nations.

This does not mean that states will become more willing to transfer any of their sovereignty to the UN or any other IGO. In all likelihood, IGOs will find it as difficult as ever, perhaps even more difficult than ever, to acquire supranational authority and capabilities. Even so, to the extent that advanced information and communication technologies increase the ability of IGOs to perform tasks that states on their own cannot successfully accomplish, advanced information and communication technologies may lead to the migration of more responsibilities from states to IGOs.

Indeed, one of the reasons the European Union (EU) has been as successful as it has been is because advanced information technologies have helped integrate the states that are members of the EU. The E. U. has even launched formal programs in information technology designed to accelerate this trend. Seeing the EU's successes, more states may become increasingly willing to allow IGOs to assume a degree of supranational authority as advanced information technologies become more capable and more a part of every aspect of human endeavor.

Buenos Aires, and Moscow. In several regional IGOs such as the Organization for African Unity (OAU), IGO headquarters are located in one city, and council meetings are rotated among cities. The leadership of organizations such as the OAU is also rotated among the leaders of member states.

IGOs have professional staffs, generally called secretariats. These staffs are expected to develop loyalty to the IGO rather than maintain loyalty to their state of origin. The long-term objectives of IGOs are debated and determined by conferences or assemblies, which are scheduled to meet at regular intervals. IGOs also have executive councils whose responsibilities include developing operational plans that reflect the long-term objectives determined by the assembly. In turn, the secretariat is to implement the operational plans developed by the executive council. For the most part, IGOs are relatively small. Their budgets average slightly over $10 million per year, and their staffs average approximately 200 people. The United Nations and its associated organs, with a budget of about $11 billion and a staff of 52,000 people, dwarf most other IGOs.[1]

IGOs perform several separately identifiable services for states. This service performance is what accounted for the proliferation of IGOs in recent years. IGOs provide a forum for communications for states; serve regulative functions; distribute scarce goods and services; offer potential for collective defense and peacekeeping; and in a few instances, provide a rudimentary regional or otherwise-defined governmental function. Indeed, in some of these areas, states expect IGOs to act for them and even argue that IGOs are the proper actors to undertake actions that in earlier eras were the domain of the state.[2]

As *forums for communications,* IGOs serve as convenient locations for representatives of states to meet informally and discuss issues that they cannot discuss elsewhere. For example, the United States in the late 1970s held a series of discussions at the United Nations with the Palestine Liberation Organization (PLO) even though the United States did not recognize the PLO. The existence of the UN made such meetings practical and possible. Alternatively, IGOs serve as formal arenas for communication between states. Many even provide mechanisms for mediating disputes. As Winston Churchill once said, "Jaw-jaw is better than war-war," and the case can be made that although IGOs such as the United Nations and the Organization for African Unity have not prevented war, they have multiplied the opportunities for countries to air their grievances and make an effort to achieve peaceful conflict resolution, even if they are not always successful.

As *regulators,* IGOs serve in a number of capacities ranging from health and postal services to meteorology and atomic energy. The World Health Organization, for example, establishes international health regulations to "ensure the maximum security against the international spread of disease with the minimum interference of world traffic." Similarly, the African Postal Union establishes regulations to improve and facilitate the movement of mail in Africa, and the World Meteorological Organization is tasked to "ensure the uniform publication of observations and statistics" on weather. The International Atomic Energy Agency establishes regulations for the transfer and use of nuclear technologies. Although one may question the degree of success that these and other regulative IGOs have achieved, it is difficult to deny that interstate cooperation has been greatly enhanced by their existence. Indeed, in some cases, such as the WHO's efforts against malaria and smallpox, the efforts of IGOs have been startlingly successful. The incidence of malaria has been sharply reduced, and smallpox has been eradicated.

Much of the same may be said for the *distributive functions* that some IGOs serve. For example, the World Bank and the International Monetary Fund distribute scarce financial funds to states that meet differing criteria of need. Similarly, the United Nations Children's Fund (UNICEF) distributes goods and services to some of the world's needy children. As distributive agents, IGOs are indispensable adjuncts for services rendered too rarely by states and condemned as costly bureaucracies that consume a disproportionate amount of the goods and services they are supposed to distribute.

IGOs have long been created to enhance the *military capabilities* of states. As long ago as the fifth century B.C., Greek city-states formed the Delian League to fight the Persian invasion, and in Thucydides' *The Peloponnesian War* formal alliance systems play a major role.[3] More recently, the League of Nations and the United Nations both sought to provide collective security for their member states, and certain regional IGOs such as NATO are predominantly military in nature.

IGOs also provide *peacekeeping services* that may not be strictly described as collective security. The United Nations and the Organization of African Unity have on numerous occasions created multinational military forces to enter areas of high tension to separate hostile forces or to quiet domestic disturbances when they threaten to disrupt the international community. UN and OAU peacekeeping operations are generally undertaken only when widespread consensus exists on a particular issue within the involved organization.

In some instances, IGOs perform what may be described as a *supranational political function.* That is, they have acquired power to make decisions that are binding on member states even if unanimous consent has not been achieved. In these cases, member states maintain that their sovereignty has not been abridged because the IGO receives its power by consent of the member states. Even so, in a functional sense, the IGO determines policy. The best example undoubtedly is the European Union, discussed later in this chapter.

 ## THE EVOLUTION OF IGOS

IGOs, particularly those whose primary function is military-related, are not new. As we have seen, the Greek city-states had formal organizations that linked them for military purposes over 2,500 years ago. However, the modern IGO is of more recent origin and owes its birth to the industrial revolution and the French Revolution.

Before the industrial revolution, trade in Europe was limited, mass production did not exist, communications were poor, and markets were small. The industrial revolution brought about mass production, improved communications, and a drive for expanded markets. It therefore promoted the establishment of transnational links and functional integration for economic purposes.

Such trends did not proceed in a vacuum. Whereas the industrial revolution tended to encourage international linkages, the French Revolution discouraged them. The French Revolution based its appeal on nationalism, and in turn evoked nationalistic responses throughout Europe. The states of Europe demanded both autonomy of action and control over the flow of goods, services, people, and even ideas. How were the economic pressures for integration to be resolved with the opposing political pressures for autonomy?

One answer was the international governmental organization, which provided both mechanisms for international cooperation and protection for national sovereignty. Indeed, the Congress of Vienna in 1815, called to create a post–Napoleonic order in Europe, also created what some have described as the first modern international governmental organization, the Central Commission for the Navigation of the Rhine. The commission's task was to provide safe and secure transportation on the Rhine. Its charter not only outlined its duties, but also promised no infringement on state sovereignty. A compromise had been reached, and the modern IGO was born.

The number of IGOs increased slowly throughout the nineteenth century. Two levels of nineteenth-century organization may be usefully discussed, one described as a "high-politics" system of negotiating institutions and the other described as a "low-politics" system of functioning institutions. The high-politics system was the Congress System, which eventually evolved into the Hague Conferences and, in a certain sense, the League of Nations and the United Nations. The low-politics system consisted of functional organizations such as the Central Commission for the Navigation of the Rhine.

Although the Congress System was not an IGO in the strictest sense of the term because it had no permanent administrative staff, the great powers of the day viewed it as an institutional mechanism to which they could turn to communicate with other powers, impose their will on smaller states, solve their own minor disputes, and seek approval for whatever new departures in policy they were contemplating. Meetings were not scheduled regularly, but from 1815 to 1900, only 36 years passed without a Congress being held.

Functional IGOs of the nineteenth century have been classified as river commissions, quasi-colonial organizations, and administrative unions; they existed both in Europe and the Americas. River commissions were exemplified by the Rhine Commission. Quasi-colonial organizations were created by European states to provide or supervise services in non–European states. Questions of health and finance in China, for example, were decided by European commissions that may be described as IGOs. Finally, many of the global or regional postal, telegraph, rail, scientific, and economic unions of today trace their lineage to IGOs created during the nineteenth century.

Even so, by the beginning of World War I, fewer than 50 IGOs existed. World War I precipitated a rapid growth in the number of IGOs, even as it did with nation-states. By 1935, nearly 90 IGOs could be identified. Although this number dropped slightly as World War II approached, the conclusion of that war ushered in an even more rapid growth in the number of IGOs than had occurred in the interwar period. As Table 3-2 shows, the number of IGOs continued to grow through the 1980s and then began to decline.

What accounted for the rapid growth in numbers of IGOs after World War I, their even more rapid increase in numbers following World War II, and their decline in numbers during the 1990s? There are several answers. As for the growth, the devastation of the two wars, and most particularly the destructive power of nuclear weapons, created a subtle psychological shift in the minds of many policy makers who slowly realized that international problems had the potential to become so destructive that increased international cooperation was a necessity for survival. Many of the IGOs created in the post–World War II era as a result addressed themselves to issues of war and peace, disease prevention, and economic development.

TABLE 3-2   The Number of International
Governmental Organizations

1909	37
1951	123
1964	179
1978	289
1989	300
1999	251

Source: Yearbook of International Organizations 2000, p. 2357.

A second reason that the number of IGOs increased so rapidly is the increased ease of international travel and communication. The mere fact that it is now possible to travel between Europe and North America in five hours instead of five days served as an impetus for governments to cooperate on solutions to issues and problems that were formerly most easily approached on a national level. Instantaneous global communications systems accelerated this trend even more markedly.

Humanitarianism provided a third impetus to IGOs. Poverty, underdevelopment, starvation, and disease have long blighted human societies, but only recently have governments involved themselves in attacking these problems on a cooperative global level. In part, these problems are tackled today because they are threats to world peace, and in part they are approached because requisite capabilities have only recently become available. Nevertheless, humanitarianism provides a definite motivating factor.

A fourth explanation for the growth in number of international organizations was the expansion of the international civil service itself. As more individuals were drawn into the bureaucracy of IGOs, more issues and problems were identified that could be approached by IGOs. Woodrow Wilson once concluded that "legislation unquestionably generates legislation."[4] It appears that his observation applies equally well to IGOs.

As for the decline in the number of IGOs during the 1990s, this can be traced directly to the collapse of communist governments in Eastern Europe and the Soviet Union. The USSR and its Eastern European communist allies created a wide variety of international governmental organizations whose members were primarily or exclusively communist states. These IGOs passed out of existence along with the communist governments that created them.

This does not mean that IGOs as a type of international actor became less important. Rather, the importance of IGOs if anything grew following the end of the Cold War, as we will see in the next two sections as we study the United Nations and the European Union.

THE UNITED NATIONS AND ITS RELATED ORGANIZATIONS

The United Nations is the most important IGO. Even before the United States entered World War II, Winston Churchill and Franklin Roosevelt agreed in the eighth point of the Atlantic Charter that a "permanent system of general security" should be created after the war. The 1943 Moscow Conference of Foreign Ministers affirmed that a new international organization should be created to regulate the postwar world, and after a number of other meetings were held, representatives from 50 countries met in San Francisco during April and May 1945 at the United Nations Conference. The conference drew up the United Nations Charter and the Statutes of the International Court of Justice.[5]

During the years since then, the UN has undertaken a host of different activities. But throughout that time, many UN activities, including its efforts to help create a "permanent system of general security," were complicated by U.S.–Soviet rivalry and the East–West conflict. Many of these complications disappeared in the late 1980s and early 1990s with the emergence of American-Soviet cooperation, the ensuing collapse of the USSR, and the end of the East–West conflict. By the 1990s, then, the United Nations had begun to play a more sizable role in international affairs than it had during its first 45 years of existence.

The UN's Structure[6]

The final organizational structure of the United Nations was the creation of the victorious Great Powers of World War II. (See Figure 3-1.) Of the six major segments of the United Nations, the **Security Council** was most reflective of the Great Powers' concerns that their voices be predominant in the new UN.

The Security Council. The **Security Council** consists of five permanent members, not coincidentally the five major victorious powers of World War II—China (before October 1971, the Republic of China on Taiwan, and since then, the People's Republic of China in Beijing), France, Great Britain, Russia (before 1992, the Soviet Union), and the

The United Nations, which has its headquarters in New York City, is the world's most prominent IGO. How effective it has been remains a matter of debate.

United States—and 10 other nonpermanent representatives elected by the General Assembly to two-year terms. Each of the five permanent members can veto any important action brought before the council; that is, for the council to take any action, the five permanent members must be in agreement on that action. At least four of the nonpermanent members must also agree to that action. The Security Council begins actions on collective security issues and economic sanctions, and authorizes deployment of UN peacekeeping forces. It also recommends candidates for the secretary-general's position to the General Assembly.

Two sidelights on the Great Powers' role in the Security Council may be instructive here. The first sidelight concerns the introduction of combat troops under the United Nations' flag to the Korean War in 1950. Ordinarily, because UN forces were to be used against communist North Korea, the Soviet Union would have vetoed the Security Council's action. However, the Soviet Union boycotted the sessions of the Security Council when the Korean action was taken, not because of the Korean action, but because the United Nations had refused to remove Nationalist China from the Security Council and give its seat to the People's Republic of China. Since that incident, the five permanent members of the Council have all faithfully attended meetings when major actions were to be taken.

The second sidelight concerns trends in the Great Powers' use of the veto. As Table 3-3 illustrates, the former Soviet Union used its veto power most frequently. However, the USSR's use of its veto declined dramatically, whereas the frequency of American and British vetoes increased dramatically during the 1970s and 1980s. Then in the 1990s, the use of the veto virtually disappeared. There are three explanations for these trends.

First, many of the Soviet Union's vetoes between 1945 and 1955 were cast to block admission of new states supported by the United States to the UN. In 1955, the two superpowers agreed to admit members from both alliance blocs. The USSR's use of its veto therefore became less frequent.

Second, as more and more states achieved independence during the 1960s and 1970s, and as these states joined the United Nations and voted in the UN's General Assembly, the United States and the United Kingdom found fewer and fewer of their allies, close friends,

TABLE 3-3   Vetoes at the United Nations, 1945–2000

State	1945–50	1951–60	1961–70	1971–80	1981–90	1991–00	Total
China[a]	0	1	0	2	0	2	5
France	2	2	0	7	7	0	18
USSR (Russia)	47	45	13	9	2	2	118
United Kingdom	0	2	2	13	15	0	32
United States	0	0	1	21	47	3	72
Total	49	50	16	52	71	7	245

Source: United Nations

[a]Until October 25, 1971, the Chinese seat on the Security Council was occupied by the Republic of China (Taiwan). After that date, the Chinese seat was occupied by the People's Republic of China, which cast both Chinese vetoes during the 1970s.

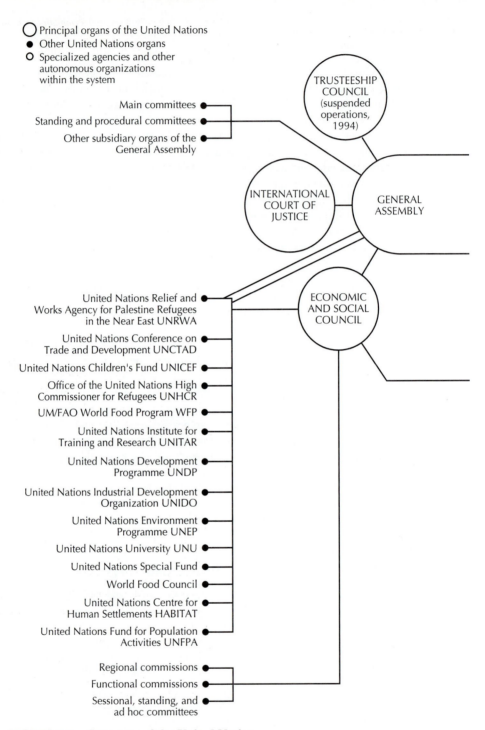

FIGURE 3-1   Structure of the United Nations.

Source: United Nations, Department of Public Information, *Basic Facts about the United Nations,* 1989. Revised by the author, 1996.

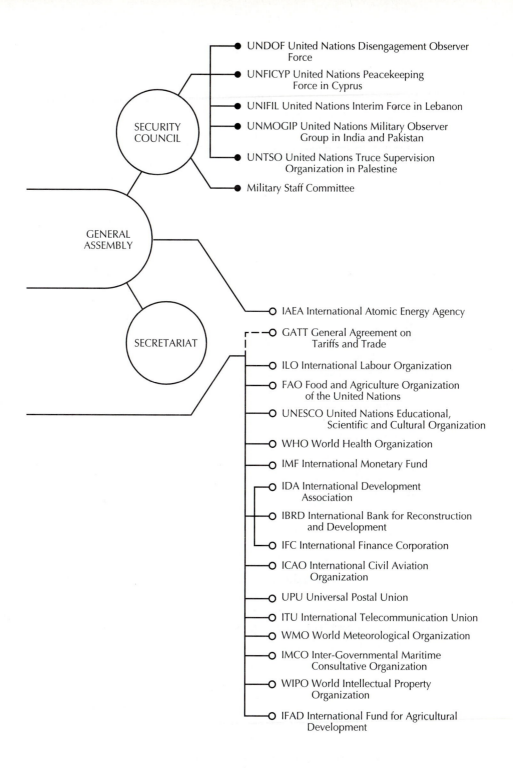

SECURITY
COUNCIL

- ● UNDOF United Nations Disengagement Observer Force
- ● UNFICYP United Nations Peacekeeping Force in Cyprus
- ● UNIFIL United Nations Interim Force in Lebanon
- ● UNMOGIP United Nations Military Observer Group in India and Pakistan
- ● UNTSO United Nations Truce Supervision Organization in Palestine
- ● Military Staff Committee

GENERAL
ASSEMBLY

SECRETARIAT

- ○ IAEA International Atomic Energy Agency
- ○ GATT General Agreement on Tariffs and Trade
- ○ ILO International Labour Organization
- ○ FAO Food and Agriculture Organization of the United Nations
- ○ UNESCO United Nations Educational, Scientific and Cultural Organization
- ○ WHO World Health Organization
- ○ IMF International Monetary Fund
- ○ IDA International Development Association
- ○ IBRD International Bank for Reconstruction and Development
- ○ IFC International Finance Corporation
- ○ ICAO International Civil Aviation Organization
- ○ UPU Universal Postal Union
- ○ ITU International Telecommunication Union
- ○ WMO World Meteorological Organization
- ○ IMCO Inter-Governmental Maritime Consultative Organization
- ○ WIPO World Intellectual Property Organization
- ○ IFAD International Fund for Agricultural Development

or dependents being elected by the General Assembly to the nonpermanent positions on the Security Council. More and more frequently, the United States and the United Kingdom were faced with situations in which at least four and even five or six of the nonpermanent members opposed American or British interests. Thus, to protect their interests, the United States and Great Britain found it increasingly necessary to resort to the veto.

Third, the sharp reduction of the use of the veto during the 1990s can be traced directly to the end of the East-West conflict and the realization by developing countries that the United States and the Western world had become the only major sources of international aid and support. Thus, from the U.S. and British perspective, reasons to use the veto declined.

The General Assembly.   The second major segment of the United Nations is the **General Assembly,** which consists of representatives from all governments that have ratified the UN Charter. As of 1995, 185 states had membership in the General Assembly. Additionally, the Vatican, Switzerland, and the Palestine Liberation Organization have nonvoting observer status in the General Assembly. The General Assembly approves the UN's budget, acts with the Security Council to select the secretary-general and judges of the International Court of Justice, and passes resolutions on issues ranging from self-determination and colonialism to women's rights and the global distribution of wealth.

Although the General Assembly has no recognized authority to enforce its conclusions on anything other than internal UN matters, it makes its viewpoints on issues that are brought before it known in one of three ways. A General Assembly *declaration* is a broad statement of general principle such as the Universal Declaration of Human Rights, passed in 1948. Declarations are often put forward as an expression of an ideal; in practice they are regularly ignored. A General Assembly *resolution* is essentially a document that recommends that member states take a particular policy action. States claim sovereignty and make their own decisions as to whether they will follow a General Assembly resolution. In some cases, however, if many states implement a particular resolution, other states that may not wish to act on the resolution may feel themselves pressured to do so anyway. At the very least, a resolution has the effect of legitimizing the policies of those states that wish to comply with the resolution. Finally, a General Assembly *convention,* or treaty, has two meanings. The more comprehensive convention refers to multilateral treaties voted on by the General Assembly that, upon passage by the General Assembly, are carried back to the capitals of member states for ratification by whatever means each state uses domestically. In other cases, a General Assembly convention refers specifically to a treaty signed between the United Nations and the government of a nation–state.

The Secretariat.   The third major segment of the UN is the **Secretariat,** which administers the UN under the leadership of the secretary-general, who is appointed by the General Assembly for a five-year term. The secretary-general has always been from a neutral or nonaligned state; his primary responsibility is to attempt to resolve international disputes and serve as mediator.

The Secretariat also consists of a sizable staff, numbering over 5,000, which organizes conferences, collects and publishes statistics on global societal, economic, and cultural trends, administers UN peacekeeping missions, and provides others with information about the UN and its activities.

ECOSOC. The fourth segment of the UN is the **Economic and Social Council** (ECOSOC). It is an umbrella organization that loosely oversees the activities of the UN's specialized agencies, conferences, and funds such as the United Nations Development Program (UNDP), the United Nations International Children's Fund (UNICEF), and the Office of the United Nations High Commissioner for Refugees (UNHCR). ECOSOC also concerns itself with human rights, world trade, and other related issues. ECOSOC has 54 members, each elected for a three-year term by the General Assembly.

The International Court of Justice. The fifth segment of the UN is the **International Court of Justice** (ICJ). Each of the 15 judges is elected by the General Assembly and the Security Council together. No two judges may be from the same country. The court hears cases that are referred to it by members of the General Assembly or Security Council. In actuality the court hears few cases, and given the claims of national sovereignty and the inability of the court or the UN to enforce its rulings, those rulings are sometimes ignored.

Trusteeship Council. The sixth and final segment of the UN is the **Trusteeship Council,** which suspended operation in 1994 after it granted independence to Palau, the last of 11 trust territories established by the United Nations following World War II. The Trusteeship Council now meets "as occasion requires."

The UN in Action: Peacekeeping[7]

Here it may be useful to provide a detailed examination of one specific area of UN effort, peacekeeping. When all is said and done, peacekeeping, after all, was the real reason why the United Nations was created.

Since the UN has come into existence, there have been at least 150 major conflicts. Some have pitted nation against nation and others have been civil wars. In some cases, fewer than a thousand people have been killed, but in others, the casualty toll has exceeded a million people. Clearly, the United Nations has not prevented conflict and warfare.

But does this mean that the United Nations has been a failure as a peacekeeper? Despite the tensions and dangers of the Cold War, half a century has passed without a third world war. No nuclear weapon has been used in warfare. How many more lives would have been lost during the decolonization process of the 1940s, 1950s, and 1960s had there been no United Nations? How many more conflicts would there have been had the United Nations not existed? There is no way to answer these questions. Nevertheless, the United Nations' success or failure as an international peacekeeping agency cannot be judged in black-and-white terms.

Tools of Peacekeeping. The United Nations has several tools at its disposal with which to try to keep the peace. As a first step, once the Security Council determines that a threat to the peace exists or an act of aggression has occurred, it may seek to resolve the situation via discussion in the Security Council. Occasionally, such discussion serves to defuse an impending conflict as one or both sides give vent to their charges before an international audience. On other occasions, the Security Council may pass a resolution or make a recommendation concerning the crisis. Usually, it is then up to the involved parties to adhere to or ignore Security Council recommendations or resolutions.

Closely related to Security Council discussions, resolutions, and recommendations is the imposition of **comprehensive economic sanctions.** When it imposes comprehensive economic sanctions, the Security Council attempts to influence a country's policy actions by applying economic pressure on it. However, because of the difficulty of getting widespread support for such sanctions within the Security Council and especially among its five permanent members, comprehensive economic sanctions are rarely imposed. Indeed, after comprehensive economic sanctions were imposed against the minority white government of Rhodesia (now Zimbabwe) in 1966 in response to its racial policies, the UN has only imposed economic sanctions three times, against South Africa in 1977 because of apartheid, against Iraq in 1990 because of its invasion of Kuwait, and against Serbia/Yugoslavia in 1992 because of its warfare against Bosnia-Herzegovina. Even when comprehensive economic sanctions are put into effect, individual UN member states decide whether or not they should abide by them.

Beyond rhetoric and economic sanctions, the Security Council may also ask UN members to make military forces available to the UN. However, this is rarely done. Only twice in the UN's history has there been a **military enforcement action.** The first time was in 1950, when under U.S. leadership the Security Council recommended that UN members "furnish such assistance to the Republic of Korea as may be necessary to repel [North Korea's] attack" against it. A "unified command under the United States" was created, and UN forces—mostly U.S. forces, but from 16 other UN member states as well—were deployed to Korea. They remain there today. The second time was in 1990, when under Resolution 678, the UN Security Council approved "all necessary means" including military force to expel Iraq from Kuwait. Within weeks, under U.S. leadership, the 30 countries that sent military forces to the Middle East to oppose Iraq's takeover of Kuwait launched "Operation Desert Storm."

Usually, instead of military enforcement actions, the Security Council opts to place **peacekeeping operations** into areas of conflict. To begin peacekeeping operations, three informal but very real conditions must be met. First, all parties to the conflict must accept the presence of UN operations. Second, broad segments of the UN, and most particularly all five permanent members of the Security Council as well as at least four of the other 10 Security Council members, must support the operation. Third, UN members must be willing to provide the forces needed for peacekeeping operations and pay for their deployment.

As a concept, peacekeeping does not appear in the UN Charter. Rather, it has evolved over time, flowing from former UN Secretary-General Dag Hammarskjöld's idea of "preventive diplomacy." To Hammarskjöld, one of the primary purposes of the UN was to prevent wars from occurring, and if they did occur, to prevent them from becoming worse. Hence "preventive diplomacy" helped foster the UN's move into peacekeeping operations.

Traditionally, there have been two major types of UN peacekeeping operations. The first, **peacekeeping forces,** consists of lightly armed troops that are authorized to use force only in self-defense. The second type, **military observer missions,** is usually unarmed, and is authorized only to observe events.

Recently, though, UN peacekeeping operations have expanded into other areas as well. One new form of UN peacekeeping is the **transition assistance group,** which helps bring new governments into power in countries that are receiving their independence or undergoing a major change in government. As of 2000, the UN had deployed transition assistance groups or their equivalents in Namibia, Cambodia, Western Sahara, and East Timor.

UN forces also provide services beyond observing, separating hostile forces, and bringing new governments to power. UN forces have also been called on to enforce embargoes as in Bosnia, monitor elections as in Angola, verify human rights violations as in Haiti, provide humanitarian relief as in Somalia, and build domestic infrastructures as in Mozambique. Peacekeeping can also be dangerous; over 1,000 peacekeepers have been killed.

Usually, UN peacekeeping operations employ only a few hundred or thousand troops. However, on occasion, they may become sizable. For example, the UN effort in the Congo from 1960 to 1964 deployed over 20,000 peacekeepers; the transition assistance effort that began in Cambodia in 1992 was nearly as large; the 1992–1995 UN deployment in Somalia totaled over 28,000 people not including nearly 18,000 U.S. troops that remained under U.S. command; and UN forces in the former Yugoslavia grew to over 42,000 people in 1995.

Issues of Peacekeeping. When the UN was founded, its major objectives included maintaining peace, avoiding wars, and preventing the escalation of conflict. It has been far less than perfectly successful in achieving these objectives. This observation leads to three questions.

1. *Why Has the United Nations Not Been More Successful in Maintaining Peace, Avoiding War, and Preventing Escalation of Conflict?* There are several answers to this question, but none is more apparent than U.S.–Soviet rivalry during the Cold War. From 1945 until the late 1980s, this rivalry often made it impossible for the UN to undertake efforts to prevent wars and to slow or prevent their escalation. When the Cold War ended, the UN thus had more opportunities to act as a peacekeeping institution. As a result, from the late 1980s up to today, the UN has sent peacekeeping missions to Angola, Bosnia, Cambodia, Namibia, Tajikistan and elsewhere as well.

The impact that the Cold War had on UN peacekeeping operations was the most glaring example of the primary reason that the UN has had difficulty implementing peacekeeping operations—national sovereignty. Despite everything that the United Nations is, it remains an international governmental organization. Since the countries of the world, and particularly the five permanent members of the Security Council, reserve for themselves the right to undertake whatever action they see fit, they can and often do frustrate actions that the UN might undertake whenever those actions might interfere with their own interests or objectives.

"National sovereignty"—the insistence by individual countries that they themselves have the right to determine their own courses of action and defend their own interests—

has thus been the major reason that UN peacekeeping operations have not been more successful. National sovereignty dictates that the UN can undertake peacekeeping operations almost exclusively when all parties involved in a conflict as well as most of the rest of the international community support the peacekeeping operation. This occurs infrequently.

There are also other reasons why the UN has not been more successful. Chief among these is that for a peacekeeping mission to have a realistic chance of keeping the peace, all sides in a conflict must want peacekeeping forces to succeed. This situation does not always exist, as the UN's experience in Bosnia and Croatia showed.[8]

In other instances, UN members have not wanted to commit their own forces to peacekeeping operations because of fear of adverse domestic reaction, because of concern about potential casualty levels, or because they perceive no advantage to themselves. Obviously, without peacekeeping forces or observers, there can be no peacekeeping operation.

Similarly, arranging financing has complicated UN peacekeeping efforts. In each case where peacekeeping operations are contemplated, financing must be arranged. This has slowed and sometimes prevented the deployment of peacekeeping forces and military observer missions. Even where difficulties in arranging funding only slowed deployment of personnel, situations in the field sometimes deteriorated while financing was being arranged.

Another reason that UN peacekeeping efforts have not been more successful is that the art of peacekeeping is new, and new methods and ideas are continually being put into effect. In essence, peacekeeping has been and remains a trial-and-error undertaking. Unfortunately, sometimes mistakes are made. The key, however, is to learn lessons from past mistakes.

2. *How can UN peacekeeping operations be improved?* One answer is to limit national sovereignty, but there is little likelihood of this occurring. Indeed, the entire United Nations Charter was worded to allow states to defend their sovereignty. (Had it not been, there is little likelihood that the United Nations would ever have come into being.) There are few indications that states are willing to submerge their sovereignty in the UN. Conversely, since the end of the Cold War, UN members have become more willing to cooperate in peacekeeping efforts. A new aura of cooperation has thus been apparent.

Other proposals to improve UN peacekeeping efforts include the idea that UN members designate a certain part of their armed forces to be "on call" to the United Nations. These forces would remain part of each respective country's national military force but be assigned immediately to UN peacekeeping operations when such operations are put in place. Some countries—for example, Norway, Sweden, Denmark, and Finland—already have taken steps in this direction. If more countries would do this, it is argued, the UN would have what amounted to a "standby force" ready for short-notice deployment.

Similarly, it has been proposed that the United Nations develop and maintain a $1 billion "contingency fund" that would enable the UN to organize and deploy peacekeeping forces and military observer missions quickly without waiting to arrange funding. The problem with such a suggestion is that it is first necessary to convince member states to contribute to the fund.

Two controversial proposals to improve UN peacekeeping efforts are to arm UN peacekeeping forces more heavily and to allow UN personnel to use force more readily.

Proponents of these positions assert that UN forces would become more influential and more assertive if these concepts were implemented, thereby aiding peace efforts. Opponents maintain that either proposal would make it more difficult to gain approval for peacekeeping missions, fundamentally alter the nature of UN peacekeeping operations, and turn UN personnel into combatants instead of peacekeepers.

Another controversial proposal advocates consciously moving UN activities from "peacekeeping" to "peacemaking." Advocates of this proposal argue that the end of the East–West conflict has opened opportunities for the United Nations to become a forceful and active defender of human rights on a global basis, and to allow it to prevent future cases of "extreme human rights abuse" such as the genocide that occurred in East Timor before UN peacekeepers arrived in 1999 and the ethnic cleansing campaign implemented by Serbia in Kosovo before the 1999 Kosovo conflict. Others oppose the idea, arguing that the UN should not be a global police force, that it would be difficult to draw a line between "human rights abuse" and "extreme human rights abuse," that the cost in resources and human lives of using such a force would be high, and that few states would be willing to devote the necessary resources to developing, maintaining, and deploying a UN peacemaking operation.

3. *Is the UN a success or a failure as a peacekeeping organization?* How one answers this question depends on expectations. If someone began with high expectations about the UN's ability to prevent war and to stop wars from escalating, he or she is probably disappointed with the UN's performance and considers the UN a failure. If someone began with the expectation that wars could not be prevented and their escalation could not be controlled, then he or she from the outset would have concluded that the UN was doomed to fail.

But if one's expectations were somewhere between the positions that the UN could prevent all future wars and the UN was preordained to fail, then it is possible to reach a more optimistic conclusion. Even if the UN has not prevented all wars from occurring and stopped all conflicts from escalating, it has stopped some from occurring, prevented some from escalating, and even brought some to an end.

But problems remain. States will undoubtedly still oppose UN peacekeeping efforts when they conflict with their own national interests or objectives, future peacekeeping efforts will undoubtedly still require widespread international approval, and funding will undoubtedly continue to be difficult to arrange. Cynics and idealists will therefore probably continue to be disappointed by the UN's ability to keep the peace, while those with more modest expectations will point to UN peacekeeping successes with pride and expect that more will occur.

The UN's Other Activities: Problems and Successes

The saga of the UN's peacekeeping efforts does much to point out the weaknesses and strengths of the organization in other areas as well. For example, as Tables 3-4 and 3-5 illustrate, the UN often has special sessions of its General Assembly and sponsors world conferences. These special sessions and world conferences are called to discuss critical issues that confront the international community. This is a notable achievement. Often, however, concerns of state sovereignty, national security, political gain, and economic

TABLE 3-4   Recent Special Sessions of the UN General Assembly

Topic	Year
Earth Summit	1997
World Drug Problem	1998
Population and Development	1999
Small Island Developing States	1999
Women	2000
Social Development	2000
Children	2001

TABLE 3-5   Recent Selected UN-Sponsored World Conferences

Topic	Year
Natural Disasters	1999
Exploration and Peaceful Use of Outer Space	1999
Trade and Development	2000
Crime Prevention	2000
Nuclear Non-Proliferation	2000
Least Developed Countries	2001
Racism and Racial Discrimination	2001

profit or loss frustrate attainment of the objectives of the special sessions and world conferences.

Sometimes, states or groups within states believe that they have reason to be concerned about the UN's actions, activities, and attitudes. For example, some people within the U.S. believe that the United Nations may move toward supranational status, that is, a status in which the majority of UN member states grant the UN authority over states. They point out that this is in fact what occurred with the European Union, as will be discussed in the next section. However, since member states must agree to an IGO acquiring supranational authority, there is no likelihood that the UN will attain supranational status in the foreseeable future.

The extent to which the UN is dependent on member states for survival and influence is easily demonstrated. In 1985 and 1986, the United States and Great Britain withdrew from the UN Educational, Scientific, and Cultural Organization (UNESCO) because of that organization's perceived anti-American and anti-British bias. When the U.S. and Britain withdrew, UNESCO lost not only two prominent members, but also 30 percent of its annual budget (25 percent provided by the U.S. and 5 percent by Great Britain).

Indeed, the UN itself has had its funding reduced because states felt it did not serve their purposes. For years, the Soviet Union was far behind on its payment schedule. Similarly, in the 1980s, resentment in the U.S. Congress and executive branch about perceived anti-Americanism in the General Assembly and about an oversized UN bureaucracy led the U.S. to intentionally fall far behind in its payments to the UN. This U.S. financial pressure led the UN to cut staff by about 15 percent and adopt a new budgetary system in which all major budget decisions had to be made unanimously. According to some U.S. government observers, the General Assembly also restrained its anti-Americanism. Nevertheless, in 2000, the U.S. still owed the United Nations over $500 million in back dues and unpaid contributions to peacekeeping missions.[9]

Clearly, the UN remains dependent on its member states for its resources. This fact has also had an immense impact on the UN in its function as a distributor of goods and services. The UN's problem here is simply stated. Put simply, the UN's member states often have been unwilling to support the United Nations at a level that would permit its specialized agencies and other bodies to affect significantly on a global scale those issues that they confront.

That having been said, the UN has had some notable successes as well. For example, the United Nations Development Program has extended over $2 billion in development aid during its existence, and by 2000, the number of UN development experts working in developing states exceeded 15,000. In addition, the World Health Organization reduced the frequency of malaria and eradicated smallpox. More examples on both sides of the argument could be used, but an objective observer is driven to the conclusion that the UN's record as a distributor of goods and services is mottled. If there were no UN or specialized agencies, the world's condition would be worse. How much worse is a matter of debate.

The two areas where the United Nations and its related organizations have most clearly succeeded are in the regulation of certain international activities and in the production and dissemination of information. A number of specialized agencies such as the Universal Postal Union, the International Telecommunications Union, and the General Agreement on Tariffs and Trade exist within the United Nations system and have as their specific purpose the international regulation of various forms of relations between states. For example, almost all the world's states accede to the regulations put forward on the mail, telecommunications, and tariffs, recognizing the benefits that such regulation brings. States consequently have accepted the specialized agencies' regulations. Similarly, the United Nations system has had great success in compiling and disseminating statistics on the economic and social performances of its member states.

Under the auspices of the United Nations Environment Program (UNEP), the UN has also developed an international network through which it can obtain and disseminate vital environmental information. UNEP's activities include maintaining a Global Environment Monitoring System (GEMS), establishing an International Register of Potentially Toxic Chemicals, and creating Infoterra, a worldwide environmental network. Although considerations of sovereignty and national interest played a major role in limiting the results of the 1992 and 1997 UN Rio de Janeiro and Kyoto conferences on the global environment, UNEP's operations have been hampered more by limited funding than anything else.

Another area of UN operations that is the subject of disagreement is decolonization. Frequently, the United Nations receives credit for the decolonization that swept the world during the 1950s, 1960s, and 1970s. The two United Nations "tools" to which decolonization is attributed are the Declaration Regarding Non-Self-Governing Territories (Chapter 11 of the UN charter) and the International Trusteeship System (Chapter 12).[10] As we saw in our discussion of the Trusteeship Council, 11 states received their independence because of the trusteeship procedures. Little debate is possible about the importance of the trusteeship system. Clearly, the involved states received independence as a result of the procedures outlined by the United Nations. Considerable disagreement exists, however, when Chapter 11 is discussed. Proponents of the United Nations argue that Chapter 11 and its requirements, which demand that colonial powers recognize the "sacred trust" to promote "the well-being of the inhabitants of these territories," including eventual self-government, were major factors that led to the massive decolonization phenomenon of the post–World War II era. More cynical observers believe that the costs of colonization began to outweigh its benefits, and therefore old colonies became new sovereign states as the colonial powers no longer saw advantage in having colonies.

Another aspect of colonialism that the United Nations sometimes approaches is "internal colonization." Internal colonization occurs when one state has within it a number of nationalities, at least one of which asserts its desire to establish its own independent nation-state, or when one state has removed a nationality from territories that the nationality alleges are its homeland. The United Nation's record on these issues is mixed. In some cases, as with the PLO, the UN has not formally recognized the claims of the nationality for statehood, but has granted the group representing the nationality observer status at the General Assembly. In other cases, as with Eritrea, the United Nations ignored the claims of nationality groups. The United Nations is clearly in a difficult position on such cases, because to support the claims of all such groups would win for the United Nations the animosity of all states that had internal groups seeking independence. Thus, on any particular case involving potential "internal colonization," the United Nations' position is the product of a variety of political, social, economic, and military factors.

All things considered, the United Nations during its first 50 years of existence did not live up to the hopes of its founders in taking "effective collective measures for the prevention and removal of threats to the peace," in developing "friendly relations among nations," nor in achieving "international cooperation in solving international problems." As we saw, many of the UN's frustrations were caused by the East-West conflict and by the demands of national sovereignty. But throughout its existence, the UN has served as an effective forum for debating and in some instances acting upon and even solving international problems and conflicts.[11]

THE EUROPEAN UNION: A SUPRANATIONAL IGO

Despite is size and global importance, the United Nations was founded as and remains a typical IGO whose member states retain control over its activities. However, one IGO in particular, the European Union (EU), has moved beyond this to become a **supranational organization.** A supranational organization is an IGO whose member states have given it authority over some of the decisions of its members. Thus, the EU is an IGO whose member states have in essence surrendered some of their sovereignty to the European Union. The EU even has as one of its expressed objectives the unification of the political, economic, social, foreign, and defense policies of its member states.[12]

For an international governmental organization, this is an immense step. It is also an immense step for Europe as a continent and for the world as an international system. Because of its supranational nature and its global importance, the EU demands detailed attention.

What is the EU?

The European Union is the current end result of a long process. What is now the EU was conceived in the late 1940s, evolved through different stages, articulated in the 1991 Maastricht Treaty, and came into being in 1993 after twelve European states—Belgium, Denmark, France, Germany, Greece, Ireland, Italy, Luxembourg, Netherlands, Portugal, Spain, and the United Kingdom—ratified the Maastricht Treaty. Since then, three more states, Austria, Finland, and Sweden, have joined the EU. Other European states have expressed an interest in joining the EU. Membership is open to any democratic European state with a well-operating market economy, a good human rights record, ability to meet EU economic requirements, and ability to fulfill EU laws and regulations.

Integration versus Unity

As stated above, the EU's objective is to "unify" the political, economic, social, foreign, and defense policies of its member states. This is a more ambitious objective than those of most other IGOs. And it is a more ambitious objective than that of the EU's predecessor, the European Community (EC), which sought to "integrate" its members' policies.

To a great extent, "integration" is the objective of many IGOs that seek to harmonize the policies and practices of their member states. For the EC, integration was the process of reducing barriers to trade and other exchanges between EC states and of creating institutions that could aid this process. "Unity" is the objective of all EU states having common political, economic, social, foreign, and security policies. The EU has not achieved unity, but it is one of Europe's central political features. All indications are that the E. U. will become even more prominent.

Why Integration?

The road toward European integration and eventual unity has been long and difficult, and it is far from complete. Several factors influenced Europe to begin the journey.

The first was the need to prevent future wars in Europe. World Wars I and II devastated Europe twice within thirty years. Many Europeans concluded that a way had to be found to prevent future European conflicts.

Second, economic production in Europe after World War II was at a standstill, and human suffering was immense. The destruction was so great that the economy of an entire continent had to be jump-started, not just the economy of a country or two.

Third, Western European and U.S. leaders feared that Europe's sorry economic condition would provide fertile ground for Soviet expansion and communism. From the U.S. and Western European perspective, this had to be prevented.

One idea that met all three objectives was to integrate the economies of European states. British Prime Minister Winston Churchill first suggested the idea in 1946, observing that if the French and German economies were integrated, warfare between the two countries would be unlikely, economic growth in the two states would accelerate, and a political-economic counterbalance to the USSR would be created.

Nevertheless, Churchill's idea languished. Then, in February 1947, Great Britain informed the U.S. that its own economic situation was so bad it could no longer provide aid to Greece or Turkey. Suddenly, the U.S. was galvanized into action.

Integration Begins

Early in 1947, the U.S. proposed both the Truman Doctrine and the Marshall Plan. Under the Truman Doctrine, U.S. President Harry Truman promised that the U.S. would provide assistance to free people struggling against internal enemies or external subversion. Under the Marshall Plan, U.S. Secretary of State George Marshall offered economic assistance to Europe for a European Recovery Plan that was to be developed, proposed, and implemented jointly by European states.

European states met several times in late 1947 to develop a plan. The first meeting included the USSR and several of its Eastern European satellite states, but they walked out. The remaining states, all Western European, requested aid from the U.S. The U.S. eventually provided over $15 billion to Western Europe.

Three points must be made here. First, the Marshall Plan was a generous and humanitarian undertaking. Second, the U.S. provided aid not only to be humanitarian, but also to restore Europe as a trading partner and to combat communist expansion. Third, the Marshall Plan, with its emphasis on joint European development and implementation of the plan, was the first step toward Western European integration.

Other steps followed. The next was the 1951 European Coal and Steel Community under which all Western European coal and steel production were placed under one authority. Five years later, West Germany, France, Italy, the Netherlands, Belgium, and Luxembourg agreed to cooperate more fully on economic issues.

In 1957, the same countries signed the Treaties of Rome which created the European Economic Community (EEC) and EURATOM. These bodies respectively reduced barriers to trade between the six states and created an agency to develop atomic energy. In the late 1960s, the EEC evolved into the European Community (EC).

During the 1970s and 1980s, six more states joined the EC, Denmark, Greece, Ireland, Portugal, Spain, and the United Kingdom. In 1979, EC countries held the first direct election for the European Parliament. In addition, all twelve EC states during the 1980s agreed to accept the decisions of the EC's governing body, the European Council, on certain issues even if they disagreed with them. This in effect transferred limited sovereignty from EC states to the EC.

From EC Integration to EU Unity

During the late 1980s and early 1990s, EC states launched two major initiatives that fundamentally altered the European Community and led to its replacement by the European Union. These two initiatives, the Single European Act and the Maastricht Treaty, are changing the way state-to-state relations have been conducted in Europe since Westphalia.

The Single European ACT (SEA). In 1985, the EC implemented the **Single European Act,** which set 1992 as the date when all tariffs and other barriers on the movement of goods, capital, and people between states would end. The SEA eliminated over 300 regulations.

The advantages that the Single European Act provided can best be illustrated by a single example. In 1988, truck drivers in Western Europe needed as many as 27 documents to go from one country to another. In 1993, all they needed was their driver's license.

The Maastricht Treaty.   Even before the SEA was fully implemented, European leaders took a more momentous step, meeting in the Netherlands in 1991 to forge a treaty that envisioned the EC moving beyond integration to union.

This agreement, **the Maastricht Treaty,** was signed in 1992. It had ambitious goals. It proposed that the twelve EC members would: 1. join together in a political and economic union; 2. adopt a common currency; 3. share social and domestic policies; and 4. have a common foreign and defense policy. In short, the Maastricht Treaty sought to create a United States of Europe by converting the European Community into the European Union.

Before this could happen, all twelve EC states had to approve the treaty according to each state's laws. Gradually, this occurred, but not without some anxious moments. For example, French voters approved it by 1 percent, and Danish voters defeated it the first time they voted on it, but approved it the second time they voted.

European unity raised many issues. What would it mean for sovereignty? Would national identities and cultures be preserved? What impact would union have on economics? Would countries really give up their own currencies? Would Germany dominate a united Europe? Would there be too many rules? The questions were endless, and most could not be answered with certainty.

The EU Evolves

Since 1993, the EU has continued to evolve as capabilities of EU institutions are realized. In addition, the EU in 1997 revised the Maastricht Treaty with the Amsterdam Treaty, which expanded the capabilities of several EU institutions.

In its efforts to achieve unity, the EU formulates policy in agriculture, aviation, commerce, competition, culture, development, education, employment, social practices, energy, the environment, foreign and security policy, justice, regional development, research, telecommunications, and transport. The EU has five major institutions: the European Commission, Council, Parliament, Court of Justice, and Court of Auditors. It also has two other institutions, the Council of Heads of State and Government and the Central Bank.

The European Commission.   The European Commission is the most important EU institution. It proposes legislation to the EU Council, manages the budget, takes legal action against those who violate EU laws and rules, is responsible for implementing EU decisions, and assures that EU institutions run correctly.

The EU Commission consists of twenty commissioners appointed for five year terms by governments of EU states. France, Germany, Italy, Spain, and the United Kingdom each appoint two. The other EU states each appoint one. The President is appointed for five years by agreement among members in consultation with the EU Parliament.

Each commissioner is supposed to make decisions in the EU's interest, not in the interest of his or her home state, and is assigned to at least one policy area. Approximately 15,000 people work for the Commission, most in Brussels. Since the EU has eleven official languages, about 3,000 of its employees are translators.

The Council of the European Union.   Based on recommendations from the Commission, the Council of the European Union enacts laws. Made up of ministers appointed by each EU state, the members of the EU Council have a difficult task balancing national and EU interests. As Table 3-6 shows, each state has a different number of votes in the EU Council based on its population.

Most Council decisions require a qualified majority vote. This means to block legislation, at least 25 votes from five members are required. In areas such as taxation, the admission of a new member, and foreign and security policy, a unanimous vote is required. Under the 1997 Amsterdam Treaty, the areas in which qualified majority votes are permitted expand and the areas in which unanimity is required are reduced.

The European Parliament. The European Parliament has 626 members directly elected in EU-wide elections for five year terms. Parliament members form ideological, not national, political groups that stretch across the EU. The European Socialist group won the most seats, but not a majority, in both parliament elections that have been held under the EU, in 1994 and 1999.

The European Parliament does not pass laws like the U.S. Congress or other national parliaments. Rather, under a system called "co-decision," it vetoes or amends Council-proposed legislation in areas such as research, health, and culture.

The 1997 Amsterdam Treaty expands the role of the European Parliament by increasing the number of areas in which co-decision applies. In addition to its co-decision responsibilities, the European Parliament also amends or rejects the EU budget, and has the ability to dismiss the EU Commission—a power it has never used.

The Court of Justice. The Court of Justice is made up of one judge from each EU state appointed for a renewable six year term. The Court of Justice makes decisions on EU laws, rules, and regulations that are binding on all EU institutions, states, courts, citizens, and companies operating in the EU. Court of Justice decisions overrule decisions of national courts.

TABLE 3-6 Votes in the EU Council

France	10
Germany	10
Italy	10
United Kingdom	10
Spain	8
Belgium	5
Greece	5
Netherlands	5
Portugal	5
Austria	4
Sweden	4
Denmark	3
Finland	3
Ireland	3
Luxembourg	2

The Court of Auditors. The Court of Auditors is the EU's financial watchdog. It examines the legality of expenditures and receipts, and makes sure that the EU budget is well managed. It is based in Luxembourg.

Other EU Institutions. Two other EU institutions, the European Council of Heads of State and Government and the Central Bank, require special commentary. Although they are not among the "big five" EU administrative bodies, they are nevertheless important.

The European Council of Heads of State and Government brings together the leaders of EU states and the President of the EU Commission at least twice a year. It sets the EU's strategic direction and provides political guidance.

The European Central Bank was created in 1998 and became operational in January 1999 when the EU's new currency, the euro, was introduced. It works closely with the European System of Central Banks, comprising the central banks of the euro countries, in defining and implementing monetary policy in the euro-area.

EU Issues and Problems

Despite the EU's progress, a number of issues and problems complicates more rapid movement toward unity. These issues and problems can best be examined under four headings: enlarging the EU; the politics of economics; sovereignty, identity, and culture; and a common foreign and security policy.

Enlarging the EU.[13] Technically, EU membership is open to any stable democratic European state that has a well–operating market economy, a good human rights record, and the ability to meet EU macroeconomic requirements and to fulfill EU laws and regulations. Despite these guidelines, deciding which states meet EU membership standards is politically, economically, and socially sensitive.

Each year, the EU Commission reviews the status of states that have expressed interest in joining the EU to assess whether they meet EU membership requirements. The fourteen states that have expressed interest in joining the EU fall into three categories.

The first is candidate for full membership. Six states, Cyprus, the Czech Republic, Estonia, Hungary, Poland, and Slovenia, are in this category. In 1998, the EU began negotiations with all six. They are likely to accede to the EU early in the twenty-first century.

The second category includes five Central European states, Bulgaria, Latvia, Lithuania, Romania, and Slovakia, that have signed association agreements with the EU but that in the EU Commission's eyes do not yet meet EU membership standards. These states are working with the EU to improve their suitability for membership.

The third category includes Malta, Switzerland, and Turkey. Each has a separate status. Norway requires special mention as well.

In Malta's case, the EU acted positively on its application for membership in 1995, planning to include the island in its next enlargement. However, a new Maltese government came to power in 1996 and froze Malta's application; another new government came to power in 1998 and reactivated it. Malta is likely to become an EU member early in the twenty-first century.

Switzerland, by comparison, expressed interest in joining the EU, but did not apply after Swiss voters opposed membership.

Turkey's situation is more controversial. An associate member of the old EC, Turkey applied for EU membership at its inception. However, the EU decided that Turkey did not meet EU criteria. Instead, the EU reaffirmed Turkey's eligibility to join but recommended that it develop closer economic relations with the EU. This has occurred, but the EU has not accepted Turkey as a member. Many people believe that the EU's continued refusal to admit Turkey has more to do with EU concern over possible increased Turkish immigration to Europe that could occur if Turkey was an EU member than with Turkey's failure to meet EU criteria.

As for Norway, its government signed an EU accession treaty in 1994, but Norwegian voters rejected the treaty. Thus, even though it meets EU membership criteria, Norway is not an EU member.

Enlarging the EU is an open-ended issue. More states are likely to join, but Turkey's case raises questions about whether issues beyond formal criteria play a role in expansion. But as Malta and Norway show, EU membership is decided not just by the EU, but also by governments and peoples of member states.

The Politics of Economics.[14]   The politics of economics bedevils the EU in several ways. For example, some Europeans are concerned that Germany's economic strength will give it too much clout within the EU. In some countries such as Denmark, France, and the United Kingdom, this has led to concern about increasing EU integration and outright opposition to moving toward European unity.

Similarly, even though other EU countries began to accept the EU's unified currency, the **euro**, as legal tender in 1999 and will withdraw their national currencies from circulation in 2002, Great Britain is unwilling to abandon its national currency, the pound. Thus, Great Britain will remain outside the so-called Euro zone.

At the same time, as we saw earlier, some Europeans express concern that enlarging the EU will open it to unwanted immigration and cheap labor that will increase unemployment in EU states. This concern is directed toward Turkey and several other prospective candidates. Especially in Turkey's case, some believe that the concern is less about economics than about race and religion.

Sovereignty, National Identity, and Culture.[15]   The EU also faces opposition because of fears that it is undermining sovereignty, destroying national identity, and homogenizing national cultures. EU opponents point to the increase of authority the EU has attained, the gradual growth of people's allegiance to the EU in addition to their national homeland, and the creation of European wide standards and tastes as proof of their fears that the EU is the enemy of sovereignty, national identity, and culture.

Conversely, EU proponents argue that the benefits of eventual European union far outweigh any loss of sovereignty, identity, or culture that may take place. No consensus exists on the debate over sovereignty, identity, and culture, nor is one likely to emerge.

A Common Foreign and Security Policy.[16]   No area of EU effort has progressed as little as that of **common foreign and security policy** (CFSP). In part, this is because under the Maastricht Treaty, most CFSP decisions must be unanimous. Since European states, like most states, jealously guard their sovereignty in the areas of foreign and security policy, unanimous decisions are rarely reached.

The Amsterdam Treaty permits more CFSP decisions to be approved by majority vote. It also includes the possibility that the Western European Union, a Western European military organization far overshadowed by NATO, will become the EU's military arm. Even so, it remains to be seen if the EU can forge a comprehensive common foreign and security policy.

Summation

European unity is still some distance in the future. Nevertheless, because of the EU, Europe is more integrated today than it has been for centuries, and most Europeans are willing to continue the experiment in creating what might become a United States of Europe. Critical issues and problems remain, but the possibility of unity is on the horizon.

As an IGO, the EU is breaking new ground as its member states provide it the power to develop and implement supranational capabilities. Not all Europeans are pleased by this, but the EU is nevertheless an immense force for change in Europe. Whether the EU will become a model for other IGOs in the twenty-first century is less clear.

THE FUTURE OF IGOS

IGOs play an important and growing role in contemporary international relations. All indications are that their role and importance, and possibly their numbers, will continue to expand in the future. The ability of IGOs to approach, analyze, and propose solutions to problems and issues that transcend national boundaries is in most cases unequaled by any other international actor. Indeed, in the eyes of many, it is unfortunate that IGOs do not have more resources at their disposal so that they may better cope with the problems and issues they face.

With this being said, the importance of IGOs as actors in the international arena should not be exaggerated. All IGOs, even those few such as the European Union that have moved from transnational to supranational status, are careful to guarantee sovereignty to their member states. (Here it should be remembered that the EU receives its supranatural authority from its member states and therefore, at least in theory, can have that authority revoked by them.) IGOs therefore remain creations of states and as a consequence are less influential than their creators.

In addition, different states have different views of IGOs and consequently pursue different policies toward them. The general U.S. attitude toward the United Nations, for example, was supportive during the early years of the UN's existence. However, as more and more Developing World nations entered the United Nations and as more and more UN votes opposed preferred U.S. outcomes, American support for the UN cooled. In the 1990s, however, U.S. attitudes toward the UN once again became more favorable as U.S. and UN positions on many issues again coincided.

The desire of states to maintain their national sovereignty remains the most significant constraint on the growth of influence of IGOs around the world. Nevertheless, as discussed earlier, IGOs do provide services for states. It is because of those services that states have seen fit to create IGOs and to grant them whatever powers they have. As more and more issues such as environmental deterioration, drugs, and health transcend national boundaries, it is likely that states will more and more turn to IGOs to help them solve their problems.

A last point should be made concerning the role of IGOs in the twenty-first century. Although a clear relationship exists between the end of major wars and the growth in number of IGOs, analysts do not agree whether the amount of violence in the international arena has been reduced by the greater number of IGOs and the increased international interactions that they bring about. Similarly, analysts do not agree whether the performance of other tasks by IGOs leads to a more stable and just international system. As in so many other aspects of international relations, the answer to the question of whether IGOs help create an improved global community is open to debate. What is not open to debate is that international governmental organizations, although more powerful and influential today than they have ever been in the past, are still subordinate to states as actors in the international arena.

 ## KEY TERMS AND CONCEPTS

structures of IGOs   IGOs may be organized in many different ways, but virtually all meet regularly and have full-time staffs

functions of IGOs   states create IGOs to perform services for them such as being forums for communications, regulators, distributors of goods, peace-keeping, and supranational political oversight

evolution of IGOs   IGOs have existed for many years but they became more common after World War II as travel and communications became easier and as states identified issues that they could not cope with by themselves

U.N. Security Council   with five permanent members and ten nonpermanent members, the Security Council begins actions on collective security, economic sanctions, and peace-keeping

U.N. General Assembly   approves the U.N. budget, passes resolutions on many issues, and selects the U.N. General-Secretary in conjunction with the Security Council

U.N. Secretariat   the policy-implementing organization of the U.N.

U.N. Economic and Social Council   oversees the activities of the U.N.'s specialized agencies such as the United Nations Development Program and the World Health Organization

International Court of Justice   the U.N. court that hears cases referred to it by the General Assembly or the Security Council

comprehensive economic sanctions   imposed by the U.N. Security Council to get a state to change a policy, comprehensive economic sanctions block a country's trade with the outside world

military enforcement actions   use of U.N. military force against a country

peacekeeping forces   lightly armed U.N. troops put into conflict situations where combatants have agreed to a ceasefire

military observer missions   usually unarmed, U.N. military observer missions are authorized only to observe events

transition assistance groups   U.N. groups designed to help bring governments into power in countries that are receiving their independence or changing their government structure

peacekeeping issues   these include questions about why the U.N. has not been more successful as a peacekeeping body and how U.N. peacekeeping can be improved

European Union (EU)   formerly the European Community, the EU has 15 members and is trying to establish the equivalent of the United States of Europe

supranational organization   any international governmental organization that subordinates state authority or national identity to its own authority or identity

European unity   the effort to make the states of the European Union become a single cohesive political and economic body

Single European Act   concluded in 1985, this act set 1992 as the date by which all barriers to the movement of goods, capital, people, and services between European Community countries would be ended

Maastricht Treaty   concluded in 1991, this treaty envisioned political and economic unity for Europe, adoption of a single currency, and implementation of a common foreign and defense policy

European Commission   a European Union body whose members, though appointed by EU member states, are supposed to represent EU interests, identify problems that confront the EU, and propose solutions to the EU Council of Ministers

Council of the European Union   the meetings of the national leaders of European Union states designed to enact legislation and set the direction for the EU

European Parliament   the EU legislative body that is a watchdog over the European Commission

Euro   the common European currency introduced in 1999

enlarging the EU   the ongoing debate over including additional members in the European Union, with some EU members desiring more states to join and others prefering that cooperation between present EU members be deepened before the EU is widenened

common foreign and security policy   the EU effort to create a single foreign and security policy for the EU

WEBSITE REFERENCES

international governmental organizations (IGOs):   *www.uia.org/index-new.htm*   website of the Union of International Associations, which contains information and data about many IGOs

123world.com/organizations/index.html   an index of websites of many important IGOs

www.lib.umich.edu/libhome/Documents.center/intl.html   the University of Michigan's listing of international agencies and information

United Nations: *www.un.org*   the United Nation's website

European Union: *www.europa.eu.int*   the European Union's website

North Atlantic Treaty Organization: *saclant.nato.int/nato.html*   the North Atlantic Treaty Organization's home page

supranational organizations: *www.pitt.edu/~ian/resource/intorg.htm*   a listing of home pages of IGOs with supranational functions

NOTES

1. Information provided by the United Nations, April 2000.

2. For additional discussion of IGOs, see Clive Archer, *International Organizations*, 2d ed. (New York, NY: Routledge, 1992); and Paul F. Diehl, ed., *The Politics of Global Governance: International Organizations in an Interdependent World* (Boulder, CO: Lynne Rienner Publishers, 1997).

3. Thucydides, *The Peloponnesian War* (Baltimore, MD: Penguin, 1954).

4. Woodrow Wilson, *Congressional Government* (New York, NY: Meridian, 1956), p. 194.

5. For a detailed history of the creation of the United Nations, see Ruth A. Russell, *A History of the United Nations Charter: The Role of the United States, 1940–1945* (Washington, DC: The Brookings Institution,

1958). See also Donald Altschiller, *The United Nations Role in World Affairs* (New York, NY: H.H. Wilson, 1993). See also Townsend Hoopes and Douglas Brinkley, *FDR and the Construction of the U.N.* (New Haven, CN: Yale University Press, 2000).

6. For more detailed discussions of the UN and its operations, see Peter R. Baehr and Leon Gordenker, *The United Nations in the 1990s* (New York, NY: St. Martin's Press, 1992); James N. Rosenau, *The United Nations in a Turbulent World* (Boulder, CO: Lynne Rienner Publishers, 1992); and Adam Roberts, ed., *United Nations, Divided World* (New York, NY: Oxford University Press, 1994).

7. The following section is derived from United Nations, *United Nations Peacekeeping* (New York, NY: United Nations, 1995); and Trevor Findlay, *Fighting for Peace: The Use of Force in Peace Operations* (New York, NY: Oxford University Press, 2000).

8. For additional information on the Bosnian and Croatian conflicts, see United Nations, *The United Nations and the Situation in the Former Yugoslavia* ((New York, NY: United Nations, 1995); Ivo Banac, *The National Question in Yugoslavia: Origins, History, Politics* (Ithaca, NY: Cornell University Press, 1994); and John V.A. Fine and Robert W. Donia, *Bosnia and Hercegovina: A Tradition Betrayed* (New York, NY: Columbia University Press, 1995).

9. Information provided by the United Nations, April 2000.

10. The UN Charter can be found in A. LeRoy Bennet, *International Organizations: Principles and Issues* (Englewood Cliffs, NJ: Prentice Hall, 1977), pp. 400–425.

11. For other views on the UN, see Karen Mingst and Margaret P. Karns, *The United Nations in the Post–Cold War Era Boulder,* 2d ed. (Boulder, CO: Westview Press, 1999); Stephen Ryan, *The United Nations and International Politics* (New York, NY: St. Martin's Press, 2000); and Thomas G. Weiss, et al., *The United Nations and Changing World Politics,* 3d ed. (Boulder, CO: Westview Press, 2000).

12. For additional discussions of the history, evolution, and functions of the European Union, see Martin Dedman, *The Origins and Development of the European Union* (New York, NY: Routledge, 1997); John McCormick, *The European Union: Politics and Policies,* 2d ed. (Boulder, CO: Westview Press, 1999); and James Caporaso, *The European Union: Dilemmas of Regional Integration* (Boulder, CO: Westview Press, 2000).

13. See Chris Preston, *Enlargement and Integration in the European Union* (New York, NY: Routledge, 1997); and Alice Landau and Richard Whitman, *The Enlargement of the European Union: Issues and Strategies* (New York, NY: Routledge, 1999) for details of the debate over EU enlargement.

14. For discussions of the economic issues that confront the EU including issues related to monetary union, see Werner Weidenfeld, "The Euro and the New Face of the European Union," *The Washington Quarterly* (Winter 1999), pp. 67–80; Francesco Giordano and Sharda Persaud, *The Political Economy of Monetary Union* (New York, NY: Routledge, 1998); and Barry Eichengreen and Jeffry Frieden, eds., *The Political Economy of European Monetary Unification,* 2d ed. (Boulder, CO: Westview Press, 2000).

15. Alan W. Cafruny and Carl Lankowski, eds., *Europe's Ambiguous Unity: Conflict and Consensus in the Post–Maastricht Era* (Boulder, CO: Lynne Rienner Publishers); and Thomas Banchoff and Mitchell Smith, *Legitimacy and the European Union* (New York, NY: Routledge, 1999) discuss concerns in EU states related to sovereignty, national identity, and culture.

16. For details of the debate over and implications of a common European foreign and security policy, see "A Common European Military Policy: Serious at Last?," *IISS Strategic Comments* (July 1999); Peter van Ham, *Europe's New Defense Ambitions: Implications for NATO, the U.S., and Russia* (Garmisch, Germany: The George C. Marshall European Center for Security Studies, 2000)

Chapter 4

Multinational Corporations

- How are MNCs different from other corporations?
- Why have MNCs developed?
- What roles do MNCs play in the world today?
- Why are MNCs so widely praised and condemned?

In its simplest form, a **multinational corporation** (MNC) is a corporation that has its headquarters or center of operations in one country and owns and operates other corporations, or subsets of itself, in other countries. These other corporations or subsets are generally called **subsidiaries.** A multinational corporation is therefore exactly what its name implies, a corporation that operates in more than one country.[1]

Sometimes called **transnational corporations,** MNCs play a large and growing role in twenty-first century international relations. There are at least 2,000 large MNCs that operate in at least six countries, and perhaps as many as 40,000 smaller MNCs. Together, they operate over 280,000 subsidiaries.

Some MNCs are extremely large, some have immense economic impact, and a few wield sizable political clout. A few scholars even believe that MNCs in the twenty-first century will challenge the state as the primary type of international actor. This combination of size, impact, and clout has made MNCs the subjects of intense debate. Regardless of whether this occurs, the large and growing importance of MNCs makes it critically important that we understand the roles they play and the impacts they have in contemporary international relations.

THE SIZE AND SCOPE OF TWENTY-FIRST CENTURY MNCS

MNCs have an immense impact on twenty-first century international economic affairs. In 1998, 49 of the world's largest 100 economic organizations were multinational corporations, as Table 4-1 shows. This was up from 37 only four years earlier. At the same time, these 49 MNCs produced over $3.5 trillion in goods and services. This was more than

10 percent of the world's entire economic output. Perhaps more surprisingly, every one of the world's largest Fortune 500 corporations in 1998 produced more than the world's 73 smallest state economies.

General Motors, the world's largest MNC, by itself has a larger economic output than all but 23 countries. Put differently, General Motors' "economy" is larger than the countries of the Czech Republic, Hungary, and Ukraine combined. And General Motors is not the only MNC whose economic output is larger than many states. The economic output of many MNCs dwarf that of many states, again as Table 4-1 shows.

TABLE 4-1   The World's 100 Largest Economic Units 1998 ($U.S. Billions)

1. United States	7923	35. South Africa	119	68. Peru	61
2. Japan	4090	36. Iran	110	**69. US Postal Service**	**60**
3. Germany	2123	**37. Mitsui**	**109**	**70. Matsushita Electric**	**59**
4. France	1466	**Itochu**	**109**	**71. Philip Morris**	**57**
5. United Kingdom	1264	**39. Mitsubichi**	**107**	**72. Ing Group**	**56**
6. Italy	1166	40. Portugal	106	**Boeing**	**56**
7. China	929	Columbia	106	New Zealand	56
8. Brazil	758	**42. Exxon**	**101**	**75. AT&T**	**54**
9. Canada	612	**General Electric**	**101**	**76. Sony**	**53**
10. Spain	554	**44. Toyota Motor**	**100**	**77. Metro**	**52**
11. India	451	45. Israel	95	**Nissan Motor**	**52**
12. Netherlands	389	Singapore	95	Czech Republic	52
13. Australia	381	**47. Royal Dutch/Shell**	**94**	**80. Fiat**	**51**
Mexico	381	**Marubeni**	**94**	**Bank of America**	**51**
15. South Korea	370	**49. Sumitomo**	**89**	**82. Nestle**	**50**
16. Russia	338	**50. IBM**	**82**	**83. Credit Suisse**	**49**
17. Argentina	324	51. Venezuela	81	**Honda Motor**	**49**
18. Switzerland	285	52. Malaysia	80	United Arab Emirates	49
19. Belgium	259	**53. AXA**	**79**	**86. Assicurazioni Gen.**	**48**
20. Sweden	227	Egypt	79	**Mobil**	**48**
21. Austria	217	Philippines	79	**88. Hewlett-Packard**	**47**
22. Turkey	201	**56. Citigroup**	**76**	89. Algeria	46
23. Denmark	176	**Volkswagen**	**76**	Hungary	46
24. General Motors	**161**	**Nippon Telephone**	**76**	**91. Deutsche Bank**	**45**
25. Taiwan	158	59. Chile	71	**Unilever**	**45**
26. DaimlerChrysler	**155**	**60. BP Amoco**	**68**	**State Farm**	**45**
27. Norway	152	**Nissho Iwai**	**68**	**Dai-ichi Life**	**45**
28. Poland	151	62. Ireland	67	**95. Veba Group**	**44**
29. Ford Motor	**144**	**63. Nippon Life**	**66**	Bangladesh	44
30. Wal-Mart	**139**	**Siemens**	**66**	**97. HSBC Holdings**	**43**
Indonesia	139	**65. Allianz**	**65**	**Fortis**	**43**
32. Thailand	134	**66. Hitachi**	**63**	Ukraine	43
33. Finland	124	Pakistan	63	**100. Toshiba**	**42**
34. Greece	123				

Sources: World Development Indicators database, World Bank, 1999; and Fortune Global 500, 1999.

Chapter 4

IT AND MNCS: EMPOWERING INTERNATIONAL BUSINESS

Multinational corporations (MNCs) are already among the largest users of information technologies. They will continue to be at the cutting edge of the creation, application, and use of IT as the twenty-first century progresses. MNCs in the service, banking, and financial sectors distribute and exchange tremendous amounts of data and information throughout the world.

In many cases, geography has little or no impact on decisions about where service sector businesses locate their data processing facilities. Many such facilities, sometimes called back office operations, are located far distant from corporate headquarters to take advantage of lower labor and property costs. For example, it is not unusual for a company to have corporate headquarters in New York, data and information centers in Ireland or the Dominican Republic, and operations in Bangkok, Djakarta, and Manila, all linked by advanced information technologies.

The ability to transfer funds electronically throughout the world has also had an immense impact on international banking and finance. With the ability to transfer funds electronically at a moment's notice, the world is well on its way to becoming a single banking and financial market. Although no one knows the actual number, multiple trillions of dollars are transferred electronically each day across national boundaries by banking and financial institutions. Further advances in information technologies will only broaden and accelerate this trend.

The trend toward regionalization and globalization of business will also accelerate as more companies acquire cost-effective access to international communications. Advanced information technologies will therefore allow many more firms to become international and marketplaces to become regionalized or globalized.

This phenomenon was one of the factors that increased pressures in Europe for political and economic unity. Similar pressures are building in East Asia, the Americas, and elsewhere as well. Indeed, the movement toward free trade areas such as the Asia Pacific Economic Cooperation area and the Free Trade Area of the Americas may have been based on economic trends and political possibilities, but advanced in information technology helped make them—and the European Union—operationally possible.

For several reasons, then, there is little doubt that advanced information technologies will enhance the role that MNCs play in international affairs. Several decades ago, noted business professor Ray Vernon observed that MNCs had the potential to hold state sovereignty at bay. In the Information Age, that observation has greater potential than ever to become a reality.

MNCs are important not only because of their size, but also because of their global presence. Almost every country in the world hosts at least one multinational corporation or an MNC subsidiary. In some cases, MNCs are permitted full control of subsidiaries, but in other cases, host countries require some degree of control by local economic interests or even by the government itself. Nonetheless, the fact remains that multinational corporations operate in almost every country in the world today.

At the same time, most MNCs have their headquarters in economically developed countries. In 1998, 477 of the world's largest 500 MNCs were based in Europe, North America, or Japan. There are several reasons for this. Most MNCs were originally incorporated in one of these regions as a domestic company and became a multinational company over time. Thus, their headquarters often remains where the company was founded. At the same time, most MNCs require modern transportation, information, and communication infrastructures to conduct business in their multiple locations. Such infrastructures are much more frequently found in economically developed states.

This reality has led some critics of MNCs to maintain that MNCs contribute to the wealth and power of economically developed states and exploit developing states. Defenders of MNCs counter this view by asserting that MNCs provide jobs and services to developing states that otherwise would not be available. This argument will be examined in detail later.

The control that some MNCs have over certain technologies and raw materials is also worth noting, for this too has generated considerable debate about MNCs. AT&T, Boeing, Daimler Chrysler, General Electric, Hewlett-Packard, IBM, Matsushita, Siemens, and many other MNCs deal heavily in advanced technologies. Exxon, Royal Dutch/Shell, BP Amoco, Mobil, and a few other MNCs dominate oil and petroleum markets throughout the world.

This has led other critics of MNCs to assert that MNC dominance of these and other economic sectors so crucial to twenty-first economies means that a few well-positioned MNCs have a stranglehold over not only the economic well-being of developing states, but also developed states, thereby placing sovereignty at bay. Critics of MNCs point to the rapid rise of gas prices in the United States in 2000 as proof of their position. This charge is hotly denied by spokespersons for MNCs, especially those in the oil industry. This argument will also be examined in detail later.

What, then, are the realities of multinational corporations? Where did they come from, and how did they evolve? How are they structured, how do they operate, and from where do they obtain their influence? What does the future hold for MNCs? These and other issues will be discussed throughout the chapter.

 ## THE ORGANIZATION AND OPERATION OF MNCS

Multinational corporations produce a variety of goods and services. Some such as Nestle and Ford produce consumer products. Others such as Boeing and IBM deal in high technology and capital goods. Some such as Citigroup and Credit Suisse are financial and banking institutions. Still others such as BP Amoco and Mobil deal in raw materials and natural resources. Most large MNCs operate in a number of different product areas. Together, the combination of large size, diversified product areas, and multinational and perhaps global operations permit most MNCs to weather the economic storms that beset smaller corporations that operate in a single national market. Indeed, since the 1970s, the growth rate of sales for most MNCs has exceeded the growth rate of sales of nationally oriented firms as well as the growth rate of the gross domestic product of most individual states.

On many occasions, MNCs produce goods from components that are made in several countries, thereby making it difficult to say with certainty that a given product is "Made in America," "Made in Japan," or "Made Somewhere Else." Many General Motors cars, for example, have components made in Japan, Europe, and North America. The same its true for Toyota and Daimler Chrysler automobiles.

Although it might not appear important where in the world a product is made, the reality is that production creates jobs for workers, profits for companies, and economic strength for countries. Thus, even though MNCs may argue that they are only economic entities, the decisions that MNC executives make have immense national and international political importance.

Stages of Development and MNC Organization

MNCs often evolve through several stages of development. Some observers posit that there are actually three stages in the development of a multinational corporation. In the first stage, after a corporation decides to operate in more than one country, it creates a separate business strategy for each country in which it operates. At this stage, an MNC may best be described as a "multi-domestic" corporation. In the second stage, an MNC may strive to dominate a specific global market sector, but it nevertheless still concentrates much of its effort in its home country. Such MNCs are sometimes called "global corporations." In the third stage of development, an MNC draws on global resources, management, production, and other capabilities to assume the status of a "transnational corporation." Few MNCs have actually made the transition to this status, although more and more are moving in this direction. We will explore the reasons for this in the next section.

Over time, both as the international system changed and as individual MNCs moved from one stage of their development to another, the preferred **organizational structure of multinational corporations** has also changed.[2]

Before World War II, when national differences in consumer preference were large, differences in industrial standards were numerous, and governmentally created barriers to international trade were high, multinational corporations operated on a predominantly national and decentralized basis. MNCs established their foreign subsidiaries so that each subsidiary operated on its own with little or no guidance from the parent corporation. Such a structural organization, known as a mother-daughter arrangement, was requisite for operating in the international political-economic environment of the era. Most MNCs that were organized as mother-daughter arrangements were European. Figure 4-1(a) illustrates the organizational structure of these types of firms.

Following World War II, a new international global economic order was created by the victorious Western powers. Over time, differences in consumer preferences were reduced but not eliminated, industrial standards became more uniform, and governmentally created barriers to trade lessened. These gradual occurrences had an impact on the organizational

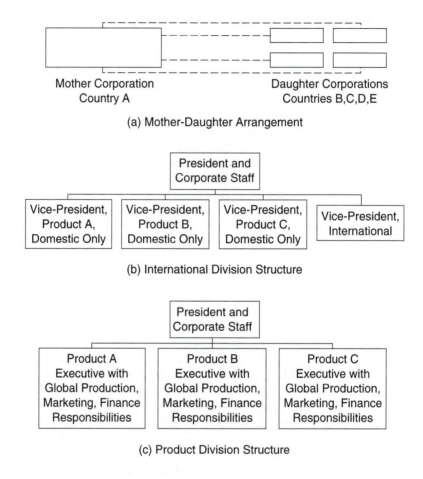

(a) Mother-Daughter Arrangement

(b) International Division Structure

(c) Product Division Structure

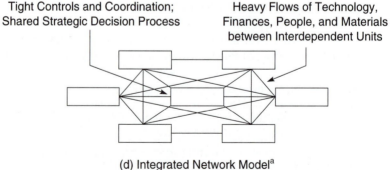

(d) Integrated Network Model[a]

FIGURE 4-1   Possible organizational structures of multinational corporations.

[a]*Source:* Christopher Bartlett, "Building and Managing the Transnational: The New Organizational Challenge," in M. E. Porter, ed., *Competition in Global Industries* (Boston: Harvard Business School Press, 1986), p.381.

structure of MNCs. Larger markets became available because of reduced barriers to trade, increased standardization, and more homogeneous consumer tastes, so economies of scale could be brought to bear. With fewer barriers to trade, the productive benefits of comparative advantage could be made an operational reality and larger corporations, with their new potential for global reach, could scan the world for the least expensive raw material and labor inputs for their products. The era of the modern multinational corporation had come.

All this took a number of years, and MNCs gradually adapted their organizational structures to take advantage of the opportunities afforded them by the new postwar international economic order. The old mother-daughter arrangements, created to allow decisions to be made individually in each unit and to allow differentiated products to be made by each unit, could not take fullest advantage of the new international economic environment. Thus, new organizational structures for MNCs were created.

U.S. firms were among the first and the most aggressive corporations to seek and find alternative structures. Many U.S. MNCs developed organizational structures based on product divisions with one division designated an international division. Thus, a single firm making products A, B, and C within the United States would have a separate domestic division for each of its three products and a fourth division for its international operations. Figure 4-1(b) illustrates this type of arrangement.

However, as MNCs expanded their operations during the 1950s and 1960s, many changed their structures to product divisions that operated on a global scale. This change was necessary because in many cases, the international divisions of MNCs had become larger than all other divisions combined and because globally oriented product divisions offered the most logical and efficient managerial structure. This trend began during the 1950s and 1960s and continued into the 1990s. Figure 4-1(c) diagrams this organizational structure.

During the 1980s and 1990s, another new organizational structure began to emerge for MNCs, the integrated network model, depicted in Figure 4-1(d). This version of organization sees the MNC as an integrated network of distributed and interdependent resources and capabilities that operate in different markets. Each unit in one way or another creates an advantage for the MNC as a whole. The activities of each unit therefore must be coordinated with those of other parts of the MNC if the MNC is to achieve the greatest possible benefits. This organizational structure places a premium on coordination and on managers who have a broad perspective.

MNC Perspectives and Operations

Indeed, an extremely subtle shift in the **perspectives of MNC management** accompanied these structural shifts. Often, the perspectives of top MNC management changed from an outlook that saw MNCs as national companies with international operations to an outlook that considered MNCs to be truly international corporations. In essence, then, at least in the minds of many corporate managers, many MNCs are now international rather than national firms. The implications of this subtle change of emphasis are potentially massive.

Before we examine these implications, we must first further examine MNCs themselves. As a general rule, MNCs prefer to have full ownership of their foreign subsidiaries because full ownership allows maximum control. To achieve full ownership, MNCs must often invest large sums of money directly in countries outside their home country. Money that MNCs—or other companies and individuals as well—invest directly outside their home country is called, aptly enough, **foreign direct investment.**

Sometimes parent MNCs share ownership of a foreign subsidiary through either public or private groups in the host country. This is called a **joint venture.** In some cases, the public group that the parent corporation shares ownership with is the government of the host country itself. Indeed, one of the major changes instituted in communist China during the 1980s and which continues in place today was the legalization of joint ventures between Western businesses and Chinese government-owned firms.[3]

There are a variety of reasons why MNCs may participate in a joint venture even though they lose some control of their subsidiaries. First, a multinational may find that public or private groups in the host country have capital or expertise without which the subsidiary would fail. Second, an MNC may view a particular market as requiring host-nation participation to reduce the political risk of having a foreign corporation operating within that market. Finally, in some states, laws require host-nation participation.

This is not to say that MNCs are willing in all cases to allow other groups or individuals to have partial control of their subsidiaries. On occasion, MNCs view joint ventures as unacceptable or consider other limitations on their operations in a particular country too serious to permit continued operation. One of the most celebrated examples of the latter situation involved the Indian government and the Coca-Cola Corporation. The Indian government demanded that if Coca-Cola wished to continue operating its subsidiary in India, it had to provide India with the composition of the closely guarded secret formula for the cola syrup that Coca-Cola used in its most famous product. Coca-Cola refused and ended its Indian operations.

Sometimes MNCs choose not to invest directly in foreign countries, but opt instead to conclude **licensing agreements** with foreign companies or governments. Under a licensing agreement, an MNC agrees to allow a foreign company to produce one or more of its products, with the MNC receiving payment from the foreign company for allowing it to produce its wares. Licensing agreements reduce the amount of risk that a company takes because it has little or no foreign direct investment in the country of the corporation with which it has a licensing agreement. MNCs and their licensing partners may also choose this form of relationship over a joint venture because of company policy preferences, tax laws, political or cultural considerations, or insufficient funds to acquire a wholly owned or partly owned subsidiary through foreign direct investment. The disadvantage of licensing from an MNC's perspective is that licensing greatly restricts the flexibility of decision making and the central control that MNCs so often prefer.

Because multinational corporations are in business to make money, their leading objective is the maximization of profit. MNCs have a number of strategies to achieve this objective. Because of their size and their global access to resources, material, and information, MNCs can maximize profits by minimizing the cost of their inputs, by dominating the market for a specific product in a particular country or a particular region, or by moving their operations to a country where the economic or political environment is more favorable to their operations.

On occasion, MNCs have actively intervened to alter what they perceive as unfavorable economic or political environments. A leading example of the **political influence of MNCs** took place between 1970 and 1973 in Chile when ITT (a large international telecommunication company) in conjunction with the U.S. Central Intelligence Agency helped overthrow the government of Salvador Allende, all in the pursuit—from ITT's perspective—of establishing a more favorable environment in which it could do business.[4] More recently, and more positively, a wide variety of U.S. firms during the 1980s acted following public urging and withdrew their investments and operations from South Africa to force the then-white controlled South African government to change its racist apartheid policies.[5]

The ethical questions raised by MNC efforts to intervene in the political affairs of host states to overthrow governments or force government policy changes are significant. In addition, other ethical questions also exist about MNC business practices in host countries that are not at the level of the "rightness" or "wrongness" of overthrowing governments or forcing policy changes. For example, if common business practice in one country requires a large upfront cash payment to guarantee the conclusion of a contract, but in the home country of the involved MNC such payment is considered a bribe, are MNC executives acting morally or immorally if such payments are made? Similarly, if the leadership of an MNC decides that operations in one country must be curtailed or eliminated to take advantage of less expensive material or labor costs elsewhere, what responsibility does the MNC have to its former employees?

These and similar questions are part of the decision-making dilemma of the multinational corporation. Other parts of the dilemma include whether an MNC should remain in a given market if it is operating at a loss there. Although a short-term assessment of the economic return may imply that an operation should be closed, the hope that future profits in that market may dictate continued operation. Coca-Cola serves as a useful example. For years, Coca-Cola's operations in Japan cost the company money, but the decision was made to continue operations there. During the 1970s, that decision was justified as Coca-Cola's Japanese subsidiary steadily increased its profitability. Small financial losses over an extended period eventually led to a major profit. In China, Coca-Cola pursued the same strategy of accepting losses in hopes of developing a long-term profitable market.

Again, however, it was the global size and overall profitability of Coca-Cola that allowed it to absorb losses for an extended period of time. Similarly, it was the centralized control of overall operations that allowed that decision to be made. Indeed, throughout the late twentieth century, size and centralization of operations were what made the MNC a significant force in international relations.

Throughout the 1990s, however, forces were at work that were changing multinational corporations. As we have already seen, some MNCs began to adopt an integrated network form of organizational structure and to become truly transnational and global in outlook and production. At the end of the twentieth century, then, the outlines of what twenty-first century MNCs might look like were beginning to appear.

 ## *TWENTY-FIRST CENTURY MNCS*

Before we examine what twenty-first century MNCs might look like, it will be useful to revisit some of the forces for change that we examined in Chapter 1. Several had immense implications for MNCs.

Forces for Change and MNCs

The collapse of communism, for example, provided large new market areas into which MNCs could expand. Admittedly, the economies of former communist states were in disarray, but from the perspective of many MNC executives, this meant that there was room for economic growth.

Similarly, the reemergence of economics as a critical factor in international relations and the accompanying emphasis by states on reducing barriers to trade provided new opportunities for MNCs to grow and reduced the problems that businesses confronted when they operated internationally.

At the same time, the wave of democratization and privatization that swept the world in the 1980s and 1990s helped MNCs by establishing an international political and economic climate that viewed private business and profit in a favorable light. This clearly helped business expansion.

So too did the movement toward regional and global integration. As the European Union and free trade areas such as the North America Free Trade Area came into existence, more and more barriers to and frustrations for corporate operations beyond a single state's boundaries were removed.

Finally, the emergence of new information and communication technologies aided and abetted the internationalization of business immensely. With advanced information and communication technologies making time and location increasingly irrelevant as barriers to business, and with all the other factors addressed above coming increasingly into play, some MNCs in the late twentieth century began to take on new characteristics. Having already examined one of those new characteristics—the integrated network structure that some MNCs have adopted—we will now examine four other prominent features of twenty-first century MNCs.

Centralized and Decentralized Decision Making[6]

Whereas twentieth century MNCs often relied on centralized decision making, 21st century MNCs will often rely on a greater mix of centralized and decentralized decision making. This trend will be driven by the need to take advantage of quickly changing local conditions while at the same time maintaining a global perspective. The move toward 24 hours a day, seven days a week markets will also accelerate this trend. It will be possible to do this because of advanced information and communication technologies, the integrated network organizational structure being increasingly adopted, greatly reduced costs of cross-border interactions, and the elimination of many policy barriers to those interactions.

Not all businesses and not all individuals will be able to mix centralization and decentralization successfully. Combining centralized and decentralized decision-making will be a difficult task to accomplish, but for those MNCs sufficiently agile and for those individuals sufficiently skillful, the rewards will be great.

Mergers and Megamergers[7]

Size will remain a critical factor for MNCs in the twenty-first century. Indeed, during the late 1990s, a wave of mergers took place between multinational corporations, some based within a single country and some between companies that were based in different countries.

Some of the world's most prominent corporations were involved in the merger wave of the late 1990s. Germany's Daimler merged with America's Chrysler to form Daimler Chrysler, in 1998 the world's twenty-sixth largest economic unit. British Petroleum and Amoco also merged, creating the world's third largest oil company and, in 1998, the world's sixtieth largest economic unit. In financial services, Citicorp and Travelers merged to form Citigroup, valued at over $140 billion, and the American bank Bankers Trust merged with Germany's Deutsche Bank. Meanwhile, in the world of information and communications, in 2000, America Online and Time Warner merged to form the world's first and largest integrated media and communications company, valued at over $350 billion.

Critics of the mergers fear that the size of the newly merged companies will act as a constraint on trade. Others fear that the size of the newly merged companies will reduce their ability to respond to changing market conditions. But from the perspective of merger proponents, these mergers, regardless of whether they were between companies based in the same country or different countries, provide companies access to markets, resources, or expertise that was required to enhance their status and profitability. To many, the mergers and megamergers that have taken place are but the crest of the wave of mergers and megamergers yet to come.

Strategic Partnering/Alliances

Mergers and megamergers are not the only trend that is gathering force among MNCs. Some MNCs, like states, jealously guard their independence and reject mergers as a strategy.

Nevertheless, many see the advantages of and the necessity for cooperation. They therefore develop partnerships with other businesses that help provide them access to markets, resources, or expertise that they require to enhance their status and profitability. Sometimes called strategic partnering or strategic alliances,[8] this form of MNC operation combines the advantages of cooperation with most of the freedom and flexibility of independent decision-making associated with competition.

Strategic alliances are particularly widespread in the international airlines, communication, entertainment, telecommunication, and travel industries. Like mergers and megamergers, they too have a downside. They require trustworthy partners and offer much less predictability and control. Nevertheless, for many MNCs, they are becoming the preferred way of doing business.

Globalist Management Perspectives

As we have already seen, the perspectives of some MNC managers even during the late twentieth century had already changed or were changing from the view that MNCs were national companies with international operations to the view that MNCs were transnational organizations whose operations and interests were global and no longer linked with those of a single state. Indeed, the perspectives of some MNC managers may be transitioning from what has been described as an internationalist or transnationalist perspective to a globalist perspective.

Given the forces for change detailed above, this trend will undoubtedly accelerate during the twenty-first century. If this occurs, it could resurrect a question that was first asked during the early 1970s, namely, "Could MNCs keep state sovereignty at bay?" We turn to that question now.

 ## MNCS AND STATES: SOVEREIGNTY AT BAY?[9]

Because of their size and wealth, MNC's wield extensive economic, political, and social power. It does not matter whether that power is sought or unsought . . . it exists.

The existence of that power and the concern over how MNCs might use it has helped make MNCs the subject of heated debate. On one level, the debate is over whether MNCs exploit developing states and their people. On another level, it is over whether MNCs challenge the state system and place state sovereignty at bay.

The MNCs' Challenge

MNCs challenge state sovereignty in several ways. Economic, security, and political challenges can all be identified.

Economically, multinational corporations can make or break a local economy, or even the national economy of a small state. Admittedly, MNCs provide investment funds, jobs, advanced technologies, and education, but they can also remove that which they bring on the basis of decisions made in corporate headquarters. With their ability to move production from high labor cost areas to low labor cost areas, MNCs have proven to be the groundworks on which several national economic "miracles" such as Singapore, Hong Kong, and Taiwan have based their prosperity. Indeed, the economic power of MNCs is such that when visiting foreign states, corporate heads often receive treatment generally reserved for visiting governmental dignitaries and heads of state. For example, when Nissan and Toyota let word out that they intended to build plants in the United States, governors from at least eight U.S. states contacted corporate headquarters to try to attract the Japanese firms to their states. And when the Japanese site teams arrived in the United States, they were treated like royalty. Regardless of whether this practice is desirable, it is understandable because MNC investment means jobs.

Equally vexing is the problem that MNCs cause for state security. There are several aspects to the problem. First, home-based MNCs may develop products useful for defense and then sell those products to potential enemies. For example, many U.S., British, French, Japanese, and German firms sold materials to Iraq that allowed Saddam Hussein to develop the well-equipped military force that he used to invade Kuwait in 1990. Similarly, the U.S. government remains concerned about the sale by MNCs—and other firms as well—of advanced nuclear, chemical, and missile technologies to other unfriendly states.

Second, with the globalization of the world economy brought about by MNCs and the accompanying free flow of investment capital, critical components of military equipment must frequently be imported. Indeed, by the early 1990s, the United States could not build a single first-line fighter aircraft without Japanese technology. Third, even under the best conditions, few countries want domestic firms vital to defense production to be owned by foreign business interests. Thus, in 1987, the United States refused to allow Japan's Fujitsu electronics corporation to buy Fairchild Semiconductor, which made computer microchips.

Similarly, because some MNCs deal in materials requisite for modern society or have cornered a product market, they are often accused of monopolistic or oligopolistic behavior. For example, during the gasoline shortages that accompanied the Iraqi occupation of Kuwait in 1990 and 1991, and again during 2000 when U.S. gasoline prices increased dramatically, many Americans believed that international oil companies were withholding gasoline so that prices for the consumer and profits for the companies would be driven up. Although such allegations were never proved, it was true that the oil corporations were collectively large enough to undertake such action if they desired.

Closely allied with the economic power of "bigness" is the political power of "bigness." We have already examined the ethical question of the intervention of MNCs in the internal political affairs of host states. The fact is inescapable, however, that the size of many MNCs means that they will have a political impact on a host country even if they do not seek such an impact. If the economic operation of an MNC is critical to the political survival of the host government, that government is inevitably pressured—unless it can provide its own expertise through alternative sources—to grant favorable concessions to guest MNCs. In what was Zaire, for example, the former government granted extremely favorable mining concessions to a number of MNCs for exactly this reason. Zaire was not unique.

Even in the United States, MNCs sometimes are seen as exerting extensive political influence. Thus, when the United States clamped an economic boycott on Libya in early 1986 in response to Libya's support of anti-Western terrorism, U.S. oil companies operating in Libya were exempted. This caused many Americans to accuse the oil companies and even the U.S. government of allowing economic profit to dominate national interest. Oil company executives and government officials asserted that oil company operations in Libya were not ended for different reasons: to prevent Libya from getting all the profits of oil extraction in Libya, which would have given Libya even more money to fund terrorism, and to protect the oil companies' long-term, large-scale capital investment in Libya. The public outcry over this issue was nevertheless sufficient that operations were cut back and negotiations begun in several cases to sell U.S. oil holdings in Libya. Despite this, the key point is that in many people's eyes, MNCs had been allowed to continue to seek economic profit, thereby endangering national interest.

In a social sense, the global marketing capabilities of MNCs have influenced and homogenized consumer tastes. Regardless of whether this is viewed as an advantage or disadvantage—an issue that will be discussed in the concluding section of this chapter—multinationals benefit from the reduction in national distinctions because they are able to sell to a more extensive market with uniform tastes. MNCs are both a beneficiary and a cause of this phenomenon, but the fact remains that MNCs, because of their size, influence international social behavior.

To take fullest advantage of the opportunities that their size and their worldwide operations afford them, MNCs in most instances have evolved a highly centralized decision-making structure. Foreign subsidiaries are closely integrated in that structure and rarely have the latitude of action that the old mother-daughter arrangements had. The purposes of close oversight of operations and centrality of decision making by the headquarters office are to allow the MNC to respond quickly to changing international political and economic situations and to prevent the firm from competing with itself. To the MNC manager, then, oversight and centralization improve the opportunity for profit.

To host nations, however, oversight and centralization imply a loss of control over their own political, economic, and social destinies. With operations overseen and decisions made for a subsidiary in a corporate headquarters that may be half a world away, the governments and peoples of a host state may question whether the decisions made by the MNCs' management have the interests of the host state and its inhabitants at heart. For example, during the 1980s, Ford, Chrysler, and General Motors moved much of their automotive production overseas as the "Big Three" sought less expensive labor and cheaper raw materials. The U.S. Congress, American labor unions, and many other U.S. citizens condemned the companies' managements for actions "not in the American interest." From the companies' perspective, however, good decisions had been made. None of the "Big Three" were—or are—in business to further "the American interest."

During the 1980s, the U.S. textile industry and computer industry fell victim to this same phenomenon—or phrased somewhat differently, took advantage of lower production costs elsewhere. By the late 1980s, the flight of jobs formerly done in the United States to other countries was so extensive that a variety of protectionist legislative measures were introduced in the U.S. Congress to deny MNCs the ability to produce goods outside the United States and then ship them back into the United States. Congress maintained that it was acting in the U.S. national interest, and domestic producers applauded Congress' efforts. Meanwhile, MNCs argued that protectionism could lead to international trade wars and would raise the price of goods to consumers. The Reagan administration, with its advocacy of free trade, sided with the MNCs.

This series of events only strengthened the arguments of those who posit that in today's world, the interests of governments (or at least the executive branch of governments) and interests of corporations are similar if not identical. Thus, the interests of an MNC with headquarters in the United States are often equated with the interests of the United States itself, and the interests of a French-headquartered MNC are equated with the interests of France. Indeed, in some cases, this perception has been strengthened both because of a government's effort to use the subsidiary of an MNC headquartered on its territory to achieve policy objectives and because of a sometimes existing willingness of governments to protect the foreign investments of its citizens.

Nonetheless, numerous examples also exist to illustrate that national interest and corporate interests often clash. U.S.-headquartered firms continued to operate in Germany during World War II even after the United States and Germany were fighting. More recently, several U.S. firms opposed the embargo of high-technology trade with the USSR that President Carter imposed in retaliation for the Soviet invasion of Afghanistan. In Europe, the European Community ended all trade with Argentina in 1982 in response to Argentina's capture of the Falkland Islands. European MNCs operating in Argentina objected bitterly. Again, in 1982, when Ronald Reagan demanded that all U.S. firms and their foreign subsidiaries terminate their cooperation with the USSR on the gas pipeline to Western Europe, U.S. firms, not to mention Europeans, were outraged. Throughout the 1980s, even with the improvement in East–West relations that marked the end of the decade, the U.S. government sought to maintain tight controls on high-technology trade with the Soviet Union and Eastern Europe. Companies that dealt in high-technology products condemned this effort as a constraint on trade. And when the Clinton administration in the mid-1990s threatened to end China's most favored nation status because of Beijing's human rights violations, many MNCs opposed the idea because it would hurt their business dealings in China.

Increasingly, then the global interests and global operations of MNCs run counter to or do not coincide with the governments of states. Corporate decisions taken in MNC headquarters can raise or lower underemployment levels within a country, compromise or enhance the security of a country, and lead to greater or lesser dependence of one country on another. A state's economic growth rate can be accelerated or retarded by corporate decisions, and it need not matter whether a country is the seat of headquarters for an MNC or host country for a subsidiary of an MNC. When General Motors or Ford decides to close a plant or reduce the operations of a plant in Detroit because of high labor costs and open a plant in Mexico City, the Michigan economy and U.S. automotive workers suffer even though General Motors or Ford is a U.S.-based company. Conversely, when the copper content of ore mined in Peru declines below that available in, say, Australia, Kennicott may close that Peruvian mine. The Peruvian economy and workers suffer, whereas the Australian economy and workers benefit. Again, a firm headquartered in the United States will have made decisions affecting the economy and social structure in two countries in which it has subsidiaries without the governments of those host countries playing a role in those decisions.

Responses of States

Because of MNCs, then, governments of states have lost some of their ability to influence and control events within their own boundaries. Not surprisingly, many resent this. In some cases, some states have moved to reassert control. The methods that they have chosen have varied.

In some cases, governments have passed laws that require that over half of a subsidiary be owned by nationals of the host country or by the host country's government itself. From the perspective of a host country, such laws are desirable because they return control of operations to the host country. Conversely, MNCs oppose such laws because their power of decision over joint venture subsidiaries is reduced or removed.

Another method through which states attempt to exert control over multinational corporations is by limiting or forbidding the repatriation of profits. For example, during much of the 1970s and 1980s, Argentina and Columbia limited how much profit could be removed, and in Brazil, all profit had to remain there for two years, after which only 5 percent could be repatriated. These and other governments hoped to keep MNC profits in the country, but frequently the result was to drive MNC investment elsewhere. As a result, this practice declined in the late 1980s and 1990s.

Another method that some governments use to try to control MNCs, also closely related to controls on profit repatriation, is governmental refusal to allow currency to be exported. Because of this type of restriction, MNCs in many cases attempt to export their profits from host nations by buying a product produced domestically within a host nation, exporting it, and selling that product overseas. In a certain sense, then, MNCs may serve as marketing agents for host countries. Thus, because the former USSR did not permit rubles to be exported, Pepsi Cola used the rubles that it made within the USSR by selling Pepsi to buy Stolichnaya vodka, made in the USSR. Pepsi then sold Stolichnaya in the West. The bottom line was that Pepsi could repatriate only the dollar value of Pepsi Cola that it sold in the USSR equal to the dollar value of Stolichnaya it could sell in the West.

Other states have taken other measures to assert their control over MNCs. In the United States, the president and Congress have legal authority to control export of certain types of capital and products, such as state-of-the-art computers and oil extraction technologies. On several occasions during the 1960s, the U.S. government attempted to block the sales of transportation equipment to China from foreign subsidiaries of U.S.-headquartered MNCs. In one case, the U.S. government intended to bring the French subsidiary of the Fruehauf Corporation to court in France to block the sale of trucks to China. Faster legal action by French citizens who opposed the sale made the U.S. action unnecessary. In another case, the U.S. government applied political pressures to Ford Motor Company to force it to prevent its Canadian subsidiary from selling trucks to China. Neither the Canadian government nor Canadian labor unions were pleased by the U.S. government's action because it cost Canadians jobs.

Some governments have opted for blacklists or embargoes in an effort to influence the sales practices of MNCs. Until recently, some Arab states blacklisted any corporation that traded with Israel, although the blacklist was less than totally effective. Similarly, just after the 1973 Arab-Israeli War, Arab members of the Organization of Petroleum Exporting Countries (OPEC) announced that they would not sell oil to corporations that in turn sold that oil to countries that supported Israel. In some cases, the threatened oil embargo influenced the MNCs to change policies. Although OPEC's objectives were clearly to alter the policies of states, it was nevertheless evident that OPEC sought to exert its influence over the multinationals.

Impressive as these efforts may be, governments still often believe that MNCs act as they choose. And for their part, MNCs often decry states as regulative interlopers that complicate the operation of legitimate business, raise prices, and reduce profits by those very regulations.

Who is correct, MNC managers who chastise government intervention and who view their corporations as being targets of costly state regulation, or the states' governmental authorities who believe that MNCs can and do have the size, flexibility, and centralization to sidestep governmental regulations? Not surprisingly, depending on the case chosen, both sides can prove their points.

MNCs can and do present challenges to the state. In a certain sense, though, they also present challenges to any group or individual viewing the world in less than global terms, because the MNCs' perspective is, in fact, global. It is this advocacy of globalism as much as anything else that arouses much of the furor over multinational corporations.[10]

MNCS AS WORLD CITIZENS: CLAIMS AND COUNTERCLAIMS

Multinational managers, as we have seen, claim to have the expertise and resources to structure a more efficiently productive world and therefore improve global living standards. Only the unique blend of size and internationalism peculiar to MNCs, they argue, can bring about the global reality of comparative advantage. As espoused by British economists David Ricardo and John Stuart Mill during the nineteenth century, the concept of **comparative advantage** posits simply that products should be produced wherever they can be produced least expensively, and that products produced elsewhere should be imported and paid for with excess internal production. As an economic theory, comparative advantage has been operationalized by MNCs.[11]

Multinational managers do not end their advocacy of their corporations with their assertions that MNCs will raise living standards. They also argue that MNCs help less developed countries modernize and industrialize by introducing technology, job opportunities, and expertise to underdeveloped economies. The benefits of economic plenty therefore will not be restricted to the industrialized countries, they assert, but would be extended throughout all human societies.

Finally, according to those who believe in the vision of a brighter future through multinational corporations, MNCs by their very nature make war obsolete. In a future world with all states and regions dependent on other states and regions for economic well-being, no sane person or government will initiate a war. MNCs bring about an interdependent world, the argument goes, and in so doing make war unthinkable. Using Western Europe, Japan, and the North American states as examples, advocates of MNCs point out that so many overseas investments exist between and among those states and their economies are so intertwined through the operations of MNCs that war among them would be virtually economic suicide.

Critics of MNCs have a different outlook. In addition to governments of both industrialized and developing states that lament that they cannot control the actions of MNCs, labor unions criticize the multinationals for their tendency to relocate in regions where labor is unorganized and inexpensive. By building plants with excess capacity, MNCs can even insulate themselves from labor's most useful weapon, the strike. When unions in one state strike against an MNC, that MNC can simply expand its production in one of its nonstrikebound plants.

Nationalists also frequently criticize MNCs, often in concert with their governments. As we have seen, most MNCs are based in the United States, Western Europe, and Japan. This has led many developing states and their citizens to condemn MNCs as exploitive and tools of imperialism. Such criticism declined during the late 1990s, but on occasion it is still evident.

But nationalist criticism of MNCs and the globalism that most espouse goes far beyond developing states and their citizens. For example, during the late 1980s and 1990s, anti-Japanese sentiment in the U.S. increased as more and more Japanese MNCs set up operations in the United States. And in 1999, riots flared in Seattle as trade union groups and others attempted to prevent the World Trade Organization, seen by many as the tool of MNCs in their effort to achieve globalization, from meeting.

Other critics of MNCs argue that MNCs use managerial expertise and technical know-how available only in the industrialized West and cheap labor and inexpensive resources available primarily in the nonindustrialized Developing World to increase their profits without making significant contributions to the economies in which they operate. Indeed, the argument goes, multinational corporations do not bring in large quantities of external capital but rather use existing capital that should be devoted to other purposes within developing countries. With their superior capital-intensive productive capabilities, MNCs drive other labor-intensive local market competitors out of business, thereby actually increasing unemployment in a host country. In addition, MNCs are accused of destroying traditional cultures by use of sophisticated advertising techniques and replacing them with local versions of U.S. and Western European consumer societies. As profit on the global level is the MNCs' primary objective, the multinationals are often accused of ignoring local questions such as environmental quality, resource conservation, and health and nutrition.

The early 1980s' efforts of the Nestlé Corporation and other international distributors of powdered dry baby formula to market their product to developing countries provide a good case in point. The MNCs argued that dry baby formula was as good or better than mothers' milk in providing the nutritional needs of infants and marketed the formula as the "modern" way to care for an infant. Unfortunately, none considered the quality of Developing World water supplies, which are often undrinkable. By mixing formula with water as is required, mothers in those areas exposed their infants to numerous diseases that they otherwise would have avoided by remaining on mothers' milk. Another grave danger to infants occurred when, in efforts to economize, mothers put too little formula into each measure of water. Widespread malnutrition among infants resulted. Only after an extensive worldwide publicity campaign including efforts at the United Nations did the MNCs reduce their baby formula marketing efforts in the Developing World.

According to critics of MNCs, continued unbridled operation of MNCs in developing countries will inevitably lead to more unemployment, more environmental degradation, poorer nutrition and health standards, and more inequitable distribution of wealth in those countries. As more and more MNCs invest outside North America and Europe, they maintain, unemployment rates will go up there as well. At the same time, as more developing countries form producer cartels to protect their resource interests against the MNCs, the multinationals will charge higher prices for their products in the developed world. Thus, in the developed world as well, critics assert that MNCs cause unemployment, inflation, and economic stagnation.

Obviously, the most ardent advocates and the most vocal critics of the multinational corporation are separated by a wide chasm. They agree that the size and global flexibility of multinational corporations give those corporations an almost unprecedented opportunity to act in the international arena, but they disagree as to the results of those actions. MNC advocates see improved living standards, more employment, and a less violent world, if only MNCs could operate in a world with less governmental intervention and a more widely accepted set of international standards. Thus, when MNC advocates favorably discuss regulation of MNCs, they mean global regulation that would enhance the operating environment for the multinationals.

Conversely, MNC critics see higher unemployment, worse living conditions, and a more elitist world with increasingly inequitable distribution of wealth if MNCs continue to operate without increased subnational, national, and supranational control. Thus, when MNC critics favorably discuss regulation of MNCs, they mean regulation that would curtail the ability of multinationals to make decisions without government control at some level.

As the debate between advocates and critics of multinational corporations makes clear, the role of multinational corporations in contemporary international relations is significant. Although the more extreme claims of both advocates and critics of MNCs can probably be safely ignored, a conflicting body of evidence exists concerning the role of MNCs in today's world. For students and scholars of international affairs, MNCs must remain a centerpiece of inquiry.

 ## *KEY TERMS AND CONCEPTS*

multinational corporation   a corporation that has its headquarters in one state and owns and operates other corporations in other states

subsidiaries   foreign corporations owned and operated by a multinational corporation

transnational corporations   another term for multinational corporations

size and scope of MNCs   MNCs range from small businesses to huge corporations, and produce a large and increasing share of the world's economic production

organizational structures of MNCs   the text discusses the mother-daughter arrangement that allowed foreign subsidiaries to operate with little guidance from the parent organization; the international division structure, in which an MNC has one division in charge of each product and an international division in charge of foreign operations; the product division structure, where an MNC gives each division global responsibility; and the integrated network model, in which each MNC unit is part of a network of distributed capabilities

perspectives of MNC management   sometimes MNC managers shift their views from seeing their companies as national companies with international operations to seeing them as truly global entities

foreign direct investment   the investment of capital directly in another country's economy

joint ventures   a subsidiary operation in which ownership is shared by the central multinational corporation and another party or group of parties, often from the host country

licensing agreements   an agreement under which a company is allowed to produce for a fee the product of another company; this is usually done in the context of one company allowing a foreign company to produce its product overseas rather than directly investing overseas

political influence of MNCs   MNC critics charge that because of their size, wealth, and centralization, MNCs have great political influence over countries in which they operate

centralized versus decentralized decisionmaking   the debate within MNCs about whether it is best to have centralized decision-making, thereby permitting MNCs to respond quickly to changes in the global marketplace, or decentralized decision-making, thereby allowing MNCs to respond rapidly to changes in local marketplaces

mergers and megamergers   the combination of two or more MNCs into a single business, with megamergers being the combination of two or more extremely large MNCs into a single company

co-op-etition   a business phenomenon which emerged in the 1990s in which competitors within a single industry find it is to their advantage to cooperate on certain aspects of business operations but continue competing in other areas

strategic partnering   a business phenomenon which emerged in the 1990s in which businesses find it to their advantage to develop formal cooperative relationships with other businesses, sometimes within their business sector and sometimes outside it

impact of MNCs on state sovereignty   MNC critics charge that because of their size, wealth, and centralization, MNCs undermine state sovereignty

impact of states on MNC operations   defenders of MNCs argue that states impede MNC operations, thereby limiting the ability of MNCs to operate efficiently

comparative advantage   the economic theory that goods should be produced wherever they can be produced most inexpensively and that products produced elsewhere should be imported

 ## WEBSITE REFERENCES

multinational corporations: *www.quickmarch.com/WorldBusinessGiants.html*   Fortune 500 listing of the 500 largest MNCs, by country, with links to corporate websites

www.essential.org/EI.html   website of a Ralph Nader initiated project monitoring the activities of multinational corporations

www.multinationals.law.eur.nl/links/index.html   website on MNCs impact on human rights, legal issues, etc.

co-op-etition: *www/warrenco.com/whtpaper/ppt5/index.htm*   a set of powerpoint slides on different types of co-op-etition agreements

strategic partnering: *www.fespa.org*   website of the Foundation for Entrepreneurship and Strategic Partnering, a not-for-profit organization assisting entrepreneurs in the global economy

 ## NOTES

1. For a sampling of the voluminous literature on MNCs and international business, see Theodore H. Moran, *Multinational Corporations: The Political Economy of Foreign Direct Investment* (Lexington, MA: Lexington Books, 1988); Robert Z. Aliber, *The Multinational Paradigm* (Cambridge, MA: The MIT Press, 1992); Donald A. Ball and Wendell H. McCulloch, Jr., *International Business: The Challenge of Competition,* 6th ed. (Burr Ridge, IL: Irwin Professional Publishers, 1995); Bruce Kogut, "International Business: The New Bottom Line," *Foreign Policy* (Spring 1998), pp. 152–165; Marina v. N. Whitman, "The Changing Role of the American Corporation," *The Washington Quarterly* (Spring 1999), pp. 59–82; John J. Maresca, "A New Concept of Business," *The Washington Quarterly* (Spring 2000), pp. 155–163;

Charles Hill, Global Business Today (McGraw Hill, 2000); and George Stonehouse, *Global and Transnational Business* (John Wiley and Sons, 2000).

2. For several different discussions of the organization of MNCs during different historical periods, see Raymond Vernon, *Storm Over the Multinationals: The Real Issues* (Cambridge, MA: Harvard University Press, 1977); Christopher Bartlett, "Building and Managing the Transnational: The New Organizational Challenge," in Michael E. Porter, ed., *Competition in Global Industries* (Boston, MA: Harvard Business School Press, 1986); and Lloyd L. Byars et al., *Strategic Management* (Chicago, IL: Richard D. Irwin, 1995), pp. 140–145. See also James F. Moore, "The Rise of a New Corporate Form," *The Washington Quarterly* (Winter 1998), pp. 167–181.

3. For a discussion of MNCs in China, see Yadong Luo, *Strategy, Structure, and Performance of MNCs in China* (Greenwood Publishers, 2000).

4. See Joan Edelman Spero and Jeffrey A. Hart, *The Politics of International Economic Relations,* 7th edition (New York, NY: St. Martin's Press, 1997) for a discussion of ITT and the CIA in Chile.

5. For a discussion of efforts to influence MNCs to reduce their investments in apartheid South Africa during the 1980s, see Kenneth Rodman, "Public and Private Sanctions Against South Africa," *Political Science Quarterly* (Summer 1994), pp. 313–34.

6. For other discussions of MNC decisionmaking, see Amir Mahini, *Making Decisions in Multinational Corporations: Managing Relations with Sovereign Governments* (New York, NY: John Wiley and Sons, 1988); Tamir Agmom et al., *Trade Policy and Corporate Business Decisions* (New York, NY: Oxford University Press, 1990); and Rajib N. Sanyal, *Managing International Business* (New York, NY: Addison Wesley Longman, 2001).

7. Mergers and megamergers are discussed in depth in Joanna Reeves, *Managing Mergers and Acquisitions* (London: Caspian, 1999); and Fay Hansen, "Global Mergers and Acquisitions Explode," *Business Credit* (June 2000), pp. 22–25.

8. See "The Latest Business Game: Joint Ventures and Strategic Alliances are Riskier than They Look," *The Economist* (May 5, 1990), p. 16; and Kalman Applbaum, "Survival of the Biggest: Business Policy, Managerial Discourse, and Uncertainty in a Global Business Environment," *Anthropological Quarterly* (October 1999), pp. 155–66 for discussions of strategic alliances.

9. This phrase is taken from Ray Vernon, *Sovereignty at Bay: The Multinational Spread of U.S. Enterprises* (New York, NY: Basic Books, 1971). See also Edward M. Graham, *Global Firms and National Governments* (Washington, DC: Institute for International Economics, 1995).

10. For additional discussions of challenges that MNCs present to states and of state responses to those challenges, see Robert Boyer and Daniel Drache, eds., *States Against Markets: The Limits of Globalization* (London: Routledge, 1996); and Herman M. Schwartz, *States versus Markets: History, Geography, and the Development of the International Political Economy* (New York, NY: St. Martin'' Press, 1994).

11. See David Ricardo, excerpts from "The Principles of Political Economy and Taxation," and John Stuart Mill, excerpts from "Principles of Political Economy with Some of Their Applications to Social Philosophy," in William R. Allen, ed., *International Trade Theory: Hume to Ohlin* (New York: Random House, 1965), pp. 62–67, 68–69.

Chapter 5

Nongovernmental Organizations, Individuals, and Other International Actors

- What is an NGO and what does it hope to accomplish?
- What role do individuals play in international affairs?
- What is a national liberation movement and what does it seek?
- What does a terrorist hope to achieve and why?
- How does religion influence international affairs today?
- Do political parties make contacts across international boundaries and what effect does this have on international affairs?

To this point, our examination of the actors in the contemporary international arena has centered on states, those international organizations that states create, and multinational corporations. The roles that these actors play in contemporary international affairs are dominant. Numerous other actors, however, also play roles in today's world that cannot be overlooked. In many instances, these other actors are not officially recognized by states, IGOs, or MNCs. Nevertheless, they often influence and sometimes determine the course of international relations.

Nongovernmental organizations (NGOs) are among the most organized of these other actors. NGOs are extremely diverse in size, composition, objectives, and influence, and include bodies such as the International Olympic Committee, Amnesty International, CARE, the International Federation of Airline Pilots' Associations, the International Red Cross, the International Chamber of Commerce, and the World Federation of Trade Unions. In 2000, the *Yearbook of International Organizations* identified nearly 19,000 NGOs, which are defined as structured organizations operating internationally without formal ties to a government.

Chapter 5

IT, NGOS, AND INDIVIDUALS: CONNECTING THE DISCONNECTED

Since nongovernmental organizations (NGOs) and individuals are so diverse, it should not be surprising that advanced information technologies will impact them in a variety of ways. Perhaps most obvious, given the fact that many NGOs have widely scattered memberships, advanced information technologies will help connect the disconnected.

As a result, many NGOs will benefit significantly from the increased speed, greater capacity, enhanced flexibility, and improved access afforded by advanced information technologies. It is reasonable to assume that many NGOs will become increasingly active, better coordinated, and more influential as advanced information technologies become more widely available and the NGOs' membership becomes increasingly able to communicate rapidly and reliably. For example, international NGOs such as Greenpeace have often used modern information technologies to marshall opposition to what they perceive as threats to the environment.

Many NGOs are not well off economically. Even this, however, should not be a barrier to expanded NGO use of IT if, as expected, information technologies continue to become less expensive. Thus, the NGOs' relative lack of resources should not necessarily put NGOs at a significant disadvantage, especially since it is not necessary for NGOs to have the absolute latest in information technology for them to benefit enormously. The huge discounts off of original prices that are given for "past generation" technology make these capabilities affordable.

As a result of the capabilities afforded by advanced information technologies, we may also expect to see not only an expansion of the international role and influence of NGOs, but also a further proliferation of NGOs and related organizations. This includes the possibility of the creation of "virtual NGO's" as well as a networking of such organizations.

Meanwhile, at the level of individuals, telephones, electronic mail, and facsimiles already link people together in ways never before anticipated. Much of the personal use of these technologies is for social, educational, and business purposes. But these technologies also have immense international political potential. Indeed, following the 1989 Tiananmen Square massacre in China and during the 1991 Soviet coup attempt, electronic mail and facsimiles provided an important link to the outside world—and vice versa—for individuals in China and former Soviet Union.

To reiterate, given the diversity of NGOs and individuals as international actors, advanced information technologies will have a diverse impact on the role that they play in international relations. Many NGOs and individuals will enhance their international roles and their international influence as a result of the increased speed, greater capacity, enhanced flexibility, and improved access afforded by advanced information and communication technologies.

But there are many unstructured or minimally structured organizations that operate internationally without formal ties to governments that also play major roles in contemporary international relations. Ethnic and national liberation organizations such as the African National Council and the Palestine Liberation Organization have had and continue to have a major impact on international affairs. So, too, have terrorist organizations such as Italy's Red Brigade and West Germany's Red Army Faction. Therefore, they must be included in our discussion as well.

Certain transnational religious movements and groups are also significant international actors. In the Christian world, the transnational impact of Catholicism, the Catholic Church, and the pope is immense. The pope is ruler of the Vatican State in Rome, but his domain extends far beyond the Eternal City. Similarly, the resurgence of Islam has altered the course of world affairs. It is important not only in the Middle East, but also in Asia, Africa, and Europe. It is also the fastest growing religion in the United States.

Transnational political parties and movements must not be overlooked as international actors either. Western European Social Democrats have forged links that transcend national boundaries, and although communism as a global ideology has been discredited, until relatively recently, communist parties appealed to their international solidarity and unity.

Finally, the role of the individual in international affairs remains significant. Prominent individuals such as Jimmy Carter after the end of his presidency, Jean Monnet following his tenure as head of the European Coal and Steel Community High Authority, and even Muhammad Ali have had some influence on policies and perceptions in the international arena. Less individually notable personages such as tourists, businesspeople, refugees, and soldiers stationed overseas may well have had a cumulative impact on international affairs more significant than their more famous counterparts.

Again, it must be stressed that the diverse actors grouped in this chapter as nongovernmental organizations, individuals, and other international actors can be and often are significantly different in size, composition, influence, and objectives. However, unless they are considered in some detail, we cannot obtain an accurate picture of contemporary international relations.

This chapter, then, examines six diverse groupings of international actors. Traditional NGOs are examined first, followed by the individual's role in international affairs. Ethnic/national liberation organizations and terrorist organizations and movements are discussed separately, as are religious movements and political parties.[1]

 ## NONGOVERNMENTAL ORGANIZATIONS (NGOS)

NGOs are not new actors in international affairs, but they have received a semblance of formal recognition as international actors only since World War II. In contrast to the League of Nations, where NGO representatives competed with tourists for seats, the United Nations has recognized the international role that NGOs play. The UN often encourages them to play active roles in the major international conferences that it holds, as evidenced at the UN's 1995 Beijing Conference on Women, the 1997 Kyoto Environmental Summit, and the 2000 Trade and Development Conference. The first of these conferences was particularly noteworthy since a separate NGO forum was held before the formal UN conference began. Over 30 thousand women attended, most representing NGOs.

Some governments have also recognized the importance of NGOs in international relations. For example, as long ago as 1945, the U.S. government designated several NGOs "special consultants" to the U.S. delegation to the UN Conference on International Organizations. More recently, in 1995, the United States decided to disperse up to 40 percent of the foreign aid that its Agency for International Development distributed through NGOs.[2]

There is no precise definition of what an NGO is, but it is nevertheless clear that the number of NGOs has increased since World War II. Their newly acquired international status, the increased volume of international interactions, and the increased ease of international travel and communications are all causes of this proliferation, even as they are for the increased numbers of IGOs, which we discussed in Chapter 3.

NGOs operate in a variety of areas of human activity. Some such as Greenpeace seek to change policies of state governments. For example, Greenpeace initiated a global "Save the Whales" campaign that was instrumental in influencing states in 1982 to agree to "harvest" only 12,000 whales per year. More recently, Greenpeace in 1995 launched a global campaign against France's resumption of nuclear tests in the South Pacific. Although Greenpeace did not stop French nuclear testing, the French government reduced the number of tests it conducted before it ended its test program in 1996.

NGO activities may also coincide with state policy. For example, within weeks of changes in governments in Eastern Europe in 1989, the American Federation of Teachers, several U.S. and Western European labor unions, and the International Bar Association dispatched members to Eastern Europe to help teach people there how democratic institutions worked. These and other NGOs have continued their efforts in Eastern Europe and expanded them into the former Soviet Union during the 1990s.

Some NGOs such as the International Red Cross and CARE undertake humanitarian efforts. Sometimes, their efforts can be quite sizable. For example, in its 50-year history, CARE has operated in 121 countries and provided over $7 billion in program aid. In 1999 alone, CARE's 9,000 person staff provided food to 21 million people, health and nutrition assistance to 3.6 million people, and medicine to 7 million more.[3]

Other NGOs monitor human rights abuses. Amnesty International's programs of investigating, pointing out, and publicizing human rights abuses around the world are particularly noteworthy. So, too, are the programs of Americas Watch, which undertakes similar activities in the Western Hemisphere.

Still other NGOs may be best described as professional organizations that seek to further the interests of their members. The International Sugar Office, the International Chamber of Commerce, the World Veterans Association, and the International Federation of Airline Pilots' Association (IFALPA) are all examples of NGOs. There is no uniform record of success or failure for these NGOs in their efforts to further their members' interests. A former Secretary of the International Chamber of Commerce lamented the dearth of publicity that NGOs receive and noted that their efforts in international affairs are generally ignored.[4] By contrast, IFALPA had a major impact on how states handle skyjacking. IFALPA members agreed to boycott all states that took ineffective antiskyjacking measures or that clearly supported skyjackers. When IFALPA called for a boycott of all flights to Algeria in August 1968 because of the Algerian government's detention of a hijacked El Al aircraft, crew and passengers, the Algerian government quickly ended the detention.[5] In 1986, IFALPA again threatened to boycott all states that supported terrorism aimed at commercial airline flights or facilities. The 1986 declaration was aimed at Libya.

Scientific organizations are also often NGOs, although they regularly find themselves in a complex web of governmental, IGO, NGO, and MNC relations. The International Council of Scientific Unions (ICSU) is perhaps the leading scientific NGO. ICSU members include the major scientific academies of the world, national research councils, and associations of scientific institutions from many countries. Its activities have included organization of the International Geophysical Year and the International Year of the Quiet Sun, and it has specialized international committees on ocean research, space research, and science and technology in developing countries, to name only a few. ICSU often cooperates with government agencies, proposes programs to IGOs and other NGOs, and seeks funding support from private corporations and MNCs. ICSU is not the only NGO that finds itself in such a complex web of interactions. It is simply one of many possible excellent examples.

A variety of international sports federations also qualify as NGOs. The International Olympic Committee (IOC) and the International Rugby Union (IRU) are of particular note because of their extreme involvement in politics between states. Although both groups maintain that politics should have no role in international sports, both are entwined in political issues that they would prefer to avoid. The IOC has been forced to decide whether the Republic of China (Taiwan) or the People's Republic of China (mainland China) should participate in the Olympic games, whether New Zealand should be excluded from participation in the Olympics because a non-Olympic New Zealand sports team competed against a South African team, whether an Olympic site should be changed because a host country (the Soviet Union) had militarily occupied a neighbor (Afghanistan), and how many if any Olympic events should be held in North Korea when the host country was South Korea. The IRU has been forced to decide whether it would permit member teams to play against the South African national team, one of the best in the world, or refuse matches because of South Africa's apartheid policy. It chose to exclude South Africa from world competition. And after South Africa abandoned apartheid, the IRU made another clear political statement, holding the 1995 World Cup of Rugby in South Africa. These issues were clearly political and had little to do with sports as such, but because of the issues at stake, athletically oriented NGOs intruded into the political domain of states.

A final type of NGO is the private foundation. Although some experts do not consider foundations legitimate NGOs because they are generally chartered under the laws of one state and operate primarily in the domestic sphere, some foundations in fact have a significant international role. Here we examine two of those.

The first is the world's largest foundation, the Ford Foundation, which has focused on international projects on developmental assistance, population studies, and European and international studies. The second is the Rockefeller Foundation, the world's third largest foundation, which has concentrated on health, population, biomedical, and nutritional projects. Together, the Ford and Rockefeller foundations have contributed extensively to the so-called "green revolution" through their funding of the International Rice Research Institute in the Philippines, the International Center of Tropical Agriculture in Colombia, the International Wheat and Maize Improvement Center in Mexico, and the International Institute of Tropical Agriculture in Nigeria. Like the scientific NGOs, foundations have interacted regularly and closely with a variety of states. Ford and Rockefeller programs are often closely coordinated with programs run by the U.S. government's Agency for International Development and the Canadian government's Canadian Development Agency. Cooperation has also been effected between the foundations and IGOs such as the Organization of American States, the United Nations Development Program, and the International Bank for Reconstruction and Development.

So far the impression may have been created that NGOs regularly cooperate effectively with states, IGOs, and MNCs. This is only part of the picture. On occasion, relations between NGOs and other actors can become quite sour. The International Olympic Committee's experience during the last several Olympic games is a good case in point.

The IOC, like many NGOs, has a central committee that acts as an administrative and policy-making body to which national sports federations can apply for membership. The IOC decides on sites for Olympic games several years in advance; the various national sports federations then send their representatives to participate in the games. Other than providing some funding in some states, national governments theoretically are in no way connected with either the IOC or the national sports federations.

However, because of the immensity of the spectacle of the international competition and cooperation of the Olympics, the games also evoke tremendous displays of national pride. Political nationalism runs rampant at the Olympic games, not only in the competition itself, but also in the international media. Host countries use the Olympics to showcase not only their athletes but also their political viewpoints, their economic successes, and their social systems.

Thus, when the Soviet Union invaded Afghanistan seven months before the 1980 Moscow Olympics and the U.S. and a significant number of other states boycotted the Moscow games, the International Olympic Committee as well as the Soviet government were incensed with the U.S. Four years later, when the Soviet Union and many communist states boycotted the Los Angeles Olympic Games, the U.S. government and the IOC was incensed with the Soviet Union. Then, in 1988, the IOC received immense pressure to allow some competitions to be held in North Korea as well as South Korea.

Although the 1992 Barcelona Olympic Games were held without political problems, the IOC later was heavily criticized for locating the 1996 summer games in Atlanta and the 2000 summer games in Sydney. Many felt that the Centennial Olympic games should have gone to Athens, Greece, and the 2000 games to Beijing. Even though the IOC prefers to avoid state-to-state politics, it can not. In this respect, the IOC is not an unusual NGO.

INDIVIDUALS IN INTERNATIONAL AFFAIRS

The **role that a private individual may play in international affairs** is often difficult to determine because of the role that that same individual may have had in an organization, agency, or government participating in international affairs. Thus, when Jimmy Carter traveled to North Korea in 1994 to talk about its nuclear weapons program, he traveled as a private citizen but was viewed both by the North Koreans and the Clinton administration as much more than a private citizen. Similarly, when during the Reagan administration, three private U.S. citizens attended the funeral of slain Egyptian President Anwar Sadat, they were accorded high honors of protocol by the Egyptians. It was also helpful that the three private citizens were Jimmy Carter, Gerald Ford, and Richard Nixon.

At the other extreme from prominent individuals are the large numbers of more obscure people who move from country to country for a host of different reasons, but who nevertheless may have a significant impact on international affairs. For example, there are millions of refugees throughout the world who for one reason or another—war, famine, drought, and so on—have chosen to or have been forced to leave their homes.

The **role of refugees** is an often overlooked human aspect of international affairs, but as Tables 5-1 and 5-2 make clear, the world refugee problem is both immense and global in scope. The most obvious aspect of the world's refugee problem is those people who move across international boundaries, as is shown in Table 5-1, but there is another dimension to the problem as well, those people who are displaced within their country, as shown in Table 5-2. The toll in human suffering exacted by the tribulations of the world's refugee population is immeasurable, and the cost to the countries that harbor and provide aid for refugees is also sizable.[6]

TABLE 5-1   Refugees Displaced Outside Their Own Countries, December 31, 1998

Palestinians	3,816,000*	Bhutan	115,000*
Afghanistan	2,600,000*	Western Sahara	105,000*
Iraq	586,000*	Cambodia	51,000
Sierra Leone	480,000*	Philippines	45,000
Bosnia and Herzegovina	424,000*	Uzbekistan	45,000
Somalia	421,000*	Algeria	40,000*
Sudan	352,000	Ethiopia	40,000*
Eritrea	323,000*	Iran	40,000
Liberia	310,000*	Mauritania	30,000
Croatia	309,000	Georgia	23,000
Angola	302,000	India	22,000
Burundi	281,000	Turkey	22,000
Vietnam	281,000	Congo-Brazzaville	20,000
El Salvador	250,000	Nicaragua	19,000
Burma	238,000*	Chad	16,000
Azerbaijan	218,000	Tajikistan	15,000*
Armenia	180,000	Laos	12,000
Guatemala	151,000	Rwanda	12,000*
Yugoslavia	145,000	Uganda	12,000
Congo-Kinshasa	136,000	Ghana	11,000
China (Tibet)	128,000	Guinea-Bissau	11,000
Sri Lanka	126,000*	Senegal	10,000

Source: U.S. Committee for Refugees, 1999.

*Sources vary widely in number reported.

TABLE 5-2   Refugees Displaced within Their Own Countries, December 31, 1998

Sudan	4,000,000	Yugoslavia	257,000
Angola	1,000,000–1,500,000*	Congo-Brazzaville	250,000
Colombia	1,400,000	Somalia	250,000
Iraq	1,000,000	Guinea-Bissau	200,000
Afghanistan	540,000–1,000,000	Kenya	200,000
Burma	500,000–1,000,000	Ethiopia	150,000
Turkey	400,000–1,000,000*	Syria	125,000
Bosnia and Hercegovina	836,000	Philippines	122,000
Azerbaijan	576,000	Algeria	100,000–200,000*
Sri Lanka	560,000	Eritrea	100,000
India	520,000	Liberia	75,000
Burundi	500,000	Croatia	61,000
Rwanda	500,000	Armenia	60,000
Lebanon	400,000–450,000	Bangladesh	50,000
Uganda	400,000	Cambodia	22,000
Russian Federation	350,000*	Ghana	20,000
Peru	340,000	Mexico	15,000
Congo-Kinshasa	300,000*	Senegal	10,000
Sierra Leone	300,000*	Papua New Guinea	2,000–6,000
Georgia	280,000	Nigeria	3,000
Cyprus	265,000		

Source: U.S. Committee for Regugees, 1999.

*Sources vary widely in number reported.

Nor can something as elementary as **the role of tourism** be overlooked. Every year, millions of people cross the Atlantic and Pacific Oceans as tourists, as Figure 5-1 shows. On an individual basis, these people play almost no role in international affairs. But on a cumulative basis, their impact is considerable, not only because of the effect they may have on the perceptions of those whose country they visit, but also because of the perceptions that they develop about the countries they visit. The "ugly American" syndrome of the 1950s and 1960s was as much the product of U.S. tourist behavior as anything else, and the "ungrateful European" viewpoint of the same era was the product of perceptions the "ugly Americans" acquired during their European visits. In the 1980s and 1990s, the "ugly American" syndrome has been increasingly replaced by an "ugly Japanese" syndrome, but the point is the same: Tourists pick up impressions of the countries they visit and in turn leave impressions of their country behind in the minds of those whom they encounter.

Between the extremes of a few past presidents and millions of refugees and tourists, private citizens engage in a variety of other significant activities in international affairs. Muhammad Ali, for example, proclaimed himself America's unofficial ambassador to Africa during the Carter administration and on another occasion was even asked by the

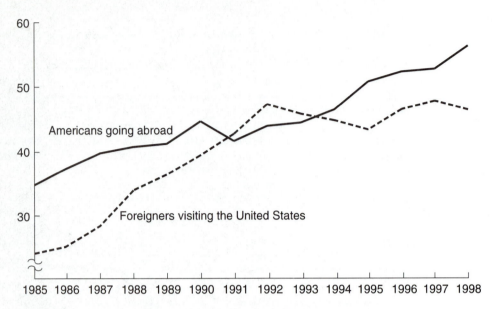

FIGURE 5-1   Comparison of outgoing and incoming travel in millions.

Source: U.S. Department of Commerce.

Carter administration to engage in formal diplomatic activity. During the hostage crisis in Iran, the Carter administration turned to private French and Colombian citizens who had contacts in the Iranian government to attempt to attain the hostages' release. During the Johnson presidency, private individuals were used on a number of occasions to attempt to open separate channels of communications between Washington and Hanoi.[7] More recently, when the U.S. Congress banned official U.S. arms sales to the Contras in Nicaragua, the Reagan administration turned to private U.S. citizens (as well as certain U.S. government employees and non-Americans) in an effort to develop private support for the Contras.

Other types of private individual contacts also play definite but undocumentable roles in international affairs. Student exchanges; foreign teaching and research; long-term job-related migration or permanent settlement; and similar activities all yield personal-level interactions between citizens of different countries. Nor can the role of businesspeople be overlooked. Indeed, as the Soviet Union and Eastern Europe changed their economic organization in the late 1980s and early 1990s, the flow of businesspeople to these countries increased dramatically. They carried with them different business practices and attitudes than those that up until that time prevailed in the USSR and Eastern Europe.

Generally speaking, private individual activities in an international context are supportive of or neutral toward the government of one's country of citizenship. However, this is not always the case. Although cases of spying or outright treason are the extremes, there are other actions that private individuals take in international affairs that can conflict with the policies of their state. Jane Fonda's trip to Hanoi during the Vietnam War was undertaken as a private U.S. citizen, and she was heavily criticized by the Nixon administration for both her trip and her statements on the war. A few years later, Nixon himself was criticized by the Carter administration for his trip to China. To Carter, Nixon had complicated the conduct of U.S. policy toward China. And in 1994, Carter himself was criticized by the Clinton administration for statements he made during his trip to North Korea. To Clinton, Carter had complicated ongoing negotiations with North Korea.

Nor should the economic impact of large numbers of individual travelers be overlooked. During the 1970s, following the murder of several tourists in the U.S. Virgin Islands and political unrest in Jamaica, tourists by the thousands changed their travel plans, avoiding not only the U.S. Virgin Islands and Jamaica, but the rest of the Caribbean as well. The economies of every Caribbean island were seriously hurt by these decisions of individual travelers. Similarly, in 1995, many tourists again changed their vacation plans after several hurricanes devastated a number of Carribbean islands, thereby unintentionally hurting the economies of the islands even more. And in 1991, fearing Iraqi-sponsored terrorist attacks against Americans in Europe, many U.S. citizens once again refused to travel overseas, as shown in Figure 5-1.

A single individual can also have an immense impact on the human side of the international community, regardless of whether that person is someone like Mother Teresa, a Catholic nun, with her compassion for the poor and homeless in India, or Ted Turner, former owner of CNN and other sports and communications enterprises, with his concern for world peace and the UN. Mother Teresa's compassion won the world's admiration. Turner's desire to improve U.S.-Soviet relations led him to organize the Goodwill Games, and his concern for the UN led him to contribute 1 billion dollars to the organization. The point is clear: Individuals can matter.

On another level, it is also instructive to speculate on the impact that different individuals with different values may have had if they had been in critical locations at crucial times in the course of international events. How would international affairs have been changed if George Washington had less of a sense of country and more of a sense of self, and decided not to step down after two terms in office? What would have happened in the USSR if instead of Joseph Stalin, Lenin's successor had been someone with a sense of human values? More recently, what would have happened in Eastern Europe if Mikhail Gorbachev had concluded like his predecessors that the USSR must dominate those countries? Would there have been a Soviet invasion and a military bloodbath? Obviously, we will never know. Washington had a sense of country, Stalin had few human values, and Gorbachev adopted a policy of nonintervention. The point is obvious: Individuals can matter.

Individuals, then, play diverse roles in contemporary international affairs. For better or worse, we form our opinions about other nationalities, about businesspeople, about military officers, and others, on the basis of our experiences with them. Also, for better or worse, they form their opinions about us. Individuals also play major roles in transmission of cultures and values, in policy formulation and implementation, and even in economic affairs. And it is perhaps at the human level where individuals are most important.

Unfortunately, however, it is difficult to assess the level of importance that should be attached to their actions. No accurate picture of the conduct of contemporary international relations can be obtained without their inclusion. All that can be safely said is that such actions form an integral part of the fabric of contemporary international relations.[8]

ETHNIC/NATIONAL LIBERATION ORGANIZATIONS

As a general rule, **ethnic/national liberation organizations** and movements have as their primary objective the establishment of a nation-state under their own government. Beyond this, they rarely have much else in common. More often than not, they have different levels of power and influence and different organizational structures. Some use nonviolent means to achieve their ends, as has the Parti Québecois in Canada, and some use violence that results in civil war or terrorist attacks, as have the Eritreans and Basques.[9]

Ethnic/national liberation movements may be divided into three types. The first we encountered in our discussion of states when we discussed certain ethnic or national groups that sought to break away from the countries of which they were a part to establish their own nation-state. The Basques of Spain, the Biafrans of Nigeria, the Eritreans of Ethiopia, and the Québecois of Canada are just a few of the many ethnic/national groups that have sought or are seeking independent statehood. Indeed, in the final analysis, the breakup of the Soviet Union was a result of the demands of ethnic and national groups for national independence.

The second type of ethnic/national liberation movement seeks to overthrow a government that it views as dictatorial, exploitive, or under the control of an external influence. In this type of liberation, the objective of the liberation movement is not the creation of a new state, but rather the creation of a new government for an old state. Political change rather than political fragmentation is sought. The Sandinistas in Nicaragua, the Contras in Nicaragua after the Sandinista takeover, the Vietcong in South Vietnam, the Mujahadeen in Afghanistan, the ANC in South Africa, and UNITA in Angola since Angolan independence are examples of this second type of ethnic/national liberation movement. The organizational structures and capabilities of these movements are as diverse as those of the first type of movement, but because of the type of political change they are attempting to initiate, violence is their most frequently used tool.

The third type of ethnic/national liberation movement pits colonial peoples against colonial powers. Colonial peoples struggle for attainment of independence, whereas colonial powers struggle for maintenance of empire. The struggle of the Mau Maus against the British in Kenya, of Frelimo against the Portuguese in Mozambique, and of the MPLA, FNLA, and UNITA against the Portuguese in Angola are examples of this type of ethnic/national liberation movement. As in the preceding typology, structures and strengths of movement differ, and the objective sought necessitates violence in most cases. Perhaps the leading example of a nonviolent national liberation movement was Mahatma Gandhi's program of civil disobedience that he unleashed against Great Britain during India's struggle for independence.

Ethnic/national liberation movements are not new arrivals on the international scene. Biblical history is replete with stories of the Jewish people's efforts to establish an independent state under their own control, and the eventual collapse of the Ottoman Empire in the early twentieth century was the final chapter of a centuries' long drama that saw Bulgars, Greeks, Romanians, Serbs, and Turks achieve their own states. The American and French revolutions were two different types of ethnic/national liberation conflicts of the 18th century, in the American case against a colonial power, and in the French case against an oppressive internal government. The revolts of South American states against their Spanish and Portuguese masters are other instances of pre–twentieth-century national liberation activities.

Ethnic/national liberation movements play important roles in international affairs, not only because of their obvious impact on nation-states, but also because of the relationships they develop with particular states. Inevitably, an ethnic/national liberation movement that concludes that it must resort to violence must have weapons and must find a source for those weapons. Private weapons merchants are one source of weaponry, but so are countries that either wish to see colonial empires dismantled, political power thrown into disequilibrium, or a particular government overthrown. Ethnic/national liberation movements therefore may turn to states for weapons and for political or economic support.[10] Given the sentiments that nationalism, imperialism, and claims of exploitation evoke, it is little wonder that ethnic/national liberation movements are extremely controversial.

 ## *TERRORIST GROUPS AND MOVEMENTS*

Depending on one's perspective, a fine line may or may not exist between terrorist groups and movements and other actors such as ethnic/national liberation groups, religious extremists, and other movements that resort to violence.

To a great extent, whether an organization is defined as a terrorist group depends on one's perspective. When seen from an American perspective, the "Indians" of the Boston Tea Party were American nationalists making a political point; when seen from a British perspective, they were terrorists destroying property and endangering life. As a general rule, if an observer agrees with the objectives of someone who employs violence, the observer considers the person a "freedom fighter"; if the observer disagrees with the objectives, that same individual is a terrorist.

Some analysts have attempted to move beyond this subjective method of defining terrorism by arguing that violence perpetrated against state institutions and other organs the state uses for control should not be considered terrorism, whereas all other forms of violence are terrorism. Under this type of definition, placing a bomb in a police station or a court building would not be terrorism. Placing a bomb in a school or a passenger plane would be.

Although such efforts to define terrorism are laudable, they are fraught with problems. For example, if a bomb is set off at a police station but happens to kill innocent passersby as well, was the bombing a terrorist attack or not? Such an event happened in South Africa in 1985, with the perpetrators of the bombing arguing that the deaths outside the police station were unintended and that therefore they were not terrorists but freedom fighters seeking to overthrow apartheid.

Another example that illustrates the difficulties of this type of a definition of terrorism was the 1995 bombing of the U.S. Federal Building in Oklahoma City. Many of those killed were government workers, the probable targets of the blast. But many others were unintended victims including many children who attended a day-care center in the building. Because their deaths were unintended, was the bombing any less a terrorist attack? Obviously, defining terrorism can present problems. There are many shades of gray, and no universally accepted definition of terrorism has yet been fashioned.

In its simplest form, terrorism denotes the use of violence to achieve a political objective. Ordinarily, the death and destruction caused by terrorism are limited, at least in comparison with the death and destruction caused by war. However, the specter lurks that terrorists will escalate their level of violence. The most feared scenario is that a terrorist group will obtain a nuclear weapon and threaten to destroy a city unless its demands are met.

Terrorism has been and is used by groups of all ideological persuasions. In El Salvador, the political right wing employed "Death Squads" to silence proponents of change, and the political left used similar tactics to foment revolution and undermine the existing social structure. Similarly, left-wing and right-wing terrorists both assaulted the social structure of Lebanon throughout the 1970s and 1980s. Even religious groups use terrorism—for instance, the poison gas attacks by the Japanese cult Aum Shinrikyo in Tokyo and Yokohama subways in 1995.

Objectives of terrorists vary and may include eventual political independence for a state, a changed social or economic structure within a state or region, maintenance of an existing socioeconomic structure, or simple publicity for a cause. Targets of terrorist groups are often highly visible individuals, prominent corporations, government buildings, or military bases that newspapers and the media deem newsworthy. Bombing, abductions, murders, hostage taking, and hijacking are all methods that terrorists employ. The 1993 bombing of the World Trade Center in New York, the 1995 and 1996 bombings of U.S. military facilities in Saudi Arabia, the 1998 bombing of the U.S. embassies in Kenya and Tanzania, and the 2000 attack against the U.S. naval vessel U.S.S. Cole in Yemen are all manifestations of terrorists attacking newsworthy targets that guarantee great publicity.

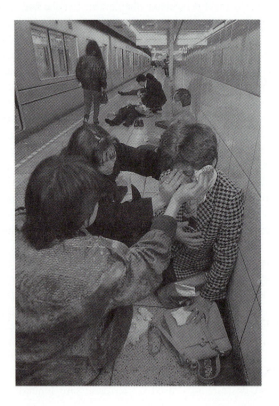

Even religious groups have used terrorism. Here, a victim of the 1995 gas attack in the Tokyo subway system perpetrated by the religious cult Aum Shinrikyo is comforted. Note the less fortunate victims in the background.

Such attacks also have a large psychological impact on the opponents of terrorist groups, because potential victims never know where or when the next attack will occur.

During the 1980s, a new phenomenon gained increased notoriety—state-supported terrorism. In simplest form, state-supported terrorism occurs when certain states for reasons of their own provide funding, training, and support for terrorist groups and movements. Libya, North Korea, and Iran all have been indicted by the U.S. and other Western states as prominent supporters of terrorist activity.[11]

State-supported terrorism presents a quandary to those who seek to combat terrorism; namely, if it is well documented that a particular state supported a specific terrorist action, how should other states respond? Should war be declared? Should a retaliatory raid be launched? Should a retaliatory raid be launched even if innocent bystanders may be killed? Should diplomatic channels, economic boycotts, or other paths be followed? Should international law be ignored if terrorists can be apprehended? What sorts of risks are acceptable to forces that are retaliating against state-supported terrorism? And if the evidence linking a particular state to a specific terrorist action is not completely reliable but only 90 percent reliable, what then?

Terrorist organizations exist around the world. In Europe, Turkey's Gray Wolves, Ireland's Provisional Wing of the Irish Republican Army, Italy's Red Guard, and Germany's Baader-Meinhof Gang all have been or are among the leading terrorist organizations. In the Americas, Peru's Shining Path, Uruguay's Tupamoros, the United States' Aryan Nation, and a variety of left- and right-wing terrorists in El Salvador have been or are prominent. In Asia, certain of India's Sikhs, Japan's Red Army Faction, and Sri Lanka's Tamil separatists have all pursued terrorism. In the Middle East, factions of the Palestinian group Hamas and several Islamic fundamentalist groups as well as the governments of Libya and Iran are among the foremost proponents of terrorism.

Because of the threat of terrorism, several Western governments have developed specially trained military forces to combat terrorist groups. West Germany's Group Nine, Great Britain's Special Air Services, and Israel's 269 Headquarters Reconnaissance Regiment all have counterterrorist responsibilities. The United States' elite Delta Team was designated to handle antiterrorist planning for the 1996 Atlanta Olympics, and elite Spanish and Australian units had the same task respectively for the 1992 Barcelona Olympics and the 2000 Sydney Olympics. In general, security has been strengthened at most airports, and international cooperation between national counter-terrorist intelligence units has been improved.

Even with these steps, however, terrorism remains a major international problem, as Figure 5-2 indicates. Given the nature of the problem and the draconian methods that would probably be required to eliminate it, it is likely that terrorism will be with the international community for the foreseeable future.[12]

TRANSNATIONAL RELIGIOUS GROUPS AND MOVEMENTS

Religious movements have played major roles in international affairs for centuries. The Christian Crusades to the Holy Land and the Muslim jihad through northern Africa are two of many examples of religious wars against "infidels," and the inter-European wars of

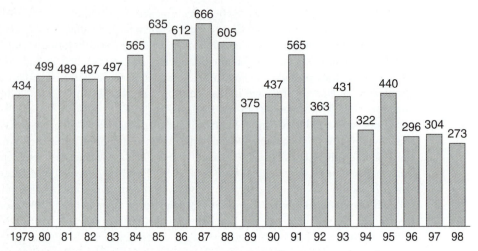

FIGURE 5-2   International Terrorist Attacks, 1979–1998.

Source: U.S. Department of State, 1999.

the sixteenth and seventeenth centuries are examples of conflicts brought about by differing interpretations of the same religion.

The impact of religious groups or movements on international affairs is not, however, limited to violence and conflicts. During the late nineteenth and early twentieth centuries, at least part of the U.S. affinity for China was the product of the efforts of U.S. missionaries to spread Christianity there. Centuries earlier, Buddhist monks traveled about China and Southeast Asia spreading their own version of peace and godliness. More recently, since the collapse of the Soviet Union in 1991, Western versions of Christianity have launched active efforts to convert those living in the former USSR to their beliefs. This has led to the hostility of many members of the Russian Orthodox faith toward the West.

Major religious movements have either made their peace with the governments of those states in which they operate or have combined their religious authority with the secular political authority of the state to create a government headed by a combined religious-political symbol of authority. In much of the industrialized world, church and state made their peace through separatism; the U.S. doctrine of the separation of church and state is a prominent example. In other cases, however, as in Western Europe during the preindustrial era, and particularly before the Treaty of Westphalia, and in revolutionary Iran today, the unity of church and state was and is the rule.

Even in those states where church and state are separated, religion may play a role in international affairs. Organized religious groups such as the World Council of Churches may take a conscious stand on an international issue, as the council did on black majority rule in Namibia and apartheid in South Africa. Conversely, less organized groups or movements such as the "Moral Majority" in the United States may seek to influence governmental policies across a wide range of international issues.

Perhaps the most prominent religious actor in the Western world in international affairs is the Catholic Church. Seated in Vatican City and headed by the pope, the Catholic

Church plays a unique role in the contemporary international arena. It is both a territorial state and a religious movement, and its influence reaches into every continent. Although the actual territory that it rules is limited today, a few centuries ago it held political control throughout and beyond Europe. Kings, princes, and lords did not act until they cleared their actions with the pope. As the secular state moved to the forefront in Western Europe following the Treaty of Westphalia in 1648, the papacy's territorial control receded.

Even so, the Catholic Church's influence remained immense. In many cases, bishops and priests accommodated themselves to whatever government was in power. The Catholic Church has survived and prospered in Western industrial democracies such as the United States, in communist states such as Poland between 1945 and 1989, and in military states such as Argentina during the 1970s and early 1980s.

In some cases, bishops and priests have seen fit to criticize governments of states in which they reside. In the Catholic Church in Latin America during the 1980s and 1990s, the "theology of liberation" was widely influential. This version of Catholicism taught peasants that they had a right and duty to better their lives. The entrenched upper classes saw this "liberation theology" as a threat emanating from the Catholic Church, which for centuries had supported the status quo in Latin America. Although not all priests subscribed to this revolutionary approach to Catholicism, enough did to make the role of the Catholic Church a political issue. The governments in Latin America—as well as the pope in Vatican City— had to decide how to respond to the challenges that the theology of liberation presented to their authority. The pope and the Vatican took the stand in the April 1986 "Instruction on Christian Freedom and Liberation" that it was "perfectly legitimate that those who suffer oppression on the part of the wealthy or the politically powerful should take action." Even armed struggle was ruled appropriate as a last resort against entrenched tyranny. Additionally, private property rights were deemed subordinate to "the higher principle that states that goods are meant for all."[13]

In the United States, religion increased its public policy role as well. The Moral Majority and other religious groups played a major role in several presidential campaigns between 1980 and 2000, and candidates for public office at all levels often identified themselves with strong religious beliefs.

Religion's role in other societies has also expanded, evidenced most clearly in Iran. There, Ayatollah Ruhollah Khomeini concluded during the 1960s that the shah of Iran was secularizing the Iranian state and destroying fundamentalist Islamic life-styles in Iran. From his headquarters in exile in Paris, Khomeini preached the overthrow of the shah and the creation of an Islamic state that would be guided by the Koran. To Khomeini, his version of Islam, Shiite fundamentalism, provided the guidelines on which policy could be formulated. After the shah's overthrow, Khomeini brought his own beliefs into practice. Most of the Western practices that the shah introduced to Iran during his rule were outlawed, and the tenets of fundamentalist Shiite Islam again ran private and public life in Iran. After Khomeini's death in 1989, a degree of religious moderation surfaced in Iran, but the country remained an Islamic republic.[14]

Other instances of the political activity of religious groups, movements, or individuals abound. Self-immolation by Buddhist monks during the Vietnam War carried an immense political message, and Pope John Paul II cannot avoid taking actions filled with political implications. His meeting with newly elected Russian President Vladimir Putin in 2000 is a clear case in point. And as noted earlier, efforts by Western Christians to convert Russians to their beliefs led to the hostility of many Russian Orthodox believers toward the West.

Clearly, religious groups and movements from the Catholic Church to Shiite fundamentalists to Moral Majority members influence and sometimes determine the course of international relations. Given their impact, it is impossible to ignore them if one is to develop an accurate understanding of contemporary international relations.

 ## TRANSNATIONAL POLITICAL PARTIES AND MOVEMENTS

As with many other international actors, transnational political parties and movements are difficult to define. To some, certain ethnic/national liberation movements are political movements, whereas others may consider them terrorist groups. Thus, depending on one's point of departure, the Palestine Liberation Organization could be described as a political movement, a national liberation movement, or a terrorist group. Similarly, supporters of the Polish trade union Solidarity were described as belonging to a political movement, a nationalist organization, and a revolutionary group. Indeed, the chameleon-like qualities of the labels we are trying to attach to different organizations, groups, and movements so that we may better conceptualize how the world works are well illustrated by Solidarity: After its 1989 election victory, Solidarity became the Polish government!

For our purposes, we define a political party as any group that seeks to obtain political power and public office by supplying its candidates for office with labels—party "identifications"—by which they are known to the electorate. They must also have a formal structure and a policy "platform." This is a broad definition and it implies that political parties are willing to participate in elections. It does not necessarily mean that those elections are impartial by Western democratic standards or that parties will not resort to means of obtaining political power other than the ballot box.

Some political parties and movements transcend national boundaries and appeal to an international clientele. Western European Social Democrats regularly coordinate and discuss their national party platforms with each other and share a political philosophy that includes equitable distribution of jobs, income, and property. Although national identities of the European Social Democratic parties remain clearly discernible, the international connections of these parties in European politics are a force to be reckoned with.[15]

Similarly, in an earlier era, the international communist movement was a major global transnational political movement and/or party. Three separate Communist Internationals (Cominterns) were formed during the late nineteenth and early twentieth centuries to aid communists in their avowed goal of uniting the workers of the world and wresting political power from the hands of the workers' "class enemies." However, following the collapse of communism in Eastern Europe and the Soviet Union and despite the continuation of communist governments in China and a few other countries, communism no longer can be said to be a global political party or movement.

Whereas communism has disintegrated as an international political movement, major U.S. political movements and parties have never become really internationalized. To be sure, both the Democratic and Republican parties have a major impact on international affairs, particularly when a member of their party is in the White House, but neither party

Throughout Eastern Europe in 1989, individuals and groups went to the streets to bring down communist governments. But were they acting as individuals, nationalist organizations, political parties, or revolutionary movements? Here, Lech Walesa and other strikers protest against the Polish communist government.

has sought to build systematic links with ideologically kindred parties in other countries. The Democratic and Republican parties are not international parties.

CONCLUSIONS

Nongovernmental organizations, individuals, and the varied array of other international actors that have been examined in this chapter have only one common denominator: They are regularly overlooked and ignored in the study of international relations. Although their impact on international affairs in most cases is not so great as the impact of states, IGOs, or MNCs, there are numerous cases to prove that if these "less significant" actors are ignored, contemporary international politics cannot be understood. Pope John Paul II captured the imagination of the world not only because of his position, but also because of his humanity, his individuality; the international power and prestige of the Catholic Church has been enhanced because of a single man. Ayatollah Khomeini's Islamic fundamentalism was a force that led not only to the collapse of the shah's government, but also to a restructuring of the entire international balance of power in the Middle East. And the whaling profession throughout the world is on the brink of extinction because of a crusade launched by a relatively small nongovernmental organization. The individual, the religious movement, the ethnic/national liberation movement, the political movement or party, the terrorist group, and the NGO can and do play major roles in today's world. Their contributions as actors to contemporary international relations must be increasingly studied and understood.

KEY TERMS AND CONCEPTS

nongovernmental organizations (NGOs)   structured organizations operating internationally without formal ties to governments

role of private individuals in international affairs   tourists, celebrities, exchange students, foreign teachers, job-related migration, refugees, and permanent international settlement all play an integral role in international affairs

role of refugees   during the 1980s and 1990s, a tide of refugees developed both internal to individual countries and spilling across national boundaries

role of tourism   millions of tourists journey oversees each year, returning to their homes with views of what other countries are like

ethnic/national liberation movements   a movement that seeks to break territory away from an established country to create a new state for those it claims to represent; or, a movement that seeks to overthrow a government which it views as dictatorial or under the control of an external influence; or, a movement fighting colonialism

terrorist groups and movements   groups that use violence short of war to achieve a political objective

transnational religious movements and groups   any religious organization whose tenets and beliefs claim to have relevance beyond national or state boundaries

transnational political parties and movements   any political organization whose beliefs and policies extend beyond national or state boundaries

WEBSITE REFERENCES

nongovernmental organizations (NGOs):   *www.uia.org/index-new.htm*   website of the Union of International Associations, which contains information and data about many NGOs

www.ngo.org/index2.htm   the home page for NGOs associated with the United Nations

www.gdrc.org/ngo   a site that serves as a "meeting place for NGOs to discuss, debate and disseminate information on their work, strategies and results."

refugees: *www.unhcr.ch*   website of the United Nations High Commissioner for Refugees

ethnic/national liberation movements: *www.knn.u-net.com/index.htm*   website of the Kurdistan National Network, a movement attempting to create an independent Kurdistan and using information technology to this end

terrorism: *www.terrorism.com/index.shtm*   homepage for the Terrorism Research Center, with articles and extensive link listings

NOTES

1. Few scholars agree on how these "other actors" should be categorized. See for example John T. Rourke, *International Politics on the World Stage,* 6th edition. (Guilford, CT: Dushkin, 1998); and Donald M. Snow and Eugene Brown, *International Relations: The Changing Contours of Power* (New York, NY: Addison Wesley Longman, 2000). See also Thomas G. Weiss and Leon Gordenker, *NGOs, the UN, and Global Governance* (Boulder, CO: Lynne Rienner Publishers, 1996); and Ann Marie Clarke, "Non-Governmental Organizations and Their Influence on International Society," *Journal of International Affairs* (1995), pp. 507–526.

2. U.S. Department of State, 1995.

3. CARE, *1999 CARE Annual Report* (Atlanta, GA: CARE, 2000).

4. Pierre Vasseur, "The Difficulties of International Non-Governmental Organizations," *International Associations,* No. 9 (1968), pp. 620–624.

5. A. LeRoy Bennett, *International Organizations: Principles and Issues* (Englewood Cliffs, NJ: Prentice Hall, 1977), p. 356. See also Peter J. Spero, "New Global Communities: Nongovernmental Organizations in International Decision-Making Institutions," *The Washington Quarterly* (Winter 1995), pp. 45–56.

6. For more detailed analysis of the role that refugees play in contemporary international affairs, see UN High Commissioner for Refugees, *The State of the World's Refugees: The Search for Solutions* (New York: Oxford University Press, 1995); Myron Weiner, *The Global Migration Crisis: Challenge to States and to Human Rights* (New York: HarperCollins, 1995); and Gil Loescher, *Rufugee Movements and International Security,* Adelphi Paper 268 (London: International Institute for Strategic Studies). See also the journal of the UN High Commissioner for Refugees, *Refugees.*

7. See David Kraslow and Stuart H. Loory, *The Secret Search for Peace in Vietnam* (New York: Random House, 1968).

8. For several different approaches to the role of individuals and individual behavior in international affairs, see Joseph H. De Rivera, *The Psychological Dimension of Foreign Policy* (Columbus, OH: Charles E. Merrill, 1968); Robert A. Isaak, *Individuals and World Politics* (North Scituate, MA: Duxbury, 1975); Otto

Klineberg, *The Human Dimension in International Relations* (New York: Holt, Rinehart and Winston, 1966); Ralph Pettman, *Human Behavior and World Politics* (New York: St. Martin's Press, 1975); and Kenneth N. Waltz, *Man, the State, and War* (New York: Columbia University Press, 1965).

9. For discussions of the role of specific ethnic/national liberation organizations in international relations, see Marina Ottaway, "Liberation Movements and Transition to Democracy: The Case of the ANC," *The Journal of Modern African Studies* (March 1991), pp. 61–82; William Cyrus Reed, "International Politics and National Liberation: ZANA and the Politics of Contested Sovereignty in Zimbabwe," *African Studies Review* (September 1993), pp. 31–59; and Oliver Froehling, "The Cyberspace 'War of Ink and Internet' in Chiapas, Mexico," *The Geographical Review* (April 1997), pp. 291–307.

10. Many ethnic/national liberation movements turned to the Soviet Union for arms during the 1960s and 1970s. Soviet objectives—the reduction of Western influence and the expansion of Soviet influence—coincided with national liberation movement objectives—the elimination of Western colonialism. Hence the USSR provided weapons.

11. There is an opposed school of thought that argues that the United States itself engages in state-supported terrorism. See Alexander George, ed., *Western State Terrorism* (New York: Routledge, 1991).

12. For several studies of terrorism and terrorist movements, see Walter Laqueur, "The New Face of Terrorism," *The Washington Quarterly* (Autumn 1998), pp. 169–78; Jessica Stern, *The Ultimate Terrorists* (Cambridge, MA: Harvard University Press, 1999); and Bruce Hoffman, *Inside Terrorism* (New York, NY: Columbia University Press, 1999).

13. See "Instruction on Christian Freedom and Liberation," released by the Vatican, April 1986. For other discussions of the theology of liberation from earlier years, see R. J. Sider, "Evangelical Theology of Liberation," *Christian Century,* Vol. 97 (March 1980), pp. 314–318; J. H. Cone, "Gospel and the Liberation of the Poor," *Christian Century,* Vol. 98 (February 1981), pp. 162–166; C. Krauthammer, "Holy Fools," *New*

Republic, Vol. 185 (September 1981), pp. 10f.; C. P. Conn, "Where the World Council of Churches Went Wrong," *Saturday Evening Post,* Vol. 254 (May–June 1982), pp. 12f.; and J. M. Wall, "Liberation Ethics: Insisting on Equality," *Christian Century,* Vol. 99 (November 1982), p. 1123.

14. For a discussion of the global political role of Islam, see Mir Zohair Husein, *Global Islamic Politics* (New York: HarperCollins, 1995). For a discussion of the broader role of religion, see Douglas Johnston and Cynthia Sampson, *Religion: The Missing Dimension of Statecraft* (New York: Oxford University Press, 1995).

15. For discussions of the international role of transnational political parties, see John Gaffney, ed., *Political Parties and the European Union* (New York, NY: Routledge, 1996); Elizabeth Bomberg, *Green Parties and Politics in the European Union* (New York, NY: Routledge, 1998); David Miller, "The Left, the Nation-State, and European Citizenship," *Dissent* (Summer 1998), pp. 47–51.

PART 2

The Systemic Framework: The Actors in the International System

All events, wherever they occur, react upon each other.

—RAYMOND ARON

International relations would be a simple subject if each actor interacted only with identical actors and if all shared similar objectives, outlooks, and capabilities. Unfortunately, this is not the case. States interact not only with each other, but also with intergovernmental organizations, multinational corporations, nongovernmental organizations, and a multitude of other actors.

Together, all international actors and their interactions with one another form an international system. Over time, as these actors, their capabilities, and their interests change, the international system changes. Simultaneously, the system influences the way the actors act and the way they view themselves and others.

Raymond Aron likened the international system that the various actors and their interactions create to a vast echo chamber in which "the noises of men and events are amplified and reverberated to infinity. The disturbance occurring at one point of the planet communicates itself, step by step, to the opposite side of the globe. . . . All events, wherever they occur, react upon each other."[1] And Aron is correct; the interrelationship of actors and their interests creates an ever-changing international system that defies simplistic explanations.

Because the international system consists of international actors and their interactions, for the first step in our analysis of the international system, in Chapter 6 we explore how international actors make their decisions about how to interact with each other and how they obtain and process information about other actors and the international system. In the case of states, this process is called the *foreign policy process.* The output from this process is *foreign policy.* In the case of other international actors, this process may be called *international decision making* or a similar term, with the output identified as *international operations, international business policy,* or something similar. However, regardless of what terminology is used, international actors must decide what they want to do in their interactions with each other, and how they want to try to do it. Thus, the first chapter in this framework studies the foreign policy process, foreign policy, and other forms of formulating and implementing international interactions.

The second step in our analysis of the international system is to explore recent international systems. We begin with an historical analysis, but we concentrate on the bipolar system that existed for most of the time between 1945 and today. Indeed, Chapter 7 takes its name from the primary characteristic of that system, the rise and fall of the East–West conflict. The East–West conflict pitted the United States and its friends and allies against the Soviet Union and its friends and allies. The East–West conflict was centered on states, but all other international actors—IGOs, MNCs, NGOs, and other actors as well—were influenced by and in turn influenced the conflict. Even though the East–West conflict is over, its impact on today's world remains immense. Thus, it is important to understand the origins and evolution of that conflict.

But the East–West conflict was not the only significant conflict that occurred during the half century after World War II. A second major conflict took place and continues today, although at a somewhat reduced level. That conflict was the North–South conflict between the wealthy industrialized countries, most of which are in the Northern Hemisphere, and the poor nonindustrialized developing countries in the Southern Hemisphere. Although the East–West conflict was, among other things, a debate over the preferred way to organize society, the root of the North–South conflict is the global inequity in the distribution of wealth. The last chapter in this framework examines the North–South conflict.

The East–West and North–South conflicts played major roles in shaping today's world, but at best, they were convenient concepts that helped order our thinking about how the bipolar international system worked. They were not perfect descriptions of that system. And we are now in a period in which the international system is undergoing revolutionary change, change that will be shaped by the decisions that policy makers in states, IGOs, MNCs, and NGOs are making each day.

What new system will emerge? We are not yet at a point in our study where we can speculate on an answer to that question; such speculation is left to Chapter 20. However, the purpose of the following three chapters is to provide information to move us in that direction and to examine the following questions:

- How do states and other international actors formulate and implement their interactions with one another?
- What types of international systems existed before the twenty-first century?
- How did the East–West conflict begin and evolve over time?
- How did the North–South conflict begin and evolve over time?

 ## *NOTE*

1. Raymond Aron, *Peace and War* (Garden City, NY: Doubleday, 1966), p. 373.

Chapter 6

Foreign Policy Decision Making

- How do states make foreign policy?
- What are the stages in a state's foreign policy process?
- How do other international actors make foreign policy?

To this point, our study of contemporary international relations has concentrated on different types of international actors and their objectives. In this chapter, we turn our attention to how the actors formulate their interactions with each other.

In the case of states, the process of formulating external actions is called the **foreign policy process.** The output from this process is called **foreign policy.** In the cases of other types of international actors, other terms are used. For example, international governmental organizations have a decision-making process that leads to their international operations. Multinational corporations engage in international strategic planning, international business, or international operations. NGOs, individuals, and other international actors also must decide what activities to pursue in their interactions with other actors, but there is little uniformity in the terms that are used to describe their decision-making processes.

In this chapter, we will first concentrate on the ways that states formulate and implement their interactions with each other. In other words, we will study the foreign policy process and foreign policy formulation. We will then discuss similar activities of IGOs, MNCs, NGOs, and other types of international actors. Our primary purpose is to develop a better understanding of how international actors formulate their international interactions.

Chapter 6

IT AND DECISION MAKING: DECENTRALIZATION AND DECISION LOOPS

Advanced information technologies have already had an immense impact on decision making, and their impact will continue to grow as the Information Age progresses. Two impacts are most apparent, and both have great relevance for international relations.

The first impact concerns decentralization. As information becomes more widely available and the need for quick on-the-scene decisions increases, decentralized decision making is increasingly becoming the order of the day. Such decentralization is most apparent in the business world.

As we saw in Chapter 3, more and more multinational corporate organizations and structures have already been networked, with direct data flow and reporting lines between operational units and decision makers. Often, driven by the need for quick decisions and the availability of dispersed information, corporate decision makers have delegated decision-making authority to operational units.

Networking has also often led to more streamlined corporate structures, with mid-level managers becoming superfluous. In the Information Age, this model of networked decentralized decision making may become the order of the day, and not just for multinational corporations.

The second impact of IT on decision making in international relations concerns decision cycles. Since advanced information technology will make more accurate information available to decision makers faster than ever before, pressures will escalate for decision makers to "get inside" an opponent's decision cycle and make decisions faster than others. The advantages of this are obvious.

Often, states, IGOs, MNCs, and NGOs that seize the initiative gain the advantage. In the Information Age, decision-makers will be able to seize the initiative on the basis of large quantities of highly accurate readily available real time information.

But there are dangers in faster decisions.

First, rapid decisions are not necessarily wise decisions. Sometimes, especially in diplomacy and strategic affairs, wise decisions evolve as a result of considerable thought, discussion, and analysis. As the ability to make rapid decisions increases, the danger lurks that speed of decision will replace wisdom of decision as an objective.

Second, as advanced IT becomes more widely available, concern will mount that other decision makers also have quick access to reliable information. This concern will further increase pressure for quick decisions. This pressure may force premature decisions to be made on the basis of inaccurate information or partial analysis. Even before the Information Age, cases of this existed, as shown when the U.S.S. Vincennes downing an Iranian passenger plane because the Vincennes' battle center believed the passenger plane to be an attacking Iranian F-14 fighter. Conversely, delaying decisions until all is known and accuracy is perfectly verified is an equally flawed approach.

In the Information Age, then decision makers must strike the proper balance, waiting when they can and acting when they must. Despite the inevitably of increased pressure for faster decisions, decision makers would do well to remember that wisdom and accuracy, not speed and rapidity, are the objectives.

THE FOREIGN POLICY PROCESS AND FOREIGN POLICY: AN OVERVIEW

The foreign policy process and foreign policy are complex concepts. As a result, people rarely agree on what the terms mean or include. For our purposes, we will consider basic definitions. The foreign policy process will be defined as the entire set of actions that a state goes through as it formulates and implements its foreign policy. Foreign policy will be defined as the goal-directed set of actions that a state takes in its efforts to achieve its foreign policy objectives. Defined in these ways, foreign policy is the output of a state's foreign policy process.

Different states have different foreign policy processes. Some countries may allow only their institutional version of the U.S. Department of State, often called the Ministry of Foreign Affairs, to participate in the foreign policy process. Other countries may allow their institutional versions of the U.S. Departments of Defense or Commerce to have a role. Some countries may have their equivalent of the U.S. Secretary of State, usually the Minister of Foreign Affairs, make foreign policy decisions, whereas others may restrict final decision-making authority to their equivalent of the U.S. president. And some countries may spend billions of dollars on intelligence collection so they can have the best and most current information available upon which to base their decisions, whereas other states may have neither the money, the skill, nor the inclination to gather up-to-date intelligence.

Obviously, potential exists for significant differences in the foreign policy processes of different states. Not surprisingly, different analysts and scholars have developed different ways to study and understand these processes. For example, some analysts and scholars believe that the best way to study and understand the foreign policy process is to use the concept of levels of analysis that we studied in Chapter 1.[1] Other analysts and scholars prefer to concentrate their study on "rings of power," a term used to describe the degree of influence that different individuals and groups may have on the foreign policy process.[2] Still other analysts and scholars emphasize the different steps that lead to the final formulation and implementation of foreign policy,[3] and some concentrate on analyzing rationality and impediments to rationality in policy making.[4]

All these approaches—and others as well—are useful. Each provides a different type of insight into the foreign policy process. In this chapter, we will examine only the third and fourth methods that are listed above, that is, the different steps that virtually every country has in its foreign policy process, and rationality and impediments to rationality. However, before we begin this study, four cautions must be added.

First, even though the foreign policy process is the primary means by which states formulate and implement the policies through which they interact, not all of the interactions that a state or its agents have with other international actors are necessarily outputs of a state's foreign policy process. Sometimes interactions are the result of spontaneous actions or chance encounters that were not expected. On other occasions, global trends in technology, economics, or culture develop that are the result of forces beyond the control of states, but that nevertheless affect states and their interactions. In still other cases, policies are not implemented as planned, or they unfold in ways that are unanticipated, unexpected, or unwanted.

The tragedies of the *U.S.S. Stark* and the *U.S.S. Vincennes* provide perfect examples. The 1986 Iraqi attack on the *Stark* was not an output of Iraq's foreign policy process. At the time when the attack occurred, it was Iraqi policy in the Persian Gulf to attack merchant vessels, especially tankers, that were going to or from Iranian ports. It was not Iraqi policy to attack U.S. warships. The entire unfortunate episode was the result of a pilot's error. Nevertheless, the attack happened, and it had a major impact on U.S.–Iraqi relations.

Similarly, the *Vincennes'* destruction of an Iranian airliner was not an output of the U.S. foreign policy process. Rather, it was the result of an incorrect interpretation of too limited an amount of data by the captain of the *Vincennes*. Nevertheless, the Iranian airliner was destroyed, and its destruction had a significant impact on U.S.–Iranian relations.

The key point here is that although the foreign policy of a state is the most important portion of a state's international interactions, not all the international interactions of a state or its agents are necessarily foreign policy. Put differently, not all international actions by states or their agents are outputs of the foreign policy process. Students and analysts of international affairs alike must be careful to differentiate between the foreign policy of states and actions that may appear to be foreign policy but that in reality are not.

A second caution is that students and analysts of the foreign policy process must not ascribe too much rationality to the foreign policy process. Although the concept of "process" brings to mind the image of a well-reasoned and logical approach to an issue, factors often intervene that make the foreign policy process less than completely rational, at least if rationality is measured in terms of planned and reasoned efforts to move toward a defined foreign policy objective. Indeed, even when rationality is desired and a logical foreign policy process is in place, impediments to rationality can easily creep into foreign policy decision making. Thus, a separate section is devoted to rationality and impediments to rationality later in this chapter.

Third, students and analysts of the foreign policy process should not ascribe too great a degree of order to the foreign policy process. Although the process described here is sequential, real-world pressures of time, politics, and money often dictate that the steps in the foreign policy process be undertaken simultaneously, with less than sufficient information or analysis, or in a different order than presented here. In certain cases, some steps may even be bypassed completely.

Finally, in every case, different people, different situations, different capabilities, and different perceptions combine in different ways to make the foreign policy process dynamic and ever-changing. This reality of constant change is one of the things that makes the study of the foreign policy process so fascinating—and so difficult.

THE FOREIGN POLICY PROCESS

As a general rule, decision makers, regardless of the type of international actor for which they make decisions, see themselves as rational decision makers who follow a logical set of steps as they make their decisions. They first identify their interests and objectives. They

In 1986, an Iraqi warplane attacked the U.S. frigate *Stark* when the U.S. ship was on patrol in the Persian Gulf. The United States later concluded that the attack was not the result of the Iraqi foreign policy process, but the result of a pilot's error. But when the attack occurred, no one knew what to think. Over 30 U.S. sailors died, and the *Stark,* shown here after the attack, nearly sank.

next assess their present situation and identify the strengths and weaknesses that they have. Finally, they determine how best to move from where they are to where they want to be, taking into account other opportunities and threats that may develop as they proceed toward their objectives.

For states, the set of procedures which decision makers follow as they develop and implement foreign policy is called the **foreign policy process.** Not all countries follow identical steps. Even so, most countries include goal setting; intelligence gathering, reporting, and interpreting; option formulation; planning and programming; decision making; policy articulation; policy implementation; policy monitoring; policy appraisal; policy modification; and memory storage and recall as steps in their foreign policy processes.[5] Table 6-1 lists these steps and identifies the purposes of and difficulties inherent to each step.

Goal Setting

Goal setting refers to the task of identifying national interests and foreign policy objectives and arranging them by order of priority. More often than not, goal setting in the foreign policy process is the task of a few senior people in the executive branch of a state's national government. The president and the secretary of state or their equivalents usually figure prominently in this process.

The degree of difficulty inherent in goal setting depends to a great extent on a state's type of government and the structure of its society. For example, authoritarian governments rarely must take public opinion into account to the extent that democratic governments do. For authoritarian regimes, aside from taking into account the ruling elite's own outlooks and priorities and settling disagreements that may exist within the ruling elite, goal setting is relatively uncomplicated.

By contrast, democratic societies often find it difficult to reach agreement on what national interests are and what foreign policy goals should be. Democratic countries also often find it difficult to assign priorities with national interests. This is because in democratic societies, many different interest groups have opportunities to make known their views on national interest, foreign policy goals, and national priorities. They also often have an ability to influence the decision-making process. As a result, goal setting is often a more complex task in democratic societies than in authoritarian societies.

Intelligence Gathering, Interpreting, and Reporting

Intelligence gathering, interpreting, and reporting are all important parts of the second step of the foreign policy process. After goals have been set, it becomes important to find out as much as possible about the issues at hand, the factors that affect the issues, and what others think about and plan to do about them. Governments typically seek information about what others can do, what others plan to do, and what impact the policies that they themselves are implementing might have or are having. These three aspects of intelligence are sometimes called intelligence about *capabilities, intentions,* and *feedback.*

As important as acquiring information is, by itself it is not enough. Information must be interpreted accurately, and it must also be provided in a timely manner to those who need it to make decisions and implement policy. A country may have the best intelligence-gathering

TABLE 6-1   Major Steps in the Foreign Policy Process

Tasks	Purposes of the Task	Difficulties of the Task
1. Goal setting	Identifying national interests and foreign policy objectives; assigning priorities to interests and objectives	Agreeing on identity of national interests, objectives, and priorities
2. Intelligence gathering, reporting, and interpreting	Gaining the most accurate information available on which to base decisions, understanding what it means, and getting it to the people who need it	Incomplete information; distortion of information; delay in information; interpreting information incorrectly; information overload
3. Option formulation	Developing choices about what to do	Limiting options too much; developing options on the basis of predispositions, groupthink, or politics
4. Planning and programming	Identifying and weighing costs and benefits of each option	Predisposition, groupthink, or politics will influence cost-benefit identification and weighting
5. Decision making	Deciding upon the proper policy option	Predisposition, groupthink, or politics will influence cost-benefit identification and weighting; deciding on proper time frame
6. Policy articulation	Effectively stating policy and its rationale to gain domestic and foreign support	Too many spokespersons; contradictions, confusion, and concern for personal image; media distortion
7. Policy implementation	Allocating resources to ensure effectiveness of policy elements; clear command and control of policy elements; decisive action	Communication problems; unclear lines of authority; organizational interests; bureaucratic politics; changing situations; and counteractions by others
8. Policy monitoring	Staying abreast of the policy and its effects as it is implemented	Gaps in monitoring; feedback failures; unclear linkages between cause and effect
9. Policy appraisal	Assessing whether the policy is having its intended effects; assessing unintended effects	Predisposition, groupthink, or politics will influence policy appraisal
10. Policy modification	Changing policy to better achieve goal	Policy inertia; insufficient resources; organizational interests; bureaucratic politics; image damage
11. Memory storage and recall	Learning from experience; improve future policy	Partial and unreliable storage and recall; "lessons" applied poorly or remembered selectively

Source: Adopted, with significant alterations made by the author, from John P. Lovell, *The Challenge of American Foreign Policy: Purpose and Adaptation* (New York: Macmillan, 1985), pp. 27, 32.

capabilities in the world, but unless the intelligence it gathers is interpreted correctly and reaches those who need it in a timely manner, intelligence is useless.

Intelligence analysis and interpretation is a difficult task. It requires familiarity with the issues and events under consideration, an open mind and a good memory, an ability to identify causal relationships, and an ability to anticipate future events. Another skill needed to analyze and interpret intelligence is the ability to sift through the immense quantity of information that is frequently available to find meaningful data.

One way that states and other international actors sometimes try to confuse foreign intelligence analysts about their real capabilities and intentions is to provide them with too much information, much of it incorrect. The rationale behind this approach, relying on "information overload" to frustrate intelligence efforts, is to hide information behind a blizzard of "noise," or misleading information. This is the technique that the Allies used during World War II to confuse Germany about where the D-Day landings would occur.

States gather intelligence in a variety of ways. Most is acquired from readily available open sources such as newspapers and magazines. Diplomats and other government employees also acquire extensive amounts of information for their country from the people they talk to and the contacts that they have. Sometimes governments also "debrief" citizens who travel abroad or who have foreign contacts. They may include businesspeople, journalists, scientists, professors, and even tourists who ventured into sensitive areas. In addition, technologically advanced countries often employ "national technical means" of intelligence gathering such as monitoring radio and telephone conversations or using satellites.

A surprisingly small percentage of intelligence is actually gathered by cloak-and-dagger undercover work, or "spying." Nevertheless, covert methods, as spying is also called, sometimes uncover extremely useful and important information.

Different states devote different amounts of resources to intelligence gathering, interpreting, and reporting. Some states with limited resources have virtually no intelligence capability. Others spend immense amounts of money on intelligence. For example, the budget for the U.S. intelligence community in 2000 was estimated as over $40 billion dollars.

Option Formulation

Option formulation is usually the third step in the foreign policy process. Although decision makers in some states sometimes simply make decisions about what they intend to do without formulating options, in most states, different policy choices are developed about what can be done about a given issue.

The purpose of this step is straightforward: to provide decision makers with choices about how to achieve the goals that they have established in light of the information available. At first blush, this seems like an easy task, but in fact it is not. Those who formulate options must be careful not to limit the range of choices they develop in light of their own predispositions. They must also avoid *groupthink,* that is, the human tendency to go along with what someone else thinks. Groupthink and other impediments to rational decision making will be discussed later in this chapter.

At the same time, those involved with the option formulation stage of the foreign policy process must try not to take political considerations into account. Assessing political considerations is more the task of planners, programmers, and decision makers. The task of those who formulate options is to provide planners, programmers, and decision makers with choices on policy that have a realistic chance of success. They must not present those choices in ways that predispose planners, programmers, and decision makers to specific conclusions or courses of action.

Different states pursue the formulation of options in different ways, with different parts of the government bureaucracy involved in the process. Many states use variations of what the United States government calls *interagency working groups.* Interagency working groups bring together people from various governmental departments and agencies that might be affected by a particular issue. These groups then formulate policy options, and present them to their superiors, sometimes accompanied by assessments about the costs and benefits of each option, thus overlapping responsibilities with the next step in the foreign policy process—planning and programming.

Planning and Programming

Planning and programming comprise the fourth step in the foreign policy process. In this step, first policy analysts and then senior governmental officials identify and weigh the costs and benefits of the options that have been developed. Factors that are considered in this step include how many resources each option will require, the length of time that an option may require to succeed, the amount of time that is available before a problem must be resolved, the political impacts that an option may have, other secondary and tertiary effects that an option might have, and the likelihood of success for an option.

Planning and programming efforts are usually undertaken by interagency working groups or their equivalents. The major pitfalls that planners and programmers face are the same as found in their primary task—to properly identify and weigh the costs and benefits of each policy option proposed. In many respects, this is more art than science.

Like those who formulate options, planners and programmers must strive to minimize the influence of their own predispositions and of groupthink. Unlike option formulators, they must also assess the political fallout that given options might have. And perhaps most difficult of all, planners and programmers must then communicate their analyses to decision makers in clear, concrete, concise, and nonconfusing language.

Decision Making

Decision making is the fifth step. More often than not the one who makes the final decision on the option that will become national policy depends on the degree of importance of the issue. Extremely critical decisions that involve options such as the use of military force are usually made by the national leader. Less critical decisions like the naming of ambassadors are often made by the secretary of state or the equivalent, although the national leader may sometimes become involved. Relatively minor decisions such as deciding whether a visa should be issued are often left to government bureaucrats such as consular officials. Such decisions rarely enter the policy process, but they are foreign policy decisions nevertheless.

Decision makers face the same problems identified in the preceding steps, but these people also need the ability to recognize when they are receiving skewed information and analysis. Skilled decision makers must have the ability to "ask the right questions" to uncover errors or omissions in the policy process.

National decision making is often a complicated and difficult task that requires input from many people. Here, President Bill Clinton meets with several of his senior advisors to discuss U.S. policy.

At this point in the foreign policy process, we must return to the levels-of-analysis problem. Will the decision maker ask the right questions, thereby uncovering any bureaucratic biases or personal predispositions that may have altered the information and analyses that he or she received? Even if the decision maker asks the right questions, will he or she make a decision on the basis of the national interest and national objectives? Or will she or he make a decision based on personal values, her or his own political future, or his or her perceived place in history? The answer to these questions depends on the individual leader, not the policy process.

Some prominent analysts argue that foreign policy decisions in the final analysis are rarely made on the basis of how a problem may best be solved. For example, Charles Lindblom argues that decision makers often have as their primary objective not the national interest or some higher concern, but the minimization of uncertainty and risk, the reduction of the number of unknowns, and the maintenance of the familiar.[6] This theory, called **incrementalism,** argues that even if earlier steps in the foreign policy process indicate that major changes in policy are warranted, decision makers prefer to make small changes that do not significantly alter policy directions. Lindblom asserts that the incrementalist approach to decision making reduces risk and danger for the decision maker and allows him or her to change course quickly if newly implemented policies appear to be bringing about undesirable change.[7]

Lindblom's analysis fits closely with Herbert Simon's observation that decision makers do not seek the "best" solution to a problem, but rather one that "satisfies," that is, meets a minimum level of acceptability.[8] Simon accepts the argument that most people try to act rationally, but he also maintains that everyone's rationality is unavoidably "bounded" or "limited" by the simplified mental images that they hold of how the world works. Thus, Simon asserts, despite the best efforts to make rational decisions, decisions that in retrospect may appear irrational are sometimes made. We will return to the question of rationality and impediments to rationality later in this chapter.

The debate over how and why people in positions of authority make the decisions that they do is not limited to the foreign policy process. But in foreign policy, with war and peace sometimes being the issue at hand, the stakes of decision making are sometimes immense.

Policy Articulation

The sixth step in the foreign policy process—policy articulation—refers to the need to state effectively what a country's policy is once it has been decided upon. The need to explain the rationale behind the policy is also a critical goal of policy articulation.

Policy articulation is an extremely important part of the foreign policy process in a democratic state because of the need for domestic public support for foreign policy implementation. But even in an authoritarian or totalitarian state, policy articulation is important. Every country, regardless of governmental type, finds the implementation of foreign policy easier if its domestic population supports its policies.

At the same time, governments of all types also find foreign policy implementation easier if foreign publics support—or at a minimum do not oppose—their policies. Governments consequently also see foreign publics as important targets for policy articulation efforts.

Like the preceding steps in the foreign policy process, policy articulation is a difficult task. Among its pitfalls are the dangers of multiple spokespersons who may inadvertently offer contradictory rationales for a policy or who may present confusing information about their government's policies or intentions. Indeed, contradictions and confusion frequently crop up in this phase of the foreign policy process even when there are only a few spokespersons. Concern for personal image on the part of government officials sometimes also complicates policy articulation. So, too, does unintended—and sometimes intended—media distortion.

Policy Implementation

Policy implementation is the seventh step in the foreign policy process. It is the first step in which a state actually attempts to move toward the goals that it identified. It is here that traditional foreign policy begins.

As a concept, policy implementation refers to the actions that a state undertakes to put into practice the policy decisions that it has made (or more accurately, that its decision makers have made for it). In many cases, these actions will be designed to move a country toward the goals that it set for itself (or once again more accurately, that its decision makers set for it). However, in other cases, factors such as personal ambition and concern, bureaucratic politics, misinformation, and faulty analysis will have intervened. In these cases, policy goals and policy actions will be less directly related.

States have at their disposal a variety of economic, military, sociopolitical, diplomatic, legal, and other instruments to pursue their goals and to implement their policies. These instruments will be examined in detail in Framework Four.

Policy Monitoring

The foreign policy process does not end with policy implementation. Because states must stay abreast of the progress of their policy and must determine what effects their policies once implemented are having, states must also engage in policy monitoring.

Sometimes it is easy to monitor the progress and observe the effect that a policy is having. But on other occasions, gaps in monitoring capabilities exist. In some cases, especially where policies are implemented with the goal of changing another international actor's intentions, it might not even be possible to observe the impact of a policy. Similarly, unclear linkages between cause and effect may exist, complicating the monitoring effort further.

Unless a country is willing to implement a policy without caring about whether it succeeds or fails, policy monitoring is a requisite step in the foreign policy process. With policy monitoring, one may fail to alter or to fine-tune a policy to achieve a desired goal. In the absence of policy monitoring, it is a virtual certainty that alterations or fine-tuning will not be undertaken.

Policy Appraisal

Policy appraisal is the process of assessing whether a policy is having its intended effect and determining what unintended side effects, if any, may be occurring. More often than not, policy appraisal is undertaken at the interagency working group level or at senior levels of government.

As with option formulation and planning and programming, policy appraisal may fall victim to the predisposition of analysts and decision makers, to groupthink, and to considerations of politics. If this happens, then policy appraisal will not be effective. Without effective policy appraisal, it is difficult to modify or change policies that are in place in ways that increase the likelihood of achieving the goals set in step one of the foreign policy process.

Policy Modification

Once policy appraisal has been completed, national decision makers may choose to modify policies that are in place so that policy objectives can be better met. This is a logical step. Nevertheless, efforts to modify policy frequently run into significant difficulties.

The most significant difficulty is often policy inertia; unless a particular policy is glaringly wrong or is rapidly worsening a country's situation, it is often easier just to let policies that are under way run their courses. Also, additional resources are frequently needed to initiate significant changes in policy. This sometimes leaves decision makers open to the charge of "throwing good money after bad."

Frequently, the biggest obstacles to policy modification are organizational interests, bureaucratic politics, and harm to the images of the decision makers who decided on the policy. Domestic and even foreign opponents of those who decided on the policy that is being modified sometimes are able to argue that a policy modification indicates that a policy in place has failed, when in fact the policy is only being modified. From the perspective of a decision maker, policy modification therefore carries with it the risk of charges of failed policy. The larger the contemplated modification in policy, the greater the possibility that such charges may be credible and accurate.

Despite the work and effort that goes into the foreign policy process, perfect policy is rarely implemented. Consequently, policy modification is an important step. States that are able to undertake this step successfully can increase the chances of achieving the foreign policy goals that they set out to achieve in the first place. Nevertheless, it is an often overlooked and sometimes ignored step.

Memory Storage and Recall

The final step in the foreign policy process is memory storage and recall. Its purpose is to help states learn from experience so that future policies can be improved.

Different states store and recall information and data in different ways. Some rely on the memories of people involved in the foreign policy process. Others use archival materials. Still others employ sophisticated information storage and recall technologies. And still others use a combination of some or all of these methods. In all cases, the purpose of storage and recall is to improve future policy.

No single level of government has exclusive responsibility for memory storage and recall. Archivists at the Department of State and its equivalents elsewhere may have responsibility for maintaining paper and electronic data on foreign policy and foreign policy issues, but secretaries of state, presidents, and their equivalents all find it useful to store mentally and recall as needed information about foreign leaders, economics, security concerns and threats, and other issues.

There are several potential flaws in any memory storage and recall system. Information may be stored incorrectly or incompletely. Lessons that are learned may be applied poorly or remembered selectively. But even if the memory storage and recall system is less than perfect, it is a useful step for all countries that intend to continue to have interactions with other states and with other types of international actors. With successful storage and recall, states do not have to begin anew when old issues reappear or when new items move up the priority list to become part of the current foreign policy agenda.[9]

 ## FORMULATING THE POLICIES OF OTHER INTERNATIONAL ACTORS

In the international arena, states are not the only international actors that interact with others and that must formulate policy. IGOs, MNCs, NGOs, and all the other actors we examined in the first framework must also decide what to do and how to do it.

Given the diversity of actors involved in the international system, it should not be surprising that other decision-making methods exist in addition to the foreign policy process of states. We turn our attention to those other methods in this section. However, to begin with, it is useful to repeat the four cautions that began our discussion of foreign policy and the foreign policy process, modified as appropriate for the "foreign policies" and "foreign policy processes" of IGOs, MNCs, NGOs, and other international actors.

First, as with states, not all of the international interactions that IGOS, MNCs, NGOs, and other international actors have with others are necessarily outputs of a policy process. Sometimes interactions are the result of spontaneous actions or chance encounters. On other occasions, global trends in technology, economics, or culture develop that are the results of forces beyond the control of any international actor, but that nevertheless affect actors and their interactions. In still other cases, policies are not implemented as planned, or they unfold in unanticipated, unexpected, and sometimes unwanted ways.

Second, again as with states, too much rationality should not be ascribed to the decision-making process of nonstate actors. Although the concept of process often conjures up images of a well-reasoned and logical approach, factors often intervene in the decision-making processes of IGOs, MNCs, NGOs, and other international actors that make them less than completely rational, at least if rationality is measured in terms of planned and reasoned efforts to move toward a defined objective.

Third, students and analysts of policy formulation in nonstate actors should not assume that there is a great degree of order in the various policy processes. Although such processes may be sequential, real-world pressures of time, politics, and money sometimes dictate that the steps in the policy process of nonstate actors be undertaken simultaneously, with less than sufficient information or analysis, or in a different order than presented here. In some cases, some steps may be bypassed completely.

Finally, in every sense, the policy process of nonstate actors is dynamic and ever-changing. Different people, different situations, different capabilities, and different perceptions combine in different ways to make the decision-making process dynamic and ever-changing.

Formulating Policy in IGOs

Because of their structures and functions, IGOs are continually involved in international interactions. More often than not, states are the primary type of actor with which IGOs interact.

Because of their structures and functions, except in rare cases where all of an IGO's members agree on a policy and provide resources sufficient to pursue it, IGOs often have a complicated and difficult task in formulating effective policies. A primary reason for this is that although the member states of an IGO may agree on an IGO's objectives, they often disagree on which policies to implement to achieve the objectives. IGO policies are thus often the result of compromises.

In a few cases, IGOs may temporarily espouse positions or undertake actions that run counter to the goals of member states. On rare occasions, a persuasive IGO secretariat may even convince member states to alter their agendas to be more in accord with those that the secretariat of the IGO prefers.

But if the IGO secretariat fails to do this, IGOs then run the risk of having their member states resign. In more extreme cases, IGOs may even be disbanded. Thus, because states create them and are their chief members, most IGOs have a more limited ability than states to set and give priority to goals.

As for intelligence, IGOs again often find themselves in difficult positions. All IGOs—and all international actors—require good data to formulate and implement effective policy. Many IGOs have the collection of data as one of their primary responsibilities. But this does not necessarily mean that IGOs can obtain the information they seek to acquire. In those instances where states fully agree with the activities of IGOs or do not see a threat to their own interests as the result of sharing information with the IGO and its other member states, IGOs may gather information to the fullest of their ability. But in cases where an IGO member state does not fully agree with the IGO's activities or sees a threat to its own interests as the result of sharing information, states may oppose IGO information-gathering activities.

Once IGOs acquire whatever information they can, they must interpret and report it. Here, IGOs face many of the same problems that states face. Too much information may be available, thereby creating noise. Information may be distorted, delayed, or misinterpreted. In addition to distortions, delays, or misinterpretations brought about by accident, bureaucratic politics, or personal agendas, IGOs may find that national predispositions or biases slant the interpretation and reporting of information.

Option formulation, planning and programming, and decision making in IGOs are often complicated political processes for which each IGO member state seeks to identify, defend, and promote its own interests. Whereas in state actors it is often possible to differentiate between these steps, in IGOs these steps often merge.

Coalition building is often an important part of the decision-making process in IGOs. This in itself can be a time-consuming and difficult task, in part because of the differing perspectives different states may hold on an issue. As noted earlier, states may agree on an IGO's objectives, but hold widely varying views on how best to achieve that objective. As a result, option formulation, planning and programming, and decision making are all often affected, especially because these tasks are usually undertaken by teams of people from two or more IGO member states.

The decision-making process in IGOs is also complicated by the need for national representatives to interact with their home governments. Depending on each country's own foreign policy process and the issue at hand, state representatives at IGOs may be required to check with their home government for guidance. For example, the United States generally grants its representatives to IGOs little discretion and requires them to check back with Washington frequently. In comparison, smaller countries grant their representatives to IGOs much greater leeway in stating positions. As a result, home governments sometimes can be surprised by the positions that they have adopted on an issue in an IGO.[10]

As with states, IGOs must also articulate their policies effectively once a decision has been reached. IGOs by definition have an international audience, with their immediate and most important target audiences being the governments and populations of their member states.

Here, IGOs face a complicated task. It may seem like a foregone conclusion that when an IGO such as the UN gains the support of a country for the UN's actions and positions, resources will be forthcoming. However, this is not always the case. Even though a country may support a policy, that country has additional uses for its resources aside from the needs of the IGO. Therefore, a country might not provide anything beyond declaratory support for an IGO's actions and positions even though it agrees with them. In addition, a country's representatives to an IGO may disagree with their own government about the IGO and its policy preferences. Even if this is not the case, a country's government may be unable to develop support for an IGO action or position among its own population. In either event, the IGO will receive little or nothing from the state in question.

Throughout the rest of the policy process, from policy implementation to memory storage and recall, IGOs remain hostage to the need for states to provide resources. Neither policy implementation, nor policy monitoring, nor any of the following steps in the policy process can proceed in the absence of state-supplied resources. This limits the ability of IGOs to interact with other actors in ways that run counter to the desires of the more influential member states of IGOs.

The problems that confronted states in these steps also confront IGOs. In the case of IGOs, these problems are complicated by the need of IGO member states to protect their own national interests and objectives within the context of IGO policy.

In summary, IGOs are more constrained than other types of actors in their interactions with others in the international system. Although they perform services for states that states either cannot perform for themselves or that they can perform better than states, IGOs are a dependent type of actor in the international system. This dependence is reflected in their decision-making processes.

Formulating Policy in MNCs

Unlike states and IGOs, MNCs have a single well-defined objective. They are in business to make money. Thus, the first stage in the foreign policy process of multinational corporations—goal setting—is a given. But from this point on, the decision-making process of MNC executives is in every respect as complicated as, and in some ways even more complicated than, the comparable processes in states and IGOs.

To make money, MNC executives must make the right decisions about what business practices and strategies to pursue and about which countries to do business in.[11] This requires accurate and timely information. Not surprisingly, MNCs devote considerable quantities of time, talent, and resources to gathering, reporting, and interpreting intelligence about factors as diverse as market size, market preference, the capabilities and strategies of real and potential competitors, host government attitudes and policies toward foreign firms, present and future political risk, labor cost, capital cost, level of capitalization, quality and reliability of infrastructure in a host or potential host country, technological inputs, one's own corporate culture, and the time frame of analysis. Only when such information has been gathered, reported, and interpreted can the leadership of a corporation begin to develop options about how and where business should be pursued.

MNCs sometimes find that gathering information is a challenge. There are several reasons for this. Competitors and governments might conceal needed information. Helpful data simply may never have been compiled. Public attitudes, political situations, and markets

Like leaders of states, executives of multinational corporations must make complex decisions about the international activities of their companies. Here, Bill Gates (CEO of Microsoft) explains his views on the international microprocessor and computer market.

might be subject to unpredictable fluctuations. The reliability of information may be questionable. Or sometimes, MNCs may simply not understand the cultures in which they are operating and as a result may ask the wrong questions or interpret data incorrectly.

Once they have sufficient information, MNC executives must try to use that information to answer questions about international business as it relates to their firm. Consequently, MNC managers may formulate several sets of options concerning their future business activities. Ideally, MNC leaders might lay out several different business strategies within each country or region in which they are doing business or planning to do business. In each strategy in each country, they may alter one or more of the factors they control that might affect their company's profitability. If done comprehensively, this can be a complex, time-consuming, and costly process.

After laying out options in each of the countries or regions in which they are doing or contemplating doing business, MNC decision makers might then determine how to weigh factors beyond their control that are important to them. These might include host government policies, social cost, projected market growth, and so on. This, too, can be a complex, costly, and time-consuming effort. For example, in the single area of MNC relations with host governments, some of the more important variables that MNCs must consider are permissible ownership levels of domestic corporations by foreign interests, tax schedules, depreciation schedules, infrastructure support, repatriation levels, duties and quotas on imports, export levels, employment levels, capital structure, debt sources, import protection, and labor laws.

At this point, MNC executives might assess the impact of these on the projected profitability of each strategy. After completing this, MNC managers might then compare the most profitable option in country *X* with the most profitable option in country *Y* or region *Z*, and on the basis of these steps (i.e., option formulation, and planning and programming) find themselves better equipped to make decisions than they were at the beginning of the process.

Firms that are just entering the international marketplace at this point might find themselves facing a difficult decision. On the basis of the just-completed steps of option formulation and planning and programming, should they pursue a global business strategy? Would a regional strategy be best? If so, which one and in which regions? Would it be better to concentrate on two or three countries or pursue a more comprehensive strategy? Might it be better to forego international activity and concentrate instead on one's own home country?

Even firms already involved in international business face difficult decisions about whether to expand or contract their activities, about whether they should alter the locations of their production or sales activities, and about the repercussions that such expansion, contraction, or alteration might visit upon them. As one pair of observers noted, the multinational corporation is continually facing the tension between its global vision and local demands.[12]

Once MNC decision makers have decided upon a business strategy, they must begin to implement it. An MNC's leadership must articulate its conclusions to the MNC stockholders and to other important publics such as its work force, the host government, consumers, and potential consumers.

Despite these complexities, MNCs enjoy an advantage over most states and IGOs at the implementation stage of their international interactions. Because of the ability of senior MNC officers to set policy directions, and because of the primacy of a single objective, MNCs often have a greater ability than states and IGOs to implement their policies with a single-minded focus.

This is not always the case. Sometimes, as during war, states demonstrate a great ability to focus their efforts in a single direction on a single objective. Similarly, when IGOs are fortunate enough to have all of their members agree on a single policy to achieve a single objective, they also are able to focus their efforts. Nevertheless, as a general rule, MNCs enjoy an advantage in this regard.

MNCs as a class of international actors also suffer from several disadvantages when they attempt to implement policies. More often than not, they must seek and obtain approval from a state to operate within the state's territories. Depending on the prevailing practices and philosophy of the government that rules a state, this may create problems for MNC operations. For example, a state may demand access to a proprietary technology or process to allow an MNC to operate within the country. Conversely, as we saw in Chapter 4, MNCs with economic clout sometimes find themselves in positions to influence the policies of states.

Like states and IGOs, MNCs also monitor, appraise, and modify their policies. In the cases of all three types of actors, the purpose of these steps is to determine whether or not the policy being implemented is achieving the desired results. If possible, the policy might be improved. Because MNCs have a single dominant objective and more often than not can be directed by senior management more easily than states or IGOs, these steps can usually be accomplished more easily in MNCs than in states and IGOs.

Information storage and recall is vitally important for MNCs as they attempt to change present policies and plan future ones. Poor information storage and recall can affect profitability and even determine whether a corporation will survive. In addition to industry and corporate data banks that most major MNCs maintain, the "institutional memory" of executives is frequently an important source of data storage and recall.

All told, then, even though MNCs have the single primary objective of making money, their interactions with the rest of the international community must take many factors beyond making money into account. As the preceding discussion shows, MNC decision-makers must take this into account throughout their company's decision-making process if their company is to be successful.

Formulating Policy in NGOs and Other International Actors

NGOs and the other international actors that we have not yet examined in this chapter often do not have a well-defined structure in their policy formulation and decision-making processes. All, to one extent or another, set goals and establish priorities. But once one moves beyond goal setting, other steps in the policy formulation and decision-making process of NGOs and related international actors are usually peculiar to the individual actor—not the type of actor—under consideration.

For example, some NGOs have a well-defined decision-making process, whereas others proceed on a completely ad hoc basis. Similarly, some NGOs place high priority on intelligence, but others either find intelligence useless or have little ability to collect it. These actors ignore intelligence out of necessity.

These observations lead to the unsatisfying statement that there is no truly useful way to describe or analyze the decision-making process for NGOs and the other international actors we have not yet examined. This does not mean that their decision-making processes are unimportant. It means that they are idiosyncratic, that is, peculiar to the individual NGO or individual other actor, not to the type of actor.

Perhaps in the future, a general pattern may become evident concerning the decision-making processes in NGOs and related international actors. But for the present, their decision-making processes can best be understood on a case-by-case basis.

RATIONALITY AND IMPEDIMENTS TO RATIONALITY

Unfortunately, regardless of what type of international actor is under discussion, following a rational decision making process is often more difficult than it appears. Impediments to rationality sometimes creep into the process, frustrating a decision maker's ability to formulate and implement rational policy. Despite a policy maker's best efforts, the likelihood of impediments to rationality entering the decision process sometimes gives policy the appearance of non-rationality at best, or irrationality at worst.

Here, several of the more prominent impediments to rationality in the decision making processes of international actors are outlined. All appear in one or more places in the third column entitled "Difficulties of the Task" of Table 6-1.

Incorrect or Insufficient Information

No matter how rational and logical a decision maker is, he or she requires accurate, sufficient, and timely information to make rational and logical decisions. Most states and other international actors recognize this. Those who can afford it spend large amounts of time and money attempting to obtain accurate, sufficient, and timely information.

The absence of such information at any stage of the decision process can lead not only to seemingly irrational or illogical decisions, but also to ghastly mistakes. The tragedies of the U.S.S. Stark and the U.S.S Vincennes were related earlier in this chapter and are recalled here.

More recently, the importance of accurate, sufficient, and timely information was driven home in 1999 during NATO's bombing attacks on Belgrade, Yugoslavia during the war over Kosovo. Acting on information from the early 1990s that was presumed to be still accurate, NATO planners targeted a building in Belgrade that they thought was a military target. Unknown to NATO, the building's occupants had changed, and it had become the Chinese Embassy. Its destruction set back U.S.-Chinese relations considerably. To reiterate—accurate, sufficient, and timely information is required for rational and logical decisions.

Cognitive Dissonance

Obtaining accurate, sufficient, and timely information is sometimes not enough to assure rational decision making. Even if enough accurate and timely information is obtained, **cognitive dissonance** can distort its meaning, preventing the formulation and implementation of rational policy.[13]

In basic terms, cognitive dissonance is the human tendency to dismiss information that is received that contradicts strongly held beliefs or desires. Cognitive dissonance can play a large role in personal decision making, and it can play a large role in foreign policy decision making as well.

Evidence of cognitive dissonance in foreign policy decision making is widely available. In 1982, Argentina's leaders convinced themselves despite evidence to the contrary that Great Britain would not fight to retake the Falkland Islands. After they invaded, they discovered they were wrong. In 1990, Iraqi President Saddam Hussein concluded—despite evidence to the contrary—that no one would respond if Iraq invaded Kuwait. He discovered he was wrong. In 1999, despite evidence to the contrary, U.S. President Bill Clinton concluded that the threat of U.S. military power would be sufficient to convince Yugoslav President Slobodan Milosevic to end ethnic cleansing in Kosovo. Clinton too discovered he was wrong as the U.S. had to commit itself to a major military operation in the Balkans.

Unfortunately, the power of strongly held beliefs and desires is so great that it is often difficult to identify the presence of cognitive dissonance before policies are implemented. Thus, cognitive dissonance will continue to plague decision makers in every type of international actor.

Conflicting Objectives

Sometimes, **conflicting objectives** complicate or prevent the formulation and implementation of rational policy. The existence of conflicting objectives may even put decision makers in the unenviable position of trying to implement policies that are contradictory. U.S.-Chinese relations again provide a pertinent example.

Throughout the 1990s, there was little doubt that the Chinese government fell seriously short of U.S. standards of human rights. For example, China abridged freedom of assembly, speech, and the press, imprisoned dissidents, and used child labor for production for profit.

Under laws passed by the U.S. Congress, these violations of U.S. standards of human rights demanded that the U.S. implement trade sanctions against China. However, throughout the 1990s, the U.S. maintained open trade relations with China.

This seeming failure of rationality and logic is easily explained. The U.S. had two other key objectives in its relations with China that contradicted its human rights position. First, it sought to maintain at a minimum a passable military strategic relationship with China. Second, it wanted to take advantage of the economic advantages that went with trade with China. To reiterate, the existence of conflicting objectives may demand the implementation of policies that are contradictory, and seemingly irrational or illogical.

False Analogy

Argument by analogy is a widely used method of decision making that takes lessons learned about what course of action to take and applies the lessons to another situation. Used properly, argument by analogy is an effective tool of decision making.[14]

However, if one situation is incorrectly compared to another situation and the lessons learned in the first situation are applied to the second, the conclusions that are reached almost inevitably will be wrong. This phenomenon, applying the lessons learned in one situation to another situation that is not the same, is a **false analogy.** It is a deadly pitfall of decision making.

The American intervention in Vietnam is perhaps the best example of the danger of false analogy. In the early 1960s, U.S. policy makers believed that one of the lessons of World War II in Europe was that if no one responded when a large power invaded a small power, the large power would inevitably invade someone else. Thus, when evidence was assembled that indicated North Vietnamese troops were infiltrating South Vietnam, U.S. policy makers applied the World War II in Europe analogy to Vietnam. As events proved, the analogy was a false one, and it was deadly.

As with cognitive dissonance, it is often difficult to identify the presence of false analogies before policies are implemented. Only extreme vigilance and critical analysis can prevent false analogies from being used. Thus, like cognitive dissonance, it is likely that false analogies will continue to plague decision makers in every type of international actor.

Groupthink

Groupthink refers to the tendency to go along with the dominant viewpoint that exists on a particular subject in a given group. More academically, **groupthink** has been defined as "a mode of thinking that people engage in when they are deeply involved in a cohesive in-group, when the members' striving for unanimity override their motivation to realistically appraise alternative courses of action."[15]

While groupthink can affect any foreign policy decision, its impact is often most apparent in military affairs. Thus, military mistakes such as Hitler's invasion of Russia, the Japanese attack on Pearl Harbor, the U.S. invasion of North Korea during the Korean War, the Bay of Pigs invasion, the U.S. intervention in Vietnam, the Soviet invasion of

Afghanistan, the Argentine invasion of the Falklands, and the Iraqi invasion of Kuwait have all been attributed to groupthink.

There is a natural human tendency to go along with a group and engage in groupthink. Like other impediments to rationality, however, it is a dangerous vice for foreign policy and other decision makers.

Cultural Conditioning

Everyone experiences cultural conditioning. Regardless of where one is born or raised, the culture that surrounds each person and which that person experiences helps shape each person's values, attitudes, beliefs, and perceptions. Admittedly, **cultural conditioning** does not affect everyone in the same way. Nevertheless, everyone, in different ways, is both a beneficiary and a victim of the culture in which they were raised.

In a general sense, cultural conditioning predisposes decision makers from the same culture to interpret and to respond to data, information, and events in a certain way. We will explore this phenomenon in detail in Framework Three, "The Perceptual Framework." Here, however, our focus is on the impact of cultural conditioning, on rationality, and on the role of cultural conditioning as an impediment to rational decision making. The point to be made is a simple one that will be revisited in our discussion on perceptions, namely, that no universally shared set of experiences exist that influence diverse decision makers to view a certain situation in the same way.

Given this reality, decision makers in one society may, because of their own cultural conditioning conclude that the decisions taken by policy makers in another society are "irrational." However, when those same decisions are viewed through the eyes of someone culturally conditioned in the other society, the decisions may be completely rational. And a third observer culturally conditioned in a third society may not agree that either side is "rational." The third observer may even conclude that in the context of the decision under review, "rational" and "irrational" are not relevant terms.

Given the diversity of cultures throughout the world, foreign policy decision makers must be attuned to the impact that cultural conditioning has on their own decision processes and on the decision processes of others. Because of cultural conditioning, what appears rational in one society may appear totally irrational in another, and vice versa. In a very real sense, then, cultural conditioning is less an impediment to rationality than it is an impediment to a shared rationality. We will return to these issues in Framework Three.

Personal Biases

Personal biases of decision makers are an even more frustrating impediments to rational decision making. While cultural conditioning presents an impediment to shared rationality, the personal biases of decision makers, and especially decision makers in totalitarian societies, are immense barriers to rationality.

The focus here is on the biases of decision makers in totalitarian societies because in democratic societies, democratic decision-making processes have a tendency to lessen the impact of personal biases. As more people have input to decisions, there is a greater chance that personal biases in the decision process will be rooted out. Conversely, in Hitler's Germany, Stalin's Soviet Union, or Saddam's Iraq, the personal biases of the leaders not only had an impact on policy, but usually drove policy.

Personal biases are dangerous in the policy world not only because they undermine rationality, but also because they reduce predictability. Even with the uncertainty that prevails in international relations, most international actors base their policies on the predicted actions of others and the predicted impacts and results that their own policies will have. Personal biases thus have potential to induce a ripple effect that increases unpredictability beyond a single international actor.

 ## THE ACTORS AND THEIR INTERACTIONS

In the first framework of this book, we studied the major types of international actors in today's world. In this chapter, we examined the ways in which these actors decide how they will interact and the impediments to rational decision making that sometimes complicate their decision-making processes.

Together, the actors and their interactions form an international system. While the actors and their interactions form the international system, the system in turn influences the way the actors act and interact. This feedback is based primarily on the way that the actors see the international system, their own role and position in the system, and the role and position of others in the system.

As actors, their interests, and their interactions change over time, so too does the international system. Indeed, three different international systems followed one after the other in the twentieth century alone, and the international community is now on the verge of the emergence of yet another new system. In the next chapter, we will examine the three international systems of the twentieth century, concentrating on the bipolar system that dominated the structure of international relations for most of the second half of the twentieth century.

 ## KEY TERMS AND CONCEPTS

foreign policy process   for states, the process of formulating external actions

foreign policy   the output from the foreign policy process, that is, the planned interactions that a state has with other international actors

goal setting   the first stage in the foreign policy process in which national interests and objectives are identified and prioritized

intelligence gathering, reporting, and interpreting   the second stage in the foreign policy process, in which accurate information is sought upon which to base decisions; this stage includes understanding what intelligence means, and getting it to the people who need it

option formulation   the stage in the foreign policy process in which choices are developed about what to do in foreign policy

planning and programming   the stage in the foreign policy process which identifies and weighs the costs and benefits of each option

decision making   the foreign policy process stage in which it is decided which foreign policy option to implement

incrementalism   the theory that decision-makers change policy in small ways rather than large ways because their primary objectives are the minimization of uncertainty and risk, the reduction of the number of unknowns, and the maintenance of the familiar

policy articulation   the stage in the foreign policy process in which the rationale for a policy is stated to gain support for it

policy implementation   the stage at which resources are allocated to a foreign policy so that its objectives can be achieved and in which the policy is put into effect

policy monitoring   the first post-implementation stage in the foreign policy process in which efforts are expended to stay abreast of a foreign policy and its effects as it is implemented

policy appraisal   the stage in foreign policy in which intended and unintended effects that a foreign policy is having are assessed

policy modification   changing a foreign policy so that it can better achieve a goal

memory storage and recall   the stage in which the results of past and present policy are stored and recalled so that future policy can be improved

coalition building   developing consensus between different individuals, groups, or actors on a policy

incorrect/insufficient information   the reality that decision-makers often must act with incorrect or insufficient information

cognitive dissonance   psychological conflict between existing beliefs and new information

conflicting objectives   on occasion, the objectives of a single international actor run counter to each other, thereby complicating rational decision-making

false analogy   the effort to reach a decision about a current issue by comparing it to an inappropriate historical example

groupthink   the human tendency to be influenced into going along with the prevailing attitude or belief in a group even though an individual may disagree with it

cultural conditioning   beliefs and attitudes influenced by cultural experiences and outlooks that influence individual views of reality

personal biases   beliefs and attitudes influenced by individual experiences and outlooks that influence individual views of reality

 # *WEBSITE REFERENCES*

foreign policy: *www.mofa.com*   index of many websites for Ministries of Foreign Affairs around the world

www.state.gov/www/regions/internat.html   the website of the U.S. Department of State

www.mid.ru/mid/eng/bod.htm   the website of the Russian Ministry of Foreign Affairs

www.fmprc.gov.cn/eng   the website of the Chinese Ministry of Foreign Affairs

www.lib.berkeley.edu/GSSI/eu.html   a list of links to the European Union, including the Ministries of Foreign Affairs of its members

groupthink: *www.abacon.com/commstudies/groups/groupthink.htm*   a brief overview of groupthink and the problems it causes

NOTES

1. See Graham Allison, *Essence of Decision: Explaining the Cuban Missile Crisis* (Boston: Little, Brown, 1971).

2. For example, see Roger Hilsman, *The Politics of Policy Making in Defense and Foreign Affairs* (Englewood Cliffs, NJ: Prentice Hall, 1993).

3. See John P. Lovell, *The Challenge of American Foreign Policy: Purpose and Adaptation* (New York: Macmillan, 1985).

4. Rationality and impediments to rationality are explored in greater depth later in this chapter.

5. The steps discussed in this section are taken from Lovell, pp. 27, 32, with adaptation by this author. The explanation and discussion of each step is this author's own, except as noted.

6. Charles Lindblom, "The Science of 'Muddling Through'," *Public Administration Review,* Vol. 19 (1959), pp. 79–88.

7. Another viewpoint on decision making called "prospect theory" argues that decision makers frame risk-taking decisions around a reference point and tend to accept greater risks to prevent losses than to achieve gains. See Barbara Farnham, ed., *Avoiding Losses/Taking Risks: Prospect Theory and International Relations* (Ann Arbor: University of Michigan Press, 1994).

8. Herbert Simon, *Models of Man* (New York: John Wiley, 1957). See also Herbert Simon, "Human Nature in Politics," *American Political Science Review,* Vol. 79 (June 1985), pp. 293–304.

9. For an excellent study of U.S. foreign and defence policy decision making, see Donald M. Snow

and Eugene Brown, *Puzzle Palaces and Foggy Bottoms: U.S. Foreign and Defense Policy–Making in the 1990s* (New York: St. Martin's Press, 1994).

10. This information was developed from discussions the author had during the 1990s with representatives from several different national delegations to the United Nations.

11. For discussions of MNC business strategy, see Kenichi Ohmae, *The Mind of the Strategist: Business Planning for Competitive Advantage* (New York: McGraw-Hill, 1982); Peter Schwartz, *The Art of the Long View; Planning for the Future in an Uncertain World* (New York: Doubleday, 1991); and Lloyd L. Byars et al., *Strategic Management* (Chicago: Richard D. Irwin, 1995).

12. C. K. Prahalad and Yves L. Doz, *The Multinational Mission: Balancing Local Demands and Global Vision* (New York: The Free Press, 1987).

13. See Leon Festinger, *A Theory of Cognitive Dissonance* (Stanford, CA: Stanford University Press, 1957), for a classic study of cognitive dissonance.

14. For an excellent study of the use and misuse of historical analogies in foreign policy decision making, see Ernest R. May, *Lessons of the Past: The Use and Misuse of History* (London: Oxford University Press, 1973).

15. See Irving Janis, *Victims of Groupthink* (New York, NY: Houghton Mifflin, 1972). See also Irving Janis, *Groupthink: Psychological Studies of Policy Decisions and Fiascos,* 2d ed., Boston, MA: Houghton Mifflin, 2000).

Chapter 7

The Rise and Fall of the East–West Conflict

- What kinds of international systems have existed before the twenty–first century?
- How and why did the East–West conflict start?
- How did the East–West conflict evolve?
- How and why did the East–West conflict end?

In Chapter 1, we saw that we live in an era of revolutionary international change. The old **bipolar system,** based on the **East–West conflict** with the United States and its allies as one pole (**the West**) and the Soviet Union and its allies as the other (**the East**), dominated international affairs for nearly half a century. Most international events that occurred during the era were interpreted from the perspective of their role in the East–West conflict. But when the USSR disappeared, so, too, did the bipolar world. No new international system has yet emerged to lend order to the way we view international relations.

The bipolar system was the longest lasting international system of the twentieth century, but it was not the first. Two others preceded it, and earlier centuries had their international systems as well. Before we begin our study of the bipolar world and the accompanying rise and fall of the East–West conflict, we will first present an overview of those earlier twentieth-century systems.

 ## EARLY TWENTIETH-CENTURY INTERNATIONAL SYSTEMS

One after another, three international systems have dominated international affairs since 1900. The international community is now on the verge of creating a fourth.

The Balance of Power System: 1870–1914

The first international system of the twentieth century carried over from the 19th century and extended until 1914. In general terms, it was a **balance-of-power system** in which flexible groupings of states altered their relationships with one another to maintain a semblance of international peace and stability. Its hallmarks were the economic dominance of European states, the maintenance of global European empires, and the functioning of a militarily based balance of power in Europe to maintain the peace.[1]

One important but often overlooked precondition for the successful operation of the system was the widespread acceptance by the actors within the system of the system's legitimacy. At the same time, while there was widespread acceptance of the system's legitimacy, the legitimacy of two of the major state actors, the Austrian-Hungarian Empire and the Ottoman Empire, was being challenged by internal ethnic groups that sought to dissolve the empires in which they lived. These groups hoped to establish their own nation-states.

In addition, other pressures had long been building that challenged the balance-of-power system's stability. As early as 1868, dissatisfied but increasingly powerful nation-states sought to reapportion colonial holdings, upset existing military balances, and otherwise challenge the existing system. Chief among these unsettling influences were Japan following the Meiji Restoration (1868) and Germany following unification (1871). Even the United States, which itself joined the rush to assemble overseas empires in the 1890s, had a role in destabilizing the balance-of-power system.

The Collective Security System: 1918 Through the 1930s

However, it was not until World War I (1914–1918) that the balance of power system collapsed. Not surprisingly, the unprecedented death and destruction of World War I caused many people to reject the system that had led to the war. Thus, when World War I ended, the victorious side, urged on by U.S. President Woodrow Wilson, created a new international system based on **national self-determination** and the nation-state in Europe, and on collective security throughout the world.

To obtain self-determination and create nation-states in Europe, the old Austrian-Hungarian and Ottoman empires were broken up. New nation-states were created out of the remains. This process was aided because both Austria-Hungary and the Ottoman Empire were on the losing side in World War I, and by the ethnic unrest that had plagued both before World War I. Albania, Austria, Bulgaria, Czechoslovakia, Hungary, Romania, Turkey, and Yugoslavia all owed their existence to this process. In addition, those territories of the Ottoman Empire that were at the eastern end of the Mediterranean Sea were given to Great Britain as the Palestinian and Iraqi mandates.

The process of creating new states based on national self-determination went even further. Although Russia had been on the winning side in World War I, the strains of the war had been more than the old Czarist empire could endure. It, too, collapsed, replaced by Lenin's communist state, the Soviet Union. The combination of Soviet weakness, mutual hostility between Russian communists and Western capitalists, and legitimate aspirations for independence by ethnic minorities that had been included within the old Russian empire made it inevitable that new states would be created out of the remains of the Czar's empire as well. Therefore, with the Soviet Union retaining the core of the old Russian Empire, the new nation-states of Estonia, Finland, Latvia, Lithuania, and Poland were all created out of the fallen Russian Empire by the victorious Allied powers following World War I.

Chapter 7

IT AND THE EAST-WEST CONFLICT: THE COLLAPSE OF THE SOVIET UNION

Usually, several reasons are put forward for the Soviet Union's collapse: The Kremlin spent too much on its military as it tried to keep up with U.S. defense spending; Soviet leaders paid too little attention to their economy; nationalism triumphed over communism; and poor policies put into place over decades of Soviet rule finally took their toll.

All of these causes, and others as well, contributed to the USSR's demise. A strong case can also be made that information technology, or more precisely the Soviet Union's inability to integrate information technology into its economy, society, and culture, played a major role in the Soviet collapse.

The lag in Soviet IT is easily documented. In 1978, the Soviet Union had about 18,000 to 28,000 computers while the United States had over 250,000. Ten years later, Soviet computer use had expanded to about 100,000 to 150,000 computers, but by then the United States had over 40 million.

Gradually, the USSR's lag in IT had a growing impact on Soviet economic and military strength. By the late 1980s, Soviet officials estimated that only 8 percent of their country's national production was up to world standards. At the same time, in the military, senior officials increasingly lamented their inability to develop smart weapons and systems.

The Kremlin's leaders faced an even more fundamental problem, the very nature and organization of Soviet society. Indeed, even when the Soviet Union developed or obtained advanced IT, it rarely could integrate it into society and culture because of the USSR's rigid political structure and authoritarian nature. With the legitimacy of the Communist Party depending upon the state maintaining tight control, the USSR could not tolerate a free flow of information among individuals or groups outside the party and state.

Mikhail Gorbachev recognized these contradictions and knew that their inevitable consequence was the decline of the USSR. Gorbachev therefore began to try to change the way Soviet society was organized and operated. As Gorbachev himself said, "Like many others, I had known that our society needed radical change." He understood that economic reform, political decentralization, and expanded IT use had to occur if the Soviet Union was to reverse its economic decline.

Gorbachev initiated his reforms, but they did not have the desired effect. As he loosened centralized political and economic ties so that information technologies could be adopted to reinvigorate the economy, ethnic nationalism was unshackled throughout the country. As he reduced censorship on Soviet media to allow a freer flow of ideas and reduced control of Soviet borders to allow a freer flow of people, many Soviet citizens asked why any controls remained at all.

The rest is history. On December 31, 1990, the Soviet Union disappeared, a victim as much of its inability to adopt to the demands of the Information Age as anything else.

Here, it is important to note that the Allies applied the concepts of national self-determination and the nation-state to Europe, not to other continents. European colonial holdings outside Europe remained European colonial holdings. Nevertheless, in the years following World War I, more and more people in European colonies outside Europe asked why they, too, could not have self-determination and their own nation-states. These questions planted the seeds that developed into many colonial independence movements in subsequent years.

However, those who were attempting to rebuild the international system after World War I had a more pressing problem, namely, what sort of system should replace the failed balance-of-power system? Their answer was a **collective security system.** Such a system relied on the belief that if one state acted as an aggressor, then other states had a responsibility and duty to act against and if need be punish the aggressor. This system again relied on the major actors within the system accepting its legitimacy and responding together to punish those who did not.

Unfortunately, however, few major states chose to follow the rules needed for the collective security system to prosper and survive. After a decade of relative success in the 1920s, one state after another abandoned the pretense of accepting collective security. First Japan and then Germany, Italy, and the Soviet Union in the 1930s invaded neighboring states. Meanwhile, first the United States and then Great Britain and France all decided that the potential costs of collective security were too high to pay and did little or nothing to counter aggression.

Consequently, by the early 1930s, the collective security system had failed. However, the dimensions of its failure did not become apparent until 1939, when Germany and the Soviet Union invaded Poland. Immediately, Great Britain and France declared war on Germany. After almost six years of fighting, World War II finally ended, and once again international actors were faced with decisions about what kind of international system they intended to create.

Some hoped to fashion an improved collective security system based on the United Nations. But events moved too rapidly for that to occur as the U.S.–Soviet cooperation of World War II broke down and as old colonial empires disintegrated. What emerged from the destruction of World War II was a bipolar system based on the East–West conflict, with a second conflict, the North–South conflict, playing a less prominent but nevertheless important role. Both the East–West and the North–South conflicts evolved over time, as will be detailed in this chapter and the next.

A Cautionary Note

Before we continue, however, a note of caution is in order. It must be recognized that constructs such as the balance-of-power system, the collective security system, the bipolar system, the East–West conflict, and the North–South conflict are convenient shorthand concepts used by analysts, academics, policy makers, and other students of international affairs to help order their thinking on international affairs. They are useful, but they are also oversimplifications. Certain international actors and international situations do not fit neatly into a given category. Perhaps the best examples of the shortcomings of the concepts of the bipolar system, the East–West conflict, and the North–South conflict are the People's Republic of China and the Angolan Civil War.

As a communist state, China had been viewed as a member of the Eastern bloc since Mao Zedong wrested control of the mainland from Chiang Kai-shek in 1949. By 1960, however, serious strains had developed in Sino–Soviet relations. Less than ten years later, China and the Soviet Union engaged in open warfare, and during the 1970s, China and the United States gradually improved relations. By the end of the 1970s, China and the United States were closely aligned on many international issues in opposition to the USSR. In addition, China undertook "punitive military actions" against a close Soviet ally, the Socialist Republic of Vietnam, and urged the United States and Western Europe to strengthen NATO. According to the East–West model of the international system, China's internal political system mandated that it be an Eastern country, but most of its external actions aligned it with the West. Clearly, China fell outside the confines of the simple bipolar system, and the East–West conflict also was inadequate to explain Chinese behavior.

China also does not fit perfectly into the North–South model. Although it is obviously a poor state that regularly puts itself forward as a spokesperson for Developing World states, other Developing World states sometimes view China's claim that it is a Developing World state with skepticism. China simply has too much potential, they believe, to be a legitimate Developing World state even though, economically speaking, it deserves membership.

If China is a good example of a state that does not fit neatly within the confines of a bipolar system, the East–West conflict, or the North–South conflicts, then the **Angolan Civil War** is a good example of a situation that defies categorization. During the early 1970s, three tribally based Angolan national liberation movements received support from various external sources in their struggle for independence against the Portuguese. When a new government in Portugal announced that it would grant Angola independence in 1975, the national liberation movements' struggle against the Portuguese increasingly became a struggle against each other, with the Soviet-backed Movimento Popular de Libertaçao de Angola (MPLA) fighting against the U.S. and Chinese-backed Frenta Nacional de Libertaçao de Angola (FNLA) and Uniao Nacional para a Independencia Total de Angola (UNITA). UNITA also received military backing from white-ruled South Africa. In addition, a fourth movement, the Federation for the Liberation of the Enclave of Cabinda (FLEC), sought to win autonomy and sovereignty for that province of Angola. Whoever won the civil war among the MPLA, UNITA, and the FNLA would become the new government of Angola.

By early 1976, the Soviet Union had helped Cuba introduce approximately 20,000 soldiers to Angola to support the MPLA. South Africa, meanwhile, sent an armored column into southern Angola to support UNITA. China stepped up its aid to both the FNLA and UNITA. The U.S. government also attempted to increase its aid to the FNLA and UNITA, but Congress prevented the United States from sending additional aid to any faction in Angola. Meanwhile, the Organization for African Unity was almost evenly divided over whether the MPLA or UNITA should govern.

The MPLA, with Cuban and Soviet backing, established a government in Luanda, but UNITA continued the struggle to gain control militarily of Angola until 1992 when national elections were finally held. UNITA lost the elections, then claimed that they were unfair, and renewed the civil war.

Throughout much of this time, the MPLA sought to attract external technical aid and financial assistance from any source. As part of this effort, the U.S.-based Gulf Oil Corporation received a concession in Cabinda, where it had been drilling before Angolan independence. The U.S. government, still seeking to weaken the MPLA, forbade Gulf to make payments to the MPLA for its drilling operations. After legal maneuvering, however, the MPLA received payment from Gulf. Throughout these proceedings, FLEC sought to disrupt Gulf's drilling by conducting terrorist attacks against its operations. Paradoxically, Cuban troops armed with Soviet weapons protected Gulf's investments.

The Angolan Civil War was in part a product of the North–South struggle and the East–West struggle, but it was also more than that. National liberation movement fought against national liberation movement. Communist sided with anticommunist against communist, and white racist sided with black and yellow against black and white. Western multinational corporations defied Western governments to obtain profits won under the protection of Soviet-supplied guns wielded by troops of an allegedly nonaligned nation against a local liberation movement. An international governmental organization found itself hopelessly deadlocked over which of two national movements should rightfully form a government. Elements of the North–South and East–West conflicts pervaded the entire struggle, but the conflicts by themselves could not explain the struggle. And the Angolan Civil War made no sense within the construct of the bipolar international system, either. It was too complicated a situation for such helpful but simplistic models.

Despite their shortcomings, the bipolar international system, the East–West conflict, and the North–South conflict explained enough about what went on in the world between 1945 and 1991 that they were accepted by most people as accurate representations of how the international system operated. And although the bipolar system has disappeared and the East–West conflict has ended, their legacies continue to play a major role in contemporary international affairs and will undoubtedly play a major role in shaping whatever new international system emerges.

ORIGINS OF THE COLD WAR AND THE BIPOLAR SYSTEM

Even before World War II ended, it was clear that the old international system had died and a new one was about to be initiated. Europe lay in ruins for the second time in a generation, and the old European powers were either weakened or destroyed. The Soviet Union's armies had swept halfway across Europe from the east, and U.S. and British armies had marched across Europe from the west. Fittingly enough, the most colossal war in recorded history was ended by the most colossal military weapon ever used in warfare, the atomic bomb. Politically and technologically, a new age had dawned, but its outlines were vague.

Expectations for the new era ran the gamut from hope for a cooperative international order run by the United Nations to fear of a conflict between the United States and the USSR. Nuclear weapons made the possibility of such a conflict terrifying. To optimists, the United Nations presented a hope for peace if the great powers were willing to seek accommodation instead of confrontation. Optimists hoped that the allies of World War II could build on the platform of cooperation established during the war. Pragmatists including Winston Churchill and Franklin Roosevelt hoped that the United States, the USSR, and to a

Churchill, Roosevelt, and Stalin, the leaders of the "Big Three" World War II allies, met at Yalta in 1945 in an effort to shape the post–World War II world.

lesser extent Great Britain, would exercise their powers within their own respective spheres of influence, thereby avoiding confrontation. Churchill was even so bold as to travel to Moscow during the fall of 1944 to propose to Stalin a formal division of Europe into spheres of influence. Only pessimists predicted confrontation, and they were correct.

The confrontation that emerged after World War II pitted the Soviet Union and its allies, known collectively as the East, against the United States and its allies, known together as the West. This East–West conflict was also called the **Cold War** for the basic reason that although everyone agreed that the two sides were locked in conflict, few shots were ever fired. It was, indeed, a cold war.

Five explanations have been advanced for the gradual slide into hostility that marked post–World War II relations between the United States and the Soviet Union. The explanations are not mutually exclusive. According to many analysts, they complement one another. The historical record, national objectives, opposed ideologies, the personalities of the decision makers of the postwar world, and differing perceptions of the international environment all explain the growth of U.S.–Soviet hostility.

Historically, relations between Washington and Moscow before World War II were coolly formal at best and openly hostile at worst. In the Kremlin, memories of the U.S. intervention in Russia in 1918 bore out the Marxist-Leninist prediction that capitalist states would seek to destroy Bolshevism. The United States did not even recognize the Bolshevik regime until 1933. In Washington, the Red Scare of the early 1920s and the fears of international communism during the 1930s created an equally pallid climate for good relations. Soviet unwillingness to repay czarist debts to external creditors added an extra dimension to U.S.–Soviet animosity. This record of mistrust continued until World War II drove the two countries into an alliance of convenience.

The record of U.S.–Soviet cooperation during World War II was scarred by mistrust. U.S. and British delays in invading Hitler's "Fortress Europa" were interpreted by Stalin as proof that the Western allies desired Germany and the Soviet Union to bleed each other to death while the United States and Great Britain stood on the sidelines. Stalin also resented Truman's unannounced termination of military aid to the Soviet Union. For its part, the United States believed that the USSR circumvented promises for free elections in Eastern Europe and pushed its political control into Eastern Europe. Consequently, at war's end, mutual mistrust and suspicion remained.

Postwar objectives of both countries may also be viewed as a cause of U.S.–Soviet animosity. Regardless of whether the USSR established governments in its own image in Eastern Europe for expansionistic reasons or out of a desire to obtain defensible Western boundaries, U.S. policy makers interpreted Soviet actions as a conscious thrust into the European heartland. Conversely, as the United States argued for free trade and free elections, Soviet policy makers believed that the United States was acting as Marxism-Leninism decreed it must, as an expansionistic political-economic system. National objectives, or rather opposed perceptions of national objectives, played an integral role in undermining U.S.–Soviet relations.

The opposed ideologies of Soviet-style Marxism-Leninism and American-style democracy also caused postwar U.S.–Soviet animosity. To many Americans, communist ideology was an expansionist, atheistic, militaristic form of social organization that presented a threat to the West. Any cooperation with such an ideology was dangerous. Conversely, to the Soviet communist, Western democracy was a threat to the survival of the Soviet state and Marxism-Leninism. Advocates of the view that different ideological outlooks caused the Cold War therefore maintained that Soviet communism defined the United States as the enemy, and the United States had no choice but to respond. U.S. foreign policy thus became an anticommunist crusade, thereby proving to the Soviet leadership the accuracy of Marxist-Leninist ideological preconceptions.

In addition, the personalities of the leaders of the era contributed to the slide into Cold War hostility. Winston Churchill, the British prime minister, was the ultimate advocate of realpolitik and spheres of influence. He did not trust Joseph Stalin or the wisdom of the U.S. leadership. Stalin, meanwhile, feared that his own domestic base of power was eroding. He also bordered on the paranoid concerning U.S. and British intentions. Although Stalin and Franklin Roosevelt had a degree of grudging but cautious mutual respect, Roosevelt was no longer alive to help fashion the postwar world. The new U.S. president, Harry Truman, had no use for Stalin and trusted him even less than did Churchill.

Perceptually, Soviet and U.S. leaders chose selectively from among the historical record, real and imagined objectives, ideological preconceptions, and their own personal biases to arrive at an image of the other that was malevolent and evil. Events were interpreted in light of expectations, and both sides had ample evidence to "prove" the worst intentions of the other. Given these different perspectives, the Cold War and the development of the bipolar international system may not have been inevitable, but only an inordinate combinational of fortuitous circumstances could have prevented it.[2]

THE EVOLUTION OF THE EAST–WEST CONFLICT AND THE BIPOLAR SYSTEM

The East–West conflict dominated international affairs from after the end of World War II until 1991, but in the years just after the war, it was not clear what type of relationship might develop between the United States and the Soviet Union. Nor was it clear what type of postwar international system might develop; uncertainty was the order of the day. The East–West conflict, then, evolved over time, as did the bipolar system that accompanied it. The relationship between the periods in the East–West conflict and the stages of the bipolar system is shown in Table 7-1.

Skeptical Cooperation and System Uncertainty: 1945–1947

Between 1945 and 1947, the United States and the Soviet Union pursued policies toward each other that could best be described as skeptically cooperative. Not surprisingly, the international system was vaguely defined as well. Throughout this period, the twin thrusts of conflict and cooperation that would become hallmarks of U.S.–Soviet relations were concurrently followed. The United Nations became a functioning reality during this period. In addition, although the USSR and the United States disagreed about the future of Europe, a postwar equilibrium was established in Europe that was not ideal from any perspective but was acceptable to almost everyone. Two essential features of this postwar European equilibrium were a divided Germany and the maintenance of spheres of influence by the superpowers—the Soviet Union's in Eastern Europe and the United States' in the West.

Even so, during this first postwar period, the seeds for future hostility continued to be planted. Communist-led insurrections developed in Greece, China, and Southeast Asia,

TABLE 7-1   The Evolution of the East–West Conflict and the Bipolar System

Years	Period of the East–West Conflict	Stage of the International System
1945–1947	Skeptical cooperation	Uncertain
1947–1955	Outright hostility	Bipolar
1955–1969	Rapprochement and confrontation	Muted bipolar
1969–1979	Detente	Debate over muted bipolar or multipolar
1979–1989	Measured confrontation	Debate over muted bipolar or multipolar
1989– ?	The end of the East–West conflict	Multipolar

and from the perspective of Western policy makers who viewed communism as a monolithic transnational political movement directed from Moscow, the Kremlin's hand was apparent. This view was strengthened by Soviet pressures on Turkey and Iran and by the creation of communist governments in Eastern Europe. Stalin reasserted the accuracy of the Marxist-Leninist tenet of inevitable communist–capitalist conflict in his February 9, 1946, preelection speech. Truman, meanwhile, told the Russians that they could "go to hell" if they chose not to cooperate with the United States. From the viewpoint of two Soviet historians, the United States during 1945 and 1946 sought to create a world "in which the USSR would be weakened and isolated . . . , in which the liberated peoples of Europe and Asia would pursue . . . an antisocialist route."[3] Despite these sentiments, both sides maintained negotiating contacts. By 1947, even that pretense ceased.

Outright Hostility and a Bipolar System: 1947–1955

By late 1947, U.S.–Soviet relations had slid into a period of clear hostility that lasted until 1955. U.S.–Soviet relations during this period were dominated by ideological rivalry, military competition, the fear of nuclear war, and mistrust and hostility as both sides consolidated their respective spheres of influence with military alliances and economic ties. All countries, with only a few exceptions such as Yugoslavia, Finland, and Switzerland, which chose to remain nonaligned for geopolitical or traditional reasons, were closely tied to either the United States or the Soviet Union. For all practical purposes, the uncertain international system that had developed after World War II had evolved into a bipolar system, with one pole based on the United States and its allies and the other centered on the USSR and its allies. This bipolar world is depicted in Figure 7-1.

For all practical purposes, two worlds existed during this period, the **First World** of the Western industrial democracies and their colonial holdings, and the **Second World** of socialist nations. The First World centered on the United States, with its global military might and massive economic strength. The Second World centered on the USSR, with its powerful army and growing economic base. This led to a classic balance of power in the international system, with the economically powerful United States, armed primarily with nuclear weapons, confronting the economically destroyed Soviet Union, with the world's largest army. U.S. nuclear weapons held the Soviet Union hostage, whereas the Soviet army held Western Europe hostage. Both sides feared the other and neither side dared to act.

In the West, the United States had moved to a position of clear and unchallenged leadership following Great Britain's 1947 realization that it no longer had the economic might to combat insurrectionist forces in Greece. In rapid succession, the Truman administration formulated the Truman Doctrine, in which the American president stated that U.S. policy was to give support to "peoples who are resisting attempted subjugation by armed minorities or by outside pressures," and the Marshall Plan, in which the United States sent billions of dollars of economic aid to Western Europe to restore Europe's war-shattered economy and to prevent communist expansion.[4] Within two years, the United States and several other countries concluded the North Atlantic Treaty Organization (NATO). Before the Cold War ended NATO grew to include 14 European states as well as the United States and Canada. By 1955, the United States had expanded its alliance system to include, the Orga-

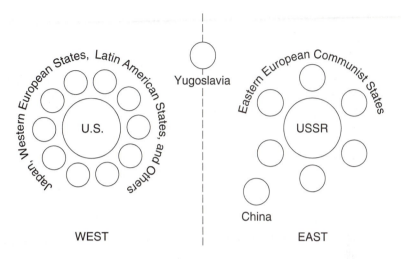

FIGURE 7-1   The bipolar world of the 1940s and 1950s.

nization of American States, the Southeast Asian Treaty Organization, the Central Treaty Organization, and the Australia-New Zealand-U.S. pact. Nearly 50 states belonged to these and other U.S.-initiated treaty organizations.

U.S. policy toward the Soviet Union during this period was based on the doctrine of **containment.** The brainchild of George Kennan, one of the leading U.S. State Department experts on the Soviet Union, containment postulated that Soviet leaders were insecure about their hold on domestic political power and fearful of foreign states. To Kennan, this meant that Soviet policies would continue to be repressive domestically and hostile internationally. Kennan's conclusion was simple: "In these circumstances, it is clear that the main element of any United States policy toward the Soviet Union must be that of a long-term, patient, but firm and vigilant containment of Russian expansive tendencies." To Kennan, such a policy would defend the West and lead over time to a Soviet willingness to accept the international status quo.[5]

In the Second World, that is, those countries in which communist governments held sway, the Soviet Union enjoyed preeminence. Few actions were taken and few speeches were given without prior clearance by the Kremlin. Economically, what remained of the industrial capacity of Eastern Europe was dismantled and moved to the USSR as the Kremlin sought to repair the ravages it had suffered during World War II. Militarily, the USSR constructed its own system of bilateral treaties with its Eastern European neighbors, concluded a mutual defense pact with China after Mao Zedong's 1949 victory, and capped its treaty system with the Warsaw Pact in 1955.[6]

By 1955, then, the world was divided into two hostile camps. The communist world viewed Western companies and multinational corporations as agents of Western and particularly U.S. expansion. Both sides in this bipolar system viewed other international actors as being either Soviet or U.S. surrogates.

Rapprochement and Confrontation in a Muted Bipolar System: 1955–1969

Even as the world was frozen into Cold War bipolarity, forces were at work that undermined the bipolar system and unleashed global trends that are only beginning to be understood now. The clarion calls of nationalism and independence increasingly were heard in the old colonial empires and the new alliance systems alike, and the growth of international trade brought about by the newly created international economic system of the First World promised both economic plenty and interdependence.

Throughout the 1955 to 1969 era, periods of accommodation followed periods of renewed Cold War tension. The opening event of this period was the first meeting in ten years between a U.S. president and a Soviet premier. Occurring in Geneva in 1955, this first summit between Eisenhower and Khrushchev accomplished little. Nevertheless, the **Spirit of Geneva** indicated a new willingness by both sides to discuss issues indicating to many observers of the time that the Cold War was finally thawing.

However, the Geneva thaw lasted only a short time. In 1956, Soviet tanks rolled into Hungary, brutally repressing an anticommunist movement that had developed there and putting in place a new government under Soviet control. At the same time, in an unrelated action, British, French, and Israeli forces invaded Egypt. The "Spirit of Geneva" had disappeared.

The following year, in 1957, the Soviet Union launched Sputnik I, the world's first satellite. This encouraged Khrushchev to increase the frequency of his missile-rattling threats. Soviet pressure on Berlin escalated in 1958 and early 1959, but by September of that year, Khrushchev had visited the United States, and U.S.–Soviet relations were once again cordial.[7] Plans were laid for Eisenhower to visit the Soviet Union.

Eisenhower's trip to the Soviet Union was shot down along with a U.S. U-2 spy plane over the Soviet Union in May 1960. The Paris summit meeting of that month between Eisenhower and Khrushchev also fell casualty to the downing of the U.S. plane. For the next two years, U.S.–Soviet relations remained tense even though a new American president was elected. In June 1961, Khrushchev met with John Kennedy, the new president, in Vienna. The result of that meeting was that both leaders returned to their respective countries and began military buildups. Shortly thereafter, the Soviets and East Germans built the Berlin Wall.

The rollercoaster of U.S.–Soviet relations continued in 1962. In October, the Soviet effort to deploy intermediate range ballistic missiles in Cuba and the American response to that effort brought the world closer to a nuclear exchange than it had ever been before or since. The aftermath of the Cuban missile crisis, however, was another period of rapprochement between the United States and the USSR. The Partial Test Ban Treaty of 1963 and the "hot line" agreement were the two most significant accomplishments of the new thaw.

After Kennedy was assassinated in late 1963, Lyndon Johnson assumed the presidency and vowed to continue Kennedy's policies, including improving relations with the USSR. U.S.–Soviet relations remained cordial even after Khrushchev's removal from power in 1964 as the new Soviet leader, Leonid Brezhnev, promised to work for friendly U.S.–Soviet relations.

Cold War summit meetings did not always reduce tensions between the United States and the Soviet Union. After the 1961 Vienna Summit between John Kennedy and Nikita Khrushchev, shown here, the Cold War heated up considerably.

However, only four months after Brezhnev took power, U.S.–Soviet relations began to deteriorate as U.S. involvement in **Vietnam** escalated. Soviet promises to send "necessary assistance" to North Vietnam were followed by Soviet warnings that "volunteers" might travel to Southeast Asia.[8] As U.S. involvement in the war increased throughout 1965, Brezhnev warned that relations between his country and the U.S. would "freeze."[9]

For four years, at least on a formal level, this is exactly what happened. But below the formal level, contacts remained and communications continued. Lyndon Johnson met with Soviet Premier Alexei Kosygin at the Glassboro Meeting in 1967, an Outer Space Treaty was concluded in the same year, and the multilateral Nuclear Nonproliferation Treaty was concluded in 1968. Despite the "freeze," cooperation remained evident.

Unfortunately for the United States and the Soviet Union, both countries found it increasingly difficult to cooperate with certain of their allies throughout the 1955–1969 period. In NATO, France questioned and challenged U.S. dominance. Not trusting U.S. guarantees of coming to Europe's assistance in the event of a war in Europe, France developed its own nuclear capabilities, exploding its first nuclear weapon in 1964. In 1966, France withdrew its forces from NATO's military command.

In the socialist world, the USSR was having even greater difficulty keeping its allies in line. Anticommunist and anti-Soviet sentiment swelled up in East Germany in 1953, in Poland and Hungary in 1956, and in Czechoslovakia in 1968. In the last two cases, Soviet and Warsaw Pact forces crushed the rebellions. Albania formally withdrew from the Warsaw Pact in 1968, although it had ceased participating in the pact five years earlier. Meanwhile, Romania refused to allow the Warsaw Pact to conduct maneuvers on Romanian soil.[10] Soviet–Chinese relations began to deteriorate in 1960. By the end of the decade, Soviet and Chinese forces were engaged in open conflict along the Sino–Soviet border. Clearly, the bipolar system was no longer as tightly structured as it had been.

In addition, as more and more colonies escaped their colonial yokes and joined the ranks of sovereign states, a **Third World** of developing states was created, separate and distinct from the First World of Western industrial democratic states and the Second World of communist central economy states.

The **impact of decolonization on East–West relations** was immense. Many Developing World states were willing to accept economic and military aid and technical assistance from whoever offered it, but chose to remain politically nonaligned. Thus, even outside the military and economic alliances of the First and Second Worlds, the post–World War II bipolar structure of world politics was breaking down.

The **breakdown of bipolarity** that occurred between 1955 and 1969 should not be interpreted as a collapse of the bipolar system. Indeed, during times of heightened international tension such as the Berlin crises, the Cuban missile crisis, and the Czechoslovakian crisis, the fundamental bipolar nature of the international system reasserted itself. During each of these crises (and others as well), most of the established states made clear their allegiance to one or another of the major poles.

The key point, however, is that during the decade and a half of this period, fundamental structural changes were altering the international system. The North–South conflict, the weakening of discipline within the established political-economic-military blocs, and the growing quantity and strength of nonstate international actors all played major roles in complicating international affairs during the 1950s and 1960s. Nevertheless, the East–West conflict predominated throughout the 1960s, even if the bipolarity that that conflict created was no longer as well defined as it had been. Bipolarity remained, but by the late 1960s, it had clearly become muted. This **muted bipolarity** is depicted in Figure 7-2.

Detente Reigns and a Multipolar System Begins to Emerge: 1969–1979

The 1970s and 1980s were decades of transition for the international system. In some respects, muted bipolarity remained in place, but in other respects, a multipolar international system had begun to emerge. The clearest indication of this was the development of new power centers on the international scene, specifically Japan, Europe, China, and to a certain extent some of the states of the Developing World. None, however, rivaled the United States or the Soviet Union in military capabilities; they were rivals in economic, ideological, and numerical senses of power. This fact led some analysts to conclude that the **multipolar system** actually signified an end to the bipolar post–World War II balance of power

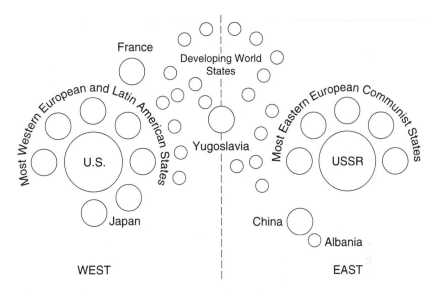

FIGURE 7-2   The muted bipolar world of the late 1950s and 1960s.

system based on military strength and ideological identification; it led others to conclude that the multipolar world was more fiction than fact. One version of the multipolar world of the 1970s and 1980s is shown in Figure 7-3.

The debate over whether a multipolar international system had superseded the muted bipolar international system coincided with the fourth major phase in East–West relations, the era of **detente,** which extended from 1969 to 1979. The period began when Richard Nixon assumed the U.S. presidency in 1969. In his inaugural address, Nixon declared that the time had come to move from "an era of confrontation" to an "era of negotiation." Gradually, over the next few years, that transformation occurred.

The changed atmosphere of U.S.–Soviet relations was best illustrated by U.S.–Soviet **summitry.** Between 1945 and 1971, the men at the pinnacle of power in the United States and the USSR met only three times (Geneva in 1955, the United States in 1959, and Vienna in 1961). Now, in the space of only four years, Brezhnev and Nixon met three times (1972, 1973, and 1974), and Brezhnev and Ford twice (in Vladivostok in 1974 and Helsinki in 1975). In 1979, Brezhnev met another American president, Jimmy Carter, in Vienna.

Detente was marked by more than summitry. Cultural exchanges, growth in U.S.–Soviet trade, technical cooperation including a joint space flight, and other manifestations of improved U.S.–Soviet relations abounded. The most significant U.S.–Soviet agreement of the period was the first Strategic Arms Limitation Treaty (SALT I), which constrained certain aspects of the nuclear arms race.

Detente witnessed not only improved U.S.–Soviet relations but also better East–West relations as both sides sought to expand confidence building measures between East and West. West Germany initiated *Ostpolitik,* a policy in which Germany improved relations with its eastern neighbors. Other Western European states followed, and by the middle

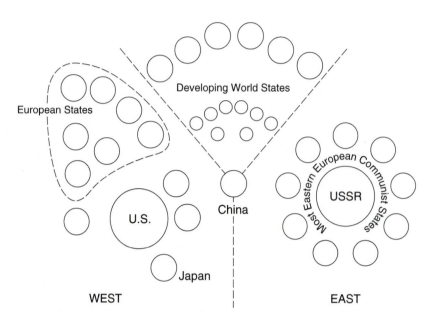

FIGURE 7-3   The multipolar world of the 1970s and 1980s.

1970s, East–West relations in Europe were better than they had been at any time since World War II. Trade and tourism expanded rapidly, Western European investments in Eastern Europe and the Soviet Union rose sharply, and the Cold War rhetoric of both sides was curtailed. Most impressively, in 1975 a meeting was held in Helsinki, Finland, that the heads of government of almost all of the states of Europe and North America attended. Called the Conference on Security and Cooperation in Europe (CSCE), the meeting heralded a new era in East–West consultation and cooperation. To many, it appeared as if a new era had dawned in international affairs.

What caused this change in East–West relations? In part, detente must be attributed to the realization that a U.S.–Soviet war would probably destroy the world as it existed. By the late 1960s, the USSR had developed a nuclear capability sufficient to devastate the United States and Western Europe; the United States had already had such a capacity to devastate the USSR. In part, the "balance of terror" led to detente.

Both sides also maintained that mutual advantages could be obtained by collaboration. For example, Western technology and investment could develop Soviet raw materials with both sides benefiting. Less tension also meant that resources formerly devoted to the military could be diverted to social needs and concerns if detente proceeded far enough. Detente was thus also the product of optimism on both sides.

Finally, detente was the product of the continuing collapse of the old bipolar international system. By the beginning of the 1970s, it was clear that the Developing World, although internally divided, had become a major actor on the international scene. In addition, the First and Second Worlds had become internally divided. A variety of economic, geopolitical, and social differences separated Western Europe from the United States, and Japan increasingly followed its own economic and foreign policy directions. In the Second World, China and the Soviet Union denounced each other almost daily, and certain Eastern European communist states increasingly asserted their independence from Soviet policy dictates. As already noted, this led some analysts to declare the old bipolar international system dead and to proclaim the birth of a multipolar world system with the United States, the Soviet Union, China, Western Europe, and Japan acting as poles. Other analysts included parts of the Developing World as potential poles.

In either event, from the viewpoint of Moscow and Washington, the result was the same: The USSR and the United States could no longer dominate international affairs as they had in the past. A new international power relationship had arisen. Detente was, at least in part, an indication of the Soviet and U.S. realization of that fact.

However, the euphoria of detente was short-lived, for many of the fundamental disagreements that caused the Cold War still existed. Historical animosities remained, as did ideological differences and conflicting national objectives. The leaders of both sides had obviously changed since Roosevelt and Stalin, but differences in perceptions continued between the new leaders. Thus, even while European and North American leaders met at Helsinki, events unfolded that brought the fourth period in postwar East–West relations to a close.

Many of these events were in the Developing World, where the United States and the Soviet Union for years had struggled to expand their own influence and limit that of the other. Before the middle 1970s, however, the Soviet Union had rarely sent large numbers of its own or its allies' military forces into Developing World areas.

Summitry was a high point of the Nixon–Brezhnev detente. Here, Nixon and Brezhnev toast the signing of the 1972 Strategic Arms Limitation Treaty.

This began to change when the Kremlin helped Cuba deploy 20,000 troops to Angola, in southern Africa. As Angola moved toward independence in late 1975, three separate national liberation movements, each of which based its political and military strength on a different tribal group, struggled with one another for the right to become the new government of Angola, and Angola was drawn into the cauldron of East–West competition.[11]

The introduction of Soviet-supplied Cuban combat forces into the Angolan Civil War during early 1976 cast a pall across U.S.–Soviet relations. U.S. leaders accused the USSR of "breaking the rules" of detente. For their part, Soviet leaders maintained that they would support national liberation movements in any way they deemed proper. Detente remained, but its luster had been dimmed.

Detente was damaged further by the Soviet-supported introduction of Cuban combat forces into Ethiopia in 1978. As in Angola two years earlier, Cuban troops won the victory for their allies.

Detente had again been traumatized. Jimmy Carter, who had assumed the presidency in January 1977, spoke of the necessity to link Soviet actions throughout the world to continued cordial U.S.–Soviet relations. According to this concept of linkage, if Soviet behavior anywhere in the world challenged U.S. interests, then the U.S.–Soviet bilateral relationship would be correspondingly cooled.

Challenges to detente emanated from the U.S. side as well, at least as seen from the Soviet perspective. Carter's human rights policy was vigorously condemned by the USSR as an unwarranted U.S. intrusion into the internal affairs of other sovereign states. Similarly, the gradual improvement in relations between the U.S. and China dismayed the Soviet Union. One analyst reported that Nixon's 1972 trip to China "stunned" Moscow.[12] And when the U.S. and China established diplomatic relations in 1979, the USSR was convinced that a U.S.-Chinese anti-Soviet alliance had been forged.

The decade of detente, then, was a period of cooperation and competition. For most of the decade, cooperation predominated, but tensions remained throughout the period, growing more serious as the 1980s approached.

Measured Confrontation: Bipolarity Triumphant? 1979–1989

As the 1970s drew to a close, debate continued over whether a multipolar system had replaced the bipolar system. This debate continued throughout most of the 1980s as East–West relations entered an era of measured confrontation even as the new centers of power that had begun to emerge during the 1970s continued to gather strength.

East–West detente finally died in December 1979 with the **Soviet intervention in Afghanistan.** Described by Jimmy Carter as "the most serious strategic challenge since the Cold War began," the United States responded by spearheading an attempted worldwide boycott of the 1980 Moscow Olympics, terminating grain and high-technology exports to the USSR, withdrawing the SALT II treaty from the Senate, and reducing the frequency of other U.S.–Soviet contacts. The U.S. president also proclaimed the "Carter Doctrine," which declared that the United States would regard any effort by any external power to gain control of the Persian Gulf region as "an assault on the vital interests of the United States of America." Carter further declared that "such an assault will be repelled by any means necessary, including military force."[13]

Other Western nations believed that Carter had overreacted and did not support the boycott of the Olympics or the curtailment in East–West trade that the American government espoused. The Soviet Union, meanwhile, claimed it had entered Afghanistan at the request of the Afghan government to help it extinguish a "reactionary counterinsurgency movement" supported by the United States and China. The Soviet claim was less than persuasive because the Afghan president who allegedly had requested the Soviet intervention was killed during the first day of the intervention.

U.S.–Soviet detente was destroyed. During the last year of the Carter presidency, the United States placed new emphasis on its military forces, both because of the perceived heightening of the Soviet military threat and because of a sense brought about by the continued captivity of U.S. hostages in Iran that the United States' military strength had eroded. Ronald Reagan, who assumed the U.S. presidency in January 1981, accelerated the U.S. military buildup. During his first press conference as president, Reagan denounced the USSR as the greatest single threat to world peace.

Heightened U.S. anti-Soviet rhetoric was matched by heightened Soviet anti-American rhetoric. The Soviet media denounced Reagan as a tool of "ultra-rightist interests" in the United States and pointed to U.S. policy as the cause of the collapse of U.S.–Soviet detente.[14] At the same time, Soviet leaders expressed the desire to continue cordial relations with other Western states. In some Western quarters, these expressions were greeted with claims of Soviet duplicity and in others as indications of Soviet good intentions. Clearly, the Western alliance was divided over what policy to follow toward the USSR.

This phenomenon of disagreement within an alliance, complicating and frustrating but not quite destroying unity within the alliance, occurred in the Warsaw Pact as well, where Romania continued its independent foreign policy line and Hungary liberalized its domestic economic organization. By far the most significant events occurred in Poland, where the independent trade union Solidarity played on Polish nationalism, a worsening Polish economy, and internal governmental corruption to challenge the legitimacy of communism in Poland. Solidarity steadily grew in influence until martial law was declared in December 1981.

Equally perplexing from the Soviet perspective was the continuing rapprochement between the United States and China. When the Reagan administration took office, the Soviets expected a deterioration of U.S.– Chinese relations because of Reagan's anticommunist rhetoric. Upon taking office, however, Reagan backed away from his previous statements on China, particularly his intention to withdraw recognition of the Beijing government. U.S.–Sino relations grew so cordial that Reagan visited China in 1984.

The Soviets themselves moved toward improved relations with China in 1982. This trend accelerated after Mikhail Gorbachev acquired the Soviet leadership in 1985, but even then, disagreement continued on many issues. To the Soviets, China remained a communist state that had lost its way. To the Chinese, the Soviets remained a major security threat.

But the most dangerous relationship to global security—indeed, to global survival— remained the U.S.–Soviet relationship; 1983 was the low point. In that year alone, President Reagan announced his "Star Wars" strategic defense plan, eliciting a harsh Soviet response; the Soviets destroyed a Korean airliner that flew into Soviet airspace, killing over 250 people; the United States invaded Grenada, a state friendly to the USSR; the United States stepped up its support for the Contras, an insurgency attempting to overthrow the Sandinista government in Nicaragua; the Soviets resorted to carpet-bombing and chemical warfare in Afghanistan; and NATO began to deploy intermediate range missiles in Europe, thereby eliciting a Soviet walkout from the Geneva arms talks. In superpower relations, 1983 was not a good year.

Fortunately, in superpower relations as in most things, conditions change. Thus, even though measured confrontation remained the hallmark of the U.S.–Soviet relationship, 1984 and 1985 witnessed a distinct improvement in relations. In July 1984, the United States and the USSR upgraded the hotline agreement. In September, Soviet Foreign Minister Gromyko met with President Reagan in the White House only five days after Reagan delivered a speech to the UN General Assembly in which he called on the two superpowers to "extend the arms control process." In November 1984, it was announced that Gromyko would meet with U.S. Secretary of State Shultz in January 1985 to begin a set of "new negotiations" on weapons in space, intermediate range nuclear forces, and intercontinental nuclear forces. Throughout 1985, U.S. and Soviet negotiating teams met in Geneva to attempt to fashion new arms control agreements.

The high point in U.S.–Soviet relations during 1985 was the November Reagan–Gorbachev summit meeting in Geneva. No major agreement came out of the summit, but the two men established a personal dialogue and had an opportunity to assess each other. Issues of contention remained over nuclear weapons, the Developing World, and a variety of other subjects.

Reagan and Gorbachev discussed these issues once again in the 1986 Reykjavik summit. Again they achieved no breakthroughs despite some progress on arms control. The

Ronald Reagan and Mikhail Gorbachev met at five summits, more than any other pair of U.S. and Soviet leaders ever. U.S.–Soviet relations improved markedly during this period.

major point of contention remained U.S. insistence on pursuing a strategic defensive program and Soviet insistence that it be stopped. However, during 1987, the United States and the USSR agreed to eliminate intermediate range nuclear weapons, and Reagan and Gorbachev met at a third summit meeting in Washington to sign the INF Agreement.

By early 1988, then, the U.S.–Soviet relationship was still one of measured confrontation. Neither side wished to compromise its positions; neither side trusted the other; and neither side wanted overt confrontation. Notably, despite the rhetoric that periodically emanated from Washington and Moscow throughout the 1980s, the United States and the USSR had not once come close to confrontation. Despite the dangers of measured confrontation, an underlying stability had entered the U.S.–Soviet relationship.

What did this mean for the international system? In certain respects, a muted bipolar system was still in place. No one doubted the centrality of the United States and the Soviet Union to international affairs. Virtually no issue in the world could be discussed without taking into account the U.S. or Soviet reaction. Clearly, the two superpowers remained the giants of the international system. But on the other hand, neither superpower dominated its alliance system as it had during earlier decades, and Japan, Europe, and China all had emerged as regional centers of power. Bipolarity remained, but multipolarity was gaining ground.

The End of the East–West Conflict: Multipolarity Triumphant? 1989–?

By the end of the 1980s, the world's movement toward a multipolar system was undeniable. Improved U.S.–Soviet relations, new policy directions in Eastern European states, the economic growth and independent course of China, the emergence of an integrated Europe planned for 1992 under the Single European Act, the rise of Japan to economic superpower status, and the division of the Developing World into regions—some of which were advancing economically and others of which were not—altered the bipolar system almost beyond recognition. This system, seen by many as multipolar, is depicted in Figure 7-4.

Few people expected the speed or magnitude of change that took place in the international system or in East–West relations between 1988 and 1991. Even fewer expected the collapse of the Soviet Union that took place at the end of 1991. In four short years, the entire face of the international system changed as the East–West conflict passed into history.

A multitude of factors contributed to the rapid improvement in East–West relations between 1988 and 1991. Cordial superpower summits occurred frequently. The Soviet Union redefined several long-held outlooks on how the international system operated. Arms control made steady progress. Several negotiations on conflicts in the Developing World achieved success.

As amazing as all these developments were, they paled in comparison to the transformation that took place in 1989 in the Soviet Union's relations with its communist neighbors. For nearly three decades, the USSR and China had reviled each other, and for over four decades, the Soviet Union reserved for itself the right to determine the course of events in Eastern Europe. Suddenly, in fewer than eight months in 1989, all this changed.

The transformation in Sino–Soviet relations was not unexpected. As early as 1982, the USSR sought improved relations with China. However, the road to rapprochement

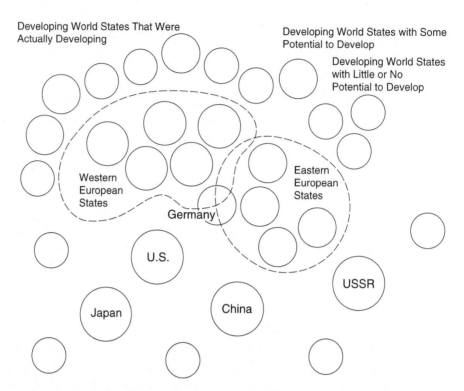

FIGURE 7-4   The multipolar world of 1989–1991.

was rocky, foundering on the Soviet military buildup on the Sino–Soviet border, the USSR's military occupation of Afghanistan, and Soviet support for Vietnam's occupation of Cambodia. Gradually, these three problems were removed or ameliorated, and Sino–Soviet relations improved. Finally, in May 1989, Gorbachev visited China. A new Sino–Soviet relationship—cordial but careful—had been forged.

The transformation in Soviet–East European relations was different; no one expected it. At first tentatively but then more forcefully, the peoples of Eastern Europe voiced opposition to the communist governments that had ruled them since the 1940s. Emboldened by Soviet declarations that the Kremlin would no longer use military force to keep governments in power and encouraged by Gorbachev's assertions that people should choose for themselves the type of society in which they lived, the peoples of Eastern Europe overthrew one communist government after another. In Poland, a free election brought the noncommunist trade union Solidarity to power. In Hungary, the Communist party and government declared itself noncommunist and prepared for free elections. In East Germany, Czechoslovakia, and Bulgaria, massive demonstrations forced communist governments to resign. In Romania, a bloody revolution toppled the communist government, and the long-time communist leader Nicolae Ceausescu was executed.

Thus, when the 1990s opened, new faces were in power in almost every Eastern European capital. Even the political map of Europe changed as East and West Germany unified in 1990. And these new faces and changes in the political map of Europe, in conjunction with all the other changes in 1988 and 1989, had completely transformed U.S.–Soviet and East–West relations. But even these transformations paled in comparison to what occurred in 1991 in the USSR itself.

By 1991, Gorbachev had been in power for six years. During that time, the reforms that he instituted had an immense impact on Soviet society. In some cases the impact was beneficial and in other cases harmful. *Glasnost,* Gorbachev's policy of opening Soviet society to greater debate and freedom of expression, had worked well and been accepted by many Soviet citizens. Gorbachev's political reform effort, *demokratizatsiya,* had also been accepted by most Soviet citizens. However, *perestroika,* Gorbachev's conception of economic reform that he had put in place to try to revitalize the failing Soviet economy, had failed. By 1991, the Soviet economy was much worse than it had been when Gorbachev assumed power in 1985.

This mixed record of success and failure caused Gorbachev's reforms to be the subject of considerable disagreement within the USSR. Some senior Soviet officials, especially conservative party members, government bureaucrats, and military leaders, strongly

George Bush and Mikhail Gorbachev continued the practice of regular U.S.–Soviet summit meetings, first in Malta in 1989, then in Washington in 1990, and again in Helsinki in 1990, shown here. They also met in other settings such as the 1991 G-7 meeting in London.

opposed Gorbachev's policies for ideological reasons. Furthermore, Gorbachev's ideas challenged their own power. Conversely, other Soviet leaders such as Russian President Boris Yeltsin criticized Gorbachev for proceeding too cautiously.

By 1991, then, Soviet society had become polarized over Gorbachev's reforms. But Gorbachev's reforms had unleashed an additional force within the USSR: ethnic nationalism. Unfortunately for Gorbachev and the Soviet Union, this newly unleashed ethnic nationalism saw people identifying themselves not with the Soviet Union, but with their own nationality groups. By 1991, all 15 of the USSR's nationally based republics declared that their own laws took precedence over those of the Soviet Union.

Recognizing that the USSR was unraveling, Gorbachev negotiated a new treaty of union with the presidents of most of the Soviet Union's republics. This new treaty gave the republics unprecedented power. Had the treaty been implemented, the entire nature of the Soviet Union would have changed. But the new union treaty was too much for conservative party members, government bureaucrats, and military leaders to accept. Already alienated from Gorbachev and his reforms, Gorbachev's conservative opponents launched a coup in August 1991 and temporarily removed Gorbachev from power.

Yeltsin and other reformers, as well as tens of thousands of Soviet citizens, rallied to Gorbachev's support and the defense of reform. Within days, the coup collapsed and its leaders were arrested.

The impact of the coup was immense. Gorbachev's authority was further undermined, the credibility of the Communist Party of the Soviet Union was destroyed, and Yeltsin and other reformers benefited from a surge of popular support for their role in defeating the coup. Emboldened by his new popularity, Yeltsin met in December with the presidents of Ukraine and Belarus, two other Soviet republics, and declared that the Soviet Union would cease to exist on January 1, 1992. Gorbachev protested, but could do nothing to stop the flow of events. And so on January 1, 1992, the Soviet Union disappeared, replaced by 15 newly independent states.

The end of the Soviet Union also ended the debate about whether the transformations in Eastern Europe and the improvements in East–West relations that had taken place in the late 1980s and 1990 had ended the Cold War. With no Soviet Union, the Cold War could scarcely continue. And more significant for our purposes here, the end of the Soviet Union also ended debate over whether the international system remained a bipolar system based on the East–West conflict.

 ## THE LEGACY OF THE EAST–WEST CONFLICT AND THE BIPOLAR SYSTEM

Before their demise, both the East–West conflict and the bipolar system had gone through several phases. (See Table 7-2.) During the late 1940s and early 1950s, the world had been divided into two hostile camps, one centered around the United States and the other around the Soviet Union. By the 1990s, this bipolarity had disappeared and had been replaced by a multipolarity that saw both superpowers unable to control their former allies. China, Japan, Western Europe, Eastern Europe, and several Developing World states all formulated their own policies and had enough power to influence the policies of the two

TABLE 7-2   Some of the Major Events and Trends in East–West Relations

International System	Period in East–West Relations	Events and Trends
Uncertain	Skeptical cooperation (1945–1947)	UN established Germany divided Eastern Europe communized Communist-led insurrections in Greece, China, and Southeast Asia Western Europe established democratic governments
Bipolar	Outright hostility (1947–1955)	Truman Doctrine Marshall Plan U.S. containment policy Czechoslovakian coup First Berlin crisis and Berlin airlift Mao victorious in China NATO formed Korean War SEATO, CENTO, ANZUS, and other Western treaty systems formed Warsaw Pact formed Franco–Vietminh War in Southeast Asia
Muted bipolar	Rapprochement and confrontation (1955–1969)	Eisenhower and Khrushchev at Geneva Taiwan Straits crisis Soviet troops invade Hungary Britain, France, and Israel enter Egypt Khruchchev's missile-rattling and Sputnik I U.S. Marines land in Lebanon Second Berlin crisis Khrushchev visits United States U-2 and the failed Paris Summit Kennedy and Khrushchev at Vienna Berlin Wall put up Cuban missile crisis Test ban treaty and hotline agreement Kennedy assassinated, Khrushchev removed United States enters Vietnam War U.S. Marines land in Dominican Republic Glassboro meeting Sino–Soviet rift widens France withdraws from NATO's military structure Nonproliferation Treaty Warsaw Pact invades Czechoslovakia Many former colonies attain statehood throughout the period

(Continued)

TABLE 7-2   Some of the Major Events and Trends in East–West Relations

International System	Period in East–West Relations	Events and Trends
Debate over muted bipolar or multipolar	Detente (1969–1979)	United States withdraws from Vietnam Six meetings between U.S. presidents and Brezhnev SALT I and SALT II Many other East–West agreements on trade, culture, science, etc. Confidence-building measures and *Ostpolitik* *Helsinki Conference (Conference on Security and Cooperation in Europe)* U.S.–China ties established Sino–Soviet hostility worsens Soviet military buildup continues Cuban troops deployed to Angola Cuban troops deployed to Ethiopia Americans taken hostage in Iran U.S. "human rights" policy
Debate over muted bipolar or multipolar	Measured confrontation (1979–1988)	Soviets invade Afghanistan United States and USSR increase criticism of each other's policies United States begins military buildup Warfare in El Salvador INF and START negotiations begin United States accuses USSR of using chemical warfare in Afghanistan, Laos, and Cambodia Brezhnev dies and triple succession begins: Andropov, Chernenko, Gorbachev in 28 months "Star Wars" strategic defense program proposed USSR shoots down KAL 747 United States invades Grenada U.S. opposition to Nicaragua increases INF deployment in Europe begins Soviets walk out of Geneva arms talks Reagan reelected Arms talks resume Reagan–Gorbachev summit in Geneva Terrorism worsens United States attacks Libya Chernobyl nuclear disaster in the Soviet Union Reagan–Gorbachev summit in Reykjavik Reagan–Gorbachev summit in Washington INF Treaty
Multipolar	End of the East–West conflict (1989–1991)	Soviets withdraw from Afghanistan Reagan–Gorbachev summit in Moscow

(Continued)

Table 7-2   Some of the Major Events and Trends in East–West Relations

International System	Period in East–West Relations	Events and Trends
		UN plays more active peacekeeping role in several conflicts
		U.S.S. *Vincennes* shoots down Iranian airliner
		United States and Soviets help arrange Angola–Namibia accords
		Nationality unrest in the USSR
		Iran–Iraq war ends
		Gorbachev's UN speech
		Reagan–Bush–Gorbachev summit in New York
		Gorbachev visits China
		Tiananmen Square massacre
		Free Polish election brings Solidarity to power
		Vietnam withdraws from Cambodia
		Hungary declares itself an excommunist state
		Communist leaders in Bulgaria, Czechoslovakia, Romania, and East Germany overthrown
		Berlin Wall torn down
		Bush–Gorbachev summit in Malta
		United States invades Panama
		Bush–Gorbachev summit in United States
		German unification
		Iraq invades Kuwait
		Multinational forces deployed to Middle East in response to Iraqi invasion
		Bush–Gorbachev summit in Helsinki
		Iraq expelled from Kuwait in Persian Gulf War
		New Soviet Treaty of Union formulated
		Gorbachev attends G-7 meeting of major Western industrial countries in London
		Soviet coup
		Breakup of the Soviet Union

superpowers. On occasion, they could even chart their own policies with little regard for U.S. and Soviet desires.

In addition, as we have seen in Chapters 3, 4, and 5, other actors had become more important between the late 1940s and the early 1990s. Multinational corporations, viewed by the Soviet Union as tools of capitalist expansion and exploitation during the 1940s and 1950s, had come to be regarded in the Kremlin as potential providers of needed investment capital and technology. First World states, meanwhile, lamented their inability to control the activities of MNCs. International governmental organizations, nongovernmental organizations, and other international actors also operated against the backdrop of international change, no longer sure of what the flow of events might bring.

The twenty-first century world is much more complicated and uncertain than was the world of the Cold War. The East-West conflict of the 1940s and 1950s, so easily represented conceptually by a bipolar world system that created a balance of power, is over. One of the chief protagonists in that conflict, the Soviet Union, no longer exists. The other, the United States, has military capabilities that remain unrivaled anywhere in the world, but also had the world's largest economic debt, suffered from serious domestic social problems, and is searching for its role in the post–Cold War world.[15] Japan has become a leading global economic power and Western Europe is forging a single economic market. China sets its own independent political and economic course and Developing World states struggle to survive. Meanwhile, MNCs invest in the former Soviet Union, Eastern Europe, and China, while civil wars, national liberation conflicts, and ethnic warfare continue in much of the world. Fundamentalist Islam rejects both communism and Western solutions to social problems.

The bipolar world that was based on the East–West conflict has clearly been relegated to the dustbin of history, but what will replace it remains unclear. Several different models have been suggested, but we are not yet ready to explore them. We will conduct that exploration in Chapter 20, after we conclude studying the international system, perceptions, power and influence, and several of today's major international issues. At that point, we will be ready to speculate on where the twenty-first century world is headed.

 ## *KEY TERMS AND CONCEPTS*

bipolar system   the international system that developed after World War II which had two major poles, one centered around the United States and the other around the Soviet Union

East-West conflict   the confrontation that set the United States and its allies against the Soviet Union and it allies for most of the period from 1945 to 1991

the West   the United States and Canada, Western Europe, Japan, Australia, and New Zealand; occasionally other states such as Israel are categorized with "the West"

the East   the former Soviet Union and its Eastern European allies; other communist and socialist-path states were sometimes considered part of "the East" as well

balance of power system   refers to the distribution of capabilities between two states or groups of states; a "balance of power" may mean that an equilibrium exists or is being created, or that a disequilibrium exists or is being created

national self-determination   when people who identify themselves as a nation are permitted to form their own nation-state

collective security system   a system in which aggression by one state brings about a response from all other states

Angolan Civil War   the civil war that began in Angola in 1975 and continued into the 1990s which played a major role in East-West relations during the Cold War

the Cold War and its origins   the reasons most often put forward for why the Cold War started are the history of U.S.-Soviet relations; differing national objectives; opposed ideologies; the personalities of post-war decision-makers; and differing Soviet and U.S. perceptions of the international environment

period of skeptical cooperation   the first period in post-World War II U.S.-Soviet relations, extending from 1945 to 1947, during which the two countries minimally cooperated even as tensions built

period of outright hostility   the second period of post-World War II U.S.-Soviet relations, extending from 1947 to 1955

First World   the industrialized West, centered around the U.S.

Second World   the communist East, centered around the U.S.S.R.

containment   the U.S. policy during the Cold War of trying to prevent Soviet expansionism wherever it occurred with a combination of political, diplomatic, economic, and military policies

period of rapprochement and confrontation   extending from 1955 to 1969, this period in U.S.-Soviet relations saw alternating cooperation and confrontation between the U.S. and the U.S.S.R.

Spirit of Geneva   after U.S. President Eisenhower and Soviet Premier Khrushchev met in Geneva in 1955, U.S.-Soviet relations improved for a period. This was called the Spirit of Geneva

Vietnam and its impact on East-West relations   as U.S. involvement in Vietnam escalated during the 1960s, U.S.-Soviet relations deteriorated. However, not all aspects of the relationship worsened

Third World   the former colonial countries that won their independence from European colonial powers after World War, also known as the Developing World

decolonization and its impact on East-West relations   as former European colonies achieved independence during the 1950s and 1960s, many became nonaligned. The U.S. and the U.S.S.R. tried to compete for influence in many of these countries

breakdown of bipolarity   in the 1960s, the alliances of the U.S. and the U.S.S.R. weakened as several countries friendly to the U.S. and the U.S.S.R. acted independently of the superpowers

muted bipolar world   as the bipolar world evolved, some states gradually became less closely connected to the United States and the Soviet Union, thereby creating a muted bipolar system

multipolar world   a system that has many centers of power

detente   extending from 1969 to 1979, detente was marked by a general improvement in U.S.-Soviet relations

summitry   the meetings that occurred between U.S. presidents and Soviet leaders during the Cold War. Summitry was a fixture of the Nixon-Brezhnev and Ford-Brezhnev years (1972-1976) and of the Gorbachev-Reagan and Gorbachev-Bush (1985-1991) years

period of measured confrontation   began with the Soviet invasion of Afghanistan and extended into the early Gorbachev years, and marked by U.S.-Soviet disagreements over Developing World events in Afghanistan, Angola, and Nicaragua

Soviet intervention in Afghanistan   when the Soviet Union invaded Afghanistan in 1979, it ended detente and began what some people called a "second Cold War"

Reasons the Cold War ended   the reasons most often listed are the end of communism in East Europe, Gorbachev's reforms in the U.S.S.R., and the economic collapse of the U.S.S.R.

 ## *WEBSITE REFERENCES*

East-West Conflict and the Cold War: *dir.lycos.com/Society/History/Twentieth_Century/Cold_War*   lists 34 websites on the East-West conflict and the Cold War

www.stmartin.edu/~dprice/cold.war.htm   another listing of links to East-West conflict and Cold War resources on the web

www.rferl.org   website for Radio Free Europe/Radio Liberty, long time observers of Soviet and Russian events

Angolan Civil War: *dailynews.yahoo.com/fc/World/Angola*   coverage of on-going events in Angola

Afghanistan conflict: *dailynews.yahoo.com/fc/World/Afghanistan*   coverage of on-going events in Afghanistan

end of the Cold War: *www.cia.gov/csi/books/19335/art-1.html*   U.S. views of the USSR at the end of the Cold War

newarkwww.rutgers.edu/guides/glo-sov.html   a collection of links on the collapse of communism

NOTES

1. For different views of events in this and subsequent periods and how they together helped define the international system, see William R. Keylor, *The Twentieth Century World* (New York: Oxford University Press, 1992); R. Ahmann, A. Birke, and Michael Howard, eds., *The Quest for Stability: Problems of Western European Security 1919–1957* (New York: Oxford University Press, 1993); Thomas J. Knock, *To End All Wars: Woodrow Wilson and the Quest for a New World Order* (Princeton: Princeton University Press, 1995); and Gordon A. Craig and Alexander L. George, *Force and Statecraft; Diplomatic Problems of Our Time,* 3rd Ed. (New York: Oxford University Press, 1995).

2. For just a few of the many views and interpretations of who caused the Cold War and of the events that occurred during it, see Gar Alperovitz, *Atomic Diplomacy* (New York: Simon & Schuster, 1965); Stephen E. Ambrose, *Rise to Globalism: American Foreign Policy 1938–1980* (New York: Penguin Books, 1981); Seyom Brown, *The Faces of Power* (New York: Columbia University Press, 1969); Herbert Feis, *From Trust to Terror: The Onset of the Cold War, 1945–1950* (New York: W. W. Norton, 1970); William L. Gaddis, *The United States and the Origins of the Cold War, 1941–47* (New York: Columbia University Press, 1972); Lloyd C. Gardner, *American Foreign Policy: Present to Past* (New York: The Free Press, 1947); Louis J. Halle, *The Cold War as History* (New York: Harper & Row, 1967); John Herz, *Beginnings of the Cold War* (Bloomington: Indiana University Press, 1966); Townsend Hoopes, *The Devil and John Foster Dulles: The Diplomacy of the Eisenhower Era* (Boston: Little, Brown, 1973); David Horowitz, *The Free World Colossus* (New York: Hill & Wang, 1965); George F. Kennan, *American Diplomacy, 1900–1950* (New York: New American Library, 1951); Gabriel Kolko, *The Roots of American Foreign Policy* (Boston: Beacon Press, 1969); Walter Lippmann, *The Cold War: A Study in U.S. Foreign Policy* (New York: Harper & Row, 1947); Vojtech Mastny, *Russia's Road to the Cold War* (New York: Columbia University Press, 1979); James A. Nathan and James K. Oliver, *United States Foreign Policy and World Order* (Boston: Little, Brown, 1976); Thomas G. Paterson, *On Every Front:*

The Making of the Cold War (New York: Norton, 1979); John Spanier, *American Foreign Policy Since World War II* (New York: Congressional Quarterly Press, 1988); William Appleman Williams, *The Tragedy of American Diplomacy* (New York: Delta Books, 1972); and Daniel Yergin, *Shattered Peace: The Origins of the Cold War and the National Security State* (Boston: Houghton Mifflin, 1978).

3. N. Sivachyov and E. Yazkov, *History of the USA Since World War I* (Moscow: Progress, 1976), p. 195.

4. See Joseph Marion Jones, *The Fifteen Weeks* (New York: Harcourt Brace Jovanovich, 1964).

5. George F. Kennan ("*X*"), "The Sources of Soviet Conduct," *Foreign Affairs,* Vol. 25 (July 1947), pp. 566–582.

6. For a detailed and balanced account of Soviet foreign policy behavior during this and other periods, see Adam B. Ulam, *Expansion and Coexistence: Soviet Foreign Policy 1917–1973* (New York: Praeger, 1974). See also Joseph L. Nogee and Robert H. Donaldson, *Soviet Foreign Policy Since World War II* (New York: Pergamon Press, 1988); and Alvin Z. Rubinstein, *Soviet Foreign Policy Since World War II: Imperial and Global* (Cambridge, MA: Winthrop, 1988).

7. *Khrushchev in America* (New York: Crosscurrents, 1960) contains all of the speeches the Soviet leader gave during his historic American tour.

8. *Pravda,* March 24, 1965, and April 11, 1965.

9. L. I. Brezhnev, *Leninskim Kursom,* Vol. 1 (Moscow: Izdatel'stvo Politicheskoi Literatury, 1970), p. 228.

10. See Robin Alison Remington, *The Warsaw Pact: Case Studies in Communist Conflict Resolution* (Cambridge, MA: The MIT Press, 1971), for a presentation of Soviet difficulties with other Warsaw Pact members.

11. For fascinating accounts of this conflict, see Arthur Jay Klinghoffer, *The Angolan War: A Study in Soviet Policy in the Third World* (Boulder, CO: Westview Press, 1980); John Marcum, *The Angolan Revolution: Exile Politics and Guerrilla Warfare (1962–1967)* (Cambridge, MA: The MIT Press, 1978); and Daniel S.

Papp, "Angola, National Liberation, and the Soviet Union," *Parameters,* Vol. 8 (June 1978), pp. 57–70.

12. Gene T. Hsiao, *Sino-American Détente and Its Policy Implications* (New York: Praeger, 1974), p. 141.

13. President Jimmy Carter, "President Carter's 1980 State of the Union Address," January 25, 1980.

14. For just a few examples, see *Pravda,* June 25, 1982; September 18, 1982; and September 19, 1982.

15. For several different treatments of the implications of the end of the Cold War, see John Lewis Gaddis, *The United States and the End of the Cold War: Implications, Reconsiderations, Provocations* (New York: Oxford University Press, 1992); Jeffrey T. Bergner, *The New Superpowers: Germany, Japan, the United States, and the New World Order* (New York: St. Martin's Press, 1991); Wayne Sandholtz et al., *The Highest Stakes: The Economic Foundations of the Next Security System* (New York: Oxford University Press, 1992); Donald Snow, *Distant Thunder: Third World Conflict and the New International Order* (New York: St. Martin's Press, 1992); Richard Ned Lebow and Thomas Risse-Kappen, *International Relations Theory and the End of the Cold War* (New York: Columbia University Press, 1995); and Brad Roberts, ed., *Order and Disorder After the Cold War* (Cambridge, MA: The MIT Press, 1996).

Chapter 8

The North–South Conflict

- What is the North–South conflict?
- How did the North–South conflict evolve?
- What are the objectives of Developing World states?
- How does economic development take place?

Throughout most of the years of the East–West conflict, another major conflict also helped shape the international system. It continues today, although at a more subdued level than during the era of the bipolar world. That conflict is the **North–South conflict.**

DEFINING THE CONFLICT

The North–South conflict derives its name from the fact that, almost without exception, the wealthy countries of the world are in the northern hemisphere and the poorer countries lie to their south. Generally speaking, **the North** includes the United States, Canada, Europe excluding Albania, Israel, Japan, Russia (although this is a matter of debate), South Africa, Australia, and New Zealand. The remaining states of the world, numbering about 150, is **the South.**

The South has been and is described by many terms—the **Third World,** the **Developing World,** and the **Less Developed Countries (LDCs),** to name just a few. Again speaking in general terms, the countries of the South share two attributes: (1) They have had a colonial past dominated by European powers and (2) they are poor—although exceptions exist. Ethiopia and Thailand were never included in European empires, and OPEC countries are usually not impoverished. Nevertheless, they are considered countries of the South.

In many respects, terms such as *South* and *Third World* are misleading, for they conjure up images of a unified group of states. Although many of the objectives these states seek may be similar or even identical to the objectives of other Developing World states, an incredible diversity exists within the Developing World states of the South. This diversity exists in political form, social structure, and economic organization. Table 8-1 provides one

Chapter 8

IT AND THE NORTH–SOUTH CONFLICT: OVERCOMING THE RIFT, OR WORSENING IT?

Historically, twentieth century information technologies such as radio and television helped make many citizens of Developing World states aware of how poorly they lived in comparison to the people of Europe, Japan, and especially North America. The growing awareness of the gap in living standards between the Developed and Developing World led directly to the "the revolution of rising expectations," that is, the desire of many people in developing states to improve their standards of living.

Will Information Age technologies help make Developing World expectations a reality? The evidence is mixed.

Optimistically, developing states will use IT to accelerate economic growth, improve living standards, and close the gap in standard of living that exists between the Developed and Developing Worlds. This is what is occurring in the newly industrialized countries discussed in Chapter 11. Similarly, libraries in 39 developing countries are aiding economic growth as a result of their ability to access commercial data bases via the Electronic Information for Libraries Direct portal (http://www.eifl.net), financed by philanthropist George Soroos. These and other developing states may even be able to move directly from an agricultural society to a post-industrial Information Age society, as discussed in Chapter 20.

But there are significant barriers to these optimistic scenarios. Some countries are not receptive to new technologies because of the level and strength of traditional values and outlooks. Other developing states suffer from a great degree of insularity or low levels of education. Others, in the absence of significant quantities of aid, will be unable to afford advanced IT. Still others will have limited human, technical, or economic infrastructures and not be able to maintain IT even if deployed. And some developing states, despite low levels of economic development, will attach high levels of priority to maintaining complete sovereignty and controlling their decision-making processes.

Thus, pessimists maintain that many developing states will be unable to take full advantage of information technologies and will enter the Information Age more slowly than developed states. Argentina, Brazil, India, several East Asian states, and a few other developing countries may successfully become Information Age states, but much of the rest of the world will lag behind. Thus, pessimists maintain, the Information Age has potential to exacerbate the North–South conflict and create a "Digital Divide" in addition to the present economic divide.

Which of these scenarios, the optimistic one or the pessimistic one, will become reality? It is too soon to tell. But it is not too soon to predict that decisions that are being made and actions that are being undertaken around the world today will play major roles in increasing the likelihood of one or the other scenario. The future is not about the future, but about the future of present decisions and actions.

**TABLE 8-1   Examples of the Political-Economic Diversity
of the Developing World**

Government Type	Level of Economic Development		
	Good Potential to Develop	Some Potential to Develop	Little Potential to Develop.
Constitutional Monarchy		Malaysia, Thailand	
Democratic	Argentina, Brazil, Chile	Barbados, Botswana, India, Philippines	Bangladesh, Namibia
Hereditary	Bahrain, Brunei, Saudi Arabia	Morocco	Jordan
Military	Iraq, Libya	Algeria, Burma, Guinea	Burkina Faso
Nonmilitary Autocratic	Iran	Congo, Cuba, Egypt, Vietnam	Ethiopia

view of the political-economic diversity of the Third World. Some Developing World states are democracies. India, for example, advertises itself as "the world's largest democracy." Other Developing World democracies include Argentina, Bangladesh, and Botswana. Some Third World states like Congo and Zimbabwe pose as democracies, but in fact have governments that are quite autocratic. Still other Developing World states such as Burma and Iraq are ruled by military dictatorships, while others like Malaysia and Thailand are constitutional monarchies. Hereditary monarchies rule Third World states such as Brunei, Morocco, and Saudi Arabia. Some states such as Nigeria are attempting to make a transition from civil unrest or authoritarian and dictatorial rule to democracy. Still other Developing World countries such as Afghanistan, Sierra Leone, and Somalia have been torn by extended civil war and have no true government. They are best described as failed states.

During the Cold War, a significant number of Third World states such as Angola, Cuba, Mozambique, and Vietnam advocated socialism and state ownership of the means of production, but after the demise of the Soviet Union, many became advocates of capitalist style private enterprise.

Economically, no single level of economic development exists within the South. Some analysts have argued that the concept of "Third World" should be supplemented by the concepts of "Fourth World" and "Fifth World."[1] According to this typology, the Third World would consist of such states as Argentina, Brazil, Nigeria, and Saudi Arabia, which have sufficiently developed economic infrastructures, resources, and/or skills of the population so that they could become industrialized in the foreseeable future. The **Fourth World,** by comparison, would comprise countries that had the potential for eventual economic development. Bolivia, Ecuador, and Thailand fall into this category. Finally, the **Fifth World** would consist of countries that have little hope for economic development because of a dearth of infrastructure, resources, and skill. Niger, Chad, Somalia, and Bangladesh represent this poorest of all classes of economic conditions. Table 8-2 lists the average per capita incomes of various developing countries, and contrasts them with the average per capita incomes of selected First and former Second World countries. A quick perusal of Table 8-2 gives an adequate overview of selected national per capita incomes, but a global statement may be more helpful in understanding the extreme maldistribution of global wealth. In simple terms, 75 percent of the world's population receives less than 20 percent of the world's gross national product.

The concept of the Third World is criticized by analysts who believe that the term hides the diversity of the poverty-stricken regions of the world. Many governments of

TABLE 8-2 **Average Annual Per Capita Income of Selected First, Former Second, and Developing World States**

	Per Capita Income in Dollars, 1998
First World States	
France	24940
Germany	25850
Great Britain	21400
Japan	32380
Switzerland	40080
United States	29340
Former Second World States	
Czech Republic	5040
Hungary	4510
Poland	4230
Russia	2300
Developing World States	
Bangladesh	350
Brazil	4570
Central African Republic	300
Ecuador	1530
Ghana	390
India	430
Kenya	330
Madagascar	260
Pakistan	480
Panama	3080
Somalia	under 100
Tanzania	210
Thailand	2200
United Arab Emirites (OPEC state)	18220
Zaire	under 100

Source: The World Bank, *Social Indicators of Development 1999,* appropriate pages.

poorer nations also criticize it because it carries with it, from their perspectives, an image of a third-rate country. Despite these criticisms, the term remains in widespread use today. For our purposes, we will use primarily the term *Developing World.*

Existent poverty, a shared colonial history, and a fear of continuing political and economic dependency are consequently three of the forces that give the Developing World a tenuous sense of self-identity. Not surprisingly, the South seeks to rectify the political-economic exploitation of its colonial past and to overturn what it perceives as an international economic system biased against newly independent or poor states. Similarly, during the Cold War, many Developing World states actively pursued a foreign policy of nonalignment, refusing to become closely associated with either the Eastern or Western blocs. However, with the demise of Soviet and Eastern European communism, it was no longer clear what nonalignment meant. As a result, the nonaligned movement became a less important factor in international affairs.

Even so, political-economic independence, political-military nonalignment, and economic-social advancement remain primary objectives of most Developing World states today. The continued fixation of most Developing World states on these objectives continues to provide a sense of solidarity, of almost a "Developing World nationalism," to many Developing World states.[2] Therefore, it remains important to understand how and why the Developing World evolved as it did.

 ## THE EVOLUTION OF THE DEVELOPING WORLD

As we have seen, Western European colonial empires began to disintegrate following World War II. This disintegration was an uneven process, proceeding as a general rule most rapidly in those colonial empires that had been the most liberal, and most slowly in those that had been the most restrictive. It was no accident that the Portuguese Empire, which had been arguably the most restrictive, was not liquidated until 1975 when Angola and Mozambique finally received their independence.[3]

The European powers also bequeathed different levels of modernization to their colonial empires. In former British colonies, for example, the transition from colony to sovereign state was often eased by the gradual absorption of more and more indigenous people into the colonial administration. In many colonies, rather extensive school systems were also established. India served as a primary example for both policies. The French, meanwhile, maintained a tighter rein on their colonial holdings. By 1930, for example, there were as many French colonial officials in Vietnam as British officials in India, even though Vietnam's population was only one-twelfth of India's. By 1940, Vietnam had only 14 secondary schools, whereas India had several hundred.[4] Although French colonial policy in Vietnam and elsewhere changed following the French defeat at the battle of Dienbienphu in 1954, historically induced differences persisted.

The lesser Western colonial powers—Belgium, the Netherlands, Portugal, and Spain—did even less than Great Britain and France to prepare their colonies for independence. Although all colonial regimes were exploitive, the lesser colonial powers were generally the most extreme. The Dutch government ran the East Indies as an enormous sugar plantation, blatantly exploiting land, labor, and capital there for the improvement of the Dutch economy. Belgium exploited the Congo's mineral resources. The Belgians went further than most powers in guaranteeing minimum wages, housing, and medical care to their colonial peoples, but they permitted little political development or education. When the Congo received its independence in 1960, there were fewer than a dozen university graduates in the country, and the new Congolese leader, Patrice Lumumba, had held no responsibility greater than postmaster. Portugal, meanwhile, fought until the mid-1970s to maintain its grip on its colonial empire. Only then did Portugal grant independence to Guinea-Bissau (formerly Portuguese Guinea), Angola, and Mozambique.

The European colonial record is not a proud one, at least in light of most late-twentieth-century values and attitudes. It is understandable why resentment lingers in the minds and hearts of many former colonial peoples against their former masters. Often, because of the United States' close political, economic, and social identity with Western Europe; because of its leadership role in the Western world; and because of its wealth and global power, Developing World countries identify the United States as a colonial exploiter as well. Inevitably, then, as the second proliferation of states brought more and more sovereign states into being, Developing World resentment of and hostility toward the West became a major force on the international political scene.

On occasion, less developed countries met among themselves to discuss their problems. The first major gathering of Developing World states was the **Bandung Conference,** held in Bandung, Indonesia, in 1955. Twenty-nine Asian and African states met to condemn colonialism as "an evil which should speedily be brought to an end."[5] Since Bandung, other conferences of Developing World states have taken place, most notably the series of conferences of nonaligned nations. More often than not, however, Developing World states have turned to the United Nations and other regional IGOs they have created to make their voices heard. Indeed, if one examines both the composition of the United Nations and the quantitative growth in IGOs, it is clear that Developing World states have become, as a group, an increasingly prominent force in international affairs despite their continuing economic poverty.[6]

In the United Nations, the Developing World has been particularly effective in using the General Assembly to attract attention to issues of colonialism and imperialism and in mobilizing the UN's specialized agencies to address its needs. One of the major reasons Developing World states have had these successes is because of their numbers. A formal coalition of Developing World states known as the **Group of 77** wields a sizable influence in UN affairs. Although the Group of 77 by 2000 numbered 129 states, it still retained its original name.

The Group of 77's quantitative growth at the United Nations is important because it can now pass any action that it chooses in the General Assembly if it can maintain its cohesiveness. Not surprisingly, then, the United Nations became as much a forum for North–South conflict as a forum for East–West confrontation during the 1970s and 1980s. During the 1990s and today, it remains a center of North–South disagreement, but the tone of disagreement became less confrontational as more and more Developing World states adopted free market and privatized economic systems similar to those in developed states.

The Developing World had also used the United Nations to push for international conferences to address specific issues of concern such as the environment, population, food, the law of the sea, disarmament, women, industrialization, desertification, technology transfer, rural development, and the role of science and technology in development. These conferences have rarely led to concrete actions.

Developing World states have also created their own regional IGOs to approach the problems that beset them. The Organization of African Unity, the Association of Southeast Asian Nations, the Arab League, the Caribbean Common Market, the Latin American Integration Association, and the Economic Community of West African States are just a few of the many Developing World IGOs. Their records of achievement are mixed.

Nevertheless, a sense of community has developed among many of the states of the South, a community brought about by shared history, objectives, and injustice. For states as disparate as those that make up the Developing World, this is a notable achievement. All seek a future of change.

THE OBJECTIVES OF THE DEVELOPING WORLD

Historically, states of the South have generally shared three objectives: political-economic independence, political-military nonalignment, and economic-social development and modernization.[7] These objectives were products of the historical experiences of most developing states; the political, economic, and social conditions that prevailed within most developing states; and the bipolar international system that existed during the last half of the twentieth century when most developing states gained independence.

As post-independence historical experiences were acquired, as internal conditions changed, and as the bipolar international system disappeared, many states of the South changed the relative emphasis they placed on these three objectives. Thus, as economic interdependence became more and more a global reality in the late twentieth and early twenty-first century, political-economic independence declined in importance in the eyes of many Developing World governments. Similarly, after the Cold War ended, political-military alignment became a less important objective of most Third World states. By the beginning of the twenty-first century, economic-social development and modernization, always an important priority in most Third World states, had become the dominant priority.

Even so, political-economic independence and political-military nonalignment remain important objectives of many developing states. Thus, despite the preeminence of economic-social development and modernization as an objective of Developing World states, only an understanding of all three objectives can provide a true appreciation of the scope and depth of the North–South conflict.

Political-Economic Independence

After obtaining formal independence, many Developing World states discovered to their chagrin that they remained economically and politically dependent on their former colonial masters. Trade ties established during decades of colonial rule were rarely terminated by the attainment of political sovereignty. From the viewpoint of Developing World countries, this economic dependence carried with it unavoidable political subservience. Thus, even though a Developing World state may have sought to establish its own political-economic independence, it could not.

Such a relationship between former colonial metropoles and their former colonies is termed **neocolonialism.** Although interpretations of neocolonialism differ on a case-by-case and region-by-region basis, a unifying thrust of the South is to escape this neocolonial relationship.

In part, the Developing World's desire to escape political-economic dependency explains its hostility toward both the West and Western institutions such as the World Bank and multinational corporations. Developing states often resent the World Bank's insistence that they provide full disclosure of financial data. Having had numerous occasions to witness the linkage between economic strength and political power, governments of the less developed states often were skeptical of the claims by Western states and MNCs that no political concessions would be sought if investment opportunities were awarded.

The South, then, was on the horns of a dilemma as it sought to achieve political-economic independence. Full political and economic independence could be achieved only if Developing World states could strengthen their economic autonomy. In most cases, however, that required increased reliance on external sources of finance and expertise. To many Developing World countries, such external economic reliance implied continued political dependence. On the basis of the historical record, this was a view with at least as much fact as fiction.

Developing World states pointed particularly to their ongoing debt problem as proof of their continuing neocolonial status. Table 8-3 shows both the total international debt of selected Developing World countries and the size of that debt as a percentage of their gross national products. Obviously, when foreign debts make up sizable percentages of gross

TABLE 8-3   International Debt of Selected Developing World States, in Billions of Dollars and as a Percentage of Gross National Product

Country	Debt in Billions of Dollars			Debt as Percentage of GNP		
	1980	**1990**	**1997**	**1980**	**1990**	**1997**
Argentina	27.2	62.2	123.2	35.29	44.06	37.91
Bolivia	2.7	4.3	5.2	98.27	87.84	65.78
Brazil	71.5	119.9	193.7	30.45	25.78	23.61
Egypt	19.1	32.9	29.8	83.49	76.39	39.48
Ethiopia	0.8	8.6	10.1		126.20	157.94
India	20.6	83.7	94.4	11.04	25.94	24.74
Madagascar	1.3	3.7	4.1	30.93	120.12	115.77
Mexico	57.4	104.4	149.7	25.67	39.71	37.15
Nicaragua	2.2	10.7	5.7	102.13	1060.89	..
Nigeria	8.9	33.4	28.5	13.90		
Philippines	17.4	30.6	45.4	53.59	117.45	55.30
Tanzania	5.3	6.4	7.2	..	152.77	101.58
Thailand	8.3	28.2	93.4	25.64	33.00	60.70

Source: The World Bank, *World Development Report* 1999/2000, pp. 270–71.

national products, prospects for repayment are not good. From the perspective of First World lenders, some bad lending decisions had been made. From the perspective of Developing World governments, economic indebtedness and accompanying high interest rates were new ways that the First World had found to continue to plunder what little wealth the Developing World had.

Nevertheless, by the 1990s, most Developing World states concluded that they had no choice other than to seek external investment from MNCs and other private and public sources. This trend accelerated in the early twenty-first century as more and more developing states accommodated themselves to the realities of international economic interdependence as they sought foreign capital, welcomed foreign investment, and adopted domestic economic policies that encouraged connections to the world economy. Political-economic independence remained an objective, but economic growth had become the primary concern of many Developing World states.[8]

Political-Military Nonalignment

Even with the end of the East–West conflict, some Developing World states consider it important to be politically and militarily nonaligned. This objective flows from one of the same motivations as the Developing World's desire to achieve political-economic independence: having achieved political sovereignty, Developing World states do not want to be subjected to another form of external control.

The **nonaligned movement** dates to the 1955 Bandung Conference. Although the role of the nonaligned movement has diminished in world affairs since the end of the Cold War, for years the movement was a major actor in the international community.[9]

The nonaligned movement is a grouping of diverse states, just as is the Developing World. Some nonaligned states, such as Venezuela, Peru, and Bolivia, are tied to the United States through the Organization of American States; other nonaligned states, such as the Philippines and Thailand, have had formal defense alliances with the United States. On the other hand, Ethiopia, Angola, Afghanistan, Yemen, and Mozambique were tied to the USSR through "Treaties of Friendship and Cooperation." In the case of Cuba, formal agreements in the past were superseded by Cuban willingness to undertake policy actions supported, sponsored, and supplied by the USSR.

Throughout the 1980s, the nonaligned movement was pulled and tugged by its internal divisions between pro-Soviet radical states, pro-Western conservative states, and legitimately nonaligned states. The first two groups sided with the blocs with which they were more closely identified, and the third group voted its mind at the UN and in other international forums on issues as diverse as the Soviet invasion of Afghanistan, the U.S. invasion of Grenada, and the international debt crisis.

As East–West tensions eased, maintaining a nonaligned status became less problematic for most Developing World states. And with the collapse of the Soviet Union in 1991, the traditional concept of nonalignment in many respects became moot. Indeed, Argentina and one or two other states even left the nonaligned movement, observing that with the collapse of the Soviet Union, nonalignment had lost its meaning.

Other Developing World states saw things differently. Despite the growing recognition in many Developing World states that they needed investment and other sources of capital from the West, they still were concerned that they might become subservient to Western interests and objectives.

Economic-Social Development and Modernization

Above all else, Developing World countries see their plight of poverty and dependence as the result of past colonial exploitation and current economic inequities in international trade, pricing, and exchange mechanisms. As a result, the South for many years called for both expanded aid from the North and a restructuring of the existing international economic order. In short, the South desired a **New International Economic Order (NIEO).**

The NIEO's roots can be traced to the first United Nations Conference on Trade and Development (UNCTAD), held in Geneva in 1964. At UNCTAD I, developing states formed the Group of 77, named after the number of developing states that attended the meeting, to articulate their objections to existing trade, development, and aid practices.

The Group of 77 eventually used its numerical advantage in the UN General Assembly to pass a resolution entitled "Declaration on the Establishment of a New Economic Order." Although the NIEO today has almost disappeared from the international agenda as an agenda for discussion, its six points reflect the complaints that Developing States have about the international economic system even today. The NIEO's six points were: 1. developed states should increase economic aid to developing states to at least 0.7 percent of their GNP; 2. developed states should reduce tariffs and increase quotas on products made in the Developing World; 3. developing states should have a larger role in decisions made by international financial organizations like the World Bank and the International Monetary Fund; 4. international economic organizations should be less intrusive in their demands for financial information; 5. more credit should be made available to developing states; and 6. technical and financial assistance from the North to the South should be redirected toward infrastructure projects.

The NIEO disappeared from the international agenda for several reasons. First, most developed states considered its demands economically and politically excessive. For example, as Table 8-4 shows, if the United States in 1997 were required to provide 0.7 percent of its GNP as foreign aid, it would have had to increase its foreign aid from 6.9 billion dollars to 53.7 billion dollars. From the U.S. perspective, this was economically and politically ridiculous.

Second, a large number of developing states—especially in East Asia, but also in Latin America and Africa—over the year improved their economies in the absence of the NIEO. This significantly reduced political pressure for continued discussions of the NIEO.

Third, analysts increasingly adopted the view that many Third World states needed to institute domestic political, economic, and social reforms before more aid and a changed international economic system would help them. This too reduced support for the NIEO.

Finally, the hard reality was that developing states had little leverage on developed states to institute or even to discuss an NIEO. Gradually, the NIEO faded from the international agenda.

TABLE 8-4 1997 Foreign Aid from Northern States and the Impact That NIEO Proposals Would Have on Foreign Aid Totals

Country	1997 Aid in Billion $US	1997 Aid as % of GNP	Billion $US Proposed Aid, 1997, at NIEO 0.7% GNP Level	Billion $US increase in 1997 Aid If 0.7% Adopted
Australia	1.1	0.28	2.8	1.7
Austria	0.5	0.26	1.3	0.8
Belgium	0.8	0.31	1.8	1.0
Canada	2	0.34	4.1	2.1
Denmark	1.6	0.97	Above 0.7%	—
Finland	0.4	0.33	0.8	0.4
France	6.3	0.45	9.8	3.5
Germany	5.9	0.28	14.8	8.9
Ireland	0.2	0.31	0.5	0.3
Italy	1.3	0.11	8.3	7.0
Japan	9.4	0.22	29.9	20.5
Netherlands	2.9	0.81	Above 0.7%	—
New Zealand	0.2	0.26	0.5	0.3
Norway	1.3	0.86	Above 0.7%	—
Sweden	1.7	0.25	4.8	3.1
Switzerland	0.9	0.34	1.9	1.0
United Kingdom	3.4	0.26	9.2	5.8
United States	6.9	0.09	53.7	46.8

But this did not mean that the North–South conflict was over. Rather, the debate over economic-social development and modernization continued, although in somewhat altered form. Thus, we now turn to that debate, for it remains a major part of the North–South conflict.

THE DEBATE OVER DEVELOPMENT AND MODERNIZATION

Virtually all scholars, analysts, and policy makers agree that economic development and modernization is difficult. They also agree that in the twenty-first century, most developing states require more capital than they currently have before economic growth and modernization can accelerate. They also agree that there are only **five ways to attain capital needed for development and modernization:** create it themselves, borrow it from public or private international financial institutions, attract private investment, develop hard currency sources by exporting domestically made products, and receive foreign aid.

Beyond this, there is little agreement on why the Developing World is underdeveloped or what should be done to remedy the situation. Some people argue that for development to occur, a technical infrastructure such as roads, harbors, and communications is a necessary first step. Others, for example, those attending the 1995 UN Copenhagen Conference on Social Development, stress the necessity of first emphasizing social issues such as education and women's rights. Some assert that external investment is required, and others say that external investment brings external control and exploitation and that economic development can best proceed with all development needs including capital accumulation being supplied locally. Marxist-Leninists advocate centralized control to bring about the elimination of the exploitation of human by human as a necessary corequisite to economic development. No one has the complete answer, and as a result, debate over economic development and modernization continues to run rampant.

Theories of Economic Development and Modernization

Over the years, several distinct schools of though emerged out of the debate over economic development and modernization. Here we will examine two of them, modernization theory and dependency theory. Both are widely accepted, modernization theory for the most part in developed states and dependency theory in developing states, but each theory has many advocates in both the Developed and Developing World. The views espoused by each theory, however, are considerably different.

Modernization Theory.   **Modernization theory** has as its basic premise the belief that economic development and modernization require the rejection of traditional patterns of behavior, value, and organization and the acceptance of new patterns of behavior, value, and organization more conducive to economic development.[10] For the most part, modernization theorists argue that those patterns of behavior, value, and organization that are required for economic development to occur are those that have emerged in countries that are economically developed—that is, the countries of Western Europe, the United States, Canada, Japan, and a few others.

Modernization theorists do not agree on the requirements for modernization. However, more often than not, they point to the need for an educated population; widespread acceptance of science, technology, and the scientific method throughout society; increased secularization and the decline of religious tradition; urbanization; division of labor in the productive sectors of society; rule by law rather than edict; the development of a system of social and economic rewards based on merit rather than station of birth or place in society; greater social mobility between and among people and classes; and a tolerance for diversity, innovation, and change as critical elements needed for economic development to take place and prosper. Not coincidentally, these are the same traits that are often viewed as required for the development of the capitalist market economies that are prevalent in Europe, North America, Japan, and a few other countries as well.

Similarly, modernization theorists do not agree on what characteristics must be eliminated from traditional societies for modernization to take place and prosper. Nevertheless, there is widespread agreement among proponents of modernization that for economic development to occur and prosper, the percentage of the population engaged in agriculture and living in rural areas must decline; feudalist social and economic organization of society must be replaced; the dominance of restrictive religious authority must be reduced;

arbitrary political decision making must be eliminated; and political, economic, and social decision making must become less centralized.

Modernization theorists proceed from the argument that because these or similar changes are what preceded or accompanied economic development in countries that are today economically developed, these same changes logically must precede or accompany economic development in countries that are today underdeveloped economically. For modernization theorists, there are many paths toward economic development, but all are paved by the abandonment of traditional ways of doing things and the acceptance of modern—that is, Western—ways of doing things.

Modernization theory has been challenged from several perspectives. Some critics point out that there may be other ways for economic development to occur that simply have not yet been tried. Others maintain that modernization theorists have an ethnocentric perspective and are too ready to dismiss and reject valuable dimensions of traditional societies. Still others argue that modernization theorists misunderstand economic development completely. Many who make this argument adhere to the dependency theory of economic development and modernization.

Dependency Theory.[11]   To those who accept **dependency theory,** modernization theorists miss two key points. First, dependency theorists point out that the twenty-first century world bears no resemblance to the world in which economic development began and proceeded in its early phases in Europe. North America, and Japan.[12] They observe that industrialization began in these locations in the absence of external competition, whereas in today's world, countries that are attempting to industrialize and develop economically face immense external competition. To dependency theorists, this competition prevents economic growth in the Developing World. What is more, they argue, the differences between the international conditions under which European, North American, and Japanese economic development proceeded and those of today are so great that the developmental experiences of the past are irrelevant to the world of today.

Second, and equally important, many dependency theorists argue that the First World's economic development was underwritten by the inexpensive raw material and labor of the Developing World.[13] Put simply, Europe and the capitalist system that developed there exploited less developed parts of the world. More extreme proponents of dependency theory even argue that industrialization in Europe and elsewhere could not have taken place without this exploitation. All dependency theorists agree that the present-day international economic system remains heavily stacked in favor of the industrialized West and that the industrialized West owes an immense debt to the Developing World for its own economic development that it is not repaying.

Dependency theorists identify many mechanisms through which industrialized states continue to take advantage of poor states. According to dependency theorists, these mechanisms include allegedly unfair foreign currency exchange rates that keep the prices of resources low and manufactured products high; the international banking and financial system, which provides loans to developing states at allegedly high and unfair rates; and multinational corporations, which allegedly repatriate profits and drive local companies out of business.

Dependency theorists also often argue that exploitation has occurred and is occurring on two levels. The first is within individual businesses, where owners exploit and profit from the labor of their workers. In many respects, this level of analysis is similar and in some cases identical to Marxist interpretations. The second level of exploitation is then between states that are economically developed and those that are not. Many dependency theorists express this relationship between economically developed states and underdeveloped states as a relationship between "the core" of economically developed states and "the periphery" of those states that are poor and dependent.

Like modernization theory, dependency theory has its critics. Some critics of dependency theory maintain that it overemphasizes the role that the international system plays in constraining development and underemphasizes the impact that policies implemented in Developing World states have on economic development. Other critics observe that dependency theory fails to explain why some states such as South Korea, Thailand, Malaysia, Singapore, and others are enjoying rapid economic growth while others are not. Clearly, then, neither modernization theory nor dependency theory provides answers to all aspects of the question, "Why and how does economic development happen?" Both provide insights to the economic development process, but both also have shortcomings.

Despite these shortcomings, it is encouraging that scholars and analysts are continuing to try to develop new ways to understand economic development more thoroughly. For example, some have begun to ask why different countries facing similar situations have chosen different developmental strategies and to explore on a comparative basis what can be learned from the experiences of these countries with their different strategies. Others are investigating the role that international trade plays in economic development. There is still much to be learned about how and why economic development takes place and how and why it does not.[14]

Policy Realities of Economic Development and Modernization

Beyond the realm of theoretical debate over economic development, numerous everyday policy disagreements about economic development have existed and continue to exist. For example, developed states that provided funds for foreign aid and assistance often disagreed over whether they should provide their assistance unilaterally or multilaterally through international organizations. The first option had the advantage, from the donor state's perspective, of allowing it to maintain some control over the direction of that aid and assistance; conversely, it had the disadvantage of appearing neocolonialistic. Multilateral aid through IGOs, on the other hand, rendered the impression of a donor state interested primarily in economic development rather than political aggrandizement.

Tied aid and assistance also became an issue of some importance. In its simplest form, tied aid and assistance referred to a donor state's requirement that aid and assistance be used only in conjunction with donor state products, equipment, and so on. To donor states, this appeared a logical policy. If aid and assistance were extended, why should a requirement not exist that it be expended in the donor country? To Developing World states, this smacked of neocolonialism.

Other developmental issues abounded. Some issues involved governments and private companies. For example, the United States was particularly concerned about formulating a policy on aid and assistance for states and nationalized U.S.-owned private property; the Hickenlooper amendment prevented the extension of aid and assistance to states that nationalized property owned by Americans. Other issues were state-related. European states, France and Great Britain in particular, targeted most of their aid to countries in their respective commonwealths. Some analysts argued that all developmental aid and assistance should be sent to those states that had the best chance for development. Other states were to be "written off," at least for the time being. A sort of economic triage would occur, with the states least capable of economic development fending for themselves until additional aid and assistance became available.

The private sector was also involved in development policy. This involvement often took one of two forms. The first was investment. Investment presented the private sector, particularly MNCs, with possibilities for profitable return, but risks were high. Nationalization and political or economic turmoil presented constant risks, and host states often viewed external investors as exploiters and colonialists (not always incorrectly). Credit was a second major form of involvement. Private banks and some Western state-owned banks extended massive credit to Developing World states. In 2000, Western banks had over $1 trillion in outstanding loans to Developing World countries.[15]

Inevitably, problems developed as Developing World states found it difficult to repay loans. Brazil, Mexico, and the Philippines were three of the many Developing World states that faced **defaulting** on foreign loans during the 1980s and even on into the 1990s. Even though the IMF and World Bank had strict performance and reporting criteria for those states to which they extended loans, default potential remained in several states.

Implications of defaulting on foreign loans are sizable. Countries near default find it difficult to import needed goods because they can rarely pay for those goods; if a country defaulted, it might find it impossible to import what it needs. Investors as well as lenders are leery of states that are near default; an actual default would make it almost impossible to attract external investment. One of the major impacts of defaulting, then, is that external sources of money would disappear. This in turn would retard economic development even more in the state that defaulted.

Defaults would also affect lending nations. One can only imagine the turmoil that would occur in Western financial markets if Developing World states defaulted on a sizable percentage of the loans outstanding to them. Probably because of this, Fidel Castro in 1986 urged Latin American leaders to default on their loans. None did, although the thought must have appeared temporarily attractive to some. Rather, during the late 1980s and early 1990s, several Latin American states suspended payment on their debts.

In a technical sense, this was not default. Indeed, if a default occurred, both lender and borrower would lose; lenders would lose their money, and borrowers would lose their ability to borrow. Thus, both borrowers and lenders in the international arena have sought ways to reschedule debts, to initiate payment moratoriums, and to employ other tactics to avoid default. These methods have successfully averted disaster, but the debt problem remains. **Politics and ideology** also enter into development decisions, both in donor and recipient states. For example, during the 1950s, U.S. Secretary of State John Foster Dulles refused to send U.S. aid to any country that would not join a U.S. alliance. His reasoning was that only those states willing to declare themselves U.S. allies should receive the benefits of U.S. largesse.

Although U.S. policy on aid and assistance has since changed several times, politics and ideology still play a role. For example, Ronald Reagan complained that the World Bank was extending too many loans to public sector projects in Developing World countries and that the United States would consider reducing its commitment to the World

(a)

In much of the world, agriculture has not been mechanized. (a) Planting, care, and harvesting often remain a by-hand activity. (b) In other cases, animals help work the field.

(b)

Bank if it did not expand its private sector loans. The former USSR also interjected politics into its aid and assistance policies by arguing that capitalists caused Third World underdevelopment and capitalist countries should therefore remedy it.

Developing World states also include politics and ideology in their development decisions. For example, the **corporatist strategy** of economic development held sway for much of the 1960s, 1970s, and 1980s in Latin America and elsewhere as well. Based on the dependency theory of economic development, corporatism argued that development proceeded best with a state-centered capitalist economy. It asserted that development could best be achieved if states pursued industrialization, central planning, import substitution, creation of state-owned enterprises, and protection of infant industries. In addition, more often than not, corporatism also meant that only a few members of a country's elite ran the economy, government, and society; in many respects, corporatism became a cover for authoritarianism.

The corporatist strategy had an immense impact in Latin America. Brazil stood out with its "economic miracle" of 1968 to 1973, even though the miracle took place under a repressive military regime. But in the 1970s and early 1980s, corporatism began to falter as OPEC increased oil prices, corporatist states raised more barriers to trade and external investment, state-owned corporations became bloated and less competitive, government regulation increased, the U.S. economy faltered slowing U.S. imports, and foreign debt grew. By the middle 1980s, many corporatist states recognized that their economies were in trouble.

Country after country in Latin America then began to abandon corporatism and institute economic reform. Reforms varied from country to country and included privatizing state-owned industries and opening economies to imports and foreign direct investment. Political democratization often led the way. But there were also liabilities as privatized businesses reduced labor costs by firing people and governments introduced economic austerity measures demanded by international lending institutions. Nevertheless, it was clear that politics and ideology plays a major role in economic development.

Another factor that slowed economic development is inadequate funding. Levels of economic aid to Developing World states have never been near the level of need. In 1999, for example, the total amount of economic aid provided to developing states by developed states was somewhere between $40 and $50 billion, far below the needs of developing states.

As distressingly, as the world's environmental situation has deteriorated, it has become increasingly clear that economic development is not necessarily a friend of the environment. This is not to say that economic development is necessarily an enemy of the environment. But it is exceedingly evident that future economic development undertakings will have to take their impact on the environment into account much more than earlier economic development efforts did.[16]

Indeed, concerns have risen so much about the extent to which economic development is ravaging the environment in Developing World states—both because of Developing World efforts and the industrialized West's demand for resources—that a new school of developmental though emerged. Called **sustainable development,** this school of thought argues that economic development must "meet the needs and aspirations of the present without compromising the ability of future generations to meet their own needs."[17] Advocates of sustainable development argue that economic development can proceed, indeed must proceed, but that it must be carefully planned and thought out so that the environment is not further degraded and so that future generations will also be able to provide for their needs.[18]

First coined as a term at the 1972 UN Stockholm Conference on the Human Environment, sustainable development is fundamentally optimistic, asserting that economic development in fact can occur without damaging the environment or compromising the ability of future generations to enjoy a high quality of life and meet their needs. As a concept, it has been widely adopted. For example, the 1994 UN Cairo Conference on Population and Development and the 1995 UN Copenhagen Conference on Social Development both called on the countries of the world to pursue sustainable development. Without exception, proponents of sustainable development agree that governments and other international actors must adopt long-range, environmentally sensitive development policies. All agree that with such policies, the world will be much better off in the twenty-first century than it would be in the absence of such policies.

The problem, of course, is to define such policies, to reach agreement on them, to convince international actors to follow them, and to develop sufficient capital to pay for them. Even then, ways must be found to assure compliance with sustainable development's precepts. As a concept, sustainable development makes sense. As a set of policies, there is still a long road to travel before sustainable development is implemented.

Regardless of the future of sustainable development, it is clear that many issues separate the North and the South concerning economic development and modernization. In addition, even though the North–South conflict in the twenty-first century has become less contentious, it still presents real dangers.

DANGERS OF THE NORTH–SOUTH CONFLICT[19]

Before we discuss those dangers, one additional fact must be identified: The gap between rich and poor states when measured either by gross national product or per capita income is in many cases still widening, or in other cases, closing so slowly that it will take over one hundred years to eliminate the gap. Only in a very few Developing World states is the gap closing rapidly enough that it will be eliminated in the next twenty years. Thus, the North–South gap will inevitably continue, and in many cases grow, if present policies and current growth rates hold.

Often, how well people live can not be accurately reflected by measuring gross national product (GNP) or GNP per capita. This is because often, just as wealth is distributed unequally between states, wealth is distributed unequally within countries. This is particularly true in many developing countries. Table 8-5 illustrates this point by listing the percentage of national income received by the wealthiest 10 percent of society and the percentage of national income received by the poorest 20 percent of society. A note of caution—this is neither a listing of all countries nor are data compared from the same year.

However, in most cases, the wealthiest 10 percent of the population in developed states generally have a lower percentage of a country's wealth than in most developing states. Just

TABLE 8-5 Wealth Distribution Within States

Country	Years Data Compiled	% National Income to Richest 10%	%National Income to Poorest 20%
Brazil	1995	47.9	2.5
Colombia	1995	46.9	3.1
Zimbabwe	1990	46.9	4.0
Guatemala	1989	46.6	2.1
Paraquay	1995	46.6	2.3
Chile	1994	46.1	3.5
South Africa	1993–94	45.9	2.9
Panama	1995	43.8	2.3
Sierra Leone	1989	43.6	1.1
Lesotho	1986–87	43.3	2.8
Mexico	1995	42.8	3.6
Guinea-Bissau	1991	42.4	2.1
Senegal	1991	42.3	3.1
Honduras	1996	42.1	3.4
Papua New Guinea	1996	40.5	4.5
Mali	1994	40.4	4.6
Nicaragua	1993	39.8	4.2
Dominican Republic	1989	39.6	4.2
Zambia	1996	39.2	4.2
El Salvador	1995	38.3	3.7
Malaysia	1989	37.9	4.6
Ecuador	1994	37.6	5.4
Gambia, The	1992	37.6	4.4
Russian Federation	1996	37.4	4.2
Thailand	1992	37.1	5.6
Ukraine	1995	36.8	4.3
Madagascar	1993	36.7	5.1
Venezuela	1995	35.6	4.3
Niger	1995	35.4	2.6
Peru	1996	35.4	4.4
Kenya	1994	34.9	5.0
Costa Rica	1996	34.7	4.0
Jordon	1991	34.7	5.9
Ethiopia	1995	33.7	7.1
Philippines	1994	33.5	5.9
Guinea	1994	32.0	6.4
Guyana	1993	32.0	6.3
Jamaica	1991	31.9	5.8
Bolivia	1990	31.7	5.6
Nigeria	1992–93	31.4	4.0
Uganda	1992–93	31.2	6.6
China	1995	30.9	5.5
Yemen, Rep.	1992	30.8	6.1

(Continued)

TABLE 8-5 Wealth Distribution Within States *Continued*

Country	Years Data Compiled	% National Income to Richest 10%	%National Income to Poorest 20%
Tunsina	1990	30.7	5.9
Morocco	1990–91	30.5	6.6
Indonesia	1996	30.3	8.0
Tanzania	1993	30.1	6.8
Mauritania	1995	29.9	6.2
Nepal	1995–96	29.8	7.6
Vietnam	1993	29.0	7.8
Switzerland	1982	28.6	7.4
Cote d'Ivoire	1988	28.5	6.8
United States	1994	28.5	4.8
Lithuania	1993	28.0	8.1
Pakistan	1996	27.7	9.4
Ireland	1987	27.4	6.7
Israel	1992	26.9	6.9
Turmenistan	1993	26.9	6.7
Algeria	1995	26.8	7.0
Egypt, Arab Rep.	1991	26.7	8.7
Lao PDR	1992	26.4	9.6
Estonia	1995	26.2	6.2
Kyrgyz Republic	1993	26.2	6.7
Ghana	1997	26.1	8.4
Moldova	1992	25.8	6.9
Spain	1990	25.2	7.5
Sri Lanka	1990	25.2	8.9
India	1994	25.0	9.2
France	1989	24.9	7.2
Kazakhstan	1993	24.9	7.5
Australia	1989	24.8	7.0
Bulgaria	1992	24.7	8.3
Netherlands	1991	24.7	8.0
United Kingdom	1986	24.7	7.1
Mongolia	1995	24.5	7.3
Slovenia	1993	24.5	9.3
Rwanda	1983–85	24.2	9.7
Hungary	1993	24.0	9.7
Canada	1994	23.8	7.5
Bangladesh	1992	23.7	9.4
Italy	1991	23.7	7.6
Czech Republic	1993	23.5	10.5
Romania	1994	22.7	8.9
Belarus	1995	22.6	8.5
Germany	1989	22.6	9.0
Latvia	1995	22.4	8.3
Luxembourg	1991	22.3	9.5

(Continued)

TABLE 8-5   Wealth Distribution Within States   *Continued*

Country	Years Data Compiled	% National Income to Richest 10%	%National Income to Poorest 20%
Poland	1992	22.1	9.3
Finland	1991	21.6	10.0
Norway	1991	21.2	10.0
Denmark	1992	20.5	9.6
Belgium	1992	20.2	9.5
Sweden	1992	20.1	9.6
Austria	1987	19.3	10.4
Slovak Republic	1992	18.2	11.9

Source: The World Development Report, 1999/2000.

as important, in most developing states, the poorest 20 percent of the population generally have a much lower percentage of a country's wealth than do the poorest 20 percent of the population in most developed states. Latin American states seem to offer the poorest people the least income. Of the 30 states whose poorest 20 percent of the population have less than 5 percent of the country's wealth, 14 are in Latin America. Notably, the United States also falls into this category.

What dangers exist because of the large differences in the distribution of wealth between North and South? One danger is that North and South may become more deeply entwined in the rhetoric of confrontation and hostility. Do the economically wealthy countries have a duty and responsibility to help less fortunate states improve themselves economically? Developing World states unequivocally answer yes, whereas wealthy states respond hesitatingly and uncertainly on both sides of the question. Even in those instances where the North extends aid, disagreement exists over what development strategy to use. The danger of allowing the North–South dialogue to move toward confrontation and hostility is that constructive action may end, thereby allowing the South to slip even more deeply into the abyss of poverty and influencing the South to take action with whatever tools it has at its disposal against the North.

Despite its poverty, the South is not without tools. Many of the resources that the industrial North requires are available primarily in the South. Realizing this, the South could turn to a strategy of resource deprivation and price increases in raw materials. So far only OPEC states have employed this strategy successfully, but their impact on the industrialized world has been immense. Although other raw material cartels would not have the same advantages that OPEC enjoyed, cartelization could appear as a useful strategy to Developing World governments. Even though the 1986 near collapse of OPEC raised questions about the effectiveness of cartels as tools that developing states could use to bring pressure on developed states, OPEC's 2000 reduction in oil output and the ensuing increase in oil prices underlined that cartels under certain conditions are effective.

Developing World governments, however, need not be the only representatives of the Developing World to act because of frustration over the distribution of global wealth. Nonstate actors such as terrorist groups or transnational ideological or religious movements may conclude that resorting to violence or terror is the key to goading the North to action or to overturning an unfair international economic system. Given the weaponry available on the international arms market and given the integrated nature of modern industrial society, a small group could terrorize a much larger organization or society. With little to lose under current conditions, resorting to violence or terror may become a preferred option for some nongovernmental actors and perhaps even for some governments. Indeed, in 1990, Iraq's leader, Saddam Hussein, argued that one of the justifications for Iraq's invasion of Kuwait was that it was not proper for Kuwait's people to be rich while many other Arabs were poor.

A more subtle effect of the continued disparity in wealth between North and South is the psychological impact that the effects of that gap may have on the collective psyche of the North, particularly in situations where starvation occurs. Whereas proponents of the "lifeboat theory" of international relations urge that the North provide only for itself,[20] others have concluded that the industrialized societies are gradually eroding their own humanity by neglecting the needs of the Developing World.

Perceived potential threats, then, are diverse: resource deprivation and price wars through cartelization, violence and terror against Northern societies and interests, and the gradual erosion of the North's humanity are three scenarios that may eventuate unless the North–South conflict is ameliorated.

 KEY TERMS AND CONCEPTS

North-South conflict   the disagreements, mostly economic, between the world's wealthy countries, most in the northern hemisphere, and the world's poorer countries, most in the southern hemisphere

the North   the world's wealthy countries, most in the northern hemisphere

the South   the world's poorer countries, most in the southern hemisphere

Third World   another term used to describe the poorer countries of the world, derived from the fact that most poorer countries obtained independence after capitalist state (the First World) and communist states (the Second World)

Developing World   yet another term used to describe the poorer countries of the world, derived from the fact that they are trying to develop economically

Less Developed Countries (LDCs)   still another term used to describe the poorer countries of the world

Fourth World   poorer states in the Developing World that have only a limited chance to develop economically

Fifth World   the poorest states in the Developing World that have almost no chance to develop economically

evolution of the Developing World   most developing states were colonies of European powers before World War II, but gradually obtained independence during the 1950s, 1960s, and 1970s, choosing different paths of political, economic, and social development

Bandung Conference   the first major gathering of Developing World states, held in Bandung, Indonesia in 1955

Group of 77   a coalition of Developing World states that has considerable influence at the United Nations and which by 2000 numbered 129 states

political-economic independence   most Developing World states seek to become politically and economically independent from their former colonial masters;   one of the three major objectives of most Developing World states

neocolonialism   the continuing political-economic dependence of some Developing World states on their former colonial masters even after they obtain independence

political-military nonalignment during the Cold War, many Developing World states tried to avoid becoming aligned politically or militarily with the United States or the Soviet Union; this political-military nonalignment was one of the three major objectives of many Developing World states and remains an objective of some today

nonaligned movement a movement begun by developing states at the 1955 Bandung Conference, many of whose members sought to stay politically and militarily nonaligned in the East-West conflict

economic-social development and modernization since most developing states are economically and socially underdeveloped, this is one of the three major objectives of most Developing World states

New International Economic Order (NIEO) begun in 1964, this is a movement of many Developing World states that seeks to change how the international economic system operates so that it favors developed states less and helps developing states more

ways to attain capital needed for development and modernization developing states can create it themselves, borrow it from international financial institutions, attract private investment, develop hard currency sources by exporting domestically made products, and receive foreign aid

modernization theory asserts that economic development and modernization require the rejection of traditional behaviors, values, and organization and the acceptance of new ones more conducive to economic development

dependency theory argues that the international political and economic system forces developing states to be dependent on industrialized states and prevents them from obtaining political-economic independence and economic-social development and modernization

tied aid and assistance when a state that donates foreign aid to a country requires the receiving country to use the aid to purchase goods or otherwise meet its needs only in the donating country

defaulting when a state fails to meet its repayment schedule on money that it has borrowed from public or private banks or other lending institutions

politics and ideology of development sometimes political outlooks and ideological positions influence the strategy and tactics of economic development pursued both by borrowing and by lending states and institutions

corporatist strategy based on dependency theory, a strategy of economic development popular particularly in Latin America in the 1960s and 1970s that had the government rather than private industry try to lead economic development; it often became a cover for authoritarianism

sustainable development a relatively new school of economic development thought that argues that economic development must lead to economic growth without damaging the environment

 ## *WEBSITE REFERENCES*

North-South conflict: *ikaoewww.unibe.ch/forschung/nordsued/nsued.html* homepage of a Canadian NGO specializing on analysis of North-South issues

ikaoewww.unibe.ch/forschung/nordsued/nsued.html a forum on the North-South conflict from the Swiss National Science Foundation

Third World: *www.twnside.org.sg/twnintro.htm* website of the Third World Network, a network of organizations involved in issues relating to development, the Third World, and the North-South conflict

www.guiadelmundo.org.uy/eng-proyecto.htm the World Guide, a reference work with text, maps, graphics, images, music, and statistics concentrating on the Third World

Group of 77: *www.g77tin.org/group77.html* website of the Group of 77

Nonaligned Movement: *www.nam.gov.za* website of the Non-Aligned Movement

NOTES

1. For example, see Hollis B. Chenery, "Restructuring the World Economy," *Foreign Affairs,* Vol. 53 (January 1975), pp. 258–263.

2. See, for example, Dawa Norbu, *Culture and the Politics of Third World Nationalism* (New York: Routledge, 1992).

3. For a discussion of the impact of colonialism on developing countries after they achieved independence, see Partha Chatterjee, *The Nation and Its Fragments: Colonial and Postcolonial Histories* (Princeton: Princeton University Press, 1993).

4. George McTurnan Kahin and John W. Lewis, *The United States in Vietnam* (New York: Delta Books, 1969), pp. 8–10.

5. Coral Bell, "China: The Communists and the World," in F. S. Northedge, ed., *The Foreign Policies of the Powers* (New York: The Free Press, 1974), p. 128.

6. See, for example, *Third World Cooperation: The Group of 77 in UNCTAD* (New York: St. Martin's Press, 1991).

7. Some analysts add a fourth factor that may be termed psychological independence. See Franz Fanon, *Black Skin, White Masks* (New York: Grove Press, 1967); and Franz Fanon, *The Wretched of the Earth* (New York: Grove Press, 1968).

8. For several discussions of the Developing World's external debt and its implications, see Martin Dent and Bill Peters, *The Crisis of Poverty and Debt in the Third World* (Ashgate Publishers, 1999); James L. Clayton, *The Global Debt Bomb* (M.E. Sharpe, 1999); and Marcus Arruda, *External Debt: Brazil and the International Financial Crisis* (Pluto Press, 2000).

9. For discussions of the nonaligned movement, see A.W. Singham, *The Nonaligned Movement in World Politics,* (Chicago Review Press, 1978); and M.S. Rajan, *The Future of Nonalignment and the Nonaligned Movement: Some Reflective Essays* (Konark, 1990).

10. For several classic discussion of modernizations theory, see Gabriel Almond and James S. Coleman, *The Politics of Developing Areas* (Princeton: Princeton University Press, 1960); Cyril Black, *The Dynamics of Modernization* (New York: Harper & Row, 1966); Alex Inkeles and David H. Smith, *Becoming Modern: Individual Change in Six Developing Countries* (Cambridge, MA: Harvard University Press, 1974); and Myron Weiner, ed., *Modernization: The Dynamics of Growth* (New York: Basic Books, 1966).

11. For several classic studies of dependency theory, see C. Furtado, *Development and Underdevelopment* (Berkeley: University of California Press, 1964); Andre Gunder Frank, *Capitalism and Underdevelopment in Latin America* (New York: Monthly Review Press, 1067); and Immanuel Wallerstein, *The Modern World System: Capitalist Agriculture and the Origins of the European World Economy in the Sixteenth Century* (New York: Academic Press, 1976).

12. Some trace the early phases of the capitalist international system as far back as the sixteenth century. See, for example, Wallerstein in the work cited before.

13. This outlook is similar to that put forward by Lenin in *Imperialism: The Highest Stage of Capitalism,* as discussed in Chapter 11.

14. See, for example, Mitchell A. Seligson and John T. Passe-Smith, *Development and Underdevelopment: The Political Economy of Inequality* (Boulder, CO: Lynne Rienner, 1993); Stephen Haggard, *Pathways from the Periphery: The Politics of Growth in the Newly Industrialized Countries* (Ithaca: Cornell University Press, 1990); and Sylvia Maxfield, *Governing Capital: International Finance and Mexican Politics* (Ithaca: Cornell University Press, 1990); for other recent studies of development and development theory, see Stuart A. Bremer and Barry B. Hughes, *Disarmament and Development: A Design for the Future* (Englewood Cliffs, NJ: Prentice Hall, 1990); Christopher Colclough and James Manor, eds., *States or Markets? Neo-Liberalism and the Development Policy Debate* (New York: Oxford University Press, 1991); and Lee A Travis, ed., *Rekindling Development: Multinational Firms and World Debt* (South Bend, IN: University of Notre Dame Press, 1989).

15. The World Bank, international debt data for 1992.

16. The World Bank, *World Development Report 1992,* entitled "Development and the Environment," is devoted completely to the impact of development on the environment.

17. This is the definition of sustainable development adopted by the World Commission on Environment and Development in 1987.

18. For discussions of sustainable development, see Olav Stokke, ed., Sustainable Development (London: Frank Cass, 1991); William M. Lafferty and James Meadowcroft, *Implementing Sustainable Development: Strategies and Initiatives in High Consumption Societies* (New York, NY: Oxford University Press, 2000); and Philip A. Lawn, *Toward Sustainable Development* (Lewis Publishers, 2000).

19. For a different treatment of these issues, see Zaven N. Davidian, *Economic Disparities Among Nations: A Threat to Survival in a Globalized World* (New York: Oxford University Press, 1994).

20. For an interesting treatment of "lifeboat ethics," see Richard J. Barnet, "No Room in the Lifeboats," *The New York Times Magazine* (April 16, 1978), pp. 32–38. See also Garrett Hardin, "Lifeboat Ethics: The Case Against Helping the Poor," *Psychology Today,* Vol. 8 (September 1974), pp. 38–43.

PART 3

The Perceptual Framework: Varying Views of the Global Community

We see . . . through the eyes of one participant after the other. Each vision is so different, so contradictory, that in the end we can never be certain of what it is that has transpired . . . the images . . . not only vary widely from one power to another but also from one period to another. The same is true of the images which the involved powers have of each other's actions and motivations.

—HARRISON SALISBURY

O wad some poer the giftie gie us To see oursel's as ithers see us!

—ROBERT BURNS

"Just the facts, ma'am." Sergeant Joe Friday repeated that famous phrase innumerable times on the old television program "Dragnet." Invariably, Sergeant Friday found that different witnesses had different versions of the same fact, and only after a long and detailed investigation was one version of events finally accepted as true.

The uncertainties of Joe Friday's investigation apply equally well to our study of international affairs. For years, the United States viewed the Soviet Union as bent on international expansion and conquest, and the Soviet Union claimed the United States sought imperial growth and economic domination. Who was right? In 1999, the United States attacked Yugoslavia because the United States maintained that Yugoslavia was pursuing a policy of ethnic cleansing against Albanians in the Yugoslavian province of Kosovo. Yugoslavia claimed its policies in Yugoslavia were not ethnic cleansing, but efforts to root out Albanian bandits. Who was right? And during the course of the U.S. air attacks, the United States bombed the Chinese embassy in Belgrade. Washington claimed the attack was a mistake, but China believed that it was intentional. Again, who was right?

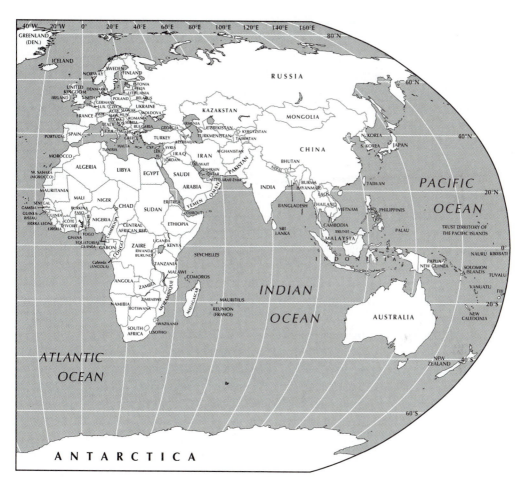

Nations of the world. (*Source: Geography* by Arthur Getis, Judith Getis, and Jerome Fellman. Copyright © 1981 by Macmillan Publishing Company, updated 1996.)

What, then, are the facts? How should they be interpreted? In the international community, a variety of answers exist to these rather simple questions. The answers differ as one moves from one capital to another capital. Even within a single capital, facts and their interpretations differ depending on whom one talks to or listens to.

Answers vary not only according to location of respondent or source of answer, but also according to time of answer. Between 1941 and 1945, Japan and the United States were avowed enemies, but after World War II, the two countries developed a close alliance. Then, during the 1990s, trade tensions introduced serious strains into the relationship, leading many Americans to become anti-Japanese. By 2000, however, as Japan's economy struggled to escape hard times, U.S.-Japanese relations were once again cordial.

Similarly, at least on the surface, China and the Soviet Union were on friendly terms between 1949 and 1960. However, by 1969, the relationship had become so bad that the two countries fought each other along their respective borders. By 1989, Beijing and Moscow had again established a cordial but careful relationship that carried over into the twenty-first century.

Perceptually, then, enemies can become friends and friends enemies as time passes. Other more subtle variations of perceptions also may occur over time, as they did in the United States during the Vietnam War. During the early years of American combat involvement (1965–1966), most Americans supported the U.S. involvement. Gradually, however, as losses mounted and success seemed no closer, more and more Americans opposed U.S. efforts in Vietnam. Perceptions had changed, and a policy change soon followed.

Differences in perceptual outlooks are therefore major contributing factors to the complications of contemporary international relations. The following three chapters offer insight into various perceptual outlooks on international relations. Chapter 9 discusses the role of perceptions in international relations and analyzes the types of perceptions that are held by international actors other than states. Chapter 10 explores some of the perceptions held by developed states and analyzes why those perceptions may be held. Chapter 11 undertakes the same tasks for developing states.

These three chapters are based on the observation that states remain the central actors in international relations, and that it is the perceptions of their governments that are the most significant. Questions that will be examined include:

- Why are perceptions important?
- How do perceptions influence policy?
- How do the states of the developed world view themselves and others?
- How do the states of the developing world view themselves and others?

Chapter 9

Perceptions and Policy in International Relations

- Why are perceptions important in international relations?
- How were U.S. and Soviet perceptions of the Vietnam War different?
- How were U.S. and Russian views of the Kosovo War different?
- Are the perceptions of international actors other than states important?

Many volumes have been written about the importance of perceptions in human affairs. Philosophers, psychologists, politicians, and social scientists have all pointed to the role of perceptions as guides to actions and to the different factors that determine how each of us views reality. Their points of departure and methods of analysis differ, but all have concluded that no universally shared set of experiences exists that influence diverse observers to view a certain situation in the same way.

Within the realm of international affairs, authors as diverse as Kenneth Boulding, David Easton, Robert Jervis, K. J. Holsti, Anatol Rapaport, Richard Snyder, and John Stoessinger have analyzed various ramifications of perceptions.[1] Their work and the work of other analysts has cast new light on, and led to additional understanding of, relations among the various international actors. In this chapter, we first examine theoretical discussions of the role of perceptions in international affairs, and then the perceptions of nonstate actors in the international system.

 ## THE SOURCES OF PERCEPTIONS

Students of perceptual analysis often identify three separate components of perceptions—values, beliefs, and cognitions. A **value** gives rank and order to conditions, situations, individuals, and objects. Thus, most people rank health better than sickness, and life as better than death. However, in some people's eyes, sickness may be preferable to health (one's ability to withstand suffering may be proved), and death may be preferable to life (one may escape suffering through death). On a less dramatic level, some people value a good book more than a good television program, or think that beef tastes better than pork. In all of these examples, an individual's values are what leads that individual to prefer one condition, situation, person, or object over another.

A **belief,** by contrast, is the acceptance of a particular description of reality as true or legitimate. An observer may believe that colonialism is repugnant because it retards economic, social, and cultural advancement. Or one may believe that dictatorships are more likely to go to war than democracies because in a dictatorship only one person makes decisions, whereas in a democracy many people share in making decisions. A belief is an effort to explain in a consistent manner a pattern of activity consisting of several pieces of information. It is an analytical answer to a stated question.

A **cognition** is any piece of information that observers receive about their surroundings that they use to arrive at a value or belief. Cognitions may be either sensory or factual inputs to our value or belief systems and are the basis for our values and beliefs. If we value health more than sickness, it is because we have seen or felt both conditions. Seeing, feeling, or experiencing these conditions were cognitive inputs.

Individual perceptions are the result of a combination of values, beliefs, and cognitions. They play off each other and influence each other continually. Values may change, or stay the same, as a result of changing beliefs and new cognitions. Beliefs may also change, or stay the same, as a result of changing values and new cognitions. And each and every one of us continually experience new cognitions that influence us to develop new or retain old values and beliefs.

At the national and international levels, these observations may be stated differently. Values and beliefs often arise from national culture. Thus, French may prefer wine and cheese, Germans beer and bratwursts, and Americans cola and hamburgers. At the same time, as people living in democracies experienced Iraq's Saddam Hussein invade Kuwait and Yugoslavia's Slobodan Milosevic order ethnic cleansing, these were our historical experiences—or cognitive inputs—from which we developed the belief that dictatorship was a less desirable form of government than democracy.

How do values, beliefs, and cognitions influence international relations? In the space available here, we discuss only two ways. First, given the vast array of cognitive information that everyone receives, it should be evident that the values and beliefs that we form, and that in turn we use both to receive and interpret new cognitive information, are highly individualized. Inevitably this leads to a wide diversity of perceptions.

Second, because perceptions are guides to actions, values, beliefs, and cognitions influence what actions we take. Thus, regardless of whether perceptions are accurate or inaccurate, the actions we take are grounded in our perceptions. In the international arena, the implications of this reality are many.

The Diversity of Perceptions

As we have already seen, there is no universal point of perceptual departure. Put more simply, different individuals see the same event or situation in different ways. As Bertrand Russell said:

Chapter 9

IT AND PERCEPTIONS:
ONE WORLD VIEW OR MANY WORLD VIEWS?

Information Age technologies provide people the ability to see, to hear, and to experience more than they ever have before. What this means is a matter of intense debate. Will people and nations develop shared perceptions as they realize that everyone is, after all, just human? Or as they see, hear, and experience more, will people's perceptions be driven further apart as they become more aware of their differences? Twentieth century television provides clues about what could happen.

Television's basic technology was invented in the 1920s. In the 1930s, U.S. corporations invested millions of dollars in TV's development. Businesses and governments outside the U.S., especially in Germany, also pursued the new technology. By 1936, German know-how had advanced so much that the Berlin Olympics were broadcast to selected sites in Berlin. In the United States, the first television broadcast was the 1939 Harvard-Yale baseball game.

Television played no role in World War II. But after the war, Americans, living in the only industrialized state not ravaged by war, led the way in adopting the new technology. By the 1960s, television had become one of the world's most influential technologies, not only in the United States but also in other industrialized states.

TV also spread into the Developing World where residents of impoverished urban tenements and isolated rural villages alike found television's lure irresistable. To a great extent because of television, the Developing World's citizens discovered what others had and what they themselves did not have. The "revolution of rising expectations" had begun.

TVs global influence grew immeasurably in the late 1960s and 1970s, especially after it was married with satellite technology. This marriage enabled people around the world to see not only what *had* happened, but also to see what *was happening as it happened*. And wherever it was introduced, TV had a dramatic effect on society and public opninon. Because of television, men, women, and children saw people and places and heard ideas and viewpoints that earlier, they might never have seen or heard.

Everywhere, then, TV became a medium for educating, informing, entertaining, and propagandizing. Television had become ubiquitous. By the end of the twentieth century, TV had carved out a place for itself in virtually every country and had penetrated virtually every realm of human activity.

But what did this really mean? Had the world truly become a "global village?" People could see the Sydney Olympics, watch the inauguration of George W. Bush, and witness the explosion of bombs in Kosovo even as they occurred. But has television brought global perceptions closer together? Suffice it to say here that the evidence is contradictory.

And what of the new Information Age technologies? As they allow us to hear, see, and experience even more than television, will our perceptions come closer together, or will they be driven further apart? The answer is one of the Information Age's many unknowns.

we cannot escape from perception with all its personal limitations. . . .
Individual percepts are the basis of all our knowledge, and no method exists by which we can begin with data which are public to many observers.[2]

A perception is thus a relative concept, determined by previous experience, present expectations, current fears or desires, and the influences of others[3]; other factors are also undoubtedly involved. The key point is the realization that another person's interpretation of a situation may be different from one's own. It may be "determined by a different frame of reference, or shaped by other sets of values and presuppositions."[4]

Anatol Rapaport stated this in a different way, declaring:

Thus, without falsifying a single fact, entirely contradictory descriptions can be and are given of persons, situations, social orders, etc., by selecting (often unconsciously) only the features which support preconceived notions. . . .
Controversial issues tend to be polarized not only because commitments have been made but because certain perceptions are actively excluded from consciousness if they do not fit the chosen world image.[5]

K. J. Holsti agreed with Rapaport and added several additional observations. As not all relevant factors influencing a situation could be known, perceptions differed from reality. Preconceived values, beliefs, or expectations often determined which factors were viewed as relevant to a situation.[6] Dean Pruitt stressed this point in his work on threat perception, noting that the stronger the predisposition to perceive a threat, the more likely it was that a threat will be perceived.[7]

These observations are directly applicable to the study of international relations. In their examinations of foreign policy decision making, Richard Snyder and Graham Allison regularly pointed to perceptual differences among American decision makers as a significant variable in U.S. foreign policy determination.[8] Given the preceding discussion concerning the diversity of perceptions, the existence of such perceptual differences within a given nation is not surprising. Even less surprising is the fact that perceptual differences exist between nations. Students of international affairs have increasingly realized this and have examined individual events not only from the perspectives of individual actors within a state, but also from the viewpoint of several of the involved states.[9] The remaining chapters in this framework are based on this, and provide differing views of contemporary international relations as seen from different parts of the international community.

Perceptions as Guides to Action

Differing perceptions would be of limited interest to us if they did not also serve as a basis for explaining human action and reaction. In his classic work *The Image,* Kenneth Boulding argued that "behavior depends on the image."[10] Similarly, K. J. Holsti observed that "man acts and reacts according to his images of the environment."[11] It is because of this linkage between perception and action that perceptual analysis occupies so prominent a place in contemporary international relations.

When international actors formulate an action or a policy, perceptions of situations, events, and other actors form the bases of those actions and policies. Thus, an actor's perceptions must be examined and understood if that actor's actions and policies are to be understood. To an extent, understanding the perceptions that actors hold at the time they undertake an action or implement a policy enables observers to comprehend why a particular action is taken or policy implemented. The way in which a state views itself is critical to its national pride, whereas the way in which a state views others is critical to its national policy.

Indeed, when studying actions of actors in the international arena, analysis of events and personalities is seldom sufficient to yield understanding of those policies. Rather, because policies are made on the basis of the "appearance of things" rather than on "objective reality," appearances *as seen by the actors* must be studied. One question that students must keep constantly in mind as they examine international affairs is, "How did different actors see a situation?"

This is not an easy task. Among the pitfalls confronting any perceptual analysis is the accurate determination of perceptions. At least two levels of problems exist when one is assessing the accuracy of perceptions. The first concerns obtaining sources that are privy to the actual perceptions held by actors. This problem exists in most societies. In the United States, for example, the analyst is faced with uncertainty as to which of several potential sources he or she should believe. Before glasnost swept the former Soviet Union, the problem in the USSR was one of finding a single worthwhile and accurate source. After glasnost, analysts of Soviet affairs were faced by a problem similar to that faced by analysts of American affairs, which of several sources should one believe? This analytical problem was further magnified by the breakup of the USSR.

The second level of problems concerns reliability of sources. International actors often find it to their advantage to have others believe that their outlooks are different than what they really are. This creates problems concerning the reliability of sources.

For example, even if the United States in 1999 did not really intend to introduce ground combat troops to Kosovo to stop Yugoslavia's ethnic cleansing there, it would have been in the American interest to have the Yugoslav government believe the United States would do so. The possibility of the introduction of United States ground combat troops would have been a real threat to Yugoslavia's control of Kosovo and would have communicated to the Yugoslav government that the United States was truly serious. However, when the United States announced that it would not send ground combat troops, the Yugoslav government perceived that the American threat had diminished and was less certain that the United States was serious about stopping ethnic cleansing.

Similarly, a multinational corporation that believes that it can make large profits in a country would find it advantageous to have that country think the MNC's operations would be barely profitable. In all likelihood, the MNC could then negotiate more favorable terms of operation within the country.

National Perceptions and the Clash of Civilizations

To this point, it has been argued that perceptions are highly individualized, that is, that no two observers see the same event, action, or situation in the same way. This is substantially true. But at the same time, within individual countries, shared values, shared cultures, and shared historical experiences can and sometimes do lead to the development of what may be called **national perceptions.**

This reality is what influences many people in one country to view another country in a similar way. For example, many French citizens believe that Germany presents a threat to France even in the twenty-first century. Similarly, despite the collapse of the Soviet Union, many Americans remain distrustful of Russia. And many Koreans and Chinese consider Japan a danger because of Japan's occupation of those countries before and during World War II.

The two following chapters are based on the argument that even though perceptions are highly individualized, widely shared—but not universal—national perceptions often exist within a country. However, the following two chapters do not carry the argument through to the conclusion that differences in national perception, along with differences in values, cultures, and historical experiences, must necessarily lead to a **clash of civilizations.**

The clash of civilizations thesis, popularized most recently by Samuel Huntington, asserts that differences in culture, values, and historical experiences lead almost inevitably to conflict.[12] The argument developed here does not deny the possibility that such differences may lead to conflict, but rejects the thesis that difference-induced conflict is almost inevitable.

Perceptions, then, are diverse, and they serve as guides to action. Unfortunately, at both the individual and national level, and at all levels that exist in between, they are also difficult to determine. To illustrate these points better, we will next analyze differing perceptions of two major international conflicts, the Vietnam War and the Kosovo War.

 ## CASE STUDIES: VIETNAM AND KOSOVO

Vietnam

From August 1950 when the first 35-member U.S. Military Assistance Advisory Group arrived in Vietnam until April 1975 when the last U.S. Marines were lifted by helicopter from the soon-to-be-captured U.S. embassy in Saigon, the United States attempted to create a viable noncommunist state in Vietnam.[13] During that 25-year period, the U.S. military commitment in Vietnam gradually escalated until by 1968, over one-half million U.S. troops were in Vietnam. Over 50,000 American lives were lost, and over $200 billion was spent on the war effort. Ultimately, these expenditures and sacrifices proved futile as North Vietnamese forces overran South Vietnam.

Why had the United States become so deeply involved in Vietnam? What convinced the U.S. leadership that Vietnam was worth so great an outlay of human and material resources? The answers to these questions were complex, and they changed over time. Nevertheless, a general outline of U.S. perceptions can be presented here.

The Early Years. The early phases of the United States' involvement in Vietnam occurred during the depths of the East–West Cold War of the 1950s. As has already been seen, U.S. policy makers viewed the world in bipolar terms during this era; they saw states and other international actors as either members of the Eastern bloc or the Western bloc. Thus, as Ho Chi Minh and his Vietminh continued their struggle against France to end colonial rule in Vietnam and as Ho's linkages to the Soviet Union and China became more widely known, U.S. policy makers concluded that the struggle in Vietnam was not between a colonial power and freedom fighters, but rather between anticommunists and communists. Given the way in which U.S. policy makers looked at the world at this time, no other alternative was possible. In the words of Dwight D. Eisenhower, during the early 1950s, the war in Vietnam began to

> *assume its true complexion of a struggle between Communism and nonCommunist forces rather than one between a colonial power and colonists who were intent on attaining independence.*[14]

Although the Vietnam conflict was viewed through bipolar binoculars, it was also seen as part of a larger strategic picture that pitted East against West in geopolitical terms. In 1953, Congressman Walter Judd headed a study commission on Vietnam that issued a report that gave birth to what became another driving force behind U.S. involvement in Vietnam, the domino theory. According to the Judd Commission:

> *The area of Indochina is immensely wealthy in rice, rubber, cork, and iron ore. Its position makes it a strategic key to the rest of Southeast Asia. If Indochina should fall, Thailand and Burma would be in extreme danger. Malaya, Singapore, and even Indonesia would become more vulnerable to the Communist power drive. . . .*[15]

U.S. Secretary of State John Foster Dulles seconded this outlook, stressing the importance of Indochina as a producer of food and pointing an accusing finger at the Soviet Union:

> *If they [the Soviets] could get this peninsula of Indochina, Siam, Burma, Malaya, they would have what is called the rice bowl of Asia. . . . And you can see that if the Soviet Union had control of the rice bowl of Asia that would be another weapon which would tend to expand their control into Japan and into India.*[16]

The U.S. involvement in Vietnam, then, was originally undertaken with the specific purpose of preventing the expansion of Soviet-controlled monolithic communism into the vital geopolitical and resource areas of Southeast Asia, at least as portrayed by U.S. leaders of that era.

It is ironic that as seen from Moscow during the early 1950s, the continuation of the Vietminh's resistance was detrimental to Soviet interests. Although the USSR condemned U.S. military adviser presence in Vietnam and U.S. assistance to the French as manifestations of U.S. imperialism, the Soviets had at least two good reasons to urge Ho to stop fighting. First, the U.S. government had unveiled its massive retaliation doctrine, in which the United States claimed that it would use nuclear weapons against any aggressor. At the time, this policy was credible; the USSR doubtless preferred not to be the target of American nuclear wrath, particularly over an issue so far removed from the USSR's primary interests. Second, the French Assembly was debating the European Defense Community proposal; the Kremlin may have reasoned that if the French Assembly perceived a reduced "communist threat" in Vietnam, it may also perceive a reduced "communist threat" in Europe and oppose the European Defense Community.[17]

In either event, the key point is that the United States perceived the Soviet Union as organizing and directing the Vietminh and formulated its policy on that perception. The Soviet Union, meanwhile, saw the conflict as dangerous to its own interests and acted accordingly. Indeed, at the 1954 Geneva Conference, the USSR and China both pressured the Vietminh to settle for less than what they could have won on the battlefield.[18] The first four years of American involvement in Vietnam were thus marked by significant differences in perception between the United States and the Soviet Union; 21 more years of differing perceptions followed.

Americanization and Escalation.   U.S. involvement in Vietnam continued to be predicated on the necessity of preventing communist expansion, but gradually other rationales were also used. By early 1965, an internal U.S. government memorandum pointed not only to containment, but also to American prestige as a significant reason for upgrading the U.S. presence there:

> *The stakes in Vietnam are extremely high. The American investment is very large. . . . The international prestige of the United States and a substantial part of our influence are directly at risk in Vietnam.*[19]

Not surprisingly, the Soviet Union had a different view of the growing U.S. involvement, which by 1965 included ground combat forces. According to the Soviets, the United States had embarked on a policy of active military suppression of national liberation movements undertaken beneath the cover of U.S. strategic nuclear superiority. To the Soviets, U.S. actions in Vietnam were a segment of a newly conceived U.S. global military doctrine. The Soviet media continually lambasted the "aggressive actions of American imperialism" and predicted that the United States could not win the war.

As the Vietnam War became Americanized between 1965 and 1968, the perceptions of U.S. and Soviet policy makers changed little. Americans by 1968 realized that communism was no longer monolithic, but the belief persisted that U.S. presence was needed in Vietnam to prevent communism's expansion. Honor, reliability, and commitment were also put forward as prominent reasons for continued U.S. involvement. Meanwhile, the Soviets pointed to Vietnam as a classic case of capitalist imperialism and U.S. aggression.

Vietnamization and Withdrawal.   By 1968 within the United States, support had eroded for the U.S. war effort. Antiwar demonstrations played a major role in driving Lyndon Johnson from the presidency, and his successor, Richard Nixon, promised "peace with honor." However, all that Nixon changed was the U.S. government's belief that a military victory was possible. As Henry Kissinger, Nixon's assistant for national security affairs, declared, the United States had to find a strategy that was "sustainable with substantially reduced casualties" so that "a genuine indigenous political process" could become established in South Vietnam.[20] That strategy was Vietnamization, the equipping and training

When North Vietnam overran South Vietnam in April 1975, many Americans and pro-American South Vietnamese were hurriedly evacuated by helicopter from the top of buildings in Saigon to U.S. Navy ships waiting offshore.

of South Vietnamese forces so that they could defend their country for themselves. For U.S. policy makers, the perception persisted that expansionistic communism had to be contained and that the credibility of U.S. power around the world demanded success in that effort. Policy had changed, but other than realizing that communism was not monolithic, governmental perceptions had changed little.

Meanwhile, the Soviet leadership viewed Vietnamization and the U.S. withdrawal as preludes to more subtle U.S. efforts to maintain influence in Vietnam. Growing Soviet military might, the strength and resilience of North Vietnam and the Vietcong, and the U.S. antiwar movement all combined to force the United States to withdraw from Vietnam, the Soviets believed, but their basic perception of U.S. expansionism had not changed.[21]

When North Vietnamese forces overran South Vietnam two years after the final withdrawal of U.S. forces from Vietnam, the U.S. government had not significantly altered its perception of the conflict in Vietnam itself or of the role of the Soviet Union in that conflict. President Ford, for one, argued that the war ended as it did because the Soviet Union and China had "maintained their commitment," whereas the United States "[had] not." At one time, the Ford administration claimed that the Soviet Union and China had poured $1.7 billion of military aid into North Vietnam in 1974 alone.[22] To the U.S. government, then, communist aggression had won out. The enemy was no longer monolithic, but it was still the same enemy as 25 years earlier.

To the Ford administration, the potential damage to the United States' reputation as a reliable ally was as dangerous as the expansion of communism. Indeed, events surrounding the *Mayaguez* ship-seizure incident of May 12–15, 1975, suggested that the United States was as much concerned with shoring up its reputation as a reliable ally as it was with rescuing the ship and its crew. A month before the *Mayaguez* incident, Ford had warned other nations that the tragedy of Vietnam was not "an indication that the American people have lost their will or desire to stand up for freedom any place in the world."[23] The U.S. effort to rescue the *Mayaguez* and its crew appeared to be an effort to prove the point.

Meanwhile, some Soviet views of the Vietnam War and the U.S. role in that war had changed, but most had not. In general, Soviet coverage of the Vietnam War became less frequent following the withdrawal of U.S. combat units from Vietnam in January 1973. In part, Soviet restraint was the product of Soviet desire to "protect" U.S.–Soviet detente, but in part it was reflective of the internal Soviet debate over whether American "imperialism" had changed.

Proponents of the view that U.S. policy had not changed pointed to continuing U.S. support for South Vietnam and to "the guise of rehabilitation" as proof of their position. Other Soviet authorities believed that "U.S. ruling circles [were taking] a fresh look at their foreign policy strategy" and "actively adapting their policy to the changing international situation." Clearly, perceptual disagreement existed within the USSR about the impact of Vietnam on U.S. foreign policy.

However, the United States and the Soviet Union still viewed their own actions and the actions of the other in considerably different terms. After 25 years of U.S. involvement in Vietnam, the U.S. government viewed the USSR as aiding and abetting aggression and itself as acting to defeat that aggression. By contrast, Soviet authorities believed that U.S. aggression had been finally overcome when South Vietnam fell and that the USSR had been instrumental in bringing about that defeat. Although disagreement was apparent in the USSR about what impact that defeat would have on U.S. foreign policy, no disagreement existed as to who caused the conflict. Clearly, after 25 years, Soviet and U.S. perceptual outlooks remained fundamentally opposed.

Kosovo

After the Soviet Union collapsed in 1991, it was replaced by fifteen independent states, the most important of which was Russia. The new Russia rejected communism, attempted to establish a democratic political system, and struggled to create a capitalist, market-oriented economy. Nevertheless, despite the end of ideological competition with the United States and the West, many Russian perceptions of foreign policy issues remained significantly different than those of the United States and other Western states. The 1999 war in and around Kosovo made this exceedingly clear.

Setting the Stage.   Kosovo is one of the regions of Yugoslavia, a multiethnic state in southern Europe in the Balkans. Created after World War I, Yugoslavia had many nationalities and religions. Orthodox Serbs, Orthodox Macedonians, Orthodox Montenegrins, Catholic Croats, Catholic Slovenes, Catholic Hungarians, Muslim Slavs, and Muslim

Albanians all lived in Yugoslavia in six provinces, Bosnia-Herzegovina, Croatia, Macedonia, Montenegro, Serbia, and Slovenia, and two autonomous regions, Vojvodina and Kosovo. Yugoslavia often had intense ethnic tension and sometimes fighting.

After World War II, Josef Tito and the Communist Party gained power and tried to unify Yugoslavia.[24] Politically nonaligned in the Cold War, Yugoslavia under Tito attained political stability and economic growth. It also linked together, apparently successfully, the region's diverse nationalities and religions into a functioning state. Many lived peacefully together, worked with each other, and intermarried. Even so, some still disliked and hated each other.

Then, in 1980, Tito died, and Yugoslavia began to drift apart. In 1987, Slobodan Milosevic, a Serb nationalist, became Yugoslavia's leader. He appealed to Serb nationalism to keep Yugoslavia together. Non-Serbian Yugoslavs saw Milosevic as a threat, and the trend toward dissolution accelerated. By the early 1990s, Slovenia, Croatia, Bosnia-Herzegovina, and Macedonia had declared independence.[25]

Milosevic and other Serb nationalists did not intend to allow Yugoslavia to dissolve. After failing to prevent Slovenia's and Macedonia's secession, they concentrated on keeping Croatia and Bosnia, where many Serbs lived. In Croatia, Serbs remembered the Croat government, the Ustache, that ruled Croatia for the Nazis during World War II and killed 400,000 Serbs. Understandably, Serbs in Croatia were terrified by Croatian independence and wanted to remain with Yugoslavia. This led to violent fighting during 1991 and 1992. Both sides were brutal and both sides massacred civilians. The fighting for the most part ended in 1992 when Croatian forces gained the upper hand and UN peacekeepers moved in.

Bosnia was less fortunate. Although almost half of Bosnia's population was Muslim Slav, Milosevic's government and Bosnian Serbs tried to expel them, using ethnic cleansing and rape as policy tools. As fighting escalated and deaths mounted, UN peacekeepers deployed to Bosnia in 1992. Although UN forces were deployed until 1995, over half a million people were killed in Bosnia as Serb forces ignored and often overran UN safe areas. Ethnic cleansing, rape, and mass executions of civilians continued, primarily but not exclusively by Serbs. UN peacekeepers were sometimes taken hostage.

In 1995, the United States brokered a peace agreement, the Dayton Accord, between Croats, Bosnian Muslims, and Serbs. The agreement arranged a division of land along ethnic lines to be enforced by NATO. In late 1995, peacekeeping in Bosnia passed from the UN to NATO as NATO deployed an "Implementation Force" (IFOR) of 20,000 U.S. troops, 43,000 French and British soldiers, and several thousand from other countries, including 2,500 Russians. IFOR in 1997 transitioned into a smaller 30,000 person NATO "Stabilization Force" (SFOR) whose mission was to keep the warring parties apart, map minefields, and destroy weapons. Warfare has stopped, but the situation in Bosnia is unsettled, with SFOR still deployed there today.[26]

The Kosovo Conflict. Then, in 1997, Albanian Muslims, who made up over 90 percent of Kosovo's population, began to push for autonomy for Kosovo. Radical elements agitated for independence and formed the Kosovo Liberation Army, taking up arms against Serb troops and police in Kosovo.

Slobodan Milosevic, still in power, directed Yugoslav forces to fight in Kosovo the same way they had fought in Bosnia, with repression, brutality, and ethnic cleansing. The United States and most Western European states at first ignored the fighting, but as it escalated in 1998 and early 1999, they attempted to change Milosevic's policies with diplomacy and negotiations. The United States and Western European states also warned that they might resort to armed force to prevent continued Serbian repression, but to no avail. Russia also urged Milosevic to change his policies, sending a former prime minister to Belgrade to talk with the Yugoslav leader. Russia's efforts did not work, either.

Finally, in March 1999, the U.S. and Europe turned to force as NATO initiated a massive bombing campaign against Yugoslavia to force Milosevic to change his policies. This was the first time NATO forces were ever engaged in full-fledged fighting. Most missions were flown by U.S. planes. Milosevic, in turn, responded by increasing Serbian brutality and repression. Meanwhile, hundreds of thousands of Kosovar refugees flooded into Albania, Macedonia, and Montenegro, destabilizing all three.

Finally, in June 1999, after three months of air attacks, Milosevic conceded. Negotiations led to the June 1999 deployment into Kosovo of a NATO-led peacekeeping force. This force remains on the ground today, but the situation remains tense and dangerous.

U.S. Perceptions of Kosovo.[27] From the U.S. perspective, Western restraint in Kosovo during 1997, 1998, and early 1999 had not succeeded and may have worsened the situation. From the viewpoint of Washington, diplomacy and negotiations had been tried time and time again. They had never worked except when Milosevic was confronted by superior military force. Milosevic played for time in negotiations, deceived Western negotiators, and lied to them, most Americans believed.

Meanwhile, Slobodan Milosevic and his Serbian supporters with their repression, brutality, and ethnic cleansing had clearly violated civilized behavior, repressed human rights, and committed war crimes, according to the predominant U.S. view. Most Americans believed that Milosevic and his supporters had undertaken these actions in Croatia and Bosnia, and had repeated them in Kosovo as the United States and the West had acted with restraint.

As seen by the U.S. administration and many Americans, then, the time had come for action. Yugoslavia's repression and brutality legitimized NATO air strikes, many Americans agreed, despite the unintended suffering and death it caused among innocent Yugoslavians. Support for the war was not unanimous in the United States, but opposition to it was muted and unfocused.

Russian Perceptions of Kosovo.[28] Viewpoints were considerably different in Russia. Most Russians, including senior Russian decision makers, saw the American-led NATO attacks against Yugoslavia as unwarranted and illegitimate, perhaps even criminal. Few Russians supported Milosevic's policies, but virtually none agreed with American policies.

On one level, many Russians saw the NATO attacks on Yugoslavia as proof of the American intention to dominate global affairs, control other countries, and contain Russia. Other manifestations of this American intention included NATO expansion into the Czech Republic, Hungary, and Poland and continued U.S. global military deployments.

On a second level, while few Russians supported Milosevic's brutality, they understood it and accepted it. Serbs, they pointed out, had suffered under Muslim rule for centuries, and Croats had killed hundreds of thousands of Serbs during World War II. As for Albanian Kosovars, many were not legitimate Yugoslav citizens at all, they asserted, having moved into Kosovo from Albania. Forced expulsion was therefore legitimate, some Russians argued.

There were other levels of Russian support for Serbia and opposition to the United States as well. As fellow Slavs, Russians had a natural empathy for Serbians. At the same time, just as many Americans harbored a lingering mistrust of Russia carrying over from Cold War days, many Russians also had a lingering mistrust of the United States.

Clearly, then, many Russians and Americans had significantly different perceptions of Serbian actions in Kosovo and of the U.S. and NATO attacks on Yugoslavia. Differences in perceptions as significant as these have potential to lead to significant policy differences as well. Such differences in perceptions will continue in the twenty-first century, and not just between Russia and the United States. These different perceptions will continue to make the world of international relations interesting, unpredictable—and sometimes dangerous.

NONSTATE ACTORS AND PERCEPTIONS

The governments of states are not the only international actors that base their actions and policies on the perceptions that they hold. All the international actors we examined in earlier chapters also undertake actions and formulate policies on the basis of their views of the international arena. Each has its own unique perspective, even as each state has its perspective. In some instances, perspectives are influenced by the type of entity that an actor is. In other cases, perspectives are influenced more by the actions that the individual actor undertakes. Often, the perceptions that nonstate actors hold are significantly different from perceptions that states have.

Given the significance of nonstate actors in contemporary international relations, it is important that some of their perceptions be examined. Given the diversity of outlooks within the broad categories of international governmental organizations, multinational corporations, nongovernmental organizations, and other international actors, only general perceptions can be addressed here.

International Governmental Organizations

As creations of states, IGOs share many of the perceptions of their state members. For example, throughout most of its existence, the Warsaw Treaty Organization, through its Political Consultative Committee and other associated bodies, viewed the United States and Western Europe as the major threats to peace, even as its member states did. Similarly, NATO through its Secretariat and the North Atlantic Council pointed to the Soviet Union and Eastern Europe as the greatest dangers to peace, even as its member states did.

In other cases, IGOs develop perceptions that are considerably different from those of member states. Such perceptions are held primarily by members of the permanent

Secretariat of IGOs and the IGOs' operational staffs. Often, these perceptions are internationalist and even globalist in nature as an individual's allegiance to his IGO transcends his allegiance to his country of citizenship. Thus, in the European Union, members of the European Council on occasion support measures that may have an adverse effect on their home countries but may be helpful for the European Union as a whole. In a sense, IGOs foster the development of international citizens.

One must be careful not to overstate the case. Although many IGOs and their secretariats and operational staffs decry the dangers of war presented by parochial state interests and the refusal of wealthy states to provide resources sufficient to alleviate Developing World poverty, their viewpoints rarely have much impact beyond the IGOs with which they are associated. One also must not assume that all IGOs, their secretariats, and staffs have acquired an internationalist perspective. Many—possibly most—have not, but remain wedded to the objectives and interests of the states that created them.

Multinational Corporations

Multinational corporations start with a single, well-defined objective: attaining profit. It is therefore not surprising that MNCs generally consider actions and policies that enhance their profitability as desirable and actions and policies that detract from their profitability as undesirable. Other factors also determine the shape of the perceptual lenses through which MNCs view the world, but profitability is invariably the dominant determinant.

As we saw in our discussion of MNCs as international actors, the corporate directorships of MNCs often consider states to be impediments to their operations. With globalist outlooks, MNCs' leaderships maintain that their activities will lead to peace, prosperity, and eventually a more equitable distribution of global wealth. The international mobility of capital and technology controlled by MNCs will benefit all humanity, defenders of MNCs argue, and any actor that hinders that flow is both shortsighted and wrong.

There are exceptions to this outlook. Smaller MNCs seek government support, defense-related MNCs recognize the necessity for government regulation of exports, and MNCs whose foreign subsidiaries are threatened by expropriation or terrorism desire state protection. Some MNCs emphasize social responsibility; others do not. In general MNCs believe that the path to world peace is world trade. And that, of course, brings profit.

Nongovernmental Organizations and Other Nonstate Actors

The perceptual outlooks of NGOs and other nonstate actors are as varied as NGOs and other actors themselves. Given the vastly different objectives, frames of references, values, and other presuppositions and experiences that these actors have, this is to be expected.

For obvious reasons, individuals hold the most diversified perceptions. Little can be or need be said about individual percepts. To paraphrase Bertrand Russell, no method exists by which the many individuals who participate in international affairs can share perceptions. Individual perceptions are widely scattered and often at odds with each other.

In contrast, ethnic/national liberation organizations usually perceive a common category of enemy, either a local government that is believed to be too closely tied to an external interest or an external colonial power that is considered oppressive. In general terms, ethnic/national liberation organizations seek friends and allies where they can find them. The Irish Republican Army, for example, accepts support from U.S. citizens of Irish descent as well as from Libya, even though it is clear that U.S. citizens and Libyans agree on little else. Similarly, UNITA, one of the Angolan national liberation movements, willingly accepted aid from South Africa, a government with which UNITA had nothing in common. For the ethnic/national liberation organization, the drive for national independence renders all other issues of marginal importance. It is therefore not surprising that from the vantage point of an ethnic/national liberation organization, any international actor that will extend military aid and/or diplomatic support is usually a friend.

The perceptions of terrorist organizations and groups may be categorized in two ways. First, terrorists recognize that they are incapable of effecting the changes they desire, given the prevailing social climate at the time they undertake their terrorist activity. Resort to terror is thus a method to maximize what may otherwise be a limited ability to affect events. Terrorists may therefore be said to recognize the limits of their own powers.

Second, terrorists more often than not have a well-defined target that they are seeking to destroy. It may be the prevailing social system, as in the case of the Red Brigade or the Bader-Meinhof Gang, which sought to undermine the capitalist system in Europe, or it may be a single individual or institution, as in the case of Mehmet Ali Agca's attempt to assassinate Pope John Paul II. Again, as cautioned in Chapter 5, it should be stressed that because of differing perceptual vantage points, a group or organization that one observer defines as "terrorist" may be termed a "national liberation movement" by another observer. This point does not refer to the perceptions held by terrorists themselves, but rather to the perceptions of those who seek to define terrorism and terrorists.

The perceptions of transnational religious movements or groups and transnational political parties or movements may be discussed together. All, to varying extents, believe that the religious or ideological outlooks that they hold have widespread applicability transcending established national boundaries. Jesus' disciples were instructed to go forward and teach all nations; Muhammad's followers were told to win converts to the true way. Marx and Engels asked the workers of the world to unite; Mao called for the peasants of the world to rise up and surround the cities. The perceptual outlook of many less renowned religious movements and political parties are similarly internationalist in content.

Again, however, the degree of internationalist outlook must not be over-stated. In many states once ruled by communist governments, local customs and interests colored and transformed what was a universalist political ideology. Similarly, religion has more than once been used by states for their own purposes. The European religious wars of the sixteenth and seventeenth centuries were ample proof that even within a universalist religion, disagreement may exist and flourish, sometimes with tragic consequences.

It should be also stressed that transnational religions and political movements and groups have found it possible to reach accommodation with national purposes of states. In reaching such an accommodation, an internationalist outlook on some questions may become captive to a more nationally oriented outlook. Communism and Christianity offer poignant examples. In Poland, for instance, the Catholic church and the communist government coexisted for four decades despite the fact that their respective religious teachings and ideological preachments mandated hostility between the two. Tension existed, but both Christians and communists perceived a necessity to coexist on the national level despite their respective teachings about the other on the transnational level.

Nongovernmental organizations are also occasionally caught between national objectives and internationalist outlooks. For example, French members of Greenpeace found themselves in a dilemma in 1995 when France decided to resume nuclear testing in the South Pacific. Should they oppose their government or should they abandon the environmentalist organization? Most decided to oppose their government.

Each nonstate actor views the world somewhat differently. Some of the actors may have similar views or even identical views on a particular situation or issue, or even on a number of situations or issues, but inevitably differences of perception exist. Because states still predominate as international actors despite the challenges to their preeminence put forward by other actors, the remaining chapters of this framework will examine the perceptions of international relations held by several major and a few minor states. As we will see, in some cases, perceptions are so different that it is difficult to believe that the same issue, event, or actor is being described.

 ## KEY TERMS AND CONCEPTS

value   gives rank and order to conditions, situations, individuals, and objects; one of three major components of perception

belief   the acceptance of a particular description of reality as true; one of three major components of perception

cognition   any piece of information that an observer receives about his surroundings that he uses to arrive at a value or belief;   the third major component of perception

diversity of perceptions   since no shared set of experiences exists that would influence observers to view an event in the same way, it is assured that in most cases, one actor's interpretation of an event will be different from another's

national perceptions   the development of shared outlooks by the people of a nation as a result of shared values, shared cultures, and shared historical experiences

clash of civilizations   the belief that differences in national perceptions, along with differences in values, cultures, and historical experiences, will lead to conflict

alternate perceptions of Vietnam   the U.S. argued that it was defending an independent South Vietnam from North Vietnamese aggression; the U.S.S.R. asserted that the U.S. was expanding its alleged colonial empire

alternate perceptions of Kosovo   the U.S. argued that it was protecting human rights and ending Serbian ethnic cleansing in Kosovo; many Russians believed the U.S. was attempting to dominate global affairs, control other countries, and contain Russia

perceptions of nonstate actors   often, perceptions that international governmental organizations, nongovernmental organizations, and multinational corporations have are significantly different than the perceptions of state, varying on an actor by actor basis

 ## WEBSITE REFERENCES

diversity of perceptions: *ajr.newslink.org/news.html*   the newslink site of the American Journalism Review, providing access to news outlets and different outlooks of global events from around the world

alternate perceptions of Vietnam: *www.yale.edu/lawweb/avalon/tonkin-g.htm#joint* the text of President Lyndon Johnson's message to Congress and the Gulf of Tonkin Resolution
www.lbjlib.utexas.edu/shwv/shwvhome.html website of the Vietnam War Internet Project, an educational organization that provides information and documents about the Indochina Wars
alternate perceptions of Kosovo: *www.kforonline.com* NATO's home page about on-going events in Kosovo
www.commondreams.org/kosovo/moreviews.htm website of views generally opposed to U.S. and NATO actions in Kosovo

 NOTES

1. Kenneth E. Boulding, "National Images and International Systems," in William D. Coplin and Charles W. Kegley, Jr., eds., *Analyzing International Relations* (New York: Praeger, 1975), pp. 347–360; Robert Jervis, *The Logic of Images in International Relations* (Princeton: Princeton University Press, 1970); K. J. Holsti, *International Politics: A Framework for Analysis* (Englewood Cliffs, NJ: Prentice Hall, 1967); Anatol Rapaport, *The Big Two: Soviet-American Perceptions of Foreign Policy* (New York: Pegasus, 1971); Richard C. Snyder et al., *Foreign Policy Decision-Making: An Approach to the Study of International Politics* (New York: The Free Press, 1962); and John Stoessinger, *Nations in Darkness: China, Russia, America* (New York: Random House, 1990).

2. Bertrand Russell, *Human Knowledge: Its Scope and Limits* (New York: Simon & Schuster, 1948), p. 8.

3. Otto Klineberg, *The Human Dimension in International Relations* (New York: Holt, Rinehart and Winston, 1966), pp. 90–92.

4. Ibid., p. 99.

5. Anatol Rapaport, *Fights, Games, and Debates* (Ann Arbor: University of Michigan Press, 1960), p. 258.

6. Holsti, p. 159.

7. Dean G. Pruitt and Richard C. Snyder, eds., *Theory and Research on the Causes of War* (Englewood Cliffs, NJ: Prentice Hall, 1969), p. 65.

8. Graham T. Allison, "Conceptual Models and the Cuban Missile Crisis," *American Political Science Review,* Vol. 63 (1969), pp. 689–718; Graham T. Allison, *Essence of Decision: Explaining the Cuban Missile Crisis* (Boston: Little, Brown, 1971); and Richard C. Snyder et al., *Foreign Policy Decision-Making.*

9. See particularly Rapaport, *The Big Two,* and Stoessinger, *Nations in Darkness.*

10. Kenneth Boulding, *The Image* (Ann Arbor: University of Michigan Press, 1956), p. 6.

11. Holsti, p. 158.

12. Samuel P. Huntington, "The Clash of Civilizations," *Foreign Affairs* (Summer 1993), pp. 22–49.

13. For a detailed study of Chinese, Soviet, and U.S. perceptions of the American involvement in Vietnam, see Daniel S. Papp, *Vietnam: The View from Moscow, Peking, Washington* (Jefferson, NC: McFarland & Company, 1981).

14. Dwight D. Eisenhower, *Mandate for Change, 1953–56: The White House Years* (Garden City, NY: Doubleday, 1963), p. 167.

15. U.S. Congress, House, Committee on Foreign Affairs, *Report of the Special Study Mission to Pakistan, India, Thailand, Indochina Pursuant to House Resolution 113,* House Report No. 412, 83rd Cong., 1st sess. (Washington, DC: U.S. Government Printing Office, 1953), p. 35.

16. *New York Times,* January 28, 1953.

17. Donald S. Zagoria, *Vietnam Triangle: Moscow, Peking, Hanoi* (New York: Pegasus, 1967), p. 40.

18. U.S. Department of Defense, *United States-Vietnam Relations 1945–1967,* Book 1, III, D, "The Geneva Accords" (Washington, DC: U.S. Government Printing Office, 1971), p. D9. See also *New York Times,* July 25, 1954.

19. *United States-Vietnam Relations,* Book 4, IV, C, 3, pp. 31–34.

20. Henry A. Kissinger, "The Vietnam Negotiations," *Foreign Affairs,* Vol. 47 (January 1969), pp. 211–234.

21. For the historical evolution of Soviet perceptions of the U.S. involvement in Vietnam, see Papp, pp. 31–48, 59–72, 102–111, 145–158, 188–195, and 207–209.

22. *New York Times,* March 20, 1974; and April 17, 1975.

23. Ibid., April 4, 1975.

24. For details of the creation of Yugoslavia and Tito's rule there, see V. Didijer, et al., History of Yugoslavia (New York, NY: McGraw-Hill, 1974); Jozo Tomasevitch, *War and Revolution in Yugoslavia, 1941–45: The Chetniks* (Palo Alto, CA: Stanford University Press, 1975); and Milovan Djilas, *Tito: The Story from Inside* (New York, NY: Harcourt, Brace, Jovanovich, 1980).

25. For details of the dissolution of Yugoslavia, see *War in the Balkans* (New York, NY: Council on Foreign Relations, 1999), a collection of eleven articles about the unraveling of Yugoslavia that appeared in *Foreign Affairs* between 1993 and 1999. See also Sabrina P. Ramet, *Balkan Babel: The Disintegration of Yugoslavia from the Death of Tito to the War for Kosovo,* 3d edition (Boulder, CO: Westview Press, 1999)

26. For details about the Dayton Peace Agreement and NATO's occupation of Bosnia, see Jane M.O. Sharp, "Dayton Report Card," *International Security* (Winter 1997–98), pp. 101–137.

27. For discussions of U.S. and European perceptions of the Kosovo conflict, see Madelieine Albright and Robin Cook, "Our Campaign is Working," *Washington Post,* May 16, 1999; William Jefferson Clinton, "A Just and Necessary War," *New York Times,* May 23, 1999; Dirk Johnson, "To Some Midwesterners, Milosevic Indictment Gives War New Meaning," *New York Times,* May 29, 1999; Robert Samuelson, "A War of Good Intentions," *Washington Post,* June 2, 1999; Mortimer Zuckerman, "A Moment to Savor Victory," *U.S. News and World Report,* (June 21, 1999); and Elizabeth Pond, "Kosovo: Catalyst for Europe," *The Washington Quarterly* (Autumn 1999), pp. 77–92

28. Russian perceptions of the Kosovo conflict are discussed in Alan Rousso, "Kosovo and U.S.-Russian Relations: The View from Moscow," Carnegie Endowment for International Peace, May 6, 1999; David Hoffman, "Attack Stirs Cold War Feelings in Russia," *Washington Post,* April 4, 1999. See also Sergo A. Mikoyan, "Russia, the United States, and Regional Conflict in Eurasia," *Survival* (Autumn 1998), pp. 112–26, for Russian concerns about U.S. interventionism that predated Kosovo.

Chapter 10

Views from the Developed World

- What views of international relations do developed countries have in common, and why do they share these views?
- How does the United States view itself and its role in the world, and why does the United States have these views?
- How do European states view themselves and their roles in the world, and why do they have these views?
- How does Japan view itself and its role in the world, and why does it have these views?
- How does Russia view itself and its role in the world, and why does it have these views?

As discussed earlier in this text, the United States, European states except for Albania, Japan, Russia (although this is a matter of debate), Canada, Israel, South Africa, Australia, and New Zealand are generally considered developed states. For the most part, all have democratic political systems, stable societies, and high standards of living.

Frequently, they also share similar although not identical perspectives on international relations, the international system, and the way the world works. These similar perspectives are the result of a surprising set of shared values, beliefs, and experiences.

However, the degree to which developed states have similar perspectives must not be overstated. There are also significant differences between the perceptions that they hold. It is a statement of the obvious that the United States, Germany, France, Great Britain, Russia, Japan, Canada, Australia, New Zealand, South Africa, and Israel view the world differently. Just as their similar perspectives are the result of shared values, beliefs, and experiences, their different perceptions are the result of different values, beliefs, and experiences.

LEVELS OF ANALYSIS REVISITED

Here, we must revisit the concept of levels of analysis that was introduced in Chapter 1. Even though this chapter stresses the similarities and differences of national perceptions of developed states, many people within those states have views of international affairs, the international system, and the way the world works that differ significantly from the dominant national perspectives that are presented here. They developed these individual perceptions because of their own individual values, beliefs, and experiences. The question we must continually keep in mind as we study perceptions and the roles that they play in international relations is, "Which level of analysis is most appropriate, the individual level, the national level, or some other level?" This is not an easy question to answer.

For example, for ease of presentation and analytical purposes, we often say, "the American view" or "the Japanese view." However, we must remember that many Americans and many Japanese do not agree with "the American view" or "the Japanese view." Not all Americans support democracy. Not all Americans are materialistic. And not all Americans like hamburgers. Yet as a general rule, it is safe to say that Americans are capitalists who are materialistic and like hamburgers. Similarly, not all Japanese are capitalists, not all Japanese are traditionalists, and not all Japanese like sushi. Yet as a general rule, it is safe to say that Japanese are capitalists who are traditionalists and like sushi.

With the importance of levels of analysis in mind, we now turn to the similarities among the perceptions of developed states about international relations, the international system, and the way the world works. We will then examine some of the major differences.

THE SHARED PERCEPTIONS OF DEVELOPED STATES

As noted above, most developed states have democratic political systems, stable societies, and high standards of living. Most also have extremely different histories and acquired democratic political systems, stable societies, and high standards of living in very different ways.

For example, the United States adopted a democratic political system over two centuries ago and gradually refined it through the years. Conversely, Japan and Germany had democratic political systems imposed on them during the late 1940s after being defeated in World War II. Both adapted to democracy and have functioning democratic political systems today. By comparison, Russia and South Africa experienced internal revolutions during the 1990s and did not become democratic states until then. Both are struggling to institutionalize their newly acquired democratic political systems.

Despite having different histories and acquiring democratic political systems, stable societies, and high standards of living in different ways, many states, as noted above, share similar although not necessarily identical perspectives on international relations, the international system, and the way the world works. For example, with few exceptions, developed states prefer peaceful resolution of conflicts, favor the prevailing international economic system, accept similar standards of individual human rights, and support the rule of international law. They also have similar perceptions on a variety of other international issues. We will concentrate here on these four.

Chapter 10:

IT AND THE DEVELOPED WORLD: A BRAVE NEW WIRED WORLD

When the twenty-first century began, much of the Developed World had already entered the Information Age. For example, in 1997, Germany had 255 computers per 1,000 people, Japan had 202 per 1,000 people, and the United States had 407. At the same time, 99 out of every 1,000 Germans had wireless phones, 304 out of every 1,000 Japanese had wireless phones, and 206 out of every 1,000 Americans. The comparable numbers in Brazil were 26 out of 1,000 for computers and 28 out of 1,000 for wireless phones, in China 6 for computers and 10 for phones, and in India 2 for computers and 1 for phones.

In addition, in most of the Developed World, major businesses relied on information technology to conduct their business, as did many smaller businesses. E-business was also growing by leaps and bounds. By many measures, the Developed World was living in a brave new wired world, perhaps not completely sure where it was going, but confident that it would get there.

At the same time, as the above statistics show, IT penetration and use in the Developed World was not uniform. Although little if any difference exists between European, Japanese, and U.S. IT capabilities in the business sector, the United States by most measures of IT presence and use is in other sectors far ahead of most of the rest of the Developed World.

More troubling, significant "digital divides" exist in Europe, Japan, and the United States. As a general rule, in Europe, northern European countries enjoy greater degrees of IT presence and use than do central European states, and central European states are further advanced than southern European states. In Japan, the digital divide relates more to a rural versus urban distinction, with urban IT presence and use being more frequent. Meanwhile, in the United States, the digital divide centers on race. Thus, a significantly lower percentage of African-Americans and Hispanic-Americans have early access to computers than do Anglo-Americans and Asian-Americans.

Unless successfully addressed, all these digital divides have potential to create domestic underclasses that will be left further behind economically and socially.

Despite the digital divides within and between developed states, the Developed World is far advanced in IT capabilities in comparison to most of the Developing World. There are significant exceptions such as in India, which is a hotbed of software development, and Singapore, which has an advanced computer manufacturing industry. But as a general rule, the Developed World has entered the Information Age, and the Developing World has not.

Obviously, most developed states already hold perceptions of day to day life, of business and government operations, and of international relations that are significantly different from those of most developing states. For at least the near term future, it is likely that differences in perceptions will increase even more as the Developed World accelerates its journey into the Information Age and the Developing World struggles to reach its threshold. It would be an irony of global proportions if the Information Age made communication between the Developed and Developing Worlds even more difficult than it already is.

Preference for Peaceful Resolution of Conflict

Often, developed states share a preference for the peaceful resolution of conflict. One reason for this is that developed states have much to lose by war, and wish to avoid it. This is not to say that developed states will not fight wars if their interests are threatened. Indeed, recent history has many examples of developed states going to war. Nevertheless, as a general rule, developed states agree that conflicts should be peacefully resolved.

A sizable body of literature also asserts that developed states are less likely to go to war because they are democracies. This, it is argued, is because in democracies, popular support must usually be developed before wars can be successfully prosecuted. In essence, many people in democracies are therefore involved in decision making about war and peace. We will return to this point in Chapter 17. However, for now, the point is that developed states, most of which are democracies, prefer peaceful resolution of conflict.

Support for the Prevailing International Economic System

Developed states also favor the prevailing international economic system because they are convinced that it is a system that assures economic prosperity both individually and globally. It also, of course, helps them obtain their high standards of living.

Developed states generally have similar views on aspects of the international economic issues as diverse as the desirability of an open international economic system, the operation of international financial institutions like the World Bank and the International Monetary Fund, and the need for market-driven international exchange rates. As we saw in Chapter 8, many also accept the wisdom of a modernization-oriented development strategy.

At the same time, developed states often disagree on specific measures and policies in international economics. Nevertheless, for the most part, they are unified in their support for the system itself.

Belief in Individual Human Rights

Most developed states also place a high value on the individual. They accept that individual human rights are universal and should not be abridged by states or other international actors. Again, while they often disagree on specific measures and policies, they are generally unified in their support for individual and universal human rights.

There is less agreement among developed states about what to do when sovereign states violate human rights. Should developed states intervene? Some argue that egregious human rights violations require intervention, as NATO countries did in Kosovo in 1999. Or should they look the other way, accepting that sovereignty is paramount? Developed states, and developing states as well, did this in Rwanda in the mid-1990s as millions were killed in ethnic conflict. To reiterate, developed states share perceptions on human rights, but they do not agree about what to do if rights are violated.

Acceptance of International Law

From the perspective of developed states, all of the above can best be accomplished when international laws are in place and operational. Most developed states accept that while they may not agree with all aspects of international law, international law nevertheless provides predictability and offers assurances that certain standards will be met. Conversely, most developed states agree that sovereign states may in specific circumstances ignore or reject international law.

Critics assert that the last point is proof that the consensus that developed states have on international law is nothing more than the developed states' way of maintaining global control. Critics argue that developed states wrote most international law and that it is slanted in their behalf, but when developed states want to ignore international law, they appeal to sovereignty. Developed states assert that there is no contradiction in their position.

Summation

In many respects, the shared perspectives of developed states on these and other issues flow from the democratic political systems, stable societies, and high standards of living that most developed countries have. To be sure, developed states often disagree on the specific policy implications of their shared perspectives. However, these disagreements should not overshadow the fundamental perceptual agreement that developed states share on these and other issues in contemporary international relations.

But there are many other issues upon which developed states have genuinely different perceptions, especially regarding how developed states view themselves and their roles in the world. We turn now to these perceptions, or at least the perceptions of the United States, European states, Japan, and Russia, and to the sources from which they spring. These differences go a long way toward explaining why states so frequently disagree with one another.

 # THE UNITED STATES' OUTLOOK

Throughout their history, U.S. citizens have believed that the United States was different from other states. Immodestly calling their country the world's "first new nation," many Americans have viewed the United States as having a special destiny, a mission. Thomas Jefferson, for example, called the United States "the last best hope of mankind" and a "barrier against the returns of ignorance and barbarism," and John Adams predicted that the United States was "destined beyond a doubt to be the greatest power on earth."

The American "Mission"

What was the U.S. mission? To Jefferson, the American mission was "to consecrate a sanctuary for those whom the misrule of Europe may compel to seek happiness in other climes." A century and a half later, President Harry Truman declared that "the free peoples of the world look to us for support in maintaining their freedoms."[1] And in 1999, President Bill Clinton announced the United States and NATO were initiating air attacks against Yugoslavia to stop Yugoslavia's ethnic cleansing in Kosovo and to defend the rights of Kosovo's peoples.[2] Almost two hundred years had passed, but the sense of mission remained.

However, in a significant way, the mission had changed. Jefferson presented the American mission as providing a model for those who sought political freedom, Truman offered American support for those who sought freedom, and Clinton undertook action to obtain freedom for others. These were significant differences.

The Roots of the American Self-Image

Despite this evolving sense of mission, the American self-image changed little before World War II. Most Americans believed their country was and always had been on the side of liberty and justice. Thus, before World War II, deep-seated perceptions that most Americans held about the role and purpose of the United States in international affairs remained constant. There were three roots to this self-image.

The first was **isolationism.** Although few Americans today would say the United States is isolationist, many Americans have a strong desire for a smaller international role. Indeed, before World War II, the United States was not closely aligned with other states, nor did it regularly intervene in the political affairs of other states. Isolation resulted from geographical, emotional, and psychological factors.

Geographically, North America was separated from most of the world by vast oceans. At the same time, little threat of invasion existed from Canada or Mexico. Emotional and psychological isolation went hand in hand with geographic isolation. Peopled by immigrants who had fled Europe's religious, social, and economic bigotry, the United States developed a new style of government in which church was separated from state, human beings were equally valued, and a social contract of justice was declared to exist between governed and government. Even if ideals were sometimes ignored, they were better than those espoused in Europe, most Americans believed.

Despite its alleged isolationism, the United States in its early years undertook many international activities. U.S. trade grew significantly during the nineteenth century, but this was not seen as a departure from isolationism. And the U.S.'s western expansion was called manifest destiny, not a departure from isolationism.

Other actions were more difficult to explain. For example, in 1801 the United States sent a naval squadron to the Mediterranean when the Barbary states captured U.S. merchant vessels, and in 1846, the United States declared war on Mexico when the Mexican government refused to acknowledge Texas' desire for independence. How could these and other American interventions be legitimized if the self-image of isolationism was to be maintained? The answer was **moralism,** the second root of the American self-image.

Especially at the end of the nineteenth century and in the early twentieth century, moralism became a watchword for intervention as the United States sent its armed forces into Cuba, Mexico, the Caribbean, Central America, China, and the Philippines. In every case, interventions were justified in moral terms. U.S. entry into World War I was similarly couched in moral terms as President Woodrow Wilson declared that the United States was fighting "to make the world safe for democracy."

Although U.S. citizens preferred to view their foreign policy as isolationist and moral, they also on occasion admitted to an underlying **pragmatism,** the final root of the American self-image. A survey of U.S. foreign policy reveals numerous instances of pragmatic national behavior.

For example, during the last decade of the eighteenth century and the first decade of the nineteenth, U.S. traders sought profit by selling to all sides in the Napoleonic wars that raged across Europe. Only when Great Britain and France interfered with that trade did the United States argue that moral issues were involved. Similarly, Americans remember the Barbary War of 1801 as a series of naval encounters that, in a moral sense, were undertaken because "Americans don't pay bribes." They forget that in a pragmatic sense, payments were made to the Barbary states until 1816. Similarly, they remember that the United States went to war with Mexico in 1846 to defend U.S. territorial claims in Texas. They forget that acquiring Mexican territory was also part of the war's objectives. Even the Civil War, fought in U.S. folklore for the moral issue of ending slavery, had as its primary objective, as far as Lincoln was concerned, the maintenance of the Union.

The twentieth century also contains numerous instances of pragmatic U.S. foreign policy behavior. The United States may have avoided the first three years of World War I because of its abhorrence of war, but its businesses profited handsomely during those years of American peace and European war. They also found it acceptable and profitable to aid Hitler's industrialization program during the 1930s while the U.S. government looked on quietly. Numerous U.S. interventions in the Caribbean throughout the first three decades of this century were explained in moral terms that smacked of the pragmatic thought that if the United States intervened, it would be better for the United States, and better for the country in which the U.S. intervened as well.[3]

American Views of the U.S. Role in the World

Times have changed since before World War II. Isolationism is no longer a major factor in the American self-image, although many Americans still long for it. But moralism and pragmatism remain pronounced.

In the years since World War II ended, American views of their country and its role in the world have gone through several periods. The first period stretched from 1947 until the mid-1960s. During this period, the United States perceived a communist menace centered in the Soviet Union that threatened to engulf the world. In response, the United States abandoned isolationism and took up a moral crusade against communism. Pursuing the policy of **containment,** the United States attempted to prevent Soviet expansion using whatever means were necessary, including military force if needed.[4] On occasion, containment dictated that the United States support dictatorships, but even this was accepted as pragmatism. Communism was the greatest danger. That, at least, is how most Americans pictured the situation.

The crusade of containment led to Vietnam and a reassessment of the U.S. role in the world. As the war dragged on, many Americans became less persuaded that their mission in Vietnam was moral or that communism was a dangerous enemy. By the time Richard Nixon was elected president in 1968, many Americans were no longer sure what role the United States should play in the world.

Nixon, however, had his own ideas about what role the United States should play. Adopting a policy firmly rooted in realism, Nixon pursued a policy of **détente,** that is, improved relations with the Soviet Union and China.[5] At the same time, under a policy called

Vietnamization, he increased aid to South Vietnam, escalated bombing of North Vietnam, and began to withdraw U.S. troops. The eventual goal of Vietnamization was American withdrawal from the country. From the Nixon administration's perspective, all of this was a careful game of balance-of-power politics in which the United States took advantage of worsening Sino–Soviet relations to pursue friendly relations with both even as it stepped up the bombing of North Vietnam with the objective of withdrawing from South Vietnam.

Nixon's realism soon gave way to Jimmy Carter's emphasis on human rights and idealism in foreign policy.[6] Most Americans at first supported Carter's new direction. However, human rights and idealism soon ran aground on the twin rocks of the capture of U.S. hostages in Iran and the Soviet invasion of Afghanistan.

These two events, and the election of Ronald Reagan as president, marked yet another new beginning for American views of the U.S. role in the world, one based on a return to the old concept of containment. Economic and military strength was rebuilt and wielded within the context of a world that the Reagan administration defined primarily in terms of the East–West conflict. It was a worldview with which many U.S. citizens had been comfortable once before, and for most of the 1980s, they were comfortable with it once again.[7]

But as the 1980s ended and the 1990s began, Americans again had to reassess their perceptions of their country's role in the world as communist governments collapsed first in Eastern Europe and then in the Soviet Union. With the Cold War over and the East–West conflict gone, an American role in the world based on anticommunism no longer made sense.

But what role should the United States play in the world? As the twenty-first century began, most Americans still had no real answer to that question. During the 1990s, under Presidents Bush and Clinton, the United States intervened militarily in numerous places including the Persian Gulf, Somalia, Bosnia, Haiti, Kosovo, and elsewhere as well. The United States also played a major role in helping the world move toward free trade areas and a more open international trading regime.

But many Americans were uncomfortable with military interventionism and global free trade. Why should U.S. boys be put in harms way in areas of the world where the United States had few well-defined interests? Why should American borders be opened and jobs put at risk to goods made overseas by underpaid foreign workers? As the twenty-first century began, the question remained, "What role should the United States play in the world?"[8] When President George W. Bush took office in 2001, the answer remained uncertain.

EUROPEAN PERCEPTIONS

Despite the European Union's efforts to unify the continent, Europe is not now and never has been an integrated whole. It is a region of diverse nationalities, ethnic groups, cultures, and languages. It is also a region of diverse perceptions.

Throughout most of the second half of the twentieth century, Europe was divided into two blocs, one substantially under the control of the Soviet Union and the other allied to the United States. Within each bloc, the differences that had divided Europe for centuries continued to exist. But to a great extent, they were concealed by the hostility that set East against West.

In 1989, this changed as communist governments throughout what was then called Eastern Europe and what is now called Central Europe were overthrown. Since then, most former communist states have put democratic political systems and free market economic systems in place. Most are still struggling to attain political stability and economic growth, but many are making progress. Meanwhile, as we saw in Chapter 3 in our discussion of IGOs, Western European states have been attempting to institutionalize the European Union.

Central European Perspectives

The euphoria that swept Central Europe in 1989 after the collapse of communism was short-lived. Central Europeans soon realized that they had an immense challenge ahead of them. Most knew that the task of constructing new political, economic, and social systems would not be easy, but not many realized how difficult it would be. For over a decade now, Central Europeans have concentrated on creating democratic political systems and free market economic systems for their countries. Few people are deeply concerned with broad issues of international relations other than obtaining aid and constructing a stable and secure homeland.

One of the most difficult challenges Central Europeans face resulted from their general lack of knowledge and experience about how democratic political systems and free market economic systems operate. For almost half a century, none had experienced democratic governance or free market economics. Communism bequeathed Central European states with a legacy of over 40 years of ignorance about democracy and free markets.

In addition, the elimination of communist attitudes was less than complete. In many countries, individuals who wanted to continue to do things the old ways remained influential. Often, they tried to retain as much of the old system as possible to hold on to their political influence, sometimes sabotaging democratic reforms.

The challenge of constructing new political, economic, and social systems was even more difficult because no country had ever tried to do what the former communist states were trying to do: create democratic political institutions, free market economic systems, and open social systems over the remains of communist structures, all at the same time. What was the best way to do it? No one really knew.

Despite these difficulties, Bulgaria, the Czech Republic, Hungary, Poland, Romania, and Slovakia all forged forward with the effort. So too did Croatia and Slovenia after they gained independence from Yugoslavia in 1993. Each faced different situations and challenges and each had a different history. As a result, each followed its own path toward democracy and marketization.

Given their recent histories and present political and economic conditions, it is not surprising that Central European states avidly seek foreign investment and aid. To acquire it, they turn frequently to Western European states, the United States, Japan, multilateral financial institutions like the World Bank, and multinational corporations. Obviously, all Central European states are favorably disposed toward investment and aid, and all also believe they do not receive enough.

Most Central European states are also concerned about their security. Having only recently emerged from Soviet domination, most are concerned that Russia at some future time might attempt to reassert its influence. Some Central European leaders are also concerned about the growth of internal antidemocratic forces.

Given these two fears, Central European states are therefore favorably disposed toward joining NATO. Indeed, in 1999, the Czech Republic, Hungary, and Poland became NATO's newest members. More have petitioned for membership.

For the foreseeable future, then, Central European states will undoubtedly continue to focus their attention on developing democratic political systems and free market economic systems, acquiring more foreign aid and investment, and improving their security situations. All are daunting tasks.[9]

The Special Case of Germany

The most unique situation in Central Europe was in East Germany. Before World War II, East Germany was not a separate country. Rather, it was part of Germany. East and West Germany were formed during the Cold War because of Eastern and Western disagreement over the country's future. As a result, Germany was divided, with each bloc building a German state based on its own values and institutions.

Even so, many Germans never gave up the hope of unifying Germany. Thus, when the Berlin Wall came down and East Germany's communist government collapsed in 1989, East and West Germany moved rapidly toward unification. In 1990, East and West Germany unified under what had been the West German government. Forty-five years of German division had ended.

But unification did not end the former East Germany's problems. The differences between East German and West German values that developed over 45 years of division were deeper than expected, and it is taking longer than expected to close the gap. For example, dependence on a state-guaranteed job undermined the work ethic in East Germany, and it is only slowly returning. In addition, East Germany's infrastructure was also more decrepit than imagined, and unemployment rates in the former East remained high, fueling Far Right political extremism.

Nevertheless, for the most part, German unification has been successful. Western values and institutions are being absorbed by former East Germans, the former West Germany pumped large quantities of economic assistance into the former East, and the East's economy has been substantially privatized. And Germany's capital has moved from Bonn back to the traditional capital, Berlin. Indeed, German unification has been successful enough that in some quarters in Europe, fears of German domination have once again emerged.[10]

Western European Perspectives

In every respect, Western Europe has made impressive strides since World War II. One reason for Western Europe's success was the region's work ethic, a second was U.S. political and economic support, and a third was Western Europe's willingness to undertake the experiments in integration and unity that led to the European Union (EU).

Not surprisingly, Western European states and the EU have developed their own perceptions on economic matters. Sometimes, significant differences exist between and among

Western European states on these issues. Nevertheless, a distinctly Western European outlook on many international economic issues often can be identified.

From the time they were first proposed, it was evident that European revitalization and integration, if successful, would lead to a European challenge of the U.S. position in the international economy. Nevertheless, the speed with which Western Europe improved its economic position and presented a challenge to the United States surprised many. The growth of Western European economic strength has led to different perspectives between Western Europe and the United States about investment and trade.

During the 1950s and 1960s, American firms invested extensively in Western Europe. By 1980, U.S. direct investment in Europe surpassed $100 billion. Much of the profit from this investment was expatriated to the United States, and U.S. MNCs prospered. However, many Europeans grew resentful about the major role played in their economies by U.S. firms. From the European perspective, U.S. direct investment meant jobs, but it also meant that foreign firms might dominate European economies.

Ironically, a countertrend developed in the 1970s as European firms began to invest in the United States. Attracted by high U.S. interest rates, European investors sent capital to the United States. At the same time, attracted by high U.S. returns on investment, firms such as Volkswagen, Bayer, and Siemens opened plants in the United States. Europeans congratulated themselves on being astute businesspeople, but many Americans became resentful of foreign penetration of the U.S. economy. Even so, they were grateful for the jobs foreign investment created. On both sides of the Atlantic, concern mounted about foreign dominance of domestic markets.

Meanwhile, the United States became concerned that the European Community's program for economic integration in 1992 would lead to the creation of a huge market that excluded outsiders. Despite European assurances that this would not be the case, U.S. firms began to seek ways to guarantee that they would have access to the post-1992 European market. On investment, Western European and U.S. perspectives had come full circle. Transatlantic economic interdependence had become a reality, but neither side was completely comfortable with it.

Contrasting Western European and U.S. views on trade also caused problems in the transatlantic relationship. After enjoying small trade surpluses with most Western European states during the 1960s and 1970s, by the late 1970s U.S. trade with the four most industrialized Western European countries showed a substantial deficit. Most of this deficit was caused by West German exports to the United States. The United States reacted to this deficit by charging that Europeans were not carrying their fair share of defense spending and by lodging claims of unfair competition. Western Europeans countered by arguing that the United States' economic decline was caused by, among other things, inefficient energy use and ineffective leadership.

During the 1980s, as the U.S. trade deficit mushroomed, Europeans developed mixed feelings about what was happening. On the one hand, they were concerned by the United States' inability to come to grips with either its trade deficit or its budget deficit. On the other hand, Western Europe benefited from the U.S. trade deficit by selling goods to Americans. Moreover, Europeans recognized that the U.S. trade deficit was probably preferable to the most likely alternative, protectionism.

Nevertheless, another serious problem remained—the issue of European Union subsidies, particularly in agriculture and the aircraft industry. To Europeans, internal politics made it necessary for European governments and the EU to subsidize certain sectors of the economy. To Americans, this unfairly lowered the price at which Europeans could sell subsidized products, and cost U.S. producers billions of dollars in sales. As a result, in 1992, the United States moved toward introducing a tariff against certain European products, including French wine. A U.S.–European trade war loomed as a distinct possibility. Hurried negotiations averted this, but U.S.–European trade tensions remained into the late 1990s.

On North–South aid and trade issues, most European states as a general rule are more favorably disposed toward developing state perspectives than is the United States. Nevertheless, Western Europe is not prepared to alter the existing international economic order to the extent preferred by Developing World countries. Although EU states and the U.S. disagree on the causes of problems in their own trade, they are united in their opposition to most Developing World proposals to change the existing international economic structure. Several European states, France and Sweden in particular, extend considerable quantities of economic aid to the Developing World when measured in terms of percentage of gross national product, but none has supported a restructuring of the international economic system to help Developing World interests.

Despite this, both Great Britain and France have managed to retain rather cordial economic relations and political accord with most of their former colonial holdings. Great Britain's global Commonwealth of Nations meets regularly, and the countries of the Commonwealth share the equivalent of the U.S. concept of most favored nation trading status. France maintains a similar relationship with the Francophone countries of Africa.

On security issues, the end of the Cold War and the East–West conflict enhanced European security immeasurably. Indeed, as we have seen, the Cold War was in many respects the result of disagreement over the future of Europe. The confidence that most Western European states felt regarding their security situation is reflected in Table 10-1, which shows the post-Cold War decrease in defense spending of Western European states measured in terms of spending as a percentage of gross domestic product. Nevertheless, several security issues still perplex many Europeans.

The first is whether political instability and economic hardship in Eastern and Central Europe, Russia and the other former Soviet republics, and northern Africa might lead to a large wave of **immigration into Western Europe.** Many Western Europeans see this possibility as a significant security threat. The fear of this has led to the growth of antiforeign sentiment in several Western European states, especially Germany and France.[11]

The second issue is German unification. Many Europeans remember that a unified Germany precipitated World Wars I and II. As we have seen, some retain fear that a unified Germany may again become expansionist despite over 50 years of peaceful relations with its neighbors.

The third issue is what to do about conflict in Yugoslavia. Again as we have seen, in the early 1990s, Yugoslavia split up along ethnic and religious lines into Bosnia, Croatia, Slovenia, and the Serbia-dominated Yugoslavia. Fighting broke out between several of the countries as well as between ethnic groups living in each. In addition, the government of

Yugoslavia and its Serbian supporters often pursued ethnic cleansing as a matter of policy. The fighting in Bosnia was especially fierce and brutal, with tens of thousands of people dying and millions becoming refugees. For several years, the international community including Europeans and NATO did little to end the fighting as millions died. Then, later in the 1990s, a similar scenario unfolded in Kosovo. This time the fighting and ethnic cleansing escalated until NATO intervened. Even after NATO's intervention, however, a question about what comes next remains.

Finally, the issue of NATO's future must be addressed. Even with the Soviet threat gone, most Western Europeans as well as many Americans believe that NATO retains immense importance as an institution that brings European—and American—defense establishments and political leaders together, and that it therefore serves a useful coordinating purpose. They also maintain that it is an institution that can militarily deter threats that may develop in the future even if such threats can not be identified now.

But some Europeans want to create within the European Union an EU defense capability that will provide both an EU and a NATO defense capability. Others see this as the first step toward the dissolution of NATO.

The issue of **NATO expansion** also must be addressed here.[12] As we have seen, most Central European states want to join the organization, and the Czech Republic, Hungary, and Poland already have. But from the perspective of Western Europe and the United States, wisdom dictates delay before further expansion is undertaken. Neither Western Europe nor the United States wants to alienate Russia, and there are questions about whether NATO has the wherewithal to take on additional commitments in an era of reduced military budgets. Because of these questions, NATO has established a series of "Partnership for Peace" agreements with prospective new members that increase military cooperation between the prospective and current NATO members and they do not provide direction about how membership might be achieved, but that do not provide security guarantees or promise future membership.

TABLE 10-1 **Defense Expenditures of Selected European States, as a Percentage of Gross Domestic Product**

Country	1984	1988	1994	1998
Belgium	3.2	2.9	1.7	1.5
Denmark	2.3	2.1	2.1	1.6
France	4.1	4.0	4.0	2.8
Germany	3.3	3.0	2.0	1.5
Greece	7.0	5.9	5.7	4.8
Italy	2.7	2.4	2.1	2.0
Netherlands	3.2	3.1	2.1	1.8
Norway	2.8	3.3	3.1	2.2
Turkey	4.4	4.3	3.2	4.4
United Kingdom	5.5	4.7	3.4	2.8

Source: IISS, *The Military Balance,* various years.

Despite these issues, virtually every Western European agrees that with the significant exception of the former Yugoslavia, the European continent at the beginning of the twenty-first century is a much safer place than it has been since the 1920s.

JAPAN'S PERCEPTIONS

Modern Japan is a country of contradictions whose economic well-being depends on continued access to reliable sources of external raw materials and stable markets. Militarily constrained because of its U.S.-created constitution, Japan relies on the U.S. military and the benign intentions of others to maintain its security. Pro-Western and modern in its cultural outlook, it nonetheless reveres old Japanese traditions and customs. The contradictions that exist in Japan and influence its perceptions of itself and the world are a mix of its values, beliefs, and experiences.

The Growth of the Japanese Empire

Japan's evolution to an industrial power did not begin until the late nineteenth century. With no scientific-technical tradition, Japan's success in transforming itself into a relatively modern industrial state by the beginning of the twentieth century was truly amazing.[13]

For two centuries before U.S. Commodore William Perry used gunboat diplomacy to influence Japan to sign an 1854 trade treaty with the U.S., Japan lived in self-imposed isolation. However, Japan soon realized that if it were to avoid the fate of dismemberment that European powers were imposing on China, it must modernize and industrialize. Thus, during the late nineteenth century, traditional Japan built the industrial basis for a modern Japan.

With modernization, Japanese nationalism increased, and Japan began to build an empire. To do this, it initiated wars with Korea, China, and Russia. The 1905 Russo–Japanese War was particularly important as Japan learned two lessons that had an immense impact on the way it viewed the world. First, Japan routed Russia at sea and on land, and now knew it could defeat European states. Second, the scope of the victory that Japan won was limited at the urging of U.S. President Theodore Roosevelt, who helped negotiate the treaty that ended the war. Many Japanese believed that the United States had taken advantage of Japan to further its own interests. They now saw the United States as a rival in the Pacific.

Japan continued its drive for empire during World War I as it acquired Germany's abandoned colonial holdings in China. Japan also presented China with the Twenty-One Demands, a thinly veiled effort to expand Japanese influence in China. As World War I ended, Japan sent an army into Russia following the Bolshevik Revolution there to try to acquire territory. Neither the Twenty-One Demands nor the Japanese occupation of eastern Russia were successful in increasing Japan's territorial holdings. Nevertheless, Japan received in the Versailles Treaty that ended World War I several Pacific islands to hold as trusteeships. Japan's empire-building undertakings resumed in 1931 when it invaded Manchuria and soon after China. And throughout the 1930s, Japan strengthened the fortifications and its military capabilities on its Pacific island territories.

Japan was on the move. As World War II engulfed Europe, Japan's military leaders concluded that with France removed as a barrier to Japanese expansion in Southeast Asia and with Great Britain pressed to look to its own survival, only the United States presented a meaningful threat to Japan's new empire. Given the history of U.S. opposition to a sizable Japanese role in the Pacific, at least as seen by the militarist/expansionists in Tokyo, U.S. power had to be neutralized. The Japanese military planned a blow designed to cripple the United States' ability to project power into the Western Pacific. It fell on December 7, 1941, at Pearl Harbor.

Four years of brutal war followed. On August 9, 1945, the war ended when the United States dropped a second atomic bomb, this time on Nagasaki. The first had been dropped on Hiroshima three days earlier. Postwar U.S.–Japanese relations thus began under a nuclear cloud with U.S. forces occupying Japan.

Post-World War II Japanese Views of the United States

The U.S. occupation of Japan lasted until 1952. During the occupation, Japan adopted a new constitution, established the political institutions and practices of democracy, and restored a healthy industrial and agricultural economy.

The United States' attitude toward Japan had also undergone a complete transformation. Whereas at the conclusion of the war the United States regarded Japan as an international pariah, by 1952, Washington considered the island nation an integral part of the U.S. security system. Mao's victory in China and the Korean War converted Japan into a crucial link in the United States' containment policy in Asia. Japan served as a valuable base for the projection of U.S. power into the Western Pacific.[14]

Japan had to pay a price for reattaining independence, and some Japanese citizens later criticized their government for its willingness to pay that price. The United States obtained bases to be used after the occupation ended, and Japan would not recognize or do business with either mainland China or North Korea, two traditional Japanese trading partners, because of its new position in the American treaty system.

Throughout the 1950s and 1960s, Japan remained an integral part of the American security system, and concentrated on building its economic strength. Under the U.S.-inspired Japanese Constitution, Japan's military was limited to territorial self-defense forces. Thus, Japan's military expenditures remained low, and the country relied on the United States to provide its defense needs. Much of the money that otherwise would have been spent on defense was devoted to industrial investment. Indeed, between 1952 and 1971, Japan's gross national product increased at a rate nearly double that of the rest of the industrialized West.

Even so, anti-American sentiment remained strong in Japan. Japanese resentment, built up over a half-century of U.S.–Japanese mistrust, a brutal war ended by atomic weapons, and six years of occupation, did not dissipate rapidly.

Nevertheless, over time, it did dissipate. By the 1960s and 1970s, most of Japan's population held favorable views of the United States. However, two noneconomic issues complicated U.S.–Japanese relations during this period, the Vietnam War and continuing U.S. occupation of Okinawa. But the end of the U.S. involvement in Vietnam in 1972 and the return of Okinawa to Japanese rule the same year removed both issues as irritants in what had become a quite close and cordial relationship. In the years since, despite additional occasional strains, U.S.–Japanese diplomatic and security relations have continued to be close and cordial.

U.S.–Japanese economic relations have been more tempestuous. During the 1950s and 1960s, most Americans had a condescending attitude toward Japan's economic capabilities, viewing Japan as little more than a country of copiers. The Japanese economy mimicked everything, Americans believed, and could produce little that was original. Further, Americans considered Japanese products inferior and shoddy; "Made in Japan" was a slogan of derision. The Japanese, historically a proud and able people, resented the United States' condescension.

As Japan's role in the world economy increased during the 1960s, signs of strain multiplied in the U.S.–Japanese economic relationship. When the U.S. deficit on the bilateral balance of merchandise trade passed $3 billion in 1971, the United States acted. The Nixon administration imposed a 10 percent surcharge on all imports for 90 days and threatened to invoke the "Trading with the Enemy Act" against Japan. Japan viewed these steps as a U.S. effort to push Japanese automakers out of the U.S. market and to force a revaluation of the yen.

Despite this, the U.S. trade deficit with Japan grew. The United States pressed Japan to restrict voluntarily its exports to the United States, to decrease non-tariff barriers to U.S. imports into the Japanese market, to reduce Japanese savings rates, and to alter the structure of Japan's domestic markets, but nothing worked. The U.S. trade deficit with Japan continued to grow, and as Japanese corporations began to buy up U.S. real estate and industry, U.S. resentment escalated further. By 1995, U.S. frustration with Japan had reached the point where the United States threatened to place a 100 percent tariff on imported Japanese luxury automobiles. Only last second negotiations averted the action, which almost assuredly would have escalated into a trade war.

But from Japan's perspective, the United States was to blame for the trade deficit. Japan argued that its businesses built better products and that the United States could not control its spending habits. It also noted that it bought one third of the U.S. government notes that funded the U.S. deficit. In addition, Japan maintained, there was little that could be done about the fact that Japanese consumers preferred Japanese products.[15]

Suddenly, in the late 1990s, Japan's economic bubble burst as super-heated economies throughout East Asia succumbed to the so-called Asian contagion. Overextended financially, Japan's business profits disappeared, real estate prices plummeted, and the stock market fell. U.S.–Japanese economic tensions dissipated as the U.S. economy soared and Japan's economy worsened. The United States still imported more from Japan than it exported to Japan, but from the U.S. perspective, Japan was no longer the economic threat that it had been only a few years before.

By 2000, then, U.S.–Japanese relations had returned to an even keel and tensions dissipated. This was well illustrated during U.S. President Bill Clinton's 2000 visit to Japan. Japan knows that it needs U.S. markets, and without the benefit of the U.S. security blanket, Japanese defense expenditures would have to be increased considerably.

At the same time, it is clear that Japan no longer trails in the American wake politically, diplomatically, or economically. During the 1990s, Japan became a country that was not afraid to say "No" to American demands. Despite its recent economic travails, Japan remains unafraid to say "No" to the United States today.[16]

Japanese Views of China and Russia

Japan's relations with and perceptions of China and Russia have varied widely over time. Parts of Northeast Asia including Korea and territories currently in China and Russia have long been subjects of dispute between Japan, China, and Russia because of resources and security concerns. Japan has not been involved in any military conflicts over these territories since World War II, but it still claims four islands currently held by Russia. These islands, called the Northern Territories, fell under Soviet control at the end of World War II as part of the peace settlement.[17] Japan has insisted that the islands be returned to Japanese rule ever since, but to no avail.

Before World War II, Japan coveted Chinese territory for its resource wealth. Following the war, as Japan became enmeshed in the U.S. security network, Japanese relations with China were proscribed by U.S. demands. Nevertheless, Japan was careful not to undertake any actions that would alienate Mao's government in Beijing. As Japanese trade with mainland China had historically been sizable, Japan's diplomacy was understandable.

During the 1960s, Japan and China implemented tentative trade contacts, but U.S. and Chinese Nationalist objections guaranteed that these contacts would achieve little. Even the beginning of the U.S.–Sino rapprochement in 1971 did little to improve Sino–Japanese relations because the Beijing regime was extremely mistrustful of Japan's support for Taiwan. But when a new Japanese Prime Minister visited Beijing in 1972 and declared that he "fully understood" China's position on Taiwan, that is, that Taiwan was and is a natural part of China, the doors opened for improved Sino–Japanese relations and trade.

Since this Sino–Japanese rapprochement of the early 1970s, Japan has had little concern about China as a threat to Japanese national security. Japan and China have no territorial disputes, and as long as Japan and the United States maintain their military security arrangement, Japan appears confident of the U.S. intent to protect it from any Chinese encroachment. Thus, as far as Japan is concerned, China is a trading partner and little more.

Japanese perceptions of Russia, and before 1992, the Soviet Union, are not so favorable. In addition to the dispute over the Northern Territories, Japan and the Soviet Union had disputes over fishing rights and Soviet violation of Japanese airspace. These and other Russo–Japanese disputes and perceived threats are, of course, additional to earlier Soviet–Japanese conflicts of this century: the 1905 Russo–Japanese War, Japanese intervention in Siberia in 1918, conflict between Japanese and Soviet troops in Manchuria during the 1930s, and the delayed Soviet entry into World War II against Japan. The last situation was particularly galling to the Japanese; the USSR, after remaining neutral for four years, declared war on Japan on August 9, 1945, the day the atomic bomb was dropped on Nagasaki. Five days later Japan sued for peace. Nevertheless, the Soviets demanded full reparations, and received as part of their settlement the Northern Territories.

During the late 1980s, Soviet–Japanese relations improved. The Soviets made it very clear that they were interested in obtaining Japanese investment capital for the Soviet Far East. With Japan's need for external resources and its surplus capital, and with the corresponding Soviet need for capital and desire to develop the Far East, the possibilities for trade and investment seemed real. The same situation applies to Russia after the collapse of the Soviet Union.

However, unless Russia and Japan settle the Northern Territories issue, only a limited expansion in Russian–Japanese trade and relations is probable. Japan insists that its lost islands be returned, and even if the Russian government were disposed to return them, Russian domestic politics would make such an action extremely difficult. Indeed, Russian domestic opposition to even the possibility of the return of the Northern Territories to Japan forced former Russian President Boris Yeltsin to cancel several trips to Japan. Yeltsin eventually made the trip, and Russia and Japan continue to flirt with the possibility of talks about the islands, but at the beginning of the twenty-first century, they remained firmly in Russia's control.

Japan's Perception of Its Role in the World

After the United States, Japan has the world's second largest economy. Yet its economy is heavily dependent on access to foreign raw materials and markets. To be denied either would be a terrible blow to Japan's prosperity. Domestic opposition to an activist foreign policy resulting from the memories of World War II also limited Japan's international activities considerably. These realities placed inevitable constraints on Japan's view of its own role in the world.

During the 1980s and 1990s, however, this began to change. Perhaps the most significant indication of Japan's changing view of its own role in the world was the Japanese government's 1992 decision to deploy Japanese military forces to Cambodia under United Nations command as part of a peacekeeping force there. This marked the first time since World War II that Japanese armed forces were stationed outside Japan.

However, this deployment also had a negative side. In many countries in East Asia, the presence of Japanese troops overseas stirs strong memories of Japan's imperial past. China, Korea, and other states waited years for Japan to apologize for its brutal invasions and occupations during the 1930s and 1940s, but until recently Japan was unable to bring itself to do so. History continues to play a huge role in Japan's views of what it can and cannot do in the world.

Japan, then, sees itself in a curious position, with a somewhat contradictory self-image. It depends on external resources and markets for its economic well-being. It largely depends on the United States for its security. But Japan is also an international economic giant that is afraid for historical reasons and for fear of raising foreign hostility to think about its global roles and responsibilities. How Japan resolves the tension between dependence and independence, between following and leading, and between the past and the present will be one of the major issues facing Japan during the twenty-first century.[18]

THE OUTLOOK FROM RUSSIA

Few countries in the world have experienced as great and as quick a change in their worldview as Russia did during the 1990s. The decade began with Russia as the dominant force in the Soviet Union, a superpower whose interests were global. The decade ended with Russia as an independent country struggling to survive. Indeed, Russia's economic struggles were so extensive that many people, but not most Russians, questioned whether Russia was still a developed country. As for Russia's role in the world, as the twenty-first century began, it had few interests beyond Central Europe and the former Soviet republics other than acquiring aid and investment.

Despite Russia's current problems, many Russians remember their country's role as a world power. It goes back centuries, long before the Soviet Union came into existence following the 1917 Bolshevik Revolution. One of the challenges facing students as they try to understand Russia today is the extent to which the viewpoints of the Russian Empire of the Czars and the viewpoints of the Soviet Union of the communists' influence present-day Russian views of Russia's role in the world.

The Russia of the Czars

The international viewpoints of the Czars' Russia were influenced by many factors, but four themes dominated.

First, Russian leaders of the Czars' court believed that Russia had a messianic mission. Successive Russian rulers used conversion of nonbelievers to the Russian Orthodox religion as a rationale for territorial expansion. Another self-perceived Russian mission was the unification of all Slavic peoples of Eastern and Central Europe, the so-called "little Slavic brothers," under Russian rule.

Territorial expansion was a second theme. Centuries ago, what is today's Russia began as the city-state of Kiev. After the Russians threw off two centuries of Mongol rule in 1480, the center of what would become Russian civilization moved from Kiev to Moscow and then on to St. Petersburg. During the seventeenth, eighteenth, and nineteenth centuries, Russia continued to grow until by the early twentieth century, the Russian empire stretched from Poland in the east to the Pacific Ocean and Alaska in the west. The Czars ruled one-sixth of all the land in the world. When Lenin founded the Soviet Union, most of this territory became the USSR.

Not surprisingly, Russians also saw their country as one of the world's great powers. This third theme was a function not only of territorial expanse, but also prowess in battle. Russia played a key role in overthrowing Napoleon, competed with Great Britain for influence throughout Central Asia, and struggled with the Chinese. By almost every measure of the eighteenth and nineteenth century world, the Czars' Russian Empire was great indeed.

Even so, despite their country's status as a great power, many Russians never believed that Russia was up to the standards of the rest of Europe, particularly France and Great Britain. The French language was used and French customs were followed in elite Russian society, and Russian leaders envied Britain's industrial might and overseas empire. They also came to envy and fear Germany's military and industrial prowess.[19]

This fourth theme of national uncertainty about Russia's real status led to a debate in Russia throughout the nineteenth century between the Westernizers and the Slavophiles. **Westernizers** believed Russia could catch up with the West by adopting European practices, while **Slavophiles** thought that Russia's national salvation lay in rejecting European thought and customs and emphasizing traditional Slavic culture. In some respects, this debate goes on today in twenty-first century Russia between those who want to modernize Russia with democracy and free markets and those who want to return to a traditional authoritarian form of government.

Despite this debate, by the beginning of the twentieth century, Russians had a fairly well defined vision of themselves and their history. Russia had historical missions, possessed vast territory, and was a great power. Its problems were great but surmountable. Few observers predicted or expected a major change in the course of Russian history. Amid the sacrifice and suffering of World War I, however, the groundwork was being laid for one of the most important revolutions of the twentieth century. In March 1917, following extensive rioting in St. Petersburg, Nicholas II abdicated, ending three centuries of rule by the Czars. A provisional government assumed power but was overthrown by **Lenin** and the **Bolshevik Party** in November 1917. For Russia, a new era was about to begin.

The Soviet Era and Soviet Outlooks

Lenin and his followers were Marxists, who as we saw in Chapter 1 believed that the course of history was determined by class conflict. Together, they created a new country called the Soviet Union based on Marx's theories as altered by Lenin. During the Soviet era (1917–1991), some Russian views of the world changed considerably and others very little. Always, however, even if it required verbal and intellectual gymnastics, the Soviet leaders tried to interpret their outlooks and actions in Marxist-Leninist terms.

The Soviet worldview was unquestionably colored by the **Russian Civil War** and the accompanying Western intervention. The Civil War and intervention followed hard on the heels of the hardships caused by Russia's involvement in World War I. Lenin, accustomed to attacking the authority of the state rather than being the authority of the state, found himself trying to cope with the problems of running the world's largest state even while he struggled against internal and external enemies to maintain Bolshevik rule.

Lenin died in 1924. After a long internal political struggle, **Joseph Stalin** won the reins of power. By this time (1928), the fundamental outline of action that guided Soviet foreign policy until World War II had clearly emerged: the primacy of state objectives over revolutionary élan; the normalization of relations with capitalist states, Germany in particular; the promotion of "peaceful coexistence"; the creation of nonaggression pacts with the Baltic and Eastern European states; the courtship of China and, to a lesser degree, the United States, for the purpose of countering Japanese expansionism; and finally, the use of the Comintern to foster external support for the Soviet Union and to foment trouble in the capitalist and colonial world.

To Stalin, Soviet survival depended on the USSR's ability to defend itself. Hence rapid industrialization became the top priority of the Soviet state. Stalin also forced peasants and farmers to work on immense collective farms. This brought great suffering to many Russians. Anyone who disagreed with Stalin was purged. Indeed, the purges were used by Stalin and his supporters to eliminate anyone for any reason. At least 15 million Soviet citizens died during **industrialization, collectivization, and the purges** in the late 1920s and 1930s.[20]

Stalin's brutality would be monumental were it not for the carnage that followed. Stalin's fear of the external world proved well founded as, on June 22, 1941, German forces invaded the Soviet Union. World War II had come to the Soviet Union. Before

World War II was over, more than 25 million Soviet citizens died. By contrast, the United States lost only 300,000 people.

During World War II, the Soviet Union, the United States, and Great Britain were allies, known as "the Big Three." Nevertheless, Stalin did nor trust the United States and Great Britain, and the United States and Great Britain did not trust Stalin. There were many reasons for this mistrust, but the largest was different views over the future of Europe. The United States wanted Western-style democratic governments established throughout Europe after the war, while Stalin wanted to maintain Soviet influence in Eastern and Central Europe to guard against invasions from Western Europe, to expand the Soviet empire, and to spread Marxism-Leninism. The disagreement over the future of Europe combined with other Soviet–American disagreements to create the East–West conflict and the Cold War, as we saw in Chapter 7.

The Rise and Fall of the USSR as a Superpower

Gradually at first, and then more rapidly, the Soviet Union recovered from World War II, during the 1950s and 1960s expanding its activities and influence beyond Europe. By the 1970s, the USSR had become a true global superpower. Wielding more military might across a greater territorial expanse than at any other time in its history, enjoying greater political influence around the world than ever before, and possessing the world's second-largest national economic base, the Soviet Union basked in its power, prestige, and influence.

But the Soviet Union also faced major problems. Economic growth had practically stopped. The USSR was beset by declining labor productivity, a failed agricultural program, overcentralized decision making, and graft and corruption. Communism as an ideology no longer inspired. Old men in their seventies who refused to transfer authority to the new generation dominated the political system. In short, the Soviet domestic situation was serious.

The Kremlin faced international problems as well. The USSR remained encircled by unfriendly states and states subservient only through force of Soviet arms. Relations with the United States, Japan, and Western Europe were at a low ebb. Even in the Developing World, the USSR for the most part was unsuccessful in its efforts to develop and maintain close long-term relationships.

Between 1982 and 1985, the Soviet Union's domestic and international position deteriorated further in all areas except the military. This deterioration was even more pronounced than it may otherwise have been as a result of the Soviet Union's leadership crisis. Between November 1982 and March 1985, four men—Leonid Brezhnev, Yuri Andropov, Konstantin Chernenko, and Mikhail Gorbachev—led the USSR, the first three dying in office. This turmoil prevented the implementation of new policies to address the USSR's deteriorating situation.

When **Mikhail Gorbachev** became general secretary of the Communist Party of the Soviet Union (CPSU) in March 1985, he took over a country careening toward crisis. He realized this and instituted policy reforms so extensive that they could only be termed a revolution. These reforms also led directly and indirectly to the collapse of the Soviet Union, the end of Soviet superpower status, the independence of the 15 republics that formerly made up the USSR, and the creation of a new Russian state that searched uncertainly for its role in world affairs.[21]

Today's Russia: What Role in the World?

During 1991, the world witnessed the demise not just of 74 years of communist rule in the Soviet Union, but also the dissolution of five centuries of Russian empire. The changes that took place and the impacts of those changes are epochal, part of an ongoing process that is still taking place.

Where is Russia headed, and what role does it see for itself in the world? Too many variables exist to answer the question definitively. Nevertheless, Russia is still a potentially rich and powerful state. It retains an immense nuclear arsenal. But its road to economic recovery, political stability, and finding a place in the world with which it will be comfortable is likely to be a long one.

Even with the successful transfer of the presidency via a generally fair election from Boris Yeltsin to Vladimir Putin that took place in 2000, Russia's political and economic reforms are on thin ice. Putin claims that he supports democratic political reform, an open society, and a free market economic system, but he also recognizes that a certain degree of discipline must be restored. How Putin will walk the fine line balancing democracy and discipline is one of the great unanswered questions for Russia in the early twenty-first century.

For Russia, the uncertainty of how domestic events will unfold plays a major role in Russia's relations with and view of the rest of the world. Russia is no longer a superpower, and it cannot act like one. During the Soviet era, the USSR could influence virtually any world event that it chose; Russia today cannot do this.

Despite its economic woes and political instability, Russia remains a regional power. It retains influence in many of the newly independent states and is a force to be reckoned with on many European and Asian issues. But the overarching reality is that beyond Europe and Asia, Russia no longer has significant influence.

Most Russians recognize this and accept this, but some do not. Even those who do recognize this do not necessarily accept it with equanimity; it is difficult to adjust to being a former superpower.

Meanwhile, the dominant foreign concerns for most other newly independent states are Russia and economics. Russia is a concern because of its fomer role in and control of the Russian and Soviet empires. Without exception, the newly independent states were part of the Soviet empire for at least half a century, and some were part of the Russian and Soviet empires for as long as five centuries. Many states remain concerned that Russia may try to reincorporate them.[22]

Many Russians are meanwhile concerned that the United States and Western Europe consider Russia a second rank international power and are attempting to further degrade their country. As if Russia's economic plight is not enough, they say, NATO's 1999 expansion and NATO's attacks on Yugoslavia in the same year were intended in part to humiliate Russia.[23] This is not acceptable, they say.

Worse yet, Russia may unravel. Ethnic groups in several areas in Russia are clamoring for independence, most notably in Chechnya where Russian forces tried unsuccessfully from 1994 through 1996 to quiet a separatist rebellion. In 1999, Russia again launched an assault against the break-away province, this time using the equivalent of scorched earth tactics to bring Chechnya back into the Russian fold.

Understandably, then, many Russians see their country as embattled and with few friends. Russia has abandoned communism and is not likely to return to it, but this does not mean that a democratic political system and a free market economic system have permanently taken hold. Nor are Russians sure of their homeland's role in the world. But they know that Russia's present situation is transitory, with an immense range of possible futures. "Transitory to what?" is the key question.[24]

PERCEPTIONS AND POLICY

The different U.S., European, Japanese, and Russian perceptions of world affairs detailed in the preceding pages, and the perceptions of other developed states not presented here because of exigencies of space, would be of limited interest to us if these perceptions did not also serve as the basis for national policies. But as we saw in Chapter 9, Kenneth Boulding observed in *The Image* that "behavior depends on the image." So too do national policies, and that is why it is critical that we have a grasp of different national perceptions.

Clearly, some of the perceptions of international relations, the international system, and the way the world works that are held in Washington, Paris, London, Berlin, Tokyo, and Moscow are similar. But many are dissimilar and sometimes outright contradictory.

This does not mean that one country's perceptions are necessarily right and another's necessarily wrong. It does mean that perceptions can be and often are different. Any policy maker who does not understand this, who refuses to accept this, or who ignores this reality places his or her country and its policies at risk.

That having been said, it is also true that the perceptions of developed states on many issues are often quite similar to each other. We saw that earlier in this chapter. Now, however, we turn to the perceptions that developing states hold of international relations, the international system, and the way the world works. They are quite different than those that we have examined to this point.

KEY TERMS AND CONCEPTS

developed states' shared perceptions   many developed states have democratic political systems, stable societies, and high standards of living, and therefore share many perceptions; most also have different histories and acquired their political systems, stable societies, and high standards of livings in different ways, and thus have many different perceptions as well

isolationism   a dominant theme in U.S. foreign policy until World War II, but abandoned following the war as the U.S. established a global economic and military presence

moralism   another dominant theme in U.S. foreign policy, much espoused as a motivating ideal

pragmatism   a third dominant theme in U.S. foreign policy that emphasizes the need to achieve common sense objectives

containment   the U.S. policy of preventing the expansion of the Soviet Union, followed from the late 1940s to the end of the Cold War

détente   the term used to describe the period of improved U.S.-Soviet relations from 1972 to 1979

Vietnamization   a U.S. policy initiated by Richard Nixon that sought to return the fighting of the Vietnam War to the South Vietnamese

Central European perspectives   Communist governments came to power in Central Europe after World War II, most with Soviet help, remaining in power until 1989, sometimes only because of Soviet interventions. In 1989, the peoples of Eastern Europe revolted against their communist leaders, establishing for the most part non-communist governments. Since then, most have struggled to create democratic governments with free market economic systems.

Germany as a special case   after East Germany's communist government collapsed in 1989, East and West Germany were unified in 1991. This was a much more difficult task than at first imagined.

immigration into Western Europe   many Europeans are concerned that the turmoil in the former Soviet Union and Central Europe, warfare in Yugoslavia, and economic problems in northern Africa will accelerate because of the immigration into Western Europe

Japanese views of the U.S.   most Japanese view the U.S. as a friend, but tension between the two countries exists because of trade issues

Japanese views of China and Russia   relations improved after the U.S.S.R. collapsed, but Japan and Russia have strained relations because of Russia's occupation of four islands it received from Japan after World War II. Japan sees China primarily as a trading partner.

Japan's views of its own role in the world   Japan is becoming more assertive in its foreign policy, but it is still trying to decide what role beyond trading it wants to play in contemporary international affairs

Russia of the Czars   under the Czars during the sixteenth through early twentieth centuries, Russia acquired an empire that stretched from Poland to the Pacific Ocean and from India to the Arctic Ocean.

Westernizers   believed that Russia's problems could be solved by becoming like Europe and adopting European ways of doing things

Slavophiles   believed that Russia's problems could be solved only by excluding outside influences and concentrating on "Russian" solutions

Russian Civil War   the internal conflict between communists and anti-communists that raged in Russia from 1918 to 1921

V.I. Lenin   Russian Marxist who led the Bolshevik revolution in Russia and who was the first leader of the Soviet Union

Bolshevik Party   Marxist party that overthrew the post-Czarist provisional government in Russia in 1917 and that later changed its name to the Communist Party of the Soviet Union

Joseph Stalin   the brutal ruler of the U.S.S.R from 1927 to 1951

industrialization, collectivization, and the purges   the drive during the 1920s and 1930s to turn the U.S.S.R. into an industrial power was industrialization; collectivization saw Soviet agriculture centralized into collective farms at the same time; and the purges were a series of trials, arrests, and murders that swept Soviet society in the 1930s.

Mikhail Gorbachev   became Soviet leader in 1985, instituting changes in policies so significant they are called the Gorbachev Revolution, including: 1. glasnost (openness in social behavior and control); 2. perestroika (restructuring in economics); 3. demokratizatsiya (democratization in political processes); and 4. new thinking in foreign policy

WEB REFERENCES

developed states' shared perceptions: *www.oecd.org* website of the Organization for Economic Cooperation and Development, whose members are developed states

www.oecd.org the University of Toronto's G-8 Information Centre, with details of past, present, and future G-7/G-8 meetings

official U.S. foreign policy perspectives: *www.state.gov* the U.S. Department of State's website

official European foreign policy perspectives: *www.europa.eu.int* the European Union's website

official Japanese foreign policy perspectives: *www.mofa.go.jp* the Japanese Ministry of Foreign Affair's website

official Russian foreign policy perspectives: *www.mid.ru/mid/eng/bod.htm* the Russian Ministry of Foreign Affair's website

NOTES

1. President Harry S. Truman, Speech before a Joint Session of the U.S. Congress, March 12, 1947.

2. President William Clinton, Address to the American people on Kosovo, March 24, 1999.

3. For more detailed views of how isolationism, moralism, and pragmatism helped shape U.S. foreign policy, see Seymour Martin Lipsett, *American Exceptionalism* (New York, NY: Norton, 1996); Robert W. McElroy, *Morality and American Foreign Policy* (Princeton, NJ: Princeton University Press, 1992); Bruce Nichols and Gil Loescher, Jr., *The Moral Nation* (south Bend, IN: University of Notre Dame Press, 1989); Amos Perlmutter, *Making the World Safe for Democracy* (Chapel Hill, NC: University of North Carolina Press, 1997); and Kenneth W. Thompson, *Tradition and Values in Politics and Diplomacy* (Baton Rouge, LA: Louisiana State University Press, 1992).

4. For the conceptual underpinnings of containment, see George F. Kennan ("X"), "The Sources of Soviet Conduct," *Foreign Affairs* (July 1947), pp. 566–582.

5. For the origins of détente, see Michael Froman, *The Development of the Idea of Détente* (New York, NY: St. Martin's Press, 1992). See also Coral Bell, *The Diplomacy of Détente* (New York, NY: St. Martin's Press, 1977).

6. For discussions of Carter's human rights policies, see Arthur Schlesinger, Jr., "Human Rights and the American Tradition," *Foreign Affairs: America and the World* (1978), pp. 503–526; J.J. Kirkpatrick, "Establishing a Viable Human Rights Policy," *World Affairs* (Spring 1981), pp. 323–334; and G.D. Loescher, "Carter's Human Rights Policy and the 95th Congress," *World Today* (April 1979), pp. 140–159.

7. For discussions of U.S. foreign and defense policy under Reagan, see Stephen E. Ambrose, *Rise to Globalism: American Foreign Policy Since 1938,* 7th ed. (New York, NY: Penguin, 1993); Steven W. Hook and John Spanier, *American Foreign Policy Since World War II,* 15th ed. (Washington, D.C.: Congressional Quarterly Press, 2000); Richard Mandelbaum and Strobe Talbott, *Reagan and Gorbachev* (New York, NY: Vintage Books, 1987); and Richard A. Melanson, *American Foreign Policy since the Vietnam War,* 3d ed. (Armonk, NY: Sharpe, 2000).

8. See Seymour J. Deitchman, *On Being a Superpower* (Boulder, CO: Westview Press, 2000); Martha Honey and Tom Barry, *Global Focus: U.S. Foreign Policy at the Turn of the Millenium* (New York, NY: St. Martin's Press, 2000); Paul Kennedy, *Preparing for the Twenty-First Century* (New York, NY: Random House, 1993); Alvin Z. Rubinstein et al., eds., *The Clinton Foreign Policy Reader* (Armonk, NY: Sharpe, 2000); and Karin Von Hippel, *Democracy by Force* (New York, NY: Cambridge University Press, 2000) for several discussions of the possible directions for U.S. foreign policy in the twenty-first century.

9. For discussions of the former communist states of Central Europe, see David S. Mason, *Revolution in East-Central Europe: The Rise and Fall of Communism and the Cold War* (Boulder, CO: Westview Press, 1992); James E. Goodby, *Europe Undivided* (Washington, D.C.: U.S. Institute of Peace Press, 1998); and Karen E. Smith, *The Making of EU Foreign Policy: The Case of Eastern Europe* (New York, NY: St. Martin's Press, 1999).

10. For details of Germany's unification and its ensuing successes and challenges, see for example Michael M. Boll, "Superpower Diplomacy and German Unification: The Insiders' Views," *Parameters* (Winter 1996–97), pp. 109–21; Philip Zelikow and Condoleezza Rice, *Germany Unified and Europe Transformed* (Cambridge, MA: Harvard University Press, 1997); and Gale A. Mattox, et al., *Germany in Transition: A Unified Nation's Search for Identity* (Boulder, CO: Westview Press, 1999).

11. For European concerns about immigration, see Che Sidanius, "Immigrants in Europe: The Rise of a New Underclass," *The Washington Quarterly* (Autumn 1998), pp. 5–8.

12. See David Calleo, "NATO Enlargement as a Problem for Security in Europe," *Aussenpolitik* (Fall 1998), pp. 24–27; and Karl-Heinz Kamp, "NATO Entrapped: Debating the Next Enlargement Round," *Survival* (Autumn 1998), pp. 170–186; John Hillen and Michael P. Noonan, "The Geopolitics of NATO Enlargement," *Parameters* (Autumn 1998), pp. 21–35; and James Sperling, ed., *Two Tiers or Two Speeds? The European Security Order and the Enlargement of the European Union and NATO* (New York, NY: St. Martin's Press, 2000) for discussions of the issues involved in the debate over NATO expansion.

13. For the history of nineteenth- and early twentieth-century Japan, see Hugh Borton, *Japan's Modern Century—From Perry to 1970* (New York: John Wiley, 1970); and Edwin O. Reischauer and Albert M. Craig, *Japan: Tradition and Transformation* (Boston: Houghton Mifflin, 1978).

14. For discussion of U.S. policy toward Japan during the 1945–1952 period, see Roger Buckley, *Occupation Diplomacy: Britain, the United States, and Japan 1945–1952* (New York: Cambridge, n.d.); Grant K. Goodman, *American Occupation of Japan: A Retrospective View* (New York: Paragon, 1968); and Robert E. Ward and Frank J. Schulman, *Allied Occupation of Japan: 1945–1952* (Chicago: American Library Association, 1974). See also Nazli Choucri et al., *The Challenge of Japan Before World War II and After* (New York: Routledge, 1992).

15. For additional details about U.S.–Japanese relations during the 1980s and 1990s, see Ralph A. Cossa, *Restructuring the U.S. Japan Alliance* (Washington, D.C.: CSIS Press, 1997); and Michael J. Green and Patrick M. Cronin, eds., *The U.S.–Japan Alliance* (New York, NY: Council on Foreign Relations Press, 1999).

16. This phrase comes from Shintaro Ishihara, *The Japan That Can Say No* (New York: Simon and Schuster, 1989).

17. The Japanese Northern Territories consist of the Habomai Islands, Shikotan Islands, Kunashiri Island, and Etorofu Island. See *Japan's Northern Territories* (Tokyo: Ministry of Foreign Affairs, 1980).

18. For additional views of Japan's international role in the twenty-first century, see Richard D. Leitch et al., *Japan's Role in the Post–Cold War World* (Greenwood, 1995); Eric Heginbotham and Richard J. Samuels, "Mercantile Realism and Japanese Foreign Policy," *International Security* (Spring 1998), pp. 171–203; and Masao Yukuwa, "Japan's Enemy is Japan," *The Washington Quarterly* (Winter 1999), pp. 13–16

19. For discussions of these viewpoints, see E.H. Carr, "Russia and Europe as a Theme of Russian History," in Richard Pares and A.J.P. Taylor, eds., *Essays Presented to Sir Lewis Namier* (New York, NY: Macmillan, 1956); and Robert F. Byrnes, "Attitudes toward the West," in Ivo J. Lederer, ed., *Russian Foreign Policy: Essays in Historical Perspective* (New Haven, CN: Yale University Press, 1967).

20. For one estimate, see Nikita Khrushchev, *Khrushchev Remembers* (Boston, MA: Little, Brown, 1970), p. 583.

21. See Geoffrey Hosking, *The Awakening of the Soviet Union* (Cambridge, MA: Harvard University Press, 1990); David Remnick, Lenin's Tomb: The Last Days of the Soviet Empire (New York, NY: Random House, 1993); and Jeffrey T. Checkel, *Ideas and International Political Change: Soviet/Russian Behavior and the End of the Cold War* (New Haven, CN: Yale University Press, 1997) for good discussions of the events that led to the decline and fall of the Soviet Union.

22. For a discussion of the concerns that states in the "near abroad" have that Russia may again become an expansionist power, see Bruce D. Porter and Carol R. Saivetz, "The Once and Future Empire: Russia and the Near Abroad," *The Washington Quarterly* (Summer 1994), pp. 75–90. See also Charles King and Neil J. Melvin, "Diaspora Politics: Ethnic Linkages, Foreign Policy, and Security in Eurasia," *International Security* (Winter 1999–2000), pp. 108–138.

23. These concerns were detailed in the discussion of Russian views of the conflict in Kosovo in Chapter 9.

24. See Nicoai Petro and Alvin Rubinstein, *Russian Foreign Policy: From Empire to Nation-State* (New York, NY: Longman, 1997); Grigory Yavlinsky, "Russia's Phony Capitalism," *Foreign Affairs* (May-June, 1998), pp. 67–79; Stephen J. Blank, *Threats to Russian Security: The View from Moscow* (Carlisle, PA: U.S. Army War College, 2000); Martin Nicholson, "Towards a Russia of the Regions, *Adelphi Paper 330* (London: International Institute of Strategic Studies, 1999); and Victoria E. Bonnell et al., eds., *Russia in the New Century: Stability or Disorder?* (Boulder, CO: Westview Press, 2000) for several discussions of Russia and its foreign policy in the late twentieth and early twenty-first century.

Chapter 11

Outlooks from the Developing World

- What shapes the perceptions of the Developing World?
- How do states of the Developing World view themselves and their role in the world, and why do they have these views?
- As the most populous state in the world, how does China view itself and its role in the world, and why does it have these views?

Before we begin our discussion of Developing World outlooks on international relations, it may be useful once again to clarify terms and concepts. As pointed out in Chapter 8, the Developing World is called by many names. Sometimes it is called the Third World, other times the South, and still other times the Less Developed Countries, to name a few.

On occasion, these terms create confusion. Should China be considered a developing state or should it be in a class by itself because of its huge population of 1.2 billion people and its nuclear weapons? Should India, with one billion people and nuclear weapons, also be considered separately? Should the rich oil-producing states be considered Developing World states or should they be moved into another category because of their oil wealth? These questions are serious, and there are no universally accepted answers to them.

For our purposes, China and India will be considered developing states. Despite China's huge population and nuclear weapons, its per capita gross domestic product measured in purchasing power parity in 1997 was only about the same as that of Botswana or Bolivia, slightly over $3,000. India's was approximately half that. Similarly, the oil-exporting states of Africa, Asia, and the Middle East will also be considered developing states because their wealth is generally restricted to a small percentage of the population and most of their citizens have yet to enjoy the benefit of wealth.

The Developing World includes about 150 African, Asian, Latin American, and Middle Eastern countries, as well as a number of island states. It is an immensely diverse grouping of countries separated not only by national boundaries, but also by differences in political outlook, social structure, economic organization, levels of stability, and standards of living.

What provides unity to this diversity is that many Developing World states share the experiences and heritages of a colonial past, sharply opposed internal social and economic

Chapter 11

IT AND THE DEVELOPING WORLD: ACCELERATING DEVELOPMENT

As we saw in Chapter 7, there are no guarantees that Information Age technology will accelerate economic growth in the Developing World. But more and more, people in the economic development and assistance community people believe that it could. Many development and assistance experts and officials believe that what must be done falls into four categories.

First, awareness must be raised in developing states that information technology could help accelerate development. This will not be easy, development experts and officials caution, since many people in developing countries think in terms of the industrial age and believe that IT has little to do with "true" development. Many in the Developing World also fear that widespread adoption of IT would lead to erosion of their local culture and the adoption of English as their primary language.

Second, many development and assistance experts and officials believe developing states must invest extensively in information infrastructure development. To many experts and officials, the correlation between economic development and information infrastructure development is compelling. The required investments, they estimate, will be sizable, probably between $70 and $100 billion per year. Investment on this scale would require both private and public funds.

To attract private investment, developing countries must have information-friendly environments. This means that information policies and telecommunications reforms must be in place and that laws protecting investment, intellectual property, privacy and data security must be passed. Open and competitive but well-regulated information and communication markets must also exist. Developing countries must also have investment-friendly environments beyond the information sector.

Third, many experts and officials maintain that developing countries must invest heavily in education, technical literacy, and computer literacy. In short, people in developing states must be "sold" on IT literacy and the need to have their country develop international connectivity. This is why the World Bank sometimes analyzes a country's ability to find, absorb, digest, and operationalize knowledge.

Finally, policies must be implemented to ensure that the poorest countries, and the poorest within those countries, are not left out. The knowledge gap between haves and have-nots must be reduced by information technology, not grow. Policies that provide universal access, rural telecommunications systems, and the provision of access to vulnerable groups that have few resources are therefore requisite. Many economic development and assistance experts and officials also believe that priority must be attached to applications of information technology that educate people, improve health, and address environmental issues.

These are not easy tasks. Nevertheless, an increasing number of economic development and assistance experts and officials believe that information technologies provide developing countries chances to grow economically and reduce poverty. Increasingly, they see IT not as a luxury, but as a crucial factor that must be integrated into development strategies.

classes, and economic underdevelopment and poverty. These shared experiences and out-looks often influence developing states to have similar if not identical viewpoints on issues as diverse as international law, multinational corporations, and human rights. Even if the De-veloping World has great diversity, this similarity of viewpoints along with their less devel-oped economies, is one of the factors that legitimizes labeling Developing World states a single group.

SOURCES OF DEVELOPING WORLD PERCEPTIONS

Before we turn to the perceptions of selected groups of developing states, it is worthwhile to examine how shared experiences and heritages unite many of the views of the states that make up the Developing World. We saw that the shared reality of democratic political sys-tems, stable societies, and high standards of living led most developed states to have similar perceptions on many issues. Much the same is true for developing states. The shared reality of a colonial past, sharply divided classes, and economic underdevelopment and poverty lead most developing states to have similar perceptions on many issues.

Several cautions are appropriate. First, not all Developing World states shared these ex-periences. Second, as with developed states, different cultural values, beliefs, and experiences within individual states sometimes lead Developing World states to have different percep-tions despite shared experiences. Third, although we will not repeat the preceding chapter's discussion about levels of analysis, the concept is important in the Developing World as well.

The bottom line is that there is often a great degree of similarity, if not perfect identity, among the perceptions of Developing World states. But diversity is also a frequent fact.

A Colonial Past

One of the factors that unifies the Developing World is a shared colonial past. Most states in South America achieved independence during the early nineteenth century. Similarly, in Africa and Asia, Ethiopia, Liberia, Saudi Arabia, Thailand, and a few other states avoided colonialism. But for most of what is today the Developing World, colonialism was a fact of life until well into the twentieth century.

It was not a pleasant life. European sates that held colonies held them for a specific reason: to extract wealth from them and to better their own economies. Few European states considered it necessary to improve living conditions or economic standards in their colonies for more than a very few of the local peoples. For example, after 70 years of French rule in Vietnam, by 1940 there were only 14 high schools and one university in the entire country.[1] In the Belgian Congo (what is today Zaire), fewer than a dozen people held university degrees when the country received independence in 1960. Throughout the colonial world, hunger, disease, and poverty were widespread. Some colonial holdings fared better than others, and certain colonial powers paid more attention to improving the lot of local peoples than others, but as a general rule the pattern was clear. Colonies ex-isted to contribute to the economic betterment of the colonial powers.

For local peoples, choices about what to do were few. Faced by superior military fire-power and, after colonial states were established, a preferential system of laws and values that gave all rights and privileges to Europeans and few if any to local peoples, local peo-ples could submit to European hegemony, move on to new locations, or fight. The choices were not appealing. Some of those who submitted became field hands on colonial plantations, miners in European-owned mines, houseboys and servants, or otherwise entered the employ of Europeans at extremely low wages. Many remained as peasants, subservient to the European overlords who supplanted local overlords. A fortunate few were selected to be educated either locally or in Europe. Those who moved on to new locations had their lives disrupted, and often came into conflict with other local peoples whose territories they were moving into. And those who fought, faced by superior European firepower, died.

From the perspective of Developing World states, then, it is not surprising that strong resentment and hostility against European states remain about their colonial experience. When seen from the viewpoint of Developing World states, Queen Victoria's definition of the imperial mission to "protect the poor natives and advance civilization" was little more than a cover to allow Europeans to exploit. Those Europeans who took the "white man's burden" seriously also contributed to the problem, for they gave colonialism a veneer of humanity. As one writer in the Malaysian newspaper, *The Straits Times,* said in a 1986 review of the movie, *Out of Africa,* the movie "distorts history by focusing on the showpiece colonials while obscuring the deeds of the more Philistine types who were more commonplace."[2]

Nevertheless, ties were created and remain even today between former colonial holdings, new states, and the European colonizers. English is spoken and cricket is played around the world within the British Commonwealth of Nations. French is the official language and schooling follows the French system in many countries in Africa. These are all ties that arose from the colonial period, which in some cases ended during the 1940s for Developing World states, and in other cases during the 1980s. Even as we recognize these ties, however, we must also recognize the darker legacy that colonialism left, for in many respects this darker legacy predominates.

Sharply Divided Classes

Most Developing World states also share the heritage of a sharply divided internal class structure. Very few people hold political power and enjoy most of the wealth of the country. Table 11-1 illustrates the disparity of the distribution of wealth in a few Developing World states.

TABLE 11-1   Wealth Distribution in Selected Developing States

Country	Year	% National Income to Poorest 10%	% National Income to Richest 10%
Bangladesh	1992	4.1	23.7
Brazil	1995	0.8	47.9
China	1995	2.2	30.9
Egypt	1991	3.9	26.7
India	1994	4.1	25.0
Indonesia	1996	3.6	30.3
Madagascar	1993	2.3	34.9
Panama	1995	0.7	43.8
Philippines	1994	2.4	33.5
Zimbabwe	1990	1.8	46.9

Source: The World Bank, *World Development Report 1999/2000,* pp. 238–239.

Most people who live in Third World countries are peasants who make their living off the land using tools and techniques similar to those their parents, grandparents, and great-grandparents used.

By far the largest group of people in most Developing World states is the **peasantry.** In some Developing World states, peasants made up as much as 95 percent of the population during the colonial era, and in many countries even today peasants make up more than 75 percent of the population. Peasants till the land, often for an absentee landlord; seldom have any education; and often survive at bare subsistence levels. For the peasant, the future has traditionally been the same as the past and present: There is no hope for a better life, because there is no thought of a better life. The peasant's great-grandparents, grandparents, and parents were peasants, and the peasant's children will be peasants, too.[3]

European colonialism did not invent peasantry. Peasantry was a global phenomenon avoided by only a few fortunate countries such as the United States, Canada, Australia, and New Zealand. According to many historians, peasantry as an institution had its roots in the feudal system that placed political, economic, and military power in the hands of a very powerful few people. Fortunately for Europe, the Renaissance ended most of the more extreme vestiges of feudalism in Europe during the fourteenth and fifteenth centuries. For the rest of the world, feudalism as an institution remained, and was not truly disrupted until the second round of European empire began in the nineteenth century.

For most peasants, European colonialism simply meant that local lords with familiar customs were replaced by foreign lords with unfamiliar customs. However, to the former ruling class, European colonialism brought immense change. Some cooperated with the Europeans, some became traders and merchants, some fought the Europeans, and most were simply supplanted by the Europeans. The key point, however, is that local rulers were replaced by Europeans.

Meanwhile, in Latin America, a rigid class structure developed following the early nineteenth-century attainment of independence by most of that region. This class structure often placed Europeans who owned land in positions of power and influence over those who did not. Thus, even though Latin America's experience with colonialism was different from that of most of Asia and Africa, a large peasantry and a small ruling class developed.

During the colonial era, two phenomena took place that had an immense impact on the Developing World once it obtained independence. The first was the development of **anticolonialism** among local peoples, especially the dispossessed former ruling class. Some of the dispossessed former ruling class espoused returning to old precolonial ways, to the reinstitutionalization of the rule of the privileged local few over the peasantry. Their thinking in many ways reflected the thinking of the peasants, but from a considerably different perspective: Our great-grandparents ruled, our grandparents ruled, our parents ruled, and had the Europeans not arrived, we would have ruled, too. Therefore, when the Europeans leave, we will rule again, or our children will.

But other anticolonials attitudes came from other sources, from European concepts such as freedom, justice, independence, and equity. Very slowly, as a fortunate few local individuals received European educations and religious training, these European values filtered to local peoples, often members of the intelligentsia, the military, and even the dispossessed ruling class. Gradually, these individuals evolved into a class of revolutionary modernizers who asserted that freedom, justice, independence, and equity were as valid for colonial peoples as for Europeans. In many countries, these revolutionaries and modernizers played a major role in ending colonialism.

The second phenomenon was **urbanization.** Urbanization was caused by many factors, but the most important were the growth of rural unemployment brought about by European expropriation of land and limited updated farming methods; population growth brought about by limited application of European medical knowledge; and the hope for employment in the cities. Table 11-2 shows some of the dimensions of urbanization since 1980. Often, hopes for employment never materialized. Thus, an entirely new class of people emerged, the urban unemployed.

But some did find jobs, occasionally in the few industries that developed, sometimes in the government or colonial bureaucracies, frequently in the military or as servants, and sometimes in other pursuits. Although not many in these groups truly prospered, all were better off than the urban unemployed whom they saw begging every day. And so, although the urban employed may not have been as well off as the privileged, they were better off than the urban unemployed or the peasants. They had developed a stake in the system.

By the end of the colonial era, and continuing on to the present day, most Developing World states have a dizzying array of opposed classes. The peasantry with its ties to the soil are quantitatively most numerous, but politically weak and economically poor. However, in some countries, segments of the peasantry are beginning to ask why life cannot be improved. In Latin America in particular, the theology of liberation encourages peasants to ask this question. The peasantry is juxtaposed in many countries to the traditional elite, who consider it their right by birth or by military power to retain political and economic

TABLE 11-2   **Urbanization Trends in Selected Developing States**

Country	Urban Population As Percentage of Total Population	
	1980	**1998**
Algeria	43	58
Angola	21	33
Bangladesh	11	20
Bolivia	46	63
Brazil	66	80
China	20	33
Egypt	44	45
India	23	28
Indonesia	22	38
Kenya	16	31
Nigeria	27	42
Panama	50	57
Philippines	38	57
Saudi Arabia	66	85
Zambia	40	44
Zimbabwe	22	34

Source: The World Bank, *World Development Report 1999/2000,* pp. 232–233.

control over other groups within the country. Their objective remains their own betterment, and the betterment of their families. Still other individuals and groups see themselves as rightful rulers because of superior moral or ethical values. These individuals and groups have opted for revolutionary modernization through autocracy, arguing that they understand the needs of society, especially the peasantry and the urban unemployed, better than others, and therefore are the right people to run the government and implement policy. In other Developing World countries, other revolutionary modernizers attempt to hold elections, improve the economy, and run the government in a more Western-oriented way. All must also cope with the facts that the urban unemployed is an abiding underclass, and that the urban employed see efforts to improve the lot of the peasantry and the urban unemployed as threats to their own well-being.

Economic Underdevelopment and Poverty

Sharply divided classes within Developing World states is one reason why economic underdevelopment and poverty have persisted in those states. In many states, this intense conflict between classes has frustrated economic development. Continual civil strife has thus been a major detriment to economic development.

The Developing World's heritage of exploitation by Europe also continues to complicate economic growth and the reduction of poverty in many Developing World state. As previously pointed out, European states held colonies to increase their own wealth and rarely took significant steps to develop extensive technical, communications, transportation, and educational infrastructures within their colonies. When Developing World states received their independence, few local people had been trained to operate and maintain those infrastructures that had been developed, and many Europeans who lived in newly independent Developing World states returned to Europe. Thus, at the outset, Developing World states were saddled with difficulties that complicated economic development.

Other problems also complicated economic development and reduction of poverty. High birth rates, often brought about because of better health care, meant that economic growth had to remain at the same level as birth rates just to maintain standards of living. This was and is a difficult task, but as Table 11-3 shows, some countries are beginning to make slow progress.

Many developing countries blame their economic problems on the international economic system. They see the system as a creation of the developed states through which those states exploit the Third World. For example, the price of a barrel of Saudi oil fell from $2.18 in 1947 to $1.80 in 1970.[4] Although it is true that in the case of oil the 1970s witnessed astronomical increases in price, the price of other raw materials that developing countries exported to the west increased at rates below that of the global inflation rate.

TABLE 11-3   A Comparison of Economic Growth Rates and Population Growth Rates in Selected Developing States, 1997–98

Country	% Population Growth Rate	% Economic Growth Rate
Algeria	2.1	2.5
Angola	2.8	9.0
Bangladesh	1.7	5.5
Bolivia	2.0	4.4
Brazil	1.2	3.0
China	0.8	8.8
Egypt	1.9	5.2
India	1.7	5.0
Indonesia	1.5	4.0
Kenya	1.7	2.9
Nigeria	3.0	3.3
Panama	1.6	3.6
Philippines	2.1	5.1
Saudi Arabia	3.4	4.0
Zambia	2.1	3.5
Zimbabwe	1.1	8.1

Source: U.S. Central Intelligence Agency, *The World Factbook 1999,* (Washington, D.C.: U.S. Government Printing Office, 1999).

Note: Economic growth rate must surpass population growth rate for the standard of living of a country to improve.

Some prices, such as those for sugar and copper, fell. From the Developing World's perspective, then, Western economic exploitation continues even though the West's political control has passed.

Nor can it be overlooked that some Developing World states such as Chad, Mali, Somalia, and Bangladesh suffer from a dearth of natural resources. They simply have too little arable land, too little water, and too few minerals to have an opportunity to develop.

Some Developing World states failed to make economic progress because they made unwise decisions. In some cases, Developing World governments sought to industrialize too rapidly and neglected agriculture, with disastrous results. Other Developing World governments borrowed too heavily, and now face immense external debts. Still others did not seek to diversify their economies; some tried and failed. Some Developing World states spent too much on their militaries and other large-scale projects such as stadiums that provided limited economic returns. And overriding all this is the fact that no one is quite sure how economic development occurs, as we saw in Chapter 8.

Thus, economic underdevelopment and poverty remain pervasive in most of the Developing World. Oil-rich states have used their oil wealth to initiate development. South Korea, Hong Kong, Taiwan, Singapore, Thailand, Malaysia, and several other states have made impressive enough strides that they are now labeled "newly industrialized countries" (NICs). But economic underdevelopment and poverty continue to unify most of the rest of the Developing World.

Even so, economic schisms are developing within the Developing World. This has led some analysts to conclude that the concept of the "Third World" should be replaced by that of "Third World," "Fourth World," and "Fifth World" divisions. The "Third World" would be defined as those states that have sufficiently developed economic infrastructures, resources, and/or skills of the population so that they could become industrialized in the foreseeable future. The "Fourth World" would be defined as those states that have potential for future economic development. Finally, the "Fifth World" would include those states that have few or no resources, infrastructures, or current skills.

Despite this differentiation, Developing World states—or if one prefers Third, Fourth, and Fifth World state—all need economic development and amelioration of poverty. This fact alone legitimizes grouping them together in a single category.

DEVELOPING WORLD VIEWS ON INTERNATIONAL ECONOMICS

Just as democratic political systems, stable societies, and the high standards of living of developed states led them to share a number of perceptions, the colonial past, sharply divided classes, and economic underdevelopment and poverty of Developing World states influence them to adopt similar views on a number of international issues such as human rights, the environment, and economic development. Not coincidentally, many Developing World perceptions on these issues oppose those held by most Developed World states. Here we will concentrate only on Developing World views of international economics, leaving our discussions of human rights and the environment to Chapters 18 and 19.[5]

During the late twentieth and early twenty-first centuries, many developing states became increasingly involved with the international economic system as they cooperated with international financial institutions, welcomed foreign investment, and emphasized privatization and private sector-led development. Nevertheless, many developing states still believed that the international economic system was unfairly structured and played a major role in preventing economic development and keeping them impoverished. Their viewpoints had—and has—six major dimensions.

Unfavorable Conditions for Infant Industries

First, the Developing World's low level of industrialization is sometimes considered a major reason that it is economically underdeveloped and that the prevailing international economic system makes industrialization difficult if not impossible. This perspective asserts, as we saw in our discussion of dependency theory, that when the Developed World industrialized, new industries could enter the marketplace and sell their products because established competitors did not exist. Over the years, those who hold this view contend, conditions changed, and it became increasingly difficult if not impossible for Developing World countries to industrialize.

Thus, advocates of this view observe, throughout most of the twentieth century on into the twenty-first century, established industries competed fiercely. New industries therefore faced—and face—intense and often unfair competition from established industries, not even having an opportunity to establish a toehold before they are forced out of business. Therefore, advocates of this view assert, few Developing World states can industrialize. Therefore, they remain underdeveloped and poor.

Single Product Economies

A second barrier to economic development caused by the prevailing international economic system, according to some, is the fact that many developing states produce few products, or even a single product, for export. This creates a chain of events that prevents economic development.

The chain is easily understood. When demand for a product falls, export earnings fall. Hence a state can no longer afford the externally produced products that it needs. This, developing states assert, undermines the ability of developing states to grow economically, preventing economic development.

Energy Dependence

Except for Middle Eastern oil producing states and a few other developing states in sub-Saharan Africa, Asia, and Latin America, most developing states depend on external sources of energy. Usually, they must pay high prices for the oil and other energy resources that they import.

Some developing states maintain that this is a reason they remain economically underdeveloped. They point out that a number of developing states enjoyed slow but real growth in the 1960s, but when oil prices increased in the 1970s, the economies of many went into a tailspin. Thus, this school of thought asserts, the dependence of many states on external sources of energy causes economic underdevelopment.

Capital Mobility

Some developing states assert that by allowing capital to be internationally mobile, the international economic system causes underdevelopment. According to this view, the political instability of many developing states leads capital flight to an inability to attract foreign investment.

An easily understood chain of events underpins this viewpoint as well. It asserts that political and social instability in developing states drives investment away. Capital flight decreases economic output and increases unemployment, which in turn heightens political and social instability, which drives even more investment away. At the same time, since few investors will invest in countries that are politically or socially unstable, many developing states have difficulty attracting new investment. Thus, supporters of this view argue, many developing states are captured in a vicious downward economic cycle resulting from capital's international mobility.

Hard Currency Payments

Some developing states point to requirements for hard currency payment as a cause of underdevelopment. Because of the uncertain economic status of many developing states, the argument goes, few other states want their currencies. This means that to purchase foreign goods, developing states must export their goods to earn U.S. dollars, French francs, Japanese yen, or another "hard currency" that people are willing to take. If they cannot export their own products, they cannot earn hard currency, and they cannot import foreign goods.

Thus, according to some, if Developing World currencies were more widely accepted, developing states could import foreign products more readily. This would make their economies would be more stable and productive, and they could develop more easily.

Debt and Interest Accrual

A final cause of economic underdevelopment, some developing states say, is debt and the accrual of interest on debt. Over the years, many developing states borrowed large amounts of money from Western banks, developed large debts, and now must pay off the debt and the interest accruing on the debt. For example, in 1998, the debt of developing African states owed to lending institutions alone totaled over $220 billion. Since surplus funds used to pay off debt and interest, they cannot be used for economie development. At the same time, knowledge that surplus funds must be used to pay off debt and interest drives investment away.

Developed states have responded to this concern by rearranging debt repayment schedules for developing states and by forgiving some Developing World debt, especially some of the debt of the world's poorest countries. G-8 countries did this, for example, at both their 1999 and 2000 summits. However, most developing states maintain that G-8 efforts in this regard are too small and too narrowly focused to have any real impact on most developing states.

Summation

To reiterate, many of the shared perspectives of developing states on the international economic system, and on other issues to be examined later such as human rights and the environment, flow from their colonial past, opposed social classes, and economic underdevelopment and poverty. But there are other issues upon which developing states have different perceptions. We now turn to these different viewpoints.

 ## SELECTED OUTLOOKS FROM THE DEVELOPING WORLD

Beyond economics, how do Developing World states view themselves and the international community? There are as many answers to this question as there are Developing World states. Most Developing World states agree on issues such as the need to modify the international economic system, moderate the activities of multinational corporations, and maintain the sanctity of international borders, but extensive disagreement exists on many other issues. These differences spring from a host of local and regional differences in history, values, cultures, and experiences.

In this section, the divergent backgrounds and viewpoints of three groups of Developing World states will be highlighted. The groups are the newly industrialized countries, because their perceptions of the international economic system are so different from those of many other developing states; Middle Eastern oil producing states, because of their often unique combinations of perceptions; and microstates, because they are so numerous. China's perceptions will be examined in the next section.

Newly Industrialized Countries

Newly industrialized countries (NICs) include a small number of developing states that have begun to industrialize and whose living standards rose rapidly during the 1980s and most of the 1990s. In 1997 and 1998, however, their economic growth stopped and in some cases reversed as questionable financial practices and economic overextension brought a temporary end to their economic booms.[6] As the twenty-first century began, however, most had resumed economic growth.

Malaysia, Singapore, South Korea, Taiwan, Thailand and a few other states are the leading examples of NICs. Unlike most other developing states, they are rarely critical of the prevailing international economic system. Rather, unlike most other developing states, they accept it and support most of its tenets. This, of course, is because the NICs have begun to reap the benefits of modernization and industrialization, and they see potential for themselves to benefit from the prevailing system.

Malaysia is a typical NIC. A constitutional monarchy that received its independence from Great Britain in 1957, Malaysia is a multiethnic Southeast Asian state whose 20 million people include Malay Muslims, Chinese Buddhists, Indian Hindus, Christians of many different ethnic groups, and a variety of tribal religions. Malaysia enjoyed an economic growth rate between six and ten percent throughout the late 1980s and early 1990s until it was beset by the so-called Asian conflation economic crisis of 1997–98. It has since recovered, and although its growth rate no longer equals the high rates that it enjoyed before the conflation, it is once again prospering. Measured in terms of purchasing power parity, its per capita GNP is over $11,000, more than twice that of Russia's.

Not surprisingly, the Malaysian government during the 1990s was rarely critical of the international economic system. Even so, it would prefer to see trade preferences and debt relief granted to developing states. As a multiethnic state, Malaysia and most of its people accept diversity easily. At the same time, it wishes to modernize but also maintain many of its traditions. This is a difficult task which it has attempted to accomplish by restricting individualism. For example, both public kissing and video games have been banned in a number of Malaysian cities.[7]

Generally, Malaysia and other NICs are among the most ardent advocates of the right of sovereign states to define and interpret human rights. East Asia NICs in particular often argue that one reason they have been so successful economically is because their societies are more disciplined and structured than Western societies.[8] This, NICs assert, allows them to have a greater degree of focus than Western societies, which in turn allegedly leads to greater economic growth. With this in mind, many NICs reject the West's emphasis on individual rights and claim that it is their right as sovereign states to defend traditional values in ways that they see fit.

Middle Eastern Oil Producing States

For most of the Middle Eastern oil producing states that form an arc across North Africa (Algeria, Libya, and Egypt) through the Arabian peninsula (Saudi Arabia, Oman, the United Arab Emirates, and Kuwait) and on into Iraq and Iran, the prevailing core of their worldview can be summed up in three words: oil, Islam, and Israel. A large percentage of the gross national product of most of these states is derived from oil revenues. Islam plays an immense role in the everyday lives and national outlooks of all. And many to one extent or another oppose Israel as well.

Saudi Arabia provides an excellent case study of a Middle Eastern oil producing state.[9] As with most of its Middle Eastern neighbors, the Saudi worldview is heavily influenced by oil, Islam, and Israel. Unlike many others, however, the United States and Iraq also figure prominently.

Oil is at the core of Saudi Arabia's "special relationship" with the United States. The United States, and more certainly the Western world, need Saudi oil. The Saudis are aware that this gives them leverage in the capitals of the West. At the same time, they are aware that their leverage is tempered by Saudi Arabia's vast holdings of dollars, its reliance on the Western-controlled international monetary system, and the more than $50 billion of investments it has in the United States alone. Stated simply, the Saudis are as dependent on the United States and the West as the United States and the West are on the Saudis.

Saudi Arabia's oil-generated wealth led to two other major connections with the United States. First, Saudi Arabia implemented a major economic development program.

Much of Saudi Arabia's development program is planned and managed by U.S. businesses. Second, because of the threat that the Saudis perceive from the several radical states that have sprung up in the Middle East, the Saudis have turned to the United States for arms. With their oil wealth and their leadership position in the Middle East, they have requested and received some of the most modern and potent American weapons as part of the "special relationship." The depth of this "special relationship" became exceedingly evident in 1990 when Iraq invaded Kuwait, one of Saudi Arabia's neighbors to the north, and posed a military threat to Saudi Arabia as well. The United States immediately sent sizable contingents of air, land, and naval forces to Saudi Arabia and surrounding waters to deter an Iraqi attack on Saudi Arabia, defend the Saudi regime, and maintain access to Saudi oil.

Islam remains the core of the Saud family's political legitimacy. The Islam/Saud alliance is an old and powerful one, but it is challenged from two directions. First, within Saudi Arabia, modernization has created social and political strains that threaten traditional Islamic values, including the role of women, sobriety, and piety. The Saud family has attempted to keep modernization within the limits of what is acceptable to Islam, but strains exist. For example, in 1992, Saudi ruler King Fahd created a 60-person Consultative Council to advise him on governance; the king subsequently guaranteed many personal freedoms to Saudi citizens and altered the way that future kings would be chosen. Modernizers praised Fahd's actions, but Islamic traditionalists and fundamentalists within the kingdom condemned the changes.[10]

Second, outside Saudi Arabia, the Saudi government sees a threat from the fundamentalist Islamic movement, most notably in Iran. Saudi Arabia believes it must arm itself against that threat and has turned to the United States and other Western states for support. In addition, to better solidify his claim as the defender of the true Muslim faith and counter Muslim fundamentalists who opposed Saudi Arabia, Kind Fahd in 1994 created the "Supreme Council of Islamic Affairs."[11]

In addition to oil and Islam, Iraq has risen to prominence in the Saudi worldview. The 1990 Iraqi invasion of Kuwait had an immense impact on the Saudi sense of security. As a result, Saudi Arabia was willing to serve as the primary staging base for the massive U.S.-led military buildup that led to Operation Desert Storm, the expulsion of Iraq from Kuwait, and the destruction of much of Iraq's military capabilities. Nevertheless, despite the Iraqi defeat, Saudi Arabia remains immensely concerned about the possibility of continuing Iraqi expansionist intentions, and has acceded to a continued U.S. military presence.

To a certain extent, then, oil, Islam, and Iraq produce a community of interests between the United States and Saudi Arabia. Shared economic needs and security concerns yield similar outlooks on a number of issues that are complicated by the fourth major determinant of the Saudi worldview, Israel.

Until recently, Saudi Arabia, like most other Arab and Islamic states, did not accept the legitimacy of the existence of Israel. Although Saudi Arabia stopped short of calling for Israel's destruction, it nevertheless made known its sympathy for the Palestinians and the PLO. Saudi Arabia thereby could argue that it was defending Arabs and Islam, and also protecting its position as a leader in the Arab world. But with the 1993 accord reached between Israel and the PLO, Saudi Arabia, as other moderate Arab states, moved to improve its relations with Israel.

Because of its high per capita income, it is sometimes difficult to remember that Saudi Arabia—and other Middle Eastern oil producing states as well—are Developing World states in the early stages of industrialization and modernization. All have oil reserves that will last well into the twenty-first century and beyond, and all remain wedded to Islam. Oil and Islam will be the constants in their worldview, but whether they remain developing states or become developed states remains to be seen.

Microstates

As the name implies, microstates are countries that have very small populations and very small territories. Although there is no universally agreed upon definition for a microstate, for our purposes, any state that has less than 1 million inhabitants and fewer than 30 thousand square kilometers is considered a microstate.[12]

It is startling how many microstates exist. The developing world alone is home to 31. (Europe has seven more.) Put differently, of the almost 200 independent countries in the world, almost one-sixth are microstates in the Developing World. Of the approximately 150 countries in the Developing World, about 20 percent are microstates.

Some microstates such as Barbados and the Bahamas are renowned vacation sites. Others such as Brunei and Qatar export significant quantities of oil. Cyprus has been the subject of a major disagreement between Greece and Turkey. Some microstates such as the Bahamas and Vanuatu have become bustling international banking centers. At one time, such "offshore banking" was notable primarily as a way that the wealthy could avoid paying taxes in their home countries, but in the 1980s and 1990s, it became a way to launder drug money. Other microstates rose to occasional prominence during the Cold War. For example, in 1983, Grenada catapulted to international prominence when a violent leftist coup precipitated U.S. military intervention. Similarly, in 1985 after Kiribati signed a fishing agreement with the USSR, the United States became concerned that the Soviet Union would next acquire a naval base there.

Most microstates present a rather mundane picture. The Solomon Islands is a case in point. Situated in the South Pacific, the Solomon Islands is a political entity significant to few people other than its 441 thousand inhabitants. It has no industry and no oil. A member of the UN, the Group of 77, and the British Commonwealth of Nations, the Solomon Islands were largely overlooked and forgotten until political turmoil disrupted the island in 1999 and 2000. This proved short lived and of little importance to anyone beyond the islands, and once again, the Solomons receded to the backwaters of international life.

Most microstates in the twenty-first century recognize and accept that they play a small and even insignificant role in international relations. While most microstates are UN and Group of 77 members, the constraints imposed by their usually limited resources mean that most participate in the international community in limited ways. They are sovereign states, but their impact is usually small, and the importance of their views outside the context of the UN General Assembly is usually limited.

Summation

NICs, Middle Eastern oil producing states, and microstates make up less than half the world's 150 developing states. Yet in our brief overview of the perceptions held by these states it should be apparent that Developing World states do indeed hold a wide variety of perceptions. And to reiterate a point made several times earlier, it must be remembered that perceptions are a guide to action, and therefore important.

While it may be safe to overlook and even dismiss as inconsequential the viewpoints held by certain developing states such as many of the microstates, the same thing cannot be said of China. With about 20 percent of the world's population, a rapidly growing economy, and nuclear weapons, China is becoming more and more a force to be reckoned with on the international scene. As we saw at the outset of this chapter, it is also legitimately described as a developing state. Given China's present and future importance, it is critically important that we understand how China views itself and its role in the twenty-first century world.

CHINA'S OUTLOOKS

China's view of the world cannot be understood if Chinese history is not taken into account. This can roughly be divided into four eras, the years of empire before 1840, the century of humiliation from 1840 to 1945, the revolutionary era of Mao from 1945 to 1976, and since then a wave of economic reforms that have had stunning results. Before we explore China's outlooks, we will therefore first examine China's history.

China's Four Eras

Until European states carved up China during the mid-nineteenth century, the Chinese knew of no other society that could rival their own. The nomadic Mongols of central Asia were considered uncultured, the civilizations of Southeast Asia were vassal possessions of China, and the Himalaya Mountains kept the advanced Indian culture to the southwest apart.

The Era of Empire. During this classical era of the **Chinese empire,** a series of dynasties ruled China. The emperor ruled by divine right as the "Son of Heaven." China's armed forces expanded the empire either by military conquest or by threatening neighbor states so they sent tribute to the emperor. Nevertheless, throughout Chinese history, the power of emperors rose and fell. In periods of decline, regional warlords played major roles in China. On occasion, such as during the "Six Dynasties" era from 200 AD to 500 AD, China was thus more an association of kingdoms than a single empire.

Traditional Chinese society was highly structured, based on obedience to authority, and emphasized the role of the elder over the role of self. Most of these practices came from the teaching of **Confucius,** a scholar and philosopher who lived during the fifth century before Christ. China was a society that was self-satisfied and confident of its place in the world. In its own eyes, it *was* the world, the Middle Kingdom.[13]

The Century of Humiliation. Then came the Westerners. By the early nineteenth century, Great Britain, France, the Netherlands, and the United States traded with China. Confined to coastal enclaves, Westerners were tolerated but little more. Unfortunately for the Westerners, they could find little the Chinese wanted, at least until Great Britain began importing opium to China from its colony in India.

By 1840, Western sale of opium to China was a major activity. Concerned that opium traffic was out of control, China sealed off the British enclave of Canton from the rest of the country. Britain objected, sent a naval squadron to Canton, fought and won the first **opium war,** and forced China to sign the Treaty of Nanking, which guaranteed British trading rights including the sale of opium. The Middle Kingdom had begun its **century of humiliation.**

Worse was to come as Westerners more and more used their superior military to force unequal treaties on China. By the early twentieth century, 80 Chinese ports were **treaty ports,** serving as centers of Western trade, culture, religion, graft, and corruption as the old Confucian order was undermined. From the 1860s on, there was a Chinese government, but it did not really govern China.

China also suffered territorially. Russia moved farther into Central Asia, France took Indochina, Great Britain acquired Pakistan, and upstart Japan defeated China in the 1895 Sino-Japanese War. Many Chinese were outraged at the "foreign devils" and what they had done to China. In 1900, outrage erupted into attacks against Christians, missionaries, traders, and other symbols of the West. Finally, Western states including the United States sent military forces into China to end the so-called "Boxer Rebellion," named after the secret society known as the Society of Harmonious Fists which led it.

China's ruling Manchu dynasty was by this time virtually powerless. In 1911, **Sun Yat-sen** succeeded in his tenth attempt to overthrow the old regime. Sun, however, could not hold China together, and the country was again run by regional warlords until 1928 when **Chiang Kai-shek,** the new leader of Sun's **Kuomintang Party,** seized power in Beijing. Even this did not bring peace to China. As Chiang consolidated his power, he turned on his erstwhile allies the Chinese Communist Party (CCP), killing over 40 thousand in just over a month. The remaining few communists retreated into central China.

As a nationalist, Chiang attempted to reduce Western influence in China. Between 1929 and 1931 he had some success, but then in 1931 Japan invaded. Meanwhile, the communists gathered strength in central China. Chiang, challenged by Japan and the CCP, turned to Germany for support. Under German guidance, Kuomintang forces attacked the communists in central China, pushing them out of the region and forcing them into their epic **Long March** to China's west during which their numbers dropped from over 100 thousand to barely 20 thousand. It was from China's west that **Mao Zedong,** who had risen to command the CCP during the Long March, would launch the campaign that carried the CCP to victory in 1949.

By 1937, the Kuomintang and the communists concluded that they were threatened more by Japan than by each other so they formed a "United Front" against Japan. But for eight more years, they proved unable to force Japan out of China. Finally, with Japan's defeat in 1945, Chiang and Mao again turned on each other. From 1945 to 1949, yet another Chinese civil war raged, with Chiang eventually being forced out of mainland China to the island of Taiwan where he established a separate Chinese government.[14]

Revolutionary Modernization and Maoism.   From the perspective of most Chinese, the Century of Humiliation was over. For the most part, Mao and the CCP emerged from World War II and the Civil War as national heroes. There were many reasons for this, one of which was the politically enlightened policies they followed in relations with the peasants. For example, whereas Kuomintang leaders often claimed fertile land for their own, communist leaders turned it over to the peasants. For land-starved peasants, few acts were more meaningful.

Indeed, Mao based his entire revolution on the peasant. With hundreds of millions of peasants in China, Mao could not have been victorious without peasant support. An avowed Marxist, Mao therefore created his own version of Marxism in which the peasant, not the industrial worker, was the center of the revolution.[15]

If the peasant was the heart of Mao's revolution, authoritarian leadership and self-sacrifice were its soul. Although traditional Chinese family and government institutions had been undermined during the Century of Humiliation, traditional Confucian values that emphasized acceptance of authority and proper behavior gave Mao a strong base on which to build a communist system. Even the Chinese extended family aided Mao in his effort to communize China.

Mao's efforts to assert control in China were abetted by another force out of Chinese history, China's unhappy relations with the West. As a Marxist, Mao accepted the concept of class conflict. As a Marxist-Leninist, he accepted Lenin's theory of imperialism. As a Chinese, he interpreted his country's history as proof of Marx's and Lenin's ideas and pointed to Chiang Kai-shek's reliance on U.S. military support as evidence that Chiang was an agent of U.S. imperialism. To the Chinese people, eager to escape their century of humiliation, Mao's views made sense. Thus, Mao accelerated Chiang's reduction in popularity by emphasizing class conflict and imperialism. He also built the groundwork for the next two decades of Chinese foreign policy, whose basic tenet was opposition to Western and U.S. imperialism, on the basis of Chinese history interpreted through Marxist-Leninist-Maoist eyes.

But Mao feared that the Chinese revolution would lose its fervor. Thus, in 1966, Mao unleashed the cultural revolution. For ten years, China was torn by continual ideological campaigns, factional political struggle and purges, and economic turmoil as Mao sought to keep China on a "true" revolutionary path.[16]

However, all they did was disrupt Chinese society. Economic growth ended. The political and social fabric of society was torn. And an entire generation of Chinese lost a decade of education. When Mao died in 1976, his militant colleagues, the Gang of Four, were arrested. China was ready to begin a new era.

The Four Modernizations. After Mao's death, China's new course was charted primarily by **Deng Xiaoping.**[17] Deng's idea of what China needed was "less empty talk and more hard work." Deng asserted that China was still communist, but he deemphasized ideology and pursued a program of **Four Modernizations** in agriculture, industry, science and technology, and defense with decidedly non-Marxist policies. For example, he created an incentive system in agriculture that allowed peasants to sell some of their crops on the open market. Deng told peasants this was their opportunity to "get rich." Chinese agricultural production jumped markedly.

During the next two decades, other reforms were also instituted as central planning was deemphasized in several industrial sectors; privately owned workers' cooperatives were encouraged in light industry; and foreign investment was actively sought. The China of Deng Xiaoping was a much different place from the China of Mao Zedong.

And China's economic reforms were highly successful. Throughout the 1980s and on into the late 1990s, China's annual economic growth rate was over 7 percent every year and sometimes ranged as high as 15 percent. Often, China's economic growth rate during this period was the highest in the world. Indeed, even though most Chinese remained exceedingly poor, Deng's reforms by the 1990s had transformed China.

But Deng's reforms were economic, not political. In marked contrast to the Soviet Union's "Gorbachev Revolution," Deng intended the party to maintain political control. Thus, when in 1989 millions of Chinese workers and students marched into the streets of almost every Chinese city demanding political freedoms and Western-style democracy, Deng acted. Although he was indecisive at first, Deng finally ordered troops to move into Beijing's Tiananmen Square against the million workers and students who were there. No one knows how many prodemocracy demonstrators died, but most estimates place the number at several thousand. The prodemocracy movement was crushed. Across China, martial law was declared, political arrests were made, and a crackdown on noncommunist political outlooks was instituted. Economic reform continued, but there would not be political reform.

The impact of the **Tiananmen Square massacre** on the outside world's attitude toward China was immense. Governments around the world, in varying degrees, condemned the Chinese government's actions, and businesses rethought their investments and their futures in China. Meanwhile, the Chinese government asserted that it had acted correctly to restore public order.

During the 1990s, China slowly overcame the impact of the Tiananmen Square massacre. Politically, other countries continued to criticize the Chinese government's control of society, criticisms which the Chinese government rejected as unwarranted foreign intervention in its internal affairs, but they nevertheless slowly restored their pre-Tiananmen relationships. Economically, China's economy continued to grow rapidly until the late 1990s when it, like the rest of East Asian's economies, slumped badly before recovering at the end of the century. But at the same time, forces of regionalism surfaced within China that raised concerns in some Chinese quarters that the country was losing its national purpose.

China Views the World[18]

When Deng died in 1997, China peacefully transferred political leadership to President Zhang Zemin. Zemin had three primary goals. First, he intended to continue China's drive for economic growth. Second, he intended to strengthen China's armed forces. Finally, Zemin intended to promote nationalism to unite China. As the twenty-first century opened, then, China viewed the world through new eyes and its future lay in new hands. But how did those eyes view the world, and in what direction would those new hands take China?

International Economics.   During Mao's era, China was one of the world's leading critics of the prevailing international economic system, viewing it as a capitalist system that exploited developing states. Not surprisingly, however, given China's rapid economic growth under Deng and Zemin, Chinese criticisms of the system abated significantly. It now views most aspects of the international economic system favorably, and ardently pursued membership in the World Trade Organization, eventually joining it in 2000.

Human Rights and Sovereignty. Conversely, China remains heavily critical of concepts of universal and individual human rights. It completely rejects the right of any country or international governmental organization to intervene in the affairs of another, especially over issues such as human rights. China was aghast, for example, when the United States and NATO in 1999 undertook military action against Yugoslavia because of Yugoslavia's ethnic cleansing policies in Kosovo. To China, state sovereignty remains supreme. Given China's nineteenth- and twentieth-century histories, this is perhaps understandable.

Russia. China's views of three states, Russia, the United States, and Japan, also warrant mention. The "Russian bear" looms large in contemporary Chinese outlooks. Despite a strained history of relations, since 1982 Chinese relations with Moscow have been cordial. Following the collapse of the USSR, China breathed even easier about its relations with its neighbor to the north. Nevertheless, with Russia's future uncertain, the Soviet collapse did not eliminate Beijing's concern about Russia. The new generation of Chinese leaders remembers history, and they know that the Russian bear and the Chinese dragon have had a long history of tension.

The United States.[19] As for the United States, Sino-U.S. relations were frozen in mutual hostility from the Korean War during the early 1950s until the Sino-American rapprochement began in the early 1970s. To the Chinese, the U.S. involvement in the Korean War and ensuing threats against China confirmed that the U.S. was a typical imperialist power. On a personal level, one can only speculate about the impact that the war had on Mao, whose son was killed during the war.

In the twenty-first century, China sees the United States as a source of investment and a market. U.S. investment in China and bilateral trade between the two countries expanded immensely during the 1980s and 1990s, interrupted only briefly by the Tiananmen Square massacre. At the same time, two major issues threaten to disrupt Sino-American relations.

The first is human rights. As we saw above, China ardently defends sovereignty and rejects the right of any country to intervene in the affairs of another, especially over human rights issues. The United States, conversely, is one of the leading advocates of universal and individual human rights. This disagreement has led to Sino-American tension in the past, and may lead to more.

The second issue is Taiwan, a residual issue from the 1945–49 civil war. As we saw, when the communists drove the Kuomintang from the mainland, the Kuomintang established their government on Taiwan and claimed to be the rightful government of all China. Conversely, the communists claimed that Taiwan was a province in revolt against the central government in Beijing. Both parties agree that Taiwan is an integral part of China, so the central issue is which is the rightful government of China.

Having supported the Kuomintang during the civil war and viewing Mao's government as a Soviet minion, the U.S. supported Chiang's government on Taiwan. From the Beijing government's perspective, the United States was meddling in internal Chinese affairs. The Taiwan issue complicates Sino-American relations even in the twenty-first century, for example during the 2000 Taiwan presidential elections when the possibility existed that Taiwan might declare independence. After some anxious moments, it did not, and the crisis was averted.

Japan.   China's relations with Japan also loom large in Beijing's view of the world. During China's century of humiliation, Japan was one of the country's primary exploiters. Japan's need for raw materials and markets drove it to expand during the 1895 to 1945 period in particular, and many Chinese remember this. They also expected Japan to apologize for this, something which Japan until recently refused to do.

As China implemented reforms and economic growth accelerated during the 1980s, China forged close but not constricting economic ties and proper but not close political and diplomatic relations with Japan. Both countries benefited from the relationship. This state of affairs continued into the 1990s and on into the twenty-first century. Unless something unforeseen happens, this is likely to continue. With China's resources and need for capital and Japan's capital and need for markets, in many respects the relationship as it currently stands is made in heaven.

Summation

China's perceptions of the world and its role in the world have changed several times since the Chinese Communist Party came to power. Undoubtedly, they will change again in the future. With China's new generation of leaders emphasizing economic growth, the armed forces, and nationalism, China could take any of several directions in the early twenty-first century.

Will China return to its imperial past, as some fear, or will it be a peaceful power that uses its prosperity to improve the life of its people? Will political democracy be in China's future, or will the Chinese Communist Party continue to dictate the country's political and social directions? Will China hold together as a single country, or will forces of regionalism win out?

As of now, there are no clear answers to these and other questions. But the way in which these questions are answered will determine the future of one-fifth of humankind and affect the lives of many others as well.

 ## THE DEVELOPING WORLD IN PERSPECTIVE

Obviously, the developing world is diverse. Its states have several shared perspectives, but they also have extremely different views about a variety of local, regional, and global issues.

As a region, overcoming economic underdevelopment and escaping the clutches of poverty remain the major task that most developing states face. Some such as the NICs and China are making progress in this regard. Others, however, remain mired in poverty. Some states that currently remain mired in poverty have sufficient internal resources and a sufficiently educated population so that they may with the right combination of foreign investment, foreign aid, insightful leadership, and appropriate policies escape their plight, but for others, there appears little hope.

It is likely, then, that the world will remain divided into developed states and developing states well into the twenty-first century. Some developing states may join the ranks of developed states, but given the different values, beliefs, and experiences that they have, it is an open question whether and how quickly those states in transition will alter their perceptions.

But many states will remain underdeveloped and in the clutches of poverty. What policies will they adopt and what actions can and will they take if the international community leaves them behind? This is one of the great unanswered questions of the early twenty-first century.

 ## *KEY TERMS AND CONCEPTS*

colonial past   most Developing World states were at one time colonies of European states that economically exploited them and rarely helped them develop economically, culturally, or politically

sharply divided classes   most Developing World states are inhabited predominantly by peasants and have a small wealthy ruling elite with other sharply divided classes such as urban workers, urban unemployed, the military, government bureaucrats, revolutionary modernizers, and the intelligentsia.

peasantry   the predominant class in the Developing World, most of whom work the land for absentee land-owners, often the same land that their parents and grandparents worked

urbanization   a dominant trend in the Developing World that is proceeding rapidly and complicating economic development

economic underdevelopment   the third element that unites the Developing World, caused by factors such as civil strife, a history of exploitation, high rates of urbanization and birth, the international economic system, unwise development strategies, and few resources

infant industries   industries that have just begun to operate

single product economies   economies in which a large share of production is the result of only one industrial or agricultural sector, usually found in Third World States

energy dependence   reliance by a national economy on external sources of energy

capital mobility   the ability of capital to move from one international actor to another, an increasingly prominent phenomenon of the late twentieth and early twenty first century

hard currency requirements   the requirement often demanded by the World Bank that developing states have money that can be converted to the world's leading currencies before they can get loans

debt and interest accrual   as developing states borrow more and more money, their debt and interest builds up, sometimes putting them into positions where they are unable to repay loans

newly industrialized countries (NICs)   developing states that have achieved significant economic growth, usually used to refer to Hong Kong, Singapore, South Korea, and Taiwan

Middle Eastern oil producing states   North African and Arabian peninsula states such as Libya, Algeria, Egypt, Saudi Arabia, Iraq, Iran, Kuwait, and the United Arab Emirates, most of which are inhabited primarily by Arab peoples who practice Islam

microstates   states that have a very small population and very small territory. Most are underdeveloped. Almost 40 exist today.

China's era of empires   China was ruled by a series of dynasties, several of which established sizable empires, from several centuries BC until early in the twentieth century

Confucius   born in the fifth century BC, Confucius founded the traditional Chinese order that taught that proper relations between children and parents were the basis for a moral society and that this had direct applicability to relations between individuals and rulers

opium wars   wars fought in the 1840s and 1850s when China tried to stop the British and French from importing opium to China

century of humiliation   1840 to 1949, when Western powers and Japan forced China to accept unequal treaties and dominated China

treaty ports   China was forced to conclude unequal treaties, primarily with European states, during the nineteenth century that ceded treaty ports and other advantages to Europeans

Sun Yat-sen   first leader of the Kuomintang Party, who overthrew the Manchu dynasty in 1911

Chiang Kai-shek   replaced Sun as Kuomintang leader, leading China until 1949, when he and the Kuomintang fled to Taiwan

Long March   during 1935–36, the Communist Chinese Party fled the Kuomintang, marching 6,000 miles to China's mountainous west

Mao Zedong and Maoism   Mao emerged as leader of the Chinese Communist Party during the Long March. Maoism was Marxism-Leninism as altered by Mao Zedong and applied to Chinese conditions. The most notable alteration was that the peasant instead of the proletariat was the base of the communist revolution in China.

Four Modernizations   the four areas that post-Mao China has emphasized in economic development: industry, agriculture, science and technology, and defense

Tiananmen Square massacre   in 1989, the Chinese government cracked down on pro-democracy demonstrators in Beijing's Tiananmen Square, killing thousands and casting a pall over China's relations with many countries

Sino-Soviet split   the dispute over ideology and the leadership of the international communist movement that shattered relations between the USSR and China during the 1960s, 1970s, and most of the 1980s

Chinese views of Russia   from the early 1960s until the late 1980s, China viewed the Soviet Union with hostility, but in 1989 with Soviet leader Gorbachev's trip to Beijing, relations improved markedly. China's relations with post-Soviet Russia have remained cordial.

China's views of the U.S.   China sees the U.S. as a source of expertise, investment, and military know-how. China also accuses the U.S. of having a "two-China" policy because of U.S. military aid to Taiwan.

China's views of Japan   Japan is important to China for trade and investment. With China's resources and need for capital and Japan's capital and need for resources, the relationship is nearly ideal.

 ## *WEBSITE REFERENCES*

colonialism and imperialism: *www-scf.usc.edu/~vasishth/Colonial_Imperial-bibl.html*   a sizeable bibliography of texts on colonialism and imperialism

Third World viewpoints: *www.twnside.org.sg/twnintro.htm*   website of the Third World Network, a network of organizations involved in issues relating to development, the Third World and the North–South conflict

newly industrialized countries (NICs):   *www.dal.ca/~finbow/nic.html*   a collection of links to websites about newly industrialized countries

microstates: *angelfire.com/nv/micronations/enter.html*   the Micronation and Sovereignty website

Mao Zedong and Maoism: *www.marx2mao.org//Mao/Index.html*   website of the Mao Zedong library

official Chinese foreign policy perspectives: *www.fmprc.gov.cn/eng*   the website of the Chinese Ministry of Foreign Affairs

NOTES

1. George McTurnan Kahbin and John W. Lewis, *The United States in Vietnam* (New York: Dell, 1969), p. 10.

2. *The Straits Times,* April 5, 1986.

3. For an interesting study of peasant culture, see Leslie E. Anderson, *The Political Ecology of the Modern Peasant* (Baltimore: Johns Hopkins University Press, 1994).

4. Peter Mansfield, *The New Arabians* (Chicago: J. G. Ferguson, 1981), p. 204.

5. For additional details on Developing World views of international economics, see Michel Chossudovsky, "Global Poverty in the Late Twentieth Century," Journal of International Affairs (Fall 1998); pp. 293–311; and T. N. Srinivasan, *Developing Countries and the Multilateral Trading System: From GATT to the Uruguay Round and the Future* (Boulder, CO: Westview Press, 1999).

6. Karl D. Jackson, ed., *Asian Contagion: The Causes and Consequences of a Financial Crisis* (Boulder, CO: Westview Press, 1998); Linda Y. C. Lim, "Whose 'Model' Failed? Implications of the Asian Financial Crisis," *The Washington Quarterly* (Summer 1998), pp. 25–36; and *Japan's Role in the Asian Financial Crisis: Hearings before the Subcommittee on Asia and the Pacific*, House of Representatives, 105th Congress, 2nd Session, (April 23, 1998,) explain the causes behind and implications of the economic downturn in the NICs in the late 1990s.

7. For additional information on Malaysia, see Harold Crouch, *Government and Society in Malaysia* (Ithaca, NY: Cornell University Press, 1996); Edmund T. Gomez and K. S. Jomo, *Malaysia's Political Economy: Politics, Patronage, and Profits* (New York, NY: Cambridge University Press, 1997); and Cecilia Ng, *Positioning Women in Malaysia: Class and Gender in an Industrializing State* (New York, NY: St. Martin's Press, 1999)

8. For example, Singapore's former Prime Minister Lee Kuan Yew often asserted that Western democratic values and governmental structures "lead to undisciplined and disorderly conditions which are inimical to development."

9. For discussions of Saudi Arabian history, see based on J. B. Kelly, *Arabia, the Gulf and the West* (New York: Basic Books, 1980); and Peter Mansfield, *The New Arabians* (Chicago: J. G. Ferguson, 1981). See also Ragaei El Mallakh, *Saudi Arabia: Rush to Development* (Baltimore: Johns Hopkins University Press, 1982).

10. King Fahd's decrees are available from the Saudi Embassy, Washington, D.C. See also *The New York Times,* March 2, 1992.

11. *The New York Times,* October 6, 1994.

12. For studies of the role of small states and microstates in the contemporary international arena, see Marshall R. Singer, *Weak States in a World of Powers: The Dynamics of International Relations* (New York: The Free Press, 1972); August Schon and Arne Olav Brundtland, *Small States in International Relations* (New York: John Wiley, 1971); and Elmer Plischke, "Microstates: Lilliputs in World Affairs," *The Futurist,* Vol. 12 (February 1978), pp. 19–25. Only the last of these discusses microstates specifically.

13. For other interpretations of classical Chinese history, see Charles O. Hucher, *China to Eighteen Fifty* (Stanford: Stanford University Press, 1978); Oun J. Li, *Ageless China* (New York: Charles Scribner's Sons, 1978); J. D. Langlois, *China under Mongol Rule* (Princeton: Princeton University Press, 1981); and John Ross, *The Manchus, or the Reigning Dynasty of China* (New York: AMS Press, reprint of 1881 edition).

14. For details of the 1911–1945 period, see James E. Sheridan, *China in Disintegration: The Republican Era in Chinese History, 1912–1949* (Exeter, NH: Heinemann, 1974); and Barbara Tuchman, *Stillwell and the American Experience in China 1911–1945* (New York: Bantam Books, 1972).

15. For an excellent explanation of Maoism, see Raymond F. Wylie, *The Emergence of Maoism* (Palo Alto, CA: Stanford University Press, 1980). See also Robert J. Alexander, *International Maoism in the Developing World* (Greenwood, 1999).

16. For an analysis of the Cultural Revolution, see Simon Leys, *The Chairman's New Clothes: Mao and the Cultural Revolution* (New York: St. Martin's Press, 1978); L. Culman, *Cultural Revolution in the Provinces* (Cambridge: Harvard University Press,

1971); and David Milton and Nancy D. Milton, *The Wind Will Not Subside: Years in Revolutionary China 1964–69* (New York: Pantheorn Books, 1976).

17. For an excellent study of Deng Xiaoping's first decade of rule, see David Wen-Wei Chang, *China Under Deng Xiaoping: Political and Economic Reform* (New York: St. Martins Press, 1991).

18. For more detailed discussions of China's global role in the twenty-first century and Chinese perceptions of that role, see Minxin Pei, "Is China Democratizing?," *Foreign Affairs* (January–February 1998), pp. 68–82; Avery Goldstein, "Great Expectations: Interpreting China's Arrival," *International Security* (Winter 1997–98), pp. 36–73; David Shambaugh, "China's Military Views the World: Ambivalent Security," *International Security* (Winter 1999–2000), pp. 52–79; "China and the World Trade Organization: Beijing Takes a Gamble," *IISS Strategic Comments* (April 2000); and Michael D. Swaine and Ashley J. Tellis, *Interpreting China's Grand Strategy: Past, Present, and Future*, (Santa Monica, CA: The Rand Corporation, 2000).

19. For different views on the future of U.S.–Chinese relations, see Michel Oksenberg, "Are America and China Diverging? East Asia and the International System," Nancy Bernkopf Tucker, "Developments in Taiwan and the Implications for U.S. Policy," and Thomas Gold, "China's Political, Economic, and Social Developments and Their Implications for U.S. Policy," all in The Aspen Institute, *U.S.–China Relations* (Washington, D.C.: The Aspen Institute, 2000), pp. 9–29. See also Paul Heer, "A House United: Beijing's View of Washington," *Foreign Affairs* (July–August 2000), pp. 18–24.

PART 4

The Instrumental Framework: The Tools of Power in International Politics

International politics, like all politics, is a struggle for power. Whatever the ultimate aims of international politics, power is always the immediate aim.

Hans J. Morgenthau

Power confuses itself with virtue and tends also to take itself for omnipotence. Once imbued with the idea of a mission, a great nation easily assumes that it has the means as well as the duty to do God's work.

J. William Fulbright

In the preceding two frameworks, we examined international actors and their interests and the views that those actors hold of themselves and others in the international arena. This framework analyzes the major instruments that the actors use in their relations with one another as they attempt to achieve their objectives. In short, this framework discusses power and its constituent elements.

Everyone recognizes and respects power, but few can define precisely what it is or what its exact ingredients are. It is a means to an end and an end in itself, the primary tool and chief objective of domestic and international political processes. Power is anything but a universal constant. Someone who is a powerful individual in one situation may find his or her power greatly diminished in another situation. For example, Mikhail Gorbachev had the power to decide to cut the USSR's defense budget in 1990 and to choose whether or not he should meet with George Bush. Yet during the same time, he could not convince Lithuanians that they should not try to secede from the Soviet Union, nor could he persuade Soviet citizens to work harder. In an equally pointed example, Bill Clinton could order the U.S. military in 1999 to attack Yugoslavia to try to end Yugoslavia's ethnic cleansing in Kosovo, but he could not convince Russian President Putin to stop Russia's attacks against Chechen rebels or the U.S. Congress to adopt many of his policy preferences.

Power depends on the context in which it is used. This is as true for state and nonstate actors in international relations as it is for individuals. The United States, for all its military and economic power, found itself virtually powerless in its relations with Iran in 1979 when Iranian radicals with the support of Iran's government overran the U.S. embassy and took Americans hostage. During the hostage crisis, U.S. nuclear and conventional weapons and American economic strength were nearly meaningless. They also were not effective in obtaining the hostages' eventual release.

Similarly, in Afghanistan from 1979 through the late 1980s, poorly armed Afghan guerrillas fought against nuclear-capable Soviet armed forces. For ten years, they succeeded in fighting off their more powerful opponent, and eventually the Soviets withdrew.

And in economics, in the early 1970s, a group of economically and militarily weak states decided they would attempt to get higher prices for their only resource, oil, from the wealthy and powerful industrial countries. They too succeeded, at least for a time.

This framework examines the instruments of power in international politics. Chapter 12 presents an overview of power in its international context, how it comes into being and is measured, and how it can and cannot be used. The subsequent two chapters examine the most prominent parameters of power—economic strength and military capabilities. The final chapter in this framework discusses international law, diplomacy, and sociopolitical elements of power. Some of the more important issues examined in this framework are

- What are the constituents of power?
- How do economic and military capabilities contribute to an international actor's power?
- Why is one type of power useful in one instance but not in another?
- What constrains the employment of power?
- How do international law, diplomacy, and sociopolitical elements contribute to an international actor's power?

Chapter 12

Power

- What is power?
- What contributes to power?
- Why is one type of power useful in one situation but not in another?
- How can power be measured?

Power has been studied from earliest recorded time. In the West, Aristotle, Plato, Socrates, Machiavelli, Hobbes, Montesquieu, and thousands of other writers, philosophers, and analysts turned their thoughts to the elusive concept of power. In the East, Kautilya, Lao Tzu, Confucius, and thousands more did the same. In our effort to understand what power means and what power is, we are following a long and illustrious line of thinkers.

Nearly as many definitions of power exist as there are writers. Some writers define power as physical force. Others see it as a more broadly based concept that includes military, economic, psychological, and social dimensions.[1] The concept of power that we will use is broadly based, but first we will examine some views of power that prevail today.

VIEWS OF POWER

Hans Morgenthau's classic text, *Politics Among Nations: The Struggle for Power and Peace,* elevated the study of power to a new level of respectability in international affairs.[2] Morgenthau's basic thesis was simple: Power is a psychological relationship between those who exercise it and those over whom it is exercised.[3] To Morgenthau, those who exercise power influence the decisions of those who have less power because the weaker individual, group, or state expects benefits, fears retribution, or respects the individuals and/or institutions exercising power. Morgenthau even went so far as to define national interest in terms of power. To Morgenthau, any action or policy that maximized a state's power was in the national interest. Actions or policies that did not maximize power were not in the national interest. Power, to Morgenthau, was both a means and an end.[4]

Morgenthau drew four distinctions about the role of power in international affairs. First, power and influence were not synonymous. Power denoted the ability to determine outcomes; influence implied the ability to affect the decisions of those who could determine

297

outcomes. To use Morgenthau's example, a secretary of state advises the president to choose a policy option, but only the president makes a decision. Thus, the secretary of state has the potential to be influential, but is influential only if the president follows the secretary of state's advice. Conversely, the president is powerful regardless of whether or not secretarial advice is followed.[5]

Second, Morgenthau differentiated between power and force. To Morgenthau, force meant physical violence, which eliminated the psychological implications of power. A powerful actor, to Morgenthau, employed force as a threat and did not need to employ it as a reality. Thus, "armed strength as a threat or a potentiality is the most important material factor making for the political power of a nation."[6]

Third, Morgenthau identified a difference between usable and unusable power. Nuclear capabilities and the threat of their use was and is a credible element of national power in certain situations but not in others. Thus, nuclear weapons may be either usable or unusable additions to a nation's power potential. In other words, power was contextual.

Fourth, Morgenthau claimed a distinction between moral power, or legitimate power, and immoral power, or illegitimate power. Political ideologies, whether they be western democracy, Marxism-Leninism, Nazism, or something else, endowed national actions with legitimacy. This legitimacy in turn made it acceptable to them to employ their power.

Morgenthau's conception of power has been criticized by many. Some critics observed that Morgenthau and other proponents of the realpolitik school of international relations emphasized the coercive aspects of power and minimized its attractive aspects. Although Morgenthau stressed that power permitted one actor to force another actor to act as the first desired and prevented other actors from forcing the first actor to act as they desired, critics of Morgenthau's emphasis on coercion pointed out that certain actors enhanced their power by attracting the loyalty or allegiance of other actors. These analysts argue that power must therefore be viewed as having both coercive and attractive components.

The complexities of the concept of power have led many analysts to maintain that power is essentially a qualitative concept that can not be precisely measured. At best, these analysts assert, power can be gauged in broad qualitative terms, not precise quantitative terms.

Others disagree. For example, Ray S. Cline, former Director of Intelligence and Research at the Department of State and former Deputy Director of Intelligence for the Central Intelligence Agency, developed a formula to measure the **perceived power** that a country has.[7] According to Cline:

$$P_p = (C + E + M) \times (S + W)$$

where P_p = perceived power
C = critical mass: population and territory
E = economic capability
M = military capability
S = strategic purpose
W = will to pursue national strategy

Cline's first three elements of power $(C + E + M)$ are tangible elements that can be objectively quantified. The last two elements $(S + W)$ are intangibles and may be only subjectively quantified.

Chapter 12

IT AND POWER: INFORMATION AS POWER

Information technologies are redefining the nature of power. As rapid advances in semiconductors, computers, fiberoptics, networks, wireless, and digital signal processing are applied to industrial control and production systems; globally integrated financial, banking, and trading systems; smart weapons; and communications and entertainment, information, information technologies, and their applications are becoming an increasingly important source of power in contemporary international relations.

IT advances have had profound effects on the global economy. Around the world, larger and larger shares of the world's production are shifting away from traditional heavy industrial production toward value-added knowledge-based manufactures. Similarly, knowledge-based service industries are becoming more important factors in the economies of developed and developing states alike. Increasingly, information is becoming a more important factor of production than land, labor, or capital.

A similar phenomenon is occurring in military affairs, where smart and brilliant weapons; advanced intelligence, reconnaissance, and surveillance capabilities; and networked command, control, and communication systems are becoming irreplaceable elements of the world's armed forces, especially those of the United States. At the same time, as information-based capabilities compress time and space, the character of military strategy is changing. As one military analyst noted, "information technology is replacing geography as the main element of national power."

Meanwhile, information and information technology are also becoming larger contributors to other elements of power. In the sociopolitical arena, the twenty-first century media plays a major role in building—or undermining—public support for government policies in both domestic and international affairs. Similarly, the entertainment industry is at least as influential in building or undermining domestic and international acceptance of a song, a movie, or more importantly, a way of life.

Nor is diplomacy as an element of power immune from the impact of information and information technologies. Advanced information technologies may tie diplomats more closely than ever to their home country, but the ability of diplomats to have an impact on the country to which they are posted, especially in the realm of public diplomacy, is greater than ever, all because of Information Age technologies.

Information technology, then, is changing the nature of power. It is increasingly becoming a component of traditional "hard" parameters of power such as economics and the military. At the same time, IT is elevating the importance of "soft" parameters of power such as sociopolitical elements and diplomacy. Indeed, in many respects, information in the context of international relations is becoming like power itself, something to be sought both for what it is and for what it provides.

An astute observer will realize that subjectivity also enters an assessment of tangible elements. Relative skills and education levels of a country's people are major factors to be considered when population is being assessed. So, too, is the physical topography of a country when territory is being considered. A skilled and educated people in many respects must be rated more highly than a quantitatively more numerous unskilled and uneducated population. Similarly, a country with few or no navigable rivers has transportational disadvantages to overcome. In the area of military capabilities, quantitative and qualitative parameters of the military balance are often subjects of heated debate. In certain instances, quantitatively more numerous weapons will overcome qualitatively superior weapons. In other cases, quality will defeat quantity. Economically, debates over questions of the wisdom of developing one's own expensive resource base or relying on relatively less expensive foreign resources are legion. Is the country that pays less for foreign resources, and is therefore dependent, in a better position than a country that pays more to develop its own resources, but is therefore self-sufficient? These and similar other economic questions make an assessment of the economic parameters of power extremely uncertain. Nevertheless, when compared to $S + W$, $C + E + M$ is a more objective set of criteria of power, at least in a relative sense.

Specific examples may clarify these points. In 1980, Cline calculated U.S., Soviet, and Chinese power potentials, as shown in Table 12-1. By early 2000, however, much had changed.

In the United States, the economy had boomed for most of the 1990s. The United States had put new weapons into its arsenal and had become more assertive in international affairs. Even though it could not dictate the direction of world affairs, it reigned unchallenged as the world's number one power.

Meanwhile, the Soviet Union had collapsed, replaced by 15 independent states, the most important of which was Russia. However, the Russian economy was in a shambles, and its armed forces were greatly weakened. In early 2000, though, a new president took power, and a new sense of purpose and direction began to emerge.

Throughout this time in China, economic growth was rapid, the Chinese military improved its capabilities, and despite the Tiananmen Square massacre, the Chinese government was still firmly in control. New leaders came to power in 1997, apparently confirming continuity in China's strategic direction.

These situations are all reflected in Table 12-2.

TABLE 12-1   Perceived Power of the United States, USSR, and China, 1980

	Critical Mass	Economic Capability	Military Capability	Partial Total	Strategy and Will	Total
United States	100	146	188	434	0.7	304
USSR	100	85	197	382	1.2	458
China	75	23	41	139	0.6	83

TABLE 12-2 **Perceived Power of the United States, Russia, and China, 2000, Version 1**

	Critical Mass	Economic Capability	Military Capability	Partial Total	Strategy and Will	Total
U.S.	100	180	220	500	1.0	500
Russia	90	70	90	250	1.0	250
China	80	80	90	250	1.0	250

But was this the way things really were? Had the United States really moved from a position 50 percent behind the USSR to a position two times ahead of Russia in only 20 years? Had China really moved from being one-sixth as powerful as the Soviet Union in 1980 to being as powerful as Russia in 2000? Or was the situation even more strikingly different than Table 12-2 indicates?

Assume for a moment that the Russian election did not signal the beginning of the growth of a new sense of purpose and direction in Russia, and that the new Chinese leaders did not succeed in maintaining China's strategic momentum. Also suppose that the United States, far ahead of Russia and China in information technology, was just beginning to reap the economic and military benefits of information technology. These situations are reflected in Table 12-3.

Obviously, assessing power even when a formula is provided is a subjective task. To Cline, the bottom line is the capacity of a state to wage war.[8] In situations where political or economic dialogue breaks down, this view is exactly correct. In other situations, the case may be overstated. In some instances different aspects of power come into play and render the superior ability of one state over another to wage war almost meaningless. We explore the contradictory aspects of power in the next section.

ASPECTS OF POWER

As the preceding section showed, power is a difficult concept to measure. In part, this is because it has so many subtle and contradictory aspects whose relationships one to another are constantly changing. These aspects of power can best be described as the multidimensional, perceptual, dynamic, relational, and contextual aspects of power.

TABLE 12-3 **Perceived Power of the United States, Russia, and China, 2000, Version 2**

	Critical Mass	Economic Capability	Military Capability	Partial Total	Strategy and Will	Total
U.S.	100	240	240	580	1.0	580
Russia	90	70	90	250	.7	175
China	80	80	90	250	.7	175

Power is Multidimensional

Power has many different dimensions, all of which have many constituent elements that in turn have many different characteristics. Some of power's dimensions such as economic strength and military capability are quite obvious. Others such as international law, diplomacy, and what is labeled sociopolitical power (Chapter 15) are less obvious but nonetheless important. All are made up by or created by constituent elements such as population, geography, natural resources, or military forces that in turn have their own subtle characteristics that add to or subtract from their overall contribution to an international actor's power.

Complicating matters still more, power is often both a **tool** and an **objective.** As a tool, power can be an instrument of **coercion, influence, persuasion, or deterrence.** Distinctions between these uses are often subtle, but they are nevertheless important, and are discussed immediately below. As an objective, power is something that many international actors seek to enable them to achieve other objectives.

As for power as an instrument of coercion, when an international actor attempts to force another international actor to undertake or not undertake actions, that is, when it attempts to control another actor's actions, it is using power as a coercive tool. In contrast, the power that an international actor has may influence another actor to undertake or not undertake an action without the first actor seeking to control the second. In such instances, power is a tool of influence.

Influence may be intentional and sought, or unintentional and unsought. If it is intentionally sought, it may aptly be described as persuasive power. Persuasive power is thus a subset of influence, that is, it is power that is intentionally used to influence another's actions but not control them. Whereas influence may be either intentional and sought or unintentional and unsought, persuasion is always intentional and sought.

Finally, when an actor uses power as a deterrent, it attempts to prevent another actor from undertaking an action that that actor may otherwise prefer to undertake.

As actors use power, and as analysts and students try to understand power, all of its many dimensions must be taken into consideration. Only then can power be most effectively utilized or most completely understood. These are not easy tasks for policymakers, analysts, or students.

Power is Perceptual

What is more, power does not consist exclusively of concrete, tangible, finite elements. It has both objective and subjective elements. Thus, at least in part, power is perceptual. Its utility lies not only in what it *can* do, but also in what others *think* it can do. An actor that is "weak" but that is perceived as "strong" has much greater leeway for action than an actor that is weak and is perceived as weak. An example may clarify the point.

During the late 1950s and early 1960s, the Soviet Union was a relatively weak state, but it was widely perceived as a strong one. Despite pronounced nuclear inferiority and a much weaker economy in comparison to the United States, the combination of the Soviet success in launching the world's first satellite and Khrushchev's missile rattling influenced many people to perceive that Soviet power was nearly equal to U.S. power. Somewhat paradoxically, Soviet power *was* nearly equal to U.S. power *simply because many people perceived it to be.*

Because of its ability to add to or subtract from an international actor's power, the perceptual aspect of power is sometimes considered a constituent element of power. This approach has merit. Here, however, because of its presence in every dimension of power, it is considered an underlying aspect of power.

Power is Dynamic

Power is ever changing and never constant. Economies grow faster, slower, or contract on a year-to-year, month-to-month, and even week-to-week basis. Today's modern weapon is tomorrow's out-of-date weapon. Diplomacy that works today may fail tomorrow. A president, prime minister, or dictator that is today's hero may be voted out of office in the next election or overthrown in a coup.

The reality of the dynamics of power makes it difficult for the policymaker to use power with certainty, for the analyst to predict the outcome of a situation in which power is used, and for the student and scholar to understand how power works.

Power is Relational

Power defines relations between and among international actors, and especially between and among states. A "powerful state" may force or influence a "less powerful state" to change its policies or objectives, and that "less powerful state" may in turn force or influence a "weak state" to alter its policies or objectives. By implication, the powerful state also can influence or control decisions made in the weak state. The weak state, in turn, is prevented from forcing or influencing the less powerful state to change its policies or objectives by its inferior power position, and the less powerful state, in turn, cannot force or influence the powerful state to alter its policies or objectives. Again by implication, the weak state cannot influence the powerful state. Thus, power defines the relationship.

Power is Contextual

Relations between and among international actors are made even more complicated by the contextual aspect of power. This means simply that the "right kind" of power must be used in the "right kind" of situation. Arguments made at the United Nations about human rights violations may influence the behavior and attitudes of delegates who hear the arguments. They may even lead the UN to deploy peacekeeping forces, as it did to East Timor in 1999. But those same arguments to those committing human rights violations on a battlefield would probably be meaningless. Words may be appropriate tools of power in the UN's chambers, but they rarely are on the battlefield.

Particular types of weapons may also be appropriate or inappropriate tools of power depending on circumstances. Nuclear weapons, the extreme tools of violence, are inappropriate instruments for use against terrorism and other types of low-intensity conflict. Even in the case of open war between a nuclear-capable country and a nonnuclear country, nuclear weapons, so far, have been deemed inappropriate. U.S. military actions in Korea in the 1950s, Vietnam in the 1960s and 1970s, the Persian Gulf War in 1991, and Kosovo in 1999 all offered proof that in certain contexts, nuclear weapons and the power they provide are not meaningfully useful. The contextual nature of power therefore frustrates simple measures of power prelationships between international actors.

Several examples may further clarify the point. Throughout the Cold War, the United States, with its large economy and powerful military, was more powerful than Cuba. However, for all its power, the United States could not persuade, influence, force, or otherwise induce Cuba to abandon its support for revolution in Africa and Latin America, nor could the United States convince Cuba to lessen its adherence to communism or its animosity toward the United States. In the context of its general relationship with Cuba, U.S. economic clout and military might added little to American power.

Similarly, in the relationship between China and Taiwan that existed from the late 1940s to the twenty-first century, China's population, economy, and military made it more powerful than Taiwan. But in most contexts, China could not bring its vast population, growing economy, and improving military to bear on Taiwan to coerce, influence or persuade Taiwan to change its policies, viewpoints, or government.

As a last example, the combined economic and military power of the UN, the European Union, and the United States was not sufficient to persuade the Yugoslav government not to carry out its ethnic cleansing program against Albanian Kosovars in 1998 and 1999. Only the direct application of military force against Yugoslavia in 1999 ended ethnic cleansing.

Power is not only contextual in interactions between states. It is also contextual in interactions between other types of international actors, at least in part because some types of actors respond more willingly to one parameter of power than to another. For example, multinational corporations respond to economic parameters of power more rapidly than national liberation movements. Negotiations and appeals to morality may prove more powerful at the United Nations than in the corporate boardroom or in the bush. Allegiance of an uneducated people in a newly independent country may render a national liberation movement more powerful, yet be meaningless for a multinational corporation or the United Nations. Power, then, is contextual not only as it applies to states, but also as it applies to other actors. The power of any actor rises and wanes depending on the context in which constituents of power are employed.

 ## CONSTITUENTS OF POWER

What, then, is power? For our purposes, we may define it as the ability of any actor to persuade, influence, force, or otherwise induce another actor to undertake an action that it would prefer not to pursue, to refrain from an action that it would prefer to undertake, or to change an objective that it would prefer to keep. One actor may achieve power over another actor through persuasion, coercion, force, or dependence. An actor may have its power enhanced as other actors enter willingly into alliance with it. Power is both subjective and objective, although its constituent elements vary from time to time and place to place. Its contextual nature complicates the ordered relations that a simple definition of power yields.

Power is nevertheless a product of many inputs. The power potential of an actor is best estimated by examining each input individually.

Population

Population is one of the most important determinants of power. Here, population refers not only to numbers but also to the training and expertise of a population. China's immense population is one reason why it is considered a major power, yet the advantages that China could derive from its population are reduced by the level of training and expertise of that population. Outside the realm of states, other actors benefit from the number, training, and expertise of their populations as well. IBM employs few people in comparison with the population of the major state actors, but the training and knowledge of IBM's "population" enhances its power. Similarly, national liberation movements increase their power as their cadre grows more numerous and better trained.

The role that population plays in enhancing or reducing the power of an actor cannot be divorced from other parameters of power such as organization, leadership, and industrial base. For example, Indonesia has a population of over 200 million, but its internal diversity and its island geography have complicated its leadership's efforts to coordinate the country's human and material resources. Bangladesh, with a population of 125 million, has had organizational and leadership problems and has too few natural resources.

Geography

Geography also plays a role in determining the power of an actor, although the importance of geography remains a matter of debate. Geography is almost exclusively relevant for determining the power potential of state actors. As discussed in Chapter 1, during the early twentieth century, the geopolitical school of international analysis emphasized the role of geography to the exclusion of other factors in determining national power potential. The advent of nuclear weapons and other high-technology armaments led most analysts to minimize the importance of geography during the first three post–World War II decades, but geography's importance was reemphasized during the 1980s when the USSR moved into Afghanistan.

Sheer size is a major geographical contributor to a country's power potential. The immense distances of the czar's Russia played a major role in defeating Napoleon in 1812 and in frustrating the Kaiser during World War I. Soviet Russia was similarly saved by its size during World War II. The incredibly cold Russian winters, a product of Russia's geographical location, contributed mightily to the defeat of all three invading armies. Switzerland's mountains have played an invaluable role in Swiss defense, and the United States has been blessed with two immense buffer zones that shielded it from invasion—the Atlantic and Pacific oceans.

Size, terrain, and location need not be advantages, however. Russia is a good example. Russia does not have an ocean port that is ice-free year round. Russian foreign trade and ocean-borne freight are thus limited. Similarly, all major Russian rivers run north and south and, with the exception of the Volga, provide limited service as internal transportation arteries. Finally, because of its size and location, Russia finds it necessary to have four separate fleets. During times of war, these four fleets, one in the Pacific, one in the Black Sea, another in the Baltic, and the fourth in the north, would not be able to link up.

A country's geography may also deny it access to the sea. A landlocked state that has the ability and desire to engage in trade must depend on its neighbors to provide it access to the sea. In some cases, this presents little problem. Bolivia has had few difficulties exporting its mineral production through Peruvian or Chilean ports. Conversely, Zambia's copper exports could no longer reach the Angolan port of Benguela when the Angolan Civil War erupted, and Zambia's political relations with white-controlled Rhodesia (now Zimbabwe) precluded egress on Rhodesian railroads.

Nonstate actors, with the exception of national liberation movements, rarely count geography as elements of power. National liberation movements may be fortunate enough to benefit from geographically or topographically provided advantages. Thus, the Vietcong used Vietnam's jungle to good advantage, thereby increasing their power, and Afghan mujahadeen used Afghanistan's rugged terrain to provide shelter and to ambush Soviet troops.

Natural Resources

Natural resources are a third element of power. At least four levels of importance—possession, exploitation, control, and use—may be attached to resources. Obviously, an actor that has large quantities of resources is in a potentially advantageous position compared with an actor that has few or none. But an actor must also be able to exploit those resources. For example, the Russian Far East and Siberia have large quantities of minerals, but Russia cannot exploit them because they are located in areas of extremely inhospitable climate and terrain. Similarly as we have seen, Zambia has rich copper deposits, but when the Angolan Civil War closed the Benguela railroad, Zambia was unable to export its copper except through Rhodesia, which Zambia refused to do for political reasons. The Chinese-built Tanzam railroad has since given Zambia a third egress alternative.

Control is a third level of importance of resources. It does little for an actor's power if the actor possesses resources that are exploited by another actor. Here, the oil-producing states of the Middle East are a prime example. Until they were able to coordinate their oil policies with each other through OPEC and wrest control of production and pricing decisions from the multinational oil companies to which they had earlier granted concessions, the oil-producing states were important, but impotent, actors on the international scene. However, when they obtained control over their oil fields, they emerged to a new powerful position in the international order of states.

Use is a final level of importance of resources. Unless an actor can put its resources to effective use for its own purposes, it adds little to its power. Use is primarily a function of an actor's level of industrial and economic development. Brazil has immense deposits of exploitable resources that it controls, yet it is only slowly developing an industrial and economic base that takes full advantage of its resources. The Democratic Republic of the Congo (the DRC, formerly Zaire) and Zambia are also resource rich, but they do not have industrial bases. In the DRC's case, multinational corporations still enjoy favorable concessions there even after the revolution and civil war, so the question of control remains pertinent. In Zambia, use is complicated because it does not have ports and other states deny Zambia access to them.

Other than states, multinational corporations are the most prominent actors that derive power from natural resources. MNCs depend on states to grant access, but on many occasions, because of the human expertise and financial income they provide, particularly to Developing World states, MNCs may exercise a disproportionate amount of influence within a state because of that state's reliance on an MNC to provide expertise and capital for resource exploitation.

Industrial Capabilities

Industrial capabilities are also major inputs to a country's power potential. Particularly during major wars, the record of the nineteenth and twentieth centuries indicates that countries with superior industrial bases and the wealth to support those bases generally emerge victorious in war. Quantitative studies tend to confirm this general observation.[9] Caution must be exercised in reaching this conclusion, however. In wars of less than major scale, industrial capabilities provide a less meaningful source of power. France, the former Soviet Union, and the United States encountered tremendous difficulties in their struggles against nonindustrial nonstate actors in Algeria, Afghanistan, and Vietnam.

Industrial capabilities are major contributing elements to a country's economic power during peace. Industrial strength contributes directly to the standard of living, which, if acceptable to a population, may lead that population to be more amenable to its government's policies. For example, the German people willingly supported Adolf Hitler's policies as he nationalized German industry, improved its efficiency, and raised Germany out of the Great Depression. Hitler's industrial successes and the support they won for him within Germany enhanced the power of the German state and led directly to World War II.

For many countries, industrial capabilities carry with them the necessity for access to external resources. Thus, industrial capabilities add to a state's power, but also make it potentially dependent on other actors. Europe's and Japan's industrial bases make them powerful actors, but their power is qualified by their extreme energy dependence, Great Britain and Norway excepted.

Military Capabilities

Military capabilities are important to an actor's power potential. In fact, some analysts of the role of power in international affairs argue that military capabilities are the only real determinants of an actor's true power. This is an extremely narrow outlook that may be legitimate during times of war, but is overly restrictive during peace. For example, Japan has limited military capabilities because of its constitutional restriction on armed forces, but it is a powerful country in economic terms. Similarly, few actors other than states and national liberation movements have military capabilities, but depending on the context of a particular situation, many have power.

Nevertheless, the military capabilities of a state are fundamental constituents of power for state actors. Qualitative and quantitative aspects of military power are variously measured, as are the varying utilities of conventional and nuclear forces. The ability to project military power far from a national homeland is one measure of military capabilities, as is the ability to defend one's homeland. Numerous other questions also must be addressed when the military might of an actor is examined: How well are an actor's military forces prepared for war during time of peace? How long would it take for an actor to mobilize for

Industrial capabilities have been major contributing elements to economic power and military power since the industrial revolution. Here, aircraft are assembled in the Boeing aircraft plant in Seattle, Washington.

war? How self-reliant is an actor on its own resources and industry? How supportive of the leadership are the people? How solid an alliance system does an actor have?

Obviously, the factors that determine an actor's military capabilities are complex and extend far beyond counting the number and quality of planes, tanks, ships, and troops. Although it is an extreme oversimplification to argue that military capabilities and the power of an actor are synonymous, in the twenty-first century, military capabilities remain a major component of power.

Will

So, too, is *will*. Regardless of the quantity or quality of the more tangible elements of power that an actor may have, an absence of will to use those elements renders them virtually meaningless. Indeed, many analysts rank will as one of the most, if not the most, important determinants of power.[10] Without will, even a massive state-of-the art military can achieve little.

Yet will is difficult, if not impossible, to measure. It cannot be quantified, and may only be estimated. Will may refer either to the intention of a particular set of decision-making elites to achieve a particular goal or it may refer to the willingness of the population to support the decision-makers' decision. During the Vietnam War, for example, the U.S. political and military elite remained committed to the maintenance of an independent South Vietnam much longer than the general population of the United States. Eventually, the population's attitude influenced the elite's attitude as well. By 1975, when North Vietnam overran South

Vietnam, neither the U.S. population nor the U.S. elite had the will to become reengaged in Southeast Asia. By contrast, in 1990 when Iraq invaded Kuwait, U.S. President George Bush successfully mobilized popular support in the United States to expel Iraq from Kuwait. American will was thus a significant factor in the 1991 victory in the Gulf War.

Will may also be ephemeral, that is, it may appear and disappear quickly. For example, when the United States launched air attacks against Yugoslavia in 1999 because of Yugoslavia's repression of and brutality against Albanian Kosovars, a groundswell of support quickly developed in the United States for the U.S. action. The United States achieved its objectives in three months without a loss of life due to enemy action. Would U.S. will have remained strong if the action had taken several years or if U.S. losses had been high? The question cannot be answered, but the U.S. experience in Vietnam implies that long wars with large losses will reduce the U.S. population's willingness to support a war.

Leadership

Leadership plays a major role in establishing will, and it also often influences how well an actor takes advantage of other parameters of power. Leadership may be either jointly managed or undertaken individually, but in either case, it is a key. Particularly during time of peace and prosperity, decision makers often prefer leadership roles to be widely shared, or at least to have the appearance of being widely shared. In many strongly authoritarian or dictatorial societies, leadership elites seek to create the image of a broad sharing of power. Despite the fact that communist "People's Republics" rarely allowed the people to share in decision making, the decision-making elite considered it necessary to maintain the fiction of popular participation. Conversely, during periods of economic and military crises, actors often opt for a more centralized form of leadership. This occurs in democratic as well as authoritarian societies. Franklin Roosevelt presided over an unprecedented accumulation of power in presidential hands during the Great Depression and World War II.

Additionally, the occasional importance of single individuals in determining the course of history has led to the development of the "Great Man" theory of history. According to this concept, the exploits of Alexander the Great, Caesar, Napoleon, Bismarck, Lenin, Roosevelt, Hitler, Churchill, and Mao occurred not because of a fortuitous combination of circumstances, but because a "great man" was in a position to take advantage of circumstances.

Leadership also influences the amount of societal cohesion that exists within a society. Although *charisma* is an overworked term, who can deny that a John Kennedy or a Franklin Roosevelt was able to mobilize large segments of the U.S. population behind him by force of personality? On other occasions, ideas or concepts may be used by leaders to achieve or seek to achieve societal cohesion. After the trauma of Vietnam, Americans responded willingly to Jimmy Carter's call for a reemphasis on human rights in U.S. foreign policy. Thereafter, as the image of U.S. impotence grew in the wake of the hostage crisis in Iran and the Soviet invasion of Afghanistan, U.S. citizens responded favorably to Ronald Reagan's call for a rearmed United States. In all cases, effective leadership abets power.

Leadership is of equally great importance in multinational corporations, IGOs, and nongovernmental organizations. Effective leadership can enhance power, and ineffective leadership can reduce power. Microsoft became a rich MNC under the leadership of Bill Gates, and Dag Hammarskjod's skills in guiding the United Nations enhanced its power in international relations.

Nevertheless, even with skillful leadership, other parameters of power are also needed. It is doubtful if any leader or leadership elite, regardless of skill, could significantly enhance the power of Chad, Niger, or Mali, three state actors that are among the world's most impotent and powerless.

Diplomacy

A country's *diplomacy* also must be considered an element of its power. Skillful diplomats can influence other countries to act in ways that will promote their own country's interests, can weave together alliances that will help defend their country, and can help establish an international climate that will abet their country's efforts to achieve its international objectives. Conversely, unskilled diplomats can allow other countries to improve their positions relative to the diplomats' own country by inattention to detail, by failing to think through implications of an agreement, by not staying attuned to ongoing events, and in many other ways. Diplomacy as a parameter of power will be examined in greater depth in Chapter 15.

Internal Organization

Internal organization is also a constituent of power. An actor whose internal organization is rigidly stratified or which disperses too many rewards to too few of its members may reduce the allegiance of its people to that actor. Power potential is correspondingly reduced. Similarly, extreme internal political fragmentation can reduce a country's political stability, thereby reducing if not its power, then at the very least others' perceptions of its power. In Italy, for example, at least six major political parties exist. Governments must be formed by coalition.

Internal organization is also important within nonstate actors in the international arena. The United Nations, for example, permits any of the "Big Five" to veto Security Council resolutions; it is not surprising that the United Nations rarely undertakes an action that will adversely have an impact on the interests of China, France, Great Britain, Russia, or the United States. Similarly, "mother-daughter" organizational structures reduced the ability of MNCs to take advantage of changes in the international economic environment and reduced the economic power of MNCs.

Strategy

The role of *strategy* in determining an actor's power has been the subject of considerable debate. As defined by Ray Cline, strategy is "the part of the political decision-making process that conceptualizes and establishes goals and objectives designed to protect and enhance . . . interests in the international arena."[11] To some analysts, strategy flows from an actor's elite and therefore must be analyzed in conjunction with the outlooks of an actor's leadership. In this view, current U.S. strategy is the product of the predominant U.S. emphasis on pluralistic political democracy and a free market economy. An opposed perspective argues that population, geography, resources, and other factors determine strategy. In this view, U.S. strategy flows from its economic interdependence, peaceful borders, and continuing concerns about world peace.

However, all concede that strategy is important. The manner in which a leadership organizes and directs capabilities toward a specific goal can add to or detract from an actor's power as much as any of the other parameters of power we have discussed. Capabilities without strategy are nearly as meaningless as strategy without capabilities.

DECLARATORY POLICY VERSUS ACTUAL POLICY

Here, the difference between the **declaratory policy** and the **actual policy** of a state or other international actor must be discussed. Declaratory policy is what an international actor says that it will do in a situation. Actual policy is what it really does or really intends to do.

Why do differences sometimes exist between declaratory policy and actual policy? In part, it is because states—and other actors—seek to add to their own power by convincing others that they will do something that they do not intend to do. If states or other actors can succeed in doing this, then another state or another actor may change its own policies.

An example may help clarify this. During the 1950s, the United States had a declaratory policy for nuclear weapons called "massive retaliation." This declaratory policy of "massive retaliation" stated that if communist forces anywhere in the world attempted to increase the amount of territory under their control, the United States would reserve the right to use nuclear weapons at times and places of its own choosing, including massive nuclear attacks against the Soviet Union. The intent of the U.S. declaratory policy was to influence the Soviet Union and other communist states to end whatever plans they had to expand.

U.S. leaders, however, did not actually intend to use nuclear weapons in every and all cases. They simply made such statements in an effort to influence Soviet and other communist policy. The actual policy of the United States remained much as it had been—conventional weapons would be used in most instances of conflict, and nuclear weapons only in extreme cases. A clear difference existed between U.S. declaratory policy and U.S. actual policy because U.S. policy makers wanted to influence the perceptions that Soviet and other communist leaders had about what the United States would do in the event of Soviet or other communist expansion. By trying to change the perception of what Soviet leaders thought the United States would do, U.S. leaders sought to change Soviet and other communist actions. Perceptions, then, are major inputs to power potential, and international actors often use declaratory policy as a way to manipulate other actors' perceptions.

Of course, when differences exist between actual power and perception of power, the actor perceived to be more powerful than it actually is, or that perceives itself to be more powerful than it actually is, may be in for a rude awakening. During the early twentieth century, Russia was generally recognized as one of the leading powers in the world. It also considered itself to be such a power. The czar and the rest of the world were shocked when the Japanese administered a humiliating defeat to the Russians in the 1905 Russo–Japanese War. Europe and Russia had deluded themselves into overestimating Russia's military prowess, a delusion that added strength to Russian power until that power was actually tested. So, too, 75 years later, Soviet leaders deluded themselves into believing that their military power was sufficient to defeat the mujahadeen in Afghanistan. The entire world believed this to be true as well—until year after year passed, with Soviet forces mired ever more deeply in Afghanistan. Thus, at first, the USSR's power was enhanced by the prevailing perception that it had the will to use its military capabilities to achieve its objectives, but as Soviet military capabilities proved unequal to the task, the perception of the power of the Soviet Union dwindled.

CONCLUSIONS

Measuring power is more art than science. Given the relational nature of power, the contextual quality of its application, and the difficulty of assigning an objective value to even its most tangible elements, it is not surprising that one of the major debates in the United States has been over power, or more specifically, over where and how to use American power. Other countries also debate their relative power positions in the world. Political elites throughout the world search for answers to the questions of where their state stands relative to the power of other regional and global actors. It was not without pride that Margaret Thatcher's government announced that it had "put the Great back into Britain" following the Falkland Islands War. Power can be measured accurately only when it is used, and for the first time since the Suez intervention in 1956, Great Britain had an opportunity to gauge the military parameters of its power.

The struggle to gauge power has led some analysts to adopt broadly based subjective judgments of global and regional balances of power, and has led others to develop concepts such as Cline's "Politectonics." The former accept measures of power as an art; the latter attempt to make it more of a science. All are attempting to answer the question, "Who, if anyone, will dominate whom?"

Given the uncertainties inherent in the study and use of power in international affairs, only one specific conclusion may be reached: "Real power—the ability to affect others— seems in fact more widely dispersed than perhaps at any time in the world's history."[12] With the end of the Cold War and the East–West conflict, that reality has become increasingly evident for all to see.

With this in mind, the next three chapters explore the most important parameters of power in contemporary international relations: economic power; military power; and international law, diplomacy, and sociopolitical power.

KEY TERMS AND CONCEPTS

Hans Morgenthau's ideas about power   Morgenthau defined power as national interest, saying that actions that maximized state power were in its national interest and that power was a means and an end

perceived power   the power that one actor believes another to have: multi-dimensional aspects of power; power as a tool and objective; coercion, influence, persuasion, and deterrence; perceptual aspects of power; dynamic aspects of power

relational aspects of power   power defines relationships between states and other international actors

contextual aspects of power   certain constituent elements of power add to an international actor's power potential in one situation but not in another, or add more to a country's power potential in one situation than in another

constituents of power   these include population, geography, natural resources, industrial capabilities, military capabilities, will, leadership, internal organization, and perception

declaratory policy   what a state says that it will do in a given situation

actual policy   what a state really does or really intends to do in a given situation

WEBSITE REFERENCES

power: *www.dal.ca/~finbow/nic.html*   quotations about power

NOTES

1. See, for example, Inis L. Claude, Jr., *Power and International Relations* (New York: Random House, 1962); and Christopher Harmon and David Tucker, eds., *Statecraft and Power* Lanham, MD: University Press of America, 1994).

2. Hans J. Morgenthau, *Politics Among Nations: The Struggle for Power and Peace* (New York: Alfred A. Knopf, 1973). The first edition was published in 1948. For a more recent and extremely useful study of the concept of power, see John M. Rothgeb, Jr., *Defining Power: Influence and Force in the Contemporary International System* (New York: St. Martin's Press, 1993).

3. Morgenthau, *Politics Among Nations*, p. 28.

4. Ibid., p. 5.

5. Ibid., p. 29.

6. Ibid.

7. Ray S. Cline, *World Power Trends and U.S. Foreign Policy for the 1980s* (Boulder, CO: Westview Press, 1980). For an update of Cline's views on power, see Ray S. Cline, *The Power of Nations in the 1990s: A Strategic Assessment* (Lanham, MD: University Press of America, 1994).

8. Ibid., p. 13.

9. Bruce Russet, *International Regions and the International System* (Chicago: Rand McNally, 1967); Harvey Starr, *War Coalitions* (Lexington, MA.: D. C. Heath, 1973); and Rudolph Rummell, "Indicators of Cross-National and International Patterns," *American Political Science Review,* Vol. 68 (March 1969), pp. 127–147.

10. See Cline, *World Power Trends,* p. 143.

11. Ibid.

12. William P. Bundy, "Elements of National Power," *Foreign Affairs,* Vol. 56 (October 1977), pp. 1–26.

Chapter 13

Economic Parameters of Power

- How does economics contribute to power?
- Why is there a new awareness of economics as a parameter of power?
- Why is international trade so important?
- How do exchange rates work?
- Why is international finance so important?
- How has the international economic system evolved?

As an element of power, economic strength is both an end and a means. As an end, economic strength allows those who have it, whether they be individuals, corporations, states, organizations, or any other type of international actor, to purchase goods and services, to produce many of one's own needs and material desires, and to improve one's quality of life. As a means, economic strength also allows one to influence and sometimes even control decisions and outlooks of others and to maintain control of much of one's own future.

This does not mean that international actors necessarily need great economic strength to be powerful. Indeed not, for as we have seen, a variety of different parameters can provide power to an actor. But at the same time, economic strength is often one of the most significant constituents of power.

Perhaps surprisingly, this was overlooked for much of the post–World War II era, at least at the state level. Although economics was never ignored as an input to power, it was frequently relegated to a second-order or third-order priority.

There were three reasons for this. First, World War II and the bipolar international system placed a primacy on military capabilities. Economic capabilities usually were and are required before military capabilities can be obtained, but given the emphasis on military capabilities that accompanied the bipolar international system, economic parameters took a backseat to military concerns.

Second, the end of World War II ushered in a new age, the nuclear era, in which many people wrongfully concluded that old truths no longer applied. Even in the military arena, many analysts at first concluded that nuclear weapons made conventional arms obsolete.

Chapter 13

IT AND ECONOMIC POWER: WORLD-WIDE MARKETS AND GLOBALIZATION

Advanced information technology is fundamentally altering the nature and sources of economic power throughout the world by creating world-wide markets and by globalizing economic practices and thinking. Although the reality of world-wide markets and globalization is only in its infancy, it is nevertheless forcing states, MNCs, and other international actors to rethink all of their economic strategies.

What does this mean in practice? There is no better way to illustrate the meaning of world-wide markets and globalization than by providing several cases in point.

In Singapore, a local IT firm obtains investment from Taiwan to purchase Israeli telephone-production technology. Still using its Taiwanese capital, the Singapore firm sets up production lines in China to take advantage of inexpensive labor there. The telephones it produces are then exported to sell in the United States and Japan. Six countries are involved in this "value chain," made possible by advanced information technology.

Meanwhile, a U.S. home improvement store chain headquartered in Atlanta with operations in Canada, Mexico, and the United States asks for bids to replenish its supplies of plywood. It receives bids via the Internet from companies operating out of Costa Rica, Indonesia, Nigeria, Panama, the Philippines, and Thailand. Bids are reviewed within hours of receipt, contracts are concluded before the day ends, and plywood begins being loaded in Manila the following day.

Recognizing the advantages afforded by world-wide markets and globalization, Ford reorganizes its worldwide operations so that it can purchase parts wherever they are cheapest, anywhere in the world. In the face of fierce international automotive competition, Ford improves its global market share of sales by announcing a reduction in the price of its cars. Ford stockholders throughout the world applaud as their stock goes up, reported on electronically interconnected stock market boards.

The same phenomena are occurring in service industries. U.S. telephone companies employ thousands of telephone operators in Barbados, the Dominican Republic, Jamaica, and St. Lucia. New York and Connecticut based insurance companies fly their paperwork to Ireland every night, where previously unemployed villagers use their newly acquired computer skills to log the paper-based data into computers. SwissAir relocates its income accounting operations from Zurich to Bombay, with all data being transferred electronically from Switzerland to India.

Everywhere, in finance, manufacture, sales, services, and elsewhere as well, world-wide markets and globalization are having immense impacts. Although it was the political will of political leaders that led to the dismantling of many of the economic barriers to trade that until recently existed, it was the technology of the Information Age that made world-wide markets and globalization economically and operationally feasible. And we are only at the beginning of the Information Age.

So, too, many analysts concluded that in the nuclear era, economic parameters of power would be less important than before.

Third, at the end of World War II, the United States enjoyed unchallenged global economic superiority. As the only major country whose industrial base had not been ravaged by the war, the United States reigned economically supreme. Little wonder that few Americans or their Western allies felt an urgency about international economics once European and Japanese reconstruction began. Peoples and governments in the Second and Developing Worlds had different views about the level of urgency of economic issues, but even there, many had been persuaded that military parameters of power reigned supreme. Thus, economics became the stuff of low politics, a significant but not dominant input to international power equations.

THE REEMERGENCE OF ECONOMICS: PRESENT AND PAST

However, as time passed, national governments in the West began to reassess the lower priority they had placed on economics. Governments in the Second and Developing Worlds did the same. By the 1990s, economics had reemerged as a first order priority for most international actors.[1] Four factors led to this.

First, the United States no longer dominated the global economy. During most of the 1950s and 1960s, the United States was the world's only economic superpower. However, as the 1960s ended and the 1970s wore on, chronic U.S. balance-of-payment and balance-of-trade deficits led many observers to conclude that the United States had entered a period of economic decline even though its military capabilities remained strong. As the U.S. national debt mounted during the 1980s and U.S. payment and trade deficits continued, it became evident that the era of U.S. global economic dominance was over.

Second, even as U.S. economic dominance declined in the 1960s, 1970s, and 1980s, other economies gathered strength. The economies of Western Europe and Japan surged ahead, and despite a variety of domestic problems, China also experienced sizable economic expansion. Similarly, a host of smaller countries on the Pacific Rim, the so-called "newly industrialized countries" (NICs), including South Korea, Taiwan, Singapore, and other states, enjoyed impressive growth during the 1980s. By the opening of the 1990s, the center of the world's economic activity had moved from the Atlantic to the Pacific basin.

Third, the collapse of the Soviet Union made it evident that economic strength remained a vital constituent of national power. Soviet emphasis on military strength to the detriment of economic strength had taken its toll. The Soviet government under Mikhail Gorbachev attempted to reverse the USSR's economic decline with extensive domestic reforms, but made little progress. Indeed, the Gorbachev reforms may even have accelerated the Soviet Union's economic collapse.

The fourth source of the international community's new awareness of the importance of economic strength was the emergence during the 1970s and 1980s of oil-rich states to positions of international prominence. Oil-derived economic wealth flowed into Saudi Arabia, Iran, Iraq, Libya, Algeria, and elsewhere. Although some states squandered their wealth on wars or ill-conceived development projects, others used their new wealth wisely. Even the downturn in the world's oil market in the middle and late 1980s did not erode significantly the positions of prominence that many oil-rich states found in the international community. Indeed, the extensive worldwide opposition to Iraq's 1990 takeover of Kuwait was the result not only of the blatant nature of Iraq's aggression, but also the concern that Iraq, in control of large reserves of oil and with a military that it clearly would use to assert its will, might try to dictate world oil prices. Thus, by the 1990s, there was no doubt that economics played a major role in determining national power.

As stated before, this relationship between economic strength and power was an old reality newly discovered. Economic theorists of the fifteenth through eighteenth centuries believed that a country's strength depended directly on how much gold and silver it had; this was the theory of **mercantilism.** Consequently, during the mercantilist era, states placed strict controls on the movement of gold and silver and on transactions in exchange markets, intervened in trading structures to attempt to develop favorable balances of trade, subsidized exploration in the hope of adding to national wealth, established tariffs and quotas, and prohibited some types of trade.

During the early nineteenth century, the European balance of power and Great Britain's control of the seas allowed Great Britain to establish an international economic system centered on Britain, based on **free trade,** that is, the ability to engage in commerce wherever one wanted without restrictions or taxes. Britain slowly reduced its **tariffs** (taxes on imports) as it developed an exchange system of domestic manufacturing for overseas raw materials. London became the world's banking and financial center so that the exchange system could be effectively and efficiently funded and overseen.

However, as the second wave of empire swept the world during the late nineteenth century, free trade was abandoned. Colonial empires were again integrated into the economic systems of the various metropoles as during the mercantilist era. Once again, colonies existed to improve the economy and enhance the power of the ruling state.

The strains of World Wars I and II undermined and then destroyed the old colonial empires. And as we have seen, a bipolar international system based on the primacy of military capabilities, the nuclear stalemate, and the economic dominance of the two superpowers in their respective blocs emerged after World War II. Therefore, economic issues became a lower-level priority.

Even so, policy makers recognized that the collapse of the international economic system prior to World War II had played a major role in beginning the war. They could not allow that to happen again. Consequently, even though economic concerns were perceived as less urgent than military ones, the construction of a stable international economic system became one of the most important agenda items for the allies even before World War II ended.

However, before one can understand the postwar economic system or the evolution of that system to what it is today, it is first necessary to provide the theoretical perspectives on which that system is based. We turn to that now.

 ## *THEORETICAL PERSPECTIVES*

International actors become involved in the international economic system because they believe they benefit from doing so. How actors engage the system can best be approached from five different theoretical perspectives.

The first perspective is from the internal economic strength of an actor. Industrial base, skills and training, internally available resources, access to external resources, accumulated wealth, organization, strategy, and leadership must all be considered here. To an extent, internal economic capabilities determine the roles that international actors play in international affairs. This perspective is crucial for understanding how an actor's economic capabilities and constraints influence its mesh with the international economic system.

The second, third, and fourth perspectives are the stuff of traditional international economics: international trade, monetary policy, and finance policy. All are key elements in actors' attempts to supplement their internal economic capabilities. International trade allows actors to acquire that which they do not have or to acquire more cheaply that which they do have. Thus, astute traders can use trade to enhance their power. International monetary policy is the mechanism that allows trade to take place. It, too, can add to an actor's strength if used wisely. International finance is the vehicle that generates investment and capital accumulation in one or another actor. International finance is also a critical component of economic strength.

The fifth and final perspective consists of the major subsystems of international trade. It includes: 1.) trade within the Developed World; 2.) trade between the Developed World and the Developing World; and (3) trade within the Developing World.

Domestic Economies and International Economics

Economic capabilities of international actors are a major factor in determining how powerful an actor is in international affairs. A single individual with limited economic resources cannot build effective modern weapons systems, and economically underdeveloped states cannot have political clout equivalent to IBM. The United Nations, aided in part by its $11 billion budget, dwarfs all other IGOs in its international operations. Internal economic realities do influence an actor's international role.

Yet given the relational and contextual nature of power, one must not overemphasize the role of economics in international affairs. A single terrorist armed with a $30 weapon nearly assassinated Pope John Paul II in 1982. Another lightly armed would-be assassin attacked Ronald Reagan the same year. Had either been successful, the course of international affairs may have been altered almost as assuredly as if a new world power had arisen.

The combination of an actor's economic capabilities and the political outlooks of its decision-making elite determine to what extent and in what ways an actor will involve itself in the international economy. Some actors have greater need than others to involve themselves in international economic transactions. Some need resources, others need markets, and still others seek to provide their populations with products not produced domestically or produced less expensively externally. For example, Europe and Japan have little choice but to seek external resources. They also need external markets for their products. On the other hand, Communist China for the first thirty years of its existence (1949–79) emphasized the development of its own internal resources and heavy industry, consciously minimizing its economic interactions with the international community. However, when Deng acquired power, this changed. From the early 1980s through today, China has actively sought international trade, exported large amounts of finished products, and imported Western technical know-how and capital.

In the industrialized West, with its emphasis on free enterprise and market economics, domestic and international economic questions often combine to create volatile political issues. For example, when the World Trade Organization (WTO) planned to meet in Seattle in 1999, many American workers and other U.S. nationalist elements attempted to block the meeting from occurring. They opposed the WTO because of its efforts to reduce barriers to international trade. Many U.S. workers and nationalists believed that such efforts actually reduced the number of jobs in the U.S. because overseas workers worked for less than U.S. workers did, thereby leading to a flow of jobs from the U.S. to foreign locations. They also asserted that the flow of jobs out of the U.S. weakened the United States' overall global economic position.

Similarly, many U.S. citizens were also concerned that the creation of the North American Free Trade Agreement (NAFTA) would lead to a flow of jobs out of the United States into Mexico where labor costs are lower. They consequently opposed NAFTA and other free trade areas such as the Free Trade Area of the Americas and the Asia–Pacific Economic Cooperation zone.

Concerns about the interrelationships between domestic and international economic questions are not unique to the United States. Indeed, one of the most urgent fears of the international trading community is that states will bow to protectionist pressure and restrict free trade. Domestic political criteria are thus mixed with economic criteria as decision makers formulate their policy on the desired interrelationship of their internal economy with international markets. Often, economically irrational decisions are politically motivated and politically necessary within an individual actor. Consequently, the political and economic situations within countries and other international actors are crucial elements in understanding the dynamics of international political economy.

Indeed, one of the most volatile issues facing decision makers in the early twenty-first century is the proper blend between **economic interdependence** and **economic independence.** The political implications of this simply phrased issue are immense, for interdependence, whatever its economic advantages, compromises national sovereignty and the ability to make decisions free of externally created constraints.[2] The interdependence/independence issue is centered around the most basic of all questions concerning domestic economies and international economics: Why is trade economically advantageous?

Trade and Trade Theory

During the early nineteenth century, English economist David Ricardo formulated the **law of comparative advantage.** In its simplest form, this law asserts that the distribution of the factors of production (land, labor, capital, and entrepreneurship) are best determined by freely operating economic exchanges. For example, Great Britain should use its land, labor, capital, and entrepreneurial abilities to produce whatever it makes most efficiently (rugby balls?), and Argentina should use its factors of production to produce whatever it makes most efficiently (bolos?). With each country specializing in what it makes most efficiently, more rugby balls and more bolos will be made than if both countries had tried to make both items. When a British need for bolos and an Argentine need for rugby balls developed, the two countries would trade bolos for rugby balls, and everyone would have more of both.[3]

The law of comparative advantage requires several preconditions before it operates well. First, both supply and demand must exist. If Britain never develops a need for bolos,

International trade has improved living standards in many countries around the world. In addition to the jobs that exports create, international trade also provides work for many people in the shipping industry in ports like Hamburg, shown here.

British–Argentine trade will not occur even if Argentina needs rugby balls. Second, products must be able to move across borders freely without economic barriers such as tariffs and import taxes or nontariff barriers such as quotas and discriminating environmental protection measures. Such barriers artificially raise the price of products and reduce or eliminate the advantages of trade. Third, competitive markets and reasonable transportation costs must exist. The intrusion of monopolies and oligopolies into international trade distorts the free trading system, and high transportation costs reduce the incentive to trade.

Advocates of free trade point out that it would allow the standard of living in involved countries to improve because all would buy their goods wherever they were produced most inexpensively and produce the goods that they could make most efficiently. Opponents of free trade point out that all the preconditions needed for perfect free trade do not exist and that the advantages allegedly derived from free trade are therefore a theoretical nicety at best. Free trade opponents further posit that the concept leads to excessive and extreme dependence on external sources for too many products. Trade, they argue, can be used as a weapon, and in some cases, extreme dependence on external products in key areas could adversely affect national security and national survival. Opponents of free trade sometimes conclude that no state can allow itself to become dependent on others for vital needs if it wishes to protect its own security and control its own decisions.

Free trade opponents also point out that an influx of cheap products from overseas can undercut the price of locally manufactured products, thereby reducing demand and leading to unemployment. In developed countries where labor unions are strong, labor often acts as an antifree trade spokesman. Labor fears that in the event of an open economy without trade restrictions, multinational corporations will relocate to less developed countries to take advantage of cheaper nonunion labor costs. "Job flight" is thus viewed as a cost of free trade, at least by labor. In addition, many nationalists in Developing World states also oppose free trade because they believe it undermines national sovereignty.

Similarly, as we have seen, many Developing World states opposed free trade, arguing that their infant industries had to be protected from the more efficient mature industries in developed states. From the Developing World's perspective, this was both a political and an economic argument. It was political since developing states sought to escape the lingering vestiges of colonialism and neocolonialism, and it was economic since developing states wanted to allow their own infant industries to become efficient producers. Although Developing World states in the 1990s and the twenty-first century now frequently accept free trade as the best way to generate long term economic development, the anti-free trade perspective has not disappeared from the viewpoint of all developing states.

In opposition to these arguments, free traders accept the arguments that inefficient industries are driven out of business by free trade and that dependence on external actors increases in a free trade regime. However, they posit that both are advantages rather than disadvantages. Supporters of free trade suggest that governments should step in with labor retraining programs and unemployment compensation for those workers who lose their jobs because of foreign competition. They also argue, as do managers of multinational corporations, that mutual dependence leads to interdependence and that interdependence leads to peace, thereby reducing national security concerns. The rationale that interdependence leads to peace flows from the belief that as countries rely more and more on external sources to fulfill their needs, they will be less and less likely to undertake actions that would jeopardize their access to those sources of need fulfillment.

But what happens if a country continually buys more from overseas than it sells overseas? Obviously, to pay for its imports, it must transfer some of its own wealth to the country from which it imported goods, or borrow money to purchase its imports. This situation is called a chronic balance of trade deficit, and it is the situation the United States has been in for most of the years since the early 1970s.

Balances of trade are different from balances of payment. Whereas a country's **balance of trade** is the receipts garnered from its exports minus the cost of its imports, a country's **balance of payments** is the total exchange of currencies that one country has with others. It includes receipts and payments for trade, tourism, travel, transportation, military expenses, foreign aid, emergency relief, capital transactions, stock and bond transfers, and savings account movements. The balance of payments is much more inclusive than the balance of trade.

If one country over time builds up a large balance of payments deficit, it gradually drains its wealth. This, too, has been the United States' situation in recent years. Conversely, when a country has a balance-of-payments surplus, it adds to its wealth. In a simplistic sense, chronic balance-of-payment deficits can lead to a decline in national power, whereas chronic balance-of-payment surpluses can add to national power.

International actors may or may not become international traders for the specific purpose of enhancing their power. But when all is said and done, at the end of a trading transaction, all trading partners should have more than they could have produced on their own, at least if they traded rationally and intelligently. Thus, international actors who trade wisely have the potential to increase mutually both their wealth and their power, even if the intention of trade has nothing to do with power. As stated earlier, economic strength is both an end and a means.

International Monetary Policy

International trade is rarely undertaken on a barter basis. Rather, countries use their own currencies, or widely accepted currencies of other countries, to buy the goods that they wish to import from foreign sources. Consequently, a standard must be established to determine the rates of exchange between currencies of different countries. This standard is the exchange rate.

The exchange rate is either "floating" or "fixed." **Floating exchange rates** exist when governments allow the market forces of supply and demand to determine the relative price of national currencies. Most exchange rates today are floating. Figure 13-1 illustrates how the value of the German Deutsche mark and the Japanese yen have changed against the U.S. dollar over time.

By comparison, **fixed exchange rates** result when two or more governments agree to set the price of their currencies in relation to each other. For example, during the 1950s, the U.S. and German governments agreed that one dollar equaled five marks, and during the 1960s, they agreed that one dollar equaled four marks.

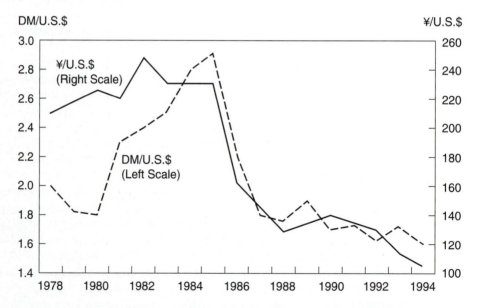

FIGURE 13-1   Exchange rates of the German Deutsche mark and the Japanese yen in relation to the U.S. dollar.

Source: International Monetary Fund, *International Financial Statistics Yearbook 1995* [Washington: International Monetary Fund, 1995], p. 4.

The value of a country's exports and imports is thus determined not only by the direction and volume of a country's trade, but also by the exchange rate. For example, in 1960, a bottle of German beer that sold for four marks in Germany, if exported to the United States, would have sold for about one dollar in the United States. In 1996, that same bottle of beer still may have sold for four marks in Germany, but because of the changed dollar–mark exchange rate between 1960 and 1996, it would have sold for about $2.50! Germany would have exported one bottle of beer to the United States in 1960 and in 1996, but in 1996, Germany (or more accurately, the German company that exported the bottle of beer) would have received $1.50 more for the bottle of beer.

In theory, floating exchange rates over time make sure that a country's balance of payments balance out. How a floating exchange rate achieves this is simple. When citizens of country A want to purchase goods or services from country B, they must first buy the currency of country B. If citizens of country A want to purchase more goods and services from country B than citizens of country B want to purchase from A, then the demand for country B's currency will be greater than the demand for country A's. The price for country B's currency will therefore go up, in turn making the price for its goods and services higher for people in country A who want to purchase them. The higher prices for country B's goods and services should therefore reduce demand for them in country A. Over time, a floating exchange rate should bring the value of a country's externally purchased goods and services more or less in line with the value of those it sells to foreigners.

Unfortunately, things do not always go as smoothly in reality as in theory. Four problems complicate floating exchange rates. First, floating exchange rates can take a long time to correct trade and payments imbalances. Thus, a country can develop chronic balance of trade and balance of payments deficits, sliding deeper and deeper into debt as it transfers its wealth overseas to pay for its imports.

Second, for floating exchange rates to work effectively, impediments to free trade and free movements of exchange rates must be removed. In the 1990s, free trade areas and the Uruguay Round of reductions in tariffs, quotas, and other barriers to free trade were significant steps toward removing these impediments, but such barriers continue to exist.

Third, floating exchange rates encourage currency speculation. Speculators buy foreign currency when it is cheap and sell it when it is expensive. This skews the exchange rate beyond what the balances of trade and payments imply it should be.

Fourth, because of uncertainties associated with a floating exchange rate, it usually discourages investment between countries. As we will see in the next section, this slows and may even stop economic growth.

Because of the problems associated with floating exchange rates, governments devised fixed exchange rates, as defined before. Fixed exchange rates ended speculation in currencies and accelerated international investment because of the certainty they introduced to international exchange markets. But like floating exchange rates, they could not cope effectively with chronic balance of trade and payments deficits.

Indeed, fixed exchange rates accentuated the problem of chronic balance-of-payments deficits. Under a fixed exchange rate, countries that have chronic balance-of-payments deficits eventually run out of foreign currencies to pay their debt, whereas under a floating exchange rate, the value of the currency of the country in debt theoretically continues to go down until the growth of debt stops.

Another method that states use to settle their foreign debts is **Special Drawing Rights** (SDRs), created by the International Monetary Fund (IMF) in 1968. The value of an SDR is based on the average value of several currencies of Western industrial states. When countries experience large unwanted declines in the value of their currency in floating exchange markets, they can borrow SDRs from the IMF to shore up the value of their currencies. SDRs are not really money and cannot be used for purchases. Rather, they are bridging mechanisms that allow countries to overcome short-term runs on their currency.

International Finance

Closely related to international trade and monetary policy is international finance. **International finance** is the movement of money among countries for the purpose of investment, trade, and capital accumulation.

During the last 20 years, the international community has removed more and more barriers to the mobility of capital and other wealth. Moreover, advances in information and communication technologies now enable international bankers to transfer funds electronically almost anywhere in the world in seconds rather than days. Indeed, by the 1990s, much of the world had become a single integrated financial market. In the early twenty-first century, this trend will progress even more rapidly as new and improved information technology enables even smaller financial markets to be directly connected to the world's large financial markets. The twenty-first century will truly be an era of global **international mobility of capital.**

To attract this internationally mobile capital, those who need funds—usually businesses and countries—issue bonds, stocks, and other financial instruments. Investors keep a close watch on which stocks, bonds, and other financial instruments offer the best rates of return, then move their money to where the best rates are. With the speed that electronic banking and other technologies afford, international finance has become a highly volatile undertaking. (Here, it should be pointed out that rate of return on investment is not the only variable investors consider. They also look for factors such as political stability, future opportunity, tax structure, and related items.)

The implications of the real-time integration of a global financial market are extensive. Rises and falls in a major stock market can trigger rises and falls in stock markets half a world away almost instantaneously. Increases in interest rates in one country could attract investors overnight, whereas decreases in interest rates could send them scurrying around the globe to find better rates of return elsewhere. Quarterly economic reports by major Western industrial countries in turn cause interest rates and exchange rates to rise and fall, sometimes with investors themselves not knowing what led to the increases and decreases.

Nevertheless, the key point here is that in the twenty-first century, international financial markets are more interconnected than ever before, more open than ever before, and can transfer funds more rapidly than ever before. Individuals, corporations, and governments all take advantage of this to find the best opportunities for their investments in a global financial marketplace.

This international mobility of capital is both a blessing and a curse. It is a blessing because investors can move their money rapidly to the best opportunities available to them. Theoretically, this should accelerate growth. But at the same time, it is a curse. Easy, rapid mobility of funds can lead to extremely volatile financial markets that rise and fall on little more than rumor and momentary perception. Over time, such volatility could lead to a growth of investor fear and reduction in the rate of global economic growth.

But how does international finance affect power? The answer to this question is both straightforward and exceedingly complex. Clearly, countries, corporations, individuals, and other organizations that have sizable financial assets have an ability to influence decisions. This does not mean that decisions are made in any arena for exclusively economic reasons, but it does imply that all other factors being equal, those with greater financial assets involved in a decision will often have a greater degree of influence on that decision. Power results.

At the same time, access to financial assets, not just ownership of assets, can enable international actors to enhance their power. For example, much of the U.S. military buildup of the 1980s was financed by deficit spending. The debt accumulated by this deficit spending was substantially bought up by Japanese investors. In a simplistic sense, U.S. access to Japanese financial assets made the U.S. military buildup possible. At the same time, Japanese investment in U.S. firms strengthened the U.S. economy and kept U.S. workers employed. The trade-offs, of course, are that borrowed Japanese capital will have to be repaid, and business decisions affecting certain U.S. firms will be made outside the United States.

Similar issues affect North–South financial relations. Because many Developing World states owe much money to Western banks and other financial institutions, Western states and banks sometimes find themselves in the position of recommending and even dictating policy to Developing World states. Conversely, some Developing World states owe so much money that if they were to default or suspend payment on their debts, significant segments of the international financial community would be shaken. Such actions on the part of any Developing World state would virtually guarantee that it not receive loans in the future. Thus, it is in the interests of international lending institutions and borrowing states to find ways that debts can be paid.

International finance, then, is tied directly to issues of power and influence, but often the tie is more complex than it appears. This is true at the individual, corporate, national, and organizational levels. In the twenty-first century, the impact of the instantaneous global international mobility of capital is a central reality of contemporary international relations.[4]

The Three Global Economic Subsystems

To complicate matters even more, many analysts of contemporary international economics recognize three **global economic subsystems.**[5] The first subsystem functions among developed Western industrial states. It is the most important economic subsystem in terms of total trade. The United States, Western Europe, and Japan are willing members, whereas Developing World states are peripherally associated. The degree to which Developing World states belong to this first subsystem is a function of both economic relationships and perceptions, and is discussed later in this chapter.

The second economic subsystem functions between the industrialized West and most of the Developing World. In the first subsystem, the dilemma is whether mechanisms can be created to manage mutually beneficial economic relations. In the second subsystem, the dilemma is whether mechanisms can be formed to *create* mutually beneficial economic relations.

Developed states perceive a common advantage in preserving the current system much as it is, while many developing states believe that significant changes are needed. From the Developed World's perspective, developed states and developing states participate in a single international trading system that provides the best chance for all to prosper on the basis of their capabilities. From the perspective of many Developing World states, they enter international trade in a subservient position and are not true partners in a trading system dominated by developed states. Rather, many Developing World states see themselves as unwilling partners in a separate subsystem, that of North–South economic relations.

Not surprisingly, separate schools of thought exist concerning North–South trade and monetary relations—three dominate. The first is the **liberal trade school,** which sees trade as a tool for growth. Trade leads to specialization, the liberal school asserts, which under the theory of comparative advantage improves a state's economic position. An improved economic position in turn leads to savings, which can be translated into investment. Investment leads in turn to further economic growth. Foreign trade and foreign investment, in the liberals' view, accelerate economic growth.

The second school is the **Marxist trade school,** which received a serious setback as a result of the collapse of communism in Eastern Europe and the Soviet Union, but which is still influential in some quarters in the West and the Developing World. Marxism asserts that the superior economic position of industrialized Western powers allows them to determine international trade patterns and rates of exchange. Marxists maintain that prices for raw materials from developing countries are artificially deflated by Western market-economy countries and that prices for finished goods produced in industrialized countries are artificially inflated. Thus, through its international trade and exchange system, the West exploits the Developing World economically even though political independence has been achieved by the Developing World. Further, foreign investment adds to local unemployment by introducing capital-intensive productive means and actually leads to a new flow of wealth from South to North as profits are repatriated. Foreign aid is similarly exploitive because "strings" are often attached to it, thereby perpetuating Developing World dependence on the West.

The third school of thought is the **structuralist trade school.** It argues that, as in Marxist analysis, the international trade and exchange system perpetuates the South's backwardness and dependence on the West. Gunnar Myrdal was a leading structuralist who posited that the market tends to favor "have" states more than "have not" states. Therefore, according to Myrdal, the gap between rich and poor tends to increase so that even in the best of all worlds, the lot of the poor improves only marginally.[6]

Structuralists further observe that although foreign investment and trade help Developing World states improve their economic status, only a small sector of a developing country's economy is aided—the export sector. Therefore, in Developing World states, investment and trade create a dual economy, one part of which is relatively developed, the export sector, and the other of which is underdeveloped. According to structuralists, the advanced export sector takes investment moneys away from the underdeveloped sector, thereby rendering the underdeveloped sector even more backward.

The debate over North–South trade and exchange relations has been long and heated. Where one comes to rest is a product of perspective and ideology. Extreme proponents of the Western subsystem of trade and exchange deny that a North–South subsystem even exists. Extreme opponents of the Western subsystem theorize that not only does a North–South subsystem exist, but that it was designed and is run by the industrialized Western states with the specific intention of exploiting the Developing World.

The third major global economic subsystem exists between Developing World states. In comparison to the first two subsystems, it is relatively minor in terms of total trade turnover. Some analysts even argue that it is so small that it should not be considered an economic subsystem, but be appended to one of the larger subsystems.

Nevertheless, the fact remains that although trade between Developing World states is relatively small, the nature of trade between Developing World states is often significantly different than the trade that takes place within either of the two larger economic subsystems. Often, it is trade in natural resources, raw materials, handmade products, or unfinished products in both directions. Frequently, it is undertaken on a barter basis. And often, despite its relatively small value in relation to the trade that takes place in other economic subsystems, it is extremely important to the states that are involved.

MAJOR INTERNATIONAL FINANCIAL AND ECONOMIC INSTITUTIONS

States also are directly involved with the international economic system through the international financial and economic institutions that they have created, most of which are IGOs. Chief among them are the World Bank, the International Monetary Fund, the General Agreement on Tariffs and Trade (which has been subsumed by the World Trade Organization), the World Trade Organization, and various regional development banks. Each requires separate commentary.

The World Bank[7]

Formally named the **International Bank for Reconstruction and Development (IBRD),** the **World Bank** was created in 1944 at the Bretton Woods Conference. (See the following section for a discussion of the Bretton Woods Conference and why it was held.) Formed originally to provide long term loans for the post-World War II reconstruction of Europe, the World Bank has become one of the primary international institutions that provides long term loans to Developing World states. It is one of the United Nations' associated agencies.

Developed countries created the World Bank, and they also provide most of the money that the World Bank has available to lend. Not surprisingly, then, the World Bank uses a weighted voting system that provides most of the votes in decision making to those countries that provide the Bank the most money. Therefore, developed states have the greatest say in where and how the World Bank makes its loans, a reality which Developing World states often criticize. In addition, the World Bank's president has always been an American.

Usually, the World Bank requires detailed economic data from countries that request loans before it grants a loan. This is to allow the Bank to assess whether a project makes good economic sense. However, this practice is often criticized by developing states because it is seen as intrusive and because World Bank criteria are frequently demanding.

The International Monetary Fund[8]

The International Monetary Fund (IMF) was also created at Bretton Woods, but its purpose was to support international monetary stability and establish stable exchange rates. The IMF was to do this by establishing exchange rates between currencies under a fixed exchange rate system. It had at its disposal a fund of gold and currencies that it could use to credit the accounts of countries that experienced chronic balance of payments deficits. Although the fixed exchange rate system was eventually replaced by a floating system, the IMF still uses its funds to credit the accounts of countries with chronic balance of payment problems. It too is one of the UN's associated agencies.

Like the World Bank, most of the IMF's funds come from developed states. Also like the World Bank, it operates on a weighted voting system, providing the most votes to the countries that contribute the most funds. To balance the presidency of the World Bank, the president of the IMF has always been a European. Because so much of the IMF's decision making power is in the hands of developed states, the IMF, like the World Bank, is often criticized by many Developing World states.

The General Agreement on Tariffs and Trade (1947–1995)

Formed several years after the Bretton Woods Conference was held, the **General Agreement on Tariffs and Trade (GATT)** was nevertheless considered one of the three Bretton Woods institutions. After efforts in 1945–46 to create an International Trade Organization failed, to a great extent because of U.S. concern over the possibility it might infringe national sovereignty, GATT was created in 1947 as a temporary organization to reduce tariffs and other nontariff barriers to trade via multilateral negotiations. GATT also sought to prevent the resurrection of protectionist trade barriers as had occurred between World Wars I and II and to establish rules for international trade and develop procedures for settling trade disputes. GATT, although formed as a temporary arrangement, remained in effect until the World Trade Organization began operating in 1995.

Over the years, GATT held eight rounds of trade negotiations, some successful, some not successful. GATT began its eighth round in Uruguay in 1986 and concluded it in 1993 with a major trade agreement that significantly reduced tariffs and created the World Trade Organization to supersede GATT.

The agreement went a long way toward creating an **open international economic system,** that is, a system in which goods and services move from one country to another with few barriers to impede them. It is extremely specific and will not be discussed in detail here. However, one measure of its importance is that the 123 countries that originally signed it (at least 20 more have since agreed to its terms) accounted for over 90 percent of the world's trade. Estimates are that the agreement will reduce tariffs by $750 billion by 2003. The Uruguay Round was a huge step toward free trade and an open and ordered international economic system.

The World Trade Organization

The Uruguay Round of GATT also created the **World Trade Organization (WTO)** to oversee and implement the reductions in tariff and other nontariff barriers that it negotiated. The WTO also provides procedures for negotiating more tariff reductions and ruling on disputes arising over trade. Indeed, the WTO superseded GATT in all of its functions, and is now the world's organization for global trade enhancement.[9]

The WTO began operating in 1995. In 2000, it had over 140 members, with several countries still considering or being considered for membership. Its chief body is a Ministerial Conference that meets at least once every two years to discuss and resolve trade policy issues. The WTO also has a General Council that oversees the WTO's operations, dispute settlement efforts, and other decisions between ministerial meeting. The General Council concentrates its activities in three areas: trade in goods, trade in services, and trade-related aspects of intellectual property protection.

In the United States and several other countries, the WTO's ability to hand down rulings on trade disputes raised concerns in some quarters that sovereignty might be compromised. However, although the WTO's dispute settlement panels can make rulings on trade disagreements, their rulings are not authoritative nor can they be enforced. Before a panel ruling becomes authoritative, it must be approved by the General Council or a Ministerial Conference without objection. Thus, no ruling can become authoritative unless the involved parties accept it. Even then, there are no enforcement mechanisms. Thus, despite its ability to rule on disputes, the WTO must rely on involved states to comply with its rulings.

Like GATT before it, the WTO provides developing countries special status in an effort to spur their economic development. Under the WTO, developing countries frequently have longer to implement trade provisions than developed states, sometimes are exempted from other trade provisions, and on occasion enjoy special protection for their exports.

The WTO in conjunction with other Uruguay Round results is a significant step toward establishing an international free trade regime and a mechanism to resolve trade disputes. It is not, however, a panacea for all of the problems that confront international trade.

Indeed, the WTO itself has been widely criticized as a tool of multinational corporations, as an institution that assaults national sovereignty, and as an enemy of the environment. These criticisms were the reasons behind the demonstrations and riots that greeted the WTO's 1999 ministerial conference in Seattle. The WTO may be the youngest and one of the most influential of today's major international economic organizations, but it clearly has its opponents.

Regional Development Banks

Throughout the years, many regions of the world have created their own regional development banks to help accelerate regional economic and social development and to ameliorate if not solve other regional international economic problems. These organizations include, for example, the African Development Bank, the Arab Bank for Economic Development in Africa, the Asian Development Bank, the Central African States Development Bank, the Inter-American Development Bank, and the Islamic Development Bank.[10]

The size and impact of regional development banks are varied. The Inter-American Development Bank has undertaken a large number of successful projects in many Latin

American countries and is one of the more successful regional banks. The Central African Development Bank has been less successful, but nevertheless has had a positive impact as well.

Summation

The World Bank, the International Monetary Fund, the World Trade Organization, and the various regional development banks all play critical roles in twenty-first century international economic relations. How well they perform the tasks for which they have been created will play a major role in determining how prosperous international actors are and how much economics contributes to an actor's power.

Both the World Bank and the International Monetary Fund were created in the waning years of World War II to help resurrect the world's economy from the destruction it had suffered in World War II. They were also created to assure that the international economic problems that helped cause World War II would not return to set the stage for another global conflict. The General Agreement on Tariffs and Trade was established for similar reasons.

Before we provide a final overview and assessment of the international economic system of the early twenty-first century, we would do well to review the evolution of the post–World War II economic system. Our objective is to understand what worked well—and what did not work so well—with the system that the Western victors in World War II created so that we may be better prepared to help the current system evolve in appropriate ways.

 ## THE EVOLUTION OF THE INTERNATIONAL ECONOMIC SYSTEM: 1945–1995

As World War II drew to a close, representatives from 44 states met in June 1944 at Bretton Woods, New Hampshire, to try to create the foundations for a new and stable post-war international economic system. Since they understood that the breakdown of international trade, the presence of high tariffs, the collapse of international exchange rates, and the development of unbridled economic nationalism and competition were primary factors that caused World War II, the creation of a stable system was one of their most important priorities

By December 1944, most states that attended the conference accepted the conference's plans for the post-war international economic system. For the next 26 years, the international economic system of the noncommunist world was based on the plans developed at Bretton Woods.

The Bretton Woods System: The World Bank, IMF, and GATT

As we have seen, the Bretton Woods negotiations established two international governmental organizations, the World Bank and the IMF, to undertake international banking and monetary functions. Also as we have seen, GATT was not part of the negotiations. It evolved from a failed post-war effort to create an international organization to negotiate tariff reductions and assure equitable international trade. Such an organization was not created until GATT in the 1990s was replaced by the World Trade Organization. Nevertheless, GATT was often considered part of the **Bretton Woods System.**[11]

Bretton Woods provided for an international financial structure based on fixed exchange rates. Most delegates to the conference were convinced that the floating exchange rates that existed between World Wars I and II contributed directly to the collapse of the international economic system during the 1930s and the growth of economic nationalism that, in part, led to World War II. At Bretton Woods, stability was a chief objective.

Under the Bretton Woods system of fixed exchange rates, all countries agreed to establish the value of their currencies in terms of gold and to maintain that exchange rate within a plus-or-minus 1 percent range. Signatory states agreed to the convertibility of their currencies into other currencies and accepted in concept free trade. The IMF was to oversee the management of the system. As the world's strongest economic power, the United States received the preponderance of influence within the IMF. The IMF had to approve any changes in exchange rate and had at its disposal a fund of $8.8 billion of gold and currencies of member countries that it could credit to countries experiencing chronic balance of payments deficits. Although IMF credits were an innovation in international economics, the Bretton Woods system placed primary emphasis on national solutions to monetary problems. Even with IMF credits and rules, it was expected that states over time would reduce imports or expand exports if they had a balance of payments or trade deficit and increase imports or reduce exports if they had a surplus.

The national representatives at Bretton Woods also recognized that economic recovery was needed before the IMF could operate successfully. Consequently, the World Bank was created. IBRD was to make loans from its $10 billion account funded by member states to underwrite private loans and to issue securities to raise new funds so additional loans could be made to speed recovery.

By 1947, however, the Bretton Woods system was near collapse. Europe's balance-of-payments deficit in 1947 alone amounted to $7.6 billion; the U.S. balance-of-trade surplus the same year totaled $10.1 billion. IBRD and IMF funds were barely capable of sustaining one year of operation, much less a long-term system. In light of this bleak economic picture and the simultaneously worsening international political situation as the Cold War began to develop in earnest, the United States stepped in to rescue the Bretton Woods system.

U.S. Intervention and Domination: 1947–1960

The international economy's major problem by 1947 was that too many people wanted U.S. goods and too few dollars were in non-American hands to pay for them. World War II had shattered the economic base of most of the world, the United States excepted, and there were too few foreign products to be imported by the United States. Therefore, U.S. dollars stayed in U.S. hands even as increasing quantities of foreign currencies came into U.S. hands. The key question was, "How could more dollars be placed in foreign hands?"

The answer was obvious—the United States deliberately created a balance-of-payments deficit for itself via foreign aid programs that allowed foreign countries to buy U.S. products with dollars. U.S. aid programs were many and varied—support for Greece and Turkey under the Truman Doctrine, Point Four program aid to underdeveloped countries, and most important, Marshall Plan aid, under which 16 Western European countries received over $17 billion in grants from the United States between 1948 and 1952. U.S. military forces overseas also contributed to the outflow of dollars, both through personnel and base operations costs.

Between 1949 and 1959, U.S. gold assets declined from over $24 billion to slightly under $20 billion, and dollars held abroad climbed from $7 billion to over $19 billion. Thus, the Bretton Woods system started to operate, based on the strength of the dollar. For all practical purposes, the dollar became the noncommunist world's currency.

The United States also encouraged European and Japanese discrimination against the dollar and trade protectionism as part of the effort to revive the European and Japanese economies. This was intended to be a temporary situation as it was expected that the European and Japanese economies would recover, thereby increasing demand for U.S. exports. Thus, the United States willingly endured a chronic balance of payments deficit. It was rich enough to do so, and it expected long term benefits. Equally important, Western Europe and Japan accepted and encouraged the U.S. role. According to one analyst, the modified Bretton Woods system had three primary political bases, the concentration of power in a small number of states, a cluster of interests shared by those states, and U.S. willingness to provide leadership. However, by 1960, the system was in trouble.

The Weakening of the System: 1960–1971

International confidence in the dollar provided the base for the international economic system of the 1950s. Confidence was assured because of the United States' vibrant domestic economy, the United States' large gold and currency reserve, the U.S. commitment to convert dollars into gold, and the global reach of U.S. economic and military power. Gradually, however, people began to wonder how long the United States could absorb significant balance-of-payments deficits without eroding the strength of the dollar. As more and more dollars became available outside the United States, the shortage of dollars turned into a glut. By 1960, more dollars were held outside the United States than the United States had gold and currency to cover. This concerned non-Americans who held dollars, and many began to convert their dollars into gold. This led to a dollar crisis that extended throughout the 1960s. In response, the United States, European states, and the international financial and banking community undertook three steps.

First, the United States joined the monthly meetings of European bankers held in Basel, Switzerland, that discussed international financial and banking problems. With this action, the United States conceded that it could no longer manage the Bretton Woods system alone.

Second, seven Western European states as well as the United States, Canada, and Japan created and maintained joint control over a new $6 billion fund to extend loans to the IMF in time of IMF need. This arrangement kept the new fund under international control.

Third, the United States tried to reduce its balance of payments deficit by making foreign borrowing in the United States more expensive, restraining U.S. investment overseas, reducing duty-free tourist allotments, and trying to expand U.S. exports primarily by reducing tariffs under the auspices of GATT. Nevertheless, the U.S. balance of trade continued to deteriorate. Between 1964 and 1971, with the exception of only one year, the U.S. balance of trade worsened annually, finally becoming a deficit in 1971. This steady deterioration combined with the glut of dollars in the international economy to further weaken the dollar's position.

The dollar weakened because of other reasons as well. In 1968, as a result of the seemingly uncontrollable flow of dollars out of the United States, the United States announced that it no longer would support gold at $35 an ounce on the free market. Gold would be allowed to rise to find its own value. This announcement had two effects. First, to maintain the value of their own currencies, other foreign governments and banks had to absorb dollars that private investors made available. Second, the United States, for all practical purposes, had abandoned the Bretton Woods agreement. Many people feared that the next U.S. step would be devaluation.

Another reason for lower confidence in the dollar was Western European and Japanese economic revitalization. By the 1960s, Western Europe and Japan again had dynamic economies. Both had less need for dollars and U.S. products. Some Europeans and Japanese viewed the abundance of dollars as an infringement on their sovereignty.

Other causes of the weakened dollar were the U.S. adventure in Vietnam and the improvement in Eastern European–Western European relations during the late 1960s. The Vietnam War led many to question the perceived wisdom of U.S. leadership, and better East–West relations lessened the need for the U.S. military arsenal. Many Europeans believed that U.S. leadership had outlived its usefulness. This view had direct impact on foreign willingness to hold dollars. Thus, during 1971, another run on the dollar occurred. It was apparent to everyone that the international trade and monetary system was in serious trouble.

Shock: NEP and OPEC

Faced with an uncontrollable outflow of dollars and equally uncontrollable inflation domestically, the U.S. government resorted to unilateral action in 1971 by suspending the dollar's convertibility to gold and levying a 10 percent surcharge on all dutiable imports to the United States. Domestically, the U.S. government instituted a wage-and-price freeze as part of its **New Economic Policy.** For all practical purposes, the United States had abandoned Bretton Woods. International efforts to resuscitate Bretton Woods failed. By the end of 1972, every major currency floated against gold. The international monetary system was in disarray.

Hopes of reinstituting some form of management of the international monetary system received another setback in October 1973 when the **Organization of Petroleum Exporting Countries (OPEC)** initiated oil production cutbacks, embargoed oil shipments to the United States because of its support of Israel in the 1973 Arab–Israeli War, and increased oil prices from $2.50 a barrel in early 1973 to $11.65 in 1974. The price increase initiated an immense flow of cash to OPEC states, with over $70 billion deposited in OPEC states' bank accounts in 1974 alone.

The flow of dollars—now called "petrodollars"—to OPEC created new problems for the international monetary system. Developing World countries were particularly hard hit by the increased price of oil. With oil imports costing more and their few exports not selling well, these countries found it increasingly difficult to get loans to finance development and oil imports. As a result, their economies suffered even more than the economies of industrialized countries. The dollar played a central role in the drama as the United States, to finance its own oil purchases, pumped still more dollars into the hands of OPEC. For those non-Americans who held dollars, this proved both a bane and a blessing. On the one hand, the continued outflow of dollars from the United States further depressed each dollar's value; more dollars meant less demand for dollars and hence less value. On the other hand, with oil priced in dollars and usually paid for in dollars, OPEC countries were more than ever tied to the dollar as their currency of exchange.

The problem created by the immense flow of dollars to OPEC states was the **recycling problem.** It was similar to the problem that confronted the United States and Western Europe immediately after World War II: How does money return to the hands of those who need it to purchase products when insufficient balancing demand exists? During the late 1940s, Western Europe bought U.S. products, but Americans bought little from Europe. Consequently, a massive flow of currency moved from Europe to the United States. During the early 1970s, Europeans, Japanese, and Americans bought OPEC oil, but the flow of dollars to OPEC states was so great that even after they had purchased their imports, large quantities of dollars remained in OPEC hands. According to one estimate, OPEC surplus income totaled $200 billion for 1974 to 1979 and over $500 billion for the 1980s.[12]

As we have seen, the recycling problem was solved during the 1940s by U.S. balance-of-payment deficits engineered through aid programs such as the Marshall Plan and through maintenance of overseas military bases and presence. Immediately following the 1973 oil shock, a number of methods were developed to address the recycling problem. None proved immensely successful. OPEC states placed sizable percentages of their surpluses in bank deposits, treasury bills, bonds, and loans in the industrialized states, particularly Great Britain and the United States. Private banks in the industrialized states then lent money to Developing World and other needy states to help them finance their oil and other purchases. Increasingly, however, as the deficits of Developing World and other needy states climbed, and as the ability of the borrowing states to repay loans grew more tenuous, private banks hesitated to make loans to high-credit-risk borrowers. In addition, OPEC states distributed their surplus to a special IMF oil fund, to be used by states to help them ride out short-term deficits caused by higher oil prices. The World Bank received development moneys from OPEC states as well. Finally, Arab OPEC states directed grants and loans to Developing World states through an Arab Development Fund. Non-Arab and non-Islamic states complained, however, that they received little support, and in some instances, accusations were made that OPEC states through their foreign aid programs meddled in the internal political and economic affairs of recipient countries.

Anarchy and Interdependence: 1974–1995

For the next 20 years, the international community struggled to fashion a viable international economic order. Developed states concentrated on exchange rate management and developing international reserve assets, and Developing World states pushed for the creation of a new international economic order that would transfer wealth to them for development and that would create preferential trade arrangements for them to facilitate sale of their products.

For 20 years, little organization existed in the international economic system because of the problems of international trade and finance and because of the collapse of consensus on leadership. For the most part, exchange rates were determined by supply and demand, although an informal agreement existed in which central banks and governments intervened to keep exchange rates within broad imprecise limits. In addition, the currencies of some countries, particularly those in the European Community (now Union) remained pegged to one another.

During the 1980s, several major economic issues buffeted the international community. The first was the continued large flow of petrodollars to OPEC coffers, at least until oil prices fell in 1986. This flow of dollars benefited not only the OPEC states, but also industrialized countries that imported little oil or that attracted OPEC moneys to their banking system.

A second major problem resulted from U.S. efforts to reduce inflation during the early 1980s. As the U.S. Federal Reserve system kept interest rates high to decrease borrowing within the United States, foreign investors moved their money to the United States. This drove up the value of the dollar and made U.S. exports more expensive for foreign consumers. U.S. exports thus decreased relative to imports, and the U.S. balance of trade declined precipitously. The negative U.S. balance of trade was also worsened by restrictive trade practices of some industrialized countries, most notably Japan. These changes are shown in Figure 13-2.

Matters were made worse by the huge U.S. budget deficit. Brought about primarily by a significant decrease in the tax structure in the early 1980s, the U.S. budget deficit helped keep U.S. interest rates high, attracted large quantities of capital to the United States as foreign investors bought up the U.S. debt, and kept the price of U.S. exports high.

East–West and North–South economic issues also were major areas of concern. On East–West issues, the U.S. position throughout the 1980s was that stricter measures had to be taken on East–West trade to reduce the flow of technology, some of which was militarily significant, to the USSR. European states were less concerned about technology transfer to the USSR, arguing that the flow was not as significant as the United States maintained. As political and economic reform swept Eastern Europe and the Soviet Union

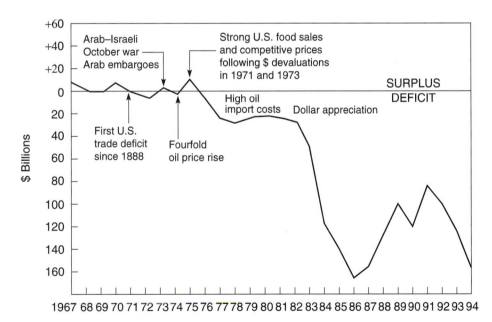

FIGURE 13-2   The U.S. balance of trade, 1967–1994.

Source: International Monetary Fund, *International Financial Statistics Yearbook 1995* [Washington: International Monetary Fund, 1995], pp. 778–779.

in the late 1980s and early 1990s, differences between the United States and the rest of the West on East–West trade issues diminished significantly.

The disagreements that existed among Western industrial states during the 1980s were mild by comparison with the discord that existed between the Developed and Developing Worlds. The combination of the oil shocks of 1973 and 1979–1980, the decreased demand for raw material exports, global inflation, and massive debt repayment schedules seriously damaged economic development in most Developing World states throughout the 1980s. Not surprisingly, Developing World states called for a restructuring of the international economic system to help alleviate their problems. Specific demands included debt rescheduling and forgiveness, a new pricing structure for finished products and raw materials, and preferential treatment for their exports. Faced by their own economic problems, few industrial states responded favorably.

 ## A NEW SYSTEM EMERGES: 1995–TODAY

When the 1990s opened, the international economic system was interdependent and anarchic. Interdependence was easily documented as the economies of almost every state relied on goods, products, raw materials, and information produced not only domestically, but also in other countries. Economic anarchy was also easily documented as no single international actor had the will or the ability to provide order to the international economic system.

Why the New System Emerged

As the 1990s progressed, this picture changed. As before, economic interdependence remained important. Indeed, it grew even more important. But by the mid–1990s, international economic anarchy began to diminish as order began to emerge. This was the result of three factors.

First, among Western developed states, consensus developed that economic growth could be accelerated and economic power shared through collaborative efforts based on an open economic system. Economic competition would continue, the consensus acknowledged, but a collective system would increase economic prosperity for all.

Second, after the collapse of communist governments in Eastern Europe and the Soviet Union in the late 1980s and early 1990s, the new noncommunist governments often wanted their economies to become integrated with the economies of Western states. They also recognized that Western states and their international economic institutions such as the World Bank were the primary source from which they could obtain investment. This trend was strengthened as most of the remaining communist states such as China and Vietnam increasingly operated their economies on capitalist principals.

Third, throughout the Developing World, more and more states in the late 1980s and early 1990s began to seek foreign investment, cooperate with international lending institutions, and emphasize privatization and development led by the private sector. Many allowed MNCs to invest capital with few or no state controls. Some also adopted World Bank and IMF suggestions about how development could best proceed. And many moved away from reliance on centralized government-controlled domestic economic development strategies. This was in marked contrast to the 1970s and much of the 1980s when many Developing World states, fearing neocolonialism and exploitation, restricted foreign investment, opposed Western economic development strategies, and emphasized state-led economic development and planning.

There were three reasons why many Developing World states changed their outlooks. First, in most Developing World states, old outlooks and policies simply had not worked. Therefore, many Developing World leaders concluded it was time to change. Second, as communist states experienced economic difficulties and finally collapsed, their model of centralized planning no longer looked attractive. Third, Western states including Japan, international lending and financial institutions, and MNCs had become the only sources of development funds and investment capital.

The changed perspectives of Western, former communist, and Developing World states on international economics were important in bringing about a new international economic system, but so too was technology. Indeed, as detailed in the accompanying box, advanced information and communication technologies played a major role in bringing about a new international economic system.

But what is that system? Today's international economic system is not a completely open system, but it has moved a long way in that direction. It can best be examined in three areas, one of which we have already explored in some detail: 1. international financial and economic institutions; 2. the increased importance of free trade areas; and 3. the continuation of G-7/G-8 meetings.

International Financial and Economic Institutions Revisited

As we saw earlier in this chapter, the World Bank, the International Monetary Fund, the World Trade Organization, and regional development banks play critical roles in the international economic system of the early twenty-first century. Their role will be only briefly reviewed here. Despite the brevity, their importance to the international economic system cannot be overstated.

The World Bank and the IMF have existed since the 1940s and continue to have major responsibilities today. The World Bank has as one of its primary responsibilities provided long term loans to developing states, while the IMF is charged with helping maintain global monetary and currency stability.

The WTO is a new entity that began operating in 1995 and replaced GATT on the international economic scene. It plays a sizeable role in twenty-first century international economic affairs by reducing trade barriers and attempting to resolve trade disputes. However, it has vocal critics who see it as a tool of MNCs, as an assault on national sovereignty, and as an enemy of the environment.

Meanwhile, regional development banks have varied size and impacts. Some have been quite successful, but others have had a much more limited impact.

The Increased Importance of Free Trade Areas

Free trade areas also play an extensive role in the early twenty-first century's international economic system. The trend toward free trade areas is based on the argument that the removal of barriers to free trade will accelerate economic growth, and it has provided a degree of order to international economic relations that was previously lacking.[13]

By the early 1990s, free trade areas or near free trade areas had been created in Europe (the European Union, with first 12 and by 1995 15 members), North America (the North America Free Trade Agreement, with Canada, Mexico, and the United States), South America (MERCOSUR, with four members), and Southeast Asia (the Association of Southeast Asian Nations, which expanded to seven states when Vietnam joined in 1995). The basis for even more extensive regional integration was laid in the 1990s as plans developed for extremely large free trade areas in the Pacific and the Americas.

In 1994, 18 Asian and American states including the Canada, China, Japan, Mexico, and the United States approved the **Asian–Pacific Economic Cooperation (APEC) agreement,**[14] which committed all developed signatory states to dismantle barriers to international trade between member states by 2010. Signatory developing states had the same objective set for 2020. By 2000, APEC had grown to 21 members which had a combined gross domestic product equal to about half the world's total ($35 trillion) and included 42 percent of the world's trade.

Later in 1994, regional integration in the Americas accelerated as 34 of the 35 countries in the western hemisphere concluded the **Free Trade Area of the Americas (FTAA) agreement** at the Miami Summit of the Americas.[15] Cuba was the only western hemisphere country that did not attend. The FTAA was formally initiated at the 1998 Summit of the Americas in Santiago, Chile when FTAA signatory states pledged to conclude negotiations by 2005 on an agreement that will put into operation in 2010 a free trade zone throughout the western hemisphere, Cuba excepted.

It is important to note that many APEC and FTAA member states are developing countries that strongly advocated protectionism during the 1970s and 1980s. At the same time, it must be recognized that neither APEC nor FTAA are in force. Many hurdles remain to be cleared before they are implemented. Nevertheless, free trade areas have gained widespread favor and are growing in importance in the international economic community.

The Continuation of G-7/G-8 Meetings

In 1975, the leaders of the world's seven largest Western industrialized countries— Canada, France, Germany, Great Britain, Italy, Japan, and the United States—began to meet regularly to discuss and act on a wide range of international economic and political problems. Known as the G-7 summits, these meetings became the **G-8 summits** in the mid–1990s when Russia became a formal regular participant. These meetings play a major role in formulating international economic policies and other policies as well.

For example, at the 1999 G-8 Summit in Cologne, Germany, the heads of state agreed to intensify their search for ways to strengthen Russia's social, structural, and economic reforms and to improve the transparency of the World Trade Organization. They also agreed to support additional teacher and student exchanges, develop ways to provide globalization a "human face" so that its negative impacts are cushioned, and improve systems that were in place that provide debt relief to heavily indebted poor countries. Similarly, at the 2000 G-8 Summit in Okinawa, Japan, the heads of state agreed to extend additional debt relief to developing states and to provide school meals for 9 million children a year in developing states. They also agreed to deposit an additional $1 billion dollars in the World Bank for loans to developing states for basic education.

Sometimes, G-8 summits are criticized for concentrating on discussions and producing few results. They are also sometimes criticized for not following through on previous promises, as when UN Secretary General Kofi Annan following the 2000 Okinawa G-8 meeting noted that the leaders did not offer as much debt relief as they had promised in 1999. There is some truth in both criticisms.

Nevertheless, it is important that the leaders of the world's developed states meet to discuss similarities and differences in their perceptions, viewpoints, and policies, and to initiate new policies at the global level. At a minimum, similarities can be solidified, differences can be prevented from growing larger, and new coordinated approaches to global issues planned even if not completely implemented. In international economics as elsewhere, this is important.

INTERNATIONAL ECONOMICS AND POWER

Today's international economic system is a far cry from that which emerged following World War II. The Bretton Woods system is gone. Exchange rates float. Capital funds are more mobile than ever. Regional free trade areas are a global trend. A new institution has been established to oversee trade disputes and to continue the movement toward free trade. World leaders meet regularly to discuss economic and other issues. And the international economic system is more open than at any other time in centuries.

To many people, these are encouraging events. A free and open trading system, a predictable system of international monetary exchange, and economic interdependence bring with them, they say, a multitude of advantages. The most prominent include increased production and higher standards of living because of efficient division of labor, incentive to invest because of a relatively certain and knowable future, and the probability of fewer serious political confrontations. In the early twenty-first century, national political and business leaders, multinational corporation executives and employees, and people living in developed states are most likely to have these views

Other people see a downside to free and open trade and economic interdependence. Primarily the wealthy benefit, they argue, as jobs go to countries where labor is paid the least. Countries also lose control of their own economies and have their national sovereignty compromised, they assert. And multinational corporations benefit at the expense of states, they charge. Those most likely to hold such views in the Developed World include nationalists and organized labor. And in the Developing World, despite significantly changed policies on the part of many governments, many people remain convinced that today's international economic system is in the hands of the wealthy Western industrialized states, and that the system is intentionally structured to favor the wealthy. And as seen through many Developing World eyes, economic might breeds political power and control. These different views are reflected in the accompanying cartoons.

What, then, does this mean for the future of the international economic system and for the relationship between economic capabilities and power?[16] First, for the foreseeable future, questions about the relationship between economic capabilities and power will be at the fore-

Economic Interdependence and Open Economies: The view at the top.

Economic Interdependence and Open Economies: The view at the bottom.

front of the international agenda. In the First World, the United States is plagued by its chronic balance-of-trade and balance-of-payment deficits. Western Europe hopes that the European Union will fuel an economic boom. Japan seeks ways to rekindle its export-driven prosperity of the 1980s. And all believe that they will benefit from free trade and an open international economic regime.

Meanwhile, in what once was the Second World, Central European states strive to develop market economies and economic ties to the West. Russia and the other states that emerged from the former Soviet Union struggle with their own immense economic and other problems. Leaders in virtually all these countries push economic reforms in efforts to revitalize their economies, but there is little agreement about how to do it. None of these states will succeed quickly in their revitalization efforts, and additional diminution in their power and influence appears inevitable.

In the Developing World, despite a new willingness to accept foreign direct investment, to cooperate with international lending and development institutions, and to adopt free market domestic economic development strategies, calls for a new international economic order that will favor the First World less and help the Developing World more, persist. A few fortunate Developing World states will enjoy high growth rates and develop economically, but most will remain economically weak. For most, change will come slowly, if at all.

But inevitably, just as the past brought economic shocks that affected the power potential of international actors, so too will the future. Few people expected American global economic domination to wane as rapidly as it did during the 1970s and 1980s, and few people expected the U.S. economic resurgence of the 1990s. Few people predicted the oil shocks of 1973–1974 and 1979–1980, the oil price collapse of 1985–1986, or the leap of oil prices in 2000. Nor did many people expect the communist world's economic crises of the late 1980s and early 1990s or East Asia's economic crises of 1997–1999. The impacts of unexpected economic shocks on the power potential of international actors can be considerable.

And what does this mean for the international system as a whole? For some time, there has been speculation that the international system that is emerging will be based on three major international trading blocs, one centered in North America led by the United States, another based in Europe led by the European Union, and a third focused in East Asia led by Japan. It remains to be seen whether this theory is accurate.

Even if such blocs do emerge, questions remain. If they develop, will these blocs be led by—or dominated by—the countries and organizations named above? Will these blocs strive for economic cooperation with one another, or will relationships between them degenerate into destructive trade wars?

These are important questions, but they are presently unanswerable. In the future, as in the past, the direction and shape of the international economy and of the power derived from economic capabilities, is anything but certain.

 ## KEY TERMS AND CONCEPTS

reemergence of economics   during the 1970s and 1980s, leaders increasingly recognized that economics played a major role in international relations. This was long understood, but for most of the post-World War II era, military and strategic affairs were of greatest importance and economic issues were lesser priorities

mercantilism   an economic philosophy that says state power comes from wealth; hence, state policy should maximize wealth through colonial acquisitions, trade, war, etc.

free trade   trade that takes place without barriers such as tariffs, quotas, etc.

tariffs   taxes placed on imports

interrelationship of domestic economies and international economics   the extent to which an international actor engages in international economic activity is a function of its needs and its desires

economic interdependence versus economic independence   interdependence exists when countries rely on other states as well as themselves to produce and furnish goods and services they require, and is in contrast to economic independence in which each state makes everything that it needs for itself

law of comparative advantage   the basis of international trade, where each country specializes in what it produces most efficiently, trading its surplus production for those items that it needs

balance-of-trade   a state's receipts garnered from its exports minus the cost of its imports

balance-of-payment   the total exchange of currencies that one country has with another

floating exchange rates   exchange rates of currencies determined by market forces

fixed exchange rates   exchange rates of currencies held at a specific value to create international exchange stability and confidence

special drawing rights   created by the International Monetary Fund (IMF) to help support currency values

international finance   the movement of money among countries for the purpose of investment, trade, and capital accumulation

international mobility of capital   the movement of capital between and among countries

global economic subsystems   1. among Western industrial states; 2. between Western industrial states and Developing World States; 3. among Developing World states

liberal trade school   views trade as a tool for economic growth

Marxist trade school   argues that the superior economic position of industialized states allows them to use trade to exploit developing states

structuralist trade school   similar to Marxist school, but argues that trade can help developing states advance economically only in the export sector

International Bank for Reconstruction and Development (IBRD)   the World Bank, set up to facilitate international financial transactions

International Monetary Fund (IMF)   established to oversee management of the international economic system

General Agreement on Tariffs and Trade   international agreements designed to reduce international tariff barriers and facilitate trade phased out in the 1990s

World Trade Organization   established in the 1990s to regulate and facilitate international trade and reduce barriers to trade

Bretton Woods   1944 meeting that established the post-World War II international economic system including the World Bank, the International Monetary Fund, and the General Agreement on Tariffs and Trade

evolution of international trading system since World War II   the Bretton Wood System evolved through several stages after World War II as detailed in the text

U.S. New Economic Policy (NEP)   wage and price freeze instituted by the U.S. in 1971 when it abandoned the Bretton Wood system

Organization of Petroleum Exporting Countries (OPEC)   a cartel of oil exporting countries whose purpose is to determine the quantity of oil pumped and set the price at which it will be sold

recycling problem (monetary)   occurred when OPEC increased oil prices so much OPEC countries had more cash than they could use

Uruguay Round the last set of meetings of the General Agreement on Tariffs and Trade which led to the creation of the World Trade Organization

open international economic system a system in which goods and services move according to supply and demand without barriers

free trade areas a zone in which there are no tariffs or other barriers to trade

Asia-Pacific Economic Cooperation (APEC) an economic association of states in East Asia, the Pacific, and the western hemisphere

Free Trade Area of the Americas (FTAA) an economic association in the Americas that intends to eliminate all tariff and non-tariff barriers to trade in the western hemisphere

G–7/G–8 meetings the meetings of the leaders of the leaders of the world's seven leading industrialized states, expanding to eight with the inclusion of the Russian leader after the collapse of the U.S.S.R.

industrialized West's views of international economics to most Western states, the current economic system provides opportunities for economic growth despite its shortcomings

Developing World's views of international economics to many developing states, international economics is based on an unfair system created by economically powerful countries to assure their continued economic pre-eminence

 ## WEBSITE REFERENCES

global interdependence: *www.interdependence.org* the website of the Global Interdependence Center, "dedicated to the expansion of global trade and finance within a free trade environment."

exchange rates: *www.x-rates.com* graphs and tables showing recent and current global exchange rates

International Bank for Reconstruction and Development: *www.worldbank.org* the World Bank's website

International Monetary Fund (IMF): *www.imf.org* the International Monetary Fund's website

World Trade Organization: *www.wto.org* website of the World Trade Organization

free trade areas: *www.ftaa-alca.org* official website of the Free Trade Area of the Americas

www.apecsec.org.sg/ official website of the Asia-Pacific Economic Cooperation zone

www.nafta-sec-alena.org/english/index.htm official website of the North American Free Trade Area

 ## NOTES

1. International economics also reemerged as a primary concern of the academic community. For several excellent studies of international political economics, see Jeffrey A. Frieden and David A. Lake, *International Political Economy: Perspectives on Global Power and Wealth,* 3rd Ed. (New York: St. Martin's Press, 1995); Joan E. Spero and Jeffrey A. Hart, *The Politics of International Economic Relations,* 6th Ed. (New York: St. Martin's Press, 1996); Thomas D. Lairson and David Skidmore, *International Political Economy: The Struggle for Power and Wealth* (New York: Harcourt Brace Jovanovich, 1993); and Theodore H. Cohn, *Global Political Economy: Theory and Practice* (New York, NY: Longman, 2000); and Robert Gilpin, *The Challenge of Global Capitalism: The World in the 21st Century* (Princeton, NJ: Princeton University Press, 2000).

2. For a more detailed discussion of interdependence, see Peter B. Kenen, *Understanding Interdependence: The Macroeconomics of the Open Economy* (Princeton: Princeton University Press, 1995).

3. Ricardo's example used Portuguese wine and English cloth. See David Ricardo, "The Principles of Political Economy and Taxation," in William R. Allen, ed., *International Trade Theory: Hume to Ohlin* (New York: Random House, 1965), p. 63. See also J. David Richardson, *The Case for Trade: A Modern Reconsideration* (Washington, DC: Institute for International Economics, 1995); and Wilfred J. Ethier et al., *Theory, Policy, and Dynamics in International Trade* (New York: Cambridge University Press, 1993).

4. For a discussion of increased mobility in the international securities market, see Andrew C. Sobel, *Domestic Choices, International Markets: Dismantling National Barriers and Liberalizing Securities Markets* (Ann Arbor: University of Michigan Press, 1994). For a discussion of the impact of information and communication technologies on global capital mobility, see Howard H. Frederick, *Global Communication and International Relations* (Belmont, CA: Wadsworth, 1993), p. 97.

5. See again Spero and Hart.

6. Gunnar Myrdal, *Rich Lands and Poor: The Road to World Prosperity* (New York: Harper & Row, 1957). See also Raul Prebisch, *The Economic Development of Latin America and Its Principal Problems* (New York: United Nations, 1950).

7. For a detailed discussion of the World Bank, see Christopher Gilbert and David Vines, eds., *The World Bank: Structures and Policies* (New York, NY: Cambridge University Press, 2000).

8. For good discussions of the International Monetary Fund, see Martin Feldstein, "Refocusing the IMF," *Foreign Affairs* (March–April 1998), pp. 20–33; Devesh Kapur, "The IMF: A Cure or a Curse?," *Foreign Policy* (Summer 1998), pp. 114–131; and Harold James, *International Monetary Cooperation Since Bretton Woods* (Washington, D.C.: IMF, 1996).

9. For additional details on the World Trade Organization, see Jeffrey J. Schott, *The WTO After Seattle* (Washington, D.C.: Institute for International Economics, 2000); and Bhagirath L. Das, *World Trade Organization: A Guide to New Frameworks for International Trade* (New York, NY: Saint Martin's Press LLC, 2000).

10. For a good discussion of the regional development banks, see Roy Culpeper, *The Multilateral Development Banks: Titans or Behemoths?* (Boulder, CO: Lynne Rienner Publishers, 1997).

11. More detailed views of the Bretton Woods system may be found in Fred L. Block, *The Origins of International Economic Disorder: A Study of U.S. International Monetary Policy from World War II to the Present* (Berkeley: University of California Press, 1977); Richard N. Gardner, *Sterling-Dollar Diplomacy in Current Perspective: The Origins and Prospects of Our International Economic Order* (New York: Columbia University Press, 1980); and W. M. Scammell, *The International Economy Since 1945* (New York: St. Martin's Press, 1980).

12. United States Department of the Treasury, Office of International Banking and Portfolio Investment, January 17, 1980; and Rimmer de Vries, "The International Monetary Outlook for the 1980s: No Time for Complacency," *World Financial Markets* (December 1979), p. 5.

13. For additional discussion of free trade areas, see Paula Stern and Raymond Paretzky, "Engineering Regional Trade Pacts to Keep Trade and U.S. Prosperity on a Fast Track," *Washington Quarterly*, Vol. 19, No. 1 (1996), pp. 211–222; Philip I. Levy, "A Political-Economic Analysis of Free Trade Agreements," *The American Economic Review* (September 1997), pp. 506–519; and Edward D. Mansfield and Helen V. Miler, "The New Wave of Regionalism," *International Organization* (Summer 1999), pp. 589–627.

14. For additional discussions of APEC, see Martin Rudner, "APEC: The Challenges of Asia Pacific Economic Cooperation," *Modern Asian Studies* (May 1995), pp. 404–37; and Nicole Gallant et al., "APEC's Dilemmas: Institution Building Around the Pacific Rim," *Pacific Affairs* (Summer 1997), pp. 203–218.

15. For additional discussion about the FTAA, see Cesar Gaviria, "The Futue of the Hemisphere," *Journal of Interamerican Studies and World Affairs* (Spring 1997), pp. 5–11; and Paulo S. Wrobel, "A Free Trade Area of the America by 2005?," *International Affairs* (July 1998), pp. 547–61.

16. For another view of the future international economic system, see J. David Richardson et al., *Why Globalization Matters Most* (Washington, D.C.: Institute for International Economics, 2000).

Chapter 14

Military Parameters
of Power

- What role does military power have in the twenty-first century?
- What is the difference between deterrence and coercion?
- How do nuclear weapons affect international relations?
- What role do conventional weapons play in a nuclear world?
- How effective is arms control?
- Do military capabilities add to the power of nonstate actors?
- How great a danger is the spread of advanced weapons technologies and weapons of mass destruction?

In the classic early nineteenth-century analysis of military affairs *On War,* Carl von Clausewitz observed that "war is a continuation of politics by other means." Clausewitz argued that although war was the ultimate form of political persuasion, the military forces so requisite during war have utility during peace as well.[1] The Prussian general was correct. During war or peace, the military capabilities of international actors make up a significant portion of an actor's power potential.

In objective terms, the power that an actor derives from its military capabilities can be determined only in actual combat. During the Cold War, the U.S. Department of Defense told its troops in Europe that superior training and superior equipment would allow them to fight outnumbered and win. Whether this was fact or fiction could have been tested only on the battlefield. So, too, with Great Britain and Argentina in the 1982 Falklands War. The British scoffed when Argentina warned that it would take over the islands if the dispute over their sovereignty was not concluded in Argentina's favor, but learned to their chagrin that the Argentine military had the capability and will to undertake such an action. Argentines scoffed when Britain sent a naval armada to retake the islands, but discovered that Britain's capability and will were sufficient for the task as well. Conversely, by assessing the volume of firepower that the United States brought to bear on Vietnam and that the Soviet Union unleashed in Afghanistan, both superpowers should have emerged victorious in short order. Neither did.

The interrelationship of military capabilities and power has both **objective and subjective components.** Quantity of military equipment alone does not determine the outcome of a battle, nor does it determine how much power an actor's military capabilities add to its overall power potential. The same is true for quality of equipment. Quantitatively numerous and qualitatively advanced military equipment adds little to an actor's power if the actor has no inclination to use its military to achieve its objectives and if the other actors are aware of that lack of inclination. However, if an actor has both numerous and modern weapons and is perceived as willing to use its weapons to achieve its objectives, then its military enhances its power *regardless* of whether the actor in reality has any inclination to use its military. From the perceptual vantage point of other actors, its power has been enhanced.

The interrelationship of military capabilities and power is rendered even more complex by other factors. How well can a military's leadership command, control, and communicate with its forces? How well can the forces be supplied, and for how long? How rapidly can losses be replaced? All these questions—and others—are important when the interrelationship of military capabilities and power is being analyzed.

Traditionally, at least since the Treaty of Westphalia, states have been the repositories of military capabilities. However, particularly since World War II, other actors have increasingly developed their own military capabilities. IGOs such as the United Nations and the Organization of African Unity have requested and received military forces from states to make up their own international peacekeeping forces, and multinational corporations have in some cases strengthened their own security forces so that they may be considered in-house paramilitary organizations. On one occasion during the 1980 Iranian hostage crisis, fearing that several of his employees also might be taken hostage, U.S. businessman (and 1996 presidential candidate) Ross Perot used his corporation's security forces to rescue employees from Teheran. NGOs such as national liberation movements and terrorist organizations use their military capabilities to strive for their desired ends, and mercenaries are again a recognized although not honored segment of the international community.

The power that military capabilities impart to an actor is the product of many factors. In our study of the interrelationship of military capabilities and power, we will examine military capabilities from several perspectives. First, we will discuss the role of military power in the twenty-first century. Second, because states possess most of the world's military capabilities, we will explore state-owned conventional and nuclear capabilities. Next, we will examine nonstate actors and military power. Finally, we will offer some concluding observations on the interrelationship of military capabilities and power.[2]

 ## MILITARY POWER IN THE TWENTY-FIRST CENTURY

After the Cold War ended and as the twentieth century wound down, some analysts speculated that the role of military power in the twenty-first century would diminish. Their rationale was straightforward. With the U.S.–Soviet confrontation over, they reasoned, the threat of war would recede and military power would lose much of its utility. Countries throughout the world could collect a "peace dividend" and divert money and men away from military pursuits.

Chapter 14

IT AND MILITARY POWER: THE REVOLUTION IN MILITARY AFFAIRS

Advanced information technologies are transforming military affairs and providing military forces capabilities that dwarf those available a few years ago. These transformations, on display in 1991 during Operation Desert Storm in Kuwait and Iraq and in 1999 in Kosovo, are so significant that they are often called "the revolution in military affairs." The revolution is taking place in four areas.

The first is in intelligence, surveillance, and reconnaissance. Some experts expect new capabilities in these areas, made possible by advanced IT, information-based sensors, and miniaturization, to provide 24 hour a day all-weather coverage so precise that the movement of every enemy soldier or piece of equipment will be known. If this happens, the battlefield will be truly transparent.

The second area is in command, control, and communications (C3). Advances in computing and other information technologies just over the horizon are so significant, some military experts believe, that C3 will be integrated to the point where commanders at all levels will be able to share information as needed, transmit orders clearly and accurately, and receive battle status and other data in a perfectly clear, accurate, and timely manner. If this occurs, proponents of the revolution in military affairs predict, military actions could be highly coordinated and virtually free of error.

The third area is precision force. Advocates of the revolution in military affairs assert that commanders will have highly accurate self-guided weapons that once fired will guide themselves to their targets. Some of these weapons like cruise missiles, TV guided bombs, smart torpedoes, and self-guided anti-tank weapons are already in the military inventory.

The final area is in information systems that enhance combat support in logistics, maintenance, and repair. Improved information systems in logistics will allow rapid transportation of weapons, supplies, replacement parts, and other required materials to areas of conflict. Once materials arrive, improved information systems will permit them to be rapidly identified, deployed, and put to use.

This vision of a revolution in military affairs is not universally shared. Some skeptics believe that the meshing of technologies required to achieve the capabilities described above is not possible. Others maintain that even if a seamless meshing is attained, enemy countermeasures will reduce the effectiveness of the revolution in military affairs. Still other skeptics argue that when potential opponents recognize they cannot win on the battlefield, they will resort to chemical, biological, or nuclear weapons, or turn to information warfare.

Is there a revolution in military affairs induced by advanced information technologies? The answer is clearly yes. However, there are unanswered questions about how great a revolution has already taken place, and about how great a revolution may eventually occur.

In a certain sense, this occurred. As will be detailed later in this chapter, in many countries, military expenditures declined and the number of people in uniform went down. But on another level, the end of the Cold War saw not a diminution in the role of military power in international affairs, but rather an increase in its importance as conflicts broke out or escalated in Africa, Asia, Europe, Latin America, and the Middle East.

This seeming paradox is easily explained. During the Cold War, a real danger existed that any conflict could escalate into a U.S.–Soviet confrontation. Although many civil wars, regional conflicts, and wars of national liberation occurred during the Cold War, decision makers usually kept the dangers of escalation in mind because, they feared, any conventional U.S.–Soviet confrontation could in turn escalate to a nuclear showdown between the two superpowers. Because of this danger, even though many conflicts occurred, most international actors consciously or unconsciously acted with restraint.

Thus, it could be argued, U.S.–Soviet rivalry had a dampening effect on conflict in the international system. Indeed, in a certain sense, the U.S.–Soviet standoff imposed a degree of restraint on international conflict during the Cold War.

When the Cold War ended, in many cases, this restraint disappeared. As a result, although the danger of a "big war" between the United States and the USSR disappeared, many "little wars" broke out or escalated. Table 14-1 lists locations where conflicts were underway in 2000. Most were civil wars or wars of national liberation, but they nevertheless required military capabilities. Military capabilities therefore remained as important as ever in international relations.

At the same time, as the threat of a nuclear war receded, the danger that a "little war" might escalate into a nuclear war receded. Thus, conventional weapons became more important than ever in many people's eyes because they might actually be used. The end of the Cold War thus brought with it, for many people, a new awareness of the importance of conventional weapons.

Even so, nuclear weapons remained important, a fact well illustrated by the large nuclear arsenals that the United States and Russia still had, the 1998 Indian and Pakistani nuclear tests, and North Korea's and Iraq's efforts to develop nuclear capabilities. In addition, fears grew that other weapons of mass destruction such as biological and chemi-

TABLE 14-1   Locations of Conflicts, 1999–2000

Afghanistan	Iraq
Algeria	Lebanon
Angola	Liberia
Bosnia	Mexico
Chechnya	Northern Ireland
Columbia	Philippines
Congo	Sierra Leone
East Timor	Somalia
Ethiopia/Eritrea	Sri Lanka
Georgia	Sudan
Kosovo	Turkey
India/Pakistan	West Bank/Gaza
Indonesia	

cal agents might be used in conflict by either state or nonstate actors. Information warfare, that is, attacks by one international actor against another's information and communication systems, also became an issue of growing concern.

At the beginning of the twenty-first century, then, conventional weapons, nuclear weapons, other types of weapons of mass destruction such as biological and chemical agents, and information warfare all either were or had potential to be important military parameters of power. Each will be examined in turn.

CONVENTIONAL WEAPONS IN A NUCLEAR AGE

Throughout the nuclear age, conventional weapons have retained great importance. Indeed, in many cases, conventional weapons have been a more accurate measure of a state's military power than nuclear weapons because nuclear weapons in many situations lose much of their political-military utility because they are so destructive. In simple terms, sometimes the use of nuclear weapons is not credible. In these situations, conventional weapons become the measure of a country's military power.

In a certain sense, conventional weapons have become even more important parameters of power since the end of the Cold War. There are two reasons for this. First, because conventional weapons can be tailored more easily to meet the demands of a given situation, they are more frequently "usable." Second, because to many people conventional weapons are not as emotionally and psychologically repugnant as nuclear weapons or other weapons of mass destruction like biological or chemical weapons, their use does not bring as much condemnation as the use of nuclear weapons or other weapons of mass destruction would bring.

This does not mean that the power afforded by conventional military capabilities is not relational or contextual. It is. U.S. conventional military capabilities are virtually meaningless as tools of power in U.S. economic disputes with Europe, Japan, or Canada, but in U.S. disagreements with Iraq, they clearly add to U.S. power potential. Again, however, it must be stressed that the subjective and objective aspects of military capabilities make it extremely difficult to estimate the relative amounts of power that states acquire because of their conventional military capabilities.

Dimensions of Military Expenditures

Between the end of World War II and the mid-1980s, military expenditures of states expanded astronomically. Between the late 1940s and the mid-1980s, global military expenditures grew by roughly 3 percent per year. Much of this expansion was fueled by the American and Soviet arms race, but very few major states did not contribute to this explosion. On a global basis, the stark fact was that by the mid-1980s, more than one out of every twenty dollars was spent on the military.[3]

As Cold War tensions eased during the late 1980s, the upward spiral in world military expenditures slowed. Then, when the Cold War ended in the early 1990s, the military expenditures of many states declined significantly. By the late 1990s, as Table 14-2 shows, the military expenditures of all regions of the world except Central and South Asia declined as a percentage of gross domestic product, sometimes significantly. In several regions of the world, expenditures on the military declined in absolute terms as well. This trend toward lower defense expenditures became known as **"the peace dividend."**

Lower defense expenditures also often led to fewer people in the armed forces. By the late 1990s, fewer people were in the armed forces in East Asia, European NATO countries, Russia, and the United States. Other regions experienced slight growth. Table 14-3 illustrates the extent to which the number of people in the armed forces of the world's states declined or grew by region between 1985, 1994, and 1998.

TABLE 14-2   Arms Expenditures in Billions of 1997 Constant Dollars, by Regions of the World

Region	Billions of US$ Spent on Defense		Percentage of GDP Spent on Defense	
	1985	1998	1985	1998
NATO Europe	206	171	3.1	2.1
United States	368	266	6.5	3.2
USSR/Russia	345	54	16.1	5.2
Other Europe	36	27	4.8	3.6
Middle East	96	61	12.3	7.4
Central/South Asia	13	21	4.3	5.4
East Asia/Australasia	108	131	6.3	3.8
Latin America/Caribbean	22	37	3.2	1.9
Sub-Saharan Africa	10	10	3.1	4.3

Source: International Institute for Strategic Studies, *The Military Balance 1999–2000* (Oxford: Oxford University Press, 2000), pp. 300–305.

TABLE 14-3   Millions of People in the Armed Forces, by Regions of the World

Region	1985	1994	1998
NATO Europe	3.1	2.5	2.1
United States	2.2	1.7	1.4
USSR/Russia	5.3	1.7	1.2
Other Europe	1.4	2.2	1.8
Middle East	2.5	2.9	2.9
Central/South Asia	2.1	2.5	2.6
East Asia/Australasia	8.0	7.0	7.2
Latin America/Caribbean	1.3	1.4	1.3
Sub-Saharan Africa	1.0	1.0	1.3

Source: International Institute for Strategic Studies, *The Military Balance 1999–2000* (Oxford: Oxford University Press, 2000), pp. 300–305.

Dimensions of Increased Conventional Military Capabilities

Despite lower levels of defense expenditures, conventional military forces improved qualitatively throughout the world during the 1990s and on into the twenty-first century. Some conventional weapons are powerful enough to destroy a square mile of a city or more. Nine of these could wreak the same nonradiation damage that the Hiroshima atomic bomb did. Other weapons called fuel air explosives are dropped by parachute and suspend droplets of flammable chemicals in the air to a radius of over one-half mile. A spark then lights the chemicals, incinerating everything in the area. Cluster bombs with over a thousand tiny bombs each were used with devastating effect in several conflicts during the 1980s and 1990s.

Conventional weapons are also becoming more sophisticated, thanks to advances in a number of technical areas. Multi-mach aircraft are now commonplace. "Smart weapons" including bombs, cruise missiles, and torpedoes are guided to their targets by televisions, lasers, computers, satellites, and microscopic wires. Surveillance and reconnaissance missions are flown deep into enemy territory by small pilotless drone aircraft that send information about what they see back to military headquarters, as they see it. Many of these weapons were displayed by U.S. forces during the Persian Gulf War during 1991 and again during the Kosovo conflict in 1999.

The availability of advanced conventional weapons is not limited to developed states. Many Developing World states either have or are developing capability to build their own advanced conventional weapons. And many of those that do not have or are not developing their own capability purchase advanced conventional weapons from developed states.

For example, the spread of ballistic missiles through the Developing World is shown in Table 14-4. As the table shows, many countries obtained their ballistic missiles from developed states and even other developing states, but some such as China and India developed their own. Ballistic missiles are dangerous not only because they can deliver conventional weapons, but also because they can deliver nuclear, biological, and chemical weapons, the weapons of mass destruction discussed in the following section, over long distances in short times with little warning.[4]

States are not the only international actors that have obtained or that are attaining advanced conventional military technology. For example, during the 1980s, the United States provided shoulder-launched "Stinger" anti-aircraft missiles to anticommunist guerrillas in Afghanistan, Angola, and Nicaragua. The United States and other states have been concerned that they may fall into the hands of people who will use them against Western aircraft. And at a different level, as will be discussed in the next section, governments throughout the world are concerned that weapons of mass destruction may be obtained and used by terrorists.

The implications of large military forces armed with better and more deadly conventional weapons are several. First, regional conflicts will become more dangerous not only to the combatants, but also to other states as the dangers of escalation increase. Increased range of aircraft and greater destructiveness of weapons also increase the chances that states not immediately involved in a conflict may be drawn in. Second, the great powers of the world will find their ability to control and influence events in other parts of the world reduced. Easily available modern weaponry will enable militarily

TABLE 14-4   Developing Countries with Ballistic Missiles, 2000

Country	Origin of Missile Technology	Longest Range Missile in KM
Afghanistan	USSR	300
Algeria	USSR	300
Argentina	Domestic	150
China	Domestic, USSR	Intercontinental
Congo	Iran	300
Egypt	Domestic, North Korea, USSR	685
India	Domestic, France, USA, USSR	3,250
Iran	China, Domestic, Libya, North Korea, Russia	5,500
Iraq	Domestic, USSR	600
Libya	Domestic, USSR	950
North Korea	Domestic, USSR	5,500
Pakistan	China, Domestic, North Korea	3,500
Saudi Arabia	China	2,600
Syria	North Korea, USSR	500
United Arab Emirates	Russia	300
Vietnam	USSR	300
Yemen	USSR	300

Source: Carnegie Non-Proliferation Project, 2000.

weak states to exact a certain toll from more powerful states even though the weaker states would undoubtedly lose in the end. However, the great powers may think twice about undertaking coercive activity if they realize that they would accrue inevitable losses. Finally, as more states acquire modern weapons, even more may be expected to attempt to attain them either through arms transfers or development of internal weapons capacity.

Most modern weapons reach the nonindustrial world via arms transfers from the industrialized world. After reaching a high of $57 billion in 1984, First and Second World arms transfers to Developing World states dropped during the late 1980s and in the 1990s. Nevertheless, in 1999, developed states still sold at least $30 billion in weapons to Developing World states. The United States, Russia, China, Great Britain, France, and Germany export sizable quantities of weapons. So too do a few developing states such as Brazil.

There are several **reasons for the international arms trade.**[5] During the Cold War, of course, the struggle for global advantage between the United States and the USSR played a major role in inducing arms sales. Both countries sought to expand their influence through arms sales, and both feared that if they did not offer weapons, the other would step into the void. Historically, at least the second part of their rationale was accurate. On a number of occasions when the United States refused to sell arms to Peru, Egypt, Ethiopia, and others, the Soviet Union stepped in. On other occasions, when the Soviets refused to continue arms aid to Egypt and Somalia, the United States stepped in. However, little persuasive evidence exists that either side over the long run enhanced its influence in one or another country by extending military aid and assistance.

Another strong motivating factor for arms transfers is money, particularly insofar as sales to the Middle East are concerned. Secretary of Defense Donald Rumsfeld put it quite bluntly, declaring that "most of these customers are ready to pay cash. They ask no gifts from the U.S." And as we saw previously, after the collapse of the Soviet Union, Russia has continued to play a major role in the international arms market because of economic needs.

Cost and obsolescence also contribute to international arms traffic. The more units of a weapon made, the more the costs of research, development, and production startup can be amortized. Thus, per unit cost for weapons is reduced as production increases. One way to increase production and bring down costs is to sell weapons overseas. Additionally, given the fact that the technological imperative drives technically advanced states to re-place their weapons with still more modern weapons, foreign sales provide a convenient dumping ground for older weapons. Old weapons thus provide income as part of their cost is recovered through foreign sale.

The flow of arms to Developing World states has been further accelerated by the widespread desire of those states to improve their military forces. The reasons for this are several. First, many Developing World states see security challenges on or near their bor-ders. India and Pakistan eye each other with uneasiness, as do China and India. Despite promises not to rearrange their international boundaries, many African states fear their neighbors do not intend to keep their promises. In the Middle East, Iraq's defeat in the 1991 Persian Gulf War has not eliminated its neighbors' concerns over its intentions, and the Iranian military buildup that began in the early 1990s once again raised concerns about Iran's intentions. Nor has South America been immune to regional rivalries. Venezuela claims territory in Guyana, and Guatemala and Belize have territorial disputes as well. The list could continue. Europe and North America, for their parts, allowed their regional disputes in this century to become world wars.

If regional rivalries provide one motivation for arming, internal security—which in some cases means the maintenance of authoritarian or dictatorial regimes—provides an-other. Weapons have many purposes, not the least of which is suppressing dissent.

A third reason developing states seek stronger conventional military forces is that, historically, the military has been the measure of a nation. Prestige thus plays a role. The more powerful a military, the more prestigious is the country, or so it is believed.

Closely linked to prestige as a motivating cause is the effort to escape vestiges of the colonial past. To many Developing World states, having one's own military forces is a vi-able proof of independence, even if one's economy is controlled or influenced by others. Several Developing World states nonetheless resent their continuing dependence on exter-nal sources for military equipment and arms and have therefore begun to develop their own domestic arms industries despite higher costs of limited production. Some have even become weapon exporters.

Even in a nuclear era, then, states recognize the utility of conventional arms and weapons and continue to purchase more weapons to add to their inventories. Although the additional power that such purchases add to a state's power potential cannot be precisely defined, conventional weapons are major instruments of power for states.

The Impact of Conventional Military Capabilities and Expenditures

Unfortunately, large-scale purchases of military capabilities carry with them sizable social costs. Critics of high levels of military expenditures point to several problems they claim are exacerbated by high levels of military expenditures. First, moneys spent on weaponry are not available for other socially useful expenditures. As all states operate more or less on budgets, moneys that are made available to the military are not available for other uses.

Second, the military produces little if anything. Soldiers and sailors may add to a state's security, but they do not add capital or consumer goods to a state's economy. The same is true for defense industries. Defense industries may produce hardware requisite for a state's defensive or offensive purposes, but they produce nothing that adds capital to a state's economy. In a certain sense, then, defense expenditures draw people and material away from economically expansive endeavors and may therefore retard economic growth.

In part, inflation also may be linked to military expenditures. Members of the armed forces and employees of defense industries draw their pay and consume products, yet they do not produce a single consumer-oriented good. Thus, more money is injected into the economy, whereas the quantity of consumer goods remains constant. Therefore, prices are bid upward, and a classical inflationary situation can occur.

A corollary of this line of reasoning is that high levels of defense expenditures may in fact *undermine* the power of a state. During Dwight Eisenhower's presidency, he made exactly this point on several occasions. Eisenhower observed that national strength was based on a variety of inputs and that emphasizing the military too much meant that other aspects of national strength would be starved. As a result of this reasoning, Eisenhower sought to reduce defense spending during his presidency.[6] Critics of the U.S. defense buildup during the Reagan presidency also used this argument. Many economists and policy analysts believe that too much defense spending was one reason that the Soviet economy collapsed in the 1980s and early 1990s.

The growth of military expenditures and the spread of advanced military technologies have had major noneconomic consequences as well. One of them, the increased ferocity of regional conflicts, has already been mentioned. Although the increased lethality of modern weapons may lead to more killing and destruction in a single war, a number of studies have concluded that the frequency of war has not increased.

Although no noticeable link exists between lethality of weapons and frequency of war, most analysts agree that increased lethality could lead to escalation of small regional wars to large ones. The rationale for such feared escalation is simple: As larger regional powers see their allied or client states suffer higher and higher casualty rates and levels of destruction, they may be more likely to step in to assist their ally/client.

The heightened lethality of Developing World arsenals may also in some cases lead to increased unwillingness on the parts of the world's Great Powers, including the United States, to intervene in the Developing World when their interests are challenged. Because of increased lethality, the costs would be higher. National decision makers may thus decide that the benefit of intervention would be less than the cost.

The final paradox of increased military capabilities is that few states have enhanced their security. More may be spent, more weapons may be obtained, and the weapons may be more deadly than ever, but the reality is that many states and their citizens feel they are more threatened than ever by the military might of potential foes. Indeed, as Figure 14-1 suggests, it may even be possible that after a certain point additional military expenditures add little or nothing to a state's military power. Experience throughout the world indicates that once a state develops an effective fighting force, a point is reached where each new division, tank, plane, or ship adds less to a state's power potential than the one that preceded it.

NUCLEAR WEAPONS AND INTERNATIONAL RELATIONS

As of 2000, seven international actors, all states, had exploded nuclear devices. The United States exploded the world's first nuclear device in 1945, followed by the Soviet Union in 1949 and Great Britain in 1952. France was the next country to detonate a nuclear device, in 1960, and China followed suit in 1964. India first exploded a nuclear device in 1973, but declared that the explosion was "peaceful" and would not be used for military purposes.

Despite fears of nuclear proliferation, no new state publicly joined the nuclear club for the next fifteen years. Then, in 1998, India and Pakistan both exploded nuclear devices clearly intended for military purposes as tensions between them escalated. As the twenty-first century dawned, then, seven states were "formally" members of the world's nuclear club.

In addition, South Africa revealed in 1993 that it had had six nuclear weapons but disassembled them in 1991. Also, most experts believe that Israel has the material and expertise to make nuclear weapons and could assemble one in a few days at most. Other

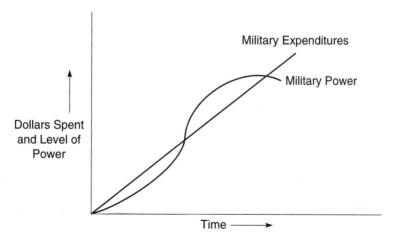

FIGURE 14-1   Military power as a function of military expenditure: A hypothetical representation.

countries such as Argentina, Brazil, Iran, Iraq, North Korea, Pakistan, South Korea, and Taiwan may also be capable of building nuclear weapons.

The United States is the only state that has ever used an atomic bomb in anger. On August 6, 1945, the *Enola Gay,* a U.S. B-29, dropped an atomic bomb on Hiroshima, leveling much of the city. Three days later, a second bomb destroyed Nagasaki. The nuclear age had arrived.

The Nuclear Arms Race

The **nuclear arms race** began slowly, with the United States retaining its nuclear monopoly until 1949 when Soviet scientists conducted their first nuclear test.

Once the U.S. nuclear monopoly had ended, the nuclear arms race had several facets. One facet was a race to develop **fusion weapons.** Both the United States and the Soviet Union had first developed **fission weapons,** that is nuclear weapons that released energy by splitting atoms. Also known as atomic bombs, or A-bombs, fission weapons were much more powerful than conventional weapons. Indeed, as postwar U.S. strategic bombing surveys revealed, it would have taken as many as 210 conventionally armed B-29s to inflict the same amount of damage on Hiroshima that the *Enola Gay* did with one atomic bomb.[7]

A second aspect of the nuclear arms race was the effort to make small nuclear weapons that could be used close to one's own troops in the field. The United States viewed the development of such **tactical nuclear forces (TNF)** as a key element for the defense of Western Europe and South Korea because the USSR and its allies had superior conventional forces. The United States reasoned that TNF would be used against hostile forces if conventional defense proved futile. The United States obtained the lead in TNF development and began moving those weapons overseas in the mid-1950s.

A third aspect of the nuclear arms race was the effort to develop superior **delivery vehicles,** that is planes, missiles, and other ways to deliver nuclear weapons to their targets. Throughout most of the Cold War, the United States had better delivery vehicles than the Soviet Union, although late in the Cold War, as Table 14-5 shows, the USSR had more.

TABLE 14-5   The Growth of the U.S. and Soviet Strategic Nuclear Arsenals[a]

	1966	1970	1974	1978	1982	1986	1990
U.S. ICBM	904	1,054	1,054	1,054	1,052	1,018	1,000
SLBM	592	656	656	656	520	616	608
Long-range bombers	630	550	437	366	316	240	360
USSR ICBM	292	1,299	1,575	1,400	1,398	1,398	1,451
SLBM	107	304	720	1,028	989	979	942
Long-range bombers	155	145	140	135	150	170	195

Source: International Institute for Strategic Studies, *The Military Balance* (London: IISS, appropriate years).

[a]Table does not include other significant quantitative and qualitative measures of strategic importance such as number of warheads, yield of warheads, reliability and survivability of systems, and accuracy.

During the late 1940s and early 1950s, the only delivery vehicles that either side had were bombers. U.S. bombers were clearly superior to the Soviet Union's, especially after the B-52 became operational in 1954. Indeed, the B-52 was such a good aircraft that 70 remain operational as of 2000.[8]

But in 1957, U.S. confidence was severely shaken when the Soviet Union launched *Sputnik I,* the world's first satellite. The degree of technical sophistication needed to launch a satellite was roughly equivalent to that needed to deliver nuclear weapons intercontinental distances. The marriage of fusion weapons and **intercontinental ballistic missiles (ICBMs)** forced a major reevaluation of strategic thinking and led the U.S. to fear that a **missile gap** had developed between itself and the USSR.

In reality, the USSR did not have large numbers of ICBMs until the mid-1960s. No missile gap existed, and the United States remained superior to the Soviet Union in all aspects of the nuclear arms race throughout the 1950s. Indeed, Soviet nuclear inferiority may be what influenced Soviet leader Nikita Khrushchev to try to deploy missiles to Cuba in 1962. This Soviet effort led to the **Cuban Missile Crisis,** the most dangerous U.S.–Soviet confrontation of the Cold War. During the crisis, the United States demanded that the USSR withdraw its missiles from Cuba. The USSR complied, thereby ending the crisis.

Meanwhile, in response to the alleged missile gap, the United States accelerated deployment of its own ICBMs and began operationalizing submarine-launched ballistic missiles (SLBMs). A new generation of U.S. ICBMs, the *Minuteman,* was deployed in underground silos, making them impervious to anything but a direct hit. SLBMs were also safe from attack because of the mobility and stealth of submarines. By the middle 1960s, U.S. nuclear superiority was greater than ever.

U.S. superiority began to diminish as the United States held its force levels relatively constant and the Soviet Union continued to try to catch up. By the late 1960s, the USSR had virtually eliminated U.S. quantitative nuclear superiority, although the U.S. qualitative lead in accuracy and reliability remained considerable.

The major technical breakthrough of the 1970s was the development of the **multiple independently targetable reentry vehicle (MIRV).** A MIRVed ICBM had several warheads atop it, each of which could be guided to a separate target. Thus, a single ICBM or SLBM could destroy several enemy targets. The United States began to deploy MIRVed ICBMs in 1970, and the Soviet Union followed five years later.

In 1972, Soviet and American leaders reached agreement on the first **Strategic Arms Limitation Treaty (SALT I).** SALT I placed a cap on the quantity of Soviet and U.S. delivery vehicles, and an accompanying protocol limited the number of antiballistic missile systems (ABMs) each side could deploy. However, no limits were placed on qualitative improvements, and the nuclear arms race continued. A **SALT II** agreement that effected some limitations on qualitative improvements was negotiated by 1979, but the U.S. Senate never ratified it.[9]

By the early 1980s, the U.S.–USSR nuclear arms race had reached a stalemate. Some Americans concluded that the Soviet Union had opened a "window of vulnerability" on the United States, and that the United States was vulnerable to a disarming Soviet first strike. Other Americans argued that U.S. forces were as safe as ever and deterrence assured because of U.S. superiority in total numbers of warheads, submarine technology, and aircraft technology.[10]

By the late 1980s, the nuclear arms race had become a confused arena for sophisticated arguments, expensive weapons systems, and bewildering acronyms. The simplistic deterrence arguments of the 1950s ("if you attack me, I will attack you, and you cannot then hope to win") had been replaced by sophisticated discussions of dynamic equilibrium, pindown, and fratricide. In the U.S. arsenal, expensive B-52s and Minutemen were replaced by more expensive B-1s, Stealth, and M-X. ICBMs, SLBMs, MIRVs, ABMs, and SALT were joined by ALCMs, GLCMs, SLCMs, MaRVs, ASAT, SDI, and START. Older strategic terminology like mutual assured destruction, counterforce and countervalue, and damage limitation were complemented by newer terms such as pop-up, precursor bursts, and interactive discrimination. Questions about nuclear superiority and inferiority, about nuclear strategy and tactics, became as complicated as the weapons themselves.

But in the late 1980s, the Soviet Union began to change its international policies and become more cooperative with the West. As a result, nuclear arms control efforts began to make rapid strides. In 1991, the United States and the Soviet Union signed the first **Strategic Arms Reduction Treaty,** also called **START I.** Under START I, each side was limited to a total of no more than 1,600 ICBMs, SLBMs, and strategic bombers. Combined, these delivery vehicles were not permitted to carry more than 6,000 "START-countable" warheads.

In January 1993, George Bush and Boris Yeltsin signed the START II Treaty, which when completely implemented will drastically reduce the strategic nuclear arsenals of the United States and Russia.

The breakup of the Soviet Union caused serious problems for START. Following the collapse of the USSR, Belarus, Kazakhstan, Russia, and Ukraine all inherited some of the Soviet Union's strategic weapons. Negotiations between these four states and the United States led to an agreement that all nuclear weapons of the former Soviet Union would be returned to Russia, with most of the returned weapons being destroyed. This occurred. In addition, all the involved states agreed that the START treaty would remain in force.

This did not end efforts to reduce the legacy of the nuclear arms race. The United States and Russia continued to negotiate further strategic nuclear weapons reductions, and in 1993, the two countries concluded the **START II** accord. START II would among other things reduce the total number of strategic nuclear warheads to 3,500 or less and ban multiple-warhead missiles.

After extensive debate, the U.S. Congress ratified START II. After even more delay caused by Russian domestic politics, the Russian parliament (the Duma) ratified the treaty in 2000. The impact of the START treaties on the United States and Russian strategic nuclear arsenals is shown in Figure 14-2. The two countries in 2000 also agreed to establish a joint warning center to exchange information on missile launches, eliminate significant quantities of plutonium and weapons-grade uranium from their stockpiles, and begin negotiating a START III treaty to further reduce the number of nuclear weapons in their respective arsenals.[11]

By the beginning of the twenty-first century, then, the nuclear arms race between the United States and Russia was for all practical purposes over. To be sure, other nuclear issues remained, including the possibilities of a nuclear arms race between India and Pakistan, a rogue state such as North Korea obtaining nuclear weapons, or terrorist groups obtaining nuclear weapons. But the good news was that the world had survived the confrontation between two nuclear superpowers.

Nuclear Strategy and Policy

Despite the end of the nuclear arms race, nuclear weapons will remain in the arsenals of the United States, Russia, Great Britain, France, and China for the foreseeable future. In addition, India and Pakistan have become nuclear capable countries, and other states such as North Korea, Iran, and Iraq are nearing the ability to produce nuclear weapons. Thus, even though nuclear strategy and nuclear deterrence is not as topical today as it was during the Cold War, they are still important considerations in international relations.[12] Here, we will explore three of the most important dimensions of nuclear strategy and policy.

What Is the Logic Behind Deterrence, Mutual Deterrence, and Mutual Assured Destruction?

The concept of nuclear deterrence is a simple one. Stated briefly, nuclear **deterrence** relies on the certainty that one country has sufficient military capabilities to convince another country that it would not be worth its while to attack.

Military analysts identify three types of deterrence: deterrence by denial, deterrence by punishment, and deterrence by defeat. Under deterrence by denial, the country that might wish to initiate a war would not do so because it is convinced that it could not obtain its war objectives. Thus, it would have no reason to begin a war. Under deterrence by

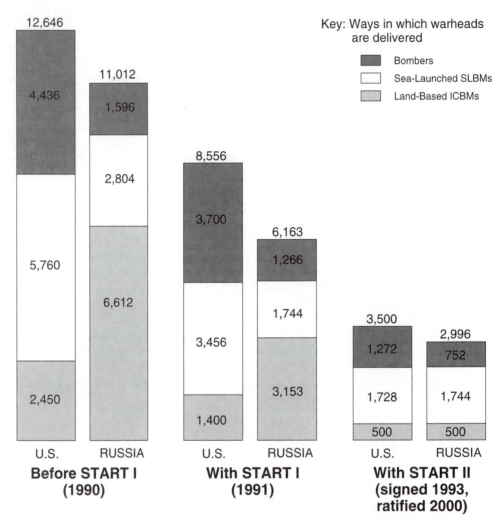

FIGURE 14-2   The impact of the START I and II treaties on the number of strategic nuclear warheads in the U.S. and Soviet/Russian strategic nuclear arsenals.

Sources: START I and II treaties, 1991 and 1993, respectively.

punishment, the country that might wish to initiate a war would not do so because it would believe that the country that is attacked could inflict unacceptable damage (punishment) to the attacking country. Obviously, the higher the level of cost tolerance that an attacking state is willing to accept, the higher the level of damage that the attacked state must be capable of inflicting if deterrence by punishment is to be effective. Under deterrence by defeat, the state that might wish to initiate a war would not do so because of the certainty that it would be defeated.

Deterrence deals in subjective aspects of military capabilities. The truth of deterrence is that if weapons are used, deterrence has failed. Thus, under any of the three versions of deterrence, the country that may be contemplating an attack must be convinced of the futility of its efforts before it initiates an attack. Under **mutual deterrence**, both sides in a potential war must be convinced of the futility of attack initiation. This is particularly true at the nuclear level where the stakes of miscalculation are so high.

Mutual assured destruction (MAD) is a variant of mutual deterrence by punishment. MAD dictates that *both* sides in a potential nuclear war must be convinced even before a war begins that the other could absorb a first strike and still have enough nuclear weaponry left to destroy the initiating side as a functioning modern society. Assuming rationality on the part of national decision makers in such a situation, no incentive to attack other than suicide could exist.

Efforts to deliver an assured second strike led U.S. and former Soviet planners to place their ICBMs in hardened underground silos and influenced U.S., Soviet, British, and French planners to place sizable portions of their nuclear strike capabilities in submarines. China has also developed SLBM capabilities. The more convinced that a state is of the invulnerability of its own nuclear forces, the more stable are deterrence, mutual deterrence, and mutual assured destruction. Any of the types of deterrence are in danger of disintegrating as soon as a state believes that it has been put in a position to "use it or lose it."

In the curious world of nuclear strategy, nuclear weapons exist so that they will never be used. They deter not only nuclear war but also, it is hoped, large-scale conventional war.

Why Do the United States and Russia Have so Many Nuclear Weapons?

There are three main answers to this question. First, since the objective of deterrence was (and is) to prevent anyone from ever employing nuclear weapons, both sides sought to convince the other through sheer quantity of weaponry that a nuclear attack was futile. Here, it should also be stressed that until recently, both the United States and the USSR claimed they were convinced that the other was seeking nuclear superiority, and therefore each continued its buildup to avoid inferiority.

Second, successful deterrence is predicated on the certainty of retaliation. As all nuclear-capable states claim to be building their forces for retaliation rather than for first strike, the prudent planner must assume that all nuclear forces will not survive an enemy's first strike. Nevertheless, that planner must be able to convince potential enemies that in a post-first strike environment, a sufficient number of operational weapons will be available to destroy the attacker as a functioning society. Given the uncertainties inherent in any war, much less nuclear war, quantity was—and is—the most effective means to provide certainty and assure deterrence.

Third, nuclear weapons provide states an aura of power. This aura may not necessarily be deserved, but it is nonetheless there. It is part of the psychological baggage that nuclear weaponry carries with it. Indeed, at the nuclear level as well as at the conventional level, a sense of "more weapons, more power" prevails. Given the relational and contextual dimensions of power, this sense is not necessarily accurate. Nevertheless, it often exists.

(a)

(b)

Despite the end of the Cold War, the United States nuclear Triad is an important element of U.S. defense policy. Views of the U.S. nuclear Triad: (a) a B-2 Stealth bomber; (b) a test launch of a U.S. Minuteman ICBM; and (c) an "Ohio" class ballistic missile submarines, built to carry "Trident" missiles.

(c)

Are Nuclear Weapons too Destructive to Have Political Utility?   Stated differently, this question asks if Clausewitz' dictum, "War is the continuation of politics by other means" is true in the nuclear age.

This question must be answered in several ways. As we saw in our discussion of the subjective aspects of military capabilities, a country that has a particular military capability adds nothing to its power potential if it does not have the intention to use that capability and if other states realize it does not have the intention to use that capability. Conversely, at the other extreme, if a state has the intention to use a particular capability and other actors realize that it will, that state may have significantly enhanced its power potential.

These observations have relevance for nuclear weapons and for the power that they bestow on actors that have them. It was widely accepted that the United States and the Soviet Union would use their nuclear weapons against the other in the event of an attack on the other's homeland. Both sides had the intention of using their nuclear weapons in this situation, and both sides realized that the other would do so. Deterrence was thus assured, and both sides used their nuclear capabilities to influence potential actions of the other. Nuclear weapons thus added power to the United States and the Soviet Union.

In other cases, nuclear weapons added little or nothing to Soviet or American power potential. The United States never seriously considered using nuclear weapons in Vietnam, and the Soviet Union never seriously considered using them in Afghanistan. Both the Vietcong and the Afghan guerrillas realized this. Nuclear weapons therefore contributed nothing to U.S. power in Vietnam nor to Soviet power in Afghanistan. The use of nuclear weapons was simply not credible; they were too powerful to be militarily—or politically—useful. All involved actors realized it.

This paradox is not limited to the U.S. and former Soviet strategic arsenals. When China, a nuclear power, launched a "punishment operation" against Vietnam in 1979, few analysts believed that China would use nuclear weapons. The Vietnamese certainly did not. Thus, given China's unwillingness to use them, nuclear weapons added nothing to Chinese power. Similarly, in 1982, if Argentina had expected Great Britain to drop a nuclear weapon on Buenos Aires, Argentina probably would not have taken over the Falklands. Argentina's estimate of Britain's willingness to use its nuclear arsenal was correct, even though Argentina's estimate of Britain's commitment to take back the Falklands was not. Argentina therefore went ahead with its invasion. British use of nuclear weapons was simply not credible, and therefore nuclear weapons added nothing to Britain's power.

Nuclear weapons, then, are situationally meaningful additions to the power that a country has at its disposal. In some cases, because of the level of destruction that they cause, nuclear weapons add little or no power to a state's account. In other cases, nuclear weapons add considerable quantities of power to a state's account. Obviously, the examples here cited are at opposite extremes of a continuum along which more uncertain situations lie.

The Perils of Nuclear Proliferation

Nuclear proliferation has long been a major concern of the international community, but in the 1990s, it reached a new level of urgency. This urgency continues over into the twenty-first century. There are four primary reasons for this. First, the dissolution of the Soviet

Union and the decline of its ability to monitor its nuclear weapons and nuclear components raised fears that the USSR's nuclear weapons, nuclear weapons components, and nuclear know-how would fuel proliferation. Second, the international community was shocked to discover in the aftermath of the 1991 Gulf War how advanced Iraq's nuclear weapons program was. Third, as already related, in 1998 India and Pakistan both exploded nuclear devices, raising fears of a nuclear arms race not only in the region but throughout Asia.[13] And finally, several other states often regarded as rogue states, especially Iran and North Korea, are also pursuing nuclear research programs that could have as an objective the development of nuclear weapons.

Seven states have proven nuclear capabilities. A seventh, Israel, is widely assumed to have them, and an eighth, South Africa, claims to have developed a nuclear arsenal but voluntarily disarmed itself. As many as 40 states may have the technical know-how to produce nuclear weapons. Many of them will doubtlessly forego production of nuclear weapons, but some will follow the lead of India and Pakistan and acquire them. A variety of states will therefore probably join the nuclear club in coming years, states that one can only hope will be as responsible with nuclear weapons as those that currently have them have been.

But there is always the concern that nuclear weapons once developed will be used. If Iraq had nuclear weapons in 1991, would it have used them against U.S. and other forces during Operation Desert Storm? If Argentina had nuclear weapons in 1982, would the Argentine government have used them to eliminate the British fleet off the Falklands? If Libya had nuclear weapons in 1986 when the United States launched two air attacks against Libya, would Libya have used them against the U.S. Sixth Fleet—or even the United States? If Pakistan had nuclear weapons in 1971, would they have been used in Pakistan's conflict with India, when Indian intervention in a civil war led to East Pakistani independence from West Pakistan as Bangladesh? In future years, would another Arab–Israeli War lead Israel to use nuclear weapons against its Islamic neighbors, or influence Libya, Iran, Iraq, or some other potentially nuclear-capable Islamic state to use them against Israel?

These are not academic questions. All the states mentioned will have the potential to develop nuclear weapons early in the next century. Some may already have them.

How have these states come close to or developed the ability to make nuclear weapons? There are several answers. In some cases, these states developed some or even most of their nuclear capabilities on their own. However, more frequently, nuclear-capable countries knowingly or unknowingly provided potential nuclear states with their nuclear know-how. In some cases, businesses and individuals worked their way around or ignored international limitations on the sale of nuclear materials and components. Some potential nuclear states stole nuclear know-how, parts, and components. But the bottom line is nevertheless easy to see. Nuclear know-how and capabilities have proliferated immensely.

The impact of the break up of the Soviet Union on nuclear proliferation warrants special mention here. With the collapse of the Soviet Union's nuclear command and control structure, former Soviet nuclear weapons, components, or materials may have been sold to countries that want to develop their own nuclear capabilities. There is also the possibility that former Soviet nuclear scientists, now unable to make a living in Russia, may have gone to work for nonnuclear countries that want to develop nuclear capabilities. Unfortunately, it is highly likely that international efforts to stem the flow of nuclear components, materials, and know-how following the Soviet collapse have not been completely successful.

Why do nonnuclear countries want to acquire nuclear weapons? In most cases, the drive to attain nuclear weapons comes from psychological and security considerations. Nuclear-capable countries are generally regarded as great powers simply because they possess nuclear weapons. This adds psychological importance to the possession of nuclear weapons. India's nuclear test in 1973 was a major factor in Pakistan's decision later in the decade to develop a nuclear research program, and when India in 1998 exploded a nuclear weapon, Pakistan followed suit in a few days.

It is not only at the state level that nuclear proliferation presents potential threats. With the expertise to build nuclear weapons easily attainable, only the availability of materials frustrates would-be nuclear-capable nonstate actors. Western leaders have long feared that terrorist groups of one type or another might gain access to a nuclear device and then engage in nuclear blackmail. A terrorist group, with little to lose, may well be able to achieve its demands if it placed a nuclear weapon in New York City or London and threatened to detonate it if its demands were not met. For the terrorist group, a nuclear weapon would have immense political utility and would tremendously enhance the power of that group.

A final chilling observation must be added to our discussion of nuclear proliferation. In many respects, those international actors that have the least to lose may be the most willing to use nuclear weapons. Historically, those actors have also had the most difficult task achieving nuclear status. However, as the twenty-first century begins, this cold solace may be less and less true.[14]

Efforts to Control Nuclear Weapons

Recognizing the dangers of nuclear weapons, the international community has long attempted to limit these weapons and prevent their spread. These efforts have not been completely successful, but neither have they been complete failures.

The United States advanced the first plan to control nuclear weapons in 1946 when it proposed the Baruch Plan, under which a UN agency would be created to oversee nuclear research programs throughout the world. Given that the USSR during this era considered the UN to be a U.S. foreign policy tool, Soviet rejection of the plan was preordained.

Subsequent nuclear arms control negotiations faltered on the issue of verification of compliance. The United States regularly proposed on-site inspections, which the Soviet Union always rejected as spying. At the 1955 Eisenhower–Khrushchev Geneva Summit meeting, the U.S. president offered his "Open Skies" proposal for reciprocal air inspections. Khrushchev countered with a proposal for ground sensor stations at areas remote from test sites, which the United States rejected as inadequate.

The 1959 Antarctic Treaty was the first major success in nuclear arms control. Eighteen states, including the United States and the USSR, agreed under the treaty to ban deployment of nuclear weapons in Antarctica. The next breakthrough came with the 1963 Limited Test Ban Treaty, in which most UN member states agreed not to set off nuclear explosions in the atmosphere, in space, or under water. As of 2000, 125 states have signed and ratified the treaty, with 11 other states having signed it but not yet having ratified it.

The two centerpiece efforts to limit nuclear weapons were and are the **Nuclear Non-Proliferation Treaty (NPT),** first signed by 43 states in 1968 and extended in 1995 at the 25-year NPT Extension Conference, and the **Comprehensive Test Ban Treaty (CTBT),** signed in 1996 by 71 states. As of 2000, 187 countries had signed the NPT and 154 had signed the CTBT.[15]

Under the NPT, signatory states agreed not to transfer nuclear weapons to any state that did not have them and not to develop nuclear weapons if they did not have them. Monitored by the International Atomic Energy Agency (IAEA), this aspect of the treaty has been for the most part successful. The NPT also committed nuclear-capable states to reduce their nuclear arsenals, a commitment that was not really fulfilled until the Cold War began to wind down in the late 1980s.

Unfortunately, the NPT has no real enforcement mechanism. This point was driven home in 1991 when in the wake of the Persian Gulf War, IAEA inspectors discovered how close Iraq was to developing nuclear weapons. Similarly, even though North Korea denies that its nuclear program is a weapons program, most external observers believe that it is.

Under the CTBT, signatory states agree not to conduct any type of nuclear explosion. As of 2000, not enough states have yet ratified the CTBT for it to enter into force. Although it signed the CTBT, the United States is one of the countries that has not yet ratified it. Some analysts are concerned that signing the treaty would weaken the U.S. ability to guarantee the reliability of its nuclear arsenal, while others argue that computer modeling of nuclear explosions has advanced so far that real testing is no longer needed.

Although the CTBT is not yet in effect, the world's seven nuclear states have put unilateral **moratoriums on nuclear tests** in place. Russia has not conducted a nuclear test since 1991, and the United States since 1992. The U.S. moratorium precludes British tests. France began a moratorium in 1992, but ended it in 1995 when the French government initiated an eight-explosion nuclear testing program cut back to six tests because of international protests at its Mururoa Atoll test site in the South Pacific. France resumed its moratorium in early 1996, the same year China placed a moratorium on its nuclear tests. Shortly after they conducted their nuclear tests in 1998, India and Pakistan proclaimed that they would undertake no further tests as well.

There have also been efforts to ban nuclear weapons from specific regions of the world. In 1967, one such treaty banned nuclear weapons from Latin America and the Caribbean; Cuba became the last regional state to sign the treaty, doing so in 1995. Similar treaties were proposed for the Middle East by the Arab League in 1994, supported by the NPT Review Conference in 1995. The UN General Assembly voted for a nuclear weapons free zone in South Asia in 1995, and the Organization of African Unity unanimously adopted a draft treaty establishing a nuclear weapons free zone in Africa the same year. In all cases, compliance is or would be left to the good will of signatory states.

Clearly, efforts to control nuclear weapons and nuclear proliferation have met with some success. In the absence of such efforts, more nuclear weapons most assuredly would exist today, and they undoubtedly would be in the hands of more international actors.

NONNUCLEAR WEAPONS OF MASS DESTRUCTION AND INFORMATION WARFARE

Unfortunately, however, nuclear weapons are not the only weapons of mass destruction. Although nonnuclear weapons of mass destruction such as chemical and biological agents are often overlooked, they too present significant dangers to the international community. In addition, as developed countries in particular grow increasingly dependent on information and communication technologies in all areas of life, many analysts have grown increasingly concerned about the possibility of information warfare, that is, attacks by one international actor against another's information and communication systems. Nonnuclear weapons of mass destruction and information warfare require separate discussion.

Nonnuclear Weapons of Mass Destruction

How serious a danger do chemical and biological weapons of mass destruction present? Two examples illustrate the case. Even though there is no concrete proof, many analysts believe that the "desert sickness" that many U.S. troops experienced after their return from the Persian Gulf War in 1991 may be the result of exposure to Iraqi chemical agents. Even more poignantly, the first major terrorist use of chemical agents occurred in 1995 when the Japanese religious cult Aum Shinrikyo released the nerve gas sarin at five places in the Tokyo subway system. Six people died and thousands were injured. A few weeks later, four more gas attacks, two of which used cyanide gas, were launched against other Japanese railway targets.

In the United States, the U.S. government takes the threat of chemical and biological attacks seriously. After the bomb explosion in Centennial Olympic Park during the 1996 Atlanta Olympics, officials were concerned that chemical or biological agents may have been involved and momentarily considered closing off Atlanta's downtown area. More recently, in 2000, the U.S. government conducted tests in several major U.S. cities on their ability to respond to biological attacks.

The international community has been aware of the dangers of chemical and biological warfare for some time and has taken a number of steps to ban chemical and biological agents. For example, in 1925, in reaction to the use of poison gas in World War I, a Geneva Protocol banned the use in war of chemical and biological weapons. More recently, the 1972 Biological Weapons Convention (BWC) banned the development, production, and possession of biological and toxin weapons, and the 1993 Chemical Weapons Convention (CWC) did the same for chemical weapons. As of 2000, 143 states are parties to the BWC and 135 are parties to the CWC.

Unfortunately, enforcement mechanisms in the treaties are weak. In addition, even if enforcement mechanisms were in place, it is virtually impossible to detect when and where many chemical and biological agents are being made. Complicating matters still more, many chemical agents are dual use products, that is, they are productively used in industrial processes, not just as weapons. Thus, the threat of nonnuclear weapons of mass destruction is real. It is and will continue to be a difficult threat to contain.[16]

Information Warfare

Increased reliance on Information Age technologies by developed states and many developing states has increased the vulnerability of many countries and multinational corporations to attacks on their information and information systems. Such attacks are called information warfare, and it could take many forms.

For example, computer hardware and software could be destroyed or degraded. Critical information could be acquired or altered. False information could be inserted. Unauthorized access could be obtained and unauthorized directions given. Important services and functions could be denied. Confidence in systems could be undermined.[17]

These dangers have led some officials to warn about the possibility of an "electronic Pearl Harbor" in which information warfare could bring a country or a corporation to a complete and devastating halt. Other observers have dismissed such warnings as overblown. Although the debate has not been resolved, a threat exists, as shown in 2000 when computers and websites used by the U.S. government as well as businesses as diverse as CNN, Home Depot, and Amazon.com came under attack from hackers. The computers and websites of non-U.S. governments and businesses have also often been attacked.

The sources of attack are many. In addition to individuals, the U.S. intelligence community estimates that more than 120 governments and nongovernmental organizations are pursuing information warfare efforts. Several of the governments are potentially hostile toward the U.S. Nongovernmental organizations that pursue such efforts include terrorist organizations, organized crime, and drug cartels.

How serious are the challenges and threats? *Critical Foundations: Protecting America's Infrastructures,* published in 1997 by a special U.S. presidential study team, highlighted the vulnerabilities of critical U.S. infrastructures including communications and telephones, banking, power grids, emergency response systems, water systems, fuel supply networks, and other systems that rely extensively on computers and information systems.[18] Vulnerabilities were further illustrated in a 1997 war game named "Eligible Receiver" in which a team of National Security Agency hackers penetrated military computer networks in Hawaii, Washington, Chicago, St. Louis, and Colorado. They also gained access to systems aboard a U.S. Navy cruiser at sea, could have closed down the United States' electric power grid, and positioned themselves to disable the 911 network in Washington, D.C. and other U.S. cities.[19]

In response to these vulnerabilities, the U.S. government expanded its efforts to improve information and communication security by changing a number of policies and by increasing its expenditures on computer security. What remains unclear is the extent to which defensive measures will lessen the dangers of information warfare given society's increased reliance on information and communication technologies.

The danger, then, both of nonnuclear weapons of mass destruction and of information warfare, is real, although the magnitude of threat is unclear. And the danger is real both to and from state and nonstate actors. With that in mind, we now turn to the military capabilities of nonstate actors.

MILITARY CAPABILITIES OF NONSTATE ACTORS

Traditionally, at least since the Treaty of Westphalia, states have been the primary repositories of military capabilities. So far, this chapter has followed a traditional approach and examined primarily those aspects of military capabilities that are directly controlled by states themselves. By itself, such analysis yields an incomplete view of the dimensions of military power in international affairs. Not only states have enhanced their power potential by attaining military capabilities. Other actors have followed and will continue to follow the path that states took. Ethnic/national liberation organizations, terrorist groups and movements, and religious movements and political parties have consciously attempted on occasion to increase their power by acquiring additional military capabilities. A few nongovernmental organizations, certain intergovernmental organizations, and some multinational corporations have also yielded to the attraction to influence actors and events through military power. So, too, have other international economic interests. For example, in 1990, rumors circulated throughout the Americas that South American drug interests had offered a $30 million contract for the assassination of President George Bush.

With the exception of a few IGOs designed specifically or primarily as military alliances and an occasional transnational religious movement or political party, nonstate actors rarely possess the wherewithal to procure and maintain military forces of great size or power. Nevertheless, the military capabilities that these other actors do possess enable them to engage in various types of nontraditional violence, including civil wars, terrorism, and other types of low intensity conflict. As we have seen, information warfare may also become a preferred tool of nonstate actors as well. Often, states, or more precisely governments of states, are the targets of nontraditional violence and other attacks.

It is difficult, if not impossible, to determine objectively the boundary between the wanton destruction and death caused by terrorists, the guerrilla war (sometimes called "low-intensity conflict") pursued by weak national liberation movements, and the civil war fought by stronger national liberation movements. Yet in each of these cases, the user of military capabilities as a tool or potential tool of violence is not a state. Nontraditional violence, then, may be most simply defined as violence between any two international actors at least one of which is a nonstate actor.

Even though nonstate actors rarely have the military capabilities at their disposal that major state actors have, their ability to influence the course of world events is sometimes considerable. George Washington and the Continental Army fought against the world's premier military power, and neither Washington nor his army represented a state actor. They won, and in so doing changed world history. Lenin and his Bolsheviks were little more than a splinter political party when they used their military capabilities to seize the Russian state in 1917; despite their limited military capabilities, they succeeded in maintaining control of the state, in part because of weak and divided opposition and in part because of Lenin's skilled leadership. Some 40 years later, Fidel Castro used military force to take over Cuba, again with startling effects for the international community. Indeed, many of the states that were formed out of the old European empires received their independence because indigenous nonstate actors, generally national liberation movements, used their military prowess to prove to their colonial masters that the costs of administering an empire were too great to bear. From Jomo Kenyatta in Kenya to Robert Mugabe in Zimbabwe, leaders of ethnic or national liberation movements have often resorted to their military arms to enhance their power. Only Mahatma Gandhi, the Indian independence leader, successfully resorted to nonviolence and passive resistance to achieve independence for his country from a colonial power that, at the outset of the struggle, preferred to maintain control.

It is a statement of the obvious that military capabilities are key ingredients of civil wars. Indeed, of the 25 conflicts listed in Table 14-1, all but one of them could be considered a civil war. And in all but two, at least one side and in some instances both sides (or more) are nonstate actors.

This is not a new phenomenon. For example, the Chinese Civil War pitted Chiang Kai-shek's government forces against Mao Zedong's nongovernment communist forces. The repercussions of this epic confrontation, civil in character, continue today. Here it would also be proper to note that at the height of the Chinese Civil War, Mao fielded an army of over 1 million men. Obviously, the military capabilities available to nonstate actors can sometimes be large.

Washington, Lenin, Castro, Kenyatta, Mugabe, and Mao were all leaders who used the military capabilities at the disposal of the nonstate actors they led to enhance the power of their respective movements. In each case, military capabilities played a decisive role in aiding the respective movements to attain their objectives. In other cases, however, the use of military capabilities by nonstate actors has strengthened the actor temporarily, even though final objectives may not be attained. Biafran secessionists, El Salvadorian guerrillas, and the PLO all turned or turn to the military as an instrument to increase their ability to influence events.

Terrorist use of military capabilities may also have great impact on world politics. (Again, please recall the difficulty in defining terrorism. The PLO, the IRA, the Mau-Maus, the Red Brigade, and a variety of organizations and groups are sometimes described as ethnic or national liberation movements, political parties, or religious movements, but are viewed by many others as terrorists.) Efforts to assassinate prominent world leaders such as Pope John Paul II have shocked the global community; if those efforts had been successful, the shock would have been magnified many times. The 1981 assassination of Anwar Sadat by religious dissidents within the Egyptian army threw much of the Middle East into turmoil, at least until Sadat's successor, Hosni Mubarak, clarified his policy intentions. The 1995 assassination of Israeli Premier Yitzhak Rabin by a right wing Israeli radical had a similar effect, at least temporarily, on the ongoing Middle East peace process.

For the most part, nonstate actors have basic military arsenals. They do not fly high-performance aircraft, use state-of-the-art land equipment, or have access to other advanced military capabilities. This detracts from their military potential. However, as they rarely seek to fight their opponent or enemy in a standing battle, this diminution of power is not so serious as may be supposed. As the 1995 bombing of the Oklahoma City federal building and gas attacks on the Tokyo subway show, the ability of nonstate actors to engage in even limited violence with unsophisticated weapons can have an immense impact on societies.

On some occasions, modern weaponry has been obtained by nonstate actors. The PLO has heavy tanks, artillery, and armored personnel carriers; the Zimbabwe Patriotic Front had surface-to-air missiles; Mao's People's Liberation Army had heavy artillery and other main force weapons; and the Afghan guerrillas acquired Stinger surface-to-air missiles. These groups and organizations had neither the industrial capacity nor the economic base to produce these weapons, so where do they come from?

Four answers are possible. First, states sometimes furnish sizable quantities of military equipment to selected nonstate actors. These arms transfers rarely appear in official statistics on international arms transfers. For example, the Soviet Union provided the PLO with virtually all of its tanks, artillery, and armored personnel carriers. During the 1980s, the United States also provided extensive support to guerrillas fighting against pro-Soviet governments in Afghanistan, Angola, Cambodia, and Nicaragua. (In the case of Nicaragua, at least some of the aid was provided illegally, as was discovered during the 1987 Iran–Contra hearings.) The purpose of these U.S. actions, as was and is the purpose of other state actors who provide weapons for nonstate actors, is straightforward: to help the nonstate actor achieve its objectives, which inevitably coincide with the objectives of the aid donor, and to strengthen political ties between donor and recipient. In more extreme cases of state support to nonstate actors, the phenomenon of state-supported terrorism develops. The state that supplies the nonstate actor in these instances may deny that it is supporting a terrorist organization, but from the perspective of the state whose interests are attacked by the nonstate actors, things look different.

A second source of weapons and arms for nonstate actors is through defection. Mao's forces were greatly strengthened by men—and the weapons they brought with them—from the Kuomintang. In Afghanistan during the 1980s, anti-Soviet forces were also strengthened by defections from the army of the pro-Soviet Afghan regime.

The international demand for arms has also led to the development of a large, illicit trade in weapons, a sizable percentage of which are purchased by nonstate actors. States have attempted to control arms trade by issuing end-user certificates and by implementing arms export control legislation, but arms dealers have used many methods ranging from forged certificates to refusing to report exports to circumvent the legislation. Illicit arms traffic to nonstate actors accelerated during the 1980s and continues today.

The final major method nonstate actors employ to acquire arms is through theft and capture. Particularly in the Developing World, theft of military equipment from state military forces presents a major problem; however, it is a problem not restricted to the Developing World. Thus, when in 1990 civil war broke out in Soviet Azerbaijan between Armenians and Azerbaijanis, both sides raided Soviet army depots to obtain weapons. Furthermore, opponents' weapons are often used by nonstate actors. The Vietcong, for example, used old French and new American weapons that they had captured during much of the Vietnam War, at least until Soviet aid was accelerated.

Perhaps the greatest fear related to nonstate actors' military capabilities is at the level of weapons of mass destruction. This problem was addressed earlier in this chapter, but must be addressed here again. It is an issue that is particularly acute in the nuclear arena, but that also extends to chemical and biological weapons. Although nuclear proliferation at the state level is an issue of concern throughout the world, an equal concern exists about the potential for terrorist groups to acquire a nuclear weapon. If it was true at the state level that those having the least to lose may be the most willing to use nuclear weapons, then it is even more true at the nonstate level. The threat of nuclear terrorism—and chemical and biological terrorism as well—is real.

At the other extreme from terrorist groups and organizations are intergovernmental organizations. Whereas terrorists seek to undermine state governments and social structures with their military capabilities, IGOs—at least those that have a military arm—attempt to defend and further the interests of member states. IGOs receive whatever military capacity they have from member states. UN peacekeeping forces, NATO, and OAU peacekeeping forces are all composed of units from member states. The units are generally employed only when widespread agreement exists within the IGO about the proposed employment. Obviously, this creates a major constraint on the use of military capabilities by IGOs. NATO countries will not designate forces for use outside European theater areas, the OAU had difficulty funding a peacekeeping force in Chad, and the United Nations Secretariat must develop not only funding sources and a political consensus in the UN before peacekeeping can begin, but also find states willing to have their troops participate in proposed peacekeeping efforts.

Quantitatively and qualitatively, the aggregate military capabilities under the control of nonstate actors is probably less than military capabilities in the arsenal of a midrank power such as Great Britain or France. (This observation excludes NATO and other defense- or security-related IGOs.) Nevertheless, because of the types of objectives nonstate actors pursue and the methods that they choose to use, the power they acquire from their weapons capabilities is disproportionately large. They rarely have territory or complex infrastructures to defend, and the threat of the use of force is, for them, perhaps even more effective than the actual use of force. At the level of nonstate actor, then, military capabilities continue to have subjective and objective components, even as they did at the state level. With few economic tools at their disposal, military capabilities remain the major parameter of power for many nonstate actors.

 ## MILITARY CAPABILITIES AND POWER

Despite the increased complexity of international relations during the twenty-first century, the military capabilities of an international actor continue to supply a major input to an actor's power potential. In the twenty-first century as before, international actors find it necessary to resort to force. They must and do prepare themselves for that contingency, even if the ethics and morality of using force or threatening to use force are sometimes open to question.

This chapter has traced the major trends in the relationship between power and military capabilities. More states are acquiring more weapons, and the quality and lethality of the weapons they attain is rising. Militarily speaking, states are becoming more powerful in absolute terms but rarely improving their power potential in relative terms. The great powers of the 1990s—France, Great Britain, China, and a very few others—would have been superpowers in the 1940s or 1950s if they had then the armaments and weapons they have now. Today, none is a military match for the world's one remaining military super-power, the United States.

Another comparison may be more telling. Before the Persian Gulf War, Iraq could put 5,500 tanks and 689 combat aircraft into the field. These totals were more than Hitler used to invade France in 1940. And their capabilities dwarfed those of Hitler's weapons. Nevertheless, in 1990, Iraq was not even considered a great power.

Even with these major trends, military capabilities do not translate directly into increased power potential. Powerful weapons used unintelligently add little to a state's power; certain types of weapons are not useful in certain situations; and the will to act must be present as well. For example, France had what was arguably the world's finest tank in its arsenal in 1940 but deployed it as an infantry support vehicle. Because of its style of deployment, it proved virtually useless. Similarly, U.S. nuclear weapons were useless in Vietnam, and Soviet tanks proved of limited utility in Afghanistan. In the U.S. case, nuclear weapons were inappropriate because of the scale and type of damage they caused, and in the Soviet case, tanks proved poorly suited for use in Afghanistan's mountainous regions. Finally, concerning will, United States armed forces were meaningless assets to effect the rescue of the U.S. hostages in Teheran once the hostages' safe return was elevated to the highest national priority. The will to use force did not exist.

The question of will returns us once again to the subjective and objective components of military capabilities. It cannot be emphasized enough that the degree of power that an actor acquires from its military abilities is a function not only of relatively objective qualitative, quantitative, and organizational parameters, but also of completely subjective parameters such as morale, cohesion, and will. These subjective parameters are rendered even more abstract because they are measured and assessed not only by the actor, but also by those that the actor is attempting to influence. Thus, the power that an actor acquires from its military capabilities is seen differently by different actors. Power, in the military sphere as elsewhere, is as much perceptual and reputational as actual.

Above the assessments of power and military capabilities hovers the reality that humans in their quest to influence others by force of arms and to prevent others from influencing them by force of arms have created and are dispersing military capabilities unrivaled in recorded history. It is disconcerting to realize that despite the death and destruction that twentieth-century wars caused, humanity has come no further than it has on arms control and arms limitation efforts.

Given the immense destructive capacity of nuclear weapons, it is even more frightening to realize that the next global war, if there is one, may end civilization as we know it. Albert Einstein once observed that although he did not know what types of weapons would be used in World War III, he could predict what weapons would be used in World War IV: sticks and stones.

Power and military capabilities, then, remain integrally related. Before the late 1980s, nothing indicated that state or nonstate actors were slowing their efforts to acquire those capabilities, both in hope of enhancing their own power and in fear that unless they improved their own capabilities, they would fall behind. But in the 1990s, East–West tensions ended, several efforts to resolve regional conflicts proved successful, and several major arms control agreements were concluded. So there is a glimmer of hope that despite the outbreak of new and serious conflicts in many regions of the world, the mad momentum to acquire more and better arms will continue to slow as the twenty-first century unfolds.

 ## *KEY TERMS AND CONCEPTS*

objective and subjective components of military power   military power has objective components such as the quantity of weapons and men as well as subjective components such as strategy and will

military power in the post-Cold War world   although some predicted military power would become less important after the Cold War ended, it has remained an important component of national strength

dimensions of military expenditures   although military spending has decreased since the end of the Cold War, it remains sizable

peace dividend   the money saved as a result of reduced military spending after the Cold War ended

dimensions of increased military capabilities   military capabilities have become increasingly more lethal and are available to more and more international actors

reasons for international arms trade   reasons to buy or sell arms include strategic advantage, profit, reducing the per unit cost of weapons to the supplying state, obsolescence of weapons in one's arsenal, and improving one's own military capabilities

impacts of military capabilities and expenditures   reasons for expenditures include national security, internal security, and prestige. Military expenditures have social costs including diverting money from other socially-useful expenditures; increasing inflation; and increasing the risk of war

nuclear arms race   the competition that developed shortly after World War II between the U.S. and the U.S.S.R. to have the best and largest nuclear arsenal

fusion weapons   thermonuclear weapons, i.e. H-Bombs, which release energy by fusing atoms together

fission weapons   atomic bombs, which release energy by splitting atoms

intercontinental ballistic missile (ICBM)   missiles capable of travelling from one continent to another

missile gap   the fear in the U.S. in the late 1950s and early 1960s that the U.S.S.R. had more and better missiles than the U.S.

Cuban Missile Crisis   a confrontation between the U.S. and U.S.S.R. in 1962 when the U.S.S.R. tried to place medium range missiles in Cuba

multiple independently targettable reentry vehicle (MIRV)   a system in which one ICBM can deliver several nuclear weapons to different targets

Strategic Arms Limitation Treaties (SALT I and II)   the 1972 SALT I limited the number of nuclear delivery platforms that each side could have. The 1976 SALT II attempted to limit quantitative and qualitative improvements in the U.S. and Soviet nuclear arsenals

Strategic Arms Reduction Treaties (START I and II)   the 1991 START I called for 30% reductions in the U.S. and Soviet strategic arsenals, while the 1993 START II, although not ratified by both sides until 2000, called for reductions in the two countries' arsenals of over 50%

deterrence and mutual deterrence   deterrence is preventing another state from attacking by having the ability to inflict unacceptable damage to the attacking state even if it attacks first. Mutual deterrence is when both sides are deterred

mutual assured destruction (MAD)   when both sides can absorb a nuclear attack and still have enough nuclear weapons survive to destroy the initiating side as a modern society

triad   three separate types of nuclear-capable delivery vehicles—bombers, ICBMS, and submarine-launched ballistic missiles

Nuclear Non-Proliferation Treaty (NPT)   signatory states to this 1968 treaty agree that they will not develop nuclear weapons, and if they have them, work to reduce the size of their nuclear arsenals

Comprehensive Test Ban Treaty (CTBT)   the 1996 treaty that bans all nuclear weapons testing, thereby broadening the 1963 NPT

non-nuclear weapons of mass destruction   chemical and biological weapons

information warfare   attacks by one state on another's information and information systems, often undertaken by computers

military capabilities of non-state actors   some IGOs like NATO are designed specifically for military purposes. Others such as the U.N. perform military "peace-keeping" functions. National liberation movements and terrorists may also have military capabilities

WEBSITE REFERENCES

military expenditures: *www.sipri.se/projects/milex.html*   website for the Stockholm International Peace Research Institute's Project on Military Expenditure and Arms Production

global military capabilities: *www.iiss.org/scripts/index.asp*   website for the International Institute for Strategic Studies

nuclear arms race: *www.fas.org/nuke/index.html*   website of the Federation of American Scientists

arms control: *www.armscontrol.org/home.htm*   webpage for the Arms Control Association

weapons of mass destruction: *cns.miis.edu*   website of the Monterey Institute for International Studies' Center for Nonproliferation Studies

information warfare: *infowar.com*   discussions of and links to articles about information warfare

NOTES

1. Carl von Clausewitz, *On War* (Princeton: Princeton University Press, 1976).

2. For an excellent series of articles on the relationship between military capabilities and power, see Robert J. Art and Kenneth N. Waltz, eds., *The Use of Force: Military Power and International Politics* (New York: University Press of America, 1993).

3. *World Military Expenditures and Arms Transfers 1988* (Washington, DC: U.S. Government Printing Office, 1988), p. 27.

4. See Aaron Karp, *Ballistic Missile Proliferation* (New York, NY: Oxford University Press, 1995).

5. For greater detail on the international arms trade, see William W. Keller, "The Arms Trade: Business as Usual," *Foreign Policy* (Winter 1997–98), pp. 113–25; and Tim Huxley and Susan Willett, "Arming East Asia," *Adelphi Paper 329* (London: International Institute for Strategic Studies, 1999)

6. For Eisenhower's own thoughts on the subject, see Dwight D. Eisenhower, *The White House Years* (Garden City, NY: Doubleday, 1963–1965).

7. As reported in Coral Bell, *Negotiations from Strength* (New York: Alfred A. Knopf, 1963), p. 141.

8. International Institute for Strategic Studies, *The Military Balance 1999–2000,* (Oxford: Oxford University Press, 1999) p. 25.

9. For the full texts of SALT I and SALT II and other related materials, see U.S. Arms Control and Disarmament Agency (ACDA), *Arms Control and Disarmament Agreements: Texts and Histories of Negotiations* (Washington, DC: U.S. Government Printing Office, 1982), pp. 148–157, 239–277.

10. See Alton Frye, "How to Fix SALT," *Foreign Policy,* No. 39 (Summer 1980), pp. 58–73; Edward L. Rowny, "Soviets Are Still Russians," *Survey,* Vol. 25 (Spring 1980), pp. 1–9; and J. Muravchik, "Expectations of SALT I: Lessons for SALT III," *World Affairs* (Winter 1980–1981), pp. 278–297.

11. For additional discussions on the debate over the ratification of START II and other arms control agreements as well as the future of arms control , see Harold Brown, "Is Arms Control Dead," James Schlesinger, "The Demise of Arms Control?," Thomas Graham, "Strengthening Arms Control," John Steinbruner, "Renovating Arms Control Through Reassurance," Stephen Cambone, "An Inherent Lesson in Arms Control," and Brad Roberts, "The Road Ahead for Arms Control," all in *The Washington Quarterly* (Spring 2000), pp. 171–232. See also Sumner Benson, "Competing Views on Strategic Arms Reduction," *Orbis* (Fall 1998), pp. 587–604.

12. For discussions of post-Cold War nuclear strategy and thought, see Robert Manning, "The Nuclear Age: The Next Chapter," *Foreign Policy* (Winter 1997–98), pp. 79–98; Thomas R. Bendel and William S. Murray, "The Bounds of the Possible: Nuclear Command and Control in the Information Age," *Comparative Strategy* (October-December 1999), pp. 313–28; and Robert Rudney and Willis Stanley, "Dealerting Proposals for Strategic Nuclear Forces," *Comparative Strategy* (January-March 2000), pp. 1–34.

13. See Francois Heisbourg, "The Prospects for Nuclear Stability between India and Pakistan," *Survival* (Winter 1998–99), pp. 77–92; Brahma Chellaney, "After the Tests: India's Options," *Survival* (Winter 1998–99), pp. 132–149; and Hilary Synnott, The Causes and Consequences of South Asia's Nuclear Tests," *Adelphi Paper 332* (London: International Institute for Strategic Studies, 1999) for further discussion on India's and Pakistan's nuclear tests and their implications.

14. The dangers of nuclear proliferation are discussed in George Perkowich, "Nuclear Proliferation," *Foreign Policy* (Fall 1998), pp. 12–23; and Therese Delpech, "Nuclear Weapons and the New World Order: Early Warning from Asia?," *Survival* (Winter 1998–99), pp. 57–76.

15. The CTBT is discussed in "Nuclear Weapons: The Comprehensive Test Ban Treaty," *Congressional Digest* (December 1999), pp. 289–314; and "Failing Grade: The Senate Rejects the Test Ban Treaty," *Amicus Journal* (Winter 2000), p.10.

16. For additional discussion on weapons of mass destruction, see Richard Betts, "The New Threat of Mass Destruction," *Foreign Affairs* (January-February 1998), pp. 26–41; Richard A. Falkenrath, "Confronting Nuclear, Biological, and Chemical Terrorism," *Survival* (Autumn 1998), pp. 43–65; and John B. Roberts, "Will Terrorists Go Nuclear?," *The American Spectator* (July-August 2000), pp. 36–41.

17. For a few of the many recent works on information warfare, see for example Roger C. Molander, et al., *Strategic Information Warfare: A New Face of War* (Santa Monica, CA: RAND, 1996); Roger C. Molander (ed.), *Strategic Information Warfare Rising* (Washington, D.C.: U.S. Department of Defense, 1999); John Arquilla and David Ronfeldt, *In Athena's Camp: Preparing for Conflict in the Information Age* (Santa Monica, CA: RAND, 1997); William A. Owens, "The Emerging System of Systems," *Military Review* (May-June 1995), pp. 15–19; Stuart J. Schwartzstein, ed., *The Information Revolution and National Security* (Washington, D.C.: Center for Strategic and International Studies, 1996); and Daniel S. Papp and David S. Alberts, *The Information Age Anthology, Volumes II and III* (Washington, D.C.: National Defense University Press, 2000 and 2001).

18. President's Commission on Critical Infrastructure Protection, *Critical Foundations: Protecting America's Infrastructures: Excerpts from the Report of the President's Commission on Critical Infrastructure Protection* (Washington, D.C.: U.S. Government Printing Office, 1997).

19. For details on Eligible Receiver, see *The Washington Times,* April 16, 1998; and John Christensen, "Bracing for Guerrilla Warfare in Cyberspace," CNN Interactive, April 6, 1999. See also the statement by Mr. Kenneth H. Bacon, Department of Defense News Briefing, April 16, 1998.

Chapter 15

Other Parameters of Power

International Law, Diplomacy,
and Sociopolitical Elements of Power

- What internal and external factors besides economics and the military add to or detract from an international actor's power?
- How effective is international law and what types of law exist?
- Who interprets and enforces international law?
- What is diplomacy and how has it changed over time?
- What are sociopolitical elements of power and how do they affect an international actor's power?

Discussions of the power potential of international actors too often are limited to the subjective and objective aspects of economic and military capabilities. Although economic and military capabilities are demonstrably important, other parameters are also crucial in determining an actor's power potential. If one measured solely the economic and military capabilities of North Vietnam and the Vietcong during the late 1960s, one would have concluded that the North Vietnamese–Vietcong tandem could not stand up to U.S. economic and military might. One would also have been wrong. Similarly, a comparison of solely the Soviet and Afghan guerrilla economic and military capabilities would lead one to conclude that the USSR would win in a conflict. One would have again been wrong. Numerous other examples exist of superior economic and/or military actors being defeated by, losing influence to, or having their policies frustrated by less capable economic and/or military actors.

Why? What enabled Mao to overcome Chiang Kai-shek, when Chiang, at least at first, had at his disposal the wealth and productive capacity of all of China's cities and the military capability of most of China's men and weapons? What enabled Gandhi to drive the British from India, and how did Khomeini undermine the shah? What gives the United Nations so prominent and persuasive a voice in international affairs when its economic and military capabilities are so limited? Why does the pope command such respect and allegiance throughout the Catholic and non-Catholic worlds? Why couldn't the United States win in Vietnam, and why couldn't the Soviets win in Afghanistan? There are no easy answers to these and other similar questions, but it is clear that the answers lie beyond the realm of economic and military parameters of power.

In this chapter, we will explore three different elements of power that for the most part lie outside economic and military affairs: international law, diplomacy, and sociopolitical elements of power. Each has the ability to constrain or add to an actor's power.

 ## INTERNATIONAL LAW

International law may best be viewed as a system of agreements between international actors, usually states, that defines how relations between and among them will be conducted. International law is not new. Rudimentary international law can be traced back to the fourth millennium B.C., when warring parties agreed to stop conflicts for holiday and celebration periods and to send and receive emissaries from each other. Ancient Greece and Rome furthered the practice of establishing rules of conduct to be followed between political groupings. Homer's *Iliad* and Thucydides' *The Peloponnesian Wars* have many references to truces, acceptance of heralds, and other standards of accepted behavior between peaceful or warring parties. (The *Iliad* and *The Peloponnesian Wars* are equally filled with instances of agreements being violated).

As a constraint on power, international law attempts to limit how an international actor may act. Admittedly, it is not always effective. For example, laws of war exist but are sometimes ignored. Similarly, it is supposedly illegal to invade and take over an embassy, but this, too, has happened.

Yet international law is also often effective in limiting the international use of power. States trade for what they want more often than they simply take it. Most international agreements are in fact respected rather than ignored, even if the agreement proves over time not to be in the interest of the "more powerful" signatory actor. Thus, although it is not always effective, international law can constrain power.

How then may international law be viewed as an element of power? If it is adhered to, international law inserts a certain degree of predictability into the international arena. Assuming that laws are followed, predictability allows international actors to plan and rationalize policies, thereby enhancing power. At the same time, international law adds to a state's power by its defense of national sovereignty, the very basis of today's state-based international system.

The Evolution of International Law

Modern international law evolved as the modern state system developed. **Hugo Grotius,** a Dutchman, is commonly considered the father of modern international law because of his 1628 publication, *On the Law of War and Peace.* Grotius' work laid the intellectual foundation for the rights and responsibilities of states to each other. It is on Grotius's work that the contemporary system of international treaties, tribunals, and codes of conduct is built. Not only states but also IGOs, MNCs, and most NGOs accept and follow these precepts.[1]

Four different major interpretations of international law exist.[2] The **naturalist school,** exemplified by Samuel Pufendorf (*The Law of Nature and Nations,* 1672), argued that all law was derived from God's law and that law was therefore universal and unchangeable.

Chapter 15

IT AND SOCIOPOLITICAL POWER: THE MEDIA, HOLLYWOOD, AND DISNEY

How will the Information age affect sociopolitical power? Will the availability of always on, always connected, use-it-anywhere IT allow only a few sources of information, news, and entertainment to set global values and outlooks? Or will advanced IT lead to a diffusion of values and outlooks? A look backwards may help guide us forward.

In the twentieth century, American television, movies, and music could be found around the world. To most Americans, this was comforting. They could watch MTV in London or Lagos, hear Madonna in Tokyo or Taipei, and see "Star Wars" in Bangkok or Buenos Aires. However, many people outside the U.S. resented this, believing that these mediums spread U.S. economic and political influence and promoted U.S. views on sex, violence, and other social norms, thereby undermining traditional values.

As a result, some developing and communist states accused the United States of "electronic imperialism." The USSR even denounced Walt Disney's cartoons as an American plot to control global culture. France also resented the dominance of U.S. media, passing laws that limited the amount of U.S. programming that aired.

The belief that TV, movies, and music spread U.S. influence and values strengthened the view in some countries that media content must be censored. Some states insisted that TV, movies, and music include values that they wanted their citizens to emulate, while others censored content to assure that it coincided with their policies.

Censorship did not always succeed. Indeed, a strong case can be made that communism's collapse was in part a result of the seepage of Western ideas and values into Eastern Europe and the USSR via the media. Western ideas and values also gained ground in developing states despite censorship by some governments. Demonstrably, the media, Hollywood, and Disney played major roles in spreading Western outlooks and values. Beholden only to themselves, they wielded considerable sociopolitical power.

What, then, may we expect in the Information Age as always on, always connected, use-it-anywhere IT becomes widely available? Two opposite trends are apparent.

On the one hand, advanced IT will allow people more frequently to see and hear viewpoints and outlooks that they find attractive. The influence of such viewpoints and outlooks may therefore be expected to grow. Conversely, with more people, institutions, and organizations able to transmit their viewpoints and outlooks, it may be difficult to gain an audience. This occurred in the United States when cable television with hundreds of channels became available, reducing the market share of ABC, CBS, and NBC.

Which trend will win? Will sociopolitical power become highly concentrated because of Information Age IT, or will it become more diffuse? The evidence is mixed, but regardless of which trend prevails, the implications for sociopolitical power and international relations are immense.

The naturalist school found its intellectual and philosophical heritage in St. Augustine, who argued that war was justifiable in self-defense or to punish evil. Naturalists sought a universally acceptable code for international law, but accepted the possibility that war could occur.

One problem with the naturalist interpretation of international law was that someone must determine what God's law is. This was no easy task. Given the record of European religious wars and the diversity of religions, cultures, and moralities that exist in the world, it was evident that those who sought to implement international standards based on natural law faced a formidable task. Naturalism also provided a ready rationale for those who wished to appeal to a higher authority to justify blatant territorial expansion and other aggressive behavior.

These problems of naturalist law led to the development of the **positivist school.** Led by Cornelius van Bynkershoek (*Forum for Ambassadors,* 1721, and *On Questions of Public Law,* 1737), positivists rejected divine authority as the basis for law and argued that the only law that existed was what its subjects agreed to. Positivists stressed that rights and responsibilities of international actors were protected by laws and standards of behavior that they themselves accepted.

The positivist position was and is criticized from two perspectives. First, states or other international actors could reject law simply by saying that they no longer agreed with it. Second, international actors could, in the absence of higher principles, declare whatever they desired to be law as long as mutual consent existed. To the naturalist, positivist law was amoral and immoral.

A third school evolved that attempted to bridge the gap between naturalists and positivists. Known as the **eclectic school** and led by Emmerich de Vattel (*The Law of Nations,* 1758), this school posited that two levels of law existed, one that was God-given, timeless, and universal, and the other that was man-made, finite, and voluntary. To the eclectic, man-made law was the natural result of man's effort to understand and interpret the meanings of natural law. To the eclectic, naturalist law and positivist law were simply different sides of the same coin.

A fourth major school of international law was the **neorealist school,** which asserted that rules were irrelevant, but policy and values were important. To the neorealist, international law was the product of the desires of the prevalent power(s). It was not timeless. It was not universal. And it might be imposed by power. To this school, international law was a product of power.

Basic Concepts of International Law

Despite the debate over the basis for international law, little disagreement exists about its sources. Article 38 of the Statute of the **International Court of Justice** lists four separate sources of law—international conventions, international customs, general principles, and subsidiary sources of law.[3]

International conventions are either bilateral or multilateral treaties and agreements that specifically commit a signatory actor to a particular type of conduct or to a particular set of standards. Of the four Article 38 sources of international law, it is the most explicit type and is valid only when two or more actors agree to abide by treaty or agreement provisions.

International customs refer to the general standard of behavior and action accepted by actors. It is a precept of international law that any widely accepted behavior or action over time becomes a part of the body of international law. Laws governing diplomatic and consular immunity and privilege as well as ocean law and high seas law evolved from the principle of international custom.

General principles of law are more vague than international customs. Expectation of reciprocal fair treatment and nonpersecution of foreign nationals, equal application of laws, and protection of personal property and life are included as "general principles of law recognized by civilized nations." They, in some interpretations, are said to be international customs. The distinction between custom and principle is difficult to draw, but may best be described as follows: Custom is practice, and principle is ideal.

Subsidiary sources are even more vague. They are generally considered interpretations of international law adopted by various courts and particularly by the International Court of Justice (ICJ). Here, a distinction between national law and international law must be made. Under most national legal systems, judicial precedence, or *stare decisis,* prevails. *Stare decisis* means that legal opinions and interpretations handed down in one case have relevance to other cases and should themselves be treated as law. Although most international tribunals accept *stare decisis,* the ICJ specifically does not.

Who are the subjects of international law? Originally, only states were. Over time, this has changed. Consequently, the current answer is more complicated. For example, although states have always been subject to international law, some states in certain situations declare that special circumstances prevail and that they therefore are exempt from the provisions of international law. For example, when the United States filed suit against Iran before the ICJ for the 1979 Iranian takeover of the U.S. embassy, Iran refused to recognize ICJ jurisdiction.

Other states have also ignored ICJ rulings. Thus, in 1984, the ICJ decided that it would accept a case filed by Nicaragua against the United States in which Nicaragua charged that the United States was arming and training rebels who sought to overthrow the Sandinista government of Nicaragua. Nicaragua requested the ICJ order the United States to end that support. The United States responded to the ICJ in 1985, declaring that it would not participate in the Nicaragua case because the case was "a misuse of the court for political and propaganda purposes." Later in 1985, the court reaffirmed its position that it had jurisdiction in the case, and the United States immediately reaffirmed its rejection of the court's position. Finally, in 1986, the ICJ ruled on the case, deciding in Nicaragua's favor and ordering the United States to stop arming and training the Contras. The United States rejected the ICJ's ruling, declaring that the court was "not equipped" to handle "complex international issues."

The Iran and Nicaragua cases raise the question of what issues that court can meaningfully decide. The obvious answer—and the correct answer—is those issues between states that states are willing to allow the court to decide. But in recent years, the jurisdiction of the ICJ has expanded to include international governmental organizations and multinational corporations. Even so, international organizations have on occasion flouted international law, but generally only with prior approval from their member states. Multinational corporations have only received widespread standing under international law since World War II. MNCs have been more successful gaining standing before regional legal bodies such as the Court of Justice of the European Community than before the ICJ.

The status of individuals under international law is expanding. Before the twentieth century, individuals were accountable to and protected by international law only through their governments. Following both World Wars, however, individuals were tried before international tribunals for acts of state and crimes against humanity, including initiating "aggressive war." A precedent was thus established for granting international tribunals jurisdiction over individuals. At the same time, as will be discussed in detail later in this book, international law is increasingly involved with defining and protecting the human rights of individuals. As we will see, however, this is an exceedingly difficult task for a number of reasons.

Other nongovernmental actors—terrorists, national liberation movements, transnational ideological and religious movements, and other NGOs—still have little access to global legal institutions, although their individual members may be subject to individual trials. At the regional level, somewhat better access exists. However, some NGOs such as terrorists and ideological or religious movements deny the legitimacy of current international legal practice. For them, access to the international legal system is irrelevant, as is the system itself.

What happens if an international actor will not comply with international law? Obviously, the situation is considerably different from that of domestic law. In a domestic case, the overriding ability of the state to apply sanctions prevails. In an international case, no entity has such overriding ability.

Traditionally, sanctions for breaches of international law have been left to the aggrieved party. In the most extreme cases, the ultimate sanction is war. But other types of sanctions are also sometimes used, especially economic sanctions. For example, in 1979 and 1980, the United States applied economic sanctions to Iran because of the hostage crisis and to the Soviet Union in 1980, 1981, and 1982 because of the Soviet invasion of Afghanistan and the declaration of martial law in Poland.

International organizations have on occasion attempted to apply sanctions when international law has been breached. Often, however, IGO-initiated sanctions fail because individual states place their own interests above those of international law. Under the League of Nations, for example, collective security was to be the guarantor of universal security. Collective security called for universal action against an aggressor. When Italy invaded Ethiopia, however, the international community conveniently found excuses to avoid action. Collective security failed, and the economic sanctions implemented proved ineffective.

The United Nations also has means at its disposal to institute sanctions, but it, too, must rely on member states to implement them. The United Nations Command in Korea became operational only because the United States footed the bill and provided most of the forces, and other UN peacekeeping missions live in continual jeopardy of supplier-nation withdrawal. UN economic sanctions have been implemented in a number of cases, notably against China in 1951 for its role in Korea, Southern Rhodesia in 1967 for its racial policy, Iraq in 1990 for its invasion of Kuwait, Serbia in 1992 for its "ethnic cleansing" campaign against Bosnia, and Khmer Rouge–held regions of Cambodia in 1992 for the Khmer Rouge's refusal to disarm as agreed under the terms of a Cambodian peace settlement. These sanctions proved of different value in different cases as UN member states pursued the policies they deemed appropriate. In the Chinese case, the Soviet Union and other communist states continued to trade with China. In the Southern Rhodesia case, the United States defined the sanctions to mean that ongoing trade was permissible whereas new trade was not. (The United States, it should be pointed out, imported most of its chromium from Rhodesia in 1967.) In the Iraqi case, almost all nations complied with UN sanctions against Iraq, and a naval and air blockade was imposed by several states including the United States to help enforce it. In the case of Serbia, many states enforced UN sanctions, but some did not. In the case of Khmer-held Cambodia, the dependence of Khmer-held regions of Cambodia on external trade was so small that the sanctions had little impact.

Obviously, sanctions that are available in the event of noncompliance with international law are weak. The decentralized mode of application of sanctions is the major drawback. And in some cases, it must be admitted that no meaningful sanctions can be applied. For example, when the United States decided that it would not comply with the ICJ's ruling that the United States must end its aid to the Contras in Nicaragua, there was little Nicaragua's Sandinista government could do to apply sanctions to the United States.

Yet to conclude that the weakness of sanctions means that international law does not exist or is irrelevant is erroneous. Although many breaches of international law are headline news, compliance with international law is by far the prevalent type of behavior in the international community. On a daily basis, far more treaties are kept than broken, whether they be extradition treaties or START treaties. For every day that an embassy staff is held hostage in contravention of international custom, thousands of days pass at embassies around the world without incident. The principle of freedom of the seas is only rarely challenged during peacetime. International law, despite it shortcomings, provides extensive predictability to today's international system.

Sovereignty, Statehood, and the Law of War

Despite the advantages that predictability affords to the international community, few states would accept international law if it undermined national sovereignty. **Sovereignty** under international law promises many rewards for states, for example, independence of action, jurisdiction over internal matters, freedom from external interference, and equality of legal standing. These rewards are sometimes more theoretical than actual, but their promise is significant, nonetheless.

Sovereignty is bestowed only on political entities that have acquired statehood. What, however, does statehood denote? Although we examined this question in some detail in Chapter 2, the question is again relevant here. When did the United States become a state, before or after it received formal independence from Great Britain? Was Guinea-Bissau a state before 1974, when it received formal independence from Portugal, simply because 81 states recognized it as independent? When did Mao's China formally join the family of states: when Mao seized power in 1949, when China joined the UN in 1971, when the

United States recognized it in 1979, or at some other time? When did Latvia, Lithuania, and Estonia cease to be states, or did they ever cease to be states? Conversely, if they did cease to be states during their time as Soviet republics, when did they become states again—when they declared their independence or when the Soviet Union dissolved? And what of East Timor? Did it become a state in 1975 when Portugal left? Or did it become a part of Indonesia because Indonesia invaded it in 1975 and occupied it until 1999? But if it were really a part of Indonesia between 1975 and 1999, why did only a handful of countries accept its incorporation as part of Indonesia?

There is no single answer to these questions. The Montevideo Convention of 1933 attempted to establish rules for statehood. It said that any political entity seeking statehood required a permanent population, a government that could rule that population, the ability to conduct relations with other states, and a defined territory. Other requirements also existed, including that the prospective state be recognized by other states.

Thus, the question of statehood is closely tied to recognition. One of the major theories of recognition and statehood is the **constitutive theory,** which argues that a state or new government is not a legal entity until it is recognized. However, a problem exists with this theory of recognition and statehood: How many states must recognize the new government or state? International law responded by answering a "reasonable" number of states, but even that response clarified nothing. In a world with over 190 states, is a majority reasonable? Is a majority still reasonable if the majority consists primarily of ministates?

A more politically oriented answer, called the **declarative theory,** rejects the Montevideo Convention's requirement for external recognition for new governments and states. Under the declarative theory, the key element for statehood is when a government can effectively rule its indigenous population. This approach solves the problem of legitimacy. Under the declarative theory, if a government can maintain control over its population, its legitimacy is proven.

Critics of the declarative theory of statehood and recognition argue that it relies too heavily on considerations of governmental power and too little on considerations of governmental quality. Some Western authorities argue that no dictatorial or repressive regimes should ever be recognized or declared states. In the past, strident communist states such as Albania rejected the legitimacy of Western governments and refused to recognize them. Other communist states extended recognition even though they denied the legitimacy of Western governments.

In practice, states may exist as sovereign entities despite a lack of formal diplomatic recognition, as China and Southern Rhodesia both did for so long. Conversely, states may disappear even when they have extensive diplomatic recognition. Latvia, Lithuania, Estonia, and South Vietnam were proof of this. At a less extreme level, a widely recognized government in one state may disappear overnight, replaced by a new government that gradually legitimizes itself by acquiring extensive international diplomatic recognition. The history of Bolivia is proof of this. Statehood, in short, is both a pragmatic and a political concept.

Nevertheless, once statehood is acquired—either through territorial and population control or recognition—international law bestows sovereignty on the new state or government. The new entity therefore enjoys the same freedom of action that old ones do, including the freedom to follow or breach international law, to apply or ignore sanctions, and to make war. With war being the ultimate sanction, it is not surprising that international law devotes much of its effort to providing rules for starting, stopping, and fighting wars.

Jus belli, or the **law of war,** evolved after international legal scholars and jurists concluded that if war was unavoidable, then its destructiveness and brutality should be limited as much as possible. International law set itself the task of creating those limits. As a result, international lawyers of the nineteenth and early twentieth centuries created wideranging laws of war. Wars should be declared, combatants should be in uniform, noncombatants should be given safe conduct out of combat areas, open cities should not be attacked, merchant vessels of noncombatants should not be attacked unless they carried military goods, prisoners of war should be treated humanely, mercy and medical personnel and equipment should be exempted from attack—the list continued. Laws of war also sought to limit the types of weapons that could be used. Dumdum bullets, mustard gas, poison darts, and other weapons were ruled illegal by the Hague Conferences of 1899 and 1907. However, as technology advanced and weapons became more lethal, the efforts to limit the brutality and destructiveness of war through international law proved futile.

The law of war also concerned itself with defining *bellum justum* (**just war**) and *bellum injustum* (**unjust war**). Increasingly, however, jurists recognized the futility of their efforts to draw clear distinctions between the two. The concepts of just and unjust war relied heavily on an adequate and acceptable definition of aggressive war, and no widely accepted definition of aggressive war could be formulated. During the twentieth century, the distinction between peace and war became increasingly blurred, and it remains so today.

International law creates a contradictory situation when sovereignty, statehood, and the law of war are viewed together. Professor J. L. Brierly summed up this contradiction concisely, observing that international law's acceptance of state sovereignty created an international system in which states were "legally bound to respect each other's independence and other rights, and yet free to attack each other at will."[4]

International Law's New Directions

As the twentieth century drew to a close, international law began to move in significant new directions that only rarely had been considered in earlier years, especially reexamining and reinforcing certain laws of war, identifying and convicting violators of human rights, and developing international environmental agreements.

International law undertook these new directions for five reasons. The first was that the Cold War had ended. During the Cold War, the ideological, policy, and perceptual differences that divided East from West and that dominated international relations were so significant that international law had no real hope to move in new directions. To begin with, international law requires a great degree of consensus, and new directions require even greater consensus. This simply did not exist during the Cold War.

Second, during the late twentieth century there were many cases of extreme inhumanity and brutality in warfare. The Khmer Rouge's genocide against fellow Cambodians in the 1970s, Iraq's use of gas during the 1980–88 Iran-Iraq War, the 1991–94 attacks by Somali factions against civilians and international relief efforts, Serbian ethnic cleansing programs in Bosnia in 1992–95 and Kosovo in 1998–99, and widespread indiscriminate use of landmines in many conflicts throughout the world slowly combined to galvanize the international community into action to improve the protection of human rights and redefine the laws of wars.

Third, information and communication technologies enabled more people to see the inhumanity and brutality. As real time global television became a reality in the 1970s and pervasive in the 1980s and 1990s, pictures of refugees, bodies, and burned out homes flooded the airwaves. The impact that such pictures had on raising public and elite awareness and mobilizing public and elite opinion in support of stricter laws of war and action against violators of human rights is hard to measure, but real.

Fourth, more and more people recognized that the global environment was deteriorating. This led people throughout the world to accept the need for enforceable international rules and laws to slow, stop, and reverse environmental deterioration. Such rules and laws proved difficult to formulate, but as the twentieth century dissolved into the twenty-first century, the awareness of this need was becoming more widespread.

Finally, nongovernmental organizations played an increasingly more active role in urging governments and the international legal community to reexamine and reinforce laws of war, identify and convict violators of human rights, formulate international environmental agreements and develop sanctions against those who ignored them. While the impact of NGOs in this effort should not be overstated, neither should it be overlooked.

International laws' new directions regarding laws of war, human rights, and the environment were not unanimously accepted or applauded. All challenged national sovereignty, an issue of great concern to countries as diverse as China, India, Russia, Syria, and the United States. They also often required the application of universal standards of human rights, a concept challenged by countries as varied as Afghanistan, Colombia, Iran, Kenya, Singapore, and Zimbabwe. Several of the new directions raised concerns in some countries including the United States about the possibility of politically motivated prosecutions. And many developing states were concerned that environmental rules and laws would constrain their economic development.

Nevertheless, to reiterate, by the beginning of the twenty-first century, international law had begun to reexamine and reinforce laws of war, identify and convict violators of human rights, and plan to develop sanctions against those who ignored international environmental agreements. These new directions are explored in greater depth in Chapters 17 (War, Peace, and Violence); 18 (Human Rights and Conflicts of Value); and 19 (The Environment and Health).

 ## *DIPLOMACY*

Diplomacy, defined here in its most general sense as the implementation of an international actor's policies toward other actors, establishes a set of expectations about what an international actor will and will not do. To the extent that expectations of others about what an actor will do limit what an actor does, diplomacy may be considered a constraint on power. Diplomacy creates expectations, and expectations can be ignored only at a cost.

Conversely, skillful diplomacy can also increase an international actor's power to the extent that it implements an actor's policies toward others in the most effective way. Not all states are equally skilled in diplomacy; inept diplomacy may weaken an actor's international position. However, this does not detract from the fact that skillful diplomacy can add to an international actor's power. Economically or militarily weak actors can and do strengthen their international positions with skillful diplomatic initiatives, and economically or militarily strong actors can and do lose standing as a result of diplomatic blunders.

More often than not, diplomacy refers to state-to-state policies. However, nonstate actors conduct diplomacy as well. For example, a diplomatically skillful leader of a national liberation movement may convince others that his or her cause is so just that it receives more support than it otherwise would receive. Here, however, we concentrate on diplomacy as a tool of state actors.[5]

The Evolution of Diplomacy

Diplomacy is an old activity, dating back to ancient Greece and Rome. As we have seen in our discussion of international law, Homer's *Iliad* and Thucydides' *The Peloponnesian Wars* contain many references to diplomatic missions, treaties, negotiations, and other concepts associated with diplomacy. Ancient Rome also engaged in extensive diplomacy, although the Roman Empire is more noted for its military conquests.

As far as is known, the first professional diplomatic corps appeared in the Byzantine Empire following the collapse of Rome. Byzantium established the world's first department of foreign affairs, developed strict and complex diplomatic protocols, and actively sought intelligence about friend and enemy alike. Surrounded by enemies, Byzantium needed all the skill in diplomacy it could muster.

The art of diplomacy was carried to the next higher (some might say lower) plane in Italy during the fifteenth and sixteenth centuries. The Italian city-states of the era engaged in constant intrigues against each other. During this era, diplomacy became identified with behind-the-scenes scheming, duplicity, and double-dealing. Niccolo **Machiavelli** of Florence, whom many consider the father of realpolitik views of the international system, stressed in his book *The Prince* (1532) that rulers should use whatever means they had at their disposal to stay in power.

Western European diplomacy continued to evolve in the seventeenth and eighteenth centuries, particularly in France. Under Louis XIV, the minister of foreign affairs became an important adviser to the King. Louis XIV also established embassies with permanent ambassadors who served as his official representatives in all major foreign capitals. For the first time, international treaties and agreements also required exact and specific wording.

The next stage in the evolution of Western diplomacy began at the end of the Napoleonic Wars with the 1815 Congress of Vienna. Throughout the nineteenth century, diplomatic practices were formalized and regularized. Ambassadors and their embassies attained an immense international importance, often creating and implementing their country's foreign policy on the scene with little control from their home capital. Diplomats were drawn almost exclusively from the nobility. Most diplomacy was conducted in secret. More often than not, diplomacy was bilateral, directly between two countries.

For the most part, nineteenth-century diplomacy sought to preserve the European balance of power as diplomats tried to maintain the status quo in Europe and in the colonial empires. Generally speaking, nineteenth-century diplomacy worked well, but it also planted the seeds for World War I.

World War I is frequently viewed as the watershed between "old" diplomacy with its emphasis on elitism, secrecy, bilateral agreements, and the importance of the embassy, and "modern" diplomacy with its emphasis on competency, openness, multilateral agreements, and personal conduct of affairs. With many people believing that nineteenth-century diplomacy's practices had caused World War I, it was perhaps inevitable that old diplomatic practices would change.

Following World War I, more and more countries began to emphasize competency as opposed to class connections in their diplomatic corps. Increasingly, diplomats came from a wider cross-section of society. This democratization of the diplomatic corps came in part from the belief that elitist diplomacy had lost touch with reality and as a result had spawned World War I. Competency—at least in theory—replaced class connections as a prerequisite for the diplomat.

In theory, **open diplomacy** also replaced secret diplomacy. Many people, particularly U.S. President Woodrow Wilson, believed that secret treaties concluded by secret diplomacy had been a primary cause of World War I. Wilson and others therefore called for "open covenants, openly arrived at." Thus, following World War I, open diplomacy became an ideal of modern diplomacy.

So, too, did **multilateral diplomacy,** in which many countries participated in diplomatic activity. Woodrow Wilson again led the way with his appeals for a League of Nations. Even after the league failed, the world's statesmen eventually created the United Nations. The states of the world also began to meet more frequently in conferences to discuss specific issues. Importantly, beyond these world bodies and multilateral conferences, an immense network of multilateral contacts developed between states following World War I, as we saw in our discussion of IGOs.

After World War I, personal diplomacy on the part of leaders of states also replaced reliance on ambassadors and embassies as a hallmark of diplomacy. One criticism of "old" diplomacy's reliance on ambassadors who operated relatively independently of control from their home government was that an ambassador might be working at cross-purposes to the home government. Some experts believed that this was one cause of World War I. Following World War I, in part because of this belief and in part because of technical breakthroughs in transportation and communications, many governments placed tighter reins on ambassadors and embassies. They relied more and more on personal diplomacy conducted by senior members of the government, usually the president and secretary of state in the United States, and their equivalents in other countries. These changes led to a new emphasis on summitry and public diplomacy, both of which are discussed below.

"Modern" diplomacy did not emerge overnight, and it did not completely replace "old" diplomacy. Even today, diplomacy often retains vestiges of elitism, secrecy, bilateralism, and ambassadorial and embassy independence. Indeed, a strong case can be made that effective diplomacy needs a certain degree of each of these. Elitism under certain conditions may abet competence, and secrecy sometimes can assist negotiations. On some occasions, bilateralism can achieve diplomatic breakthroughs that multilateralism cannot.

Similarly, ambassadorial initiatives can sometimes yield results that the personal diplomacy of senior government officials cannot.

In reality, "modern" diplomacy is a mix of new elements and old, with competency and elitism coexisting; openness and secrecy both serving their purposes; multilateral and bilateral diplomacy occurring simultaneously; and personal diplomacy and ambassador/embassy diplomacy blending together. The world of modern diplomacy is complex. We now turn to some of its specific purposes.

The Purposes of Modern Diplomacy

Modern diplomacy has six purposes, all concerned with the implementation of a state's policies toward other actors. These purposes are representing the state, gathering and interpreting information, signaling and receiving positions, conducting negotiations, managing crises, and influencing international public opinion. Each demands separate commentary.

Representation.   When diplomats are overseas, their official duty is to represent their country and its policies. Skillful diplomats project a favorable image of their country, and in so doing, aid their country in its efforts to achieve its objectives. Skillful diplomats also explain their country's policies and positions in ways that are both comprehensible and acceptable to the governments and peoples of the country to which they are assigned. When they find it impossible to present their country's policies and positions in acceptable ways, skillful diplomats attempt to minimize points of disagreement, emphasize points of agreement, and otherwise further their country's policy objectives. Obviously, in their representational capacity, skillful diplomats are a tremendous asset for a country.

Information Gathering and Interpreting.   Because good policies are usually based on good information, diplomats often find themselves gathering and interpreting information for their country. This does not mean that diplomats are spies. Rather, it is accepted throughout the world that one purpose of diplomats is to acquire and interpret information about the country in which they are posted.

There is a vague boundary between acceptable information gathering in the overt diplomatic community and unacceptable spying in the covert world of espionage. This is not the place to explore the dimensions of that boundary. Indeed, many embassies of many countries have personnel attached to them who have one overt responsibility, but whose primary responsibility is in fact the covert gathering of information.

Here, however, the emphasis is on the overt information gathering and interpreting function that all diplomats at all embassies have. It is accepted within the international community. Given the advantages that good information accurately interpreted gives to a country as it makes its own policies, a country whose diplomats are skilled information gatherers and interpreters is fortunate indeed.

Signaling and Receiving.   Sometimes, diplomats are vehicles through which their government communicates new and sometimes subtle position shifts to other countries. Similarly, diplomats are sometimes asked to float "trial balloons" to their opposite numbers to see how their opposite numbers' countries might respond to a policy or position change. Diplomats operating in this capacity serve as signaling agents for their country.

Diplomats often serve as receivers, as when a foreign government wishes to communicate information back to a diplomat's home country. Signaling and receiving are essentially opposite sides of the same coin of diplomatic communications. Seasoned diplomats frequently have well-developed signaling and receiving skills.

Negotiating.   All diplomats must engage in negotiations to some extent. At the highest levels, presidents and foreign ministers negotiate the final details of weighty international issues like arms control agreements and free trade agreements. At the lowest levels, consular officials decide who will receive travel documents. In between, diplomats negotiate a host of other issues. But in all cases, diplomats must be able to negotiate.

International negotiating is an art and a skill in which representatives from two or more countries meet to find or create areas of agreement among two or more different positions. Most international negotiating is done by ambassadors and their staffs, by senior government officials, or by national delegations with expertise on specific issues who attend international conferences and meetings. Often, international governmental organizations play important roles in organizing, sponsoring, moderating, or mediating such conferences and meetings.

A country whose diplomats are capable negotiators often is in an advantageous position relative to other international actors even when the strengths of its other parameters of power imply that it should be weaker. Negotiating is thus a key element of diplomacy and of national power.

Crisis Management.   When international crises break out that affect their own country and the country to which they are posted, diplomats sometimes find themselves on the front line of crisis management. In these situations, diplomats must use all their skills as they seek to defuse the crisis while simultaneously achieving their country's objectives.

As a general rule, the more serious a crisis is, the more likely it is that a senior official in the home capital, perhaps the national leader, the minister of foreign affairs, or even the entire senior executive branch, will focus on the problem and assume primary responsibility for crisis management and resolution. But even then, diplomats remain crucial. Even in crises, it is frequently through the ambassador or the embassy staff that representation, information gathering and interpreting, signaling and receiving, and negotiating take place. In crises, these functions are collectively elevated to a higher level of importance.

Public Diplomacy.   Finally, public diplomacy has become a critical part of the diplomatic repertoire. As a result of the communications and transportation revolutions, diplomats from national leaders on down can be seen and heard by more people in more places than at any previous time. Skillful public diplomacy can influence public opinion beyond one's own country to support one's country's policies and positions and can influence foreign peoples to have a favorable view of one's country. Conversely, blundering public diplomacy can undermine even well-conceived policies and positions and can project a negative image of a country.

At the highest level, superpower summitry must be viewed as the epitome of public diplomacy. Whatever the substantive content of such summits, most negotiations have been concluded by lower-level diplomats before the summit takes place. Without denying the importance of personal relationships that develop at superpower summits (both the Nixon–Brezhnev and Reagan–Gorbachev relationships come to mind), and recognizing that only national leaders can untie certain policy knots that may exist, one of the primary purposes of summitry is public diplomacy. Both sides seek to project a favorable image of themselves and their policies to domestic and international publics through summitry.

Public diplomacy is important at other levels as well. Diplomats often seek and accept speaking engagements, media interviews, and other ways in which they can obtain the opportunity to influence others to view their country and its policies favorably. At some times, such diplomacy may be considered by host countries as meddling in their internal affairs. At other times, such public diplomacy may be almost identical to a diplomat's representation function. Nevertheless, regardless of the level, public diplomacy is a central function of diplomacy and diplomats today.

SOCIOPOLITICAL ELEMENTS OF POWER

As different as law and diplomacy are from economic and military parameters of power, they are similar in that they are tangible, that is, they can be easily defined and identified. In this section, we explore a set of more intangible elements of power such as will and morale, character, and the ability to attract external support to one's own cause. These elements of power helped Gandhi drive the British from India, enabled Mao to attract more and more Chinese to his cause, and give the United Nations whatever degree of prestige it may have. These intangible elements are defined here as sociopolitical parameters of power.

Determinants of sociopolitical strength are diverse: ethnic and religious identity, legitimacy of cause, linguistic background, reputation, will and morale, character, ability to attract external support, cultural or conceptual integration or diversity, leadership, political strategy and tactics, and life-style are just a few of the more readily identifiable determinants.

They are also ever-changing. For example, Americans have become more willing to accept cultural diversity in the United States than they were during the 1950s. During the 1950s, cultural integration was extremely important. Cultural diversity was often viewed as "un-American" and shunned. Diversity was also believed to reduce U.S. sociopolitical capabilities. By the 1990s, however, cultural diversity was considered natural and even desirable, at least within certain bounds. Cultural integration became less important, and the prevalence of diversity was believed by all but the extreme political right to have little adverse impact on U.S. sociopolitical strength. What, then, is the **nature of sociopolitical parameters of power?**

Sociopolitical parameters of power are psychological in nature. The role of ethnicity as a determinant of sociopolitical power offers the best example. Ethnic *uniformity* has often been alluded to as a factor that enhanced national identity and hence national will in Germany, France, and Japan. Even today, citizens of these countries point to their ethnic uniformity as a symbol of national pride. Yet in the United States, ethnic *diversity* is often presented as an element of U.S. strength. Clearly, the part that ethnic uniformity or diversity plays in the international arena as a sociopolitical parameter of power is far from well defined.

Sociopolitical parameters of power are also often ephemeral; that is, they may appear and disappear rapidly. U.S. will in Vietnam during the 1960s and U.S. will to rearm during the 1980s provide examples of the ephemeral nature of sociopolitical parameters of power. Following attacks on U.S. destroyers in the Gulf of Tonkin in August 1964, U.S. sentiment strongly supported U.S. military action against North Vietnam. Within three years, however, mounting U.S. losses and growing uncertainty about U.S. war objectives led many U.S. citizens to question the wisdom of the war. The Johnson administration had lost one of the most crucial elements of power available to a democratic government—support of the population for its international policies.

Similarly, in the case of the Reagan rearmament program of the 1980s, domestic support for rearmament grew rapidly in the wake of the capture of U.S. hostages in Teheran and the Soviet invasion of Afghanistan. Ronald Reagan used this sentiment to good advantage during the 1980 presidential elections and during his first year in office, but discovered by 1982 that public support for large increases in defense expenditures was soft. Many citizens began to question whether the United States could afford the massive defense expenditure increases Reagan proposed, and others questioned the need for such increases in light of significant reductions in U.S. governmental social expenditures. Reagan thus found it necessary to nurture the intangible sociopolitical element of popular support for his defense program so that the more tangible military elements of power could be acquired. For the most part, his efforts to maintain popular support for his defense program succeeded.

Sociopolitical parameters of power are not confined to domestic concerns. Actors also gain—and lose—sociopolitical strength in the international arena. The United States and the Soviet Union again offer excellent cases for study.

Through most of the post–World War II era, the United States prided itself on its reputation of being a fair and stalwart ally, opposed to communism and external interference in the internal affairs of others. Whether this was an accurate reputation is beyond the scope of this chapter; what is relevant is that that was the U.S. image and reputation held both by the United States of itself and by many other international actors. U.S. prestige and power were enhanced by this image and reputation. However, with Vietnam, this began to change. Increasingly, the United States was seen as a traditional imperial power, seeking to control lesser actors to its own advantage. As a result, U.S. prestige and power were undermined. A change in intangible sociopolitical parameters of power, image, and reputation contributed to an overall decrease in the United States' global position.

The Soviet Union was a short-term beneficiary of this deteriorating U.S. image and reputation. During the 1960s and early 1970s, the USSR moved rapidly to cement its reputation throughout the world as a proponent of nonintervention and disarmament and as an opponent of imperialism and expansionism. The Soviet message sold well, particularly in the Developing World. The USSR's reputation and image improved tremendously, and the USSR's ability to influence world events expanded. Although the Kremlin's military capabilities grew rapidly during this period as well, it is an arguable point that, because of the USSR's improved reputation and image in the Developing World, the sociopolitical parameters of its power had grown equally rapidly. In short, the USSR had done well in its efforts to win the hearts and minds of the global community.

It also began to overplay its hand during the 1970s and to consume the sociopolitical parameters of power it had acquired. Intangible elements of Soviet power, image and reputation among them, began to deteriorate as one country after another told Soviet advisers to leave. Egypt, Nigeria, Sudan, Iraq, and Somalia were the more prominent ones. Other countries asked for Soviet support and assistance. Nevertheless, Zambian President Kenneth Kaunda's warning that "the marauding tiger with cubs" (i.e., the Soviet Union and Cuba) should not be allowed to enter the African back door while other dangers (the United States and Europe) were being barred from the front pointed to new Developing World uncertainties about the legitimacy of the USSR's reputation and image. The Soviet invasion of Afghanistan added to these uncertainties as the Soviet Union was increasingly viewed as just another great power pursuing its own interests. As a result, the USSR's image and reputation was tarnished, and the Kremlin lost an important sociopolitical element of power.

Internal Sociopolitical Factors

Of the many factors that may be included among those elements that constitute internal sociopolitical parameters of the strength of international actors, we concentrate on only four: will and morale, character, leadership, and degree of integration. These four factors have been selected for two reasons. First, they apply to all the actors we have examined. Will and morale are as important for an IGO as for a state in the success or failure that it has in attaining its goals. Similarly, an IGO or an MNC with ineffective leadership is less likely to achieve its objectives. The same is true for a state or NGO. The same may be said for character and degree of integration.

Second, each of these factors includes diverse items that may be important for one set of actors, but less so for another. Will and morale include internal public opinion, a factor of considerable importance for a democratic government or an IGO that needs unanimity of opinion before action can be taken. Public opinion is of less importance but not inconsequential in an autocratic state or an MNC. The character of an international actor may be the product of its historical experiences, its geographical and environmental location, or its technical orientation. Although history is important for all actors when character is discussed, geographical and environmental location may be expected to be more important for a state than an MNC, whereas technical orientation may be more important for an MNC.

It should be further noted that divisions between sociopolitical factors are somewhat artificial. Will and morale influence character, leadership, and integration, even as each of the other three influences all. Nevertheless, for clarity, their interrelationships have been minimized in the following discussions.

Will and Morale.   Hans Morgenthau defined national morale as "the degree of determination with which a nation supports the foreign policies of its government in peace or war."[6] For our purposes, this definition is accurate, but overly restrictive. **Will and morale** are viewed here as the degree of determination that any actor has in the pursuit of its internal or external objectives.

Within an international actor, will and morale need not be identical at all levels of society. Leadership will and morale (as apart from leadership capability) may be strong, as was the case in Russia during 1916 and early 1917, whereas the masses may be defeatist. The Russian nobility and military continued to plan for and believe in new offensives against the Germans even while Russian troops were laying down their weapons and walking away from the front. Similarly, the final withdrawal of the United States from Vietnam resulted primarily from a conviction on the part of U.S. citizens that the war should be terminated. Only slowly did the U.S. decision-making elite adopt this attitude.

Different levels of will and morale also exist in other actors. The chief executive officer and board of a multinational corporation may bask in the confidence and assurance generated by a record profit year for the MNC as a whole, whereas at the same time a single division may be laboring under loss, impending leadership changes, and layoffs.

But what creates will and morale? No one can say with certainty. The will and morale of the British, the Germans, the Japanese, and the Vietnamese remained strong, according to most estimates, despite the large-scale conventional bombing raids they experienced during World War II and the Vietnam War. Would they react the same way to similar experiences today? Would other peoples react with heightened will and morale if they were subjected to similar bombing? How would any society react to a nuclear bombing exchange as opposed to a conventional one? The answers are unknown.

Here, the role of **nationalism** as a significant input to the will and morale of state actors must be stressed. As discussed in Chapters 1 and 2, nationalism has been and remains an important force in bonding people together within the nation-state. By psychologically providing people with a sense of attachment to an entity beyond themselves and by providing people with a sense of pride in their nation, nationalism often adds an immense measure of will and morale to the capabilities of state actors in the international arena.

Nevertheless, nationalism, like all aspects of will and morale, is a psychological phenomenon. Why do so many Central Europeans and former Soviet citizens still have high hopes for the future when their economic situations are disastrous and their political systems are in disarray? The answer is that despite their problems, they believe that the future will be better than the past. Similarly, why during the height of the Cold War did so many members of the UN's Secretariat continue to have high hopes for the future of the organization as a peacekeeping body when time after time states appealed to their sovereign rights and frustrated UN peacekeeping efforts? They, too, believed the future would bring better times. And why do the employees and management alike of some MNCs maintain appearances of high dedication to the company under even the most trying circumstances? The answers, again, are not known, but are clearly psychological.

Character. The **character** of an international actor is a subject of more debate than will and morale. Some analysts deny the existence of a national, organizational, or corporate character. Others argue that certain emotional, intellectual, or human qualities occur more frequently and are valued more highly in one actor than in another. Germans are more philosophic and militaristic than the French, who are in turn more emotional and sensual than the English. Russians are stoic and persistent; Americans are industrious and pragmatic. UN employees are idealistic internationalists, whereas IBM employees are efficient and methodical. Critics of the concept of character dismiss these and other categorizations as meaningless stereotypes. Adherents to the concept accept them as generalizations that may have exceptions.

Given the insights to societies and organizations provided by cultural anthropology and related disciplines, it is difficult to dismiss the concept of national, organizational, or corporate character in totality.[7] Russian mistrust of the external world is historically documentable. Regardless of whether its cause is the centuries of Tatar rule, three invasions from Western Europe in little more than a century, or something else, it is a part of the Russian character. Russian stoicism, regardless of whether caused by Russian Orthodox Christianity, communism, or long and cold Russian winters, is equally real. Similarly, regardless of whether the successful "IBMer" is fashioned by the demands of the corporate environment or selected for employment because his or her character fits the employer's preferences, a certain style of corporate personality emerges. Many exceptions exist, but enough evidence exists to accept a generalized rule.

How does character relate to power? Certain policies, strategies, or tactics may be favored or proscribed by character. For example, Americans are impatient for results, or so the North Vietnamese believed. As seen by the North Vietnamese, the United States could not fight a protracted war successfully. At least in Southeast Asia, events proved them right as American impatience effectively reduced U.S. power and forced the United States to withdraw.

Similarly, Americans like to justify their actions. Thus, the United States did not enter World War I until after U.S. ships and lives were lost, and it did not enter World War II until after Pearl Harbor. The United States legitimized its original bombing of North Vietnam by claiming North Vietnam had attacked U.S. destroyers. More recently, the United States invaded Grenada in 1983 only after internal disorder in that Caribbean island dissolved and the lives of U.S. students there were endangered. The United States also sent troops into Panama only after General Noriega's forces stepped up harassment of Americans living there and killed a U.S. citizen. In 1990 and 1991, the United States moved against Iraq after its invasion of Kuwait only after it obtained UN approval. Similarly, the United States intervened in Somalia in 1992, in Haiti in 1995, and in Kosovo in 1999 only after the UN approved the interventions.

British determination provides another good example of national character. This national trait, often mentioned in commentary on individual Britons, was somehow overlooked both by Hitler in 1939 and Argentina in 1982. This determination, according to some, was the sole factor that allowed Great Britain to fight on alone against the Nazi juggernaut for over a year and was a major factor in convincing the Thatcher government to undertake an expensive military operation for the purpose of recapturing a few bleak South Atlantic islands. Russian stoicism and persistence in turn may be best exemplified by Soviet Marshal G. K. Zhukov's response to the question of how the Soviet army would clear a minefield: by marching a division across it!

As in the case of will and morale, the causes and sources of character cannot be specifically delineated. Historical experiences and traditional values undoubtedly play a role, as do geographical location, environment, organizational structure, and a country's economic and technical base. Other sources undoubtedly exist as well. But in the final analysis, character's contribution to the sociopolitical parameters of power can be only roughly estimated.

Leadership. Few analysts deny the necessity of effective leadership. Effective **leadership** permits an actor to take advantage of its economic and military capabilities. In some instances it may allow an actor to overcome shortcomings in one or another parameter of power. An absence of leadership inevitably detracts from an actor's ability to achieve its ends.

Three separate aspects of leadership must be discussed. First is the organizational structure of an actor, for it is within this milieu that leadership must function. Different types of organizational structures have certain strengths and weaknesses, whereas other structures have different strengths and weaknesses. At the state level, for instance, a totalitarian system cripples individual freedom and initiative, but permits formulation of a highly organized state strategy. Totalitarian systems rarely can rely upon significant levels of popular support for their policies simply because the decision-making process is tightly controlled and does not permit interchange of ideas. Democratic systems, by comparison, require policy formation by consensus building and persuasion. A policy, at least initially, may have significant support from wide segments of the state's population. However, it is extremely difficult to develop and implement a long-range state strategy or to change policy direction. Clearly, although both the totalitarian and democratic systems have their advantages, the type of leader that each system demands is quite different.

Quality is a second aspect of leadership. Often, the power potential of an international actor is increased in proportion to the capabilities that that actor's leadership possesses. A mesh between type of system and type of leader is important, but quality of leadership is also important. Thus, Franklin Roosevelt could not only operate effectively in the U.S. political environment, but he could also make that environment serve his purposes. By exercising his leadership gifts and position, he not only succeeded in building his own personal prestige, and therefore power, but also strengthened U.S. morale and will. Roosevelt's ability to mobilize the American people behind his policies proved a tremendous asset. Under Roosevelt, presidential leadership and U.S. will and morale were integrally related both during the depression and during World War II.

Ronald Reagan played a similar role in his administration. Whatever the criticisms that may be levied against Reagan's grasp of the issues, few can deny that Reagan's leadership helped rekindle U.S. patriotism and rebuild a sense in many U.S. citizens that the United States had an important and assertive role to play in world affairs. Once again, leadership was demonstrably important.

Roosevelt and Reagan, successes in the U.S. system, would probably have been failures in the Soviet system in which Joseph Stalin so ruthlessly succeeded. By contrast, Stalin would have failed in the U.S. system. Nevertheless, Stalin's ruthlessness provided the Soviet people with a strong central authority in the tradition of Ivan the Terrible, the Romanov dynasty, and Lenin. His methods proved workable within the Soviet system.

The ability of leaders to formulate and implement a strategy to achieve its objectives is a third aspect of leadership. Although this third point is a subset of quality of leadership, it is significant in its own right. Regardless of the quality of leadership, if a strategy is not formulated that is meaningful and workable in relation to an actor's objectives, leadership quality means little. A national leadership may be capable enough to tap all the measures of economic, technical, and sociopolitical parameters of power, but if it has no strategy, its chances of success are diminished.

Even though he failed to achieve his objective of a more humane and efficient Soviet Union, Mikhail Gorbachev and his efforts to revitalize the Soviet Union provide a useful example. Early on, Gorbachev concluded that the changes that would have to take place in the USSR to renew the country were so significant and would arouse so much opposition that he would have to launch a comprehensive revolution that would change Soviet political, economic, social-cultural, and foreign policies. He implemented this strategy of comprehensive revolution first via *glasnost,* and then in economic restructuring, political democratization, and foreign policy new thinking. Although the tactics he employed were ad hoc, and the changes that eventuated were not those that he envisioned, he nevertheless had an overall strategy to bring about change within the USSR.

Leadership is also important in diplomacy, which in its most elemental form is the art of conducting relations between governments of independent states. Although diplomacy is sometimes viewed with derision, effective leadership can transform diplomacy into a meaningful instrument of state power. Effective leadership defines for diplomacy the objective that it is to pursue, the strategies that it is to employ, and the instruments that are available. Without effective leadership, diplomacy can achieve little. With effective leadership, it can enhance a state's power.

An example or two may help clarify the importance of leadership for diplomacy. During the nineteenth century, Otto von Bismarck strengthened Germany by weaving a subtle pattern of alliances across Europe. Without an overall strategy, Bismarck could never have created his treaty system. Between 1969 and 1974, Richard Nixon and Henry Kissinger also formulated U.S. foreign policy toward China and the Soviet Union on the basis of a comprehensive strategy. Nixon and Kissinger forged a policy that made China and the Soviet Union consider cordial relations with the United States to be of paramount importance. Such a policy increased U.S. freedom of action in the international community and limited Chinese and Soviet options.[8]

Leadership is also important within international actors other than states. Dag Hammarskjöld's optimism about the United Nations, his ability to convince others that peacekeeping was a legitimate function of the UN, and his willingness to have the UN accept international responsibilities were all trademarks of his secretariatship; they have remained trademarks of the UN to this day. With a lesser leader, the UN may not have acquired the prestige that it has.

Degree of Integration.   Will and morale, character, and leadership are clearly important elements in an actor's sociopolitical strength, but another factor, **degree of integration,** adds a significant dimension to sociopolitical strength as well. Stated differently, degree of integration refers simply to the sense of belonging and identification of an actor's people. At the state level, this often translates into nationalism.

In most cases, the greater the degree of homogeneity and uniformity, the greater the degree of perceived integration. This, in turn, contributes to a sense of belonging, of citizenship. Homogeneous ethnic, religious, linguistic, or cultural backgrounds add to a sense of identity and integration. Shared values are also important. For states, national liberation movements, and other actors whose members share one or more of these identities, a significant parameter of power has been acquired. Technical and organizational identity are also important, particularly for MNCs, IGOs, and certain NGOs. An MNC whose employees are unsure of the contribution they make or role that they play in the company's overall operations is less likely to have the allegiance of its employees than is an MNC whose employees recognize that their abilities are valuable assets to the MNC, and that the MNC appreciates those assets. The same is true for IGOs and NGOs.

Although it is generally true that great integration leads to an enhanced sense of identity between an actor and its people, a lack of integration need not necessarily imply a lack of identity. For example, France has a high degree of integration. Ethnic origins, language, religious preference, cultural heritage and values, and historical background are all widely shared. The same is also true of Japan. Switzerland, by contrast, has little integration. Shared values are offset by ethnic diversity, disparate languages and religious preference, different cultures, and in many cases, different historical backgrounds. Yet the Swiss view themselves as a separate entity as surely as the French view themselves as a separate entity.

There are numerous cases where a low degree of integration leads to an uncertain or questionable degree of unity. Yugoslavia and the Soviet Union are two cases in point. In both countries, immense internal diversity led many citizens to identify more with their own ethnic group than with the state itself. In Yugoslavia, Serbs, Croats, Bosnians, Macedonians, and others all insisted on their own national identity. Similarly, in the Soviet Union, Latvians, Lithuanians, Estonians, Moldavians, Armenians, Azerbaijanis, Georgians, and others wanted their own national identity, too. In both Yugoslavia and the USSR, this sense of allegiance to a group other than the Yugoslav or Soviet state led to secession, the collapse of the Yugoslav and Soviet states, and warfare between ethnic groups. Both cases prove that too low a degree of integration can be disastrous for a state.

It is impossible to specify how and why a sense of identity develops, or what the key factor or factors are in leading to a sense of belonging. In some cases, a low degree of integration across a wide number of variables will be sufficient to lead to a sense of belonging. In other cases, a high degree of integration in a single area will be sufficient. In either case, the sense of identity may be long-lived or ephemeral. To use the Swiss as an example again, Swiss unity has continued across the centuries despite low degrees of integration in ethnicity, language, religion, and so on. The Angolan national liberation movements by comparison had a shared enemy in Portugal, but little else. They shared the objective of driving the Portuguese out of Angola, but, with that single integrative factor removed, they plunged into civil war. Japanese multinational corporations provide yet another type of example. Japanese industrial workers identify themselves as much with their corporation as with their nation. Although several causes for this identity exist, it is nonetheless a unique phenomenon.

All the sociopolitical parameters of power addressed to this point—will and morale, character, leadership, and degree of integration—evolve from considerations internal to an international actor. All also are important aspects of an actor's overall power potential, but are at the same time intangible elements whose composition cannot be precisely defined or measured. The sociopolitical parameters of an actor's power are not, however, limited to internal considerations.

External Sociopolitical Factors

Many international actors appeal to the "good of the people" to justify their international actions. The Soviet Union claimed that it was fighting against imperialism for the "good of the Afghan people" when it sent its combat forces into Afghanistan in 1979, and the United States argued that it was opposing communism and supporting freedom for "the good of the Vietnamese people" during the war there. Ayatollah Khomeini overthrew the shah for "the good of the Iranian people," and the UN sent relief and developmental teams into Somalia for "the well-being of those who have little." The World Council of Churches sends money for food and medical aid, some of which is diverted into weapons purchases, to a variety of national liberation movements, all in the name of humanity, whereas those national liberation movements fight for independence for "the good of the peoples" of a variety of territories. Even multinational corporations justify their global reach by arguing that they will bring better living conditions to more people than ever before, if only they can operate unfettered by national and international restrictions. "The good of the people," it seems, is everywhere.

"The good of the people" plays a dual role in international affairs. It may serve as either the ultimate objective of an actor or it may serve as a pretext behind which an actor pursues its real objectives, one of which may or may not be "the good of the people." "The good of the people" is variously defined by actors to mean national independence, improved living conditions, equitable distribution of resources, freedom of religion or dominance by a specific religion, or any of a variety of other "goods." In addition, actors have found that they are able to broaden their own appeal and therefore add to their own power if they can convince not only their own citizens, but also those of other actors, of the accuracy of their own interpretation of good and of their own honesty in pursuing it.

Examples of this abound. The Soviet Union represented the vanguard of communism for years, and as a result of its preeminence, won the allegiance of communist parties throughout the world. As a result, Soviet power was enhanced. When Mao took power in China with his own variant of communism, Soviet preeminence in the international communist movement was challenged. The ensuing Sino–Soviet ideological dispute hence revolved around more than esoteric interpretations of Marxist dogma. To an extent, it was a dispute over sociopolitical parameters of power. Clearly, if a large number of communist parties adopted pro-Chinese as opposed to pro-Soviet stances, the external sociopolitical parameters of Soviet power would have been diminished.

Supranational Appeal. Religious movements and organizations also depend on their **supranational appeal,** that is, their appeal that extends beyond a single state to several states, to strengthen their international positions. The Vatican, Israel, and Iran are three examples in which religions have combined their spiritual aspirations with the secular realities of a state. The Vatican, the heart of Catholicism and the earthly seat of power of the pope, is a microstate not unlike the Solomon Islands in terms of its economic and military capabilities. Yet because of its religious importance and historical background, it plays a role in international affairs far above what its economic and military capabilities would imply. The Pope may not have many earthly divisions, but he wields considerable influence.

Israel, by comparison, is the strongest military power in the Middle East. But even its military capabilities are enhanced by its stature as the Jewish state, the spiritual home of the Jewish people. Jews throughout the world extend their moral support and financial aid to Israel, and on occasion actively seek to influence the policy of other actors on issues that concern Israel. Thus, Israel's power is strengthened by its supranational appeal as the Jewish homeland. This is obviously a sociopolitical factor contributing to Israeli power.

Iran is similar. Revolutionary Iran purports to be a fundamentalist Shiite Islamic state that follows Allah's teachings in the Koran precisely. The Iranian clerics hope to attract fundamentalist Shiites throughout the Islamic world to their revolutionary cause. Moderate Arab states, including Saudi Arabia, Jordan, Oman, and the United Arab Emirates, fear that Iran's call for revolution may fall on receptive ears. Iran became a potentially powerful center for revolution in the Middle East, not necessarily because of its economic or military capabilities, but because of religion.

Communism and religion are not the only sources of supranational strength. Other concepts, like human rights, noninterference, nonalignment, and economic betterment, also attract external support for those actors that claim to support them. Jimmy Carter's human rights policy was undoubtedly a sincere statement of Carter's beliefs, but it also allowed the United States to assert that it was on the side of justice and morality.

International Public Opinion.   **International public opinion** is thus an important element of an actor's sociopolitical strength. Some actions such as withholding food from a starving population to prove a political point or using nuclear weapons when anything less than national survival is threatened are usually viewed by international actors as so certain to evoke an international backlash that they are usually excluded as policy options. Similarly, for multinational corporations, international public opinion is a critical variable. Fear of adverse public opinion was a major reason that baby formula producers curtailed their marketing efforts in the Developing World in the early 1980s. The involved MNCs concluded that the long-term impact of adverse international public opinion was more important than the short-term economic advantage that might be gained by continuing sales. Consequently, favorable international public opinion may be seen as a critical component of sociopolitical power for MNCs as well as states and other international actors.

Sometimes, international actors who have no clear claim to external sociopolitical appeal through ideology, religion, human rights, or the like, seek to enhance their stature by claiming to be leading spokesmen for other concepts of international appeal. Yugoslavia and India both did this with nonalignment, and both states acquired sociopolitical strength and prestige that they had not previously had.

We have to this point concentrated on states and their efforts to acquire external sociopolitical parameters of power. Other international actors also attempt to improve their power potential by seeking external support. There are many examples. Multinational corporations seek to persuade others not associated with MNCs that they bring economic advantages not available elsewhere. Nongovernmental organizations regularly appeal for support for their causes from external sources. The World Council of Churches asks others to remember their religious morality, hoping that such remembrances will yield additional support for WCC causes. Greenpeace begs others to observe the brutality against whales, hoping that such observers will become more opposed to the slaughter. The United Nations Charter is the source of much of the UN's reputation as an international beacon of morality and justice. National liberation movements the world over claim their struggle is a just one against colonial oppression, hoping to acquire added external support and legitimacy.

It is in this light that the success of South African blacks in their struggle against the white South African government's policy of apartheid can be understood. Over time, much of the international community accepted the morality of the blacks' cause: the elimination of apartheid and the institutionalization of majority rule in South Africa. This acceptance added a significant but immeasurable amount of sociopolitical power to calls by the African National Congress, Nelson Mandela, Bishop Desmond Tutu, and others to change the system in South Africa. Under a combination of internal and external sociopolitical pressures, the South African government dismantled apartheid.[9]

External sociopolitical parameters of power are no more easily defined or categorized than are their internal counterparts. It is equally obvious that no guarantee exists that they will be long-lasting or easily regained if lost. The United States squandered much of its international appeal in Vietnam; Carter's calls for human rights only regained a portion of what had been lost. Before its collapse, the Soviet Union too found its external sociopolitical parameters of power rendered less persuasive by a combination of poor economic performance, adventurous foreign policy, and ideological stultification.

Nevertheless, international actors of all types are aware that their overall power potential can be increased if they influence others to support their causes. As we move further into the twenty-first century, the efforts of international actors to enhance their external sociopolitical parameters of power will not diminish and may well increase.

Nelson Mandela symbolized the struggle of black South Africans against apartheid. Mandela's leadership of the African National Congress even from prison played a major role in gaining international recognition for the ANC's cause. Mandela was elected the first post-apartheid president of South Africa.

INTERNATIONAL LAW, DIPLOMACY, AND SOCIOPOLITICAL ELEMENTS OF POWER: AN ASSESSMENT

Throughout this chapter, we have seen that not all dimensions of power can be categorized or quantified easily. International law, diplomacy, and sociopolitical elements of power are all important factors that must be considered when an international actor's capabilities are being assessed, but there is no foolproof way to measure their contributions to an actor's power potential.

International law's relationship to power is complex. On the one hand, it limits power by establishing certain standards of behavior. If adhered to, international law thus constrains the application of power. On the other hand, international law also provides a degree of predictability for the international community, enabling international actors to rationalize their policies. International law thus enhances power by helping to create an international environment in which actors can plan and implement future-oriented policies.

At the same time, for state actors, national sovereignty is rooted in international law. Obviously, states benefit immeasurably, although not equally, from the concept of national sovereignty.

Skillful diplomacy also enhances an international actor's power potential. Although our discussion in this chapter has centered on the importance of diplomacy for states, all international actors can benefit if their diplomats represent their policies and positions well, gather and interpret information effectively, signal and receive communications accurately, negotiate persuasively, manage crises intelligently, and engage in effective public diplomacy.

As for sociopolitical elements of power, for the most part, they are psychological factors that are difficult to categorize and quantify. How an actor's will and morale will hold up under adverse conditions cannot be predicted. How well an actor's leadership will respond to a crisis is similarly unknown. Although an actor's character may provide an observer with some clue as to how the actor will react in a given situation, it is usually impossible to predict with certainty whether an actor's degree of integration will add to or detract from its overall power. And the power that an actor acquires through its external appeal is even more difficult to gauge.

One of the most frustrating aspects of sociopolitical parameters of power is that, in many cases, they are more significant factors in determining an actor's overall power potential than the actor's more tangible economic and military capabilities. As an example, Ray Cline's work on "politectonic" measures of national power that we examined in Chapter 12 extends most importance to strategic purpose and national will, two elements that we have called sociopolitical parameters of power.[10]

Too often, because they are not easily categorized or quantified, international law, diplomacy, and sociopolitical elements of power are ignored or overlooked as parameters of power. International actors that ignore or overlook these elements almost inevitably weaken their own international standing and position.

KEY TERMS AND CONCEPTS

Grotius   a seventeenth century Dutchman generally considered the founder of international law

naturalist school   argues that all laws are derived from God's laws; law is therefore universal and unchangeable

positivist school   maintains that the only legitimate law is that which those who are subject to it agree to follow

eclectic school   says that two levels of law exist, one God-given and the other man-made

neorealist school   asserts that law is a reflection of the desires of the prevalent powers and that law is not a constraint on power but a product of power

International Court of Justice (ICJ)   the UN court that hears cases referred to it by the General Assembly or the Security Council

sovereignty   the concept that no international authority higher than the state exists

constitutive theory of statehood and sovereignty   no state or government is a legal entity until it is recognized

declarative theory of statehood and sovereignty   if a government can control its population, then it is a sovereign government

law of war   the extensive body of international law defining codes of conduct in war, just and unjust war, and related issues

just and unjust wars   international law's effort to define "legitimate" reasons to go to war and "illegitimate" reasons to go to war

international law's new directions   at the end of the twentieth century, international law increasingly began to enforce certain laws of war formerly ignored, identify and convict violators of human rights, and develop international environmental agreements

diplomacy   the implementation of an international actor's policies toward other actors

evolution of diplomacy   "old" diplomacy emphasized elitism, secrecy, bilateral agreements, and the importance of the embassy and ended after World War I, while "new" diplomacy emphasizes competency, openness, multilateral agreements, and personal leadership

Machiavelli   sixteenth century Italian considered the father of realpolitik

open diplomacy   carrying out diplomacy without secrecy

multilateral diplomacy   diplomatic activities undertaken by several international actors

purposes of diplomacy   representation; information gathering and interpreting; signaling and receiving; negotiating; crisis management; and public diplomacy

nature of socio-political parameters of power   intangible elements such as will, morale, and character that contribute to power

will and morale   sociopolitical parameters of power

nationalism   the psychological force that binds people who identify with one another together as a nation

character   although it is debated whether there is such a thing as "national character," it is frequently viewed as a sociopolitical parameter of power

leadership   widely recognized as a critical sociopolitical parameter of power

degree of integration   the sense of belonging and identification that an actor's people have with that actor

external sociopolitical factors   the ability of an actor to attract external support for its causes

supranational appeal   the ability to gain support that extends beyond a single international actor

international public opinion   the attitudes of the international community toward a given issue, actor, or situation.

 ## WEBSITE REFERENCES

international law: *www.ilrg.com/nations*   a legal research tool index linked to a directory of LawRunner home pages for every state in the world

www.asil.org   website for the American Society of International Law

www.soas.ac.uk/Centres/IslamicLaw/Materials.html   a directory of Islamic and Middle Eastern law materials on the net

International Court of Justice (ICJ):   *www.lawschool.cornell.edu/library/International_Resources/icj.htm* the official mirror site for the Americas for The International Court of Justice

diplomacy: *cfdev.georgetown.edu/sfs/programs/isd*   website of Georgetown University's Institute for the Study of Diplomacy

 ## NOTES

1. For a recent study of Grotius' work, see Hedley Bull et al., eds., *Hugo Grotius and International Relations* (New York: Oxford University Press, 1990).

2. For more detailed explanations of these schools, see J. L. Brierly, *The Law of Nations: An Introduction to the International Law of Peace* (New York: Oxford University Press, 1963). For additional discussions of international law, see Lori Fischer et al., eds., *Beyond Confrontation: International Law for the Post-Cold War Era* (Boulder, CO: Westview Press, 1995); and Rosalyn Higgins, *Problems and Process: International Law and How We Use It* (New York: Oxford University Press, 1994).

3. See S. Rosenne, *Documents on the International Court of Justice* (Dobbs Ferry, NY: Oceana, 1979); and R. Bernhardt et al., eds., *Digest of the Decisions of the International Court of Justice, 1950–1975* (New York: Springer-Verlag, 1978). See also Paul Reuter, *Introduction to the Law of Treaties* (Leicester: Leicester University Press, 1992).

4. For more extensive discussions of the law of war, see William Ballis, *Legal Position of War: Changes in Its Theory and Practice from Plato to Vat-*

tel (New York: Garland, n.d.); Julius Stone, *Legal Controls of International Conflict* (New York: Garland, n.d.) and Peter D. Trooboff, ed., *Law and Responsibility in Warfare: The Vietnam Experience* (Chapel Hill: University of North Carolina Press, 1975); Peter Rowe, ed., *The Gulf War and International Law* (New York: Routledge, 1993); and Geoffrey Best, *War and Law Since 1945* (New York: Oxford University Press, 1994).

5. For more detailed views of diplomacy, see Adam Watson, *Diplomacy: The Dialogue Between States* (New York: Routledge, 1992); and Robert Hopkins Miller, *Inside an Embassy: The Political Role of Diplomats Abroad* (Washington, DC: Congressional Quarterly Press, 1992).

6. Hans J. Morgenthau, *Politics Among Nations: The Struggle for Power and Peace* (New York: Alfred A. Knopf, 1973), p. 135.

7. See R. P. Anand, *Cultural Factors in International Relations* (Columbia, MO: South Asia Books, 1981); Frederick H. Hartmann, *Relations of Nations* (New York: Macmillan, 1978); Hans J. Michelmann, *Organizational Effectiveness in a Multinational Bu-*

reaucracy (New York, Praeger, 1979); Luc Reychler, *Patterns of Diplomatic Thinking: A Cross National Study of Structural and Social-Psychological Determinants* (New York: Praeger, 1979); and Kenneth N. Waltz, *Man, The State, and War* (New York: Columbia University Press, 1959).

8. For Nixon's and Kissinger's views on global strategy, see Henry Kissinger, *The White House Years* (Boston: Little, Brown, 1979); idem, *Years of Upheaval* (Boston: Little, Brown, 1982); idem, *Nuclear Weapons and Foreign Policy* (New York: W. W. Norton, 1969); Richard Nixon, *The Real War* (New York: Warner Books, 1980).

9. For recountings of the end of apartheid, see Nigel Worden, *The Making of Modern South Africa: Conquest, Segregation, and Apartheid* (Blackwell, 2000); and Elisabeth Jean Wood, *Forging Democracy from Below* (New York, NY: Cambridge University Press, 2000).

10. See again Ray S. Cline, *World Power Trends and U.S. Foreign Policy for the 1980s* (Boulder, CO: Westview Press, 1980), pp. 16–25.

PART 5

The Argumentative Framework: Issues of International Politics

. . . human rights and economic and social progress are inextricably linked. For far too long we have looked at development and human rights separately . . . they are two sides of the same coin.

—*MARY ROBINSON,*
UNITED NATIONS HIGH COMMISSIONER FOR HUMAN RIGHTS, JUNE 29, 2000

Many of the issues that confront the international community, from political economic issues to issues of war, peace, and violence to issues of human rights and conflicts of values to questions about the environment and health, are inextricably linked. Each impacts the other, and in turn is impacted by the others.

At the same time, many of the issues cannot be fully understood in local or regional contexts. Issues such as population growth, skewed distribution of wealth, environmental problems, and so on obviously have local and regional impacts, but they are problems that can be fully understood only on the global level.

To this point, we have examined different types of international actors and their interrelationships, the system in which the actors operate, the dominant perceptions those actors hold, and the major instruments with which those actors pursue their objectives. We have not analyzed the preceding issues in their global contexts. This framework makes that analysis.

Global issues may be categorized in many ways. In this framework, we examine them in four chapters. The first, Chapter 16, concentrates on issues of international political economy. It explores basic inputs to the global standard of living such as population, food, energy, mineral resources, and technology. (Two other critical issues of international political economy, economic development and the global distribution of wealth, were studied in Chapter 8.) The second chapter, Chapter 17, discusses problems of war, peace, and violence. The reasons why war and peace occur are central features in this chapter. Chapter 18 examines human rights and conflicts of values. The final chapter in this section, Chapter 19, looks at international questions about the environment and health.

This framework by no means presents a comprehensive discussion of the preceding issues, nor does it maintain that it covers all issues. Rather, it highlights several of the international community's major concerns. How well the international community resolves these concerns will determine how well—indeed, whether—humanity lives in the twenty-first century. This framework examines such questions as the following:

- How serious are the world's population and food situations?
- Why do resource shortages exist and can their impacts be reduced?
- What role does technology play in today's world, and why do some countries have developed technical capabilities, while others do not?
- What causes war, what causes peace, and can wars be avoided?
- What is the international community doing to protect human rights?
- What steps are being taken to safeguard women's rights?
- What types of conflicts of values exist and why?
- How serious are the world's environmental problems, and what is the international community doing about them?
- What can be done about international health problems?

Chapter 16

International Political Economic Issues

- What are the implications of world population growth?
- Is world hunger caused by an absolute shortage of food or by poor distribution of food?
- What is the world's energy situation?
- How long will the world have adequate mineral resources?
- What role does technology play in today's world?

Throughout history, but particularly since World War II, international actors—especially states—have been joined in what may be called a "standard-of-living race." Disagreements over which state had the best quality of life and over which sociopolitical-economic system provided higher standards of living and better quality of life to more people were central to the East–West conflict throughout the Cold War era, and disagreement over the causes and cures of the economic gap between North and South remains a major international issue today.

Beyond the parochial economic concerns of individual state and nonstate actors loom issues of importance for the international system at large. On a local and regional basis, international actors continue to undertake policies that run contrary to what most analysts would consider to be the global interest. Global population continues to grow, but some states continue to provide economic and noneconomic incentives for large families. World food production barely meets need, yet some governments pay their farmers to produce less. Governments pursue economic development in different ways, but no one is really sure how and why it occurs. And the simmering resentments caused by uneven distribution of wealth may explode into violence at any time.

Much of the debate that the "standard-of-living race" has generated intertwines international political issues and international economic issues. This intertwining is so complex that most analysts and policy makers call the issues that are included in the debate issues of **international political economics.** No definition of international political economics is universally accepted, but there is general agreement that population growth, food availability, energy, mineral resource availability, and technical capabilities are included within the term. So too are economic development and the global distribution of wealth, two issues which we examined in depth in Chapter 8 during our study of the North–South conflict.

All of these issues of international political economy are significant enough to warrant volumes, and the connections between several are exceedingly complex. However, since this is an introductory course, we will concentrate in this chapter on only the most critical dimensions of and the most evident connections between population growth, food availability, energy, mineral resource availability, and technical capabilities.

 ## *POPULATION*

The central problem for the twenty-first century may be nothing so esoteric as combating terrorism or coping with the Information Age. Twenty-first century humanity's central problem may be the mundane issue of assessing the earth's carrying capacity for human beings and then determining how to stay within that capacity. The population explosion may have slowed down somewhat, as Table 16-1 indicates, but the world's population is still growing.

In quantitative terms, the earth's **population growth** sped up in the nineteenth century, accelerated significantly during the early and middle twentieth century, and then slowed somewhat at the century's end. Nevertheless, by 2000, world population exceeded six billion people. The locations where the earth's population lives is shown in Figure 16-1.

TABLE 16-1 Past and Future World Population Growth

Year	Population in Billions
1000	.31
1250	.40
1500	.50
1750	.79
1800	.98
1850	1.26
1900	1.65
1950	2.55
1960	3.04
1970	3.71
1980	4.46
1990	5.28
2000	6.08
2010	6.82
2020	7.52
2030	8.14
2040	8.67
2050	9.10

Source: Before 1950: UN Population Information Network 1950 and After: U.S. Bureau of the Census

Chapter 16

IT AND INTERNATIONAL POLITICAL ECONOMY: THE IMPACT ON FOOD, POPULATION, AND RESOURCES

Carefully applied and intelligently used, advanced information technology could help the world better understand its food, population, and resource situations. IT would not "fix" problems in any area, but the information IT provided could allow policy makers to formulate and implement more timely and more effective responses to food shortages, population pressure, and resource needs.

For example, space based remote sensing devices coupled with computers on the ground could enable policy makers to track food production more effectively, identify food reserves more readily, and engage emergency food distribution resources earlier. This would allow quicker and more effective responses to food shortages, minimizing the impact of drought and other natural disasters and reducing the prevalence and impact of famine. Of course, such responses would require the mobilization of political will to remove barriers to the rapid movement of food reserves, but that is beyond the realm of information technology.

At the same time, population projections and demographic studies enabled by advanced information technologies could enable policy makers earlier to understand population trends that are developing in their countries. Early identification of significant trends in birth rate,

educational level, employment, transportation usage, consumption patterns, and health could help policy makers implement policies that might significantly improve standards of living. The impact of IT on health in particular will be examined again in Chapter 19.

Finally, the identification, extraction, and exploitation of fuel and nonfuel mineral resources could benefit greatly from Information Age technologies. Again, space based remote sensing devices coupled with computers to correlate disparate data provide the ability to identify new potential locations of resources, to assess the environmental impact of extraction, to improve the exploitation of resources throughout their product life, and to enhance the likelihood of recycling reusable resources. At the same time, IT applied to the environment will allow managers to better assure that the replacement rates of renewable resources are in line with use rates.

To reiterate, IT will not eliminate any of the problems associated with food shortages, population pressures, or resource needs. It will, however, help policy makers better understand food, population, and resource situations, thereby enabling them to formulate and implement more timely and more effective policies.

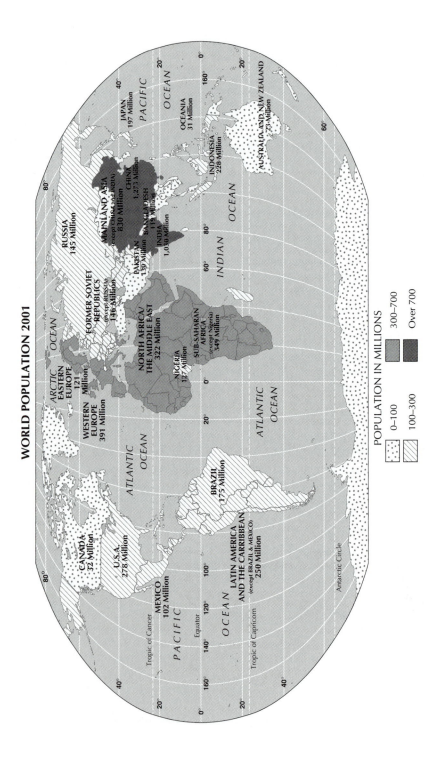

FIGURE 16-1   World population.

Most of the world's rapid population growth has been the result of impressive improvements in health and medical services throughout the world. Death rates declined precipitously and life expectancy increased, but birthrates remained relatively constant. Inevitably, population totals grew rapidly.

The problem of population growth is compounded by the location of that growth. According to the UN Population Information Network, about 95 percent of the world's population growth between 1992 and 2042 will take place in the Developing World. In 2000, about five billion of the world's six billion people already lived in the Developing World, over two billion in China and India together. At least 37 countries could not feed their own populations.[1] Equally distressing, most of the Developing World's population is in or near their offspring producing years. Thus, even though projections show that population growth will slow, it will continue. This has important political and economic implications, as we will see.

Historically, urbanization has accompanied population growth. This phenomenon continues today. In 1960, the world had 111 cities with over one million people. In 1990, that number had leaped to 288, one third of which were in the Developing World.[2] Table 16-2 provides historical trends and future projections for several cities in the Developing World. Most are already larger than New York City, and all are growing more rapidly than New York. Continued urbanization means that sanitation, water, health, and food delivery in cities will have to be substantially expanded as well. More housing must be constructed, and more jobs must be created.

For Developing World governments that find themselves hard-pressed to maintain satisfactory living conditions in urban areas today, this task may prove insurmountable. Distressingly, rural areas of Developing World states are often less well off than the urban centers.

Population pressures, along with warfare, are also primary causes of a growing world refugee problem. Some estimates place the world's refugee population at over 20 million people, and others go as high as 40 million. In some locations, warfare is the chief cause

TABLE 16-2   **Urban Population in Several Major Developing World Cities, in Millions**

City	1960	1975	1997	2015(est.)
Bombay	4.1	7.1	15.7	26.2
Calcutta	5.5	8.1	12.1	17.3
Cairo	3.7	6.9	9.9	14.4
Delhi	2.3	4.5	10.3	16.9
Jakarta	2,7	5.6	8.8	13.9
Karachi	1.8	4.5	10.1	19.4
Manila	2.2	4.4	9.6	14.7
Mexico City	4.9	10.9	16.9	19.2
Seoul	2.4	7.3	11.8	13.0
Sao Paulo	NA	NA	16.8	20.3

Sources: 1960 and 1975: The Carter Center, *Global 2000 Report,* 1982; 1997 and 2015: The United Nations, *Urban Agglomerations,* 1997.

of the refugee problem. In others, population has simply grown so rapidly that land can no longer support the number of people that are present. Thus, as we will see later, population pressure leads to overuse of land, which in turn leads to land degradation and desertification, which in turn forces population migration. Hence, more people are added to the world's refugee population. This can lead to international tension and conflict as refugees move across national boundaries to seek better land or more food.

All is not necessarily gloomy, however. As we have seen, population growth has slowed. Indeed, during the 1950s, population experts predicted that the global population would top 7.5 billion people by 2000. As Table 16-1 showed, this did not happen. Several possibilities exist for the slowdown.

One possibility may be as simple as greater awareness of the problem. For example, the UN has held three major conferences on population: one in Bucharest in 1974, the second in Mexico City in 1984, and the third in Cairo in 1994. These conferences did much to highlight world population pressures even though few concrete steps emerged from them. Indeed, at the Bucharest Conference, Western states proposed a series of family planning efforts that were rejected by most Developing World states, which argued that "economic development is the best contraceptive." By Mexico City, the two sides had essentially reversed their positions. Not until the Cairo Conference did the Developed World and the Developing World reach consensus that both family planning and economic development had merit as ways to curtail population growth.

Indeed, in some regions of the world, artificial or natural birth control methods and family planning efforts are becoming effective as a way to reduce population growth rates. Governments are often integrally involved in such efforts, as are IGOs such as the UN's World Health Organization and NGOs such as the International Planned Parenthood Federation. Throughout the Developing World, the rate of contraceptive use climbed from 40 percent in 1980 to 49 percent in 1990.[3] In certain countries, according to the UN, contraceptive use is extremely high. In Costa Rica, 75 percent of all incidents of sexual intercourse reportedly use contraceptives, in Botswana 76 percent, and in South Korea 79 percent.

Often, however, social or cultural custom frustrates birth control efforts. The depth of such opposition is well illustrated in China, which as long ago as 1989 reported that its population in 2000 would exceed the planned target of 1.2 billion people by at least 100 million despite extensive governmental birth control efforts.[4]

Religious organizations can also frustrate birth control efforts. The Catholic Church, for example, has long opposed them. It was primarily because of the Catholic Church's opposition to birth control that the issue of population was not directly addressed at the 1992 UN "Earth Summit" in Rio de Janiero.[5] The Catholic Church also raised vocal opposition to family planning and other items on the agenda of the UN's 1994 Conference on Population and Development in Cairo. Many Islamic countries held positions on population control issues that were extremely similar to those of the Catholic Church. Several Islamic states such as Saudi Arabia and Sudan refused to attend the conference.[6]

Governments have also on occasion opposed family planning. Under the Reagan administration, for example, the United States switched its emphasis from family planning as the best way to reduce birth rates to economic development. The Reagan administration also ended U.S. support for international birth control programs that supported abortion.

Social change and revolution may be another way to lower birthrates. This position was put forward not only at the three UN population conferences, but also at the 1995 UN Copenhagen Conference on Social Development and the 1995 UN Beijing Conference on Women. There is in fact evidence from the field to support this perspective. For example, both Sri Lanka and Thailand attribute some of the decline in their birthrates to this factor. In addition, as old attitudes about the superiority of male children over female children are displaced, fewer and fewer couples have children simply to assure a male heir.

The education level of women also has a direct impact on population growth. UN data from many countries indicates that where women receive no secondary school education, the average woman has seven children. But in countries where 40 percent of all women have had secondary school education, the average drops to three children.[7]

Historical data also show that higher standards of living lead to lower birthrates. For example, as of 1998, Austria, Belgium, Denmark, Finland, France, Germany, Great Britain, Italy, Norway, Portugal, and Spain all have population growth rates under 0.5 percent per year. Japan's population growth rate is 0.2 percent, and the United States' growth rate, although higher than most developed states, is still only 0.9 percent.[8]

More pessimistic reasons for lower population growth rates have also been advanced. Over time, poverty and malnutrition may lead to lower population growth rates. Historical data indicate that in some extremely poor areas of Indonesia and Brazil, this has already happened.[9]

Despite this, the world population is continuing to grow. Even this fact, however, does not concern some people. Technological optimists maintain faith in the ability of science, technology, and humanity to provide for the world's population, almost regardless of number. Religious optimists express a similar faith in God's ability to provide for humankind. These optimists are offset by population pessimists who predict a future of Malthusian pestilence, famine, and war, all brought about by rising population pressure. Even the experts disagree about whether the earth has a finite capacity to support human beings, and if it does have one, what that capacity is.

FOOD

The world's population problem is closely linked to questions about food. This linkage and the concern that it evokes are not new. As early as the eighteenth century, British clergyman and economist **Thomas Malthus** postulated that global food production would expand arithmetically, whereas global population would grow exponentially. The disparity in growth rates of food and population would lead to disease, hunger, and conflict on an unprecedented scale, Malthus believed.[10]

Malthus's dire prediction did not happen, and the growth of world grain and meat production has for the most part outpaced the world's population growth, as Figures 16-2 and 16-3 show. Nevertheless, there is little room for complacency since global grain reserves have

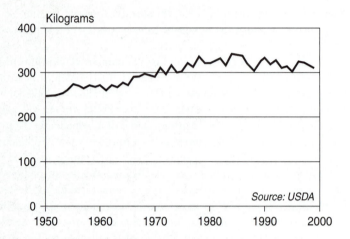

FIGURE 16-2　World Grain Production Per Person, 1950–99.

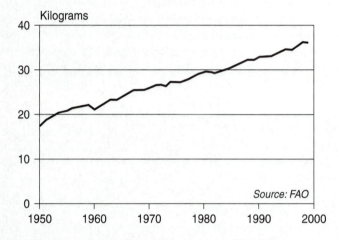

FIGURE 16-3　World Meat Production Per Person, 1950–99.

declined since the late 1980s. Although global famine is not imminent, the world's margin of safety is such that a few years of drastically reduced food production could spell disaster.

Given that the world's population is continuing to grow, the question of where increases in the world's food production will come from must also be raised. Outside North America, most of the world's arable land is already in agricultural use, so little increased production can come from increasing the area under cultivation. Much of the future's expanded agricultural production must come from the use of better farming methods and more extensive and intensive use of fertilizers, herbicides, pesticides, and irrigation. But as we will see in Chapter 19, these latter efforts to increase food production often damage the environment.

Other solutions may also increase the world's food production. Bioengineering may provide new strains of disease-resistant and insect-resistant crops that have higher yields than present-day crops. More fallow land may be put into production for a short time to help lessen short-term food shortages. But to reiterate, humanity has only a narrow margin of safety in its food supply situation.

The total level of global production is not the only food-related problem the world faces. Distribution is also a problem. In the late 1990s, only Europe, North America, Australia, and New Zealand were grain surplus areas. This pattern has not changed in the years since then. Indeed, if North America is excluded, the world's grain situation appears dire. And it is extremely perplexing that most of the countries in food deficit areas are economically underdeveloped. Many will be forced to rely on assistance from wealthier states to import food.

In some countries, famine has already been and is now present. During the 1970s and 1980s, famines killed somewhere between 2 and 3 million people.[11] In the 1990s, famine struck again in Ethiopia, Mozambique, Somalia, and Sudan. In Somalia alone, as many as 3 million people were in danger of starving to death. Before the UN-authorized U.S.-led military intervention took place in 1992 to create a secure situation in which emergency food rations could be distributed, over 200 people per day died of hunger and malnutrition.

What is worse, in all four states listed, governments, other political authorities, and gangs used hunger and famine as weapons of war to increase their own power and influence.[12] Although most people condemn the use of hunger and famine as a weapon of war, it is a fact of international life that such actions occur.

Obviously, the uneven global distribution of food leads to uneven levels of food consumption. Even so, the magnitude of this unevenness is surprising. For example, North Americans consume about 1 ton of grain per capita per year, 200 pounds directly in grain,

Too often, U.S. citizens think hunger and homelessness is "only" a problem in the Developing World. They are wrong. It is also a U.S. problem, as this recent photo taken in Manhattan illustrates.

and the remainder indirectly through livestock and dairy products. In Developing World countries, average annual per capita consumption is about 400 pounds of grain per year. According to the UN Food and Agricultural Organization (FAO), individual Developing World caloric intake during the 1980s and 1990s averaged 94 percent of the minimum FAO requirement. When it is realized that the rich eat much better than the poor in Developing World states, the 94 percent figure appears greatly overinflated.

Undernourishment carries with it a hidden cost. Underfed youth never develop their full mental or physical capabilities. For example, in Africa, over 40 percent of the children under age five are malnourished to the degree that they experience actual physical or mental damage. For a continent seeking to modernize and industrialize, this is a considerable blow. Undernourishment in no uncertain terms hampers economic development.

Questions of food are clearly among the most important that humanity will face in the twenty-first century. The international political economy of food is complex, and the complexity of the food equation is a large part of the reason why global maldistribution of food remains a problem.

In addition to political and economic issues, population and food issues pose moral dilemmas. Is it moral to practice birth control? If so, what method(s) is (are) acceptable and successful? If not, is it moral to bring a child into the world if the world's population is nearing its limits and insufficient food supplies appear a possibility? Is it moral to deny a hungry person food for political or economic reasons?

These and related questions have no universally accepted answers. Nevertheless, as the world's population increases and its food situation remains precarious, humankind must begin to address and solve such questions.[13]

 ## RESOURCES

For centuries, humans have used and abused nature's resources as if these resources were limitless. When one valley was overhunted, tribal humans simply moved on to the next valley. Slash-and-burn agricultural methods destroyed acres of forestland. Wide areas of forestland and savannahs were stripped of wood for construction and fuel. These and other cases of human assaults on nature pale in comparison with the ravishes visited upon nature following the industrial revolution. Strip mining, industrial production, sedentary agriculture, and extensive fishing improved life either directly or indirectly for millions, even billions, of people, but during the last three decades, humans became widely aware that resources were not limitless. By the late 1970s, resource depletion was an issue of widespread global concern, especially in the industrialized countries of Western Europe, Japan, the United States, and the former Soviet Union. For our purposes, resource concern will be examined as concern over energy resources and nonfuel mineral resources.

Energy

Global energy consumption expanded tremendously with the industrial revolution, and has continued to expand ever since. Some analysts have been predicting for years that humanity's rabid consumption of fossil fuels would deplete those resources, but few paid serious attention to their prediction. However, following the 1973 OPEC price increases and boycott, the Western world listened anew to those who foresaw future fuel shortages. For the first time, widespread segments of the West saw their visions of a future utopia clouded by the prospect of an energy shortage. For most, that energy shortage revolved around oil.

The rise of oil to the central position in the world's energy picture is a relatively recent phenomenon. At the beginning of the twentieth century, coal occupied the dominant position; at the beginning of World War I, as much as 75 percent of the world's energy consumption came from coal. Coal's preferred position deteriorated rapidly during the next 40 years as more and more oil was found. Given oil's relative cleanliness, ease of production, and relatively low cost during this period, and given the invention of the internal combustion engine, oil gradually surpassed coal as the world's dominant energy source. By 1965, oil had supplanted coal as the world's most important energy source, and by 1980, oil met nearly one-half of the world's energy needs.

The specter of oil depletion arose from the simple fact that until the worldwide economic recession of 1981–1982 reduced demand for oil, global petroleum producing capacity was not increasing as rapidly as demand. In addition, fewer oil reserves were being discovered. On the positive side, more efficient use of petroleum and petroleum products during the 1980s and 1990s lent credence to the technological optimists' claims that global petroleum reserves could be extended. Nevertheless, even to the optimist, it was clear that the earth's oil reserves were finite. Table 16-3 shows estimates of oil reserves in a number of locations, and gives their expected life at current rates of extraction.

Impending oil scarcity was not the only reason oil became a source of concern. Much of the Western world's prosperity of the 1950s and 1960s was built on the availability of inexpensive oil. Indeed, from the late 1940s through the early 1970s, oil declined in price relative to most other commodities. Depressed oil prices for this 25-year period may be attributed both to favorable concessions gained by the major oil companies from their sources of production and to their success in keeping independent producers out of the market. When OPEC, whose member states had recently gained control of production and pricing decisions over the oil they produced, quadrupled the price of oil during 1973–1974, the entire noncommunist world felt the shock. OPEC raised prices again in 1979–1980. Not until 1985–1986 did oil prices fall significantly, from roughly $30 per barrel to about $15.

However, this respite proved short-lived. Following the Iraqi invasion of Kuwait in 1990, world oil prices shot up temporarily to over $35 per barrel as Iraqi and Kuwaiti oil disappeared from the market and as fears of war swept world oil markets. Following the 1991 Persian Gulf War, oil prices dropped to about $20 a barrel, only to rise to over $30 a barrel in 2000 as OPEC states again cut back production. This was about 15 times higher than oil prices had been in 1970. This roller coaster ride of oil prices between the early 1970s and the beginning of the twenty-first century created economic uncertainty and at times decline in many oil importing countries in both the Developed and Developing Worlds.

In the Developed World, in addition to paying higher prices for oil, the habits, technologies, and investment patterns that had been established during the 1950s and 1960 when oil was inexpensive could not be changed overnight. For example, in the United States, the automobile played a dominant role in social, cultural, and economic life. In industry, inexpensive oil led to lack of concern about efficient energy use. And the long availability of inexpensive oil had discouraged investment in non-oil sources of energy.

TABLE 16-3   Global Oil Reserves and Production Rates

Region/Country	Estimated Proven Reserves Jan. 1995 (billion bbl)	Estimated Oil Production in 1994 (1,000 bbl/day)	Years of Production Remaining at 1994 Rate
Total Asia–Pacific	44.5	6,687	18
China	24.0	2,950	22
India	5.8	622	25
Indonesia	5.8	1,329	12
Malaysia	4.3	642	18
Total Western Europe	16.6	5,581	8
Norway	9.4	2,499	10
United Kingdom	4.5	2,504	5
Total Middle East	660.3	18,595	97
Abu Dhabi	92.2	1,840	137
Iran	89.3	3,573	68
Iraq	100.0	520	527
Kuwait	94.0	1,845	140
Oman	4.8	804	16
Qatar	3.7	407	25
Saudi Arabia	258.7	7,818	91
Total Africa	62.2	6,247	27
Algeria	9.2	745	34
Egypt	3.3	893	10
Libya	22.8	1,368	46
Nigeria	17.9	1,930	25
Total Latin America	129.1	7,644	46
Argentina	2.2	657	9
Brazil	3.8	673	15
Mexico	50.8	2,684	52
Venezuela	64.5	2,463	72
Total North America	28.0	8,383	9
Canada	5.0	1,743	8
United States	23.0	6,640	9
Total Eastern Europe and Former USSR	59.2	7,276	22
Former USSR	57.0	6,990	22
Romania	1.6	136	32
Total World	999.8	60,412	45

Source: Oil & Gas Journal, December 26, 1994.

Most developed states accommodated themselves to higher oil prices by improving efficiency, developing alternate energy sources, and increasing the price of their exports. Developing states were not as fortunate. Their consumption of oil was lower because of their lower level of development, but they had no way to generate more hard currency to

MAJOR SOURCES OF PETROLEUM PRODUCTION

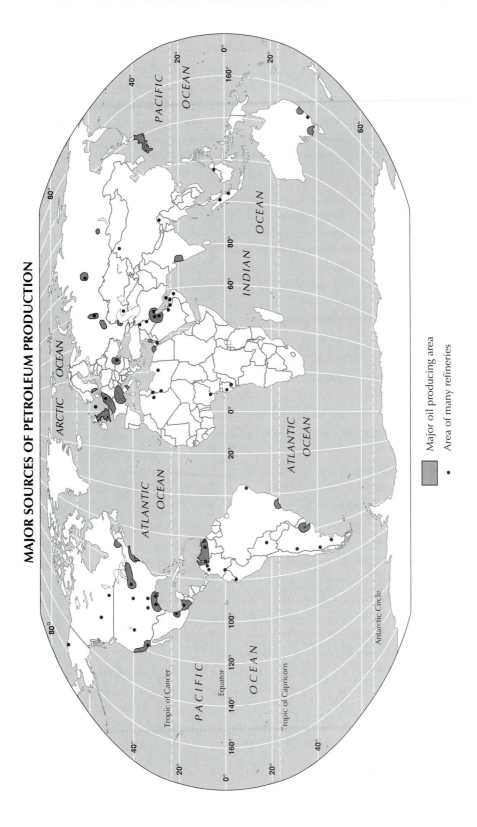

FIGURE 16-4 Major sources of petroleum production and refinery operations of the world.

(*Source: Geography* by Arthur Getis, Judith Getis, and Jerome Fellman. Copyright © 1981 by Macmillan Publishing Company. Updated in 1993 by the author.)

pay for more expensive oil. Consequently many were forced to use hard currency formerly available for food purchases or investment to purchase oil, and their peoples and economies correspondingly suffered.[14]

Political uncertainty also reduced oil's attractiveness. OPEC states had used oil as a weapon, and they understood that the more oil they left in the ground now, the wealthier they could become in the future. To developed and developing states alike, then, the threat of reduced availability of oil was a real economic danger. In many cases, severe economic disruption could result from a sizable reduction in the amount of oil imported. This fear was one reason that the United States and other developed states reacted so quickly and so emphatically when Iraq invaded Kuwait in 1990.

Slowly and sporadically, then, alternate sources of energy such as wind power, geothermal power, solar power, and nuclear power grew in importance. However, as oil prices rose and fell, no real momentum developed to move away from oil as the preferred energy source. Thus, excluding important energy sources that are not traded commercially such as wood and peat, the world still depended on oil for almost 40 percent of its annual energy needs at the end of the twentieth century, as Table 16-4 shows.

TABLE 16-4   1998 Global Energy Consumption of Selected States, in Million Tons of Oil Equivalents

Country	Oil	Natural Gas	Coal	Nuclear Energy	Hydro Electric	Total
Algeria	8.4	19.4	0.4	0.0	0.0	28.2
Argentina	23.1	26.7	0.9	1.9	2.5	55.0
Brazil	83.2	5.8	11.1	0.8	25.0	126.1
Canada	83.2	63.3	25.9	18.5	28.6	219.3
China	190.3	17.4	615.4	3.9	17.1	844.0
Egypt	27.3	11.0	1.0	0.0	1.1	40.3
France	94.5	33.7	15.1	100.0	5.7	249.1
Germany	136.6	71.6	84.7	41.7	1.8	336.3
Great Britain	80.5	79.9	40.7	25.8	0.6	227.5
India	86.1	20.9	153.6	2.8	7.2	270.6
Indonesia	43.7	28.7	7.6	0.0	0.8	80.8
Iran	58.0	46.5	1.0	0.0	0.6	106.1
Italy	94.7	51.5	11.8	0.0	4.1	162.1
Japan	255.0	62.5	88.4	84.0	9.3	499.2
Malaysia	19.0	18.4	1.5	0.0	0.4	39.2
Mexico	81.9	32.6	6.0	2.4	2.1	125.1
Russia	122.3	328.3	102.8	26.9	13.6	593.8
United States	852.4	551.2	533.7	183.0	26.7	2,146.9
Venezuela	18.4	26.9	0.0	0.0	5.0	50.4
World Total	3,389.0	2,016.4	2,219.4	626.6	226.4	8,477.4

Source: BP Amoco, *Statistical Review of World Energy 1999.*

Note: This chart includes only commercially traded fuels, thus excluding fuels such as wood, peat, and animal waste.

Often, government policies have a major impact on national and world energy situations. For example, the United States deregulated the price of oil and gas in an effort to spur more production, whereas France opted to emphasize nuclear power. Japan stressed conservation. The former Soviet Union sought to bring more oil and gas production sites into production in the Soviet Far East and Siberia. Although few of these efforts proceeded independently of other energy-related efforts, energy decisions made in the recent past and made today will play a major role in determining the world's energy future.

Humankind's use of energy has led to adverse environmental consequences. We examine those consequences later, but here it must be pointed out that such consequences are both global and local in nature. Global consequences of humankind's energy use can be seen in concerns over global warming, but on a local basis the quest for energy has already had sizable impact. For example, wood is used as a major fuel throughout much of the Developing World today. Local scarcities of fuel wood already exist, particularly in West Africa's Sahel region, in India's Ganges plain, and in regions of South America's Andes Mountains. Deforestation will inevitably continue, making fuel-wood gathering a major task in many areas of the world. Environmental degradation will assuredly accompany deforestation.

The shape of humankind's energy future may also go a long way in determining how international actors, particularly states, define their international interests. For Japan, Western Europe, and to a lesser degree the United States, the Middle East must be a central area of concern as long as it remains the source of so much oil. Thus, the United States, Europe, and Japan were all vitally concerned throughout the 1980–1988 Iran–Iraq war that oil production in and around the Persian Gulf not be closed down. Similarly, in 1990, Iraq's takeover of Kuwait raised concerns in industrialized countries—and in other states as well—that Iraq could determine both the price and production level of Middle Eastern oil.

One last point must be made about the world's energy and oil situations—namely, that global energy consumption is extremely uneven. Developed countries as a general rule use much more energy on a per capita basis than do developing states. Table 16-5 illustrates this. Much of the developed world's higher standard of living is the result of higher rates of energy use, so at least two questions must be asked concerning that energy use. First, ethically, one must question the morality of so few of the world's inhabitants using so much of the earth's scarce energy resources. Second, in a pragmatic sense, one must wonder where additional energy will come from if energy and development are as integrally linked as they appear to be. Both questions have within them the seeds for future conflict over energy.

However, conflict over energy is far from certain. As we have seen, the world's energy future is murky at best. How well will government policies, technical innovations, and changed living habits succeed in making alternate energy sources more attractive? Can efficiency and conservation extend the time that currently utilized energy sources, particularly oil, can be exploited? How much more oil, gas, and coal remain to be discovered? How much will the Chernobyl nuclear disaster influence countries to stay away from nuclear energy? These questions are unanswerable, but their answers hold the key to the world's energy future.

Nonfuel Minerals

Worldwide consumption of nonfuel mineral resources has steadily increased throughout the twentieth century except during economic recessions. Between now and 2010, nonfuel

TABLE 16-5   **Per Capita Energy Consumption in Selected States, 1998**

Country	Energy Consumption, in Millions of Tons of Oil Equivalents (MTOE)	Population in Millions	Per Capita Energy Consumption, in MTOE
Developing Countries			
Algeria	28.2	30	.94
Argentina	55.0	36	1.53
Brazil	126.1	170	.74
China	844.0	1,237	.68
Egypt	40.3	66	.61
India	270.6	984	.27
Indonesia	80.8	213	.38
Iran	106.1	69	1.54
Malaysia	39.2	21	1.87
Mexico	125.1	99	1.26
Venezuela	50.4	23	2.19
G-8 Countries			
Canada	219.3	31	7.06
France	249.1	59	4.22
Germany	336.3	82	4.10
Great Britain	227.5	59	3.86
Italy	162.1	57	2.84
Japan	499.2	126	3.96
Russia	593.8	147	4.04
United States	2,146.9	270	7.95

Source: Energy Consumption—BP Amoco, *Statistical Review of World Energy 1999.* Country Population—U.S. Central Intelligence Agency, *The World Factbook 1999.*

mineral consumption is expected to increase about 2 percent annually. Thus, many of the same concerns addressed in the previous discussion of energy resources—depletion, cost, and access, to name three—are relevant for nonfuel mineral resources as well.

Mineral depletion is a particularly vexing issue, if only because it is so difficult to come to terms with. Depending on the resource examined and the assumptions made, enough reserves are available for centuries—or barely enough for a decade. The severity of the problem presented by those minerals that may be depleted is difficult to gauge. Resource substitution (e.g., fiber-optic cable for silver or copper wire for communication purposes) and improved efficiency of use may greatly alter consumption rates for various minerals.

Conclusions about mineral depletion are difficult to reach, but conclusions about resource location and the political implications that may be derived from them are more obvious. Many resources are concentrated in a few countries or regions. For example, in the early 1990s, 93 percent of the world's platinum production and 63 percent of its chromium production came from South Africa and Russia. Similarly, Australia, South Africa, and Russia together produced 54 percent of the world's diamonds, and Canada by itself produced 30 percent of the world's nickel and 20 percent of the zinc. Generally, Australia, North America, Russia, and southern Africa are four of the major locations for many non-fuel mineral resources. Many industrialized states, particularly Japan and those in Western Europe, are highly dependent on nonfuel mineral imports. Thus, as in the case of oil, a very few areas of the world are of critical importance to mineral-importing states.[15]

Because production of several of the most important nonfuel minerals is concentrated in a few locations, fears are occasionally expressed that mineral resource cartels modeled after OPEC may be formed to control mineral production and prices. To date, no successful mineral cartel has been formed. Mineral substitutability is one reason for the failure of mineral cartelization; few nonfuel minerals are as critical to industrialized societies as oil. Thus, in the event of cartel-induced price increases or production cuts, less expensive minerals may in many cases be substituted for the cartelized ones.

A second reason that mineral cartels have not been successful is that many production sites are still under the control of foreign firms by virtue of concession. Host states have as a result denied themselves a voice in production and pricing decisions, at least until concessions expire. Stockpiling is a third reason that nonfuel mineral cartels have been less than successful. For example, the United States has maintained strategic stockpiles of a variety of minerals since 1939. U.S. stockpiles have rarely reached levels the U.S. government wanted, but the stockpile program nevertheless serves as a buffer against price and supply disruptions.

A final cause of the futility of nonfuel mineral cartels is recycling. Oil, when it is used, is gone, but many minerals may be used again and again. And even in the case of OPEC, as the 1986 collapse of oil prices indicated, holding a cartel together once it is formed is a difficult task.

As in all facets of our examination of the international political economy of resources, Western industrialized states consume and use a disproportionately large percentage of the world's nonfuel minerals. The same ethical and pragmatic questions that were asked about food, wealth, and energy could be asked about nonfuel minerals, but the points will not be belabored further.

 ## TECHNOLOGY

Often, the role that technology plays in the political economy of international relations is overlooked or restricted to only its military implications. This is unfortunate, for in nonmilitary as well as military issue-areas, technology's role is vitally important. Indeed, in every chapter of this book, we have explored some of the impacts that advanced information and communication technologies are having on all aspects of contemporary international affairs.[16]

The role of technology in military affairs is discussed elsewhere in this text and will not be repeated here. Beyond military affairs, technology is a key input to a country's economy. Often, technology is a major factor in determining a country's level of production, labor productivity, and standard of living. As a general rule, the greater the quantity of technology that a country has and the more sophisticated that technology is, the higher the country's standard of living will be.

Unfortunately, there are several downsides to technology. For example, technology is often expensive, and not all countries have the wherewithal to acquire the types of technology that they need. Thus, the use of technology can sometimes lead to greater differences in the standard of living both within and between countries. At the same time, under some conditions, increased use of technology can also lead to unemployment as technical advances reduce the number of people needed to perform an industrial or agricultural function.

In addition, to be effectively employed, technology usually requires an educated and disciplined labor force. Not all countries have or can develop such a labor force. Indeed, the combination of the cost of technology and the requirement that many technologies have for an educated and disciplined labor force goes a long way to explaining why advanced technologies in particular are so unevenly distributed around the world.

Also, technology frequently disrupts traditional social relationships and patterns of behavior. Therefore, those who wish to defend traditional values and ways of life sometimes oppose technological advance. Much of the conflict between tradition and modernization is driven by efforts to apply technology to society. Nor can it be overlooked that some types of technology degrade the environment, again as we will discuss later. Nevertheless, despite the drawbacks of technology, virtually every country in the world has sought and continues to seek to introduce more and more technology to its economy and to develop and apply new technical breakthroughs.

International actors do not limit their efforts to acquire technology to developing their own technologies. Because of the advantages that technology can bring, all types of international actors, especially states and multinational corporations, seek to acquire technical know-how from others. Consequently, the flow of technology between and among international actors is an issue-area of major importance in contemporary international relations. This flow of technology between and among international actors is called **international technology transfer.**

Sometimes, international actors acquire foreign technology openly and legally. Other times, they engage in covert or illegal efforts to acquire foreign technology. Indeed, the importance of technology as a factor in international economic competitiveness has led many international actors to spy on others to acquire technical secrets from their competitors.

Not surprisingly, because of the advantages that technological superiority may impart to those who have it, some international actors including the United States have sought to restrict international technology transfer in certain critical areas. The extent to which these efforts have been successful is a matter of debate.

Beyond the impact that technology has on individual international actors, technical breakthroughs and applications have altered the way in which the entire international system is shaped and has operated. As we already have seen, the advent of nuclear weapons played a major role in the creation of the bipolar system that existed between the late 1940s and the early 1990s. Nonmilitary technologies have played an equally important role in shaping the international system and influencing how it operates.

Transportation and communication technologies lead the way. The abilities to travel quickly to any point on the globe and to know almost immediately what is happening half a world away have changed the way people look at the world, creating a sense of a "global village." Transportation and communications advances have also given a sense of immediacy and urgency to events in the most remote corners of the world. A few years ago, many events could have gone unheeded for months, perhaps permanently. Now they become headline news almost as they occur.

Transportation and communication breakthroughs have also changed political, social, and economic relations within and between international actors. New transportation technologies enable major countries to intervene rapidly in far-distant places and allow countries throughout the world to trade with one another. New communications technologies make it almost impossible for a government to cut its citizens off from information from and about the outside world, and the pervasiveness of the international news media has influenced the behavior of some governments toward their people. For example, the presence of the international media played a major role in the failure of the 1991 coup attempt against then Soviet President Mikhail Gorbachev. And as we have seen, the failure of the coup played a major role in the collapse of the Soviet Union.

Transportation and communication breakthroughs have also altered perceptions of peoples around the world about other peoples and events. People-to-people contacts lessened U.S. views of Russians as enemies and lessened Russian views of Americans as enemies as well. Advances in transportation technologies helped make this possible. Advances in communications technologies allowed anyone who had a television to see what life is like in other countries, to witness the bombing of Baghdad at the beginning of the Persian Gulf War even as it occurred, and to observe the horror of famine in Somalia.

Advances in communications technologies also revolutionized the world of international finance and banking, as we have seen. The ability to transfer funds globally on a

New communication technologies enable us to see events on the other side of the world as they happen, as CNN's reports of the Persian Gulf War showed. Will instantaneous global communications change the way we look at the world?

moment's notice has integrated the international banking and financial community to an unprecedented extent. It has also raised questions about whether states and even multinational corporations including banks can control their economic and financial affairs. For example, in 1995, stock speculation undertaken completely by computer by one banker in Singapore on the Japanese financial market led to the collapse of Great Britain's oldest investment bank and sent tremors through the entire British financial community.

In addition, one can only guess what the international impact of the **Internet** will be over time. A global network of interconnected computers, the Internet allows people around the world to electronically send messages, pictures, data, and information to each other virtually instantaneously. As Figure 16-5 shows, the growth of the Internet has been phenomenal. This growth has been concentrated in industrialized countries, as Table 16-6 shows, but Internet connections are becoming increasingly available in developing states as well. The implications of the Internet for international relations are immense.

Nor can we overlook the impact that the international media has had on the behavior of nonstate international actors such as terrorist groups, national liberation movements, and others. The availability of worldwide publicity via the international media on at least some occasions has served to goad certain international actors to action.

Transportation and communications breakthroughs have also revolutionized diplomacy by tying ambassadors more closely to their home capitals. In earlier eras, ambassadors often acted on their own discretion. But today, with rapid transportation and instantaneous communications, ambassadors often are called home for consultation, receive immediate instructions from their home government, or both.

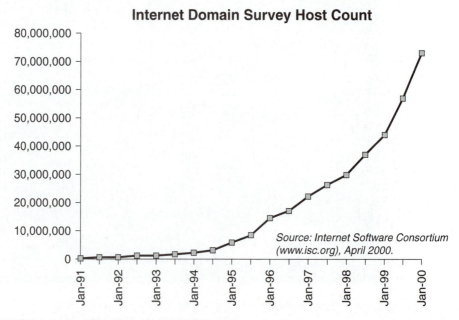

Internet Domain Survey Host Count

Source: Internet Software Consortium (www.isc.org), April 2000.

FIGURE 16-5   The Growth of the Internet.

Source: Internet Software Consortium (www.isc.org), April 2000.

TABLE 16-6   **A Country-by-Country Sampling of Computer Networks on the Internet, 2000**

Country	Initial Internet Connection	Number of Networks on the Internet, 2000*
Algeria	4/94	26
Argentina	10/90	142,470
Australia	5/89	1,090,468
Belarus	2/95	901
Belgium	5/90	320,840
Brazil	6/90	446,444
Burkina Faso	10/94	211
Canada	7/88	1,669,664
Chile	4/90	40,190
China	4/94	71,769
Denmark	11/88	336,928
Ecuador	7/92	1,922
Egypt	11/93	4,640
France	7/88	779,879
Germany	9/89	1,702,486
Ghana	5/93	110
Hungary	11/91	113,695
India	11/90	23,445
Indonesia	7/93	21,052
Japan	8/89	2,636,541
Kazakhstan	11/93	3,750
Kenya	11/93	602
Mexico	2/89	404,873
Morocco	10/94	961
Mozambique	3/95	162
Norway	11/88	401,889
Poland	11/91	183,057
Russia	6/93	214,704
Singapore	5/91	148,249
South Africa	12/91	167,635
Thailand	7/92	40,176
Turkey	1/93	90,929
United Kingdom	4/89	1,901,812
United States	7/88	1,875,663
Uruguay	4/94	25,385
Vietnam	4/95	126

Source: Internet Software Consortium (www.isc.org), April 2000.

*Note: The domains com, net, edu, and mil are respectively the first, second, third, and seventh most widely used domains with respectively 24.9 million, 16.9 million, 6.1 million, and 1.8 million hosts. By far most of these in all four domains are in the United States. They do not appear, however, in the above sampling because they are not identified by country.

Other scientific-technical breakthroughs, sometimes even the potential of break-throughs, can also alter political, social, and economic relations among international actors. The emergence of technical capabilities to initiate deep seabed mining made that issue one of the most bitterly contested items in the United Nations Law of the Seas negotiations in the late 1970s and early 1980s. Developing World states feared U.S. hegemony over the seabed, whereas the United States feared Developing World appropriation of U.S. technology. Thus, a scientific-technical advance became an issue that separated the United States and the Developing World.

But scientific-technical breakthroughs need not be the source of discord. The Green Revolution allowed many countries to avoid famine, and improvements in health care and immunization have increased life expectancy throughout the world. Manufacturing and agriculture have also benefited from a multitude of technical innovations.

There is no doubt that the importance of technology in contemporary international relations will continue to expand. For example, in addition to the continued advances in information and communication technologies that are revolutionizing and will continue to revolutionize human affairs, one can only speculate about the impact that advances in biotechnology, genome research, and other life sciences will have on international relations and other aspects of human affairs in the twenty-first century. All indications are that they will be immense.

Whatever the technological advances of the future are, however, the issues that emerge from the international political economy of technology are not simple. Technology has tremendous potential to bring great benefits to humankind. Unfortunately, technology and its imbedded issues also carry risks and dangers.[17]

 ## NET ASSESSMENT

In this chapter, we have examined five of the most important issues of the international political economy. As we have seen, the questions that these issues raise are exceedingly complex. What are the implications of the world's population growth? Can the world's population growth be controlled? If it can be, should it be? Why is there hunger, and can hunger and starvation be prevented? How long will the world have adequate fuel and mineral resources? What impact will today's technological advances have on tomorrow's world?

The answers to these questions are subjects of considerable debate and disagreement. It is likely that there will be no simple or widely accepted answer to any of them any time soon. Nevertheless, finding answers to these questions—and then beginning to implement them—may well be the most important task for humankind if the race is to survive and prosper in the twenty–second century.

 ## KEY TERMS AND CONCEPTS

international political economics   examines political aspects of international economics and economic aspects of international politics

population growth   on a global level, the result more of declining death rates without a corresponding decrease in birth rates

Thomas Malthus   an eighteenth century British clergyman who predicted that food production would expand arithmetically and population would grow exponentially, leading to hunger and famine.

trends and patterns in global food production and consumption   surpluses in global food production are often concentrated in a few areas which frequently do not coincide with locations where need is the greatest

role of oil in the world energy picture   oil is the most important single energy source in much of the world

trends and patterns in global energy production and consumption   global energy production varies widely according to the type of energy source while the largest percentage of global energy consumption occurs in the industrialized world

trends and patterns in global mineral production and consumption   global mineral production is concentrated in a variety of different sites, while the largest percentage of global mineral consumption occurs in the industrialized world

role of technology in international affairs   technology has played and is playing an immensely important role in shaping the international system, for example through information and communication technologies, transportation technologies, and weapons

international technology transfer   the flow of technology between and among international actors

Internet   the world wide network of computer networks that allows computers around the world to communicate with one another

 WEBSITE REFERENCES

international political economics: *www.csf.Colorado.EDU/ipe*   website of the International Political Economy Network

international development: *www.devdir.org*   a directory of international development organizations

global food production and consumption: *www.fao.org*   website of the UN's Food and Agriculture Organization

global energy production and consumption: *www.eia.doe.gov/oiaf/ieo/index.html*   the international energy outlook as seen by the U.S. Department of Energy

technology in international affairs: *www.ipef.org*   website of the International Political Economy Forum, which explores the impact of the Internet on international politics and economics

 NOTES

1. 2000 UN Population Information Network data.

2. U.S. Department of State, *Focus on Population and Development: The U.S. and the UN Conference on Population and Development* (Washington, DC: U.S. Department of State, Office of Public Communications, Bureau of Public Affairs, 1994), p. 8.

3. The World Bank, *World Development Report 1992* (Washington, DC: The World Bank, 1993), p. 29.

4. Ann Scott Tyson, "China, UN Join Forces to Reshape Population Policy," *Christian Science Monitor,* January 27, 1989, pp. 1–2.

5. "Population Control: The Issue that Got Scuttled," *Atlanta Journal,* May 23, 1992, p. E1.

6. For just a few of the many articles that covered these controversies, see *Time,* September 5, 1994, p. 52; *Time,* September 12, 1994, p. 56; *New York Times,* September 4, 1994, p. A1; and *New York Times,* September 6, 1994, p. A1.

7. The World Bank, *World Development Report 1992,* p. 29.

8. U.S. Central Intelligence Agency, *The World Factbook 1999* (Washington, DC: U.S. Government Printing Office, 2000), appropriate pages.

9. Ronald Freedman, "Theories of Fertility Decline: A Reappraisal," in Philip M. Hauser, ed., *World Population and Development* (Syracuse: Syracuse University Press, 1979); and John C. Caldwell, "Toward a Restatement of Demographic Transition Theory," *Population and Development Review* (September/December 1976). See also Gerald O. Barney et al., *The Global 2000 Report to the President,* Vol 1 (Washington, DC: U.S. Government Printing Office, 1980), p. 12.

10. See Thomas Malthus, *First Essays on Population, 1798* (New York: St. Martin's Press, 1966).

11. "Not By Bread Alone," *The Economist,* January 13, 1990, p. 65.

12. "Hunger as a Weapon of War," *The Economist,* December 2, 1989, pp. 50–52.

13. For other discussions of the political economy of the contemporary global food situation, see Peter Uvin, *The International Organization of Hunger,* (London: Kegan Paul International, 1994); and Jean Dreze et al., eds., *The Political Economy of Hunger* (New York: Oxford University Press, 1995).

14. For another view of the world's oil situation, see Georgia Philip, *The Political Economy of International Oil* (Edinburgh: Edinburgh University Press, 1994).

15. Kenneth A. Kessel, *Strategic Minerals: U.S. Alternatives* (Washington, DC: National Defense University Press, 1990), p. 207. See also World Resources Institute, *World Resources 1994–95* (New York: Oxford University Press, 1994).

16. For further analysis of the role of technology in international affairs, see Eugene B. Skolnikoff, *The Elusive Transformation: Science, Technology, and the Evolution of International Politics* (Princeton: Princeton University Press, 1992); Dominique Foray and Christopher Freeman, *Technology and the Wealth of Nations: The Dynamics of Constructed Advantage* (Pinter Publishers, 1992); Dennis Pirages, *Global Technopolitics: The International Politics of Technology and Resources* (Pacific Grove, CA: Brooks-Cole, 1989); and John A. Alic et al., *Beyond Spinoff: Military and Commercial Technologies in a Changing World* (Boston: Harvard Business School Press, 1992).

17. For several discussions of the role of technology in international relations, see Frank Barnaby and Marlies ter Borg, eds., *Emerging Technologies and Military Doctrine: A Political Assessment* (London: Macmillan, 1986); David S. Alberts and Daniel S. Papp, *The Information Age Anthology, Volumes I–III* (Washington, D.C.: National Defense University Press, 1997, 2000, and 2001); and Lloyd J. Dumas, *Lethal Arrogance: Human Fallibility and Dangerous Technologies* (New York, NY: St. Martin's Press, 1999).

Chapter 17

War, Peace, and Violence

- What are the boundaries between war and peace?
- How serious a problem is war and international violence in the twenty-first century?
- What are the different types of war and international violence?
- What causes war and international violence?
- What causes peace?
- Can war and international violence be avoided and peace assured?

No issues present greater challenges to humankind than war, peace, and violence. Energy and resource shortfalls present the unwelcome alternative of a deteriorated global standard of living, and environmental deterioration, in its most extreme form, offers the specter of a future earth made unlivable by humans. War and violence, however, present the threat of immediate death and destruction. Although the end of the East–West conflict and the breakup of the Soviet Union immensely reduced the possibility of large-scale nuclear war, the hard reality remains that thousands of nuclear warheads still exist, any one of which could devastate an entire city. Thus, without minimizing the severity of problems relating to international political economics or other global problems, humankind must successfully address the issues of war, peace, and violence, both on a short-term basis and over the long term.

War and violence are nothing new to the human experience. The fourth chapter of the Bible records man's first murder, and the ancient Hindu classic, *The Bhagavad Gita,* opens with a chronicle of the "heroic warriors, powerful archers, . . . and the chariots of war" of two great armies about to lock in combat.[1] Man's violence against man has ranged from confrontations between individuals armed only with their bare fists to confrontations between armed forces several million strong, equipped with nuclear weapons capable of destroying civilization. Violence and war, it would seem, are part of the human condition. Since the end of World War II alone, there have been at least 140 wars. Over 45 million people died in these conflicts, approximately 28 million in the fighting and another 17 million because of war-related famine or illness.[2]

Historically, war and peace have been viewed as mutually exclusive. Cynics considered peace to be merely a respite between wars, simply a period of time to prepare for war.

Other analysts were more optimistic, arguing that war was the aberrant condition. To optimists, peace could be preserved only if the right combination of factors could be found. And so, at least until recently, a distinction was drawn between peace and war. By definition, war was the absence of peace, and peace the absence of war.

This overstated dichotomy between war and peace has been relegated to the dustbin of history as extended periods of **neither war nor peace** have become increasingly common. Leon Trotsky's famous dictum may have been considered ridiculous by Germany in 1918, but it is an apt description of the state of much of international relations since World War II.[3]

Indeed, if only industrialized states are examined, none have been formally at war since World War II. Nevertheless, many instances of First and Second World violence and threatened violence have been evident. Throughout the Cold War, the United States and the USSR each feared violence would be unleashed by the other and built their militaries accordingly. On a more active plane, the United States fought in Korea, Vietnam, Grenada, Panama, and the Persian Gulf; bombed Libya and supplied the Contras in Nicaragua; and participated in a number of covert actions throughout the world. Even so, the United States never declared war. Similarly, the former Soviet Union fought in Afghanistan, sent troops into Eastern European states on two occasions, supported national liberation struggles throughout the world, and funded terrorist organizations, but never declared war.

Examples of the "neither peace nor war" status of contemporary international relations are not limited to the superpowers. Since World War II, Great Britain has fought in Malaya and the South Atlantic, and France has fought in Indochina, Algeria, and sub-Saharan Africa. China has struggled with the United States, India, the former Soviet Union, and Vietnam, but never declared war. Indeed, as shown in Table 17-1, 25 conflicts, each of which had over 1,000 deaths, were underway in 2000 alone. The locations of these conflicts, not a single one of which was a formally declared war, are shown in Table 17-2,

TABLE 17-1   Number of Conflicts, 1950–2000

Year	Number of Conflicts with Over 1,000 Dead	Number of Conflicts with Over 100,000 Dead
1950	11	6
1955	10	4
1960	12	7
1965	17	10
1970	17	8
1975	20	8
1980	26	7
1985	33	11
1990	33	9
1995	28	7
2000	25	6

Sources: 1950–1994: Lester R. Brown et al., eds., *Vital Signs 1995* (New York: W. W. Norton, 1995 and 2000), p. 111. 1995: Compiled by the author.

Chapter 17

IT, WAR, AND PEACE: INFORMATION WARFARE

As more and more countries, corporations, organizations, and individuals become dependent on information and information technology to conduct their activities, "information warfare" is becoming a main focus of military affairs. Information warfare could be directed against states, IGOs, MNCs, NGOs, or even individuals. In short, anyone or anything that uses information or information technologies could be the target of an attack.

As we saw in Chapter 14, information warfare could take many forms. Hardware and software could be electronically destroyed or degraded, with no physical sign of attack. Critical information could be acquired or altered, endangering national security or personal identity. False information could be inserted into information systems, again threatening national security or personal identity. Unauthorized access could be obtained and millions of dollars stolen. Unauthorized orders could be given and international tensions escalated by mistake. Important services could be denied, as occurred in 2000 when amazon.com, e-bay, and other electronic businesses were the targets of denial-of-service attacks. Confidence in systems could be undermined and banking systems closed down.

These are not hypothetical situations. All have occurred. Indeed, businesses and governments around the world are especially aware of the threat of attack against information and information systems. In the twenty-first century, protecting information security is a multibillion dollar a year business. Nevertheless, security is far from guaranteed, and information warfare and information attacks remain immense dangers.

Who might launch such a war or an attack? One study by Sandia National Laboratory identified 37 types of actors that might launch such an attack. Such actors included insiders, especially employees who had legitimate access to information technology; hackers, that is, people who enjoy using computers and exploring the information infrastructure and systems connected to it; and crackers, that is, people who maliciously break into information systems and intentionally cause harm. They also included criminals who break into systems for profit; vandals who damage things for fun; activists who take actions they believe might forward their ends; drug cartels; terrorists; foreign governments; infrastructure warriors who attack information at the behest of foreign governments; private paramilitary groups; and extortionists.

Not all information attacks can be described legitimately as "warfare." Some are pranks, and others are initiated for profit, revenge, or political purpose. Nevertheless, the increasing dependence of all parts of society on information technologies is expanding the vulnerabilities of whomever uses information and information technology. Information warfare and information attacks, coming from anywhere in the world with no real notice, are everyday realities of twenty-first century international relations. They are as much a threat to international actors as weapons of mass destruction.

TABLE 17-2   Locations of Conflicts, 1999–2000

Afghanistan	Iraq
Algeria	Lebanon
Angola	Liberia
Bosnia	Mexico
Chechnya	Northern Ireland
Columbia	Philippines
Congo	Sierra Leone
East Timor	Somalia
Ethiopia/Eritrea	Sri Lanka
Georgia	Sudan
Kosovo	Turkey
India/Pakistan	West Bank/Gaza
Indonesia	

which has already appeared in Chapter 14. With only three or four exceptions, each may also be described as a civil war or a war of national liberation. The definitions of such wars are discussed in the next section.

The distinction between war and peace is made difficult not only by the reluctance of states to declare war formally, but also by the proliferation of types of international actors that occurred in the late twentieth century. After the Treaty of Westphalia, war was traditionally a condition of large-scale violence between two state actors. However, as different types of international actors gained prominence in the late twentieth century and acquired weapons, conflicts between state actors and nonstate actors, and conflicts between nonstate actors and nonstate actors as well, became inevitable. The U.S. involvement in South Vietnam; U.S. support for the Contras in Nicaragua; the Soviet involvement in Afghanistan; British actions in Malaya; and French involvement in Algeria, Indochina, and in several locations in sub-Saharan Africa were all instances of conflicts between states and nonstate actors.

Terrorism again requires brief mention here. More than any other form of international violence, terrorism blurs the distinction between war and peace. Whether terrorism is a form of warfare is a matter of debate, but no doubt exists that it is a form of violence that plays a large role in contemporary international relations. As Figure 17-1 shows, terrorist attacks fell to a twenty year low of 273 in 1998. However, the 1990s saw an average of about 381 terrorist attacks per year, more than one terrorist attack every day somewhere in the world.[4]

The difficulty in distinguishing between war and peace in the twenty-first century is more than a semantic problem emanating from the reluctance of states to declare war, the proliferation of the number of types of actors, and the uncertainty created by terrorism. Low-intensity conflicts and civil wars also increased in number and scope in the late twentieth century. An increased numbers of parties who consider themselves in some way aggrieved, the greater international availability of weapons, and the ease of international movement are all factors that contribute to the increase of violence in the international arena. To be accurate, questions of war and peace must be realistically discussed as questions of war, peace, and violence.

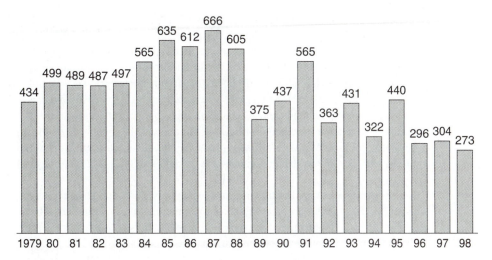

FIGURE 17-1   International terrorist incidents, 1979–98

Source: U.S. Department of State

   Diplomats, theologians, military officers, academics, and other men and women from all walks of life have regularly addressed themselves to issues of war, peace, and violence. On occasion, their efforts to reduce or eliminate the incidence of war and violence have succeeded. More often, they have not. War and violence continue to plague humankind, seemingly without respite. Peace often seems the aberrant condition. Nevertheless, with the awesome growth in destructive power of nuclear *and* conventional weapons, and with increased availability of those weapons throughout the world, the urgency of reducing or eliminating the incidence of war and violence has acquired a new poignancy. Humankind's survival as a species may be in the balance.

   However, efforts to enhance the prospects for peace must be predicated on an accurate understanding of what causes war and violence, and on how war, peace, and violence fit within the international community. Therefore, before we examine the causes of war, peace and violence, we will identify and discuss five major categories of international conflict.

 ## TYPOLOGIES OF INTERNATIONAL CONFLICT

War and international violence take many shapes and forms. In their efforts to better understand war and violence, scholars and analysts have developed many different categories, or typologies, of international conflict. For the most part, five categories of international conflict predominate: 1. international crises; 2. low-intensity conflict; 3. terrorism; 4. civil war and revolution; and 5. international war. Each requires separate commentary.

International Crises

Sometimes we seem to live in an age of continual crisis. For example, during the 1990s, news accounts have applied the term *crisis* to a wide variety of international events: The

Persian Gulf crisis, the Somali crisis, the Kosovo crisis, the debt crisis, the food crisis, and the environmental crisis are a few examples. Some included violence, as in the Persian Gulf and Kosovo. Others did not, as in the debt crisis and the food crisis.

For our purposes, a more restricted definition of crisis is requisite. One of the most useful definitions demands that four sets of circumstances prevail: (1) high priority goals of an actor must be threatened; (2) a limited amount of time is available before action must be taken; (3) the situation must be for the most part unanticipated; and (4) the situation must not escalate into armed conflict.[5] When many of the benchmarks of East–West relations since World War II are listed—for example, the Formosan Straits crisis, the Berlin crisis, and the Cuban Missile Crisis—it is evident that crisis was central to the East–West relationship.

But crises were not limited to East–West relations, even under the restrictive criteria just set forth. The Iranian hostage crisis, for example, met the requirements for a true crisis. A high-priority U.S. objective, the safety of its diplomatic legation in Iran, was threatened. The Carter administration believed the situation was time sensitive. The capture of the hostages was generally unanticipated. And the situation did not escalate into armed conflict.

Because crises, under the definition we have adopted, preclude war and most types of violence, the question may legitimately be asked, "Why are crises included in a typology of war and violence?" The answer is because many crises escalate into war and violence. Although quantitative evidence suggests that crisis escalation to warfare has become less frequent, possibly because of the increased cost of war, crises nevertheless must be viewed as a special stage in the relationships between international actors. They are manifestations of a condition of "neither war nor peace."[6]

International crises may be considered a type of negotiation or communication between international actors that arises when neither side desires war or violence, but considers its own goals important enough to risk war or violence. For example, former U.S. Secretary of State John Foster Dulles believed the United States should follow a policy he called **brinkmanship,** that is, the art of being able to move closer to the brink of war than one's potential opponent. The more skilled an actor is in practicing "brinkmanship," the more successful he will be in resolving crises to his advantage.[7] Crises may in this light be viewed as situations in which one's resolve and intent are communicated to potential opponents.

This method of negotiation or communication carries with it the danger of sliding over the brink into war and escalating into violence. Often, as in World War I and the Vietnam conflict, no sharp distinction between crisis and conflict is apparent. The "brink" in fact may not be a brink, but rather an ever steeper incline that precludes a reversal of policy. Negotiation by crisis is therefore an extremely risky way to achieve one's objectives.

Nevertheless, international actors and states in particular continue to engineer crisis situations in efforts to achieve their objectives. For example, in 1982, Argentina did not expect Great Britain to mount an effort to recapture the Falkland Islands following the Argentine takeover. Great Britain in turn miscalculated the Argentine seriousness of purpose. Both sides sought to move closer to the brink of conflict without actually initiating conflict in an effort to make the other side back down. Both sides failed. By the time the British task force reached the Falkland Islands, the brink—or was it an ever steeper incline?—had been passed. Armed conflict broke out.

In the West, and particularly in the United States, some analysts have developed a degree of confidence in human ability to "manage" crisis. **Crisis management** has become a major conceptual tool of Washington's national security community. Basing its appeal on the assumption that war and violence are not rational or cost-effective responses to disagreements between international actors, crisis management theorists have developed techniques of bargaining, signaling, and nonverbal communication that, they hope, will prevent actors from taking the last step into war and violence. Little evidence suggests that their methods have been successful. Indeed, by wrongly assuring decision makers that their lines of logic are clearly evident to others and by incorrectly persuading decision makers that a particular action will send an unambiguous signal to others, crisis management techniques may have precipitated the transition of some situations from crisis to war and violence.[8]

Low-Intensity Conflict

Relations between and among state and nonstate actors are often marred by small skirmishes along borders or at sea, by individual or small group violence, or by other forms of sporadic violence. Conflict as diverse as ethnic cleansing in Kosovo, guerrilla warfare in Colombia, border fighting between Ethiopia and Eritrea, and exchanges of gunfire along the 38th parallel between North and South Korea fit within the broad heading of low-intensity conflict. Crises may escalate to low-intensity conflict, or move beyond **low-intensity conflict** directly to full-scale warfare.

Low-intensity conflict may be limited either in frequency or in level of violence. Fighting along the Sino-Soviet border, for example, occurred rarely after the two communist powers had their falling out, and with the exception of a period during 1969, was not large-scale. Similarly, the signing of the Korean Armistice ended main force engagements between North Korea and United Nations forces, but gunfire often erupts along the demarcation line, often with no damage and no loss of life.

Low-intensity conflict has long been a part of international affairs, but its importance has only been recognized in the relatively recent past. A number of reasons exist for its newfound notoriety. First, low-intensity conflict presents the danger of escalation to a higher level of violence. Once violence has been initiated, a significant psychological inhibition has been overcome, and escalation to more extreme levels of violence becomes more probable. Second, with the spread of modern weapons, low-intensity conflict has the potential to become extremely destructive. Closely related to this, and the third reason for the notoriety of low-intensity conflict, is global interdependence. In an interdependent world, the effects of a temporary disruption of peaceful activity in one location ripple out to other areas. For example, when low-level fighting first erupted in the former Yugoslavia in the early 1990s, not only European states, but also the United States and the UN soon became involved.

Low-intensity conflict may be used as a tool of policy by a state actor or a nonstate actor, or it may on some occasions spontaneously erupt. As a tool of state policy, it may be used to drive home a point. For example, in 1999, few people doubted that the Indonesian government supported and perhaps initiated the wave of violence directed against pro-independence groups and individuals in East Timor by gangs and militia groups. Indonesia clearly intended to maintain control of East Timor, or failing that, to depart leaving behind a trail of blood and destruction.

Nonstate actors may use low-intensity conflict in the same way. For example, the Palestinian movement Hamas used low-intensity conflict throughout most of the middle and late 1990s to try to disrupt the Palestinian-Israeli peace process. In addition, low-intensity conflict can erupt spontaneously from the flow of events rather than planned policy. Thus, the skirmishes along the Sino–Soviet border in the 1960s were the result of neither Soviet nor Chinese policy, but rather local military responses to local stimuli. The same is true of some of the sporadic gunfire and shelling between North and South Korea.

Low-intensity conflict is one of the most prevalent forms of violence in the international arena. In the eyes of some, terrorism is one form of low-intensity conflict. Given the specific objective of terrorism, however, and its increased use as a peculiar form of international violence, terrorism is here categorized as a distinct form of international violence.

Terrorism

Lenin summed up the purpose of **terrorism** as concisely as anyone: "The purpose of terrorism is to inspire terror." Despite the fact that the political, economic, or social objectives of terrorists range across all fields of human endeavor, terrorism must be listed in any typology of war and international violence either as a subset of low-intensity conflict or as a separate category. The problem with terrorism is defining it. As we saw in Chapter 5, in many cases, the difference between a freedom fighter and terrorist depends on one's perspective. Yet Lenin's stark description of terrorism permits distinctions to be drawn even within the shadowy world of the terrorist. Thus, when Hamas bombed several Israeli buses in 1998, there was no doubt that this was terrorism. But had Hamas attacked an Israeli army depot, a Palestinian might describe the actions as low-intensity conflict.

As a form of violence, terrorism generally causes few casualties. There are exceptions, however, as when the U.S. federal building in Oklahoma City was bombed in 1995 with almost 200 people being killed or when Pan Am 103 was blown up by a terrorist bomb in 1988 with over 250 deaths. Nevertheless, terrorism has a psychological impact far beyond the death and destruction that it causes. One excellent example of this was the 40 to 50 percent drop in U.S. tourism to Europe that took place in 1986 following a number of terrorist attacks in Europe and the U.S. retaliatory strikes against Libya. Another excellent example is the increased level of tension evident throughout New York City in 1993 following the terrorist bombing of the World Trade Center, which killed six people.

Terrorism is an extremely useful tool for those elements of international society that find themselves unable to influence events in the way they desire. For the most part, terrorism is therefore a tool of violence used by nonstate actors against state authority.

Sometimes, however, states also use terrorism. During the Cold War, the United States and USSR accused each other of fostering state-supported terrorism. More recently, the United States has accused Iran, Libya, Iraq, and North Korea of being terrorist states. All deny the charge, but defend their right to fight "U.S. imperialism" in any way they see proper. Indeed, the concept of "state-supported terrorism" has become one of the hallmarks of contemporary international relations.

Terrorism is common in international life because of a number of reasons. The first is the widespread availability of arms. It is not difficult to purchase or steal arms in most international cities. A second cause of terrorism is the growth of interdependence. With more and more economic, social, and political events and endeavors being connected to each other, terrorists see many secondary targets that can be attacked in the hope of bringing pressure to bear on their primary target. Third, the lack of international consensus about the future of the international community may also lead to terrorism. Ideology and frustration can serve as powerful goads to violent action. A fourth cause is the information and communication revolution. With today's almost instantaneous global communications, the impact of terrorist action is worldwide whether it is a small pipe bomb in Centennial Olympic Park in Atlanta or simultaneous large truck bomb explosions at U.S. embassies in Nairobi and Dar es Salaam. Terrorism as a form of international violence has come of age.

Civil War and Revolution

In general terms, civil wars are conflicts within a state between two or more groups fought because of disagreements over the future of that state. At least one of the groups at war must be a nonstate actor; the other group(s) may be either the state's government or additional nonstate actors. Civil wars may be massive upheavals including millions of men and women, as were the American Civil War and the Chinese Revolution, or they may be more limited. All levels of violence may be included. The American Civil War was fought between full armies, as was the Chinese Revolution during its later phases. Guerrilla warfare must also be considered civil war, for movements internal to a country are here seeking to overthrow a government. At the opposite extreme from conflicts such as the American Civil War, certain forms of terrorism may be described as low-intensity civil war. The terrorist, after all, has a different view of the desired future of the state structure he or she is attacking.

The frequency of civil war appears to be increasing. One study analyzed the wars that occurred between 1900 and 1941, and found that over 80 percent of them were traditional wars between the armed forces of two or more states. Another study examined wars that took place between 1945 and 1976, and discovered that over 85 percent of them were either "internal antiregime" or "internal tribal" wars, that is, civil wars. This study did *not* include terrorist-oriented activity.[9] As was indicated earlier in this chapter, of the conflicts under way in the world in 2000, all but three or four were civil wars or wars of national liberation. The conclusion to be reached is simple—since World War II, state authority has been challenged more often from *inside* the state than from *outside* it.

Civil wars often have international dimensions, either because one or another of the parties involved in the war receives support from external sources or because an external actor is vitally concerned with the outcome of the war. This is not a new phenomenon, but a rediscovered one. The two "civil wars" that the United States has fought provide ample proof of the international relevance of civil wars. During the American Revolution (a civil war in the sense that British subjects were fighting for their independence from British rule), France helped the revolutionaries because of a French desire to weaken the British Empire. Poles and Germans also came to the aid of the North Americans on an individual basis because of their support for the ideals that the revolution espoused. During the War Between the States, Great Britain lent support to the South, primarily because Britain saw its economic interests tied more closely to Southern cotton and timber than to Northern industry.

During the twentieth century, ideology, economics, power, and religion have internationalized virtually every civil war. The Russian Civil War saw British, French, American, and Japanese intervention. The Spanish Civil War included elements from Italy, Germany, France, Great Britain, the Soviet Union, and the United States. The Chinese Revolution also was internationalized. During the Cold War, internal conflicts without fail were analyzed by Washington and Moscow on the basis of which side was more "democratic" or more "procommunist." Even during the height of East–West detente, the Angolan Civil War, the Ethiopian conflicts, and the racial strife in Zimbabwe, all of which began as civil wars, rapidly took on significant international import. The United States often interpreted Latin American events in light of their East–West implications. The Nicaraguan, Grenadan, and El Salvadoran situations, to Washington, presented a threat of communist penetration of the western hemisphere, and the frequent government changes in Bolivia and Peru caused consternation in Washington and elsewhere whenever a too radical public policy line was adopted by the new government.

Since the end of the Cold War, several "old" civil wars that once were interpreted in East–West terms have continued, such as the conflicts in Afghanistan, Angola, and Cambodia. Although they have lost their "headline" quality, they have retained many of their international characteristics. Islamic fighters from around the world are involved on one side or another in Afghanistan, and the UN has sent peacekeeping forces into both Angola and Cambodia.

In addition, several "new" civil wars have broken out in the former Yugoslavia, Rwanda, and Somalia. In all of these cases—and in others as well—there is a significant international component. In the early twenty-first century, it is very difficult to confine a civil war to a single state. Most civil wars either are or have potential to become "International Civil Wars."[10]

Civil wars occupy a curious place in any typology of wars and violence. On the one hand they are quite often destructive. Because of their inordinate violence, civil wars have been condemned as needless and senseless destroyers of life and treasure. Advocates of "evolution, not revolution" base their arguments on a solid body of evidence as to the destructiveness of even limited civil war. On the other hand, civil wars have been defended as the last recourse of action against corrupt, outdated, or unyielding social systems and governments. The American, French, Russian, Chinese, Cuban, and other revolutions all have been defended on exactly these grounds—the entrenched order refused to permit orderly change, and the violence of civil war and revolution was the only recourse available.

International War

International war is conflict between or among states carried out by their armed forces.[11] It is an accepted form of conducting relations between and among states, and has been accepted by international law as an inevitable if not desirable element of state interaction. It is distinct from low-intensity conflict only in its level of violence. However, in some cases this may be misleading. "The Phony War" period of World War II, for example, was a period of extremely low-intensity conflict as each side prepared for battle, and yet it was also a period of war inasmuch as Great Britain and France had declared war on Germany, and vice versa. Conversely, the Korean conflict was officially labeled a "police action" by the United States and the United Nations despite its extreme level of death and destruction; it was a war in everything but name.

For our typology, all declared wars and all periods of extensive military engagement between and among states even if not declared as war will be considered war. A state may have a number of reasons for not declaring a major military conflict a war. A declaration of war may break treaties a state is committed to, prove constitutionally illegal or politically unpopular within the initiating belligerent state, reduce or eliminate the element of military surprise, draw forth neutrality and neutrality regulations from other states, or widen rather than localize a conflict. If one examines those military confrontations fought by the major world powers since World War I, it is startling how seldom war was declared. Instead, terms such as intervention, reprisal, embargo, pacification, blockade, and police action were all used as euphemisms to describe military conflicts as diverse as the Japanese campaign against China between 1931 and 1941, the Soviet actions in Afghanistan between 1979 and 1989, the U.S. involvement in Vietnam between 1965 and 1973, and the Chinese and Indian border conflict of 1962. Although none was a formally declared war, they all must be viewed as wars.

As recently as the late 1980s, Yugoslavia was a country where Bosnian Muslims, Croats, Serbs, and Slovenes lived with each other in peace. Civil war erupted there in the 1990s, leading to thousands of deaths and immense destruction, such as this mosque in Bosnia.

Similarly, at least in theory, wars may be "just" or "unjust." Humanity has long struggled with the question of what constitutes a just war. Plato thought that just wars were those fought for the benefit of the state and that war against non-Greeks was acceptable regardless of purpose. Aristotle accepted three types of wars as just—wars of self-defense, wars to control others for their own benefit, and wars against peoples that deserved to be enslaved. Early Christianity rejected all wars as unjust, but gradually changed its viewpoint as it became the state religion of many European courts. Following the 1648 Treaty of Westphalia, war increasingly was regarded as the right of all states, and questions about the "justness" or "unjustness" of war gradually were relegated to the background.

The twentieth century witnessed a resurgence in interest over the distinction between just and unjust wars. A major reason for the increased interest is the destructiveness of modern weapons and the inability of those weapons (or more accurately, the users of those weapons) to discriminate between military and civilian personnel and targets. The Covenant of the League of Nations and the United Nations Charter both include efforts to allow states to judge whether an international conflict is just or unjust, and the Tokyo and Nuremburg trials at the end of World War II both attempted to define "just" and "unjust" actions by individuals and states during war. In 1983, Catholic bishops in the United States concluded that any use of nuclear weapons was unjust. More recently, Stanley Hoffman argued in 1995 that under certain conditions where human rights were being violated or other generally accepted standards of civilized behavior were being egregiously violated, it was morally and ethically necessary to intervene in other states.[12]

The United States' and NATO's attacks on Yugoslavia in 1999 were undertaken for exactly such reasons in response to Yugoslavia's ethnic cleansing campaign against Albanian Muslims living in Yugoslavia's province of Kosovo. Was the United States and NATO assault against Yugoslavia just or unjust? If defense of human rights is of paramount importance, it was clearly just. If the protection of sovereignty is of paramount importance, it was clearly unjust. Obviously, no consensus exists on what is a just or an unjust war.[13]

 ## *THE CAUSES OF WAR AND INTERNATIONAL VIOLENCE*

What causes war and international violence? Perhaps even more importantly, how can war and international violence be averted and peace achieved? The answers to these questions have been and remain a matter of dispute. As we have seen, there are several categories of war and international violence, and one of the few items upon which there is agreement regarding their causes is that there is no agreement.

For centuries, scholars, analysts, policymakers, theologians, philosophers, and others have debated the causes of war and international violence. Consensus is no nearer today than it was in ancient China, Greece, India, Rome, or elsewhere as to why war and violence occur. Nevertheless, the questions persist, and they are more than rhetorical or philosophic. To provide answers is to imply that certain actions should be taken or policies adopted to reduce, minimize, or eliminate the possibility of war and international violence. Almost all the reasons that have been advanced as to why wars and international violence occur fall within five broadly defined categories: 1. human nature; 2. human perceptual limitations; 3. poverty and disparities in wealth; 4. the internal structure of states; and 5. the international system itself.[14]

Human Nature

Perhaps the most widely accepted interpretation of the cause of war is human nature. Western intellectuals as diverse as St. Augustine, Reinhold Niebuhr, and Benedict de Spinoza all concluded that the source of international conflict springs from within people. Outside the West, Confucius and the unknown authors of the sacred scripts of Hinduism, among others, reached similar conclusions. Although these and other similarly disposed thinkers disagreed as to the type of fatal flaw within us, they all concurred that human nature caused war.

For example, St. Augustine posited that wars were a manifestation of original sin. "Perfectly good men," St. Augustine argued in *City of God,* "cannot war." Unfortunately, however, perfectly good men do not exist, at least if one accepts the concept of original sin. Therefore wars are inevitable.

Existing hand-in-hand with original sin in St. Augustine's worldview was human fear of death, inability to reason logically, and flawed will. The contradiction between fear of death and willingness to wage war was explained by the inability to reason logically. At the same time, although humans were cognizant of the immorality of warlike behavior, St. Augustine maintained that their flawed will rendered it impossible for them to control their actions even when they were aware of the immorality of their behavior and feared death. To St. Augustine and many others, "love of vain and hurtful things" was the source of human conflict, whether it was on the individual scale of murder or the state-sanctioned scale of war.

Benedict de Spinoza argued that people were led by simple passion to undertake acts that defy reason. People are slaves to their passions, Spinoza argued, and because of this, conflicts have occurred as individuals and groups sought to assuage the demands of their passions. In Spinoza's view, passion and reason were at odds. If humans followed reasonable courses of action, passion would become slave to humans and wars would be less frequent. Spinoza, however, was no naive idealist. Whoever believed that people could be "induced to live according to the bare dictate of reason" was "dreaming of the poetic golden age, or of a stage play," as Spinoza said in *Political Treatise.* One of the roles of the state, Spinoza maintained, was to promote peace. Not surprisingly, however, inasmuch as states were subject to the conflict between passion and reason that rages within humans, they could become warlike if they fell prey to human passion.

Spinoza's dualism of passion and reason was rejected by Reinhold Niebuhr. Nevertheless, Niebuhr's view of international conflict still placed its cause within human nature. To Niebuhr, people were flawed. As he said in *Beyond Tragedy,* war stemmed from "dark unconscious sources in the human psyche." Niebuhr further argued in *Christianity and Power Politics* that exploitation, class division, conquest, and intimidation stemmed from "a tendency in the human heart." To Niebuhr, human nature was the cause of war.

Similar conclusions were also reached in Asia. In China, Confucius concluded that "there is deceit and cunning in man, and from these wars arise." Wars could arise between feudal barons or between emperors and kings, but Confucianism still attributed them to human "deceit and cunning." In *The Bhagavad Gita,* the answer to the question of what caused war and violence was pronounced to be a fatal flaw in human character. As Krishna revealed to Arjuna, people are driven to act sinfully and to conduct war by "greedy desire and wrath, born of passion . . . wisdom is clouded by desire, the everpresent enemy of the wise . . . which like a fire cannot find satisfaction."

Ethnic conflict and the more extreme forms of nationalism are often seen as a product of humankind's flawed nature. The inability of many humans to accept those who are not the same as themselves as human beings who have value and worth, and in some cases to dominate or to kill them, according to this view, is a result of flaws in human nature. China's ancient repression of Cambodia and Vietnam, Rome's enslavement of captive peoples, Spain's destruction of the Aztec empire, the United States' Indian Wars, the Franco-English conflicts of the eighteenth and nineteenth centuries, Hitler's effort to dominate Europe and to exterminate the Jews, the Khmer Rouge's assault against fellow Cambodians, genocide in Rwanda, and ethnic cleansing in Bosnia and Kosovo all occurred, according to this viewpoint, because of flawed human nature.

Perceptual Limitations

As we discussed in Chapter 9, humans are limited beings. They are limited in their ability to comprehend natural phenomena, to understand and relate data, and to perceive from more than a single viewpoint. These facts of human existence have led some to conclude that war and violence are the result of human perceptual limitations.

John G. Stoessinger's *Nations in Darkness* is one of the most thoughtful and thought-provoking discussions of the role of human perceptual limitations in war and international violence. In *Nations in Darkness,* Stoessinger posits that because people are limited in their ability to comprehend and perceive, they most naturally seek to justify that with which they are most familiar and that with which they are identified. This leads to their rejection of and opposition to less familiar and less identifiable elements of life. In the context of human relations, this rejection and opposition leads to conflict. Using case histories from the U.S.–Soviet–Chinese triangle, Stoessinger argued that perceptual limitations have led to various conflicts and near-war situations.

This second outlook on the cause of war and international violence is less optimistic than the first. In the first, at least in the eyes of some of its proponents, religion, values, or human reason could overcome human passion and human flaws, thereby limiting warfare and violence. In the second, human perceptual limitations are unavoidable and inevitable, given the biophysical limitations of the species. People are victims of their own perceptual limitations, this view argues, and war and violence therefore must result.

Poverty and Disparities in Wealth

In his classic 1942 work, *A Study of War,* Quincy Wright presented evidence that industrialized states with relatively high standards of living were generally less likely to initiate war than were poorer states.[15] Significant exceptions to this rule, such as Germany in 1939, existed during Wright's time, but it is noteworthy that 56 years later, the Worldwatch Institute made a similar observation—over 90 percent of the conflicts and casualties of warfare since World War II occurred in developing states.[16]

To some, this is persuasive evidence that poverty, either in a relative or absolute sense, induces war. Poverty-stricken countries, frustrated in their efforts to "keep up with the Joneses" of the international community, may lash out at neighbors in an effort to meet needs or to overcome a sense of impotence. Alternatively, war in the Developing World may be brought about by poverty-produced political instability. Governments of Developing World states, seeking to quell domestic hostilities brought about by poverty, may cast about for an external enemy in an effort to defuse resentment directed at the government itself. A key point in the argument that poverty leads to war and violence is that either absolute or relative poverty may generate hostilities. Thus, the point is more aptly phrased that poverty and disparities in wealth cause war.

The Internal Structure of States

Another explanation for war and international violence argues that they are the result of the internal governmental, social, cultural, or economic structure of the state. Proponents of this perspective are as diverse as Immanuel Kant, Woodrow Wilson, and V.I. Lenin. All agreed that one kind of internal state structure led to war and that another led to peace, but their approaches and conclusions were decidedly different.

Late in the eighteenth century, German philosopher Immanuel Kant observed that states were neither wholly good nor wholly bad, but that when bad predominated, wars were inevitable. Wars were more likely to occur, Kant reasoned, when heads of state were authoritarian, made decisions on their own, and did not have to take public opinion into account. Thus, Kant wrote in 1795 in *Eternal Peace and Other International Essays* that states must actively seek to improve themselves internally or wars would result. The ideal state structure, he declared, was the republic, a state form which he believed was "unable to injure any other by violence."

Slightly more than a century later, Woodrow Wilson followed in Kant's liberal intellectual tradition, arguing that the absence of political democracy increased the chances of war and international violence. Wilson even advocated that states which achieved what he deemed was the superior statehood of democracy should actively encourage the establishment of governments in other states based on self-determination and democracy. Wilson urged states to create a world confederation of states that would operate on a democratic basis and provide collective security to prevent war and international violence. The key to the success of Wilson's plan was the widespread acceptance of political democracy, which was not forthcoming. Even so, to Wilson, the absence of democracy and the right of self-determination increased the likelihood of war.[17]

As we saw in Chapter 1, Lenin also believed that war and international violence resulted from the internal structure of the state. Unlike Kant and Wilson, who emphasized politics and values, Lenin emphasized economics. As a Marxist, Lenin believed that private ownership of the means of production was the cause of class conflict within a state. Capitalism also led to imperialism, Lenin believed, and imperialism inevitably led to war, in his eyes, as capitalist states struggled to find and control inexpensive resources, cheap labor, and external markets to increase their profits.

The International System

Still other observers and analysts reject the internal structure of states as the cause of war and international violence and suggest instead that the anarchical international system in which each state must fend for its own survival was the primary cause of war. States, or more accurately the leaders of states, were bound by no code of conduct other than that which they established for themselves and then chose to follow. Despite international law, no established pattern of international behavior existed that was both universally applicable and universally enforceable. Thus states, and the leaders of states, sought to achieve their goals and objectives through whatever means they deemed appropriate, including force of arms. This outlook flowed directly from the realpolitik interpretation of international relations advocated by Hans Morgenthau.

Morgenthau had many predecessors. In his *History of the Peloponnesian War,* Thucydides observed that Agamemnon "raised the force against Troy" because he was "the most powerful of the rulers of his day." In the ancient world, Thucydides believed, might made right. The anarchy of the international system permitted and encouraged the outbreak of conflict.

Jean Jacques Rousseau viewed the Europe of his era in a similar light. European laws were contradictory rules from "which nothing but the right of the stronger" could produce peace. Self-interest, Rousseau claimed in *A Lasting Peace,* would produce wars as long as states sought to preserve their identities and expand their powers. The culprit, Rousseau maintained, was neither humans, their perceptions, nor the internal structure of states, but rather the international system of states itself. An imperfect international community existed in Europe, and "the imperfections of this association make the state of those belonging to it worse than if they formed no community at all." To Rousseau, inasmuch as no authority existed above the state to control the state, states could and did act in their own selfish interests to promote their own self-defined objectives. War was the end result.

To those who see the international system as the primary cause of war, the structure of that system is of paramount importance. A first viewpoint argues that an international system that has one dominant power is the least likely to lead to war. Others maintain that such a system, in the absence of a benevolent dominant power, would lead to exploitation of all other international actors by the dominant power. A second point of view asserts that a bipolar system with two dominant powers is the least likely to lead to war as long as rough parity of power exists between the two. This type of system existed for most of the period since World War II, as we saw in Chapter 7. A third point of view maintains that a multipolar system with many centers of power is the most stable and the least likely to lead to war. Here, the rationale is that international actors will maintain flexible policies and attitudes so that a rough balance of power will always exist and war will be avoided.

For our purposes, it is worth noting that during the late 1990s and the early years of the twenty-first century, the international system appears to be moving from a bipolar system to a regionalized or multipolar system. We will explore these alternatives in the final chapter of this text. For now suffice it to say that despite disagreement over which system tends to be the most prone to induce war and international violence, the transition from one type of international system to another appears beyond the control of any single international actor.

One final systemic view of the cause of war and international violence must also be addressed, the **long-cycle theory.** There are various types of long-cycle theory, but all suggest in one way or another that large scale general wars occur over more or less regular periods of time. Some scholars argue the cycle is fifty years, others believe it is 100 years, and still others maintain it is as long as two hundred years. Quantitative evidence presents widely different results depending on the assumptions and arguments that are made.[18]

ALTERNATE PATHS TO PEACE

Clearly, there are many views about what causes war and international violence. Similarly, there are many views about how peace can be attained and maintained. Interestingly, although two individuals may disagree about what causes war, they sometimes can agree on how best to seek peace. Conversely, those who agree on why wars and international violence occur can and do have extensive disagreements about how peace can be attained and maintained.

Most views about alternate paths to peace can be grouped into one of ten different categories: 1. accept a set of religious or philosophical values; 2. maintain military power and deterrence; 3. control arms and disarm; 4. pursue economic interdependence; 5. create a system of international institutions that promote peace and conflict resolution; 6. institutionalize democracy; 7. institutionalize communism; 8. eliminate poverty and unequal distribution of wealth; 9. institutionalize and enforce international law; and 10. develop a world federation or world government.

Religion and Values

The view that war and international violence are caused by human nature paints an unpleasant picture of the species, but not all is necessarily gloomy. Few who assert that war and international violence are the products of human nature believe that human nature can be changed, but many believe that the excesses of human nature can be controlled or limited by religion or other philosophical values that oppose war and international violence.

For example, many religions and humanistic philosophies and ideologies argue that even if permanent peace is not possible, periods of peace can occur if humankind follows their beliefs and teachings. St. Augustine, Spinoza, Niebuhr, Krishna, Buddha, and Confucius would all, to one extent or another, accept the proposition that war and international violence would be less likely if their religions or philosophies would be accepted.

Military Power and Deterrence

Maintaining peace by preparing for war is a widely accepted and often followed prescription for keeping the peace and reducing the frequency of war and international violence. Regardless of whether military power is pursued on a national basis or achieved via collective security in alliances, and regardless of whether it is at the conventional or nuclear level, it is a key element in many people's eyes in keeping the peace.

Military power can deter war and violence, or so it is argued. The basis for deterrence, as we saw in Chapter 14, is the fear that if an individual, state, or group undertakes an action that harms another, then severe adverse consequences will befall the individual, state, or group that initiated the original action. Since individuals, states, and groups usually wish to avoid severe adverse consequences, they will therefore refrain from initiating the original action. Deterrence is achieved, an action that would have harmed another will have been averted, and peace will prevail.

Arms Control and Disarmament

However, others argue that weapons contribute to warfare and violence, and that weapons therefore should be quantitatively or qualitatively limited. Proponents of arms control also on occasion push for the elimination of certain types of weapons, for example, nuclear weapons. Arms control and disarmament are thus often viewed together as ways to try to prevent war and international violence.

Again as we saw in Chapter 14, the international community has initiated a number of arms control and disarmament efforts at the conventional and nuclear level. Some have been more successful than others. Two of the successful arms control efforts of the Cold War era were the 1972 Anti-Ballistic Missile (ABM) Defense Treaty, in which the United States and the Soviet Union agreed to limit the number of ABM systems that they deployed, and the 1986 Intermediate Nuclear Forces (INF) Treaty, in which the same two countries agreed to dismantle all their INF capabilities. Both treaties remain in force today, although the United States in the late 1990s began pushing for a modification of the ABM Treaty.

Economic Interdependence

Some economists, business leaders and MNC heads, national policymakers, and others argue that war and international violence can be reduced if not eliminated by reducing barriers to trade and commerce. In addition to its economic benefits, then, economic interdependence is seen by some as a major contributor to world peace. At its extreme, this school of thought asserts that "world peace through world trade" is possible.

Belief in economic interdependence as a critical element in maintaining peace has had a sizable policy impact. As we have already seen, it was one factor that led to the creation of the European Iron and Steel Community after World War II as European leaders struggled to find ways to prevent the continent from sliding over time back into another destructive war. Belief in the potential of trade and commerce to overcome political animosity and reduce the possibility of war was also one of the factors that led U.S. President Richard Nixon to initiate détente with the USSR in the early 1970s. In both examples, policymakers hoped that as countries linked their economies through trade, relationships would be created that lessened the likelihood of war.

International Institutions

Some scholars and policymakers believe that the chances for peace are best promoted by establishing a set of transnational political and economic institutions that help states work together to achieve their objectives and overcome their differences. Called **functionalism,** this belief relies heavily on international governmental organizations such as the World Bank, the International Monetary Fund, various regional bodies such as the Organization of African Unity and the Organization of American States, and of course the UN to promote international amity and peace.

Functionalism proceeds from the assumption that while states will rarely surrender their sovereignty, they will share it if the objective is achievement of a common good. Further, functionalism assumes that states under most conditions prefer to avoid war and international conflict and that "the right kind" of transnational political, economic, and social institutions will help achieve these objectives. It also hopes that shared cooperative behavior in areas in which transnational institutions operate will spill over into other areas as well.

Democracy

Following in the footsteps of Kant and Wilson, a number of scholars and policymakers in the late twentieth century increasingly accepted the thesis that democracy is the underlying element behind peace. Termed the **democratic peace,** this view stressed that "established democracies fought no war against each other during the entire twentieth century." This was because, as one noted scholar maintained, democracies have a tendency to "live-and-let-live" in their relations with each other because of shared cultural values, internal institutional restraints on war-making, the presence of alternative means of dispute resolution, and relatively slow decision making processes.[19]

These observations must be qualified. Democracies may not initiate wars against each other, but they do initiate wars and undertake violent actions against other international actors. Sometimes such wars, actions, and interventions are extremely violent. In addition, new and poorly established democracies sometimes slide back to previous modes of behavior. If one goes back to the nineteenth century, the American Civil War was in fact between two democratic entities that had similar views on many things, but disagreed on how centralized power should be and how broadly human rights should be extended. But they were still democracies.

Despite these qualifications, the weight of scholarly opinion, policy preference, and recent history leans heavily in the early twenty-first century on the side of those who argue that at a minimum, democracies rarely go to war with each other. Indeed, U.S. President Bill Clinton in his 1994 State of the Union address used this observation to justify U.S. support for democratization around the world. In addition, international institutions as diverse as the European Union, the International Monetary Fund, NATO, the UN, and the World Bank all laud democracy for the same reason.

Communism

Proponents of communism also believe that they have the solution to the problem of how to prevent war and international violence and instill peace: eliminate capitalism and institute a communist society. To communists, the elimination of capitalism would both end the exploitation of human by human within a state and remove the cause of the external conflicts of capitalist states that led to war and international violence. To Lenin and other communists as varied as Mao and Castro, capitalism brought war and violence and communism would bring peace.

Redistributing Wealth and Eliminating Poverty

At a less extreme level than communism, many people from developing states, religious organizations, humanitarian groups, and elsewhere argue that redistributing wealth and eliminating poverty would help reduce war and international violence. Remedies as different as foreign aid, humanitarian assistance, technical training, a restructured international economic system, and outright direct transfers of wealth from the Developed to the Developing World have all been proposed.

None have been implemented at levels large enough to lessen the concerns of those who maintain that poverty and disparities of wealth lead to war and international violence. Thus, UN High Commissioner for Refugees Sadaka Ogata spoke for many people in December 1997, arguing that "to establish a more peaceful, prosperous, and secure world, poverty must be eliminated and income differentials reduced."

International Law

Going back to the time of the Treaty of Westphalia, international law has been used to try to regulate, modify, and control the behavior of states. Given that states have until recently jealously guarded their sovereignty in virtually every instance, international law has had little impact on curtailing the frequency of war. It may be argued, however, that it has had occasional impact on the way wars have been fought. Laws of war have mandated how prisoners and civilians should be treated, what weapons could be used, and how neutral countries should act and be treated. But whether laws of war have limited violence in wars is another matter.

Nevertheless, it would be unwise to dismiss the possible impact of international law on war and international violence too quickly. As we saw in our discussion of international law, many more international laws are followed on a daily basis than are broken on a daily basis. At the same time, the creation and acceptance of international law helps establish a set of norms that help regulate international behavior. While it is naive to believe that world law may lead to world peace, it may not be overly optimistic that international law over time may lead to the acceptance of standards of international behavior that will lessen the likelihood of international actors resorting to war and to other forms of international violence.

World Federation or Government

A world federation or world government is one of the more enticing prescriptions for world peace. If the United Nations or some other international organization were given authority over global affairs and were also given the ability to enforce that authority, it is sometimes argued that war and violence would be curtailed, regardless of cause. A world government would theoretically be able to prevent human flaws (if those are the causes of war) from leading to conflict and would eliminate international anarchy (if that is the cause of war). Global standards of equity and justice could also be enforced, as could global standards of perception. In many respects, a world state appears an ideal solution to the problems posed by war and violence.

But many problems exist with such a solution. Aside from the obvious difficulty of how states can be persuaded to renounce their sovereignty and the independence of action that it affords them, no guarantee exists that war and violence would be eliminated by a world government or federation. Since World War II, it will be remembered, over 85 percent of all wars were civil wars. Governments of states in today's world have clearly shown their inability to eliminate domestic strife; why would a world state be any different?

Advocates of world peace through a world state or world law also often assume that a global order of either type would find most people willing to accept international law and that those who would not accept it would be easily and readily apprehended. This again may not be the case. Again using current states as examples, what guarantee is there under a world state or world law that a lawbreaker would, for example, resign his office as Richard Nixon did? Is not the Indian experience equally plausible? In India, when a court ruled that Prime Minister Indira Gandhi had violated election laws and requested that she resign, she refused and imprisoned her opposition.

WAR, PEACE, AND VIOLENCE IN THE TWENTY-FIRST CENTURY

In the twenty-first century world, boundaries between war and peace, and war and violence, are more blurred than ever. While the frequency of declared wars between states is decreasing, the frequency of civil wars with international ramifications remains high. At the same time, sub-state violence such as terrorism has become a hallmark of contemporary international relations.

Although it is a relatively simple task to group wars and international violence according to type if one is not too concerned about precise definitions, little consensus exists about the causes of war and international violence. Nevertheless, the search for reliable paths to peace continues, often simultaneously on different tracks.

Sometimes, these tracks may even appear contradictory. In many cases, contradictions may be less real than apparent. Advocates of military preparedness and disarmament may be equally committed to the pursuit of peace; they simply have different views on how it can be achieved. Military preparedness advocates argue that if one wants peace, one must prepare for war; disarmament advocates maintain that the chances for peace are diminished by the existence of arms and weapons. Similarly, both military preparedness proponents and world government proponents desire reduced international conflict; they simply disagree on how best to achieve it. Balance-of-power proponents see a match of countervailing capabilities as the best guarantee of peace; world government advocates rest their hopes for peace on the creation of a transnational body that will overcome petty parochial disagreements and enforce peace.

Peace and stability, then, remain elusive goals. World order, whatever its form, is no nearer a reality now than it was at the beginning of the last century. With the proliferation of international actors and the end of bipolarity, one may argue it is further from reality now than earlier. Nevertheless, the search for peace and stability continues. As long as the search continues, there is reason for optimism that humankind may someday successfully meet the challenges raised by war, peace, and violence.

 ## *KEY TERMS AND CONCEPTS*

neither war nor peace   first put forward by Leon Trotsky to describe relations between the U.S.S.R. and Germany in 1918, it also describes the state of much of international affairs since World War II

international crisis   any unanticipated situation where high priority goals of an actor are threatened; limited time is available before action must be taken; and the situation must not escalate into war

brinkmanship   in diplomacy, the art of being able to move closer to the edge of war than one's potential opponent in the hope of gaining diplomatic advantage

crisis management   the ability to manage and defuse tense international situations without going to war

low-intensity conflict   international violence limited in frequency or level, often used to describe small skirmishes, individual or small-group violence, terrorism, and guerrilla warfare

terrorism   violence initiated by groups of all ideological persuasions for a variety of objectives against innocent targets

civil war and revolution   any conflict within a state fought between two or more groups because of disagreements about the future of that state, with at least one group being a non-state actor

international war   any conflict between or among two or more states

causes of war and violence   almost all reasons advanced as to why war and violence occur fall within five categories: human nature, human perceptual limitations, poverty and disparities in wealth, the internal structure of states, and the international system itself

paths to peace   most views about paths to peace fall within ten categories: accept religious or philosophical values, maintain military power and deterrence, control arms and disarm, pursue economic interdependence, create international institutions that promote peace, institutionalize democracy, institutionalize communism, eliminate poverty and unequal distribution of wealth, enforce international law, and develop a world federation or government

functionalism   the theory that chances for peace are promoted by creating transnational political and economic institutions that help states work together to achieve objectives and overcome differences

democratic peace   the thesis that democracy is the underlying element behind peace

 ## *WEBSITE REFERENCES*

international wars and conflict: *www.ploughshares.ca/content/ACR/ACR99.html*   discusses armed conflicts underway in 1999, with links to earlier year's lists

international crisis: *www.crisisweb.org/default.cfm*   website of the International Crisis Group, dedicated to analyzing and resolving international crises

crisis management: *www.osce.org*   website of IGO devoted to early warning, conflict prevention, and crisis management in Europe

low-intensity conflict: *www.ndcf.org/Home3.htm*   website of the National Defense Council Foundation, specializing in studying low-intensity conflict, etc.

terrorism: *www.terrorism.com/index.shtm* homepage for the Terrorism Research Center, with articles and extensive link listings

democratic peace: *www2.hawaii.edu/~rummel* R.J. Rummel's website, with extensive documentation on democratic peace and war

 ## NOTES

1. *The Bhagavad Gita* (New York, NY: Penguin Books, 1962), pp. 43–47.

2. See also Lester R. Brown, et al., eds., *Vital Signs 2000* (New York, NY: W.W. Norton, 2000).

3. In 1918, Leon Trotsky proclaimed that a condition of "neither war nor peace" existed between Germany and the new Bolshevik government of Russia. After some hesitation, Germany attacked Bolshevik Russia despite Trotsky's slogan, and the Bolsheviks were forced to accept the humiliating Treaty of Brest-Litovsk.

4. See U.S. Department of State, *Patterns of Global Terrorism 1999* (April 2000).

5. For varied discussions of crises, see T. Clifton Morgan, *Untying the Knot of War: A Bargaining Theory of International Crises* (Ann Arbor: University of Michigan Press, 1994); Charles F. Hermann, ed., *International Crises* (New York: The Free Press, 1972); and Richard Ned Lebow, *Between Peace and War: The Nature of Individual Crisis* (Baltimore: Johns Hopkins University Press, 1981).

6. See Gerald W. Hopple, Paul J. Rossa, and Jonathan Wilkenfeld, "Threats and Foreign Policy: The Overt Behavior of States in Conflict," and Robert B. Mahoney, Jr., and Richard P. Clayberg, "Images and Threats: Soviet Perceptions of International Crises, 1946–1975," both in Patrick J. McGowan and Charles W. Kegley, Jr., eds., *Threats, Weapons, and Foreign Policy* (Beverly Hills: Sage, 1980), pp. 19–53, 55–81, respectively. See also John A. Vasquez et al., *Beyond Confrontation: Learning Conflict Resolution in the Post-Cold War World* (Ann Arbor: University of Michigan Press, 1995).

7. According to John Foster Dulles, brinkmanship was "the ability to get to the verge without getting into the war . . . if you are scared to go to the brink you are lost." See James Shepley, "How Dulles Averted War," *Life,* January 16, 1956, p. 70.

8. For a further discussion of "crisis management," see A. N. Gilbert and P. G. Lauren, "Crisis

Management: An Assessment and Critique," *Journal of Conflict Resolution,* Vol. 24 (December 1980), pp. 641–682.

9. Wright's *A Study of War* contains the data on traditional wars, whereas the "internal antiregime" and "internal tribal" data are from Istvan Kende, "Wars of Ten Years (1967–1976)," *Journal of Peace Research,* Vol. 15 (1978), pp. 227–241. See also William Eckhardt and Edward Azar, "Major World Conflicts and Interventions, 1945 to 1975," *International Interactions,* Vol. 5 (1978), pp. 75–110; Evan Luard, *Conflict and Peace in the Modern International System* (Boston: Little, Brown, 1968); Melvin Small and J. David Singer, "Conflicts in the International System, 1816–1977; Historical Trends and Policy Futures," in Charles W. Kegley, Jr. and Patrick J. McGowan, eds., *Challenges to America* (Beverly Hills: Sage, 1979), pp. 89–115; and Melvin Small and J. David Singer, *Resort to Arms: International and Civil Wars, 1816–1980* (Beverly Hills: Sage, 1982).

10. Pierre Hassner, "Civil Violence and the Pattern of International Power," *Adelphi Papers No. 83* (London: International Institute for Strategic Studies, 1971), p. 19.

11. For a more detailed definition, see Wright, *A Study of War,* pp. 8–13.

12. Stanley Hoffman, "The Politics and Ethics of Military Intervention," *Survival* (Winter 1995–1996), pp. 29–51.

13. For views opposed to intervention to protect human rights, see Christopher Layne, "The Case Against Intervention in Kosovo," *Nation* (April 19, 1999), pp. 11–16; and Ted Galen Carpenter, ed., *NATO's Empty Victory: A Postmortem on the Balkan War* (Washington, D.C.: The Cato Institute, 2000).

14. For other views on the causes of war, see Greg Cashman, *What Causes War? An Introduction to Theories of International Conflict* (New York, NY: Lexington Books, 1993); Lawrence Freedman, ed.,*War*

(New York, NY: Oxford University Press, 1994); David W. Ziegler, *War, Peace, and International Politics,* 8th ed. (New York, NY: Longman, 2000); and Joseph S. Nye, Jr., *Understanding International Conflicts: An Introduction to Theory and History,* 3d ed. (New York, NY: Longman, 2000).

15. Quincy Wright, *A Study of War* (Chicago: University of Chicago Press, 1942).

16. Lester R. Brown et al., *Vital Signs 1995,* p. 110.

17. See, for example, Bruce M. Russett, *Controlling the Sword* (Cambridge, MA: Harvard University Press, 1990); Gregory A. Raymond, "Democracies, Disputes, and Third-Party Intermediaries," *Journal of Conflict Resolution* (1994), pp. 24–42; and Margaret G. Hermann and Charles W. Kegley Jr., "Rethinking Democracy and International Peace: Perspectives from Political Psychology," *International Studies Quarterly* (December 1995), pp. 511–533.

18. For more detailed discussion of long-cycle theories, see Lois W. Sayrs, "The Long Cycle in International Relations: A Markov Specification," *International Studies Quarterly* (1993), pp. 215–238; Brian M. Pollins, "Global Political Order, Economic Change, and Armed Conflict: Coevolving Systems and the Use of Force," *American Political Science Review* (1996), pp. 103–117; and George Modelski and William R. Thompson, "The Long and the Short of Global Politics in the Twenty-First Century," *International Studies Review* (Summer 1999), pp. 109–140.

19. See Margaret Hermann and Charles W. Kegley, Jr., "Rethinking Democracy and International Peace: Perspectives from Political Psychology," *International Studies Quarterly* (1995), pp. 511–533; Edward Mansfield and Jack Snyder, "Democratization and War," *Foreign Affairs* (May-June 1995), pp. 79–98; Michael E. Brown et al., eds., *Debating the Democratic Peace* (Cambridge, MA: MIT Press, 1996); Steve Chan, "In Search of Democratic Peace: Problems and Promise," *Mershon International Studies Review* (1997), pp. 59–92; and Joanne Gowa, *Ballots and Bullets: The Elusive Democratic Peace* (Princeton, NJ: Princeton University Press, 1999), for different views on the democratic peace.

Chapter 18

Human Rights and Conflicts of Values

- Why do conflicts over human rights and values occur?
- Are there universal human rights?
- How well are human rights protected internationally?
- What happens when some states value individual freedom and others value collective rights?
- Must conflict between material values and spiritual values, modernization and traditionalism, and centralization and decentralization cause international problems?
- Can the conflict between political democracy and political authoritarianism/totalitarianism be resolved?
- What happens when there is disagreement on fundamental human values?

During the twentieth century, human rights and conflicts of values gradually became important international concerns that gained more and more of the attention of the international community. Everything indicates that they will become even more important and noticeable concerns during the twenty-first century.

But the increased attention that human rights and conflicts of values gained during the last century does not mean that there is widespread agreement about them. Many of the most significant international disagreements that exist today are over human rights and conflicts of values. Both remain evolving concepts that have potential to unite or divide the international community. We will begin with human rights.

 ## HUMAN RIGHTS

What exactly is meant by "human rights"? Where do they come from? How can they be protected? These three questions generate immense disagreement in the international community. The best way to understand the sources of that disagreement and what prevents a resolution is to first explore the origins of the concept of human rights.

Origins of the Concept

For most of recorded history, kings, queens, emperors, and other rulers did what they wished with their subjects, limited only by their personal preferences, their religious or philosophical beliefs, or the power of others. When political, economic, or social conditions became too burdensome, subjects on occasion rebelled against their rulers, but individual freedom and the natural rights of human beings, that is, the core of what is today most widely recognized as human rights, rarely caused rebellions. Except for a few religious leaders and philosophers, human rights was simply not a part of human consciousness. For centuries, rulers ruled and the ruled were ruled. That was the way things always had been and always would be, or so it seemed.

This began to change in the seventeenth and eighteenth century as British philosophers like John Locke and John Stuart Mill wrote about political democracy, equal opportunity, individual rights, and limited government while Adam Smith and other economists developed ideas about free market economics. Gradually, the ideas of these **classical liberal philosophers** and economists found a wider audience in Europe, especially within a small middle class that resented the inherited control and authority of the aristocracy and that was appalled by the living conditions of peasants and, by the nineteenth century, the growing proletariat industrial worker class.

It was in Great Britain's colonies in North America where the ideas of the classical liberals in the late eighteenth century first found their way into widespread national policy. The American Declaration of Independence in 1776 and the U.S. Constitution in 1789 put forward as the new nation's founding concepts the ideas—political democracy, equal opportunity, individual rights, limited government, and free market economics—that the classical liberal philosophers and economists had developed years before. In Europe, as we saw in Chapter 2, the ideas of the classical liberals and the American Revolution paved the way for the 1789 French Revolution, although the French Revolution eventually took a different course than its American counterpart.

By the beginning of the nineteenth century, then, the core ideas of what would become human rights were well established in North America and beginning to make inroads elsewhere in Europe. During the nineteenth century, more and more people became persuaded about the legitimacy of classical liberal thought. Nevertheless, few governments translated those thoughts into policy. The expansion of political democracy, equal opportunity, individual rights, limited government, and free market economics was slow.

The pace accelerated during World War I as U.S. President Woodrow Wilson announced that the United States was entering the war to "make the world safe for democracy." After the war, the Versailles Peace Treaty gave human rights another boost as it accepted national self-determination for the peoples who lived in the defeated countries. Conversely, many European leaders considered these ideas hopelessly naive.

With World War II and its accompanying violence and atrocities, human rights became an increasingly recognized international concern. The 1941 **Atlantic Charter,** for example, signed by U.S. President Franklin Roosevelt and British Prime Minister Winston Churchill, was a practical document pledging U.S.–British cooperation.[1] However, it also pledged support for national self-determination, collective security, economic collaboration leading to "social security," and a future in which "all the men in all the lands may live out their lives in freedom from fear and want." In 1942, 26 states

Chapter 18

IT, HUMAN RIGHTS, AND VALUES: QUESTIONS OF RIGHT AND WRONG

With its great mobility and global reach, advanced information technology could have an immense impact on the future of human rights and conflicts of values. But as with its application to many other international issues, the impact that IT will have on these issues is far from clear. "Technology is the answer," historian of technology Melvin Kranzberg once observed, "but it is not the question."

Information Age technologies have potential to cast the glare of global publicity on violators of human rights. The mobility of wireless transmitting systems with direct broadcast capabilities to satellite based global networks enables reporters and observers to communicate with a global audience from virtually any location on earth. This broadcast-from-anywhere capability often can serve as a deterrent against violations of human rights.

But other times, this is not the case. Ethnic cleansing in Bosnia and Kosovo and genocide in Rwanda continued even after the glare of global publicity had been turned on the atrocities. Earlier, in Somalia, pictures of a dead U.S. serviceman being dragged through the streets led not to a greater resolve to end the fighting, but to a greater resolve to end the U.S. intervention, the original purpose of which was to create conditions for the peaceful distribution of food.

Information Age technologies, then, may publicize human rights violations better, but they will not end such violations in and of themselves. Technology is the answer, but it is not the question.

Similarly, in the area of values, information technology plays a less than decisive role. Take, for example, the issues of freedom of the press and freedom of expression, and extend the issues to international values and the Internet.

Some governments use licensing and regulations to limit access to and activity on the Internet, filtering content and restricting or denying access in different ways. As of 2000, at least 20 countries completely or extensively controlled access to and activity on the Internet. Their declared intent was usually to "protect traditional values," "defend national security," "promote morality," or "prevent the spread of subversion," according to *Censor Dot Gov,* published by Freedom House. In 1996, the U.S. government also tried to censor the Internet by removing pornography with the Communications Decency Act, which was eventually ruled unconstitutional. And in China, the government has permitted only one gateway to the World Wide Web, monitors and controls use of that gateway, and censors domestic websites at the source.

These efforts and undertakings clearly fly in the face of time-honored American values such as freedom of the press and expression. But are such efforts and undertakings wrong?

Given the global reach of Information Age technologies, what rights or powers should governments, religions, political parties, or other organizations have to limit access to the data and information that IT can provide? Or should all data and information be readily available to anyone, and should everyone be able to connect to the global information infrastructure? The answers to these and related questions will be critically important as we try to sort out global conflicts of values in the Information Age.

signed the Declaration of the United Nations, which pledged cooperation in achieving the aims of the Atlantic Charter.

After World War II, the United Nations provided the first major forum for furthering human rights, especially with its 1948 adoption of the **Universal Declaration of Human Rights.**[2] The Universal Declaration proclaims that it identifies and states a "common standard" of human rights "for all peoples and all nations." By the second half of the twentieth century, then, human rights has become a widely accepted international concept.

Defining Human Rights

Despite the Universal Declaration of Human Rights and the many international agreements that have been concluded to carry it out and expand its meaning (see Table 18-1), international disagreement exists over many aspects of the definition of human rights. This disagreement primarily lies in four areas.

Broad versus Narrow Definitions. Scholars, analysts, and policymakers alike have struggled with whether human rights should be broadly or narrowly defined. The Preamble to the Universal Declaration of Human Rights states that "recognition of the inherent dignity and of the equal and inalienable rights of all members of the human family is the foundation of freedom, justice, and peace in the world," but what this means in practice is a matter of considerable debate.

Many people prefer a narrow definition of human rights. They restrict their definition primarily to political and legal rights such as freedom of religion and speech, maintenance of democratic political systems and practices, equality of opportunity, opposition to racial and ethnic discrimination and violence, prevention of imprisonment without fair trial, and opposition to other abuses of individual freedom associated with classical liberal political thought.

Others believe that definitions of human rights that concentrate only on political and legal issues are inadequate. They instead opt for a broader definition that includes economic and social quality of life concerns. Sometimes called the **basic human needs**

TABLE 18-1   Major Multilateral Human Rights Agreements

Agreement	Year
Prevention and Punishment of Genocide	1949
Status of Refugees	1951
Elimination of All Forms of Racial Discrimination	1965
Civil and Political Rights	1976
Economic, Social, and Cultural Rights	1976
Elimination of Discrimination Against Women	1979
Against Torture and Other Cruel, Inhuman, or Degrading Treatment or Punishment	1984
Rights of the Child	1989
Rights of All Migrant Workers and Members of Their Families	1990

approach to human rights, this interpretation includes availability of food, health services, education, and a clean environment as human rights.[3]

The debate over narrow versus broad definitions of human rights has policy implications. For example, the United States historically has accepted the narrow political and legal definition of human rights, but at the 1993 Vienna Conference on Human Rights expanded its definition to include economic and social rights as human rights "goals." It did this to gain Developing World support for its view of universal as opposed to relativist human rights.

The approach that this text takes to human rights in this chapter is very close to the U.S. government's approach. It considers political and legal human rights current issues and examines them in this chapter as human rights. It examines economic and social rights elsewhere under the heading of economic and social development, the environment, and health.

Universal or Relativist Human Rights. A second debate is over the issue of whether human rights are universal or relativist. Many Developing World states such as Burma, China, Cuba, Iran, Iraq, Libya, North Korea, Singapore, and the Sudan argue that universal human rights are a creation of the developed Western world in which the West is attempting to impose its values on developing states. They point out that Western states were the primary authors of the Universal Declaration of Human Rights, and observe that what are today developing states had no input to its writing because at the time almost all were colonies of European states. Universal human rights rarely if ever exist, many argue, because in their eyes human values are culturally determined.

For example, in preparation for the 1993 Vienna Conference on Human Rights, developing countries held three separate regional meetings to formulate their positions for Vienna. The Asian meeting, held in Bangkok, Thailand, issued a statement called the **Bangkok Declaration,** signed by 40 Asian states, which declared that the definitions of core human rights concepts such as freedom and democracy flowed from "regional particularities and various historical, cultural, and religious backgrounds." To these states, human rights were clearly relativist.[4]

Critics of this perspective include not only Western states but also former UN General Secretary Boutros Boutros-Ghali, who observed that most states that argue for culturally created relativist human rights as opposed to universal human rights are generally authoritarian states that "cloak their wrong doing in terms of exception." Be that as it may, many developing states still assert that national cultural practices determine human rights, and that human rights are therefore relative, not universal.[5]

An example may help illustrate the point. In 1994, Singapore caned an American teenager for vandalism. This was a typical sentence for the crime in Singapore, but it caused an immense uproar in the U.S. where caning is considered cruel and unusual punishment. To most Singaporeans, the caning was a culturally acceptable punishment that was an everyday event. To many Americans, it was an unacceptable and reprehensible punishment that became a major international incident.

Lest one think that the debate between proponents of universalist and relativist human rights divides only the Developed and Developing World, we hasten to point out that such disagreement exists in the Developed World as well. For example, capital punishment is supported by many Americans and is legal in many U.S. states. Most Europeans and most European states consider capital punishment barbaric and a clear violation of human rights.[6] To reiterate, then, are human rights universalist or relativist?

Sovereignty and Human Rights.   The debate over universal versus relativist human rights is closely associated with the relationship between sovereignty and human rights. Clearly, if human rights are relative, then, states have as part of their sovereign power the ability to define and protect human rights as they see fit within their own borders. Conversely, if human rights are universal, how human rights are defined and protected is the concern not only of individual states, but also of the broader international community.

The world's major states have been particularly sensitive to the relationship between human rights and sovereignty. Until recently, China, Russia, and the United States all opposed the creation of transnational legal institutions that had authority to try cases involving human rights. China and Russia often claimed that international criticism of their domestic human rights practices and records was tantamount to meddling in their domestic affairs.

The U.S. position took a somewhat different line. It was especially interesting since the U.S. accepted the concept of universal human rights. The United States claimed that its opposition to creating international institutions that had authority to try cases involving human rights was not based on concern about abridged sovereignty, but over the possibility that human rights courts might be used for political purposes against Americans and American interests overseas. Despite increased U.S. support for the creation of international institutions with authority over human rights cases, this remains a major American concern.

Enforcing Human Rights Standards and Agreements.   Questions also arise over the extent to which human rights standards and agreements can be enforced even when there is widespread agreement that human rights have been violated. Sovereignty is of course a primary issue here, but so too are questions of power and intent. Enforcing human rights standards and agreements requires not only the existence of standards and agreements, but also the existence of mechanisms and institutions that will carry out punishment as well as the will to use them.

Historically, the UN at the end of World War II played a role in establishing the **Nuremburg and Tokyo trials** as forums to enable the international community to judge war crimes and other crimes against humanity for their actions during the war. Condemned by some as "victor's justice," the Nuremberg and Tokyo tribunals sentenced some to death, gave others life in prison, levied extended sentences against still others, and acquitted only a few.[7]

After the Tokyo and Nuremberg trials, the international community did little to punish those who violated human rights, even when there was widespread agreement that rights had been egregiously violated. For example, few could deny that the 1993–94 genocide in Rwanda and the Serbian ethnic cleansing campaigns against Bosnian Muslims and others in 1991–95 were reprehensible. But no mechanisms or institutions were in place to punish those responsible, nor was it clear that the international community had the will to undertake action against those responsible. By the early 1990s, then, international law still had a long way to go to protect human rights and to punish those who violated them.

Toward a New International Human Rights Regime

But a new international regime for action against those who violated human rights was on the horizon. The atrocities in Rwanda and Bosnia combined with other earlier egregious assaults on human rights such as the Khmer Rouge's genocidal campaign against fellow Cambodians in the late 1970s, Iraq's use of gas during the 1980–88 Iran-Iraq War, the 1991–94 attacks by Somali factions against civilians and international relief efforts, and widespread indiscriminate use of landmines in many conflicts throughout the world to galvanize the international community into action to improve the protection of human rights, especially during time of war.

International Criminal Tribunals. Responding to rising international concerns, the UN established in 1993 the **International Criminal Tribunal for the former Yugoslavia (ICTY)** and in 1995 the **International Criminal Tribunal for Rwanda (ICTR).**[8] There were key differences between the Tokyo and Nuremberg trials of the 1940s and the new tribunals of the 1990s. Whereas the Nuremberg and Tokyo tribunals were concerned only with punishing German and Japanese leaders for war crimes and crimes against humanity, the 1990s tribunals intended to punish anyone who committed such crimes. Also, the 1990s tribunals explicitly excluded the death penalty.

At first, it was not clear that the Yugoslavia or Rwanda tribunal would be effective. But gradually, especially between 1996 and 2000, the NATO led peacekeeping forces in Bosnia began to arrest more people accused of crimes and bring them before the ICTY. The ICTY in turn began to adjudicate the cases. It also in 1999 indicted Yugoslav President Slobodan Milosevic for Serb actions in Kosovo, and in 2000 concluded that there was no evidence that NATO in its 1999 bombing attacks against Yugoslavia had violated international law.

Meanwhile, the Rwanda tribunal also became more effective as it began to hear and adjudicate more and more cases. It even convicted a Rwandan of genocide in 1998. This was the first time that an international court had handed down a genocide conviction. Even so, by 2000, more suspects had been detained by the Rwandan national courts for genocide than had been detained by the ICTR.

The International Criminal Court. In 1998, the UN went even further than the tribunals as delegates from 160 states and observers from 135 NGOs adopted the Rome Statutes of the **International Criminal Court (ICC).** The ICC, once in operation, would have jurisdiction over crimes against humanity, war crimes, and genocide.[9]

The effort to create an effective International Criminal Court dated all the way back to a 1947 proposal at the UN. The Cold War; disagreements over definitions, especially of aggression; questions about the extent to which human rights were universal; and concerns about infringement of sovereignty and politically motivated prosecutions prevented any real action on the ICC until the 1990s. Then, with the Cold War over and an agreement reached to delay defining aggression to a future time, the Rome Statutes moved the ICC closer to reality. By 2000, 93 states had signed it.

But the ICC still has immense hurdles to overcome before it becomes meaningful. Before it enters into force, it requires 60 states ratify it. As of 2000, only six states, Fiji,

Ghana, Italy, San Marino, Senegal, and Trinidad, had done so. Several major states including the United States, Russia, and China, had not even signed it. Given its extensive overseas military presence, the U.S. remained concerned about politically motivated prosecutions. China and Russia were most concerned about the possibility of infringement of sovereignty.

By the beginning of the twenty-first century, then, the international community had begun to create enforcement mechanisms and institutions for both the laws of war and humanitarian laws. Issues still remained, especially over sovereignty, definitions, politically motivated prosecutions, and the extent to which human rights are universal. Nevertheless, the new century dawned with new possibilities for the protection of human rights, especially during war and conflict.

Women's Rights

The world also has a long way to go to assure women their rights. Although significant strides have been made in recent years, as Table 18-2 indicates, in many parts of the world, especially developing states, women and girls are fed less, receive less medical care, work longer hours for less pay, and withdraw from school earlier, if they attend at all. The UN estimates that women perform 60 percent of the world's work, own only 1 percent of its land, and earn just 10 percent of its income. In many countries, women have few if any legal or social rights, are denied education, and are at best second-class citizens. In some countries, social values accept female infanticide if no living male heir has been born. Girls and women are often forced into prostitution in Thailand, the Philippines, and elsewhere. Bride

TABLE 18-2   Life Expectancy, Education, and Employment Comparisons by Gender Over Time

Country or Type of Country	Life Expectancy				1997 Adult Illiteracy Rate		Employment (Female % in Labor Force)	
	Female		Male					
	1970	1997	1970	1997	Female	Male	1970	1998
Low income except China and India	47	64	45	62	42	22	32	41
China	63	71	61	68	25	9	42	45
India	49	64	50	62	61	33	30	32
Lower middle income	63	71	58	65	18	11	NA	40
Upper middle income	64	74	59	67	13	9	25	40
High income	75	81	68	74	Low	Low	36	43
United States	75	79	67	73	Low	Low	37	46

Source: The World Bank, World Development Report 1999/2000 (Washington, D.C.: The World Bank), pp. 232–233, 234–235.

burning still takes place in India, although it is no longer condoned. In some Islamic countries, a man can legally kill his wife if he finds her committing adultery, but if a female kills an adulterous husband, she may be convicted of murder. And in Bosnia and Kosovo, Serbs used rape as a weapon of war to intimidate the Muslim population.

As a general rule, women on a global basis fare better in developed industrialized states than in developing countries. Even in developed states, however, women are underrepresented as a percentage of the population in certain professions and decision-making positions in business and government. For example, in the developed industrialized states, only 18 percent of all management level positions are held by women. Equally telling, during the 1990s, only 25 countries at any time ever had a female prime minister, president, or reigning monarch; there are over 190 countries in the world. Even so, on the positive side, the number of female decision makers who led countries in the 1990s is higher than for any preceding decade. Some progress is taking place.

Gender inequity and abuse are harmful and destructive in human terms, but they also have sizable social and economic costs. For example, poorly educated and uneducated women on a global basis earn less, are restricted to poorer paying jobs, and have more children than educated women. Thus, poorly educated women held 63 percent of the low paying clerical jobs in developed industrialized states during the 1980s. Similarly, women in industrialized states, who generally have more education, gave birth to approximately two children apiece during the 1980s, whereas women in developing states, who generally have less education, averaged approximately six births apiece.

Overcoming gender inequity and abuse is a difficult task. Often, inequity and abuse are held in place by a combination of social values, cultural practice, historical precedent, and religious teaching. Indeed, especially in many traditional societies, gender inequity and abuse frequently are not even recognized as problems. Obviously, this makes efforts to overcome gender inequity and abuse all the more difficult.

IGOs and NGOs have often led international efforts to attain women's rights. The UN has been particularly active, having held four conferences that specifically focused on women and many more that concentrated on women's related issues. For example, the 1993 UN Vienna Conference on Human Rights, the 1994 UN Cairo Conference on Population and Development, the 1995 UN Copenhagen Conference on Social Development, and the 1995 UN **Beijing Conference on Women** all included extensive and sometimes exclusive discussions on women and women's rights. The Beijing Conference was particularly noteworthy not only because it was held in China, a country with an extremely poor record of guaranteeing women's rights, but also because over 30,000 women gathered outside Beijing the week before the conference started to attend an NGO Forum on Women.[10]

But have the conferences actually achieved anything? At a minimum, they have significantly raised public awareness of the problems that women face. They have also provided hope for thousands of women that change may come. A number of international conventions have also been approved to protect women, such as the 1979 Convention on the Elimination of All Forms of Discrimination Against Women, signed by 120 countries as of 2000.

Nevertheless, it is clear that the international community has a long way to go to eradicate gender inequity and abuse. Women's rights, like all of the other human rights issues

Women from around the world gathered at the 1995 UN Beijing Conference on Women and an NGO Forum on Women that immediately preceeded it. Although the UN Conference went well, the Chinese government did as much as it could to make life difficult for the estimated 30,000 women who attended the NGO forum.

examined in this chapter, are higher on the international agenda now than they were a few years ago, but they are nowhere near being solved.[11]

The Future

What is the prognosis for the protection of human rights in the twenty-first century? As a general rule, despite the issues of definition, universality, sovereignty, and enforcement that were discussed earlier, it appears reasonably good. There are four reasons for this.

First, many are appalled by the violence and brutality of human against human that occurred in the last quarter of the twentieth century and support international action to curtail human rights violations. Atrocities such as the Khmer Rouge's genocide against fellow Cambodians in the late 1970s, Iraq's use of gas during the 1980–88 Iran-Iraq War, the 1991–94 attacks by Somali factions against civilians and international relief efforts, ethnic cleansing in Bosnia in the early 1990s, genocide in Rwanda in 1994, ethnic cleansing in Kosovo in 1998–99, Indonesia's 1999 assault against East Timor's independence movement, and widespread indiscriminate use of landmines in many conflicts throughout the world have raised international consciousness about human rights violations of all types.

Second, the electronic media with its global presence and its ability to record and transmit in real-time images of human rights abuses that occur almost anywhere in the world to people who live almost anywhere in the world virtually assures that the level of international awareness of human rights abuses will increase. Just as the media has played a major role in building such awareness, it most assuredly will play a major role in maintaining and expanding such awareness in the twenty-first century.

Third, many NGOs such as Amnesty International and Human Rights Watch play a global watchdog role in highlighting and publicizing human rights abuses and the status of human rights throughout the world. The number of human rights oriented NGOs increased dramatically in the late twentieth century, and many are now armed with their own sophisticated electronic communication capabilities. Like the traditional media, many of these NGOs are adept at identifying and publicizing human rights abuses.

Finally, prominent world leaders as diverse as Pope John II, Jimmy Carter, and Nelson Mandela have stepped to the foreground in condemning human rights violations and abuses. With well-respected men and women in leadership positions taking strong stands against such violations and abuses, action against those violations and abuses becomes more likely, as eventually occurred in Kosovo and East Timor. As we learned in our discussion of power, if the possibility of action exists, deterrence is more likely.

None of this suggests that human rights violations and abuses will disappear. But it does suggest that constant attention with new tools can bring continued progress.

CONFLICTS OF VALUES

Beyond this optimistic view of the future of human rights lies another reality. The diversity of the world's languages, societies, foods, music, and lifestyles is often praised as one of the most valuable assets of humanity. Few would deny that the overall quality of life is greatly enhanced by this variety. Nevertheless, despite the advantages that the international community derives from diversity, diversity is sometimes the source of considerable hostility and disagreement. This is particularly true when international diversity includes differences in the value systems that prevail within and between individual actors.

Several major clashes between value systems in the international arena have already been discussed in some detail: capitalism versus communism, one national viewpoint versus another, debates over the global standard of living, issues of war and peace and violence, and others. However, a number of other major conflicts of values in the international arena have not yet been discussed. Indeed, in most introductory international relations texts they are ignored. This is unfortunate, since many of the less discussed international conflicts of values play prominent roles in shaping the current and future world.

In this section, six of the most prominent global conflicts of values are discussed: individualism versus collectivism, materialism versus spiritualism, modernization versus traditionalism, centralization versus decentralization, political democracy versus political authoritarianism/totalitarianism, and moral value versus opposed moral value. Often, these conflicts are closely interrelated. For example, in Western Europe, Japan, and the United States, individualism and materialism are closely related, whereas in the former Soviet Union, Eastern Europe, and China, until recently, collectivism and materialism were closely connected. Certain forms of collectivism may also be categorized as traditionalist, as in many African states, whereas other forms of collectivism are termed modernist, as in China. Similarly, spiritualism and traditionalism are often equated in Christian, Islamic, Buddhist, and Hindu societies, whereas materialism is viewed as a force of modernization. Decentralization and individualism are also often considered to be integrally related, as are centralization and collectivism. However, despite these and other interrelationships, this chapter examines each of the six major conflicts of values individually.

Here, it is useful to differentiate between the concept of conflicts of values discussed in this chapter and the concept of differences in national perceptions explained in Chapter 9 and detailed in Chapter 10 and 11. As discussed in this chapter, conflicts of values refer to differences between people's views of how human affairs and relations *should* be conducted and organized. In contrast, differences in perceptions refer to contrasting viewpoints about the way human affairs and relations *are* conducted and organized. This is a significant difference, and both types of differences are extremely important in international affairs. Sometimes the two overlap and are intertwined, but often they are separate.

We must also differentiate between the concept of conflicts of values put forward in this chapter and Samuel Huntington's concept of the **clash of civilizations** discussed in Chapter 9.[12] The clash of civilizations thesis, it will be recalled, argues that differences in culture, values, and histories almost inevitably will lead to conflict; and that the culture, values, and history that dominate a given civilization serve as the defining characteristics of that civilization. They change rarely if at all.

The conflicts of values perspective presented here makes no such claim. Rather, it sees values as potentially transitory rather than inevitably permanent. It argues that the culture and values of a society can change over time. (Historical experiences are more permanent, but even they can be reinterpreted over time.)

This leads to a significant difference between Huntington's clash of civilizations perspective and the conflicts of values outlook presented here. To Huntington, clashes of civilizations are virtually inevitable. However, in the perspective presented in this chapter, clashes of civilizations are not inevitable, but conflicts of values are.

Individualism Versus Collectivism

Throughout human societies, tensions exist between value systems that emphasize the responsibility of individuals to themselves and those that emphasize the responsibility of the individual to society. This tension may be described as the conflict between **individualism** and **collectivism.** Throughout the world, in developed and developing states alike, tensions exist between these two opposed values, often with important ramifications for international relations.

The conflict between individualism and collectivism takes many forms. Throughout most of the post–World War II period, East–West rivalry, with the East emphasizing collectivism and the West individualism, was the most visible such conflict. That conflict pitted the West's emphasis on self against the East's emphasis on society. In the context of the East–West struggle, this was an ideologically derived conflict.

Beyond the East–West clash over individualism and collectivism, there is also a disagreement between the West and many East Asian states, particularly those known as the "Four Tigers" (Hong Kong, Singapore, South Korea, and Taiwan) over the concepts. All four of the Tigers are societies based on Confucianism, and many people in these countries attribute the incredible economic growth that they experienced during the 1980s and 1990s to the superiority of that philosophy of life, which stresses responsibility to family and society over responsibility to one's self. There are many people even within the Four Tigers who disagree with that assessment and who attribute the Tiger's growth rates to other causes, but nevertheless, a fundamental conflict of values is evident between the Tiger's stress on collective responsibility and the West's emphasis on personal aggrandizement.

Other aspects of the conflict between individualism and collectivism also have important ramifications for international affairs. In a certain sense, the struggle to impose some form of world order on the anarchic international system is a form of conflict between individualism and collectivism. State actors, seeking to protect their individual claims to national sovereignty and independence, have been unwilling to subordinate their individual desires and actions to the needs of the broader global community. International governmental organizations such as the United Nations have discovered this on regular occasions. But conflict between individualism and collectivism need not exist only at the international system level to have an international impact. State and nonstate actors throughout the world find themselves torn by internal tensions between individualism and collectivism. Only rarely have international actors achieved an internal balance between collectivism and individualism, with Japan being perhaps the best example.

Developing World states are often caught in the individualism/collectivism clash. In the traditionalist societies of many Developing World states, life revolves around a collective body. In some cases, that body is the tribe or village; in other cases, it is the extended family. In all cases, however, the desires of individuals, as well as their rights and needs, are subordinate to the interests of the collective. Often, rigid formal or informal rules and customs have been developed to assure primacy of the collective. In societies such as these, Western conceptions of individualism often have little relevance. This has portentous implications for Western relations with Developing World states.

But traditional societies are breaking down, succumbing to pressures of urbanization and development. Together, urbanization and development disrupt traditional collective societies by challenging or rejecting old rules and customs and by weakening or destroying links within the collective. Within many Developing World states, masses of the population are adrift, their old traditional collective attitudes disrupted and replaced by little or nothing.

Developing World governments have reacted to this phenomenon in various ways. Some, such as Tanzania, Nigeria, and Ghana, have sought to transfer the old uprooted traditionalist collective consciousness to the state, thereby developing what may be called a "new national collectivism." Such efforts continue, but to date have yielded limited success. A few states such as Kenya and Sri Lanka have attempted to instill a degree of Westernized individualism, at least within their urban populations. Their success has also been slight. Other states like Cambodia and Iran have tried to reinculcate old collective values, often agrarian in form. The Cambodian effort resulted in genocide and the Iranian effort remains embroiled in strife. Most Developing World governments followed a fourth pattern and appeared unsure what steps to take concerning the contradictions between individualism and collectivism.

Developing World states are not alone in their quandary. In the industrialized West with its emphasis on individualism, concern is often expressed that excessive individualism may undermine the societal cooperation that is necessary in an industrialized society. Although few advocate abandoning individualism, many believe that more social consciousness, that is, a greater sense of collectivism, must eventuate if Western societies are to overcome the challenges that confront them. Collectivism is rarely held up as a model in industrialized Western states, but its ideal of social cooperation is often praised.

In the pre–1989 communist world, collectivism was the idealized objective of the communist governments, but among the populations, considerable sentiment existed for individual fulfillment and identity. A large number of youth in Eastern Europe asserted their individualism through Westernized dress and manner, and the former Soviet Union's *stilyagi* (Soviet youth who adopted "stylish" Western patterns of dress and action) offered a more subdued version of Western individualism. Soviet and Eastern European governments condemned these displays of individualism as "decadent" and "antisocial," but despite government condemnations—and in some cases, more severe penalties—the displays continued.

The depth of rejection of collectivism as a value in the former Soviet Union and Eastern Europe became increasingly apparent in the late 1980s and early 1990s as revolution and change swept these countries. Individualistic social, political, and economic behavior became increasingly accepted and increasingly apparent. The collapse of communism in Eastern Europe and the USSR accelerated this trend.

But even in Eastern Europe and the former Soviet Union, the collapse of communism did not eliminate collectivism. And in many other countries throughout the world, collectivist values continue to hold sway or play an important role. Indeed, conflicts between individualism and collectivism remain in most societies. These conflicts have been sources of both mistrust and animosity among international actors and tension and instability within actors. Aside from the other nationalistic and ideological baggage included in the East–West conflict, the governments on both sides fundamentally disagreed on the value of individualism and the value of collectivism. Individuals on both sides of the East–West boundary, however, identified elements of attraction in the value that the other side espoused. Not surprisingly, the governments on each side often viewed those individuals as threats to the dominant internal value system.

But what of the Developing World? Although Developing World states may individually be deciding whether to cast their lots with individualism or collectivism, or to follow their own line of thought to resolve the individual/collective dilemma, they are at the same time seeking to establish their own internal identities, called into question by the disruption of their traditional collective societies. With their traditional collective heritages disrupted, a natural response to that disruption may be an effort to institutionalize an allegedly "modern" version of collectivism. In a certain sense, developing societies may be predisposed to adopt a more socialistic, that is, collectivist, social organization than the West would prefer.

This observation is far from an ironclad rule, but it is sufficiently valid to argue that some Western disagreements with Developing World states are in part the result of a clash in values—individualism versus collectivism—as well as products of the colonial past and disparities in wealth. Although empirical proof for this line of reasoning is difficult to provide, it merits careful consideration by policy makers and students alike.

Materialism Versus Spiritualism

Like the conflict between individualism and collectivism, the conflict between **materialism** and **spiritualism** is global in scope and affects internal and external dimensions of international actors. In Iran, Ayatollah Khomeini condemned U.S. capitalism, Soviet communism, the shah's modernism, and most of the rest of the Islamic world's version of Islam as perversions of the true spiritualism of Allah. In the United States, Ronald Reagan reached back to the Cold War rhetoric of the 1950s to chastise "Godless communism," even while critics in the Developing World, and in the United States and Western Europe as well, criticized the United States for being too materialistic. Several Developing World states such as Zambia and Tanzania that had opted for collective approaches to societal organization also stressed a need to remember spiritual values.

Materialism had its proponents as well. Marxist states throughout the world including China continued to stress materialism as the preferred value. Even in these societies, however, the old Marxist mandate that spiritualism in general and religion in particular were nothing more than the "opiate of the proletariat" and therefore to be shunned was increasingly abandoned as spiritual values and religious beliefs became more acceptable in the 1990s. Meanwhile, some Developing World states, Angola and Mozambique included, emphasized materialism at the expense of spiritualism, although no economic improvement resulted. And in the United States and Western Europe, materialism remained the dominant feature of life.

How does the conflict between materialism and spiritualism affect international relations? The East–West struggle again provides a useful example. U.S. criticism of Soviet materialism did little to raise Soviet ire against the United States; the Soviets probably viewed such criticisms as compliments. U.S. criticisms of Soviet materialism, however, raised in some quarters U.S. consciousness of the differences between the two systems and made a U.S.–Soviet modus vivendi more difficult to arrange. This same observation applied to Soviet criticism of spiritual values in the West and elsewhere. Although spiritually oriented and religiously oriented people regarded such criticisms as compliments, Soviet attacks on religious and spiritual values raised consciousness of intersystemic differences. These observations should be regarded neither as supportive of nor opposed to U.S. or Soviet pronouncements on materialism and spiritualism.

Probably the best and most poignant recent examples of the impact of the conflict between materialism and spiritualism on international relations are events of the late 1970s and the 1980s in Iran. Here, an ascetic fundamentalist Muslim cleric, exiled from his home country for his criticisms both of his government's blatant materialism and its modernization program (we will return to this later) appealed to Allah's higher authority to restore Iran to a straight-and-narrow Islamic path. While factors additional to Khomeini's spiritualism were also at work, the Iranian people accepted Ayatollah Khomeini's arguments, overthrew the shah, and brought Khomeini to power. Although Khomeini's actions while in power left many both inside and outside Iran uncertain about the sincerity of his spiritualist appeals, no doubt existed that the inherent conflict between materialism and spiritualism was manipulated brilliantly by Khomeini and his lieutenants in their pursuit of political power. The impact of the success of their spiritual appeal was immense—ruptured U.S.–Iranian relations, the hostage crisis, an abortive rescue mission, possibly the Soviet invasion of Afghanistan, the seizure of the Great Mosque in Mecca, the Iran–Iraq War, and worsened U.S.–Western European relations, to name but a few. The conflict between materialism and spiritualism was not the only cause of these events, but had the shah's government not fallen to Khomeini's spiritual appeal, the course of events in Southwest Asia would have been considerably different.

Without doubt, the late twentieth century witnessed a resurgence of the role of spiritualism and religion in the international community. The self-immolation of Buddhist monks in South Vietnam sent searing images of the meaning of religious commitment to materialistic Americans. Less than 30 years later the Catholic Church played significant roles in bringing down a communist government in Poland and challenging a right-wing government in El Salvador. Khomeini's Islamic revival has already been discussed, but even it is only a part of a broader global resurgence of Islamic vitality. In the United States, the spiritual revival manifested itself first in the conservative politics of the Moral Majority, but soon expanded to include reassertion of the merit of "family values" across a broad spectrum of the U.S. body politic. And in Europe, many clergymen in the 1980s used their spiritual appeal to lend weight to their support of nuclear disarmament. Similarly, in the United States, Catholic bishops supported the antinuclear movement, maintaining that no Christian could support the annihilation of humanity. And with revolution sweeping the USSR and Eastern Europe, many observers noted increased interest in religion and greater attendance at churches. Indeed, in 1990, the Soviet government granted freedom of religion, a freedom that continued in Russia and most of the other newly independent former Soviet republics. After the collapse of the Soviet Union, religion expanded considerably in Russia.

In recent years, then, searches for and adherence to spiritual values have expanded considerably. The implications of this trend for international affairs are several. During the 1990s alone, appeals to higher moral authority were used to justify wars, to support calls for peace and disarmament, and to legitimize demands for alternate economic systems and pleas for more equitable social orders. In many cases, spiritual and religious explanations are also used to justify traditionalist positions in struggles against modernization.

Thus, the struggle between materialism and spiritualism continues. In many societies, materialism remains or is becoming the dominant force, but in others, spiritual values are gaining strength and becoming dominant. In the twenty-first century, the potential for conflict between materialist and spiritualist values remains high. If present trends continue, the potential for conflict will increase.

Modernization Versus Traditionalism

The conflict between modernization and traditionalism takes on many faces and has many impacts in contemporary international affairs. In Poland before 1989, the Catholic Church defended what it considered traditional Polish respect for church, family, and state, and often found itself in conflict with the Polish Communist Party, which viewed itself as a force for modernization. The implications of this church/party conflict—which may be viewed as either a modernization/traditionalism struggle or as a materialist/spiritualist conflict—extended far beyond Poland to Moscow, Washington, and the Vatican. In Japan, proponents of traditional Japanese customs and values decry the Westernization that has sped throughout society. Old customs and values have been lost, they say, and disservice to Japan's heritage has been committed. Other Japanese argue that the post–World War II Japanese economic miracle would have been impossible had not forces of modernization swept aside Japanese traditions. The fact that modernists retain the upper hand in Japan has had tremendous importance for international economic affairs, at least if their explanation of the cause of Japan's economic successes is accurate.

Meanwhile, in other East Asian states such as the Philippines, Indonesia, Singapore, Malaysia, and Hong Kong, governments either restricted or banned the use of video games because, as one Malaysian newspaper said, "video games [were destroying] traditional games and children [were] no longer interested in flying kites or top spinning." Since then, Burma banned rock music, and Malaysia outlawed public kissing and refused to permit Madonna, LaToya Jackson, and others to give concerts in Kuala Lumpur, Malaysia's capital, because their songs "promote values alien to Malaysian traditions."[13]

Obviously, modernization and traditionalism have several meanings. **Modernization** may mean "progressive" change; it does not necessarily mean change alone. On many occasions, modernization implies opposition to entrenched religion, if only because religion often defends traditional values. In preindustrial societies, modernization is regularly

The conflict between modernization and traditionalism is frequently strong and sometimes violent, but sometimes old and new can coexist in harmony. Here, modern conveyances meet traditional garb in Lahore, Pakistan.

defined as the series of processes that lead to industrialization, whereas in industrialized societies, it is often viewed as the introduction of state-of-the-art productive capabilities or the transformation of society from an industrial to a postindustrial phase.

By contrast, **traditionalism** may be defined as the desire to maintain values, customs, mores, and living patterns that have been established over time. Traditions usually take centuries to develop, although sometimes their history is much shorter. Many Jewish traditions are twenty or more centuries old. By comparison, the U.S. tradition of two political parties is barely two centuries old. At the short-term end of the scale, cartoons on Saturday morning and college football on a fall Saturday afternoon are becoming U.S. traditions, although a purist would argue that both phenomena are too recent to be called traditions.

In its more extreme forms, traditionalism dictates continuation of the past. Extreme traditionalism is unalterably opposed to all forms of modernization simply because modernization may challenge or change established societal values, relationships, and patterns of behavior. "Conservative" governments that seek to maintain established values may find themselves in conflict with other segments of society that seek change. Ethiopia's Haile Selassie opposed modernization in Ethiopia and found opposition to his rule steadily mounting. Eventually, he was driven from his throne by forces that labeled themselves "modernists." China's Sun Yat-sen led modernist forces against traditional Chinese society and unleashed a revolution that continues today. In Africa, Julius Nyerere tried to create a modern state by transferring the traditional collectivist allegiance of Tanzania's citizenry from tribes to the government in Dar es Salaam.

But traditionalism does not necessarily mean blind acceptance of everything in a country's history. For example, in Russia after the collapse of the Soviet Union, Vladimir Zhirinovsky and other right-wing nationalists urged the promotion of "traditional Russian values" such as strong political rule, a powerful state, the Russian Orthodox church, the good of the collective, defense of Russian culture, and the rejection of Westernization. However, they rejected communism. Ironically, the new Russian Communist Party also promoted all of these traditional Russian values with the exception of religion.

Governments that emphasize modernization often find themselves in conflict with traditional elements of society. Khomeini's opposition to the shah was the result not only of conflict between Khomeini's spiritualism and the shah's materialism, but also from conflict between their visions of what Iran's future should be. To the shah, the Iran of 2000 would be a modern, Westernized, industrial state. To Khomeini, the Iran of 2000 would be a traditional, fundamentalist Islamic state.

Similarly, in Cambodia, the Khmer Rouge in the 1990s continued their assault against Prince Norodom Sihanouk's government not only because of ideological antipathy and desire for power, but also because they wanted Cambodia to return to its rural agrarian past. Sihanouk, by comparison, accepted at least some vestiges of Westernization, although he by no means intended to abandon all Cambodian traditions.[14] Traditionalism and modernization were once again in conflict.

Some states have sought to balance pressures for adherence to traditional values, relationships, and patterns of behavior with policies of modernization in industry and other sectors of society. Saudi Arabia is perhaps the leading example of those states that have attempted to balance traditionalist/modernist tendencies in this way. The future of the Saudi and other similar experiments is not certain.

In most cases, the conflict between traditionalism and modernization has greatest impact within a state. But the conflict has two types of relevance for international relations as well. First, when transnational religious, ideological, or other movements assume the mantle of traditionalism or modernization, the international community is immediately affected. Thus, the Islamic revival supports traditional values, relationships, and patterns of behavior and is therefore a force that all Islamic states must reckon with. Similarly, for decades, Marxism purported to be a force for modernization, given its claim to be a higher form of social organization. Therefore, states wishing to "modernize" sometimes looked to Marxism.

Second, the conflict between traditionalism and modernization has relevance for international relations when traditional/modernization struggles within a state affect external actors. This occurs often. Indeed, every example used in this section falls within this category, with the two exceptions of Southeast Asian attitudes toward video games and U.S. views of cartoons and football. In Poland, Japan, Israel, the United States, Ethiopia, China, Tanzania, Iran, Cambodia, and Russia alike, domestic tensions between traditionalist and modernist forces spill into the international community. Some are more explosive and more important than others, but they cannot be overlooked as conflicts that help shape contemporary international affairs.

Centralization Versus Decentralization

In most cases, international actors have developed internal organizational structures to enable them better to make and implement policy decisions. States have their governments, multinational corporations have their corporate organizations, and intergovernmental organizations have their own structural forms. Nongovernmental organizations usually have internal decision-making and policy-implementing structures as well. Despite the diversity of internal organization in all these actors, a common issue confronts all: How much authority should be concentrated in a single central location, and how much should be dispersed to secondary and tertiary sites?

Many arguments have been advanced to defend both centralization and decentralization. Advocates of **centralization** argue that more efficient decision making and policy implementation can be achieved if authority is concentrated. If need be, decisions can be reached quickly and policy can be implemented with fewer people working at cross-purposes. Under a centralized regime, international actors can more readily function as a single unit, thereby displaying unity of purposes and allowing pursuit of a single goal. Centralization also frustrates tendencies toward actor fragmentation, or so centralization proponents assert.

Advocates of **decentralization** counter that decentralization is more democratic because it brings more people into the decision-making and policy-implementing processes, thereby frustrating the potential for dictatorship and/or authoritarianism that centralization carries with it. Moreover, decentralization advocates argue, expanding the number involved in the decision-making process multiplies the perspectives from which an issue is viewed, thereby minimizing the possibility of a decision-making error. Proponents of decentralization concede that their preferred system is less efficient than a centralized one, but maintain that the advantages their preference carries with it outweigh its decreased efficiency. In addition, decentralization enhances the probability of grass-roots support for a particular decision because more people are involved in arriving at that decision.

Clearly, many of the arguments advanced by both centralists and decentralists are diametrically opposed and rest on considerably different sets of assumptions and expectations. Generally, centralists value efficiency more than do advocates of decentralization. Similarly, decentralists fear dictatorship more than do advocates of centralization. Proponents of both schools of thought have numerous historical examples to prove the superiority of their preferred model. Centralists point to Stalin and his ability to rally the Soviet people to the anti-Nazi cause as proof of the advantages of centralized authority; conversely, decentralists point to the national consensus of the American people that built slowly but relentlessly in support of Great Britain during 1940 and 1941 as proof that a less centralized system has advantages.

The clarity of the debate between advocates of centralization and advocates of decentralization is clouded by the fact that defenders of both positions may seek nothing more than to strengthen their own positions. Some centralization–decentralization debates are therefore more related to questions of power than value. It should also be evident that when centralization and decentralization are at issue, two extremes on a spectrum are being discussed. Many degrees of difference exist between those two extremes. Indeed, it is doubtful whether a totally centralized or a totally decentralized system ever existed. Nevertheless, as concepts, the impact on international affairs of the conflict between centralization and decentralization is considerable. Generally, that impact is more evident within actors than between them.

At the level of the state, many separatist movements interpret alleged usurpation of authority by a central government as a primary cause of their struggle for autonomy. Many separatists maintain that the central government that they oppose has taken decision-making powers unto itself. Separatists therefore claim that they are seeking a return of centralized power to local authorities. Thus, a struggle between centralization and decentralization is joined.

And it is a struggle that is joined on every inhabited continent in the world. French-speaking Canadians in Quebec decry the control that Ottawa has over their lives, even as Western Australians argue for fewer rules and regulations from Canberra. Basque separatists threaten to assassinate the Pope to make known their displeasure with Madrid's rule, and Eritreans, before they achieved independence from Ethiopia in 1993, fought the armies of whoever controlled the Ethiopian government in Addis Ababa. In India and Brazil, state governors make known their opposition to the New Delhi and Brasilia governments. Demands for sovereignty in Latvia, Lithuania, Estonia, Georgia and other Soviet republics in the late 1980s and early 1990s tore the USSR apart. Similar demands for sovereignty and independence on the parts of different ethnic groups in Yugoslavia and Czechoslovakia also led to the dissolution of those countries. Obviously, when the conflict between advocates of centralization and decentralization becomes severe, the internal stability of a state may be destroyed, often with international ramifications.

Debates over the proper degree of centralization and decentralization also take place in transnational political and religious movements. Such debates may play a significant role in shattering the unity of those movements. Soviet insistence that only the Communist Party of the Soviet Union (CPSU) could provide accurate ideological guidance to the world communist movement was one of the factors that alienated the Chinese, Yugoslav, and Albanian Communist parties. Although the CPSU eventually accepted the inevitability of decentralized decision making in the international communist movement by recognizing "national paths to communism," its recognition came too late to repair the damage done by a debate over degree of centralization.

IGOs, MNCs, NGOs, and other international actors are not immune to conflicts over centralization and decentralization. Should the UN Secretariat strictly oversee the operations of UN field operations? If it does, rapid response to changing needs in the field may be stifled. If it does not, individual field operations may be directed to purposes other than those for which they were intended. Should IBM run its foreign subsidiaries from corporate headquarters? If it does, individual initiative within the subsidiary structure may be reduced, but if it does not, subsidiary managers, not knowing the global picture of operations, may undertake actions not in the company's overall economic interest. The centralization/decentralization question may be most critical for NGOs. As essentially voluntary organizations, too much decentralization could lead to the dissolution of an NGO. Paradoxically, too much centralization could have the same effect.

Political Democracy Versus Political Authoritarianism/Totalitarianism

In some respects, the clash between political democracy and political authoritarianism/totalitarianism is a subset of the clash between centralization and decentralization.[15] As a concept, **political democracy** argues for a decentralized political system in which all citizens have a say in decisions that affect them, whereas **political authoritarianism/totalitarianism** argues that only one person or a small portion of the citizens of a society, because of birth, control of the elements of power, or an allegedly superior view of the direction in which society should be heading, should make decisions for that society. Even though the democracy versus authoritarianism/totalitarianism conflict is a subset of the centralization versus decentralization conflict, it is of sufficient importance to be examined separately.

The democracy versus authoritarianism/totalitarianism conflict is exceedingly old, going back at least as far as the wars between Athens and Sparta in ancient Greece. More recently, much of the East–West conflict was centered around the clash between political democracy and political authoritarianism/totalitarianism. The United States and its industrialized allies claimed to be democratic, and chastised the USSR and its allies for being authoritarian or totalitarian states controlled exclusively by a small portion of society, the Communist Party. The USSR and its allies rejected the Western charges, claiming in turn that Western political democracy was a sham and a coverup of the fact that the wealthy few dominated Western political processes. Further, Communist parties maintained that only they spoke for all the working class even though only a few of the working class were actually party members.

The collapse of communism in Eastern Europe and the Soviet Union eliminated one of the most visible clashes between political democracy and political authoritarianism/totalitarianism, but it did not mean that the conflict between political democracy and political authoritarianism/totalitarianism had ended. In China, the Communist Party of China insisted on maintaining a monopoly of political power. This insistence led directly to the Tiananmen Square massacre of 1989. And in many Developing World countries, authoritarian or totalitarian regimes continued to rule.

Interestingly, however, in one Developing World region, Latin America, political democracy during the 1980s and early 1990s won victory after victory over political authoritarianism/totalitarianism. Democratic governments came to power via open elections throughout the continent. By the middle 1990s, 32 of the 33 states in Latin America and the Caribbean were ruled by democratically elected government. Cuba was the only exception. A large wave of democratic elections also swept Africa during the 1990s.

But given the serious economic problems and social cleavages that dominated these regions, how long could political democracy last? The same question could be asked about the democracies that emerged from the wreckage of communist governments in Eastern Europe and the former Soviet Union. Although there is no doubt that the 1990s witnessed a pronounced growth in strength of political democracy over political authoritarianism/totalitarianism, that growth was far from a final victory. Thus, the struggle between democracy and authoritarianism/totalitarianism, as old as recorded history, will continue, both within and among the various international actors.

Moral Value Versus Opposed Moral Value

On other occasions, conflict in national and international communities is more elemental, stemming from disagreements over what is morally right and what is morally wrong. For example, in South Africa before the dismantling of apartheid, many white South Africans believed that they were in fact a superior race and therefore should rule; many probably still believe that today. To them, nothing was wrong with apartheid. However, most of the rest of the international community disagreed, believing that apartheid was morally repugnant. There are few starker contemporary examples of opposed moral values than this.

There are many other examples of opposed moral values. For example, before World War II, most Europeans saw nothing wrong with imperialism; it was simply the established way to run the world. Many people in the colonies disagreed with this belief and struggled for independence, eventually achieving it in most cases during the 1940s, 1950s, and 1960s. Similarly, even today, authoritarian and totalitarian leaders find it completely acceptable to imprison those who disagree with them. They feel that it is a right that comes with the position. On an economic level, in many states, bribery and payoffs are accepted and acceptable ways of conducting business. The people in power there feel that nothing is wrong with these practices.

From the prevailing North American and Western European perspective, however, apartheid, imperialism, political imprisonment, and bribery are not acceptable. They are morally wrong. Even so, the fact remains that in some areas of the world ruling by race is considered morally acceptable; imperialism is morally legitimate; political imprisonment is not a moral issue; and bribery is a way of life. These conflicts of moral value versus opposed moral value sometimes serve as a cover for other conflicts, but no analyst can deny that few universal moral standards exist.

The West itself receives its share of moral criticism from the Developing World. What right does the West have to challenge and criticize the moral values of others when people are unemployed, without adequate food, and in need of shelter even in the richest Western state? How can Western states speak of morality when Western consumers each year spend three times as much on cosmetics as their governments do on food aid and technical assistance to developing states?

Obviously, opposed moral values raise difficult questions. And the answers are even more difficult.

Conflicts of Values and World Order

Assume, for a moment, that all the world's outstanding problems had somehow been solved—that population pressures and food shortages had dissipated, that all states were satisfied with their respective levels of economic development, that economic dependence and resource scarcity had been overcome, and that the problems of war and violence had been solved. Assume further that individuals and societies continued to disagree over individualism and collectivism, materialism and spiritualism, modernization and traditionalism, centralization and decentralization, political democracy and political authoritarianism/totalitarianism, and the legitimacy of opposed moral values.

How long would the idyllic world just depicted last?

The definitive answer, of course, will never be known, because such an idyllic state of world affairs will probably never exist. Nevertheless, the scenario should provide considerable food for thought. How long would a near-perfect world exist if men and women as individuals and in groups continued to have different values, different approaches to life, and different ideas about what was right and wrong? The answer in all probability would be, "Not long at all."

This is a chilling realization that reaffirms the oft-made assertion that humankind's technical accomplishments have outstripped its ability to deal with social relationships. But it is a realization that must be dealt with in realistic terms. The question is, "What will those terms be?"

Many different proposals have been advanced to enable humankind to deal more effectively with social relationships at the international level. Some proposals stress a unitary world government. Some suggest an international federalist governmental structure. Others suggest world law as a solution to international problems. Still others call for universal social justice as a prerequisite for improving our ability to live with one another.[16]

The objectives of all these proposals are laudable, but they all ignore the fundamental conflicts of values that continue to divide humankind. Is it realistic to propose a unitary world government when proponents of decentralized government remain influential throughout the world? How likely is it that any government, particularly those that are militarily or economically strong, would accept even a federated world governmental structure? What foundation exists for world law when forces of modernization oppose forces of traditionalism, and vice versa? How can universal social justice be achieved when some people advocate individualism and others collectivism? In short, given the many conflicts of values that exist in today's world, how can we move from where we are to where we want to be, when no consensus exists on where we want to be?

These are pessimistic thoughts, but they at least offer an insight to one of the major problems confronted by all forms of world order proposals: Given the diversity of human values, comprehensive global solutions to humankind's international problems stand little chance of success until greater global consensus on values exists. Building that consensus may be humanity's most important—and most challenging—future task.

 KEY TERMS AND CONCEPTS

human rights   the right of all persons to be free from abuses such as torture and imprisonment for political beliefs and to have minimum standards of economic and social security

classical liberal philosophers   philosophers like John Locke and John Stuart Mill who wrote about political democracy, equal opportunity, individual rights, and limited government, and economists like Adam Smith who developed ideas about free market economics

Atlantic Charter   1941 document signed by U.S. President Franklin Roosevelt and British Prime Minister Winston Churchill pledging U.S.-British cooperation and support for national self-determination, collective security, and economic collaboration leading to "social security"

Universal Declaration of Human Rights   1948 UN document identifying and stating a "common standard" of human rights "for all peoples and all nations"

debates over human rights definitions   issues of debate include broad versus narrow definitions, universal or relativist definitions, and the relationship between sovereignty and human rights

basic human needs approach   the belief that the primary responsibility of governments and others is to meet human need for adequate shelter, food, health care, sanitation, and education

Bangkok Declaration   1993 statement by 40 Asian states declaring core human rights concepts such as freedom and democracy flowed from "regional particularities and various historical, cultural, and religious backgrounds"

Nuremburg and Tokyo trials   tribunals at the end of World War II at which the international community tried German and Japanese officials for their actions during the war

International Criminal Tribunals for Yugoslavia and Rwanda   1993 and 1995 UN tribunals to try anyone who committed war crimes and crimes against humanity during the conflicts in either country

International Criminal Court   established under the 1998 Rome Statutes, it has not yet begun to operate because of concerns about sovereignty issues on the part of several states including the U.S.

Women's Rights   an area of human rights that is gradually receiving increased recognition under international law

Beijing Conference on Women   a UN conference held in Beijing that cast an international spotlight on women's issues

clash of civilizations   a theory developed by Samuel Huntington that argued that different civilizations have different values and different styles that lead them into conflict with each other

individualism   emphasis on individual human beings, often linked to Western political, economic, and social development and values

collectivism   emphasis on groups of human beings, often identified with the tribe or extended families in developing states and the state in communist countries

materialism   emphasis on material goods, again often linked with Western political, economic, and social development and values

spiritualism   emphasis on spiritual values, often identified with religion and traditional societies

modernization   "progressive" change, often implying opposition to religion and other entrenched ways of organizing society

traditionalism   the desire to maintain values, customs, mores, and living patterns that have been established over time

centralization   the concentration of authority at a single location

decentralization   spreading authority among several locations

political democracy   a decentralized political system in which all citizens have a say in decisions that affect them

political authoritarianism/totalitarianism   a centralized political system in which only a few people make decisions that affect all

conflict of moral values   disagreements over what is morally right and what is morally wrong

 ## *WEBSITE REFERENCES*

human rights: *www.amnesty.org*   website for Amnesty International, a prominent human rights NGO

www.hrw.org   website for Human Rights Watch, another prominent human rights NGO

www.state.gov/www/global/human_rights/hrp_reports_mainhp.html   the U.S. Department of State's annual report on global human rights

basic human needs: *worldbank.org/poverty/strategies*   a World Bank website directed toward poverty reduction strategies to meet basic human needs

women's rights: *www.research.umbc.edu/~korenman/wmst/links_intl.html*   a listing of international women's websites

 ## *NOTES*

1. The Atlantic Charter may be found in David R. Facey-Crouther, *The Atlantic Charter* (New York, NY: Saint Martin's Press LLC, 1994).

2. The Universal Declaration of Human Rights may be found in Johannes Morsink, *Universal Declaration of Human Rights: Origins, Drafting, and Intent* (Philadelphia, PA: Iniversity of Pennsylvania Press, 2000).

3. For more discussion of basic human needs, see Bruce E. Moon, *The Political Economy of Basic Human Needs* (Ithaca, NY: Cornell University Press, 1991); and Len Doval and Ian Gough, *A Theory of Human Need* (New York, NY: Guilford Publishers, 1991).

4. A Chinese view of the Bangkok Declaration can be found in "Bangkok Declaration," *Beijing Review* (May 31, 1993), pp. 9–11.

5. For a variety of views on different approaches to human rights, see Jack Donnelly, *International Hu-*

man Rights, 2nd edition, (Boulder, CO: Westview Press, 1997); Seyom Brown, *Human Rights in World Politics* (New York, NY: Addison Wesley, 2000); and Wm. Theodore de Bary, *Asian Values and Human Rights: A Confucian Communitarian Perspective* (Cambridge, MA: Harvard University Press, 2000)

6. For a European perspective on capital punishment, see "The Cruel and Even More Unusual Punishment: Capital Punishment in the U.S. and the World," *The Economist* (May 15, 1999), pp. 95–97.

7. The stories of the Nuremberg and Tokyo trials may be found in Robert E. Conot, *Justice at Nuremberg* (New York, NY: Carroll & Graf, 1984); and Antonio Cassese and B.V. Roling, eds., *The Tokyo Trial and Beyond* (Malden, MA: Blackwell, 1994).

8. For details on the Yugoslavia and Rwanda Tribunals, see "The Evolution of International Criminal Law," *Strategic Survey 1999–2000* (London: Oxford University Press, 2000), pp. 29–37. See also

"Prosecuting Heads of State," *IISS Strategic Comments* (July 1999).

9. Excerpts from the statutes of the International Criminal Court may be found in "Rome Statutes of the International Criminal Court," *Social Justice* (Winter 1999), pp. 125–43. See also Helen Duffy, "Toward Eradicating Impunity: The Establishment of the International Criminal Court," *Social Justice* (Winter 1999), pp. 115–24.

10. See *The Beijing Declaration and the Platform for Action: Fourth World Conference on Women* (Collingdale, PA: Diane Publishers, 1996) for documents from the Beijing Conference on Women.

11. For additional discussion of efforts to protect women's rights, see Marsha A. Freeman, "International Institutions and Gendered Justice," *Journal of International Affairs* (Spring 1999), pp. 513–532; and Arvonne S. Fraser, "Becoming Human: The Origins and Development of Women's Human Rights," *Human Rights Quarterly* (November 1999), pp. 853–906.

12. Samuel P. Huntington, "The Clash of Civilizations," *Foreign Affairs* (Summer 1993), pp. 22–49. For other discussions of clashes of civilizations and conflicts of cultures and values, see David I. Hitchcock, *Asian Values and the United States: How Much Conflict?* (Washington, DC: Center for Strategic and International Studies, 1994); William Zimmerman and Harold K. Jacobson, eds., *Behavior, Culture, and Conflict in World Politics* (Ann Arbor: University of Michigan Press, 1994); John L. Esposito, *The Islamic Threat: Myth or Reality?* (New York: Oxford University Press, 1995); Bernard Lewis, *Cultures in Conflict: Christians, Muslims, and Jews in the Age of Discovery* (New York: Oxford University Press, 1995); and Frederick Buell, *National Culture and the New Global System* (Baltimore: Johns Hopkins University Press, 1994).

13. "An Asian Assault on Video Games," *Newsweek,* October 11, 1982, p. 38; *Atlanta Journal-Constitution,* January 19, 1986; and *The Indonesian Observer (Jakarta),* April 14, 1986. For other interesting articles on these and related issues, see "East Asia Spurns West's Cultural Model," *International Herald Tribune,* July 13, 1992; and "Why Is Black Africa Overwhelmed While East Asia Overcomes?" *International Herald Tribune,* July 14, 1992.

14. See Gareth Porter and G. C. Hildebrand, *Cambodia: Starvation or Revolution* (New York: Monthly Review Press, 1978); Francois Ponchaud, *Cambodia: Year Zero* (New York: Holt, Rinehart and Winston, 1978); and Norodom Sihanouk, *War and Hope: The Case for Cambodia* (New York: Pantheon Books, 1980), for discussions of the Khmer Rouge's assault on Cambodia.

15. As used here, *authoritarianism* refers to a government that exerts extensive control over society. *Totalitarianism* refers to a government that exerts extreme control over society. These definitions may thus be viewed as different points along a continuum depicting governmental control of society. Authoritarianism at some point may therefore evolve into totalitarianism, as the government in question exerts greater and greater control over society. These views of authoritarianism and totalitarianism are fundamentally different from the views that argue that authoritarianism refers to "right-wing dictators who can be influenced to accept democratic principles," and totalitarianism refers to "communist dictators who will never accept democratic principles."

16. See Louis René Beres and Harry R. Torg, *Reordering the Planet: Constructing Alternative World Futures* (Boston: Allyn & Bacon, 1974); Howard O. Eaton, ed., *Federation: The Coming Structure of World Government* (Norman: University of Oklahoma Press, 1944); Lester R. Brown, *World without Borders* (New York: Random House, 1972); Philippe de Seynes, "Prospects for a Future Whole World," *International Organizations,* Vol. 26 (1972), pp. 1–17; Grenville Clark and Louis B. Sohn, *World Peace through World Law* (Cambridge, MA: Harvard University Press, 1966).

Chapter 19

The Environment and Health

- How serious are the world's environmental problems?
- Can anything be done to stop and reverse environmental degradation?
- Can global health be improved?
- Can the international flow of drugs be curtailed?

The questions and issues explored in the preceding two chapters have been with humankind for some time. During the late twentieth century, however, two other sets of international issues emerged that had potential to significantly affect the future of humankind.

The first set of issues centered on global environmental problems. Environmental degradation at the local level had been recognized as a problem in some countries for some time, but during the last quarter of the twentieth century, more and more people realized that many environmental issues crossed national boundaries. Some environmental issues were even global in scope. Thus, the environment became an issue in contemporary international relations.

The second set of issues centered around health problems. Health issues had long been a concern of the international community. However, in the three decades after World War II, the successes of health-oriented IGOs and NGOs such as the World Health Organization as well as improved health conditions in a number of countries gradually reduced the attention the international community gave to international health issues. Then, in the last quarter of the twentieth century, two new health problems arose, AIDS and drugs, again focusing the global community's attention on international health issues. Other health issues connected to the environment also vied for international attention.

By the beginning of the twenty-first century, then, global environmental and health issues had become first-order priorities for the international community. They are distinct issues, but they also are often interconnected. At the same time, the resolution of many international environmental and health issues is affected by other issues that we have previously explored such as national sovereignty, uneven distribution of wealth, and differing views of economic development. International environmental and health problems, like issues of war, peace, violence, human rights, and conflicts of values, are not easy problems to solve.

THE ENVIRONMENT

Population growth, increased food production, and accelerated energy and nonfuel mineral use have all taken their toll on the world's environment. The earth enjoys an amazing capacity to replenish itself, but that capacity is not limitless. Several unalterable facts exist: The environment has a finite capacity to absorb pollution and to overcome pollution-caused damage; most resources are not renewable, and those that are require time to replenish themselves; no one knows what the earth's limits are; and environmental damage often does not appear until long after the damage-inducing agent is placed in the environment.

Humanity's degradation of the environment is not new, but its pace has accelerated as humans multiplied and as the industrial revolution proceeded. As more human beings consumed more food and needed more resources, more land was tilled, more animals were killed, and more resource sites were more heavily exploited. The industrial revolution led to an explosion of per capita energy use and resource consumption in the industrialized areas of the world, accompanied by new and previously unknown types of environmental pollution.

Here, humanity's assault on the earth will be considered in four categories: (1) land degradation, desertification, and deforestation; (2) water degradation and depletion; (3) atmospheric pollution and climate change; and (4) species and gene pool extinction. Many of these phenomena are interrelated, but for ease of analysis, they are treated separately here.[1]

Land Degradation, Desertification, and Deforestation

Most U.S. citizens are familiar with stories of the erosion and the dust bowls that ravaged U.S. agricultural lands during the 1920s and 1930s. Most also know that erosion and dust bowls were the result of, among other things, overfarming and poor land-use practices. Fortunately, a combination of good luck, good weather, and improved land use resurrected U.S. farmlands. Today, the United States leads the world in agricultural production.

This impressive U.S. recovery pushed the ominous reality of global soil loss and deterioration into the back of most U.S. citizens' minds. But the reality is that soil loss, soil deterioration, and desertification are proceeding more rapidly now than at any time in recorded history. Each year, according to the United Nations Environmental Program, an area of land about the size of Austria, approximately 31,000 square miles, turns into desert. More insidiously, even where desertification is not a problem, erosion continues and topsoil depth decreases. In certain areas of Nebraska and Kansas, topsoil loss exceeds one-half inch per year, giving rise to fears that in their foreign sales efforts, U.S. farmers in effect are exporting their most important commodity, their topsoil.

In most cases, soil-related problems are directly traceable to population growth and poor soil use. More people need more food, and hence even marginal agricultural areas such as the former Soviet Union's "Virgin Lands" territory of Central Asia must be brought into production. More extensive use of rich croplands degrades the soil, and in

Chapter 19

IT, THE ENVIRONMENT, AND HEALTH: IMPROVING THE WORLD'S FUTURE

Information technologies will provide no magic bullet guaranteed to improve the world's deteriorating environment or improve the world's health situation. Nevertheless, carefully and intelligently applied and used, IT can help improve the world's future in both arenas.

Globally, IT can help address a major problem that environmental protection efforts face, developing and cataloging information about what is actually happening. New information technologies such as tele-detection and computerized databases can be of enormous help in this area. Remote sensing technologies aboard orbiting satellites, for example, fed data to earth-bound computers to help detail how much the Aral Sea in Russia and Lake Niger in Niger had receded. Similarly, a land-resource database of the Arun River Basin of Eastern Nepal produced the first basin-wide mosaic of land use and capability, with detailed maps of deforestation.

The marriage of global positioning systems and high speed wireless data and information transmission capabilities will also help protect the environment and increase food production. By remotely sensing the nutrient needs of a specific square meter of cropland and transmitting that information to sensors on farm equipment in real time just before the equipment spreads fertilizer, exactly the right amount and type of fertilizer can be dispensed. The environment will benefit, crop yields will increase, and farmers might reap greater profits as well. The implications for international relations could be considerable.

In health, the most important application of information technologies with international ramifications is preventive as opposed to curative healthcare. Information technologies properly applied could lead directly to better nutrition, greater immunization rates, access to clean water, improved disposal of waste, and other benefits. In all these areas, information must both be gathered and disseminated. In many developing countries, poor communications and limited access to information technology have deprived health care programs of their effectiveness and limited their reach. This leads directly to problems such as difficulty controlling communicable diseases, not training enough health workers, and difficulty in keeping health care workers current.

Two areas where information technologies are already making major contributions are in surveillance and control of epidemics and contagious diseases and in the dissemination of information on best health practices to doctors, nurses, health agents, community leaders, and women's groups. For example, the Global Health Network, an Internet-based global medical information system, helps doctors, researchers, and health practitioners throughout the world interact and learn together in an organized way.

To reiterate, information technologies will not be a magic bullet. They will not guarantee improvement of the world's deteriorating environment or health situation. Nevertheless, careful and intelligent application and use of IT can help improve the world's future in both arenas.

many areas of the world, neither chemical fertilizers, crop rotation, nor fallow-year practices are used to replenish it. Urbanization presents another threat to good cropland. Major urban and industrial centers are often located near rivers. The rich alluvial river valley soils therefore fall victim to the concrete, asphalt, and high population densities that accompany urbanization.

Forest degradation is a serious problem as well. Deforestation occurs because of urbanization, farming, industrial and private consumption of wood, and the need for fuel. In many cases, deforestation leads to desertification or destabilized water flow, which in turn causes siltation of streams, intensified flooding, and worsened water shortages during dry periods. Deforestation is particularly rapid in tropical forest areas; the UN Food and Agriculture Organization estimates that the world lost about 8 percent of its tropical forests during the 1980s alone.[2] But as Table 19-1 shows, deforestation is a widespread phenomenon.

Until the 1990s, land degradation, desertification, and deforestation were rarely major international issues. One reason why was because most states and businesses emphasized

TABLE 19-1   Deforestation in Selected Countries During the 1990s

Country	Annual Deforestation 1990–95 Square Kilometers	Average Annual Percent of Forest Lost, 1990–95
Algeria	234	1.2
Bangladesh	88	0.8
Brazil	25,544	0.5
China	866	0.1
Colombia	2,622	0.5
Costa Rica	414	3.0
France	1,608 planted	1.1 gain
Germany	0	0.0
Honduras	1,022	2.3
India	72 planted	0.0
Madagascar	1,300	0.8
Malawi	546	1.6
Morocco	118	0.3
Panama	636	2.1
Philippines	2,624	3.5
Russia	0	0
Tanzania	3,226	1.0
Thailand	3,294	2.6
United Kingdom	128 planted	0.5 gain
United States	5,886 planted	0.3 gain
Venezuela	5,034	1.1
Vietnam	1,352	1.4
Zambia	2,644	0.8
World	101,724	0.3

Source: The World Bank, *World Development Report 1999–2000* (Washington, D.C: The World Bank), pp. 246–247.

economic development over protection of land and forests. When the two were in conflict, land and forests generally lost. And when industrialized states complained to developing states about the destruction of the rain forests, developing states often accused the industrialized states of seeking to slow their development.

Today, however, there is wider recognition of these problems, and as we have seen, the concept of sustainable development is increasing environmental sensitivity. In some countries, again as Table 19-1 shows, reforestation programs are even restoring small quantities of lost forest. Nevertheless, there often remains a conflict between economic development and protection of land and forests. When that occurs, land and forests still frequently lose.

A second reason that land degradation, desertification, and deforestation rarely became major international issues was that many of those people who were immediately affected were at the lower end of international society's structure. They were pastoralists and subsistence farmers, for the most part outside the channels of local, national, and regional political influence.

However, as all three problems worsened, it became increasingly apparent that land was being degraded, that the desert was gaining, and that forests were disappearing. In the twenty-first century, even though no solution is in sight, these issues have moved higher on the international community's agenda.

Water Degradation and Depletion

Water degradation and depletion is also a significant problem throughout the world. Overpopulation, industrialization, and urbanization contribute to both parts of the world's water problems. In many areas of the world, but especially in the Middle East, water table levels are going down simply because of overuse. Too many people are using water resources.

Urbanization also creates major problems for water table levels, and widespread use of pesticides and industrial use of water for cooling and waste disposal pollute large quantities of water daily, although many First World states have reduced their use of long-lived "persistent pesticides" and are trying to limit industrial water pollution. Even so, in many Third World states, persistent pesticides are still widely used. Planners there often show little interest in water quality control measures.

Irrigation also adversely affects water quality. In areas downstream from large irrigation projects, water salination often climbs to levels that make agricultural production difficult and even impossible. In addition, fresh groundwater use in coastal areas is often so extensive that seawater is now intruding into the water table. More generally, coastal ecosystems are important to fisheries, but development of coastal communities and off-shore oil drilling have put many coastal ecosystems at risk.

Water degradation is not limited to Developing World states. In the United States, industrial pollution and irrigation have put water resources at risk. In Russia, several major lakes and other water resources have been seriously damaged by industrial waste. Irrigation has also used so much of the water from the tributaries to the Aral Sea that it lost one-third of its total surface area between 1960 and 1990.[3] Japan has also polluted many of its water sources. And in Western Europe as elsewhere, industrial emissions released into the atmosphere have led to acid rain, which is poisoning many lakes, rivers, and streams.

As was the case with land degradation, desertification, and deforestation, many of the causes of water degradation—and water shortages as well—cross national boundaries. In some cases, water degradation and water shortages are so severe that there is fear that they could lead to war.[4] Indeed, it is imperative in these cases, many of which are in the Middle East, that multilateral action be taken to ameliorate water shortage and water quality problems. Successful actions by individual states to solve water degradation can be undertaken only rarely. More often, regional or even global solutions may be necessary. But to do this, humankind must begin to recognize and accept the need for transnational solutions to problems of declining water quality. Such a fundamental reorientation of thinking may be difficult to achieve.

Atmospheric Pollution and Climate Change

During the 1980s, it became increasingly clear that the large quantities of nitrogen dioxide, carbon monoxide and dioxide, sulfur dioxide, chlorofluorocarbons, and other gases and particulates that humankind was releasing into the atmosphere were having an effect on the atmosphere and on climate. Industrialization, the industrial processes that go with industrialization, and the internal combustion engine are the chief culprits in atmospheric pollution and climate change. Although these culprits may have additional effects on the atmosphere and climate, here we concentrate on only two, the "greenhouse effect" and the deterioration of the ozone layer.

The **greenhouse effect** refers to the dangers of global warming brought about by greater concentrations of carbon dioxide and other "greenhouse gases" in the atmosphere. These gases, produced primarily by burning coal and other carbon-based fuels such as oil, hold heat in the atmosphere. Deforestation also contributes significantly to the quantity of carbon dioxide in the atmosphere. Other greenhouse gases like methane, nitrous oxide, and chlorofluorocarbons (CFCs) enter the atmosphere from other sources, but in all cases, the rate of emission of the greenhouse gases into the atmosphere has risen steadily.

Although there has been debate over the greenhouse effect's contribution to global warming, more and more scientific evidence supports the thesis that human-induced atmospheric changes are in fact leading to global warming.[5] There is no doubt that the global average temperature has been generally climbing, as Figure 19-1 illustrates. The consequences of global warming are considerable. Glaciers will melt, oceans will rise, rainfall patterns will change, crop locations will shift, and climate will change. These consequences will be accompanied by social problems and human dislocations.

Indeed, 37 island states, home to 23 million people, have already expressed their fears to the United Nations that unless global warming is curtailed, they may disappear altogether. They fear that global warming will melt the polar ice caps, raising the level of the oceans. If this occurs, this aspect of global warming will also have an immense impact on nonisland states. For example, a 3-foot rise in ocean levels would drive 72 million people from their homes in China, 11 million in Bangladesh, and 8 million in Egypt.[6] Clearly, even a slight rise in global temperatures has significant implications for humankind.

Closely related to the greenhouse effect is **ozone depletion,** caused primarily by CFCs used as refrigerants, propellants, solvents, and insulators. CFCs rise into the upper atmosphere and attack ozone molecules that reside there, molecules that shield the earth's surface from too much ultraviolet solar radiation. During the last half of the 1980s, scientific observations confirmed that human-made CFCs in the atmosphere had created a "hole" in the earth's ozone layer over the South Pole. Subsequent observations verified that the earth's overall ozone layer was thinning as well.

The consequences of a weakened ozone layer are severe. With more ultraviolet radiation able to reach the earth's surface, the incidence of cancer and other skin diseases is likely to increase. Equally unsettling, CFCs are extremely stable gases; even if production were stopped, it would take a century for CFCs to settle out of the atmosphere.

Can anything be done about the greenhouse effect and the deterioration of the ozone layer? Under the auspices of the United Nations Environment Program, countries of the world in 1987 signed the **Montreal Protocol** on Substances that Deplete the Ozone Layer, which was strengthened in 1990 and again in 1992. Signed by 165 states as of 1999, the Montreal Protocol and its follow-on agreements committed industrialized states to stop producing CFCs by 1996 and gave Developing World states another 10 years to halt production.[7] Since the protocol went into effect, world CFC production has declined by 75 percent.[8] International efforts can have an impact on the world's environmental situation.

Once again, though, it is evident that the world's atmospheric pollution and climate change problems cannot be successfully approached only on a local or national basis. Solutions to these problems must be undertaken on a regional or global basis. It is encouraging that the international community recognizes this.

Species and Gene Pool Extinction

Species and gene pool extinction is often overlooked when human impact on the environment is addressed. When it is examined, it is often viewed in terms of an aesthetic or moral loss, as were the extinction of the passenger pigeon and the dodo bird and the near-extinction of the whooping crane.

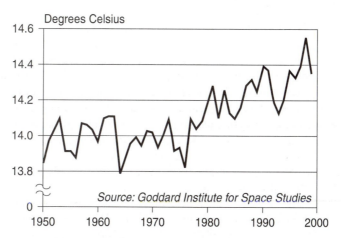

FIGURE 19-1 Global average temperature, 1950–1999.

Source: As reported in Lester R. Brown et al., eds., *Vital Signs 2000* [New York: W. W. Norton, 2000], p. 65.

These were tragedies in their own right, but today, species and gene pool extinction is proceeding faster than at any time in history. Environmental scientists estimate that before the twentieth century, species became extinct at the rate of about 10 per year. By 1972, the rate had climbed to about one per day. In 1992, according to environmental scientists' estimates, 100 to 300 species died out. About one-fourth of the earth's remaining species are under risk of extinction by 2025 as the result of human activities.[9]

Many environmentalists believe that the accelerated rate of species and gene pool extinction indicates that the ability of the earth to support life is diminishing and that the decline in the number of species carries immediate dangers for humankind as well. Their point of view can be easily illustrated in agriculture.

Today, as much as 80 percent of the world's food comes from fewer than two dozen plant and animal species. Subspecies variation within these species assures some degree of survivability in the event of disease or sickness, but the movement toward monoculture high-yield varieties of grains reduces the number of subspecies available and increases the chance of crop blight. The blight that ravaged U.S. corn production in 1970 is ample proof that high-yield monocultural agriculture carries with it significant dangers. Therefore, it should not be overlooked that monoculture is taking place concurrently with the extinction of many genetic variants. The dangers this portends for the future are clear.

Solutions to species and gene pool extinction problems are as difficult to find as with any of the preceding environmental problems we discussed. First, a political consciousness must be built to convince people that a problem exists. Then, transnational action must be decided upon, implemented, and enforced. But in the area of species and gene pool extinction, there remains debate. This was shown by the United States' original refusal under the Bush administration to sign the Biodiversity Treaty concluded at the June 1992 Earth Summit in Rio de Janeiro and the reversal of that position less than a year later by the Clinton administration.

 ## GLOBAL RESPONSES TO ENVIRONMENTAL DETERIORATION

The countries of the world have recognized that the earth's environment is in trouble. For example, in addition to the 1987 Montreal Protocol on Substances that Deplete the Ozone Layer discussed earlier, the international community has concluded many other environmental agreements as shown in Table 19-2. Several of these agreements were concluded at two key UN environmental conferences held during the 1990s, the 1992 **Rio Earth Summit** and the 1997 **Kyoto Environmental Summit.** We turn to these crucial global meetings on environmental issues now.

The Rio Earth Summit

Held under UN auspices, the Rio Earth Summit brought together thousands of delegates and representatives from hundreds of states, IGOs, and NGOs. Over one hundred heads of state attended, including President George Bush of the United States, Chancellor Helmut Kohl of Germany, and Prime Minister John Major of Great Britain. According to one observer, the Earth Summit was "the largest and most complex conference ever held—bigger than

TABLE 19-2   Selected International Environmental Agreements

Agreement	Year Concluded	Number of Parties, 1999
Basel Convention on Hazardous Waste Movement	1989	118
Convention on Biological Diversity	1992	173
Convention on Long-Range Transboundary Air Pollution	1979	43
Convention on the Regulation of Whaling	1946	57
Convention on Trade in Endangered Species	1973	134
Convention on Wetlands	1971	97
International Tropical Timber Agreement	1994	51
Kyoto Protocol to the UN Framework Convention on Climate Change	1998	7
Montreal Protocol on Substances that Deplete the Ozone Layer	1987	165
UN Convention on the Law of the Seas	1982	125
UN Convention to Combat Desertification	1994	124
UN Framework Convention on Climate Change	1992	174

the momentous meetings at Versailles, Yalta, and Potsdam."[10] But did the Earth Summit accomplish anything? To a great extent, the answer depends on one's perspective. The summit's legacy covered five areas.

First and second, the 178 states that attended the conference signed two treaties, the UN Framework Convention on Climate Change, which addressed global warming issues, and the Convention on Biological Diversity, which sought to protect endangered species and biodiversity. The United States at first opposed the biodiversity treaty because of its provision that research, technology, and profits from genetic engineering be shared with countries where the original genetic material were produced. But when the U.S. administration changed from President Bush to President Clinton, the U.S. position on the treaty changed. It was signed in 1994.

Third, the conference issued a Declaration on Environment and Development that sought to balance the needs of humans and nature. As discussed earlier, this treaty provided the concept of sustainable development considerable impetus by committing, at least in principle, all signatory states to pursue 27 nonbinding provisions that would encourage economic development that does not compromise the ability of future generations to meet their needs.

Fourth, the Earth Summit adopted a vaguely worded nonbinding pledge to protect the earth's forests and woodlands. Its objective was to minimize the impact of economic development on forests and to seek ways to limit damage to forests.

Finally, the Earth Summit adopted *Agenda 21,* a document that stressed the need to forge a global partnership between developed and developing countries to combat environmental deterioration. This document addressed many issues, including changing patterns of consumption, transferring appropriate environmental technology from developed states to developing states, and creating a Commission on Sustainable Development to help implement the actions agreed to at Rio.[11]

Some participants and observers considered the conference a success. They pointed out that so many people from so many parts of the international community, including many heads of state, had never before assembled to discuss a particular issue. In this respect, the Earth Summit raised global consciousness about environmental issues. They also pointed out that industrialized countries of the world pledged over $11 billion to help clean and protect the environment, $7 billion from Japan over five years and $4 billion from the European Community (now Union).

Others believed the conference accomplished little. They pointed out that because of U.S. insistence, the climate treaty was so diluted that it had no meaningful effect on reducing carbon dioxide emissions. The agreement on forest and woodland protection was also watered down, this time because of the insistence of many Developing World states who feared that stronger wording might adversely affect their economies. Throughout the Rio meeting, a conflict between environmental protection and economic development was evident.

Critics of the Rio meeting also minimized the importance of the new commitments for environmental programs and sustainable development taken on by Japan and the European Union, noting that the United Nations estimated that as much as $125 billion per year were needed for the next decade for environmental cleanup on a global basis. They asserted the new environmental aid was much too little to have any meaningful impact. They also noted that the United States pledged only $150 million in new money for global environmental improvement, to protect forests.

The Kyoto Environmental Summit

Following the Rio Earth Summit, the international community moved forward on several environmental fronts, some of which will be discussed in the next section. But it was not until 1997, in Kyoto, Japan, that the states of the world met again in another environmental summit. This meeting specifically targeted global warming. Despite reductions in the emission of greenhouse gases such as carbon dioxide, chlorofluorocarbons, methane, and nitrous oxides mandated by the Montreal Protocol and the Rio agreements, the states of the world continued to release too many of these gases into the atmosphere. As a result, the earth's atmosphere remained at risk. The **Kyoto Environmental Summit** intended to address this problem.[12]

It quickly became apparent that a serious rift existed between developed and developing states. As a general rule, developed states intended to reduce their greenhouse gas emissions to 1990s levels and committed themselves at Kyoto to a set of emission reduction standards that would last well into the twenty-first century. Developing World states refused to accept these standards, however, believing that the stringent reductions required would prevent them from developing their economies. An impasse soon developed.

Careful diplomacy and the creation of an innovative standard for international emissions trading broke the impasse. The final **Kyoto Protocol** included terms that committed the European Union to reduce greenhouse gas emissions to 8 percent, the U.S. to 7 percent, and Japan to 6 percent below 1990 levels by 2008–2012. The protocol also allows countries with emissions targets to trade greenhouse gas allowances by purchasing permits from countries that meet their targets. This innovation adds an economic incentive for developing states to meet their targets. Another innovation, the Clean Development Mechanism, allows developed states to use emission reductions from project activities in developing states to contribute to compliance with their own targets. This innovation adds incentives for developed and developing states to cooperate in developing "environmentally clean" projects. Subsequent meetings in Buenos Aires, Argentina in 1998 and Bonn, Germany in 1999 added additional detail to the broad agreements concluded in Kyoto.[13]

Nevertheless, ratification of the Kyoto Protocol is proceeding slowly. In 1999, 84 countries had signed the protocol. However, only seven had ratified it, all of which were small island or low lying states particularly concerned by global warming and the possibility that global warming could melt the polar ice caps, thereby raising the sea level and submerging them. But other countries less immediately threatened fear that the protocol's standards will adversely affect economic development or performance. Thus, despite progress, the conflict between industrialization and the environment addressed earlier in this chapter remains a very real problem for the environment.

Other International Environmental Efforts

In addition to Rio, Kyoto, and the other agreements listed in Table 19-2, the international community has moved forward with several other concepts designed to protect the environment. These other efforts have had mixed success. For example, the Rio Earth Summit's *Agenda 21* created the **Commission on Sustainable Development (CSD.)** Given the task to ensure followup of Rio Conference decisions and to enhance international cooperation on environmentally sound economic development, the CSD has held annual meetings since 1994 to achieve these ends. However, even though it has an ambitious agenda, it has limited oversight and implementation capabilities and few resources.

Multilateral agencies such as the World Bank are also playing a larger role in global environmental affairs since Rio. For example, the Rio Convention on Climate Change and the Convention on Biological Diversity designated the **Global Environmental Facility (GEF),** established in 1991 as a pilot program under the auspices of the UN Development Program, the UN Environment Program, and the World Bank, as their funding mechanism. Between 1991 and 1994, the GEF dispersed $750 million in four focal areas, climate change, biological diversity, international waters, and stratospheric ozone, as well as moneys to combat desertification and deforestation. Reorganized and refinanced with $2 billion in 1994, the GEF now disperses much of its funding to projects undertaken by governments and NGOs.[14]

One final point must be reiterated about efforts to find solutions to the earth's environmental problems. In the past, most if not all of the environmentally related problems in the categories we examined here were localized or national in scope. Within the last decade or two, however, they have been increasingly recognized as international in scope. Acid rain caused by Russian industrial production damages Norwegian as well as Russian lakes and streams. U.S. topsoil loss threatens not only U.S. but also Japanese nutrition. French industrial production brings smog and air pollution to Germany, and German industrial production does the same to France. Dam construction and irrigation in the Sudan affect Egyptian agriculture, and deforestation in the Ivory Coast, Ghana, Togo, and Benin accelerates desertification in Mali, Upper Volta, and Niger.

Environmental challenges have become international in scope, and solutions to them must also be international. The good news is that the international community increasingly understands this. The bad news is that fears over compromised sovereignty and slowed economic development continue to prevent more rapid progress.[15]

HEALTH

After years of often slow but very real progress on global health issues, the emergence of acquired immune deficiency syndrome (AIDS) as a global health problem refocused international attention on health as a critical global issue. Even as AIDS gained notoriety, more people realized that drugs were also an international issue. Our discussion of international health issues will focus on AIDS and drugs before turning to other international health issues. First, however, it will be useful to provide a background to the international community's concern about international health issues.

Health as an International Issue

AIDS is not the first disease that has had global implications. When Europeans moved to the Western Hemisphere during the fifteenth, sixteenth, and seventeenth centuries, they brought with them measles, typhus, yellow fever, and smallpox, diseases that were until that time unknown in the Western Hemisphere. These diseases ravaged much of the Western Hemisphere's indigenous population. More recently, extensive international campaigns have been undertaken against smallpox and malaria under the auspices of the **World Health Organization (WHO).**[16] The WHO eliminated smallpox throughout the world and had a major role in reducing the frequency of malaria, although as we shall see later, malaria is making a comeback as a global health threat.

The WHO was specifically created by the states of the world to monitor, treat, and prevent diseases and health problems that confronted the international community. Given that today's rapid transportation capabilities and mobile populations make it possible for diseases to spread very quickly, there is a demonstrable need for the WHO and similar bodies. Highly infectious diseases and new diseases without known antidotes have a greater probability of affecting more of the world's population than in years past. The international community has already taken some steps to meet this challenge.

Given rapid transportation and mobile populations, the resolution of global health issues in certain ways requires transnational approaches similar to those demanded by global environmental problems. Nevertheless, despite the WHO's several successes, the world still has a long way to go to cope with its international health problems.

AIDS and HIV

The dimension of the world's AIDS epidemic is truly staggering. In 1999, as Table 19-3 shows, almost 34 million people were living with AIDS or the human immunodeficiency virus (HIV) that causes AIDS. An estimated 16.3 million people had already died from the disease. By the end of 1999, the epidemic had orphaned 11.2 million children under the age of 15.

What is more, approximately 95 percent of the infections and deaths from AIDS are in the Developing World, as Figures 19-2 and 19-3 show. Africa is particularly hard hit, with over 23 million people infected. Over one half of Africa's HIV infections are in East and Central Africa. The Democratic Republic of the Congo, Kenya, Malawi, Rwanda, Tanzania,

TABLE 19-3   The Growth of HIV and AIDS

Year	Millions of Estimated HIV Infections	Millions of Estimated AIDS Deaths
1980	0.1	0.0
1981	0.3	0.0
1982	0.7	0.0
1983	1.2	0.0
1984	1.7	0.1
1985	2.4	0.2
1986	3.4	0.3
1987	4.5	0.5
1988	5.9	0.8
1989	7.8	1.2
1990	10.0	1.7
1991	12.8	2.4
1992	16.1	3.3
1993	19.7	4.4
1994	23.8	5.7
1995	28.3	7.3
1996	33.5	9.2
1997	38.9	11.3
1998	44.1	13.7
1999	49.9	16.3

Source: Lester R. Brown, et al., eds., *Vital Signs 2000* (New York: W.W. Norton, p. 101).

Uganda, and Zambia all have high incidence rates. In some cities, 30 percent of the population is infected. The AIDS epidemic has profound economic and social implications for the Developing World, and especially for Africa. It has already significantly diminished the intellectual and skilled labor force and raised health care and social services costs.

Recognizing this, the World Health Organization in 1987 formed the Global Program on AIDS (GPA). With GPA support, over 120 countries developed short-term anti-AIDS plans. This proved insufficient to combat the disease, and in 1999, several UN agencies such as the WHO and the World Bank in 1999 established the International Partnership Against HIV-AIDS. The partnership works with governments, health deliverers, donors, non-governmental agencies, and AIDS victims to control and halt the spread of AIDS. No cure for AIDS has been found, and much remains to be done.[17]

Drugs

Like AIDS, drugs emerged as an internationally-recognized health problem in the 1980s. Again like AIDS, drugs remain an immense international problem today. But unlike AIDS, the contemporary era is not the first time that drugs have created problems in international relations.[18]

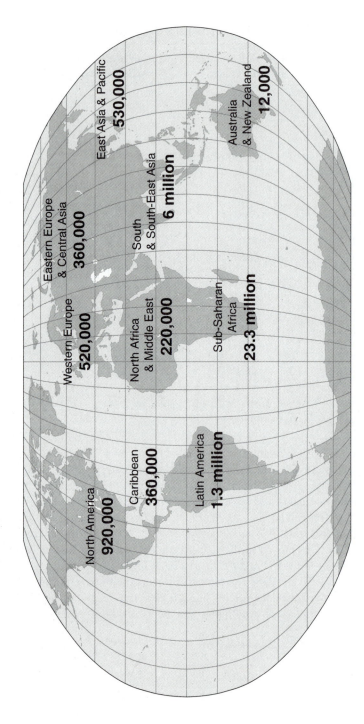

North America
920,000

Caribbean
360,000

Latin America
1.3 million

Western Europe
520,000

Eastern Europe
& Central Asia
360,000

North Africa
& Middle East
220,000

Sub-Saharan
Africa
23.3 million

South
& South-East Asia
6 million

East Asia & Pacific
530,000

Australia
& New Zealand
12,000

FIGURE 19-2   Adults and children estimated to be living with HIV/AIDS as of January 2000

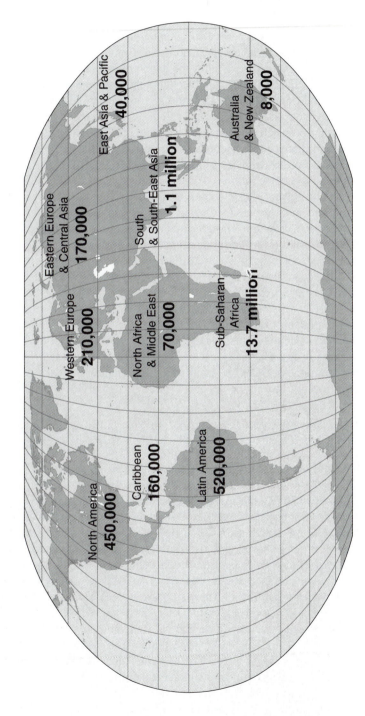

FIGURE 19-3 Estimated adult and child deaths due to HIV/AIDS from the beginning of the epidemic to January 2000

During the nineteenth century, European powers sold large quantities of opium to China, disrupting the normal functioning of Chinese society. When the Chinese government tried to stop the opium trade, Great Britain and France went to war with China to force China to continue to allow the import of opium. Opium addiction remained a significant problem in East Asia until well into the twentieth century.

In the United States, today's drug problems are not the first time society has shown concern about addictive substances. In the early twentieth century, many U.S. citizens developed a cocaine habit, using cocaine imported from South America. New food and drug laws and changed societal outlooks helped reduce cocaine use in that earlier era, but new laws did not decrease U.S. citizens' love for alcohol during prohibition in the 1920s. Many people made millions of dollars smuggling alcohol into the country, and U.S. relations with several states, notably Canada, became strained because of the U.S. government's attempts to stem the flow of illegal liquor.

Today's drug problems are immense in scope and global in nature. Although it is difficult to measure the magnitude of drug problems, the United States probably has the worst one, followed by Western Europe. However, drug addiction does not stop there. Russia, Japan, Eastern Europe, and most Developing World states admit that drug addiction is on the rise there as well.

The sources of drugs are widespread. Cocaine comes primarily from South America; marijuana from South America, the Caribbean, and North America; heroin and opium from Southeast Asia and the Middle East; and other drugs from elsewhere. Many of these drugs, especially cocaine, must first be processed. In a fascinating twist that points out the complexities of the international drug trade, U.S. businesses provide up to 90 percent of the ethyl ether and acetone needed in South America to make cocaine out of coca leaf.

International drug traffic is big business. Some estimates place the earnings of international drug traffickers at between $30 and $60 billion per year. In some countries like Peru, Colombia, and Bolivia, drug profits allow drug barons to fund private armies, bribe public officials, and otherwise operate as if they were sovereign rulers. Their great wealth allows the drug barons to extend their influence beyond their home countries, keeping people on their payrolls in the United States and Europe and buying property there as well. Indeed, when it was charged in 1995 that the Cali drug cartel had made large contributions to the election campaign of Colombia's president, no one was really too surprised.

In many instances in Latin America, Asia, and elsewhere, drug lords rely on local peasants to provide them with the labor to grow, harvest, and process drug-producing crops. Living on the edge of subsistence, peasants frequently view drug traffic as the only way to earn a livelihood. Thus, an intricate relationship exists between drugs and economic underdevelopment. Without the substitution of crops whose payoff is better than drug crops, there appears little hope of stemming the flow of drugs at their sources. But the difficulty of relying on crop substitution as a solution to the drug problem was underlined in the late 1980s and early 1990s when international coffee prices fell precipitously. As the price of coffee, one of Colombia's primary non-drug exports, fell, more and more Colombians turned to drug production for their livelihood.

Meanwhile, in Bolivia and Peru, an alliance developed between drug lords and revolutionary groups. The drug barons provided money and weapons to the guerrilla bands for protection, and the revolutionary groups then protected drug production as they ran their military campaigns against the national governments. In some cases, the governments were less well financed than either the drug barons or the guerrillas.

Not surprisingly, the flow of drug money into several countries is sizeable. This is especially true in South America where much of the economies of Bolivia, Colombia, and Peru are based on drug trafficking. These three countries in the 1990s were the world's three largest producers of coca, a statistic unlikely to change in the early years of the twenty-first century.

International traffic in drugs has also had an impact on a number of smaller countries, for example, the ministates of the Cayman Islands, the Bahamas, and Vanuatu, in which prosperous banking industries have sprung up. Often, these banks also launder drug money. Although most of the banks in these countries operate legally and most were established for the purpose of providing tax shelter locations for large offshore investors, large quantities of drug money move through these offshore banking sites.

Can anything be done about international drug traffic? Given the scope and magnitude of the problem, only multifaceted international cooperative efforts have a chance to have a serious impact. Within user countries, demand-reduction programs must be put in place. Within producer countries, economies must be strengthened and alternate crops must be established to reduce drug sources and profits. Governmental institutions in producer states must be strengthened as well. Interdiction efforts must be undertaken with an understanding of national sensitivities about neocolonialism and imperialism. Indeed, when in 1990 the United States announced its intention to deploy an aircraft carrier off the Colombian coast in international waters to help that country in its war against drugs, almost every sector of the Colombian body politic denounced the U.S. move as an intrusion into Colombian affairs. The deployment did not take place.

Nevertheless, military cooperation between the United States and the governments of Colombia, Peru, and Bolivia to combat the drug industry and drug trade has grown significantly. For the most part, U.S. forces provide information and act as advisers to local militaries in coca crop eradication, processing plant destruction, and interdiction efforts. The U.S. Drug Enforcement Agency has also played a major role in these efforts in these countries. During the 1990s, the United States provided these countries with over $10 billion in military and economic aid to help combat drugs and improve local economies. In addition, in 2000, President Clinton journeyed to Colombia to announce the U.S. was providing that country with $1.3 billion and military assistance to help it in its fight against drug trafficking.

Thailand's experience with its campaign against drugs is also noteworthy. Long a source of the poppy plant from which heroin and opium is made, Thailand with U.S. help began a campaign in the 1980s to eradicate poppy cultivation. The campaign was successful, at least until those who were growing poppies moved their fields across the border into Burma. In the absence of Burma's cooperation, the regional poppy crop was almost undiminished.

Obviously, multifaceted international cooperation is needed to combat drugs. For a variety of political and economic reasons, this has been difficult to arrange. When cooperation does occur, it often takes a long time to have the desired impact. Antidrug efforts also are costly in terms of money, time, property, and sometimes lives. Much of the cost must be born by developed countries including the United States. Developing countries in

South America and elsewhere have few spare resources to provide in the war against drugs. But unless such steps are taken, the international drug situation will likely only grow worse. Over time, it is a problem as dangerous and deadly as AIDS.[19]

Other International Health Issues

In addition to AIDS and drugs, the international community is also confronted by a host of other health issues that will be addressed here only in their broadest outlines, concentrating on the Developing World. These health issues can be best viewed as other major diseases, the impact of malnutrition and economic underdevelopment, general health care practices, and the colonial legacy.

Other Major Diseases.   Malaria, spread by mosquitoes and once thought defeated by insecticides and antimalarial drugs, has reemerged as the second most deadly disease after AIDS in much of the Developing World. Malaria reemerged as a world health threat because it developed resistance to antimalarial drugs. According to the WHO, malaria caused over 1 million deaths in Africa alone in 1998. About 50 percent of Africa's population has the disease.

In 1997, the WHO, the World Bank, and other international agencies launched the Multilateral Initiative on Malaria, with a priority focus on Africa, to promote research on malaria and to develop strategies to control it. In addition, a number of governments, pharmaceutical companies, and private financial backers formed the Medicines for Malaria Initiative to develop antimalarial drugs and make them affordable in poor countries.

Many Developing World states also face other diseases such as river blindness, caused by the larvae of the black fly when they invade a person's body causing extreme itching and then blindness; sleeping sickness, transmitted to humans by the tsetse fly; and guinea worm, transmitted by drinking water that has the worm larvae. Most are usually not fatal, but all are severely debilitating.

In the case of guinea worm, the WHO together with national governments eliminated it as a threat from Asia and the Middle East. Guinea worm may soon be gone in Africa as well as a result of a WHO program launched in 1995. Cases of the disease in Africa declined from 3.5 million in 1985 to 150 thousand in 1998.[20] As previously shown with the example of smallpox, international collaborative efforts can have major positive results in health.

Malnutrition and Famine.   Malnutrition and famine are also widespread and represent immense health challenges in the Developing World. For example, as long ago as 1989, the World Bank noted that one fourth of sub-Saharan Africa's population was under-nourished, with enough food for only 80 percent of its requirements. Since then, food production in many countries has declined, with countries like Ethiopia, Somalia, and Sudan experiencing famines that killed hundreds of thousands.

Malnutrition also contributes to the high incidence of deaths in the Developing World from diseases that are seldom fatal in the Developed World. It contributes especially to deaths from childhood diseases like measles, whooping cough, and diphtheria. Malnutrition also contributes to a large percentage of maternal deaths.[21]

Economic Underdevelopment and Health.   Health and development, and poor health and underdevelopment, are related in several ways. First, high levels of development allow better health care to be provided. Second, good health reduces production losses caused by illness, thus aiding development. Third, good health increases the ability of children to learn, thereby providing a better educated and more productive population.

Many developing states are thus caught in a vicious cycle. Their health problems impair their ability to develop, and their low level of development impairs their ability to improve health care delivery. Without wise domestic policy and external help, this is a difficult cycle to escape.[22]

Health Care Practices and Education.   Malnutrition, disease, and underdevelopment are not the only reasons that the Developing World's health problems are so persistent. Many developing states devote an insufficient portion of their budget to health care delivery and education. Good health practices and good health delivery systems can reduce health problems, as demonstrated in China, Sri Lanka, and elsewhere. For example, three times the number of children under five die in Tanzania as in equally poor areas of China. Many experts attribute China's better performance to superior health practices and health delivery.

The World Bank and other international lending agencies have tried to force some developing states to increase the percentage of their budgets they expend on health care by including it as a measure to qualify for loans. However, this has not overcome the problem. In addition, even those developing states that devote a significant portion of their budgets to health care often find it difficult to attract doctors.

The Impact of Colonial Health Practices.   To a great extent, the pattern of present-day health care in many Developing World states was created during the colonial era when medical service was available in cities but not rural areas. Men could receive health care but rarely women and children, and the rich had enough money to pay for care, but not the poor. Many of these practices exist in health care in developing states to the present day.

How these practices developed is easily traced. For example, the first physicians in colonial Africa were military doctors who had European soldiers as their chief concern. The health of Africans received little attention. As a rule, health care in the colonial era treated epidemic diseases rather than endemic diseases, ignored women's and children's issues, and concentrated on European enclaves in cities. Different colonial states had different health care practices, but in general practices were similar.

Health practices in the colonies thus reflected the political, economic, and social inequities of the colonial system. Not surprisingly, the same often remains true in many developing states long after colonialism ended.

CONCLUSIONS

What do the international environmental and health issues that we examined in this chapter imply for the future of the international system? In almost every case, these issues force the international community, and particularly states, to think in terms that go beyond national boundaries. Many of the interrelationships that exist among the environment, health, and drugs are exceedingly complex, just as they are with population, food, energy, resources, economic development, and the distribution of wealth. It is not clear that any of these issues can be resolved successfully working exclusively within national borders.

One of the major challenges for the twenty-first century, then, is for humankind on at least some issues to make the transition from narrowly defined national thinking and solutions to more broadly defined transnational and perhaps even globalist thinking and solutions. This is not a call for globalism or world government, however. Rather it is a recognition that the extent to which this transition is successful may determine not only the quality of life in the twenty-first century, but also whether Homo Sapiens as a species survives into the twenty-second century.

 KEY TERMS AND CONCEPTS

land degradation   soil quality is worsening in many locations of the world because of over-use, fertilizers, and poor land management

desertification   the growth of deserts and sand areas throughout the world, claiming about 43,000 square kilometers per year

deforestation   the destruction of forestlands around the world, with tens of thousands of kilometers lost each year

water degradation and depletion   water quality and availability is worsening in many regions of the world because of factors such as acid rain and overuse caused by industrialization

greenhouse effect   as carbon dioxide and other "greenhouse gases" are emitted by industrial processes into the atmosphere, they trap heat in the atmosphere, leading to global temperature increases

ozone depletion   as chlorofluorocarbons are released, they move to the upper atmosphere where they deplete the earth's ozone layer

Montreal Protocol   1987 agreement between over 45 countries to reduce the production and use of chlorfluorocarbons

species and gene pool extinction   each year more species become extinct, thereby depleting both species and gene pools

Rio Earth Summit   held in 1992 under UN auspices, was the world's first major environmental summit, bringing together thousands of delegates from hundreds of states, IGOs and NGOs

Kyoto Environmental Summit   the 1997 UN environmental meeting, in Kyoto, Japan, that sought to reduce the world's emission of greenhouse gasses to slow global warming

Kyoto Protocol   negotiated at the 1997 Kyoto Summit, the protocol has terms that commit industrialized states to reduce greenhouse gas emissions, allows countries to trade emission allowances by purchasing permits from other countries, and provides chances for developed states to use emission reductions from project activities in developing states to contribute to compliance with their own targets

Commission on Sustainable Development   created at the Rio Summit to follow up on Rio Summit decisions and to aid international cooperation on environmentally sound economic development

Global Environment Facility   created in 1991 by the UN to disperse funds to state governments and NGOs to study climate change, biological diversity, international waters, and ozone depletion

World Health Organization the UN agency charged with improving the world's health standards and combating disease

trends and patterns in global Acquired Immune Deficiency Syndrome (AIDS) problem emerged as a leading international health problem in the 1980s affecting millions around the world and hitting Africa and certain other locations very hard

role of drugs in international relations drugs are often produced in developing countries and consumed in developed states, thereby requiring international rather than national attention to the problem

malaria and other global health problems malaria is one of the world's most frequent diseases with, like many other diseases, widespread international implications

economic underdevelopment and health many factors contribute to underdevelopment, but the very poor health conditions found in many developing states is a major contributor

 ## WEBSITE REFERENCES

environmental issues: *www.webdirectory.com* an extensive directory of environmental websites

global warming: *www.globalwarming.net* website of the Global Warming International Center, established to disseminate information on global warming science and policy

sustainable development: *www.foundation.novartis.com/nfhome.htm* home page of a foundation devoted to furthering sustainable development

Greenpeace: *www.greenpeace.org* the website of perhaps the world's most influential environmental NGO

global AIDS problem: *www.209.27.118.7* a database of thousands of policy statements on HIV-AIDS from national policies and international resolutions

World Health Organization: *www.who.int* website of the UN agency tasked with improving global health

 ## NOTES

1. Unless otherwise noted, much of the following discussion is taken from Marc Levy, "Time for a Third Wave of Environment and Security Scholarship?," *Environmental Change and Security Project: Report, Issue 1* (Washington, DC: Woodrow Wilson Center, 1995); Marc A. Levy, "Is the Environment a National Security Issue?," *International Security* (Fall 1995), pp. 35–62; Marian A. L. Miller, *The Third World in Global Environmental Politics* (Boulder, CO: Lynne Rienner, 1995; Karen T. Liftin, *Ozone Discourses: Science and Politics in Global Environmental Cooperation* (New York: Columbia University Press, 1995); and Alan Thein Durning, "Redesigning the Forest Economy," in Lester R. Brown et al., eds., *State of the World 1994* (New York: W. W. Norton, 1994).

2. UN Food and Agriculture Organization, *Forest Resources Assessment 1990: Tropical Countries, Forestry Paper 112* (Rome: UN FAO, 1993).

3. See William S. Ellis, "A Soviet Sea Lies Dying," *National Geographic* (February 1990), pp. 73–93.

4. Peter H. Gleick, "Water and Conflict," *International Security* (1993), pp. 79–112.

5. See, for example, the draft report from the UN's International Panel on Climate Change (IPPC), as discussed in "Heading for the Apocalypse?," *Time* (October 2, 1995), pp. 54–55.

6. *New York Times,* February 16, 1992. These outlooks are substantially confirmed by the 1995 IPPC draft report.

7. Number of signatory states from *The World Factbook 1994,* p. 489. Terms of the revised protocol from *The New York Times,* November 26, 1992; and "Ministers Approve Stepped Up Timetable to Phase Out Ozone Depleting Substances," *International Environmental Reporter,* January 13, 1993.

8. Lester R. Brown et al., eds, *Vital Signs 1995,* (New York: W. W. Norton, 1995), pp. 62–63.

9. *The Atlanta Journal-Constitution,* May 16, 1992.

10. Philip Elmer-Dewitt, "Rich vs. Poor," *Time,* June 1, 1992, p. 42.

11. See Caroline Thomas, ed., *Rio: Unraveling the Consequences* (Ilford, Essex, England: Frank Cass, 1994); and Lawrence E. Susskind, *Environmental Diplomacy: Negotiating More Effective Global Agreements* (New York: Oxford University Press, 1994).

12. For the results of the Kyoto Summit, see R. Coppock, "Implementing the Kyoto Protocol," *Issues in Science and Technology* (Spring 1998), pp. 66–74; B. Bolin and A.P. Loeb, "Act Now to Slow Climate Change," *Issues in Science and Technology* (Fall 1998), pp. 18–22; U.S. Department of State, "The Kyoto Protocol," Fact Sheet Released by the Bureau of Oceans and International Environmental and Scientific Affairs, (November 2, 1998); United Nations Press Release, "84 Signatories to the Kyoto Protocol," (March 16, 1999).

13. For the results of the Buenos Aires meeting, see "Turning Down the Heat," *America,* December 12, 1998, p.3; G.S. Becker, "What Price Pollution? Leave the to a Global Market," *Business Week* (October 18, 1999), pp. 26; and A.D. Sagar, "A 'Polluters Get Paid' Principle?," *Environment* (November 1999), pp.4–5.

14. Information obtained in January 1996 from the Global Environment Facility Secretariat, Washington, DC.

15. For additional discussions of the responses of the international community to global environmental issues, see Hilary French, *Vanishing Borders: Protecting the Planet in the Age of Globalization* (New York, NY: W.W. Norton, 2000); Paul Diehl and Nils Gleditsch, eds., *Environmental Conflict* (Boulder, CO: Westview Press, 2000); and Gareth Porter, et al.,

Global Environmental Politics, 3d ed. (Boulder, CO: Westview Press, 2000).

16. For the early history of the WHO, see World Health Organization, *First Ten Years of the World Health Organization* (New York, NY: The United Nations, 1958); and WHO, *Second Ten Years of the World Health Organization 1958–67* (New York, NY: The United Nations, 1958).

17. For more detailed discussions of the international implications of AIDS, see World Bank, *Confronting AIDS: Public Priorities in a Global Epidemic* (Washington, D.C.: The World Bank, 1998); and Jonathan Mann and Daniel J. Tarantola, eds., *AIDS in the World II* (New York, NY: Oxford University Press, 1996).

18. Much of this section is developed from news reports. For more academic-oriented views on the international drug situation, see LaMond Tullis, *Unintended Consequences: Illegal Drugs and Drug Policies in Nine Countries* (Boulder, CO: Lynne Rienner, 1995); and Bruce M. Bagley and William O. Walker III, *Drug Trafficking in the Americas* (Miami, FL: North-South Center Press, 1994).

19. For additional discussions of the international drug situation, see Raphael Peri, ed., Drugs and Foreign Policy: A Critical Review (Boulder, CO: Westview Press, 1994); "Narcopolitics," *Current History* (April 1998), pp. 145–88; and "U.S. Anti-Narcotics Strategy: At War with Reality?," *IISS Strategic Comments* (March 2000).

20. See The Carter Center's reports, 2000, for details of the international community's efforts to eradicate guinea worms.

21. The impact of malnutrition and famine on health is explored in World Bank, *Health, Nutrition, and Population,* (Washington, D.C.: The World Bank, 1997).

22. For discussions of the negative impacts of economic underdevelopment on health, see S.K. Adijiboloso, ed., *International Perspectives on the Human Factor in Economic Development* (Westport, CN: Greenwood, 1998); and Randolph Quaye, *Underdevelopment and Health Care in Africa: The Ghanaian Experience* (Lewiston, NY: Mellen University Press, 1996).

PART 6

The Futuristic Framework: Where Is the World Going?

The question at issue is therefore the ultimate end of mankind.

—HEGEL

Man had acquired a past, and he was beginning to grope toward a future.

—ARTHUR C. CLARKE

The twentieth century was a century of immense change for the international community. As the century opened, a few states and their empires dominated the international landscape. Today, over 190 states exist and overseas empires are gone. Only a few decades ago, states were the sole actors of international consequence. Today, so many other types of actors exist and wield so impressive an array of capabilities that some serious observers question whether states will remain viable entities very far into the twenty-first century. Economic and military issues remain as important now as they were at the turn of the century, but they have become increasingly complicated. Economically, questions of dependence, interdependence, distribution, depletion, and development demand answers. Militarily, nuclear proliferation and increased destructiveness and availability of conventional weapons call into question the continued political utility of military solutions to the world's problems. Even so, the frequency of violence has not diminished.

All these changes also altered the international system. As we saw in Chapter 7, the twentieth century opened with international affairs organized into a balance-of-power system. World War I—and the changes in international actors and their relationships that preceded and accompanied that conflict—brought the balance-of-power system to an end. The international actors of the day then created an international collective security system that proved ineffective and unstable. It, too, ended in a global conflict. And at the end of World War II, yet another international system formed—a bipolar system—that went through various shapes and forms, but for the most part survived intact until the beginning of the 1990s.

Today, the international community is experiencing another period of systemic change. The East–West conflict is over. Economic issues have gained new prominence as additional centers of economic power developed and gained strength. New global issues are emerging to join older transnational concerns. Old ways of looking at the world and the international community in many cases are outdated.

Can a new international system emerge without the international community resorting to global violence? What will its shape and form be, and how will it affect international actors and their interactions? How can the actors influence the shape and form of that system as it emerges?

These are difficult questions, made all the more problematic because indications are that the rapidity of change will increase as the twenty-first century progresses. Present day international actors find themselves increasingly challenged. The international economic system is in transition. The arms race has been globalized. Scientific and technical advances have potential to revolutionize international affairs. Conflicts of values remain as prominent, perhaps more prominent, than ever.

The impact that these and other forces will have on international affairs will be immense, and the shape that the future world will take is not yet evident. Will increased economic interdependence accelerate a trend toward world order or will it precipitate a move toward increased protectionism? Will affordable energy and materials alternatives be found or will energy and materials availability decrease, thereby heightening the chances of "resource wars"? Will scientific and technical breakthroughs enable the Developing World to accelerate its pace of development and reduce the North–South gap, or will the industrialized world reap most of the advantages of future advances and widen the gap still further? Will the state, today's dominant international actor, survive the challenges presented from within and without? Even more centrally, will humankind survive, given existing stockpiles of nuclear weapons and other weapons of mass destruction and the virtual inevitability of their proliferation?

Answers to these questions are at best speculation. But even so, given our understanding of the past and present international system and the forces that shaped and are shaping it, such speculation may prove useful in preparing us for change. This concluding chapter is a primer on "future shock" in the international system. Although future shock cannot be avoided, it can be prepared for, even if projections of change prove less than totally accurate. In this final chapter, we look at some of the most important issues we need to examine:

- Where is the international community heading?
- Where do we want it to go?
- How can we help it get there?

Chapter 20

Toward 2100

- What forces are changing today's international system?
- What type of international system do we want?
- How can forces of change be used to create the international system we want?

International actors rarely remain static. Neither do the systems that they help create, the perceptions that they hold, the instruments that they use, or the issues that they face. In the last ten years alone, all have undergone major changes. Obscure actors have attained prominence, and prominent actors have become obscure. Allies have become enemies, and enemies allies. Resources increase and decrease in value, weapons change, and the world economy surges and falters. Equitable distribution of resources, economic dependence and interdependence, nuclear proliferation and the environment, and international health and human rights have joined more traditional issues on the international community's agenda. The international arena is a world of change.

On occasion, these changes individually and collectively may be unexpected and go in directions few imagined or planned for. As aware as people were in 1941 that World War II would bring incredible change to the international arena, few predicted that events and inventions would shift the center of world power from Europe within six short years. Yet that is exactly what happened. In the early 1960s, many knowledgeable people predicted "an American century" that would rival the eras of Roman and British global dominion. Twenty years later, by 1980, U.S. citizens wondered what had happened to their clear-cut economic and military preeminence. More change would come as at the turn of the century, the United States once again was militarily and economically preeminent in comparison to all other states, its one-time rival, the Soviet Union, having collapsed amidst economic and political turmoil and disarray.

However, by the turn of the century, some scholars were pondering whether being the preeminent state meant as much as it once did. With the European Union having been established as a "United States of Europe" and with large free trade areas emerging on the Pacific rim and in the Americas, perhaps large transnational groups of state would be the wave of the future, they posited. Or perhaps advanced information and communication technologies would couple with a coming revolution in biogenetics to move the international system in other new and unexpected directions.

Major changes can truly come rapidly and unexpectedly to the international arena. And what is more, they are constant. The purpose of this concluding chapter is to explore where some of those rapid, unexpected, and constant changes may take us.

 ## THE INTERNATIONAL SYSTEM IN TRANSITION

One of the major themes running throughout this text has been that the international system is in a state of flux, and it is changing to a new system that is as yet vague and undefined. This text has also implied that the broad outlines of several alternative systems that may emerge are beginning to become discernible.

Because the international system is not only formed and shaped by international actors and their interactions, but also in turn helps form and shape those actors and their interactions, the views that the major actors hold about the constraints and opportunities they will have in the emerging international system will be critical variables in determining what that system is like. For example, if the major economic powers see the emerging international system as one in which economic well-being mandates cutthroat economic competition and protectionism, the emerging system will doubtlessly have those characteristics. Conversely, if the major economic powers see the emerging international system as one that requires cooperation for economic well-being, the emerging system will probably have those characteristics.

The key point here is that in the midst of systemic change, old expectations and patterns of behavior of international actors are themselves more likely to change. This does little to help us predict in which direction systemic change will move. But it is beyond question that systemic change is taking place. Developing an international consensus on the direction of preferred change remains an immense challenge.

At least three different models of the next international system have been put forward by analysts, policy makers, journalists, politicians, and other observers of contemporary international affairs. These three models are a unipolar world based on U.S. military and economic might, a regionalized world organized around three economic trading blocs, and a multipolar world based on several measures of national and international capabilities.

A Unipolar World?

Throughout most of the years of the post–World War II bipolar international system, military strength was the primary measure of national power. To be sure, economic strength was almost always a major component of an international actor's ability to develop and maintain military strength, but military capabilities were nevertheless the foremost measure of national strength in most observers' eyes.

Given this emphasis, it was not too surprising that when the Soviet Union collapsed, some people concluded that a unipolar world had emerged, with that one pole being the United States. These observers argued that the United States was now the only country that could project large quantities of military power anywhere in the world, that the United States had far and away the world's single largest national economy, and that the United

Chapter 20

IT IN 2100: PREDICTING THE FUTURE

The Information Age, like the agricultural and industrial ages which preceded it, is a global phenomenon. Also like the agricultural and industrial ages, Information Age changes are not equally present everywhere. Change induced by Information Age technologies is taking place in different countries at different rates of speed, with different types and different depths of impacts.

How will these different rates of change induced by different rates of absorbing information technology affect the international system? Here, we present the views of Alvin and Heidi Toffler, futurists who emphasize the role of information technology in shaping the twenty-first century's international system.

To the Tofflers, the world is moving toward a global socio-economic revolution that will result in a global "trisected power structure." This structure will replace the Industrial Age's two part structure in which states with industrial economies had economic, military, and social superiority over agricultural societies.

In the Information Age, the Tofflers say, states that use information technology the most effectively will be at the top of a global power structure dominated by information and information technology. They will have superior capabilities in comparison to states that retain an industrial or agricultural economy. To gain the advantages of information technology, some states may attempt to bypass the industrial stage of development, moving directly from an agricultural economy to an information economy.

Because they are more dependent on information technology than states with industrial or agricultural economies, states that use information will be more vulnerable than those societies to alteration, disruption, or destruction of information technology. In much the same way, industrial societies are more vulnerable to the disruption of energy supplies than agricultural societies.

As the trisected structure emerges, capabilities provided by information technology are likely to further blur boundaries between domestic and international affairs. Some states will try to control access to information, as China has with access to the Internet. However, few will succeed unless they impose extreme social or technical controls. Such solutions might include capital punishment for accessing information sites deemed unacceptable or restricting Internet access via licenses to loyal subjects.

Advanced information technologies are also likely to increase the international role of nonstate actors. Multinational corporations have long been major actors in the international scene, but they are likely to become even more influential. Similarly, the influence of nongovernmental organizations will increase.

To the Tofflers, the emerging international system will be more complex than today's. More fissures of change and conflict will divide the global community than today as information technology will be absorbed, diffused, and operationalized at different speeds and with different results in different countries.

Given the potential provided by Information Age technologies for like-minded people to articulate and act on their viewpoints, and contrary to those who argue (or fear) that the Information Age will bring with it an era of global homogeneity, the Tofflers believe that the international system of the Information Age will be more complex than those that preceded it.

States was now the focus of global affairs. Most observers who adopted this viewpoint were U.S. citizens, and their outlook of U.S. dominance is reflected in Figure 20-1.

These were persuasive arguments. However, by concentrating on military might and diplomatic positioning, they tended to overlook several important issues. Could the United States maintain its military might given that some quarters in the U.S. doubted the value of continued large scale military spending? Would military might remain the most meaningful measure of national power in the twenty-first century, or was economic strength becoming more important? Were issues emerging on the international scene that could not be readily solved by either military might or economic strength? Because of the probable answers to such questions, most people rejected the unipolar world as the most likely model of the new international system.[1]

A Regionalized World?

A second model of the new international system was based on the assumption that the collapse of the Soviet Union and the end of the Cold War had relegated military capabilities to a less important place in international affairs and had elevated economic strength to preeminence. Many people therefore concluded that the new international system would be based on three regional economic blocs: in the Americas centered on the United States, in

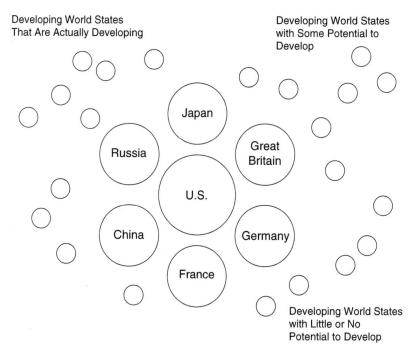

FIGURE 20-1   **One version of what may emerge as the New International System in the twenty-first century: A unipolar world based on military and economic power; most scholars and analysts do not believe this is the most likely model.**

Europe centered on the European Union, and in East Asia centered on Japan, as shown in Figure 20-2.

There were actually two variants of this model, one based on the assumption that the economic blocs would cooperate with each other and the other on the assumption that they would be extremely competitive with each other. But both variants of this second model also had critics who maintained that the second model overlooked the continuing importance of military capabilities and national aspirations. They argued that factors beyond economic strength were extremely important in international affairs and that military strength remained an important tool of state power.

In addition, critics of the regionalized world model insisted that such a world was unstable and dangerous because it could lead to economic warfare and trade restrictions like those that contributed to the onset of World War II. If this was the direction in which the new international order was heading, they insisted, the international community should do everything in its power to change directions.

A Multipolar World?

Still other observers believed that the next international system would be a diffuse world order, with the United States, the European Union, Russia, Japan, and China all continuing

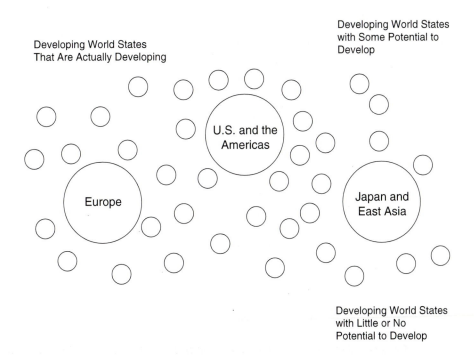

Developing World States That Are Actually Developing

Developing World States with Some Potential to Develop

U.S. and the Americas

Europe

Japan and East Asia

Developing World States with Little or No Potential to Develop

FIGURE 20-2 **A second version of what may emerge as the New International System in the twenty-first century: A regionalized world based on economic trading blocs.**

to play major roles, but with other states and other types of international actors also, on occasion, rising to prominence on a case-by-case or issue-by-issue basis. This outlook is depicted in Figure 20-3.

Proponents of this perspective more often than not saw economic strength growing in importance. However, they also believed that military strength would continue to play an important role in contemporary international relations. Often, they pointed to the collapse of the Soviet Union as proof of the growing importance of economics and the 1991 Persian Gulf War as proof of the continuing importance of military power. But they also stressed that measures of national power in addition to economic capabilities and military strength were extremely important. These other measures included but were not necessarily limited to law, diplomacy, and sociopolitical parameters of power discussed in Chapter 15.

This third perspective on the emerging international system is extremely diffuse. Some of its critics asserted that it underplays the importance of economic capabilities and military strength as well as the continued importance of traditional actors and issues in contemporary international affairs. Other critics argued that it is so diffuse a model of the emerging international system that it is not a model at all, but rather a refusal to create a model of what the new international order will become. Nevertheless, its proponents believed that it provided the most accurate representation of what the emerging international system will be like.[2]

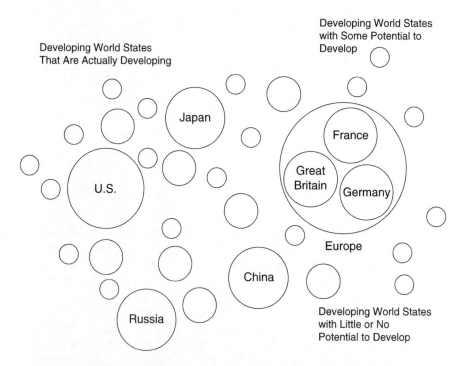

FIGURE 20-3   A third version of what may emerge as the New International System in the twenty-first century: A multipolar world based on multiple parameters of power.

CRITICAL AREAS OF INTERNATIONAL CHANGE

Which system will be the one that emerges? Most indicators seem to point toward the third model. However, as noted in the beginning of this chapter, major change can come rapidly and unexpectedly to the international arena.

Although the exact nature of change and the exact shape of the emerging international system cannot be foretold with certainty, several critical areas of international change are evident. Each could have immense and unpredictable impact on international affairs and the future international system. Here, five of the most significant areas of change are discussed with the purpose of providing a better outline of possible alternative futures. The importance of providing such an outline is best deduced by paraphrasing management consultant Peter Drucker: Planning the future does not deal with future decisions, but with the future of present decisions.

Present-Day Actors Under Assault

This book opened with a detailed analysis of the most prominent categories of actors in the international arena: states, intergovernmental organizations, multinational corporations, nongovernmental organizations, and individuals. Although it was pointed out on several occasions throughout the opening framework, a rather startling fact may nevertheless have been overlooked: Several of the categories of actors, and even more specifically several prominent actors, are under internal and/or external assault. Although their survival may not currently be in question, their legitimacy and raison d'être are.

The state is the leading example. In most cases no longer able to provide as much economic independence or to offer as much physical security as it has in the past, the state has seen two of its fundamental reasons for existing thrown open to question. Some states have sought to overcome their problems by adhering to supranational alliances or economic communities, whereas others seek to enhance their own military credibility or attempt to erect trade barriers. But the fundamental fact remains that the state, as Henry Kissinger said, is "inadequate" to meet many of the challenges of the twenty-first century.

Other actors realize this and seek to turn this to their own advantages. Executives of multinational corporations promise higher living standards and eschew state protectionism. The secretariats of IGOs seek to strengthen their own organizations' positions vis-à-vis states. A variety of nongovernmental organizations, particularly national liberation movements that seek to break away from existing states and transnational movements that purport to have supranational appeal, similarly argue that the state in its present form is obsolete. They propose respectively to replace states with more localized forms of governance, with large governmental units, or with large free trade areas.

The decline and fall of the former Soviet Union deserves special mention here. Recognized as one of the primary actors in the international arena for half a century, the USSR proved unable to cope with the combination of the need for internal political and economic reorganization and the demands by internal national movements for their own independence. Despite its global military reach, it was unable to survive as an international actor.

Similarly, Yugoslavia and Czechoslovakia were also unable to survive internal ethnic, political, and economic tensions, and also dissolved as states.

What of the states of Western Europe as they unite in a continentwide union? Will national identities remain or over time will a supranational identity emerge, a type of "citizen of Europe" regional mentality that will overshadow old national identities?

The state is not the only international actor under assault. Multinational corporations, viewed by their advocates as purveyors of economic plenty, are criticized by state governments, national groups, IGOs, and NGOs alike for their perceived efforts to dominate the economies of others. Several states have taken active steps to limit activities of MNCs within their borders and to prohibit the export of profits. National groups, some of which seek independence from the state taking such action, have applauded these restrictions, as have a variety of IGOs including the UN. NGOs, as would be expected given the variety within the category, hold disparate views.

As the most prominent IGO, the United Nations has received its fair share of criticism. Developing World states resent the great powers' ability to veto in the Security Council, and the United States has evidenced similar resentment toward the General Assembly and several of its associated agencies.

States, MNCs, and IGOs are thus all under assault from internal and/or external forces. None of this is to say that any category of actor or individual actor is in danger of extinction. However, it is to point out that the precarious balance of capabilities, power, influence, and importance that exists among and between these actors is by no means a given. The state will maintain its position of preeminence. Nevertheless, because few states exclusively control their own destiny, even that is a statement of faith.

The International Economic System in Transition

Until recently, the international economic system was in turmoil. However, by the mid-1990s, a degree of stability and order unseen for years began to appear in the system as major free trade areas or the precursors of free trade areas were formed in Europe (the European Union), the Americas (the Free Trade Area of the Americas), and the Asia–Pacific region (the Asia–Pacific Economic Cooperation forum). In addition, smaller trade zones such as the Association of Southeast Asian Nations and the Andean Pact continued to operate or were formed within the major areas and elsewhere as well.

At the same time, the Uruguay Round of GATT ended with a major world trade agreement that significantly reduced tariffs and other non-tariff barriers to trade. It also created a World Trade Organization to oversee international trade, adjudicate trade disputes, and work for additional reductions to trade barriers. Today's international economic system is a much different one than existed in the early 1990s.

But this does not mean that everything is well within the system. Even though they are less strident than in the past, Developing World states continue to call for a more equitable international economic system that provides fewer advantages to industrialized developed states. The industrialized world itself asserts that free trade and market access will solve many Developing World economic problems. Developing World states respond that this is a cover for industrialized economic interests, represented primarily by MNCs, to further penetrate and dominate their economies.

Despite the successful conclusion of the Uruguay Round of GATT, international economic problems also exist between and among industrialized states, which still accuse one another of enacting unfair trade laws, instituting nontariff barriers to free trade, dumping, and other practices designed to generate economic advantage. Threats of protectionism continue. And in Eastern Europe, Russia, China, and elsewhere as well, governments search for ways to attract external capital to accelerate economic growth there. Meanwhile, capital and stock markets around the world become increasingly bound together because of the ability of investors and speculators to shift funds from one location to another on virtually a moment's notice.

This tension in the international economic system is even more striking because of the growth of global economic interdependence. What will happen in a world where interdependence exists, but where disagreement exists over the advantages that each side derives from that interdependence? What will happen if one side believes it is overcharged for resources that it desperately needs? How will international actors react when their needs are met by uncertain external sources of supply? Three scenarios seem most probable.

First, international actors may realize that global interdependence dictates that precepts of cooperation and mutual advantage be followed. Given the proliferation of trade areas and the successful conclusion of the Uruguay Round, this is in fact what appears to be happening as negotiations and discussions gradually moved to the fore as a way to solve and prevent trade disputes. Optimistically, each actor will realize that its own welfare depends on the welfare of others in the international economic system. This is a strategy that has a rational appeal.

However, rationality can be seen from a number of perspectives. A second rational alternative is possible, one in which international actors, particularly states, see increased interdependence as a threat to economic well-being. Thus, they may seek to reduce dependence on outside sources to satisfy internal needs. This phenomenon has already taken place in certain areas. For example, dependence on imported oil led the French government to emphasize nuclear power. Similarly, the Japanese government decided to expand its nuclear power program to decrease its dependence on imported oil.

At the same time, sentiment grew within some sectors of industrialized countries for protectionist economic measures. For example, in the United States, Congress introduced legislation for domestic content of finished products, and quotas on iron, steel, and automotive products were negotiated. U.S.–Japanese trade negotiations in the late 1980s and early 1990s became particularly rancorous as the United States accused Japan of unfair trade practices and Japan accused the United States of overconsumption and inattention to its economic base. Protectionist sentiment proliferated in Europe as well. Meanwhile, Developing World states argued that they had to develop indigenous industry before they could participate in anything other than a dependent economic relationship.

The third and final scenario is the most frightening, particularly in a world made more dangerous by more and more powerful weapons. Given the continuing differences in perceptions and conflicts of values that exist throughout the world, the possibility exists that international actors may decide to meet their needs by using armed might. Resource-starved actors may engage in "resource wars" to satisfy their requirements, and capital-starved actors may opt for terrorism to meet their needs. This is not a pleasant scenario. But in a world where national sovereignty and freedom of action remain chief objectives of the still preeminent category of actor, it is a realistic one.

The Global Availability of Advanced Weaponry

Despite the end of the East–West conflict and a slowdown in the growth of spending throughout the world on arms, in 2000, states still spent about $800 billion on weapons. This is over $1.5 million per minute. These expenditures bought many weapons, many of which were more powerful than ever before. In addition, more countries had access to highly sophisticated and more lethal weaponry than ever before. This was true at the nuclear as well as conventional level. The U.S. government estimates that nearly 40 countries have or soon will have the ability to make nuclear weapons. Nor can increased access to chemical and biological weapons be overlooked.

Clearly, the availability of greater quantities of increasingly lethal weaponry make the world a more dangerous place in which to live. More hands will be on more triggers. Optimists hope that the increased lethality of the weapons in various arsenals will introduce elements of caution and restraint into the foreign policies of newly potent states. Pessimists fear that more weapons in more hands will merely add more deaths to the over 40 million that have occurred in wars fought since World War II alone.

Wider availability of more lethal weapons will inevitably make wars more costly in terms of human life. Will that realization be a deterrent, or will it be irrelevant to policy makers caught in the web of past practice and history? No one knows the answer to that question, but if the answer is the former, international affairs could be transformed by the lethality of modern war. Even as nuclear war has been avoided because of its lethality, conventional war may become obsolete.

Unfortunately, events suggest otherwise. During 2000, conflicts raged on every inhabited continent except North America and Australia. Nor has the frequency of wars and the number of casualties they cause declined. As we saw in Chapter 17, at least 25 conflicts were under way in 2000. Clearly, suggestions that military force had lost its utility in international affairs were premature.

Nuclear war is of course the greatest threat. Although the United States and Russia have significantly reduced their nuclear arsenals with more reductions still to occur, they still have many more nuclear weapons than other states. Even so, the probability of nuclear proliferation looms large. Indeed, India and Pakistan joined the nuclear club in the late 1990s.

What impact will additional nuclear proliferation have? The question is difficult to answer, but a few additional questions will illustrate the potential impact that nuclear proliferation could have. If Iraq had had nuclear weapons before the 1991 Persian Gulf War, would the United States have deployed forces to the Persian Gulf? Would Iraq have used nuclear weapons in the war if it had had them? Would Egypt or Israel have used nuclear weapons if either had had them during any of their several conflicts? And would India or Pakistan have used nuclear weapons if they had had them during their several wars? In the last case—and probably in the case of Israel as well—the question is nor longer merely rhetorical. It has become a policy issue.

Military research and development could further alter international relations in ways not even dreamed of, just as nuclear weapons and long-range aircraft and missiles did. Lasers in space may become practical. Their impact on international affairs could be immense. "Hold the high ground" could take on an entirely new meaning if domination of space meant domination of earth. On earth itself, improved remote control and sensing capabilities could give rise to a true automated battlefield that would be extremely expensive but result in few casualties. Defense against ballistic missiles may become a possibility. The United States has already worked on lasers and other defensive technologies. The list could continue.

But here, the point to be made is a simple one. With many countries spending large sums of money on their militaries and with revolutionary new military capabilities on the horizon, the possibility of a military induced change in the international system remains great.

Scientific and Technical Advances: Their Potential to Revolutionize International Relations

When the roles of science and technology in international relations are discussed, their impacts are too often restricted to their military implications. Although scientific-technical contributions to military advances cannot be overlooked, neither should they be overstressed, for scientific-technical breakthroughs and applications have altered the conduct of international relations in many other ways as well.

Agricultural, health, transportation, and communication advances lead the way. All have been discussed in earlier chapters and that discussion will not be repeated here. Advances in these and other scientific-technical areas have allowed more people to eat better and to live longer than ever before, to travel faster and farther than any previous generation, and to know more about what is going on in the world than their forebears.

Scientific-technical advances often create problems as well. The population explosion and the arms race are partially attributable to scientific-technical advances. Science and technology drove the industrial revolution onward, but industrial pollution has also contributed extensively to environmental degradation. Whether science and technology can be harnessed to improve the environment is likely to be one of the major issues of the next century. Furthermore, industrial processes remain potentially dangerous, as proved by the explosion at a chemical storage tank in Bhopal, India, in 1984 that killed over 2,000 people. In 1986, the USSR and the rest of the world suffered through the Chernobyl nuclear disaster.

Even when science and technology bring potential for benefit to humanity, questions must be asked about the use that will be made of scientific-technical advances. Will they be used to improve the living standards of the billions of Developing World citizens who live in poverty, or will they lead to increased concentration of wealth and capital in the hands and countries of the affluent? In international affairs, as in domestic affairs, scientific-technical advances do not occur in a vacuum. The Green Revolution provides a perfect example. On the one hand, it allowed many people to avoid starvation. On the other hand, it also led to greater concentration of wealth in the hands of a few in several countries.

Scientific-technical breakthroughs have the potential to revolutionize international affairs. (a) The U.S. space shuttle at liftoff. Will easier access to space lead to greater incentives to cooperate internationally or greater political and military rivalry in space? (b) Earth stations for satellite communications. Will better international communications lead to a greater sense of global community or make humankind more aware of its differences? (c) An artist's rendition of NASA's "Landsat" in orbit. Will the ability of remote sensors in space to identify resources lead to international agreements on resource identification and use or to greater rivalry to exploit newly identified resources?

Improvements in health care and immunization also provide poignant examples. These improvements not only lengthened lives, but they also increased population, thereby resulting in a decreased standard of living in those countries in which economic growth rates fell behind population growth rates. Scientific-technical advances may therefore be seen as a mixed blessing.

However, the emphasis here is on change. No doubt exists that scientific-technical advances, innovations, and breakthroughs have major effects on international affairs. They will continue to do so. Imagine, for a minute, a major breakthrough in alternate energy sources. Such a breakthrough could significantly degrade the importance of Persian Gulf oil to Western Europe, Japan, and the United States. How different would the foreign policies of all these states be in the absence of need for external sources of oil? No specific answer is possible, but major changes in their foreign policy would inevitably occur.

Or contemplate the impact on international actors of the ongoing revolution in information and communication technologies. The possibilities are truly immense. For example, current power relationships between and among types of international actors are already being disrupted. Multinational corporations already electronically transfer large quantities of funds and information across national borders with little regard for state sovereignty, and nongovernmental organizations have increased their importance in and impact on international affairs as well. The role of MNCs and NGOs in international affairs has often expanded at the expense of states and intergovernmental organizations, witness the NGOs women's conference outside Beijing and NGO efforts to stop French nuclear testing in the Pacific.

What changes in the international system will these scientific-technical advances induce? We can only speculate, but the changes will come.

Resurgent Conflicts over Human Rights and Other Values

Chapter 18 detailed some of today's major conflicts over human rights and other values, and on more than one occasion concluded that the potential for severe conflicts was possible. The consequences of worsened conflict are discernible: multiplied instances of civil strife within countries, increased senses of jingoism and economic protectionism, and a general decrease in international cooperative efforts.

In many ways, each pole of the conflicts over human rights and other values that we observed may be considered an ideology. All are belief systems that maintain a degree of internal consistency and assert their own primacy. This is an important realization in that many intellectuals speculated during the 1960s and 1970s that the world was entering an era that would see the end of ideology. The collapse of communism in the 1980s and 1990s gave rise to such speculation once again.

The prediction that ideologies would soon die away was premature in the 1960s and 1970s, and it is probably premature once again today. A more accurate assessment may be that specific ideologies are less and less able to hold sway over masses of peoples, but other ideologies remain of major importance. Ideologies have fragmented and mutated, but they have not disappeared.

Ideologies—and conflicts over human rights and other values—therefore remain potent forces for change in the international arena. But as we saw in the cases of the other forces for change discussed here, the shape of ideologically or value-induced change is not predictable. Who would have predicted in the early 1970s that revolutionary Islam would be a major force in world politics only 10 years later? Who in the early 1980s would have predicted that only 10 years later, communism as an ideology would have been rejected throughout Eastern Europe and that nationalism as an ideology would tear the Soviet Union apart? Ten years from now, conflicts over human rights and other values may be less important international causes of change, but for the present, they cannot be ignored.

 ## *TOWARD 2100*

Too many forces for change are at work in the international system to allow anyone realistically to believe that the current global status quo will be preserved. Similarly, given the uncertain nature of change, no one can accurately predict the world's future. Despite the proliferation of communication and information technologies that allow us to know more and more about the world we currently live in, the shape of the world in 2100 is increasingly unknown and unknowable.

Nevertheless, a number of clear challenges confront the human race. These challenges range across a wide spectrum of issues: Population growth, food production, nuclear and conventional arms races, the environment, drugs, health, human rights, equitable distribution of wealth, trade and exchange, mineral and energy scarcity, development and developmental aid, and value conflicts are just a few. Failure to initiate actions that come to grips with any single one of these challenges could seriously degrade the quality of life on earth in the twenty-first century. Efforts to come to grips with these challenges must be initiated now, or in the relatively near future, and they must be undertaken on a widespread and even a global basis.

A skeptic might ask, "What actions could be undertaken now or in the relatively near future on a widespread basis to cope with the challenges that face the world? With so many international actors of so many different types, each of which perceives its own interests as special, can any global solutions to global challenges ever be implemented? Is not the anarchy of the current global system severe enough to preclude any widespread consensus on how best to cope with global issues?"

As we have seen, the current international system, with its variety of actors and interests, its diversity of perceptions, its imbalance of capabilities, and its multitude of issues, gives cause to be skeptical about the feasibility of instituting solutions to global problems. Remember, however, that actors are under assault, that the very legitimacy and utility of states, IGOs, MNCs, and NGOs are being questioned. All may survive as actors, but all may also change. Although the possibility of a global government appears as remote as ever, the possibility of actors recognizing the severity and the scope of the challenges they confront is increasing. Leaders and peoples throughout the world acknowledge the necessity of avoiding nuclear war; perhaps someday they will acknowledge a need to avoid all war. They also avow desire to improve the economic and human conditions of everyone on earth; perhaps someday they will agree on how to attempt to do this. Increasingly, international actors recognize environmental issues as global problems that need international solutions.

So there is room for optimism about the twenty-first century. Some significant advances have been made in the recent past. For example, less than sixty years ago, colonialism and imperialism were widely accepted and respectable. Today, they are almost universally decried and reviled. Thus, there is reason to hope that today's problems and challenges will be met and overcome as well.

Change, then, is inevitable. Nothing can escape its all inclusive net. What the world will be like in 2100 — or even in 2010 — is not what the world is today. Change will come, and it can come rapidly. Our responsibility is to be ready for it and to shape it so that the challenges that the world faces can be met better in the future than they are being met today.

KEY TERMS AND CONCEPTS

international system in transition: the international system is in a state of flux, and it is changing to a new system that is as yet vague and undefined

unipolar world: an international system in which one state dominates international affairs to the extent that no other state or actor rivals it

regionalized world: an international system in which power is concentrated in several distinct parts or regions of the world

multipolar world: an international system in which several states, empires, or alliances have the preponderance of power and are recognized as poles in a balance of power system

assaults on present-day actors: the continued existence of states, multinational corporations, and international governmental organizations in their present forms are challenged by internal and external forces

transition in the international economic system: after a period of turmoil during the late twentieth century, the international economic system during the late 1990s and early 2000s began to gain a certain degree of stability and order

increased availability of advanced weapons: military capabilities have become increasingly more lethal and are available to more and more international actors

impacts of scientific-technical change: technology has played and is playing an immense role in shaping the international system, for example through information and communication technologies, transportation technologies, and weapons

resurgent conflicts of values: conflicts in values ranging from differences over religion, ethnic nationalism, and political ideologies continue to play a major role in international affairs

WEBSITE REFERENCES

www.geocities.com/~acunu   website for the Millennium Project of the American Council for the UN University, a think tank of futurists, scholars, businessmen, and policy makers who work for IGOs, governments, corporations, NGOs, and universities

www.wfs.org   website of the World Future Society, a clearinghouse devoted to understanding how social and technological developments shape the future.

www.geds.umd.edu/geds   the Global Events Data System of the Center for International Development and Conflict Management (CIDCM) at the University of Maryland

www.ksgnotes1.harvard.edu/bcsia/bcsia.nsf/www/home   website of the Belfer Center for Science and International Affairs, which examines issues where science, technology, and international affairs intersect

NOTES

1. For discussions of a unipolar system, see David Wilkinson, "Unipolarity Without Hegemony," *International Studies Review* (Summer 1999), pp. 141–172. See also Lea Brilmayer, *American Hegemony: Political Morality in a One-Superpower World* (New Haven, CN: Yale University Press, 1996); Ethan B. Kapstein and Michael Mastanduno, eds., *Unipolar Politics: Realism and State Strategies After the Cold War* (New York, NY: Columbia University Press, 1999); and William C. Wohlforth, "The Stability of a Unipolar World," *International Security* (Summer 1999), pp. 5–41.

2. For an interesting view of multipolarity and peace, see Charles A. Kupchan, "After Pax Americana: Benign Power, Regional Integration, and the Sources of a Stable Multipolarity," *International Security* (Fall 1998), pp. 40–79. For other views of the future of the international system, see Curt Gasteyger, "The Future Shape of the International System," *Internationale Politik,* Transatlantic Edition, (Spring 2000), pp. 69–74; Stuart J. Kaufman, "Approaches to Global Politics in the Twenty-First Century: A Review Essay," *International Studies Review* (Summer 1999), pp. 193–221. For a computer-based simulation with text that allows users to develop their own conceptions of future worlds, see Barry Hughes, *International Futures,* 3d ed. (Boulder, CO: Westview Press, 1999).

Index

Photo Credits

p. 8, Corbis Sygma; p. 43, North Wind Picture Archives; p. 52, AP/Wide World Photos; p. 72, United Nations Photo Library; p. 128, AP/Wide World Photos; p. 133, AP/Wide World Photos; p. 144, (top) Corbis Sygma; (bottom) Corbis; p. 149, Corbis Sygma p. 156, Craig L. Noran/Corbis Sygma; p. 171, Corbis; p. 177, The John F. Kennedy Library; p. 181, Corbis; p. 184, Corbis; p. 187, Archive Photos; p. 211, (top) John Isaac/United Nations Photo Library; p. 211, (bottom) United Nations Photo Library; p. 233, Corbis; p. 274, Lee Day/Black Star; p. 308, Stock, Boston; p. 320, Magnum Photos; p. 340, World Future Society/The Futurist Magazine; p. 341, World Future Society/The Futurist magazine; p. 358, Corbis; p. 362, (top) Corbis Sygma; (middle) Corbis; (bottom) US Dept of Defense; p. 401, AP/Wide World Photos; p. 417, United Nations Photo Library; p. 427, Dennis Brack, Ltd./Black Star; p. 443, Corbis Sygma; p. 466, Corbis Sygma; p. 473, Viviane Holbrook/United Nations Photo Library; p. 518, (a) Photri, Inc.; (b) Courtesy of NASA; (c) Courtesy of NASA.